The White People Show

How To Understand Racism and Still Be Wrong About It

Kamau Kenyatta

Songhai Publications

Also By The Author

Black Folk's Hair Secrects, Shame & Liberation (co-authored)

The 7 Most Dangerous Pitfalls Threatening Your College Success and How To Avoid Them

Get a sneak preview of the author's next book at
www.theWillCWrightFiles.com

The White People Show: How To Understand Racism and Still Be Wrong About It

Library of Congress Control Number: 2021942374

10 digit - ISBN 0-9650653-7-5

13 digit - ISBN 978-0965065375

Printed in the United States of America

Photo by Tobias Tullius on unplash.com

Songhai Publications

165 Winona Street

Easton, PA 18040

Dedicated to my maternal grandparents
Elvie Davis, Sr. and Amanda Davis
Thank you.

Contents

Acknowledgments

Every book is written with the help and input of many people. Their contributions are provided in both intellectual and spiritual ways. Those who have assisted in clarifying my own thinking on this subject include students I've taught over the years. They have helped me to refine my thinking through their questions, insights, and challenges. They are of course too numerous to mention here.

However, the students at William Paterson, where I taught Racism and Sexism classes for many years, deserve a mention. They were instrumental in the nascent stages of my thinking on the subject. As I developed and refined my approach, other students there helped me to mature in my thinking. This would include those students who took the following courses with me: Racism & Sexism, Introduction to Africana Studies, African History 1 & 2, African American History 1 & 2, and African American Social Thought. For all of them I am grateful.

Students at Northampton Community College and Lafayette College continue to influence my thinking with the passage of time and with the invasion of social media in all of our lives.

I'm thankful to the many colleagues who helped sharpen and shaped my understanding. While there are many, Victor Vega, Ph.D. of Middlesex County College, who has been a friend and colleague for many years, has contributed to this work in many ways from our long talks on just about everything. I appreciate your intellect and steadfastness.

The editors at THPeditingServc helped make the book readable. Their promptness and professionalism were invaluable. Thank you.

My family, including my wife Janice, son Shaunte and daughters Aliya and Ayanna, could be counted on to engage me in lively debate and bringing insights that I would otherwise have missed. They challenge me without fear. Thank you.

Introduction

Let's start with a question: Can you define racism correctly? Furthermore, what is it and how do most people understand it?

When I began teaching college racism classes, I mistakenly assumed that students knew what it meant. But to my surprise, I found that more than 99% of students held an incorrect definition of its meaning. It did not matter their race, gender, or age. Even more surprising was that after a few semesters of teaching these classes, I discovered that students usually gave similar definitions of the term. And they were always wrong. Given that this popular idea was widespread, I wondered where they had learned this incorrect information. Paying closer attention, I soon found that this mistaken definition of racism was not confined to just college students. It spills out into the larger population in general.

For example, as I watched television programs, I observed people of different races, ages, and backgrounds get into arguments about racism simply because they did not understand the term and used it inappropriately. In most cases, they were speaking about two different things but believed they were talking about the same thing They would confuse it with other terms like prejudice and discrimination. I noticed that news pundits and talk show hosts' attempts at discussing racism with guests or audiences would, after a while, have nothing to do with racism. But if you quizzed them, they would swear they are discussing racism. Politicians remain the worst offenders because they tend to pontificate and posture in ways that avoided answering questions put to them about racism. Some of the answers they give on the topic seem almost deliberate misdirection and concocted misunderstanding of the concept.

I have been invited to speak in places where you would think that those in attendance would know what racism meant. In many cases, however, I would discover their ignorance on the subject during the question and answer section of my presentation.

This has led me to one ultimate conclusion. Most people do not know what racism means. I ask again, can you define it correctly? Where did you get that definition? When you talk with others about racism, are you both referring to the same thing? Does it cause conflict and pain? What does that do to your ego? That's what this book is about.

I have written this book to help bring clarity to the discussion of racism. I delve into its meaning, its origins, the desired outcome, and the result of its impact. My purpose here is to help shine light on that which has become muddy, unclear, and crammed with confusion. In so doing, I hope to help you be more informed on the topic so you can talk about it intelligently and from an informed position. As a result of reading this book, you will be able to identify the mistakes others make when you hear them discuss it. The newfound understanding received from reading this content, will prevent you from being wrong when you discuss racism. It will also help you avoid useless and frivolous arguments about racism because you will have the information that will help put it into proper context at your fingertips. The bulk of the information you will discover as a result of my research and experience will help you understand why there is so much confusion about the term and where it runs off the rails and into the ditch.

Some who read the pages of this book will find themselves feeling uncomfortable admittedly, because it will challenge their long-held, cherished, but erroneous notions of racism. Others will feel confirmation. This is not a book for those who prefer wishy-washy double talk over fact. As the great sangoma, Vasamazulu Credo Mutwa, has stated, *"You cannot fight an evil disease with sweet medicine...and one cannot hope to cure a putrid malady like inter-racial hatred and misunderstanding by mincing words."* [1] In that spirit, this book will shatter many fallacies about racism which have become accepted as facts over the years simply because few have questioned their accuracy.

I write this book primarily to black people. As such, the redundancy to constantly use the term black is abandoned except where distinctions are necessary for clarity. My rationale is that there has been the tendency among too many of our writers to write as if they are speaking to a white audience primarily and a black audience incidentally. The directive of the sage, Dr. John Henrik Clarke, comes to mind when he stated, *"Write first to your own people "* Poet bell hooks is more pointed on the matter when she complains: *"We produce cultural criticism in the context of white supremacy. At times, even the most progressive and well-meaning white folks, who are friends and allies, may not understand why a black writer has to say something a certain way, or why we may not want to explain what has been said as though the first people we must always be addressing are privileged white readers."* Those of us who write to white audiences on this topic do so, I surmise, in the hopes that somehow the message, the moral message, will get through to them. This is not such a book. I do not write in hopes that white people will hear and repent of the wrongs they and their ancestors have done against us. That day has passed.

My interest is not, "How do we get through to these people (white people)?" We cannot, at least not enough of them to matter. The issue, the question is "How can we live victoriously along with them?" If we are seeking change, the ones among us who are ready to see through the smoke and mirrors of racism are the ones we can influence the most. In the meantime, we do so while enduring and experiencing the presence and influence of those who embrace and practice the doctrine of racism whether wittingly or not.

 Occasionally you will see the Aya Adinkra symbol. It symbolizes our endurance, independence, defiance against difficulties, hardiness, perseverance, and resourcefulness.

You will also notice that throughout the book I use the terms racism and white supremacy synonymously. That is deliberate, and I discuss it in detail in Chapter Three.

I opine that if such clarity as set forth herein is not brought to the surface of our consciousness, as a people, we risk being tricked into a slavery worse than our ancestors previously endured.

—*Kamau Kenyatta*—

Part 1
Center Stage

humiliation

I grew up in South Carolina when overt racism/white supremacy existed in the USA. It was humiliating and dangerous for us. I remember how my grandfather and all the men in our community were expected to behave in the presence of white males.

"You ready to take your 'bacco (tobacco) *to market, Elvie?"*

The little white boy who asked my grandfather that question was no more than twelve or thirteen years old. My grandfather, a man in his fifties at the time, removed his hat and put on a big smile and answered, *"Yes, sir, Mr. Hally.* That was the expected, accepted and normal response to an inquiry from any white person regardless of age, education, or status. Instead of referring to my grandfather as Mr. Davis, the little white boy, and others his age, would call him by his first name as if he were a child of their age. The same was true of white women and little white girls regarding the men and women of our community. If these social rules of conduct were not strictly followed by our people, or if they dared to challenge the norm, the results would be further humiliation that could open the door to more degrading and devastating consequences that would be decisive, swift, and, in some cases, deadly.

As I watched this customary exchange for the first time early in my life at the age of five or six, it confused me. Reason being that in my family and the families of our community, all children were taught that it was a sign of great disrespect to call an adult by their first name. This lesson was engrained into us by my grandparents and every adult in our community. So, when we spoke with an adult, regardless of their color, we would call them *Mr. This* or *Mrs. That*. We were never allowed as children to call any adult by their first name. But here was this young white boy addressing my grandfather by his first name, and my grandfather spoke back to the boy as if the little boy was older than him—like he was an adult.

This was one of the many lessons I learned early in life about the mores of racism/white supremacy in the town and state in which I grew up—Timmonsville, South Carolina. [1] I later learned that racism/white supremacy was not something unique to our town, but it was state and nation-wide. In fact, I would later discover that it was world-wide and like volcanic lava, it is a destructive force designed to destroy all in its path.

Chapter 1

The Gospel of Racism

WE ALL AGREE THAT racism/white supremacy is a problem. But it is not just *a* problem. It is *the* problem—an uncomfortable one at that. I have, in fact, identified it as the number one problem facing our people worldwide. It is the problem that, if seen properly and addressed correctly, will significantly solve all other problems. Those things that we commonly identify as problems are actually symptoms of the problem. The symptoms I speak of include the issues regarding inequality and inequity that we experience in education, economics, housing, health, law, labor, religion, politics, and entertainment. The problems we encounter in all those areas find their roots in racism/white supremacy.

For example, we have been led to believe that if we could change the laws and have more of our people in political offices, or if we obtained better jobs, things will be better. Presumably, some things might get better. Laws, however, have been changed, but they are not enforced, or they get reversed. In essence, they do nothing in eliminating racism/white supremacy. Many of us have super great jobs but we still encounter racism in the workplace regardless of the position or the industry. We have more college educated graduates than ever, and still we are confronted with the ubiquity of racism/white supremacy. When we attempt to address any of the singular symptoms thus mentioned, we miss the mark. To use a trite expression, it's like putting bandages on a gunshot wound. It may look as if you're attending to the wound while not really addressing *the* problem—the bullet and the shooter.

How Is Racism/White Supremacy the Problem?

Racism/White Supremacy is the problem we are faced with regardless of our achievements or lack of achievements. It is what we encounter at all levels of life everyday no matter where we may go from the halls of political power, supreme courts, classrooms, or jailhouses. Many of us have wrongly equated positions with power. We have mistakenly identified status and wealth as eliminators of racism/white supremacy. The truth is, it does not matter what our educational and economic status, or our religious and political affiliations are in life. It matters not whether we're healthy or sick, young or old, tall or short, fat or skinny, single, married or divorce. It does not matter if we are a felon, or if we are famous. It matters not the shade of our complexion whether it is light, dark, or somewhere in between. We are all faced with the problem of racism/white supremacy. It does not matter if we're in the USA, England, France, Germany, China, Japan, the Caribbean, Brazil, Argentina, Columbia, Australia and anywhere on the continent of Africa. It does not matter how much we smile and agree or how much we shuck and jive, how high we jump and run, or how much we sing and dance to get along, racism/white supremacy is the one constant that threads through it all. It is at the root and the gospel of life as we know it in the western world.

We are denied employment, housing, and loans because of it. If we have a job, all too often we are denied equitable promotions or skipped over because of it. Our fight to gain and maintain the right to vote in the USA was and is because of it. The denial to be part of labor unions was because of it. The necessity to fight to have laws enacted for our benefit is because of racism/white supremacy. The denial to live in the house of any neighborhood of our choice and income ability is connected to it. The denial of bank loans and credit for housing or to open a business or to pay for higher education is because of it. The fact that our mortality rate is higher due to either no health care, insufficient health care, or living in polluted environments where we are susceptible to life threatening diseases are the results of racism/white supremacy.

The reality that we are the products of an educational system designed to intentionally mis-educate us about ourselves is a factor of racism/white supremacy. The certitude that we are some of the biggest proponents of the two religions, Christianity and Islam, that first proclaimed to the world that we were savages and brutally enslaved us for hundreds of years is a testament to the diabolical efficiency and insidiousness of racism/white supremacy. The fact that some of the most well-paid and famous among us acquired their wealth by being entertainers who either ran fast, jumped higher, hit harder, sang louder, danced better, or told jokes that humiliated themselves and our communities and at the same time made white folks laugh while posing no threat to their comfortable lifestyles and privileges is all the result of racism/white supremacy.

In the words of the late eminent law scholar and civil rights activist, Derrick Bell,

> *"Racial bias in the pre-Brown era was stark, open, unalloyed with hypocrisy and blank-faced lies. We blacks, when rejected, knew who our enemies were. They were not us! Today, because bias is masked in*

unofficial practices and "neutral" standards, we must wrestle with the question whether race or some individual failing has cost us the job, denied us the promotion, or prompted our being rejected as tenants for an apartment. Either conclusion breeds frustration and alienation—and a rage we dare not show to others or admit to ourselves." [1]

We Used To Be Clear About Racism

The intentional message conveyed to my grandfather by reducing him, other adult men, and women in our community to the status of children was that they were inferior to whites. By inferior, I mean that they were thought of as less valuable, not as important, and not worthwhile as humans who felt love, pain, rejection, happiness, or respect as do all humans. They were depicted as lazy, shiftless, and having no aspirations or dreams for themselves and their families. They did not matter to white people. Their feelings and well-being did not matter. As white people saw it, they were put on the earth only to serve them, their interests and well-being. And the reason being is that white people believed themselves to be more important, more valuable, and worthwhile humans who deserved respect, privilege and status simply because they possessed skin that was white. That is racism in its purest form. As such, the treatment of our people as equals deserving of respect was non-existent and, in the minds of whites, impossible and undesirable.

The message that was sent to both black and white people was unambiguous and crystal- clear racism. Neither group was confused about what it was, who was responsible for it and who perpetrated it upon the other. That undebatable message communicated that those who classified themselves as white people were superior to (i.e., better than) those who were not white-skinned people. As a result, white-skinned people were rewarded, and their assumed superiority, however false, was approved, accepted, and applauded. We, on the other hand, were put upon, punished and penalized. Our supposed inferiority was reinforced and embedded both to us and white people by every institution encountered within the system.

For added emphasis, during that time and before, there was no confusion about who was racist or what racism meant. Since that time, however, there has been an ongoing attempt to confuse us on both points— what is meant by racism and who is racist. Additionally, we are told that there are many different definitions of the term, and that everyone can be racist. I have watched with amazement over the years how too many of us have fallen prey to these bogus claims. Too many of our supposed intelligent and highly educated people capitulate to this sleight of hand. In so doing, it is (1) a disservice to our community and, (2) however wittingly or unwittingly, supports the gospel of racism/white supremacy, and (3) adds more confusion in the minds of our people.

Considering this, we must, like Dorothy in the well-known movie, The Wizard of Oz, look behind the curtain and find out what's really going on. What is racism anyway? Although you most likely know of it through private experience, let me show you.

separation

I remember it well. I was a small child. We lived in the "country" not in town but on a sharecropping farm. I recall going with my grandmother to the doctor's office in our town. At the entrance of the doctor's office, there were two doors where patients could enter. One had a sign that read, FOR WHITES ONLY and the other had a sign that read FOR COLORED ONLY. Once we entered the office through the FOR COLORED ONLY door, everyone was expected to register with the receptionist announcing their arrival. The receptionist's booth was in the center of a large waiting room that had clearly been setup to separate black and white people. She sat in a small booth that divided the two waiting rooms, but we could see those on the white side just as they could see us on our side.

When names were called, whether black or white, everyone went into the same examination room to be examined by the only doctor in our town, Dr. Davenport.

Sometimes when we visited Dr. Davenport's office, my grandmother would often see someone she knew on the other side of the divide—usually a white woman. With me sitting at her side, my grandmother and the white woman would engage in rather loud small talk due to the distance created by the divide. Neither of them would ever think of going to the forbidden side where they could sit beside each other and chat. They carried on their chatter at a "respectable" distance. To do otherwise, would invite...I don't know...because it never happened.

This was not an uncommon occurrence and I remember asking my grandmother after one such encounter how she knew the lady. Our conversation went something like this:

> *"How do you know her, Grandma?" I asked.*
>
> *"That's Mrs. ______," she replied. "We grew up together and use to play together as children."*
>
> *You did?!" I exclaimed, amazed and curious at the same time.*
>
> *"Oh, yeah," she said as a matter fact. "All us young'uns use to play together growing up. Didn't matter back then if you were colored or white. We were all the same."*
>
> *"What happened?" I asked in my innocence. "Why don't you see her more now?"*
>
> *"Oooh, no," she said somewhat animated. "Can't do that. When we got older, her mother told us we couldn't play with her any more cuz she said we were "niggers" and white children can't be seen playing with "niggers." Her mother told her she had to learn her proper place and so did we. And that was the end of that." She paused for a moment and then said, "We never played together no more." She stopped walking and then turned to me with a stern look on her face shaking her finger at me and said, "And don't you ever use that word!" It became part of the mental signature that is me. It stuck in my mind.*

That was one of the very rare occasions, if not the only one, I ever heard my grandmother use the term, "nigger." It was not an accepted thing to say in our household and wasn't a part of her or my grandfather's vocabulary. The story she told me was one repeated several times throughout my childhood by some of her brothers and other adults in our community. They had similar stories of playing with white children when they were small, and how the relationship was 'nipped in the bud' as they grew older. It was a common and prevailing practice that was etched into my memory although I didn't have one of those relationships, because there were no white children that I played with as a child.

Along with the above conversation, my grandmother informed me that when this breakup of black and white children happened, the black children were required to start using Mr. or Misses when speaking with their former playmates—the white children. This signified that the white child was to be respected and valued as an adult even though they were the same age and, in some cases, younger. Those relationships, and the behavior, was a life-long practice. This and other practices of that nature have a long and ugly history, that as I learned later, appears to have been a common practice in most parts of the country.

> *"Today one can travel for thousands of miles across this country and never see a public facility designated as "Colored" or "White." Indeed, the very absence of visible signs of discrimination creates an atmosphere of racial neutrality and encourages whites to believe that racism is a thing of the past."* [1]

> — *Derrick Bell* —

Chapter 2

The Big Misunderstanding

That Won't Go Away

RACISM/WHITE SUPREMACY IS A problem. But to solve a problem, one must first recognize that a problem exists. Not only must one recognize this fact but there should also be an agreement with others regarding that reality.

While we might agree that racism/white supremacy exists, there is confusion about what it means. It's in the USA. It's in the world. The demonic results of its influence and impact are felt on a global scale. Almost no one on planet earth is exempt from its impact. We African/Black people have been its direct target, its bullseye for over 500 years. Here in the United States of America, except for the native people of the land, the so-called Indians, all other people of color have been peripheral targets. The consequences, however, on all groups impacted by it are deep, devastating, and lasting.

Many white scholars, pundits, and the like, however, attempt to confuse us on the matter of racism. They downplay it and even attempt to deny it. When we point it out, they claim we're playing what has become known as the *"race card."* [1] Despite their attempts to convince us otherwise, we know the truth all too well. Unfortunately, even some of our own misguided people, as well as other people of color, fall into that camp. As a counter to our valid observations and recognitions of racist behavior and acts, these misguided folks are often paraded out. We must ignore both their attempts and the attempts of whites who deny racism/white supremacy as a factor. We must also ignore those who question its existence, and those who attempt to redefine it to suit their narratives. Denying it does not diminish its ramifications. Questioning its existence is an exercise in first-class folly. Redefining it, to include everyone as perpetrators, is an attempt to ignore the historical record and to create further confusion. To give any of these notions attention is to give them credence. Doing so may be likened to giving credibility to those who would deny, question, or redefine the law of gravity. Presumably intelligent people would not engage in serious discussion, deliberation, or debate with anyone over the validity of the law of gravity.

The visits to Dr. Davenport's office with my grandmother came with a clear and unmistakable message. That message, which was conveyed to me, my grandparents and everyone else in our community was that white people were to be regarded as superior because they had white skin. There was no confusion or ambiguity about it, no double message to decipher, and no hidden meanings to discover. Racism/white supremacy was the sole and unequivocal domain of white people.

So Why Is There Confusion About Racism?

Racism/white supremacy is an emotionally charged and fragile topic. It is emotionally charged because of a history full of real-life consequences that, like hot lava, has spilled over into present-day realities. Although most people have very strong feelings about it, their knowledge or the lack thereof concerning its meaning, origin, and purpose is problematic. Additionally, there is a massive gap in most folk's understanding of the historical practice of racism and its relationship to the contemporary world. Many speak of racism without any substantial historical reference regarding its long-range consequences, which are dangerous to say the least. As far as whites are specifically concerned on the matter, while they have proven to be great practitioners of racism, most of them remain woefully ignorant on the topic. Writer Barbara Trepagnier aptly shines light on the issue observing that,

"The reason well-meaning white people do not notice their own silent racism is because they presume that they are not racist...their white perspectives tell them so. However, the presumption is faulty, and this aspect of silent racism—that is hard for white people to detect in themselves—allows it to do its damage undisturbed." [2]

And because they don't see themselves as racist, Trepagnier correctly adds that,

"White people who see themselves as "not racist" are unlikely to see their connection to race or racism." [3]

This "detachment" from issues of racism enables white people to benefit from the racial status quo without taking any responsibility. In other words, their denial of racism and its impact on us allows them to freely enjoy the rewards they receive because of racism.

Meaning

To better understand racism, there must first be a meeting of the minds of what it actually means as opposed to what one may think it means. If two people were discussing dogs, for example, and one person thinks that dogs are cats and the other person thinks that dogs are elephants, they can never have a meaningful or insightful discussion about dogs. Until they clearly define what each means by a dog, the result will be confusion.

Imagine the confusion that would ensue if car manufactures could not agree on a definition of what is meant by a car. Or if there was no definitive agreement of what constituted the meaning of day or night. A world without agreed upon definitions is a world designed to either confuse or control others. All too often the two complement each other because the more you can confuse people the easier it is to control them. The same applies to the meaning of racism. If we are confused about what racism means, it becomes difficult, if not impossible, to identify it, confront it, or curtail it.

Consequently, when racism is discussed, problems arise because, in most cases, there is not an agreed upon definition of the term. If there is not an agreement of its meaning between two or more persons, discussions about it can lead to extreme levels of stupidity. The results lead to flawed and false statements that in turn lead to confusion that produces invalid conclusions.

Origin

The inception of an idea or the origins of something tells us a lot about that idea or thing. It helps us understand it in a way that would otherwise escape our attention thereby leaving severe blind spots in our understanding of the thing. The origins of racism, at least in its current codified manifestations, provides us with insights that help prevent confusion.

Purpose

The purpose of racism helps us understand its goal, its reason for being, its motive and its intention. Purpose helps us understand the "why" of something. When we understand the purpose of racism, we are given insights of how to identify it, how to measure it, and how to effectively deal with it. It is the purpose of racism that has all too often left us baffled and without a plan to handle it. When we understand the purpose of racism/white supremacy, it doesn't catch us off our guard or by surprise. It helps us to anticipate. When we anticipate, we foresee; we predict, and we can prepare. If I know what you're going to do before you do it, I can prepare myself to defend against it. Better yet, if I know what you're going to do before you do it, I can launch an offensive to undermine your attack. The next few chapters will examine each of the following areas: the meaning of racism, the origin of racism and the purpose of racism.

denial

I had just graduated from college. Having earned my bachelor's with a dual major in both music performance and business administration, my top priority was to find a full-time job. Like any young man, there were things I wanted; a car, an apartment, and clothes—- you know, "things." I was resourceful and began to apply for jobs that offered Management Trainee positions.

After several weeks of applying for jobs and with a few unproductive interviews here and there, I finally scheduled an appointment with a company that looked promising. During the interview, I was informed that they did not have any management trainee positions available even though that was the position they had advertised. They informed me, however, that they did have a position available in their accounts payable department. My resume had revealed that I had taken several accounting courses for my business degree and so they asked if I would be interested in taking that position until a management trainee position became available. Although I had not thought of specifically taking an accounting job, I accepted the offer with consideration for the next available management trainee position.

In the new position, I was responsible for the accounts payable of the entire company. This covered three regions—Northern, Mid-Atlantic, and Southern regions from Maine to Virginia Beach which consisted of twenty-three locations. The other accounting department employees consisted of mostly women who were in the accounts receivables department. The general ledger department was handled by my immediate supervisor, Bruce, the only other male in the department. He and I were also the only two people with college degrees in the entire accounting department. I was the only black male at the corporate headquarters.

I loved the job and the challenges it gave me. It spurred my creative juices and my left-brain inclinations at the same time. I felt that I was on the right track and had made a good decision in accepting the job. So, I dug in, learned my responsibilities and excelled.

When my first six-months review was conducted, I received flying colors on my assessment. Naturally, I asked about the status of a management trainee position. I was told that none were available. Additionally, they informed me that they weren't sure when one would open but assured me that when one was available, I would be at the top of the list. These reviews occurred at six months intervals and at every review, I received rave assessments and the same answer to my inquiry about a management trainee position; none were available.

After about a year and a half, the company was expanding and opened several new offices. The southern region was experiencing tremendous growth which increased my workload exponentially. The decision was made to hire another person in account payables to help with the growing southern region while my duties were to maintain the northern and Mid-Atlantic regions. The person hired was literally a young white girl out of high school. Let's call her, Kathy. Kathy possessed virtually no work experience in general, no accounting experience, nor any college. Coupled with her lack of experience was the fact that she knew absolutely nothing about accounting—zero. I was given the additional responsibility of training her. In that role, I taught her the very basics of accounts payables and supervised her work. After six months of hand holding Kathy to get the basic procedures down, I turned the third region books over to her. Under my supervision, I had to double check her work for accuracy which became almost like another part-time job. In my opinion, it was more productive for me to maintain all the regions as I had because the added responsibility of double checking and redoing some of her work required more time and energy than it was worth.

During this same time, the company hired Tom, a young white man about my age, in the General Ledger department, which is a slight notch above accounts payables. It was a newly created position of which I was not aware was available until the new hire. Tom had a basic liberal arts college degree with no business background and no accounting background either. We had the same basic work background, except for my business degree and almost two years of accounting experience at that point. Tom had no accounting experience but was taught by our supervisor, Bruce. I didn't think too much of it because I was waiting for a management trainee position to open.

Around the time I finished training Kathy, Tom had been there for approximately seven months or so. A short time later, I remember coming to work and discovering a company-wide inner office announcement informing us that Tom was being promoted to the new management trainee position. As you can imagine, I was stunned. Shocked. Floored.

I remember sitting at my desk seeing red and trying to make sense of what had happened. I went to my supervisor and asked him why I had not been considered for the position. His response was that it was out of his hands and that I should speak with his supervisor, Stu, the vice-president of finances. I then went to Stu's office and asked him the same question. His response was that it was a decision made by the Operations Manager, Bruce (a different Bruce). As I started toward his office, a reality slowly dawned on me that I was being given the run around. With that realization, I stopped in my tracks, turned around, and headed back to my desk. I was seething with anger and could not think straight for the rest of the day. I was forced, however, to watch as a parade of other employees came into our office area throughout the day congratulating Tom on his promotion. Many of them naively commented to me, *"It's such a great opportunity, isn't it? He'll do a great job."* I sat there mulling over what was happening and how it happened.

The next day, I went to my supervisor's office and asked when Tom would begin the management training program. I was told in a few weeks. I then asked that since Tom was leaving the General Ledger position making it vacant, that I would like to be considered for the position. He looked me squarely in the eyes and said that I did not have enough experience for that position and that it required more attention and detail than I was used to handling. This was the same man who praised my work and the great job I was doing for over two years. The same man who had repeatedly led me to believe that when a management trainee position opened, I'd be the first considered! The same man had taken Tom, who had zero accounting background or experience, under his wings and taught him the ABCs of accounting. As you can imagine, I was furious.

After I returned to my desk, I considered the possibility of filing a formal legal complaint. While I sat there and looked around, the reality of my vulnerability dawned on me with the impact of falling bricks. There was no one that I could turn to that could make a real difference. It occurred to me like the impact of the sun on a new day that I was the mythical token black guy of whom I had heard about; you know, the one who makes a company look like a diverse and equal opportunity employer. I also grasped how expendable I was and that if I decided to quit, they would simply hire another "token" to replace me.

For the first time in my life, the sheer bitter truth of racism/white supremacy gushed through my mind and my being like never before. I immediately started searching for another job, founded one and left. On my final day, as was the custom of the company, they purchased a cake and held a small going away celebration for me. I listened as my immediate supervisor, the vice-president of finance, the operations manager and others in the company talked about how valuable my contributions were to the company, how difficult it would be to find someone to take my place, and how much they would miss me. Blah, Blah, Blah.

Approximately three weeks later, I received a phone call from one of the two black women I had worked with in the accounting office. Let's call her Sylvia. After exchanging greetings, she said, "Guess who they gave the General Ledger job to that you wanted but was denied?

"Who?" I inquired.

"You have no idea?" she asked.

Pondering her question but coming up blank, I said, "No."

Sylvia replied slowly and sarcastically, "Your little trainee, Kathy."

We were both silent for a moment. Not believing what I had heard, I finally asked, "Are you kidding me?"

"You think I'd call you to joke about something like this?" was her reply. I was speechless.

That kind of event or one similar has happened to all of us at some point in our working careers. The location and particulars of the job varies but the results are the same. You, or someone you may know, was overlooked and replaced by someone white who was less competent and less qualified. If it hasn't happened to you personally yet, I'll bet that you know someone or know of someone to whom it has happened.

Chapter 3

What You May Not Know About Racism

I HAVE ASKED STUDENTS in my college classes for over twenty years to define the term racism. During that time and out of a few thousand students, only four or five were able to define it correctly. Most have a total misconception of what it means. As such, they represent a microcosm of the macrocosm. Said another way, those few students, out of a couple billion people on the planet, represent the reality that many people are ignorant of what racism is or is not. This is not an accident.

There are two reasons why a discussion about racism leads to misguided conclusions and confusion. Those who discuss it either (1) use different definitions of the word or (2) they use a wrong definition of the word. In simple terms, they have not come to an agreement of what they mean as they are discussing the concept. Interestingly, in either case, if asked, most people cannot properly define the term.

For example, regarding point number one above, some incorrectly use the words prejudice or discrimination when they should use racism instead. It has become the normal and accepted state of dialogue around the topic. The result is utter chaos because they believe they are talking about racism. The problem is that neither the word prejudice nor the word discrimination correctly defines the term racism. In other words, it is incorrect to use the terms prejudice or discrimination when what one really means is racism/white supremacy. Doing so weakens the impact and the historicity of racism/white supremacy. It neutralizes the stench of its consequences and diminishes its offensiveness. Using the terms prejudice or discrimination as synonyms for racism/white supremacy misses the bullseye. Neither term is synonymous with racism.

But What About Racial Discrimination and Racial Prejudice?

Yes, there is racial discrimination and racial prejudice, but those terms without the adjectival modifier (racial) have little to do with racism and may be applied to a variety of topics. The adjective qualifies the type of prejudice or discrimination one has in mind such as racial prejudice or racial discrimination. However, to use the word prejudice or discrimination as a substitute for racism creates confusion, whether intentional or not. Neither prejudice nor discrimination means racism/white supremacy. They are completely different terms all together.

Decoding Racism/White Supremacy

Perhaps the following analogy will help in understanding racism. Law enforcement officers using forensics can identify criminals using fingerprints because fingerprints have patterns. Those patterns vary from person to person and are exclusive to an individual. They help eliminate innocent persons as suspects and narrows the search to a specific person. Every human has a fingerprint pattern unique to themselves.

Likewise, DNA is used in a similar manner as fingerprints but tends to be even more definitive in its conclusions of distinguishing one individual from another.

In the same way that fingerprints and DNA have patterns that identify or distinguish them, racism/white supremacy has patterns that identify and distinguishes it. There are markers that provide us with clear evidence of what racism/white supremacy is by definition. It also has historical markers that provide us with concrete and irrefutable examples.

By definition, and in a nutshell, racism is the belief that white-skinned people are superior to those who are not white-skinned. This belief is held by white-skinned people, and as such they believe they are better than those who do not possess white skin and because they have white skin, they consider themselves as more valuable than those who are not white-skinned. It is not based on merit, achievement, or accomplishment. It is based solely on the belief, held by white-skinned people, that they and their type are more valuable, more worthy, and more important simply because of the color of their skin. The result for whites who capitulate to this belief is that they gain a feeling of superiority (however false) resulting in an unmerited sense of entitlement to dominate all arenas of life: economics, law, labor, politics, education, religion, entertainment, sex and war. It results in them thinking that, as a group and by extension as individuals, they deserve certain privileges, and they expect special treatment because of their whiteness.

Let me say it another way: Racism is the belief that one or one's group is superior to others based solely on skin color and that belief is held only by those who classify themselves as white-skinned. What accompanies this definition is the idea that white-skinned people feel they have the natural and God-given right to subordinate, marginalize and control those who are not white-skinned.

A more nuanced definition of racism says that it is the doctrine or belief that one or one's group is superior to others based solely on skin color. That definition, while correct, is slightly flawed in that it leaves room for speculation by not explicitly pointing a finger. Consequently, it leads one to conclude, erroneously of course, that anyone might be a practitioner of racism. In other words, it leaves room for too much speculation about the meaning. It also lessens the historical connections making it more difficult to point the finger. And so, in this muddled fashion and through other garbled ways, whites, who have been the creators and practitioners of racism, find a loophole of sorts allowing them to escape a full-frontal indictment. In the end, it's designed to distract our attention from racism and creates a straw man. However, the bottom-line regarding racism is that it is about how white people see themselves in relation to those not white and not the other way around. But some claim that the term has multiple meanings. Is that true?

Are There Multiple Meanings of Racism?

Can racism mean more than one thing? There are those who would argue that there are multiple meanings for racism. Those arguments are attempts at blurring the substance and unadulterated meaning of the word. Those arguments also aim to obscure and down-play the historical origins of the racism construct as well as the implementation of that construct. Whether feigned or true, we must consider the argument because, if left unaddressed, more confusion may result for the uninitiated. And what do the dictionaries have to say on the matter?

When we consult most reputable dictionaries, we find that the claim of multiple meanings is not supported. In fact, most dictionaries are clear and precise about the meaning of the term. Here are a few examples.

Merriam-Webster

A belief that race is the primary determinant of human traits and capacities and that racial differences produce an inherent superiority of a particular race.

Merriam-Webster *(for children)*

Belief that certain races of people are by birth and nature superior to others.

Oxford English Dictionary

Prejudice, discrimination, or antagonism directed against someone of a different race based on the belief that one's own race is superior.

b.   The belief that all members of each race possess characteristics, abilities, or qualities specific to that race, especially so as to distinguish it as inferior or superior to another race or races.

Dictionary.com

A belief or doctrine that inherent differences among the various human racial groups determine cultural or individual achievement, usually involving the idea that one's own race is superior and has the right to dominate others or that a particular racial group is inferior to the others.

The belief that races have distinctive cultural characteristics determined by hereditary factors and that this endows some races with an intrinsic superiority over others.

b. Abusive or aggressive [sic] behaviour towards members of another race on the basis of such a belief.

These definitions are unambiguous, unequivocal, and clear. They are not multivalent, multifarious, multivariable or multifactorial. They all emphasize that there is the element of assumed racial superiority over other races. If there is fault to be found in the definitions usually given in dictionaries and in discussions, it is that they do not include the historical reality associated with the term. The theoretical and historical origin of the practice as already mentioned is excluded. In addition, when we read phrases like, "a belief or doctrine," "the belief," "abusive or aggressive behaviour," the subject or actor is not identified. The question of "Who holds this belief?" or "Who is doing the believing?" is left open to speculation. Furthermore, such language leaves the impression that this is a ubiquitous phenomenon practiced by all peoples of all races. The historical record, again, does not confirm this impression.

Despite the clarity surrounding the term derived through experience, as outlined here, and as seen in dictionaries, there are those in the academy and other elite circles who argue that there are multiple meanings of the word. According to them, not only does the term have multiple meanings, but its meaning is subject to change over time. This is merely an attempt to further confuse and at the same time minimize the indictment against white people.

For example, Pooja Sawrikar and Ilan Katz from the Social Policy Research Centre at the University of New South Wales wrote the following on the matter:

Disagreements in the definition of racism have long plagued the research and policy discourse on race relations. Such tensions have emerged because researchers, policy makers, and activists from different disciplines are interested in different aspects of racism. For example, definitions in the sociological literature (e.g., Cazaneve & Maddern 1999; Carmichael & Hamilton 1992) tend to focus on differences in social power as explaining the nature and scope of racism, as well as the factors that sustain or reinforce its occurrence. Definitions in the psychological literature (e.g., Allport 1979) on the other hand tend to focus on cognitive processes for explaining the emergence and entrenchment of racism. Legal definitions (e.g., United Nations (UN) Convention on the Elimination of all forms of Racial Discrimination, http://www2.ohchr.org/english/law/cerd.htm) are generally interested in how institutional practices and policies contribute to or perpetuate racism, and definitions in the economics literature (e.g. Blalock 1967; Sivanandan 1993) stress the role of competition over limited resources as a primary reinforcer of racism.

1

Their assertion is misguided and misinformed. While it may be true that different disciplines might approach the topic with a particular emphasis, it does not mean there is not a definitive definition by which everyone operates. For us as a people, we have always been clear about that definitive definition despite some of us not having the adequate language to articulate it. The exceptions to this rule, are those of us who are attempting to curry favor with the white supremacist system. This would include those of us who are circumscribed from speaking truth to power because our employment, housing (and our overall safety and our family's well-being) may be jeopardized if we step out of "our place." And that "place" is one where we do not challenge white people, contradict them, or question their conclusions about things especially those things pertaining to how we really feel or think about race matters. On some level of that continuum, all of us can, at one time or another depending on the situation, fit into one or more of those exceptions as a survival tactic.

Authors Sawrikar and Katz's are wrong in their belief that the definitions of racism of necessity must also change over time via discipline or political bent. Except in the arena of armchair scholars it has no traction. In the real world where we live, there is no such change. It is only true if there is not a definitive definition especially in intellectual circles. The result and impact of racism/white supremacy for us, however, is the same—violence, repudiation, nullification, marginalization, dehumanization, and brutalization. It is constant. And it is constant because white people believe themselves to be innately superior to black people in every arena of life.

The problem that the authors, and many like them, have with a clear unambiguous definition of racism is the indictment it brings upon white people. The clear unambiguous definition is seen as too harsh, too candid, one-sided, etc., and as an indictment against white people. We, and by extension all people of color, know that when we properly define the term it does bring that indictment against white people. We also know that defining it properly invites the wrath, anger, and vengeance of white-skinned people upon us and our community. To avoid that wrath, anger, and vengeance, we "stay in our place." Therefore, we observe intellectual acrobatics of this type by the likes of these authors and others like them who attempt to change the meaning or create new meanings that fit the worldview that avoids that indictment. Additionally, by their own admission, Sawrikar and Katz admit that "The aim of this paper is not to take these various elements of racism and propose a unified definition that reconciles these differences…" In the end, their conclusion is neither helpful nor informative, and that last statement is simply a weasel clause.

Is Racism an Indictment Of Whites?

When we fail to approach the discussion of racism/white supremacy with the above meaning and understanding, we fall prey to the diversion trap. The purpose of the diversion trap is to move our attention away from deeper and revealing discussions and implications about racism/white supremacy. It is a distraction. For example, the historical record demonstrates that the only group to hold the belief, that they were superior to others based on their skin color, are those who classified themselves as white-skinned. Likewise, historically, they are the only group that engaged in this practice as seen in their own historical behavior. In our long history, we African/Black people have never made such a claim. Yellow people have never made such a claim and neither have brown people. When half-assed definitions or incorrect definitions of racism are used, discussion of those more revealing points are lost and can lead to incorrect and unacceptable conclusions.

Although other groups or races have made claims of superiority in terms of their culture, their military might, or being the chosen of God, etc., none, however, except those classifying themselves as white skinned, have ever claimed superiority because of their skin color. That designation belongs exclusively to those who classify themselves as white-skinned people. And that is known as racism.

In summary, because of that understanding, whites believe they therefore have the right to dominate and subordinate those others; namely us. Additionally, to assert that simple fact is to invite the wrath and anger of white people who are historically prone to exhibit violent behavior toward those who challenge their notions of racial superiority because it squarely shines the spotlight on their nefarious actions and behavior both historically and contemporarily. This, for them, must never happen. Said another way, it is expected that we must never point the finger at them as being the racists. It's why we hear some of our own people saying crazy things like, we all can be racist. In fact, if we say that whites are racist, we are accused of being racist for correctly saying they are racist! And it's true, for the most part, we don't call them racists despite them saying and doing racist things.

White people inevitably think they have a monopoly on putting other groups, especially us, under the microscope of examination while they remain exempt from such scrutiny. In general, they love to be in the spotlight. They love to have their accomplishments and achievements glorified, whether true or not, at the expense of others. Having those accomplishments examined and questioned by one of us, as they see it, is an attack upon them. When that happens, their tendency is to resort to violence against us. Their propensity for violence toward us manifests itself in overt and covert ways, physically, politically, economically, and socially. It's known as keeping us in our place. That place is a creation in the minds of white people to maintain their invented superiority. If they can keep us in our place, they can continue living the illusion of being superior.

Racism as a term has a definitive historical origin and context. That origin and context is in the western (white) world. Phenotypically it is known in the world of those who classify themselves as white-skinned. It has an historical record that can be summoned. Once summoned, that history will; (1) testify as a witness to its origin and meaning, (2) identify those who practiced it, (3) show who were its victims, and (4) reveal its intended purpose.

Again, in the world of my grandparents and in the community in which I grew up, not very long ago, there was no such ambiguity, confusion or muddling about what was/is racism.

Is Racism Like White Supremacy?

Racism is not *like* white supremacy. Racism *is* white supremacy. While racism is a dirty word in the United States of America, and indeed most of the western (white) world, its equivalent, White Supremacy, is just as dirty. The term white supremacy is erroneously used by many to distinguish it from racism. When this is done, one may be left with the conclusion that, on the one hand, you have racism and, on the other hand, you have white supremacy. In other words, most people believe that racism is one thing and white supremacy is something altogether different. Here, too, the historical record is clear. It does not support such a dichotomy. These terms are not separate or different from one another neither in substance, degree, nor practice. They are synonymous. Neely Fuller, Jr. is correct when he asserted that *"Racism is white supremacy. White supremacy is racism. There is no other form."* White supremacy describes one "who" is practicing racism.

Therefore, to say racism or white supremacy (racism/white supremacy) is to say the same thing using different terminology. It means that if you say either one of them, you would be correct in definition and description. To say "white racism" then, is redundant. and superfluous. There is only one kind of racism and that is white supremacy. White people have been the only group in the USA, the world, and history who has been inclined to effectively discriminate against others racially, i.e., deprive and punish other races who are not white skinned because they are deemed inferior due to their skin color. They are also the only ones who have systems and institutions in place that were created to sustain and maintain their notions of white superiority. This imbalance is evidenced in systems of economics, education, entertainment, labor, law, politics, religion, sex, and war.

It might be helpful to think of it this way. Racism is the behavior and white supremacy is the foundation for those who carry out the behavior. Therefore, what we are dealing with is a structure (racism) whereby whites, who deem themselves superior to those without white skin (white supremacy), can systematically deny rights and benefits to non-whites in every area of human activity. Again, those areas include economics, education, entertainment, labor, law, politics, religion, sex, and war. This is all done out of the belief, by whites, that they are superior to non-whites solely because of their white skin color.

Simple observation reveals that white people control all the major areas of human activity in the USA, and for that matter the world. It is then accurate to define racism as white supremacy. There is no black supremacy, yellow supremacy, nor brown supremacy. There is only white supremacy/racism. As such, there are no competing supremacies. White supremacy AND Black supremacy cannot simultaneously exist in the same space and time. Both can never occupy the same space. It is either one or the other. Either you have white supremacy, or you have black supremacy. You cannot have white supremacy and black supremacy.

This clarification is necessary and important so that the targets of racism/white supremacy do not become confused about their relationship to the history of the term. It is imperative that we realized that it is intrinsic and necessary of racism/white supremacy to create confusion about its identity when exposure of that identity threatens its existence. As a consequent, the confusion surrounding the term racism is not by accident; nor is it just a historical etymological development. British author and historian, Basil Davidson, clarifies it as follows:

"By racism I mean the conscious and systematic weapon of domination, of exploitation, which first saw its demonic rise with the onset of the trans-Atlantic

trade in African captives sold into slavery, and which, later, led on to the imperialist colonialism of our yesterdays.

This racism was not a "mistake," a "misunderstanding" or a "grievous deviation from the proper norms of behavior." It was not an accident of human error. It was not an unthinking reversion to barbarism. On the contrary, this racism was conceived as the moral justification—the necessary justification, as it was seen by those in the white man's world who were neither thieves or moral monsters—for doing to black people what church and state no longer thought it permissible to do to white people: the justification for enslaving black people, that is, when it was no longer permissible to enslave white people."[2]

snubbed

By the time I entered the tenth grade, the schools in my state and town were racially integrated. As a result, our elementary school, Brockington—the black school— was closed and all elementary students in the town went to Timmonsville Elementary—the white school. Our high school was Johnson High School home of the mighty Panthers. It was relegated to the position of middle school. The white high school, Timmonsville High became *the* high school. Both the white elementary and the white high schools were elevated because someone had deemed them to be superior, and both the black elementary and the black high schools were demoted because someone had deemed them to be inferior.

Prior to this so-called integration of the schools, and despite the unequal distribution of state and federal school funding between the black schools and the white schools, our community thrived educationally, and we were proud of our schools. Our teachers were great, but more importantly, they cared, and it showed in their dedication. We were self-contained and had our own principals and administrators, who were all black people. Since then, the number of black teachers in the district has dwindle to somewhere south of five percent. Most of the jobs for teachers and administrators are now held by whites. The rationale is that there are not enough qualified black teachers to fill the spots.

I say all that to say that when I was in the ninth grade, we had been given the choice of following the college track or the vocational track for the rest of our high school career. Along with my family, I had chosen the college track and the classes I took reflected that choice. The schools were integrated the next year. At the end of my tenth-grade year, we were advised to make appointments with the student career counselor of the high school to discuss our college choices so we could receive information and begin preparing for the college application process. As instructed, I went to the school's career counselor, Mrs. McCloud—a white woman. I informed her that I had decided I wanted to attend Florida A & M University (FAMU) in Tallahassee, Florida to major in music. In the way of background, I had been playing drums since age twelve and was a member of the school's marching band. By this time, I had risen to the rank of lead drummer. My goal was to become a member of the well-known and prestigious Marching 100 at FAMU. Mrs. McCloud informed me that she would request the information and we would discuss it when the material arrived.

After some time had passed, I stopped by her office to inquire if she had received the information. She let me know that she had not, but that it should arrive soon. I inquired several more times throughout the year to no avail. To my knowledge, it never came. At the time, I did not know the process, or that I could have requested the information for myself. I had been led to believe that the only way to get the information was through the counselor.

Needless to say, I never attended FAMU. It wasn't until years later as an adult with a couple of college degrees under my belt that I revisited that episode in my life. It was then that I realized how a simple thing as seeking information about college entrance could have racist implication. That snub had come out of her belief that I and some other black students were not college material even though

I graduated from high school a year ahead of time. The racist undertones of this incident did not become apparent to me until years later when I realized that racism was at play.

Chapter 4

The Demonic Invention

*"If you do not understand White Supremacy /Racism—
what it is, and how it works—everything else that you
understand, will only confuse you."*
—Neely Fuller, Jr.—

THE ONGOING AND NEVER-ENDING crisis surrounding racism suffers from a lack of attention given to the root cause(s) and thereby creates a lack of understanding. Those root causes are found in Europe, and what follows is a brief summation of its origin and development.

Swedish botanist, Carl Linnaeus (1707-78), is best known for developing the classification of plants, but he expanded it and created a system of classifying humans. In so doing, he laid the foundation for other "researchers" to build on theories of classifying people according to race.

One notable person who expanded on the work, among others, was German anthropologist, Johann Fredrich Blumenbach, who, in 1775, developed a substantial racial construct of humans with the publication of his book, *Degeneres Humani Variegate Nativa (On the Natural Varieties of Mankind)*. The construct he formulated consisted of three races; Caucasoid (whites), Mongoloid (yellows) and Negroid (blacks) with Caucasoids being purposefully placed at the top of this fabrication. Every subsequent such construct has expanded upon this list. All of them, however, without exception, place the Caucasoid (whites) at the top of the construct, and the Negroid (blacks) decisively at the bottom of this racial invention. [1]

Blumenbach, and those after him, created a hierarchic construct based on contrived notions and outlandish opinions of race that were accepted and promoted as scientific research. The aim and the result appear to have been to develop a scientific rationalization for the imagined superiority of whites over all other races. He did not provide any credible evidence and therefore arrived at this conclusion devoid of any merit attributed to Caucasians. Up to that point in the history of the world, no other people had imagined, let alone invented, such a thing. No other people had ever thought to create and codify such an idea. While it is true, as I mentioned earlier, other groups of people may have considered themselves superior to others, but it was based on military might, culture, and other forms of meritorious achievements. None of them, however, had ever generated a classification of the races for the purpose of making themselves preeminent based on skin color alone and that again, without merit.

The racial constructs created by Linnaeus and Blumenbach served as the paradigm for how discussions surrounding racial identity and roles would be conducted for centuries to come. Their construct represents the beginning of a vile and destructive force in the world.

Within its creation were planted the seeds for the justification of the savagery against Black people, and by extension, other people of color. This brutality would be used to justify, sustain, promote, and maintain the existence of racism/white supremacy. But the brutality and savagery were not enough. They took it a step further and vilified us as no other branch of the human family has ever incurred in the history of the world.

How Our People Were Demonized

Almost sixty years after Blumenbach's publication, J.C. Nott & George Gliddon in their 1854 book, *Types of Mankind*, referred to the Khoikhoi people in Southern Africa with the offensive term Hottentot. Despite that, they went further by referring to them and virtually all Africans as monkeys and orangutans. According to them,

> *"...it is here that we find the lowest and most beastly specimens of mankind: viz., the Hottentot and the Bushman. The latter, in particular, are but little removed, both in moral and physical characters from the orangutan. They are not black, but of a yellowish-brown (tallow-colored, as the French term them), with woolly heads, diminutive statures, small ill-shape crania, very projecting mouths, prognathous faces, and badly formed bodies; in short, they are described by travellers [sic]as bearing a strong resemblance to the monkey tribe."* [2]

A little more than two decades prior to Nott and Gliddon's statement, a German philosopher admired by whites, Georg Wilhelm Hegel in a lecture in Berlin in 1831, made the following statement:

> *"… the Negro exhibits the natural man in his completely wild and untamed state… There is nothing harmonious with humanity to be found in this type of character… Africa should never be mentioned for it is not a historical part of the world…what we properly understand by Africa is the Unhistorical, Underdeveloped spirit, still involved in the conditions of mere nature…Africa had to be presented here only as on the threshold of the world's history…the Negro has no movement or development to exhibit."* [3]

None of the statements made by the above-mentioned men (who are highly respected by whites) provided a single piece of evidence supporting their claims. There were no facts, nor truths or verifications in what they declared. Despite that, their opinions took root and, through repetition, were spread far and wide throughout the white world as facts. In the end, their works represented deception, fraud, and wickedness. It is the writings of these men, and others like them over an extensive period, that helped spread the engrained belief that white-skinned people were superior to black people especially, and then to other people of color. Their ill-founded and ill-informed presumptions helped embed false impressions of us in the minds of everyone including our own people. The perception they embedded demonized us and designated us as inferior beings who were not deserving of treatment as humans. As a result of the perpetuation of their lies and false ideas, we have endured centuries of untold physical and psychological harm that continues unabated. [4]

Freeing A Demon - The Results of Their Works

The work of Linnaeus, Blumenbach, J.C. Nott and George Gliddon helped spawned false notions about Africa and its people. Those false notions were then replicated and repeated through books, pamphlets, newspapers, magazines, articles, journals, lectures, radio, television, and movies. These false notions gained ground not for their validity but more because of who repeated them. The lies are now broadcasted via the internet in ways never imagined. What follows are transcripts of statements made by very influential white men that helped spread the false idea that white people were superior and that we were inferior. They are just a small sample of derogative statements made for centuries against our people.

"It is impossible for us to suppose these creatures to be men, because, allowing them to be men, a suspicion would follow that we ourselves are not Christians."
— Montesquieu, Charles Louis de Secondat, French Philosopher, (1748)

"It is true that the centre [sic] *of the continent is filled with burning sands, savage beasts and almost uninhabited deserts. The scarcity of water forces the different animals to come together to the same place to drink. It happens that finding themselves together at a time when they are in heat, they have intercourse one*

with another, without paying regard to the difference between species. Thus [sic] are produced those monsters which are to be found there in greater numbers than in any other part of the world."
— Robert Hallet *(Geographer) The Penetration of Africa,* An African map published in Paris (1761)

"I am apt to suspect the Negroes [African] and all other species of men…to be naturally inferior to the white. There never was a civilized nation of any other complexion than white, nor even any individual eminent either in action or speculation. No ingenious manufactures amongst them, no arts, no sciences."
— Dave Hume, Scot philosopher "Of National Character," in his *Essay and Treaties* (1768)

"I advanced it, therefore, as a suspicion only, that the blacks, whether originally a distinct race or made distinct by time or circumstance, are inferior to the whites in the endowments of both body and mind."
—Thomas Jefferson, US President (1801-1809)

"Pass as severe laws as you will to keep these unfortunate creatures in ignorance. It is in vain unless you can extinguish that spark of intellect which God has given them… we have, as far as possible, closed every avenue by which the light might enter their mind; we have only to go one step further—to extinguish the capacity to see the light, and our work would be

completed; they would then be reduced to the level of the beast of the field, and we should be safe."
—Henry Berry, Virginia House of Delegates (1832)

"We come among the Africans as members of a superior race and servants of a government that desires to elevate the more degraded portions of the human family."
—Dr. David Livingstone (1813 - 1873)

"The study of the Negro is the study of man's rudimentary mind. He would appear rather a degeneracy from the civilized man than a savage rising to the first step, were it not for his total incapacity for improvement..."
—Richard Burton, Explorer & Writer (1821-1890)

"A Black skin means membership in a race of men which has never created a civilization of any kind. There is something natural in the subordination of an inferior race even to the point of enslavement of the inferior race..."
—John W. Burgess (1844-1931) Columbia University "Scholar"

"I have no purpose to introduce political and social equality between the white and black races...There is a physical difference between the two which, in my judgment, will probably forever forbid their living

*together upon the footing of perfect equality;… and I,
as much as any man, am in favor of having the
superior position assigned to the white race."*
—Abraham Lincoln, US President, Debate with
Stephen Douglass (1858)

*It is now quite plain to me — as the shape of his head
and the way his hair grows also testify — that he is
descended from the negroes who accompanied Moses'
flight from Egypt (unless his mother or paternal
grandmother interbred with a nigger). Now, this blend
of Jewishness and Germanness, on the one hand, and
basic negroid stock, on the other, must inevitably give
rise to a peculiar product. The fellow's importunity is
also nigger -like.*
—Karl Marx, Letter to Friedrich Engels (1862)

*"Almost all civilized people belong to the white race.
The people of other races have remained savage or
barbaric, like the men of prehistoric times."*
—Charles Seignobos (1854-1942) University of Paris
History of Ancient Civilization

*"When we Westerners call people 'Natives,' we
implicitly take the cultural color out of our perceptions
of them. We see them as trees walking, or as wild
animals infesting the country in which we happen to
come across them. In fact, we see them as part of the
local flora and fauna, and not as men of like passions*

with ourselves, and seeing them thus as something
infra-human, we feel entitled to treat them as though
they did not possess ordinary human rights."
—Arnold Toynbee (1889-1975)

"Having demonstrated that the Negro and Caucasian
are widely different in characteristics, due to a
deficiency in the Negro brain, a deficiency that is
hereditary…we are forced to conclude that it is useless
to try to elevate the Negro by education or otherwise."
—Dr. Robert Bennett Bean "Some Racial Peculiarities
of the Negro Brain" Journal of Anatomy, Sept. 1906,
Anthropologist and descendant of Thomas Jefferson

"Africa had no history before the coming of the
Europeans. History only begins when men take to
writing. And since Africa had no knowledge of writing,
information on African History could be found only in
material remains, in language and in primitive culture.
These are the concerns of linguists, archaeologists and
anthropologists and not the concern of historians."
—Professor A. P. Newton (1923)

"When we classify mankind by color, the only one of
the primary races…which has not made a creative
contribution to any of our twenty-one civilizations is
the black race."
—Arnold Toynbee (1889-1975) From A Study of
History (1934)

"The Negro is a child, and with children nothing can be done without the use of authority. With regard to the Negroes then, I have coined the formula: I am your brother, it is true, but your elder brother."
—Albert Schweitzer, MD, On the Edge of Primeval Forest (1961)

"Nowadays, undergraduates demand that they should be taught African History. Perhaps in the future, there will be some African History to teach. But at the present there is none; there is only the history of the Europeans in Africa. The rest is darkness, and darkness is not a subject of history… The present world is one that is dominated by European techniques, European examples, and European ideas. It is these, which have shaken the non-European world out of its past, out of barbarism in Africa. The history of the world, for the last five centuries, in so far as it has significance, been European history. The study of history, must therefore, be Europa-centric. We cannot, thus, afford to amuse ourselves with the unrewarding gyrations of barbarous tribes in picturesque but irrelevant corners of the globe."
— Professor Trevor Roper (1963)

"Whites are more intelligent than Negroes; intelligence is overwhelmingly the result of genetic inheritance rather than environmental influence…"

—Arthur Jensen, University of Berkeley, Psychologist, Saturday Review Magazine (May 17, 1969)

"Since Negro intelligence is naturally…low…let's give blacks cash incentives not to breed."
—William B. Shockley, Stanford University, The National Review Magazine, "Lesser Breeds" (December 7, 1973)

"…savages, including the whole Negro race, should on account of their low mentality and unpleasant nature, be painlessly exterminated."
—Professor Raymond Bernard Cattell, British & American Psychologist (1905-1998)

"America's blacks could only marginally benefit from federal programs because 'blacks are genetically inferior to whites'."
—Richard Nixon according to a top advisor, John D. Ehrlichman (New York Times, Friday, December 11, 1981)

"It's not that the dedication is less. In fact, it's greater. They lack the intellectual capacity to succeed, and it's taking them down the tubes…one of the best things (slave traders) did for you was to drag your ancestors over here in chains."

> —William K. Coors, Adolph Coors Brewing Co. Told
> to a group of minority business owners attending a
> seminar (Jet Magazine April 19, 1984)

> *"Today's young players should lynch Tiger Woods in a*
> *back alley."*
> —Kelly Tilghman, Anchor for the Golf Channel
> (2008)

These statements represent the substance of racism/white supremacy. The significance they have in dehumanizing us and our rich and beautiful past is nothing short of demonic. They are inhumane, savage, and wicked statements. They were statements meant to destroy us, demolish us, ruin us, and kill us. We must never forget this. These words and these people represent the sentiments of those who are racist/white supremacists. Those who elevate, uplift, admire, endorse, commend, approve, applaud or praise them and their words are also racist/white supremacists. It matters not how much they attempt to evade the obvious racism of these people. Their attempts to do so reveals the truth that they themselves are consciously or unconsciously attempting to excuse and justify their own racist/white supremacist thinking.

The following explanation by writer and deep thinker, Neely Fuller, Jr., sums up the matter.

> *"At some point in the past, an effective number of persons classified as "white" began promoting the idea of dominating all of the "non-white" people of the known universe, entirely on the basis of "color" and/or factors "associated with" color."*

"These persons developed ways and means of establishing the domination through trial and error, based primarily, on the use of deceit and violence. The skillful use of these methods proved to be totally effective in dominating all of the non-white people of the known universe, in all of the Nine Major Areas of (People) Activity, including economics, education, entertainment, labor, law, politics, religion, sex, and war." [sic] [5]

But What Happens When…?

Given this elaborate fabrication concocted and believed by generations of white people, what happens when white people encounter non-white people who have more advanced and superior cultures? Asked another way: What did white people who claimed color superiority do when they met non-white people who were demonstratively superior to them? According to the historical record, they did one of two things. They either (1) laid claim to those cultures and the achievements associated with them. Or (2) they destroyed and/or distorted the records of those cultures and killed the people who might contest their bogus claims.

First, let's look at number one. Many whites, especially some scholars, have claimed that the accomplishments of the western Sudan empires of Ghana, Mali, and Songhai were the achievements of someone other than our ancestors who lived there. They have claimed that the achievement of the magnificent enclosure in Zimbabwe was the result of someone other than our people who lived there for thousands of years. In those cases, and others, they suggest that mysterious groups of white people were in fact responsible for those, and other achievements found in our traditional lands.

Many parts of Africa's history and cultural achievements have been claimed by Europeans as belonging to their ledger of achievements, but none stands out as a more excellent example of their thievery than that of ancient Egypt. The accomplishments of this African civilization are mind-boggling and without parallel. It is one of Africa's quintessential civilizations representing the greatest achievements of black people and continues to influence humanity like no other civilization before or after. It clearly towers above European achievements and stands as an unequivocal challenge to all notions of white people's superiority. But white historians and scholars have claimed, without evidence and in the face of an abundance of proof to the contrary, that the Ancient Egyptians were white people.

As an example, the following words of the American Egyptologist, James H. Breasted claimed that the origin and development of the ancient Egyptian civilization belonged to what he called the "Great White Race":

> *On the south of the northwest quadrant lay the teeming black world of Africa, separated from the Great White Race by an impassable desert barrier, the Sahara, which forms so large a part of the southern Flatlands. Thus, isolated and at the same time unfitted by ages of tropical life for any effective intrusion among the white race, the Negro and Negroid peoples remained without any influence on the development of early civilization. We may then exclude both these external races—the straight-haired, round-headed, yellow-skinned*

Mongoloids on the east, and the woolly-haired, long-necked, dark-skinned Negroids on the south — from any share in the origins or subsequent development of civilization. [6]

This is typical of statements found in textbooks during Breasted s life as well as in many current textbooks on the topic. Additionally, there are dozens of films about ancient Egypt where the inhabitants are depicted as white people rather than black people. And to further scrutinize his statement, the dictatorial nature of Breasted's assertion is equated only by the absence of any proof, verification, or corroboration. And because of this lack of evidence, he gets caught in his own contradiction by claiming, on one hand, that the Sahara has always separated Blacks from the Nile and, on the other hand, that this valley was their only road to the north. A glance at the map of Africa shows that our people could easily go from any point on the continent to the Nile Valley by; (1) not crossing the desert, (2) by walking right through the desert as our ancestors have done for hundreds and perhaps thousands of years, or (3) they could simply walk or build a boat, a canoe, or a raft and sail up the Nile River into Egypt.

What is even most revealing about Breasted assertion, as it is with most racist statements, is he provides no supporting evidence of when, where, and how this "Great White Race" arrived on the continent of Africa. Lastly, the African character of Egyptian civilization, as recognized today in reputable circles, rules out any possibility that this civilization was monopolized by the white race. But Breasted's account of this matter, and others like him, has been accepted and repeated far and wide as fact for almost a century.

Regarding point number two, the destruction of the libraries by both Europeans and their Arab allies is well documented. It may be seen in the destruction of knowledge in Egypt, Ethiopia, Carthage, the Congo, eastern Africa, the Western Sudanese empires of Ghana, Mali, and especially the Songhai empire all of which represented hundreds, if not thousands, of years of accumulated knowledge by our people. [7] The same destruction and obliteration of knowledge can be seen on the continents of Australia, and North and South America. The extent to which white people have gone to destroy any competing cultures that would rival, challenge, or refute their claims of racial superiority has known no limits.

imposition

When I was an undergraduate student at Essex County College in Newark, New Jersey, I majored in music. One of the courses required of music majors was a class in music appreciation. It was a class that should be more appropriately titled Appreciation of White People's Music. That's because the only body of music we were given to appreciate was European classical music from various time periods of European history. There was no appreciation of African music, Indian music, nor Asian music, only European music. This included music by Mozart, Beethoven, Bach, Handel, etc.

The reality of this did not dawn on me until on one occasion when I mentioned to the instructor, an older white man, that I had plans of attending a music concert over the weekend to see one of the popular acts that was coming to the area. It was to complete a written assignment which he had given the class of a music appreciation experience. He asked who it was I intended to see. I told him it was Teddy Pendergrass. He gave me a condescending look with a dismissive wave of his hand and said, *"That's not REAL music, you know. It's not going to help your music career. I'll read your paper but don't expect that it will fulfill the requirement."* I was baffled by his comments and asked what if I went to see James Brown? *"Same thing,"* he said. *"It's not real music."*

Although I was a little baffled and slightly offended at his response, I didn't understand the racist gravity of what he was saying until much later. He had declared that the music I grew up listening to and loved, music by black people, was not really music that held appreciative musical qualities. The only "real" music, as he and the western academy saw it, was music done by white people. It is still the same today with minor modification in attempts to appear egalitarian. For example, white people have attempted to usurp the intellectual space on everything. The result is that when classical music is mentioned, there is no attempt to clarify whose classical music is in view. It is assumed that only those of European descent have classical music. No one else.

Chapter 5

White People's Fantasy World

AS WE HAVE SEEN, racism/white supremacy is a concept that is the creation of the European world that was imposed on us and the rest of the world. But why? What was its purpose then and what is its purpose now? What is the end game of racism/white supremacy and what should we know about it as a people? When we can begin to grasp this concept, our understanding and approach to the matter should be altered for the better.

The purpose of racism/white supremacy is an attempt to elevate white people to an imaginary position of superiority. The continuation of racism/white supremacy helps maintain that elevated and imaginary position of superiority. Its role is to make white people feel superior to all others especially to black people. The converse role is to make black people, and other people of color, feel inferior. Armed with this skewed and distorted perception of themselves along with the invention of the gun, it was used by white people to help them gain control of the economic resources of Africa and the resources of the rest of the world that they invaded outside Europe. The question then becomes...

How Did They Do This?

An example of how they accomplished this may be seen in how white people tend to write about, speak about, or portray their ancestors. In books and other media, they refer to their early ancestors who went to Africa, the Americas, Australia and parts of Asia as settlers and explorers. They taught, and in most cases forced others to digest this and other such white supremacist ideas through their educational, religious, and media systems. As a result, we as a people have been indoctrinated through these systems to view white people as superior and ourselves as inferior. Given the nature of the systems, it could not be otherwise. That system is designed to give them an air of decency, honorability, and nobleness. But what it does is distract our people from a very simple and clear truth, that their ancestors invaded our lands, murdered us, and enslaved our people. They were not settlers. They were invaders, marauders, looters, and thieves.

Stepping outside of the indoctrination would allow us to think logically. We would ask, for example, how does someone, uninvited, settle into someone else's house? You don't. Imagine if someone, whom you did not invite, barged into your house, took over the house, and killed most of your family members. Would you consider them as settlers? Of course not! It would be absurd, illogical, and unreasonable. Yet, we have been taught to believe that white people who came uninvited to Africa, the Americas, and Australia were simply explorers and settlers rather than thieves, invaders, and murderers. It is a fact, by any reasonable measure, and fully documented in their books that they were invaders, thieves, and killers. They were not settlers, but euphemistically refer to themselves as such.

Additionally, when the people whom they invaded resisted their advances, they were either killed or enslaved. The invaders then labeled us and other people of color, whom they invaded, as savages and heathens. By hiding behind the cloak of respectable sounding names such as settlers and explorers, white people have conferred upon themselves and their history an unmerited air of virtue and decency. When this scheme is understood, all declarations and proclamations of their alleged superiority become empty and allows us to see them without the security of smoke and mirrors that blind and misguide us. By using terms such as settlers and explorers instead of invaders, thieves, or murderers we witness a gigantic cover-up of the insidious, barbaric, and heinous acts resulting from racism/white supremacy. Their systems of education, religion, and media help teach and solidify those claims in both their minds and ours.

Through military might, religious subjugation, depravity and violence, white people were not only able to gain control of the resources of those they encountered in Africa, Asia, and the Americas, but they also destroyed those cultures, traditions, and histories. They later either rewrote, eliminated, or falsified the histories and replaced the histories and cultures of those people with a series of vicious lies. In the case of our people, Africans, they went so far as to create lies which claimed that our people were not even human beings. Recall, for example, the words of the European philosopher George Wilhelm Hegel, previously mentioned, who said the following of African people:

> *"There is nothing harmonious with humanity to be found in this type of character...Africa should never be mentioned for it is not a historical part of the world."*

Hegel is an indispensable pillar of European educational thought. His philosophy facilitated the foundations of the educational system as we know it today. The weight of his words and his influence on tens of thousands of decision makers are woven into the fabric of western (white) thought and institutions. In other words, if you take him out of the equation of the educational system that exists today, it would be significantly crippled.

Another, among many, who told vicious lies about our people is a Columbia University "scholar," John W. Burgess who said, *"Black skin means membership in a race of men which has never created a civilization of any kind."* He clearly did not know or pretended not to know anything regarding the great civilizations of Kush, Kemet (Egypt), ancient Ghana, Mali, Songhai, and Segu all African civilizations, some of which predated Europe by thousands of years. Ironically, Burgess fought on the Union side of the American Civil War, yet he held these beliefs about our people.

While white people, using the doctrine of racism/white supremacy, dismantled and disfigured the history of Africa and our people, they endeavored to enlarge and falsify their own history. For example, they placed themselves in historical places that predate their emergence on the stage of world history. In so doing, they have painted themselves as heroes and heroines of everything good and right. They have attempted to give themselves special importance when and where they have no importance because they were not in those places at the time. They have credited themselves with accomplishments created by others whom they classified as savages, heathens, or worse. As it relates directly to us, they invaded Africa, kidnapped, and enslaved our ancestors using their military might, deception, and sadistic violence. They then rewrote the history of the world leaving African Civilizations out of the equation. African heroes and heroines, in some cases, were made to have white skin as seen with Egyptian civilization. In other places, Arabs and Europeans are credited with African achievements, not Africans.

This rewriting of history, as they believed, would ensure that we would view ourselves as inferior and would ultimately neutralize us giving whites a sustained degree of security and would place them at center stage. It was designed to cripple us economically, mentally, politically, militarily, socially and to circumscribe us physically. Former assistant Secretary to the U.S. Department of Commerce and author, Dr. Claud Anderson, puts it in perspective when he asserts,

> *"The sole purpose of racism is to support and ensure that the White majority and its ethnic subgroups continue to dominate and use Blacks as a means to produce wealth and power. Centuries of Black enslavement and Jim Crow semi-slavery resulted in the majority society becoming 99-foot giants and Blacks one-foot midgets. This massive inequality in wealth and resources made Blacks non-competitive and totally dependent upon Whites for the necessities of life. True racism exists only when one group holds a disproportionate share of wealth and power over another group then [Sic]uses those resources to marginalize, exploit, exclude and subordinate the weaker group. In America, it is Whites who use wealth and power to marginalize, exploit, and subordinate Blacks."[1]*

To Dr. Anderson's cogent assessment, I would only add that the behavior he describes goes beyond the borders of America extending throughout the globe.

Once crippled as such, we would pose no challenge or threat to the well-being of whites as they pillaged, killed, and looted without restraint. It would later enable them to build institutions and create a twisted and perverse logic to cover it all up with lies and weak justifications. At the same time, it gave whites a head-start to position themselves for control using our economic resources and the resources of other people of color. This was done in North America, South America, Central America, Australia, and in Africa. The genocide of the North, South and Central American populations gave resourced-poor Europe access to unimagined accumulation of assets consisting of land and riches.

The same can be said regarding the genocide of the original people of Australia by Europeans. Africa, however, represented the motherlode in both unlimited and untold land, minerals, diamonds, gold, and a myriad of other riches, but none was more valuable than the kidnapping and the psychological damage done to Africa's greatest resource—the people. We the people, African people, Black people along with the vast amounts of knowledge we had accumulated over millennia, helped position Europeans/white people to ultimately gain control of the world. This was accomplished by enslaving us and provided them with hundreds of years of free labor that lifted them out of relative obscurity and poverty at our expense. Racism/white supremacy enabled and sanctioned the entire enterprise.

In summary, the purpose of racism is to elevate white people to an imaginary position of superiority. It has been used to justify the mistreatment of African peoples as they were conquered, raped, and pillaged in their home countries and as they were kidnapped and forced into enslavement. Once this precedence was set, racism was used incessantly as a means of maintaining a social, political, economic, and psychological hierarchy where African/Black people were at the bottom. This allowed for the legalization of a detrimental state that worked for white people but worked against all other races.

Given this background, we must ask the question, how is it that we, black people, are now called racist in any capacity, under any circumstance, or any condition?

Part 2
Back Burner

liars

A few years ago, I saw a television commercial that made my blood boil. It contained short clips of ethnically diverse people and of different genders, including black people. They were uttering words to the following effect, *"We are all responsible for racism and we must all help solve it."* I stood up and yelled, "HELL NO!" at the television. Here is why.

I was raving because the commercial was telling a blatant lie. It was instilling the idea that all people are racist and responsible for racism. It helped spread the untrue idea that the targets of racism are just as guilty of racism as the perpetrators and that the victims are equally as responsible for solving the problem. This and other ahistorical racial messages have created much confusion. We, African people, have been fighting against racism/white supremacy for centuries both on the continent of Africa and in the diaspora. That was the legacy of Nzingha, Shaka, Lumumba, Tubman, Garvey, Nkrumah, Kenyatta, King, Parks, Malcolm X, and countless others. They were fighting against it then and we are still fighting against it as I write this. So, how is it that we get labeled as racist?

Chapter 6

Remember: We Are Not The Racists

I NEVITABLY IT HAPPENS. WHETHER in my classes, listening to a news program, or if I'm engaged in discussions about racism, someone makes the statement that "Blacks are racist, too." Or they will ask the question, "Are Black people racist?" In either case, it is evident that they are confused about the meaning of racism because when the meaning of the term is understood, as I explained earlier, such statements and questions become irrelevant and quite frankly, unintelligent. Additionally, it insults our intelligence. But the question remains, "Are Black People Racist?"

There is a danger in allowing discussions of more than one definition of what racism is or is not. It opens the door for whites and their cronies to point the finger at other racial groups as practicing racism when those groups have historically been the targets and victims of racism/white supremacy. To say that we, black people, are racist, whether by whites or even those of our own kind, is absurd and is the ultimate epitome of an attempt at deception. The same can be said regarding the contrived and ludicrous phase "reverse racism" that became vogue a few years ago. Both are preposterous.

By way of comparison, no one in their right mind would conclude or accept the idea that a woman who has been raped is just as guilty of the crime as the one who raped her. All too often, women who have been raped have been equated with having as much to do with being raped as does the rapist. Words are twisted to construe that she is the perpetrator of her own rape! She is seen as being just as guilty as the rapist. It's often pointed out that if she were not in the situation, or if she had not been wearing a certain type of clothes, or if she had been more careful about how much alcohol or drugs she consumed, it would not have happened. Such justifications for blaming the victim are well known in rape cases and those same justifications are not only flawed, illogical, and incorrect but they demonize rape victims while normalizing the rapist.

This same distorted logic is exactly what we are expected to accept as logical, coherent, and truthful when we hear it said that black people are racist, or that black people can be racist. It is assumed that we as the victims and target of racism/white supremacy are somehow responsible for perpetrating it.

Let's Set the Record Straight

The simple fact of the matter is this: we are not racist and have never been racist. Additionally, other people of color are not racist either and have never been racist. The answer to the question of whether we are racist is an unequivocal NO. The definition of the term and the historical record confirms this and argue against such a conclusion. What many, in error, often identify as racism in our people is in fact our response to racism not the practice or instigation of racism. On this point, author Claud Anderson correctly concludes that,

> *"Black people cannot be racists. No group of Blacks has the power or exclusive control of resources to the degree that they can educationally, politically, economically, and socially exploit and marginalize the White race. Blacks can only react to racism and try to alter the conditions that racism creates…Blacks have a reason for their feelings about Whites based on how they have been treated by Whites. The White race, on the other hand, has never been marginalized by the Black race."* [1]

The crime of racism was committed against us and is still being committed against us, not the reverse. The expansive and exhaustive works of Dr. Paula Rothenberg, out of many others who have written on this topic for decades, points out that we, black people, may be prejudice against white people but that is not racism. This is what she says on the matter.

> *"While an individual person of color may discriminate against white people or even hate them, his or her behavior or attitude cannot be called "racist." He or she may be considered prejudiced against whites, and we may all agree that the person acts unfairly and unjustly, but racism requires something more than anger, hatred, or prejudice; at the very least, it requires prejudice plus power. The history of the world provides us with a long record of white people holding power and using it to maintain that power and privilege over people of color, not the reverse."* [2]

Author and scholar, Dr. Molefi K. Asante, has said this on the question:

> *"The language of the exploiter is vile, corrupt, and vulgar. For him racism is non-existent because it is not merely discrimination or pragmatically the inequality of opportunity. We cannot permit this easy slide into exploitative rhetoric. There is no such thing as black racism against whites; racism is based on fantasy; black views of whites are based on facts."* [3]

Author, Joel Kovel, agrees with Asante and states that "racism is a set of fantasies." Regarding whether we can be racist or not, Kovel adds:

> *"But whatever black people may do in the way of a racism response, there is no such thing as black racism. The response is to white racism and is part of its unfolding dialectic. There can be no black racism so long as the dominant institutions of Western society are shaped according to white interests and organized symbolically about whiteness...it remains White racism, and its primary object is the black, for the basic reason that it arose out the enslavement of millions of Africans over three centuries. Our racism is white because our social production came so extensively out of enslaved black bodies."* [4]

Kovel also acknowledges that we black people cannot escape the whiteness of society except by denying who we are which is not an actual escape. With respect to this idea of us escaping our blackness, Kovel asserts the following:

> *"It does not matter if he makes a million dollars a year for leaping high above a ten-foot basket; or accumulates many more millions by selling records; or constitutes a technical-professional elite in a city like Atlanta; or even gets to sit on the board of directors of truly white corporations, or in the Cabinet or Supreme Court—he, or she, will still be defined by an order whose power and dominion are white."* [5]

Racism is not my problem nor is it "our" problem as Black people. We, like a raped woman, have been and continue to be the targets of racism. Racism is a white people problem. Kovel correctly lays the blame of racism at the feet of white people when he stated:

> *"The White Problem is… the problem of those children of history who created the situation of racism and therefore bear responsibility for it."* [6]

These assertions clearly put the blame of racism at the doorsteps of whites and makes it illogical and ahistorical to suggest that black people can be racist. Barbara Trepangnier confirms the point as she discusses the everyday racism practiced by whites in what she has identified as silent racism when she says,

> *"Ignoring racism that is not hateful and intentional effectively hides the fact that white people daily perform acts of everyday racism."* [7]

Her statement also inadvertently, but correctly, places the blame of racism on whites and not on black people. On this topic, clinical psychologist, Dr. Bobby Wright, has said,

> *"... it is very clear that at this point in time Blacks cannot be racists because of their lack of power to oppress anybody; White, Indians, Chinese, etc."* [8]

Racism is what we as a people have endured at the hands of white people. White people are the racists and the only racists. In the history of the world, there is no other group of people who has ever made such a claim and then created an economic, political, social, military, and religious system to solidify and practice it except those who classify themselves as whites. You will not find such a belief or practice anywhere in the long history of the African world, the Indian world, the Chinese, Japanese, or Korean world. No people of color anywhere on the planet in my research have ever made such a claim or created a system reflecting such a claim except white people.

But where you do have instances of what might be called racism by us is a response to it and/or the negative impact it has had and continues to have on us. As mentioned earlier, other societies have made claims of superiority about their culture but not about skin color superiority. Those other claims of superiority were made based on some meritorious accomplishment. We and everyone else who is not white have been the expressed target and victims of white people's racist behavior. That simple fact sums up the meaning and reality of racism. For whites, and the misinformed among us, to then turn the table and say that we, or anyone other than whites, are racist is pure fiction and the ultimate insult. It is just as insulting to claim that a woman is just as guilty of rape as the one who raped her.

What About Light Skin Versus Dark Skin In Our Community?

What about those other than whites who do practice some form of what appears to be racism? It is correctly known as infra-racism—racism practiced within a group against themselves. What it is and what we see, and experience is all part of the aftermath of racism inflicted upon us by whites. What we see is a response or the results that have occurred on account of the condition of racism/white supremacy. In other words, those who practice this are like a person who after having been held as a hostage for a long period of time eventually takes on the characteristics of their kidnappers and even identifies with their kidnappers. It has more recently been classified as the Stockholm Syndrome. The literature on the psychological impact of being held hostage is plentiful. [9]

There is an interesting thing about studies and discussions around the Stockholm Syndrome. Rarely, if ever, is it applied to what happened to us—the longest kidnapped victims in the history of the world. It is never employed as an attempt to understand our situation or more correctly what our ancestors endured as kidnapped hostages. The trauma to the first and the subsequent generations who also endured the continued abuse for a few hundred years has no parallels in recorded history. Despite that, the definition and the results of the syndrome have much in common with our experience. I would, in fact, argue that we are exhibit A of the symptoms that embody the Stockholm Syndrome. According to an abstract on the topic from the National Criminal Justice Reference Service (NCJRS), the following is concluded:

> *"The Stockholm Syndrome is the positive bonding that hostages often develop with their captors. This bonding may be the result of an effort to deal with the anxiety and stress caused by being taken captive. The body goes through three stages in its reaction to stress: alarm, resistance, and exhaustion. Constantly facing a hostile and uncontrollable environment may lead to helpless and self-defeating behavior and ultimately to depression. Society cannot prevent all kidnappings or hostage incidents, but brief intervention with victims and their families may prevent or control lifelong difficulties. Counseling and the offer of psychological assistance and information for victims, employers, and their families are increasingly regarded as essential parts of the response to hostage and kidnapping incidents. Family members and employers should be prepared for the victim's reactions. Victims themselves need confidential counseling that is separate from the effort to gather evidence."* [10]

White society can clearly see the need for psychological assistance in those instances of the syndrome as pertaining to themselves. What is interesting regarding the indispensable need for counseling and psychological assistance for victims of kidnapping is that white people cannot see, nor do they apply the concept to the trauma we have endured. There has never been any such counseling or psychological assistance provided for our ancestors who were "set free" from hundreds of years of bondage and abuse at the hands of whites. Neither have the subsequent generations of the enslaved descendants been offered counseling or psychological assistance. The fact that our ancestors who were "freed" after the American Civil War were not given any counseling or psychological therapy after generations of bondage and abuse is reflected in some of the ongoing dysfunctionality evident in our communities today. Clinical psychologist, Na'im Akbar, notes that,

"There is a certain hesitation about dwelling on events of the past. On the one hand, it creates an atmosphere of determinism which removes the volitional possibilities of people to alter their condition. It tends to excuse the perpetuation of past events which could be altered simply by initiative. It preoccupies people unnecessarily and purposelessly with old hurts, tending old wounds. It is an emotional tirade that ultimately provides no constructive solutions for the present. But those who deny the lessons of the past are doomed to repeat it. Those who fail to recognize that the past is a shaper of the present, and the hand of yesterday continues to write on the slate of today, leave themselves vulnerable by not realizing the impact of influences which do serve to shape their lives." [11]

Speaking to the kidnapping and enslavement of our ancestors, Akbar reveals that,

> *"The tales of this period of our history are so morbid that they will arouse vehement hostilities at the very thought of what occurred. The level of cruelty was incomparable to anything recorded in modern history, including the Nazi atrocities at Auschwitz which were fleeting and direct, destroying bodies, but essentially leaving the collective mind intact. The protracted and intensive atrocities of slavery have had a lingering effect, and the pain of times past continues to call out from the genetic memories of those whose ancestors survived the test of slavery."* [12]

Lastly, Akbar observes that,

> *"As cruel and painful as chattel slavery was, it could be exceeded only by a worse form of slavery...The slavery that captures the mind and imprisons the motivation, perception, aspiration, and identity in a web of anti-self images, generating a personal and collective self-destruction, is more cruel than the shackles on the wrists and ankles. The slavery that feeds on the psychology, invading the soul of man, destroying his loyalties to himself and establishing allegiance to forces which destroy him, is an even worse form of capture."* [13]

In this last statement, Akbar pinpoints the problem that some of us have when we insist that we are racist. Rather than recognizing that our behavior is a response to racism, we erroneously conclude that we are racist. Those who fall into this trap exhibit anti-self-images of ourselves and destroy our loyalties to ourselves. Additionally, it inadvertently plays into the hands of racists/white supremacists by absolving them of the indictment that they are the racists and not us.

The following words of South African writer, Sobuantu Mzwakal, sums up the question of whether we are racist or not. He says,

> *"Black people can never be racist – we never had the tools or power to institutionalise [sic] racial oppression. The exclamation of such bigotry that blacks are also racist is incited both by white arrogance and ignorance. A subjugated group cannot be racist – they can only be prejudicial. The colour [sic] of my skin does not discount me from being racist, but the very society that we as blacks find ourselves in – where we are automatically inferior due to the continuous systemic support of white privilege – discounts us from being racist. Due to the fact that we find ourselves in this inferior position, it is impossible for us to be racist."* [14]

White people are the racists. We are not the racists. These two statements cannot be said loud enough nor too often. Any deviation from these two facts is dishonest. The acceptance of them are the first two steps towards resolving the issue of racism.

rude

The class was small with only nine or ten students. We sat around a
large square table. The professor would sit at the head of the table. I
was one of two African Americans in the class. To protect his
identity, I'll call the other African American student Ralph. This was
a Biblical Aramaic class at Princeton Theological Seminary.
Admittedly, we were an elite class of students who had survived the
rigors of several Biblical Greek and Hebrew language classes. Most
students at the seminary didn't even take basic Greek or Hebrew let
alone the advance classes in language studies. But we had taken the
basic and advance courses, and this was the pinnacle of those
studies.

It became clear very early on in the class that the professor had
racist assumptions about me and Ralph. One of them was that he
thought we should not be in such a class. Despite the evidence of our
transcripts which clearly showed we were more than qualified for the
class, he would ignore us. And when I say ignore us, I mean he
literally acted as if we were not there. On several occasions, if we
raised our hands in response to a question he asked, he would
deliberately look at us and then call on one of the white students. It
didn't happen all the time, but it happened enough for us to know it
was not an oversight. If we approached him at the end of class to get
clarification about something, we would get terse responses that
bordered on rudeness. It was designed to make us appear as if we

were stupid for asking questions. When the white students would ask questions, he was the most affable and kindest person you ever wanted to meet, a complete Jekyll to Hyde transformation and suddenly a virtual walking encyclopedia of information and assistance.

I recalled seeing this professor and a few students from the class congregating in the cafeteria. Thinking nothing of it, I decided to go over to the table and join them. This was not an uncommon practice for students to sit with professors during lunch discussing the class and other matters. However, as I walked toward the table ignorantly smiling, the professor turned and gave me a look that said: how dare you think about sitting at this table? It spoke volumes; loud and clear. I detoured and went to another table.

Ralph and I watched these displays of rejection knowing exactly what was happening. We knew what was at the root of it—racism. But we were basically helpless to do anything meaningful because there was no one to whom we could complain that would make a difference. And if we did, we feared it would appear that we were protesting that the work was too hard and that we would be perceived as wanting an easy way out. For us, that was completely out of the question! Ralph and I would talk about it and knew that if we were going to survive the class we needed to buckle down and really master this language.

The professor continued to throw monkey wrenches our way that would require us to readjust. For example, we would come to class having prepared to translate a particular section of which he had assigned only to find that he had changed the lesson. All the other students had received the "memo." We didn't. And so, at times, we were forced to sit through an entire class looking as if we were not studious enough to prepare for class.

These antics by the professor were not lost on a few of the other students whom we had befriended or knew from other classes. With their help we were kept in the loop. Without their help, he would have failed us. I say that because he tried to pull a fast one on us for the final exam. Again, we were told which passages of Aramaic we were expected to know for the exam. The only thing is that we were not given a few of the passages that the white students were told about. They shared that information with us. And because of their help, we passed the class. Without their help, we would have failed that class without a doubt. And it would have confirmed to that professor the validity of his racism.

The story of what Ralph and I encountered is not an unusual story. Every person (black person) who is reading this book almost without exception has a similar story of sorts. It's the kind of story where you encounter racist behavior that is so subtle and disguised that it's hard to put your finger on it. At least, where you can make a point about it because it's hard to prove and to do so seems almost petty. This is the kind of racist behavior that we encounter on a regular basis that white people claim they don't see. They don't hear about it because if we spent time on every racist act and behavior we encountered daily and weekly, we would get nothing else done.

Chapter 7

The Era of White Kidnappers

IT IS A WELL-KNOWN fact that Europeans enslaved our people. However, there is more to the story that has been deliberately left out. As the lands of Africa and the lands of other indigenous peoples with unlimited resources were being stolen by the Europeans, they began to model the Islamic-Arabic long-standing practice of enslaving African people. Ultimately, our ancestors were used as free labor to work and cultivate the lands the whites had stolen from the indigenous people of the Americas. But here's the other part of the story that gets swept under the rug, so to speak.

Before the kidnapping and enslaving of our ancestors, it is important to understand that white people first enslaved the indigenous people of the American continents—the so-called Indians. However, due to the excessive labor demanded of them, the insufficient diet, the white man's diseases, and their inability to adjust to this new abnormal way of life imposed upon them by the white invaders, the indigenous people rapidly succumbed. Since they proved to be unsuitable for sustained use as slaves due to their familiarity with the land and the resistance they posed by waging war against the invaders, the Europeans realized that another source of free or cheap labor would be necessary. For that source of free and cheap labor, they next turned to their own people, other whites.

In the end, Indian slavery, as the New England colonies saw it, was unprofitable because it was not suited to the diverse agriculture of the colonies. Additionally, it wasn't until after the decimation of the indigenous people's populations over a very short period that whites considered the idea of using Africans. That suggestion came from, of all places, a prominent member of the church when in 1517 Bishop Bartolomé de Las Casas suggested that our people be used to replace the so-called Indians.[1] But it must be noted that before this happened, the Chinese and the people of India were the options that were first considered. In the long run, that idea was dismissed due to the rigors of the long and hazardous sea journeys that would be involved. Thus, Africa and its people became the target primarily because of its proximity to the Americas. It had nothing to do with the supposed inferiority of African people—nothing. It had more to do with the prospect of cheap or free labor regardless of skin color.

White Slavery and Its Relationship To Racism Exposed

It will surprise most people to learn that the immediate successor of the so-called Indians for slave labor was not Africans but poor whites from Europe. These white slaves included a variety of types. Some were indentured servants who had signed contracts which stipulated service for a period agreed upon before leaving their homelands. They are the ones most often pointed to by whites when this subject comes up. That's because it's made to appear that white people were too good to be slaves. We shall see that this is not the case. Others known as redemptioners made arrangements with the ship captains to serve a period of time in return for their ride over to the so-called "New World." If they did not keep their end of the bargain, they were sold into slavery by the captain to the highest bidder.

More sources of white slave labor from Europe included kidnapping adults and children which became a regular source of business in places like London and Bristol. Adults would be made drunk with liquor and taken as hostages. Children were enticed with sweets and other goodies. Eric Williams tells us that captains of ships trading to Jamaica would visit places like the Clerkenwell House of Corrections and give intoxicating drinks to the girls who had been imprisoned there as disorderly, and "invite" them to go to the west Indies. By such trickery, husbands were induced to leave their wives and wives to leave their husbands. [2] The misery and oppression of the conditions, economic and political, of the Germanic states promoted the same types of enslavement of whites.

Perhaps the most telling source of white slavery was that of convicted criminals who were released from jails and sent to the so-called New World. This allowed much of Europe to rid itself of its convicted criminal populations. Proposals were made in 1664, which allowed all vagrants, rogues and idlers, murderers and petty thieves, gypsies and loose persons who visited unlicensed brothels to come to the "New World" as slave labor. Without these convicts, the early development of Australian colonies in the nineteenth century would have been impossible. The political and civil disturbance in England between 1640 and 1740 also augmented the supply of white slaves. [3]

In the United States, white people were slaves during the colonial period, after the revolutionary war, and during the entire period slavery existed in the United States. There is overwhelming evidence to support the fact that whites were still slaves in the U.S. as late as

1858 three years before the American Civil War. What follows is a brief sampling of the evidence supporting this claim.

The New York Gazette dated September. 4, 1732 carried this advertisement:

"Welshmen, Englishmen, Negroes, a Negro girl, and Cheshire cheese."

Incidentally, this was an advertisement on Wall Street in New York, which was the location of one of the first slave markets in the USA.

Gottlieb Mittelberger, who came to America in 1750, describes the plight of other whites making their way from Europe to Philadelphia. His description of these whites being sold into slavery, and in some cases indentured servitude, are as follows:

> *"When the ships have landed at Philadelphia after their long voyage, no one is permitted to leave them except those who pay for their passage or can give good security; the others, who cannot pay, must remain on board the ships till they are purchased, and are released from the ships by their purchasers. The sick always fare the worst, for the healthy are naturally preferred and purchased first; and so, the sick and wretched must often remain on board in front of the city for 2 or 3 weeks, and frequently die, whereas many a one, if he could pay his debt and were permitted to leave the ship immediately, might recover and remain alive."*

"The sale of human beings in the market on board the ship is carried out thus: Every day Englishmen, Dutchmen and High-German people come from the city of Philadelphia and other places, in part from a great distance, say 20, 30, or 40 hours away, and go on board the newly arrived ship that has brought them and offers for sale passengers from Europe, and select among the healthy persons such as they deem suitable for their business, and bargain with them how long they will serve for their passage money, which most of them are still in debt for." [4]

White children were not exempt from enslavement either. Regarding this, Gottlieb Mittelberger wrote the following: *"Many parents must sell and trade away their children like so many head of cattle."* He estimated that during the four years he was in Philadelphia, 25,000 of his compatriots [other whites] were sold into slavery. [5]

White slaves who ran away were advertised for in the newspapers. If caught, they were branded with the letter "R" for Runaway. Those who stole flour, meal and other foodstuffs had their ears clipped to distinguish them from other free whites. George Washington, America's first president, advertised for two of his white runaway slaves who worked on his plantation at Mount Vernon.

James O'Neal, writing about a sale of whites in 1826, made the following observation when he stated:

"A half a century had passed since the adoption of the Declaration of Independence which declared all men free and equal and yet the purchase of white flesh had not become extinct." [6]

But O'Neal reveals more about this white slavery than is currently acknowledged or admitted in school history books. He reveals that "the American colonies were regarded as a convenient dumping ground" for England's homeless populations who had become a "problem" for its ruling class. As a result, various proposals were made between the years 1661 and 1668 to the king for *"transporting to the American plantations all vagrants, rogues and idle persons… felons… and such as were convicted of petty larceny."*

In other words, these proposals were seen as a way for England, and by extension other European nations, to rid themselves of their criminal populations. O'Neal goes on to point out that,

> *"It was the poor wretches like these in England, Germany and other countries who were seized upon to provide white slave labor for the colonies."* [7]

Pointing to a historian whom he refers to as McMaster, O'Neal further unveils that *"The felons formed the great source of supply and had been sent over in very considerable numbers from the earliest days of colonization."*

What kind of numbers did he have in mind? O'Neal exposed that between 1650 and 1745, *"As many as four thousand are known to have been sent over to this country."*

He then informs us that a Maryland historian divulged…

> *"That up to the Revolution [American Revolution] twenty thousand came to that colony and half of them after 1750. Additionally, he says, "Another authority…*

asserts that between 1715 and 1775, ten thousand felons were exported from the Old Bailey Prison in London..." [8]

Lastly on this point, O'Neal reveals the following:

"When a ship laden with one to three hundred such persons arrived, we will say at Philadelphia, the immigrants, arranged in a long line, were marched at once to a magistrate and forced to take an oath of allegiance to the king or, later, to the United States, and then marched back to the ship to be sold. If a purchaser was not forthcoming . . . they were frequently sold to speculators who drove them, chained together sometimes through the country, from farm to farm, in search of a purchaser.

"The contract signed, the newcomer became in the eyes of the law a slave, and in both the civil and criminal code was classed with negro slaves and Indians...They were worked hard, were dressed in the cast-off clothes of their owners, and might be flogged as often as the master or mistress thought necessary. . .. Father, mother and children could be sold to different buyers...The only difference between these white slaves, sold in American ports, and the blacks was that the slavery of the whites was limited, and the blacks were slaves for life.

"The white slaves were sold in all the colonies…It may be said with truth that both black and white slaves formed the basis of the landed aristocracy of the colonies before and long after the Revolution. Yet this fact is suppressed by most historians in order that historic figures, who witnessed the auction of white laborers without a protest, and some of whom were interested in the traffic, might be glorified. It was a modified form of chattel slavery and admirably served the purposes of the classes who confiscated the land or inherited it from those who did. With the resources of life in their hands and whites and blacks held in servitude, the ruling classes had all the advantages that the masters of any age might wish." [9]

The sale of white orphans continued in New York as late as 1858, seven years before the end of the civil war. They were offered for sale in churches at $10 each. Congressman W. Jacobs writing in 1859, quotes an advertisement of these white children in the New York Journal of Commerce dated May 6, 1858. One sale is described as follows:

"The price of each slave was $10 each. The Free Church was then thrown open. The young females occupying the front seats in rows, some of them crying. Customers walked among the ranks with perfect coolness examining their condition one by one. As they found one suitable, they planked the cash and carried off the piece."

What Does This Have to Do With Racism/White Supremacy?

What this has to do with racism/white supremacy is that it reveals the hypocrisy of the belief and practice. It reveals how the doctrine of racism is a charade used by the wealthy to maintain their wealth without threat. Wealthy whites have, through the racism doctrine, convinced poor whites that their interests are the same when in fact they are not. But the poor whites, however unwittingly, capitulate to this chicanery and have become the accomplices against themselves and us. In other words, most of them have become victims of racism/white supremacy as much as we have. The difference is they are rewarded more handsomely for their surrender to it than we. Additionally, they have allowed themselves to become the battering ram by placing themselves as a buffer between us and against the rich white wealthy class. We, both blacks and poor whites, are given meaningless trinkets and gadgets by the wealthy class to keep us distracted.

While arguing that whites are superior to blacks, on the one hand, the record shows that what upstages the notions of white superiority is the accumulation of just enough wealth that allows both blacks and poor whites to reside at the lower realm of white supremacy with enough riches to think themselves above it. This gives them, these newly rich folks, a false sense of inclusion so that they continue to serve as buffer and defender of the wealthy class. The distinguishing factor that helps poor whites stay in their place is the delusion that because they are white in skin color, they are better than us—racism. They believe this as a fact of the divine order. It's been engrained and branded into their psyche.

Poor whites who live in Appalachia, for example, could proudly claim during the administration of President Barack Obama, that they "might not be president but at least they were not black." It did not matter that he was a Harvard graduate or that he was president of the prestigious Harvard Law Review. It mattered not that he had been a US Senator and a definitively dully twice elected President of the country. They still believed that, despite all those accomplishments, they were superior to him simply because of their white skin.

parade

It was only a few days before final exams. My final semester as a student at Princeton Theological Seminary in Princeton was coming to a welcomed end. I was enrolled in a class entitled World Religions Through World Literature.

The professor was conducting a review of the materials covered during the semester. He was standing in front of the class using a world map pointing to the various parts of the world that we had surveyed and the literature we had read from those places. As I watched him point to various parts of the world we had covered, I noticed that he was pointing everywhere on the map except Africa which was in the center of the map. He pointed to South America (skipping over Africa) and then to parts of Europe. He then moved to the so-called Middle Eastern area, to China and the Asian countries, and then to the Pacific islands and Australia.

It suddenly dawned on me with alarm that we had not covered any of the religions or literatures of Africa with its more than fifty countries. I turned to a fellow African American student and said, *"We didn't cover anything about Africa."* Her response was both succinct and dismissive as she grimaced and said, *"So?"* As if to ask why would we? It's not important. Then she asked, *"What's the point?"* Bewildered I replied, *"The class is supposed to be about World Religions through World Literature,"* with an emphasis on the word "world," thinking she would see my point. She responded with, *"It doesn't bother me as long as I graduate. Why are you all concerned?"*

I looked at her dumbfounded.

Something went silent in me, and a light came on. I looked back at the professor who was giving himself a tacit congratulatory pat on the back for what he thought was an expansive and inclusive presentation of materials. He did not have the faintest idea how racist the entire semester had been or that he had, by virtue of his education, engaged in a racist pedagogy.

As for me, in those few moments, I realized how not only that class but my entire education up until then had been nothing but a relentless exposure to the white people show. I was completing my master's degree at one of the most prestigious schools in the world and I knew absolutely nothing about Africa—home of my heritage. Something was drastically wrong with that. I also realized that all our people are subjected to this parade of whiteness from kindergarten to graduate school. The appalling thing is we don't realize that it's happening and most of us never even question it, because we send our children through the same racist system.

Chapter 8

What Happened To White People?

WHEN THE TOPIC OF racism is discussed, especially in the manner that I've presented it here, inevitably, someone will ask, "Are you saying that all white people are racist?" I reply in the words of an anonymous writer who made the following scrupulous observation, *"All white people are not racist, but all racists are white."*

Molefi K. Asante, Ph.D., has recognized that *"the condition of evil in whites is not inherent, but inherited through history and environment."*[1] The evil practiced by whites against our people was a result of the choices they have made and continue to make. It is, therefore, not our responsibility as African people to rehabilitate or even educate them on the topic. All too often when issues of race or racism emerge, we African people are tacitly appointed as the spokespersons. By some arbitrary means, we are viewed as the defacto to whom the responsibility falls of providing solutions to the so-called "race" problem. It's like asking a rape victim to be responsible for helping rehabilitate the rapist. In this setup white people are let off the hook and it makes it appear as if they have no responsibility for racism/white supremacy.

Believe it or not, the racism problem is not a racism problem but a white people's problem. As already noted earlier, it was created by whites, carried out by whites, and is carried on by whites. In any event, it is not our responsibility to help them come to the realization of the error of their ways. We have, for nearly five hundred years, attempted to do just that with minor results to show for the effort. They have little, if any, shame for their behavior in the world for the last five hundred years. During that time, we have relentlessly preached to them about the evils of racism, the inappropriateness of racism, and the deleterious ramifications of racism. But it has been as if we were speaking to blind people who could not see the disastrous impact racism/white supremacy has had on we African people. All our appeals have had virtually little impact and have, for the most part, fallen on deaf ears. When we think we have made some progress with one generation of white people, or with a region of the country or the world, or when there is some life defying event that makes it appear as though some progress in race relations is advancing, they inevitably revert. Their regression seems to be the default position on the matter. They tend to embrace the rhetoric and symbolism associated with diversity and equity, but seldom do they accept the substance.

And so, there is always that starting over that occurs due to lack of honesty when racism is discussed between the races. The integrity of the discussion is flawed because white people have the advantage of sabotaging the discourse as has ultimately been the historic case. Consequently, appeals to their moral sensitivity is not the wisest use of our time. Racism/white supremacy is a permanent social phenomenon. That fact, and it alone, is a difficult thing for us to accept and at the same time the source of much misery. It proves to be the one lesson we seem to fail repeatedly regardless of geographical location, economic status, religious affliction, or political bent. We do not wish to accept what five hundred years of historical experience shows us.

In order to better understand this point, it is imperative that we recognize the early historical development of Europeans to gain better insight into whom it is with which we're dealing.

How Did White People Become Racist?

The eminent Senegalese scholar, Cheikh Anta Diop, has posited the two-cradle theory. [2] The theory consists of a Southern Cradle representative of Africans (Blacks) and a Northern Cradle representative of Europeans (Whites). It explains why each group behaves in certain ways under certain conditions. He has pointed out how early African and European development provides evidence of historical realities that were shaped by environment and climatic conditions. That early development, in two different environments, shaped the instincts, temperament and values of each, and the environment determined those long-lasting characteristics found in each. It has nothing to do with race, inferiority, or superiority. As Diop characterized it, what we're dealing with is the accident of birth.

The Southern Cradle - Africa

The Southern Cradle is where African people developed (Blacks). Living there in an abundant, warm, salubrious environment would result in the development of us having a gentle, peaceful spirit and personality. Such an environment made it possible to develop relationships that resulted in understanding the value of other humans. Because of climatic conditions, African people did not stay inside their homes for extended periods of time. Instead, we intermingled with others in an open and free manner of exchange just for the sake of socializing or being with each other. Through this socializing element, we learned to relate to each other as human beings and came to understand and accept the value of other humans. We consequently developed an understanding for the equality of all people and that it was important to treat others morally and humanly. That development makes it difficult for us to accept the amoral and inhumane treatment we have received and continue to receive at the hands of white people. Because of African peoples optimistic perspective of life born out of our early development, we expect and anticipate that they will at some point change and conduct themselves morally and humanly. The historical record has shown this to be a flaw in our thinking.

The Northern Cradle - EuroAsia

The Northern Cradle is where European people developed (Whites). Forced to live in a cold, harsh, hostile environment with limited food resources would create in them a survivalist personality which focused on developing better weapons to kill food. The significant factor about this point is that such an environment made it difficult to develop relationships with other humans. The extremely cold weather forced them to spend vast amounts of time alone isolated in their caves. This forced seclusion, for the sake of survival, prevented and limited their social interactions. Consequently, living in an environment that restricted social interactions retarded their social skills. When they did emerge from their caves, it was usually to search for food. Any contact with other people was incidental and not of a social nature. The extent of those social interactions were outgrowths of searches for food. That being so, they began to associate economic interests as paramount to human interaction and that those economic interests mattered more than social relationships.

In other words, the climatic conditions prevented them from developing a healthy appreciation for other humans. That environment, due to the competition for limited resources, made it difficult for white people to develop a healthy understanding of human relationships. In the end, they developed a value for things over humans. Joel Kovel has termed this phenomenon as *thingification.* [3] Therefore, in their communities, humans were viewed as either an asset or a liability. If others could help them obtain more resources/things/items for survival, they were viewed as an asset. If others competed for those limited resources, they were viewed as a liability and therefore had to be neutralized or eliminated.

This isolation of white people from the rest of the world lasted for hundreds, if not thousands, of years. During that time the rest of the world, which was older to begin with, had matured and developed to such a degree that when the Europeans encountered them, they were dumbfound.

The Unexpected Consequence of European Isolation

The isolation that Europeans were forced to endure created an unexpected development that would later negatively impact the entire planet. Having been shut away from the rest of the world in a cold, harsh, and unfriendly environment, forced them to develop better methods of hunting in order to survive. Over time they became highly proficient in hunting and their skill sets of building better weapons for that end improved dramatically. Ultimately, the gun became the apex weapon in that development. While it is known in most circles that the Chinese had used gunpowder for hundreds of years prior to the Europeans, they had not used it for destructive purposes especially in destroying human lives. That is a development that can be attributed to white people.

In any event, they (whites) would first use those weapons on each other as a means of eliminating their economic competitors. When they moved beyond their geographical confines, they stumbled upon a much bigger world that was culturally more advanced than them; a world that was much older than them; and a world that contained an abundance of resources they never imagined existed. Christopher Columbus in speaking of the indigenous people of the Americas pointed out in his diary that, *"they are destitute of arms, which are entirely unknown to them... they are very guileless and honest, and very liberal of all they have."* [4] This was the case of not only the people that Europeans met in the Americas, but of those they encountered in Australia, Asia, and Africa. In all those places, the people they met treated white people with hospitality, friendliness, and civility.

The fact that the people who greeted white people treated them civilly is of special importance because it reveals that these people were civilized, contrary to what Europeans have taught the world. The white people would later say, as they do now in their writings and other media, that we, and others they encountered, were uncivilized savages. Despite their well-known civility, the people in those places were massacred by white people on a scale of genocidal proportions that has no historical parallel. Additionally, our people were kidnapped and enslaved on a magnitude that has no historical equivalent. White people's excessive attention to creating more proficient killing weapons grew out of a necessity for survival in the cold climates of their early development. That would later position them to use those weapons against Africa and the rest of the world. This in turn, propelled them to gain dominance over the resources which they have stolen and hoarded primarily for themselves. By using their advanced military weaponry, they were able to conquer the world geographically and culturally. It is that military technology that has given them the decided advantage.

James W. Loewen gives us insight on the matter when he says,

> *"Around 1400, European rulers began to commission ever bigger guns and learned to mount them on ships. Europe's incessant wars gave rise to this arms race, which also ushered in refinements in archery, drill, and siege warfare. China, the Ottoman Empire, and other nations in Asia and Africa now fell prey to European arms, and in 1493 the Americas began to succumb as well."* [5]

The following statement by Loewen correctly informs us that the European nations still dominate the military landscape.

> *"We live with this arms race still. Since the demise of the Soviet Union, the nuclear arms race may have come to a temporary resting point. But the West's advantage in military technology over the rest of the world, jealously maintained from the 1400s on,*

> *remains very must contested. Western [white] nations continue to try to keep non-Western [non-white] nations disadvantaged in military technology."* [6]

Loewen's point is not a minor one because it goes to the crux of the matter revolving around issues of race and racism. Namely, white people's inordinate control over much of the world's resources has given them an economic advantage that enables them to establish and perpetuate the notion of their superiority via skin color—racism/white supremacy. This position is what prevents an honest discussion of what racism is and who is responsible. They bring to bear the full weight of their economic and military might down upon those who would speak, write, or broadcast their complicity in the matter.

So, we see that differing climatic conditions affected the nature of black people and white people in radically different ways. The results were that Black people grew to develop a high regard for human life and a repugnance for human suffering. White people, on the other hand, regarded human beings in primarily economic terms and not humane terms. Therefore, they developed a capacity and willingness to mercilessly destroy humans and cause humans to suffer if economics demanded it.

A proper understanding of these early developments gives us an understanding about how and why things are, in part, the way they are racially. Seen through this lens we can begin to understand why white people's behavior as it pertains to racism can be viewed as evil and why appeals to their morality in the matter falls on deaf ears. As Maya Angelou has instructed us, *"When someone shows you who they are, believe them the first time."* We must recognize them for who they are and let them be themselves. Let the people in their community—their neighbors, teachers, friends, and children who realize the truth about their nature—deal with it.

This analysis tells us that what is at the core of white people's evil behavior is a fight for economic survival. Due to their early development in scarcity, they fostered an extreme fear of economic annihilation. This gave them a view of the world as a place with limited resources, and they must therefore gather those resources for themselves and the survival of their group. Encounters with others outside their group compels them to exploit and handicap outsiders economically, culturally, socially, and politically. Ironically, it is from the exploitation of the resources of these other people that they have derived their economic dominance in the world. All the people they met outside of Europe were wealthy in resources, traditions, and culture.

Realizing that they were lacking in those things especially resources, they concluded that all competition for the resources must be destroyed without mercy or consideration. Additionally, as they murdered and stole our ancestors and our resources (along with other people's cultures), they attempted to destroy our traditions and cultures. As they see it, they cannot allow any African/Black person to become a symbol of cultural power, political power, or a social force. To allow such would be a direct threat to their economic security. They must therefore eliminate or reduce the demand on what they view as the "limited" resources.

The Road To The Dehumanization Of Our People

For them to accomplish this, it became necessary for them to dehumanize our people. They classified us as non-humans or only partial humans. The constitution of the United States of America reflects this fiction by quantifying enslaved Africans as three-fifths of a human for purposes of voting representation for the enslaving kidnappers. [7] Doing so would mean that we would not be worthy of any of the "limited" resources even when those resources were found in our own lands. Conversely, whites had to portray themselves as being worthy of the "limited" resources, which they see as survival of their species issue. The brutal enslavement and colonization of Africans, the genocidal elimination of the Native peoples of North and South America, the isolation and murder of the Aboriginal people of Australia are all evidences of their attempt to gain control of the resources in those areas for their economic survival.

What makes it egregious is that in all the places where white people intruded, they were welcomed, and the people of those lands willingly shared their resources with them and would have gladly set up equitable trade with them. The whites, however, interpreted those events from a completely different point of view and later justified their actions despite how inhumane they may have been. Additionally, the treatment they meted out to our people and other people of color was justified using the same reasoning. To maintain control over those resources, they must continue the brutal treatment of our people and other colored peoples that we see daily. The aim of racism/white supremacy is to never allow us to be able to challenge, threaten, or oppose them. So how do they rationalize it?

The Emergence of Human "Thingification"

Based on their early development, white people have historically shown that they prefer things over humanity. In other words, property, which tends to be an extension of one's perception of oneself, i.e., the body, was more important to whites than the value of humanity in and of itself. The acquisition of property, therefore, became the identifying marker of a more expansive or bigger self for whites. It allowed them to conclude that their body could be extended to include other things and thereby enlarge themselves. For them, this distorted image of the white self, and indeed white culture in general, is evident in the fact that when the Europeans first encountered what they called the "barbaric" African states, they were, at the time in their homelands, giving death sentences to petty thieves. For example, at the time, a child in England could be put to death for stealing a scrap of cloth. [8] This demonstrated their already developed preoccupation with things or property over humans. Conversely, that same crime in Africa (stealing a scrap of cloth) only warranted a public shaming.

In order for the whites to "own" another human as "property," it became necessary to dehumanize us by denying our human qualities which reduced us to a *"thing."*

This Is How They Dehumanize Our People

Ancient slavery was primarily based on rules of war wherein the victors had the right to enslave the losers. The labor of the losers was the spoil given to the victor. In this setup, the humanity of the loser was never called into question nor even considered as an option. The losers maintained their family, religion, culture, language, and traditions as well as, and more importantly, their humanity. They were able to keep all the things that helped them retain their identity and control of themselves. Christianity and Islam changed that setup by enslaving those who did not accept their religions. This was a break from the old traditional rules; one that has had long-term and devastating consequences. Regarding our people, both Christianity and Islam took it a step further. They proclaimed to the world that African people were savages. Others have subsequently followed their lead, but they were the first to make such a proclamation and by so doing they opened the door of the destruction of African people.

The white kidnappers/enslavers in the USA, weighted down with their notion of things or property being more important and more valuable than humanity, went further still. They dehumanized our people. They first reduced the African person to a body, a black body. They then reduced the body to a *thing*. Thus dehumanized, the *thing* qualified as a commodity which could be bought and sold just as any other "thing." Our people became chattel *(a personal possession)* just as a pair of shoes, a pen, a book, or a dog. African humans were thus reduced to things, black things, or African things, and were included with other non-human things that could be bought and sold as chattel property. This concept was both theoretical and pragmatic. By that I mean, it was conceptualized and then put into practice. It was engrained in the psyche of white people as part of the natural order of things. It was acclaimed and established as sacred in white people's theology. For them, God had ordained this order of things which they saw as irreversible—permanent.

This is the prevailing thinking in the entire European world. In the United States of America, this belief was so engrained that the country was divided to the extent of having a civil war. This means that the country was so convinced of this order that white people were willing to kill other white people

and, if necessary, die themselves to prevent it from being changed. Said another way, the white people in this country were willing to kill other white people in order to keep our people enslaved forever. It must be noted that the North (Union) was fighting the Civil war to expand the on-coming industrial revolution more than to emancipate our people from enslavement. This point often gets lost in discussions about the Civil War. Their Southern counterparts

(Confederates), as the North saw it, were in the way of that progress. In August 1862, Lincoln stated:

The Battle of Gettysburg left approximately 7,000 corpses in the fields around the town. Family members had to come to the battlefield to find their loved ones in the carnage. (Civil war photographs, 1861-1865, Library of Congress, Prints and Photographs Division.)

"If I could save the union without freeing any slaves I would do it; and if I could save it by freeing all the slaves I would do it; and if I could save it by freeing some and leaving others alone, I would also do that."

9

Our emancipation from enslavement was a collateral benefit of the Civil War.

For our part, we want to believe, by virtue of what we've been taught within the educational system, that (1) the war was primarily fought to free our people, and (2) the war ended racism/white supremacy. Regarding point number one, it is true to an extent that the American Civil war was fought to free our people—African people—from enslavement. However, the underlying purpose, which is either overlooked or not known by most, is that it was a war that was about helping the North accomplish its goal of forcing the South to capitulate to its industrial revolution ambitions. Regarding point number two: despite the short-lived reconstruction period where the country attempted to live up to its ideals, and to right the wrongs that had been committed against us up until that point, racism/white supremacy has never ceased. There is no period in American history, and for that matter the western world's history (the white world) in general, where racism/white supremacy has not been the prevailing belief and practice.

Characteristics of the Two-Cradles:

Southern Cradle	Northern Cradle
Matriarchal	Patriarchal
Sedentary	Nomadic
Agricultural Development	Hunters
Socialization	Isolation
Buried their dead	Cremated their dead
Territorial State	City State
The emancipation of women	The subjugation of women
Ideals: peace & justice	Ideals: moral & material solitude
Favorite literatures: novels, tales, fables, & comedy	Favorite literatures: tragedy, ideals of war, violence, crime & conquest.
Valued other humans	Valued things
Xenophilic	Xenophobic

appointment

It was my second semester as a college professor. My area of expertise is African World Studies. It's what many commonly call African American Studies. My classes have always had a diverse student population with many students coming from the African world: African Americans, Haitians, Jamaicans, Puerto Ricans, Brazilians, Columbians, and several nationalities from Africa— including Ghana, Kenya, Nigeria, Angola, South Africa, Burkina Faso, Egypt and many others. They have also included other international students from China, Japan, Germany, Italy, etc.

At the end of that second semester of teaching, I was asked for an appointment by one of my white male students. I scheduled the appointment and meet with him a few days later.

When we met, I discovered that he wanted to apologize to me for, what had been for a while, his hostile behavior in the class. I was certainly aware that he had been aggressive with his questions and statements throughout the semester, but I had politely answered his questions and addressed his concerns. He then revealed that early in the semester he had issues and disagreed with the material being taught in the class. Additionally, he divulged that he had made it a practice of going to other white history professors in the department telling them what I was teaching and asked for their help to gather information he hoped would disprove what I had presented on various topics in the class. What he discovered was that they did not have any such information, but as he, along with them, searched for counter evidence, they ran into brick walls. Instead, what they found buttressed my positions on topics they were considering. He disclosed that he decided somewhere in the semester that the information I was giving was accurate and he became more studious.

He continued to divulge that I was the first black teacher he had ever had in his life, and that he just could not believe a black person's information. He apologized to me for his behavior and said he was thankful that he had the chance to attend the class and study with me. I could tell that he was both sincere and embarrassed. He thanked me for the appointment and the semester.

Our education has by default taught all of us three things: (1) what white people say is correct and to be trusted as valid; (2) that what black people say is incorrect, not to be trusted and suspicious; and (3) what black people say can only be seen as correct when white people confirm it.

Chapter 9

The Backdrop

At The Mercy of Beasts

"All the world's a stage, and all the men and women merely players: they have their exits and their entrances…"

—Sakespeare—

E VERY MORNING WHEN YOU awake, the white people show begins to play automatically. The channel has already been set. It's your life but in the white people show. Everything you see, hear, touch, feel, and do is within that show. You don't have to touch any dials, turn any knobs, or even touch a screen for it to begin. You simply wake up on the stage of the white people show. Your room? Compliments of the stage and set hands. You're in the white people show and they would have you believe that your role is just supporting cast. So, you're not supposed to forget your role. But don't worry. You will barely have to lift a finger because the producers of the white people show will take care of everything.

They have taken care to design the bed you're in. The sheets, pillowcases, and covers have all been designed by white people. You get up and step out onto a floor that has been designed, manufactured, and installed by white people. You step into a bathroom that has been designed, manufactured, and built by white people. Everything in the bathroom the toilet, the towels, the shower, the tub, the shower curtains, the soap, the toothpaste, and the tooth brush all compliments of the white people show. You look in the mirror, which by the way is one of the prompts complements of the white people show. It's been put there to help you remember but you forget as you look at you stare back and you see your black, brown, beige, tan skin staring back at you. You see the beauty of your afro, locks, braids, and twists; now mangled and adjusted by curling irons, straightening combs, dyes and chemically treated hair made with just the right tweak so you don't completely lose yourself as you prepare to play your role in the white people show. You try to hold onto as much of you as you can, your identity, your heritage, your history but most of all your sanity.

Many of us get lost on the white people show and forget our roles. Those who do that forget they are supporting actors on the stage of the show meant to highlight and glorify whiteness. Thinking that they too are white, they go out of character. "Cut!" says the director taking a moment to remind you of your part. But the director doesn't use words to remind you. Remember this is a stage and a show and so it's acted out by shooting one of you down in the streets, or choking another, or hunting another and then hanging them. Sometimes, the reminder takes the form of overlooking you for a deserved promotion, denying you access to quality education, housing, and health care. At other times, they get another actor, white of course, to shoot you down in the street in the back where you have no weapon and with hands in the air. It's a reminder for you to play your part and not forget your role. Stay on script is the message. They're trying to get you to understand you're in the white people show. And you stand there wondering why someone doesn't help as these horrid scenes play out. You must understand that in the white people show, you are not human. Your role, for them, is the backdrop to the main event. They are set on winning at all costs. But we won't let them because we assert our agency, our dignity, our humanity. We must always remind them. But more importantly, we must always remember who we are and remind each other.

typical

At one point in my early tenure as a professor, I was asked by the department chairperson to develop an additional course, Introduction to African Civilizations. The request came about because of two things: (1) a demand by students for an additional course in African American Studies since there was only one. (2) The one class I taught on the subject was filled to capacity. This prevented many students from enrolling in the class.

I set about putting a proposal together which needed the department's approval. When I met with the committee, one of their primary concerns (objections) centered around why I was proposing books by all African or African American authors. They wanted to know why I did not include any white authors. I knew that none of them used black authors in the Introduction of Western Civilizations courses which they taught. When I ask them why they didn't use any black authors in those courses, they looked at me surprised but unfazed. They insisted that at least one white author be included. I strongly objected.

One of the professors on the committee, a Jewish fellow, who taught the course prior to my replacement of him, felt that it was his place to teach the course instead of me. He suggested some of the books he used when he taught the course be considered. They were all by white authors. As I understood it, he had earned only a bachelors in history, not a master's or a Ph.D., which is usually required to teach college level courses. I mentioned this because part of their resistance revolved around the fact that I had not yet received my Ph.D. It did not matter that no one else on the committee or in the department held a Ph.D. But that's a side issue which I'll return to in a moment. This Jewish fellow, along with others on the committee, continued to give me a particularly difficult time. They questioned my intention, the credentials of my proposed authors, and my methodology for the course, etc. Some of their questions were legitimate, but the sticking point was my use of only black authors.

In essence and in retrospect, they were preoccupied as to why I was leaving white people out of the white people show. For them, black authors who were authorities in the field were not as competent as white authors who had, in most cases, only a tangential connection to the disciple.

Long story short, the course was ultimately accepted as I presented it. But the time in which they took to pass it, was dragged out over a year. At that time, they wanted to hire someone on a full-time basis and required that they possess a Ph. D. I was still working toward my degree at the time. In the end, they hired a black woman with a Ph.D., and I was no longer needed to teach the course. In doing this, they in essence, killed three birds with one stone to check off the boxes that made them appear diverse and unbiased. They (1) hired a black person, (2) they hired a woman, and (3) they hired someone with a Ph.D. She was the only person in the department with such a degree, more qualified than all of them. They rewrote the course and presented it to her as part of the curriculum. Included were white authors that she was required to use in the course materials.

Chapter 10

The Black White Supremacists

T OO MANY OF OUR people want to pretend that the history of this country is not the history of this country. Some of us have forgotten that when our ancestors were kidnapped and brought to this hemisphere, they were not immigrants seeking a better way of life. They seem to have forgotten, or want to forget, the essential fact that our ancestors were kidnapped and dragged to this stolen land.

You might hear some of our people say things like, "our constitution," "our military," and "our educational system." They have forgotten, or maybe they never knew, that their ancestors were literally treated like animals for hundreds of years in this and other countries that Europeans invaded. Or if they do remember, they have convinced themselves that "slavery wasn't that bad," which was told to them by a segment of the white people show. And so, they have fallen victim to the suggestion of ideas that subscribe to the fantasy version of history—the white people's show version. The fantasy is rooted in the belief that there was some utopian period of racial harmony in the United States or for that matter in the western world.

Some of our people have said, like white people, that there is no racism or that by talking about it, we're stirring up the races, creating division by creating something that isn't there. They are in a total state of denial and represent the damage that racism/white supremacy can have on the psyche. Their position might be compared to a woman who has been physically and mentally abused for years by her mate. Many women who have endured this sort of abuse are often heard making statements like, "He doesn't abuse me. It only happens when I don't do what I'm supposed to do or if I don't do something correctly." In most cases, the abused woman puts the blame of her mistreatment upon herself, not the abuser. As outsiders listening to her, we have psychological distance. This perspective enables us to easily see and hear how what has happened to her has caused her to believe that she is not abused. In the end, she has convinced herself that, whatever it is, she's responsible for it. She does not blame her abuser for his role in it at all. Doing so allows the abuser to escape responsibility and the consequences of his actions. The similarities between that and what has happened to our people and our resultant behavior is startling when first realized.

We have suffered physical, mental, and sexual abuse for generations at the hands of white people. Following that abuse, we have not received any therapy to help us readjust, nor have we received compensation—reparations. In fact, for us, the abuse has never stopped. It perseveres unabated and unrestrained generationally. The abusers, white people, now blame us for some of the deficiencies and dysfunctional behavior we see in our communities. Unfortunately, some of our own people, like an abused woman, blame ourselves for our condition. So, when we hear those from our own community making statements to the effect that there is no racism or that we must look at ourselves and what we're doing to ourselves, we must remember that we're watching the long-term impact of generational abuse that has been left untreated. When our people engage in such activity, however, we in fact become supporters and enablers of racism/white supremacy. We become, in effect what I call Black White Supremacists.

Black white supremacists are people from our community who support white supremacy wittingly and for a pat on the back from the producers of the White People Show. They want to maintain the status quo of race relations. Like most white people, these black white supremacists claim they don't see any racism. Like most whites, they tend to think that when we talk about racial issues, we are stirring up division between the races. They think that to bring attention to the racial injustices we receive is a misreading of the situation. They think that when we point out the disparities between us and white people as seen in health care, education, housing, and employment it is an attempt on our part to play the so-called "race card." They will defend white people who have been caught making racist statements or behaving in ways that are clearly racists. They are the ones whom the white media will parade out to help put a happy face on what we know are obvious racist words and behavior. They are the ones that are also used to refute others within our community who would dare speak truth to power.

Derrick Bell provided remarkable insight to this phenomenon when he stated the following:

> *"When a black person makes a statement or takes an action that the white community or vocal components thereof deem "outrageous," the latter will actively recruit blacks who are willing to refute the statement or condemn the action. Blacks who respond to the call for condemnation will receive super standing status* [emphasis mine]. *Those blacks who refuse to be*

recruited will be interpreted as endorsing the statements and action and may suffer political or economic reprisals." [1]

When our people do this type of thing, they effectively become black white supremacists. What I mean by that is their behavior is that of being racist against themselves and their own people. They have become black people who are white supremacists. They help further and strengthen racism/white supremacy.

For example, we have been conditioned to think that only one group of people who hold certain features are, therefore, the most favorable to the world. This is a very faulty view of the definition of beauty and falls under the white supremacist delusion that white features are the best features. The world needs to expel the idea that only a small variation of physical features is beautiful, and the rest are not. There are still too many people who think that Eurocentric features are superior. [2]

It appears the Black White Supremacists are what white people want, and have always wanted—assimilation, the demand to reject our own culture, heritage, appearance, etc., and adopt theirs as better instead.

The Permanence of Racism And What's The Solution?

The other day, I observed some fish swimming in water. I stopped to look and one of the friendly fish popped its head out the water and said to me.

"Hey, how are you today, buddy?"

"I'm doing fine. It's a lovely day," I replied. "How about you?" I ask.

"Oh, just another day chasing minnows," says the fish.

I then asked the fish, "How's the water?"

The fish looks at me clearly puzzled by my question and then asks, "What water?"

I was stunned by his question and apparently it showed on my face as I searched for an answer that was not forthcoming.

Puzzled by my reaction, the fish shrugs his shoulders, shakes h's head in disbelief, and dismisses me mumbling, "Humans. I'll never figure them out." With that he disappears under the water leaving me perplexed.

We, you and I, —Black people— are not responsible for solving the problem of racism/white supremacy. It is a white problem. However, like fish who do not see the water that they live in, most whites are just as oblivious to racism/white supremacy that they live and breathe every day. Trying to teach white people about racism is, in many ways, like trying to explain water to a fish. In most cases, it's a no-win situation, unless they are at a place where they are ready to learn; otherwise, it's a waste of time and energy. In most cases, it's easier to explain water to a fish. For four hundred years, we have been trying to explain it to them; trying to make them understand it and they still don't get it. The native people of these lands tried to explain it to them, and they didn't get it. The aboriginal people of Australia tried explaining it, and it didn't work there either. I won't belabor the point.

It does not mean I am completely pessimistic on the matter because despite the racism and injustices I have faced and endured individually, there have been whites whom I know that have genuinely come to full grips with their racist/white supremac_st tendencies—their personal racism. They are the first to admit that it's ugly and difficult because it's easier to be white in a racist/white supremacist society where they can reap all the privileges and benefits that come with it than it is to buck the system. But they somehow have come to see the light, and there have been those whites throughout every generation who come to grips with it and join us in combating it. There are many of them and their numbers are growing. However, remember that they are relatively few. The spectrum of these whites is on a continuum of sorts that includes those who are at the early stages of recognition of their racism to those who have faced their demons and moved to a place of action to help other whites understand it. This does not mean that racism will disappear simply because those numbers increase.

Many of us are too willing and are too quick to believe that whites mean us good when they help us in some way or when they may express their sorrow for what might have been done to us because of racism/white supremacy. Derrick Bell left us with a reminder of something we ought never forget on this matter. He stated,

> *"Black people will never gain full equality in this country. Even those herculean efforts we hail as successful will produce no more than temporary "peaks of progress," short-lived victories that slide into irrelevance as racial patterns adapt in ways that maintain white dominance. This is a hard-to-accept fact that all history verifies. We must acknowledge it, not as a sign of submission, but as an act of ultimate defiance."* [3]

While on the surface his statement appears pessimistic, Bell adds this in the way of explanation.

"...African Americans must confront and conquer the otherwise deadening reality of our permanent subordinate status. Only in this way can we prevent ourselves from being dragged down by society's racial hostility. Beyond survival lies the potential to perceive more clearly both a reason and the means for further struggle." [4]

There is a documentary entitled, *The Color of Fear,* that comes the closest to anything I've seen that shows what will be necessary to begin a path to anything in any semblance of addressing or resolving racism/white supremacy. White people are under a hypnotic spell with their belief in their superiority and everyone else's inferiority. As already stated, it is engrained, embedded, and established in such a way that it is consciously and subconsciously passed from one generation to the next.

That hypnotic state is further sustained in whites when there is no honest discussion between black and white people about racism. Again, as noted earlier, the discussions are dishonest. We do not tell white people the truth about racism because it is an indictment against them. We don't tell them the truth because we do not want to be the subject of their retaliation against us as they can in the form of unemployment, housing, demonization, etc. White people do not want an honest discussion because they will be forced to deal with the reality that racism/white supremacy is in fact their problem. They are to blame for its creation and its consequences. As a result, both groups continue to lie about it and continue to be confused by what happens because of it. When we are pushed to the brink, we protest and march to demonstrate our rage. We beg for them to see us, hear us, and acknowledge what they have done to us. But they don't. They retaliate by appearing to be sympathetic by implementing new measures, programs, and trainings. They want to avoid the guilt and shame of what their ancestors did to us and what they inherited and continue to do to us. It's like a rapist who wants to live in harmony with their victim without acknowledging the crime they committed and the pain they caused.

As far as racism is concerned, all this is done to avoid the truth about racism and if that truth is avoided, it will be like a cancer that eats away at us all. Make no mistake about it, if it is not addressed correctly, it will destroy the world as we know it. That may or may not be a bad thing. Nevertheless, for those who must have solutions, I offer the film mentioned above, The Color of Fear, as a starting point.

In the 1994 documentary, *The Color of Fear*, directed by Lee Mun Wah, race relations in America is seen through the eyes of eight American men of Asian, European, Latino and African descent. They meet in an undisclosed location and have agreed to stay for the duration no matter what transpires. At first, we see the usual behavior that we see in society where everyone is polite, living behind a thin veil of rage kept at bay. As the men get past the preliminaries and politeness and into more substantive conversations, the heat begins to rise and ultimately explodes in a combustion of fury, anger, bitterness, and hostility.

As you watch, you can only cringe as they wade through this lake of fear that we never have the courage to venture into when it comes to the topic of racism/white supremacy. The brutal honesty that comes through is painful, unpleasant, and gut-wrenching. The anger that spills out would be dangerous in an uncontrolled environment.

But these men jump in, taking the plunge that will be required to simply peak behind the door of what it will take to consider just talking about solving the racism problem. Spoiler Alert: They don't solve it. They do, however, recognize it and just recognizing and acknowledging it in its totally repulsiveness opens a door for honest discussion. That is the first critical step toward any notion of a solution. Talk of resolving racism/white supremacy without white people acknowledging it for what it is, is a waste of time.

Part 3
Close Up

Chapter 11

Where Are All The Racists, Anyway?

P ICTURE THIS: SOME WELL-KNOWN white person is caught on either audio or video saying something that's clearly racist. When we hear it, we know without a doubt that IT IS RACIST AND THE PERSON IS A RACIST. Up to that point, we may have only had our suspicions about them being racist. But this confirms it beyond a doubt. We know, too, that this is not a one-time incident with the person. It's more likely, they have been saying things of this nature behind closed doors to family and friends for a large portion of their life perhaps their entire life. But now they have been caught publicly.

> *"For every tree is known by his own fruit…The good person out of the good treasure of the heart produces good, and the evil person out of evil treasure produces evil; for it is out of the abundance of the heart that the mouth speaks."*

Luke 6:44-45 (KJV)

After such occurrences, white people, (at least the white media and its pundits) run around trying to figure out why the person would say or do such a thing; how could they? Everyone pretends as if it is an aberration and a deviation from the norm. Everyone except us of course. We know it is not a deviation but the norm. The white people's show sets out to convince us that what this person said or did was not racist; that it's just an isolated episode in an otherwise atmosphere of racial harmony.

One of their well-known tactics when faced with such occurrences is to find one of our people to vouch for the supposed non-racist character of the racist. It's a childish masquerade that is part of the white people's show of which we are not supposed to be aware. The thinking, as far as they're concerned, is we don't have the intelligence to see through the charade. And so, they reward one of our own people (usually a celebrity type) who comes forward and says of the racist *"He doesn't have a racist bone in his body."* Or *"I've known her for years and never heard her say a racist thing."* They will be heard saying something like that or a variation of it. For their part, white commentators and pundits will ask, with a straight face mind you, *"Do you think what so and so* (the white person who has his nuts in a grip) *said is racist?"* Then they will follow up with an even more absurd question, *"Does that make him a racist?"* The whole thing would be laughable if it wasn't so serious.

Whenever these public cases were showcased in the past, it usually consisted of a group of white men having a discussion among themselves wherein it is assumed that they themselves are not racist. Occasionally, they might invite one of our people into the discussion to back up their attempt to acquit the currently accused racist. The all-white men show, however, has been updated in recent years to include a multicultural group of talking heads, who do the exact same thing as in the past. In the end, they all lament how horrible what the guy with his nuts in a grip said. But then they opine that he's not a racist. Along with that conclusion, they will admit that *"Yes, there is racism out there, and there are racists, but this is clearly not one of them."* Case closed…as far as they are concerned.

Next, they cut to a scene where a white cop has recently gunned down an unarmed black man. And so, they have the same conversation and debate, but in the context of whether the cop was racist are not. Meantime, we watch the white people show and shake our heads.

They Went That-a-Way

In view of this charade, the question we must ask is where are all the racists if racist speech and behavior is deemed non-racist? If we listen to and accept the uncut adaptation of the white people show that is shoved down our throats daily, we will have to arrive at the preposterous conclusion that there are no racists. That's because every incident of clear unadulterated racism is made to appear as if it is not racist because of either who the person is or the circumstances under which they are caught saying and doing racist things. The attempt is presented in such a way as to confuse us about the matter of racism.

Remember These Seven Things About Racists:

1. Racists don't admit that they are racist.

2. Racists all claim that they are not racist.

3. Racists try to convince us that there is no racism.

4. Racists tell us racism has many meanings.

5. Racists try to persuade us that everyone is racist.

6. Racists say racist things then pretend that it wasn't racist.

7. Racists want us to feel comfortable with their racism.

When racist words are uttered or racist behavior is identified, they act as if what was said or done has been taken out of context. In the attempts to eliminate racism, we are told that there is some other explanation for the behavior. They remove racism as a factor when it is the only factor. These are not the facts, and it is done for our benefit in that it is designed to move us away from any talk of racism/white supremacy. When and if we do allow our attention to be diverted, racism/white supremacy wins the day by sleight of hand.

Slaveholders Were Not Racist?

Believe it or not, even those who kidnapped and enslaved our people and held them in slavery for hundreds of years did not believe themselves to be racist/white supremacists. They made the same claims of not being racist as we hear many white people say today. They justified the enslavement of our ancestors on the following three rationales which Dr. Maulana Karenga has identified as absurdities. They are (1) religious absurdities, (2) biological absurdities, and (3) cultural absurdities.

Religious absurdities were used to argue that "God" had ordained white people to conquer, civilize, and Christianize African people. The biological absurdities were used to redefine our people out of the human race. In so doing, they denied our history and our humanity and gave our people animal characteristics when speaking about us. Since they viewed us as non-humans, they reasoned that treating us as beasts was justified.

Regarding the cultural absurdity, they claimed that white people were culturally superior to black people not by virtue of merit but simply because of their skin color. As a result, they elected themselves as having the natural God-given right and responsibility to conquer and use our human labor along with our material resources for their sole benefit. [1]

Armed with this heinous and evil view of us, they established a blueprint of behavior toward us that endures until today. No amount of legislation nor social integration has been able to undo what was put in motion by those absurdities. To undo them would require a mass reeducation of white people in particular but would also require a psychological reeducation of our people with regard to our history and the history of what has happened to us. The problem with that, however, is the educational system is controlled by white people who, in general, have no interest in changing things. Why would they? As things stand, they derived a privileged status psychologically, economically, socially, and politically. To undo this whole thing would mean their undoing as it currently stands.

Racists are not ready to be identified as racists. Their best card is to pretend that racism doesn't exist. And if it does exist, then, for them, it's not that bad or they construe and consign it to the category of just an "isolated incident." They try to reassure us that it's all in our heads, that we are seeing shadows in the night where there are none.

Racism does not go away. It does not disappear just because white people, along with some of our own dimwitted people playing the buffoon, try to convince us otherwise.

As we gain clarity about what racism is, the less we will be hoodwinked into the diversion set by racism to convince us otherwise.

Racists would have us believe that since the advent of the Civil Rights movement, the voting rights acts, school integration and the election of President Barack Obama racism has died. That is not true on any account. Most white people feign ignorance of racism. It is a distraction tactic designed to divert attention. When we hear this, we often go into a teaching mode. We feel it's our responsibility to educate them. And we think that if we educate them, then they will see, know, and understand. They already see, know, and understand. It works in their favor and their role is to make sure you and I do not come to an unequivocal conviction of this realization.

Racists envision a world where there are no Black people. Or one where Black people are subservient to them and serving their needs. The health and well-being of Blacks in a racist world is that which is equivalent to a pet who is dependent upon an 'owner' for food clothing and shelter.

They have painted themselves to be the heroes and heroines of everything good and right. They have projected themselves into places and times of history where they did not exist. They have attempted to give themselves special importance when and where they have no importance. They have credited themselves with accomplishments made and created by others whom they classify as savages, heathens, or worst.

Chapter 12

How Has Racism Damaged Our People?

An Example

THE RESULTING HARM AND damage of racism is death and destruction. We have been abused and maligned by white people and the rest of the world more than any other people in the history of humanity. They have enslaved us for hundreds of years. They have dehumanized us, raped us, removed us from our homeland and enslaved us in our own land which is given the fancy name—colonialism, just enslavement by another name. They have hung us for entertainment, hunted us for sport as they would wild animals, roasted us for fun, and staved us to death. They have conducted experiments on us without our consent or anesthesia. They have worked us to death without pay for hundreds of years. They have abused our women and fathered children by them whom they seldom acknowledged. They took our names, our religions, our families, our history, and our humanity and then blamed us for the shortcomings we now see in our communities.

Their actions and behavior toward us are the epitome of what can only be characterized as that of a devil or a senior demon. And after all of that, and more, they feign astonishment to find a few of us who have the guts to say it loud and unfiltered. And so, they, who have hated us for centuries, expect for us to love them, to overlook the evil they have relentlessly inflicted upon us, and to forgive them. We do not and we must not!

There has been no therapy for us after enslavement which included several hundred years of the cruelest abuse known in history. And yet, we're expected to behave and operate as if the trauma had no consequences upon our wellbeing. Author, Ruby Shivers, illuminates this when she says,

"We have never been given any treatment to cure the mental damage that has been done to us by white supremacy indoctrination."[1]

We live daily lives within the reality of the damage done to us and that has been left untreated. As expected, some of the damage is overt and in plain sight. However, most of it is not acknowledged as damage resulting from generational abuse. Instead, it gets characterized as "our culture" and other such nomenclatures that pass for normalcy. Other elements are hidden. We see it in the distorted behavior of our people. We see it in the attempts to lighten our skin, straighten our hair, the wearing of blue contact lenses, calling each other by the "N" word, and the overall disorganization we witness. There are many aspects of the damage done to us as result of racism/white supremacy that go beyond the scope of this book. Each of them deserves deep structural considerations. For purposes of this writing, I will deal with only one such aspect, namely the N word.

The Social Engineering of The N Word

As stated earlier, I grew up in a home and during a time when the N-word was not acceptable nor widely used especially in mixed company or as openly as is today. However, the development over the last four decades has seen an inordinate rise and use of the word in most aspects of our lives. Most notably in our conversations with one another and in our music, comedy, and movies. I think it's important to give a brief background on how social engineering by racism/white supremacy has manipulated this evolution. I do not use the term in any situation at any time except for purposes of explanation in discussion and in my classes. I will use it here for demonstrative reasons in the next section.

This emphasis on the N word is by no means exhaustive of the damage done to us but is only a small but significant part of the damage. Molefi Asante has correctly identified the significance of language when he says,

> *"Our liberation from the captivity of racist language is the first order of the intellectual...language is essentially the control of thought. It becomes impossible for us to direct our future until we control our language. The sense of language is in precision of vocabulary and structure for a particular social context. If we allow others to box us into their concepts, then we will always talk and act like them. Black language must possess instrumentality, that is, it must be able to do something for our liberation... Liberation is fundamentally a seizure of the instruments of control. If the language is not*

functional, then it should have no place in our vocabulary. In every revolution, the people have first seized the instruments of idea formation and then property production." [2]

First, it must be understood that we —black people— did not make the N word ours as some have declared. That is a false narrative that was born out of racism, but it is believed and repeated by those of us that are gullible especially to the significance and impact of words.

The reason and rationale of why millions of our people now refer to themselves as n*ggers is testament of the immense power of racist media social engineering. Those that control the media images of a people can control the culture of those people. People often become replicas of those repeated media portrayals of themselves which, if not critically accessed, are accepted as being true representations. This is done through what is known as social engineering—those who attempt to manage social change by regulating the development of a society. The resultant outcome of social engineering may either be negative or positive. In the case of our people, whose cultural identity has been manipulated for centuries, the susceptibility to its programming is increased. For example, a better understanding of social engineering as applied to us, helps us have a clearer understanding of why many of our people now calls themselves n*ggers, b*tches, hoes, and thugs.

Presently there are media social engineers and propagandists controlled by white people who work relentlessly behind the scenes influencing the minds of our people on a massive scale. In such positions of power, they are uniquely situated to control the media images of our people. By virtue of their miseducation about us combined with the environment of racism, they can use those positions to unfavorably steer Black culture. For example, most people unsuspectingly believe that the media reflects our reality, but in truth, it is more often that we imitate what we see and learn from the media. In today's world, a group's identity is greatly shaped by how they repeatedly see themselves depicted in the media. As a result, people—our people in this case—often imitate media depictions of themselves that they accept as being their reality. This ability is immensely powerful and dangerous for us because it enables a racist/white supremacist society with that kind of control to adversely influence the behaviors and the culture of black people through the images and information they routinely project.

For instance, if these social engineers wanted our youth to start putting yellow Afro combs in their left rear pocket, they would need to do no more than place that image in several rap music videos, movies, and TV shows exhibiting it as very cool and trendy. In so doing, our Black youth would then see the image, imitate it and adopt it as being of their own making although it is in fact not of their own making. The style and behavior were learned from what they repetitively saw in the media.

When white social engineers create trends and customs for our youth to imitate, they deliberately create images that tacitly direct them to act and dress as caricatures that reinforces resentment and anti-black perceptions. Furthermore, those images reinforce many negative and racist stereotypes about our people. Our youth consequently become mimics of those derogative images and stereotypes which they have accepted as part of their culture when in fact they are nothing more than engineered affectations.

Because we African Americans were stripped of our identity and culture during the enslavement of our ancestors, we are much more susceptible to negative media social engineering. We did not make the N word into our own word. That again is a false narrative created by white propagandists and believed by those of us that are naive and gullible! It was, more correctly, through white media social engineering that white oppressive forces manipulated millions of us to call ourselves N*ggers.

The POWER of Words

During the Vietnam war, to ease the American soldiers' anxieties about torturing and killing the Vietnamese, they were taught to refer to them as Chinks and Gooks. This dehumanized them and made it easier to kill and torture them. They saw them not as fellow humans but as something other than human. In similar fashion, white oppressive forces socially engineered millions of our people to call themselves n*ggers through media manipulation.

Words affect and influence our behavior. They also shape how we think of others and how we think of ourselves. We conduct ourselves out of the well-spring of the words we have ascribed to our ourselves about ourselves. And we treat others based upon the words we assign or ascribe to them. As an example, it becomes easier for many men to mistreat women when they refer to them as bitches and hoes. Men who proclaim themselves as dogs begin to behave in ways that are doggish. Those who claim they are thugs are more likely to engage in thuggish behavior. This is not rocket science. When you can get a person, a group, or a people to accept and apply those kinds of terms to themselves, the resultant behavior is not a mystery. When it is intentionally used, it is a psychological phenomenon used by social engineers to obtain the desired result. Noted psychiatrist Dr. Frances Cress Welsing observed the following: *"We wonder why we're not making progress? I can't call myself a bitch, hoe, gangster, thug, [and nigger] everyday then get up and do something constructive.*

That's impossible." The reason it is impossible is because it is the self-image that the individual or group has accepted as the truth of their reality, and therefore, they cannot rise to a level beyond their belief. For those who are religious the Bible says it this way: *"For cs he thinks in his heart, so he is.* Proverbs 23:7 (New King James Version).

Consequently, we have heard terms like "Bad Bitch" added to lyrics accompanied by an irresistible beat along with an image that appeared to be empowering. Before long, our people were proudly calling themselves and each other bad bitches, thugs, hoes, ard n*ggers. The reality is this. When we call each other by harmful terms such as these, we dehumanize ourselves and each other. This in turn makes it easier for us to mistreat one another just as American soldiers behaved in Vietnam and in other wars.

The Evolution Of The N*gger Campaign

White social engineers took the word "nigger," a word once reviled and deemed deeply offensive by millions of African Americans, and not only desensitized our people to the word, but also convinced millions of us to favorably perceive the word as a term of endearment. When our people accept that they are n*ggers, they are subconsciously programmed to believe the worse about themselves and others like them. The prison industry complex, especially in the USA, is filled with our men who have been programmed to believe that they are real "n*ggas" if they have traversed the prison system. Through media manipulation, prison life has been glamorized. This does not excuse the racist bent of the society to control our people by containing them in these "institutions." It explains, in part, how they are maneuvered into playing a role that fulfills the agenda of a racist society.

The Role of The Arts And The Rise Of The N Word

The Arts are not exempt from this scheme. The same racist music companies that claim, "Black Lives Matter," are the same companies that will record, produce, and mass market some of our artists who say, things such as, "Die N*gger Die" or "Kill that N*gger" in their music. Those companies make millions, if not billions of dollars and we don't bat an eye. We don't see the exploitation and the contradictions associated with this. Or if we do, we excuse it because the artists are "getting paid."

The reason why many of our rappers succeed within white society is because they help benefit the system of white supremacy. White oppressive forces secretly perceive Black rappers, and indeed black art in general, as useful to the ends of white supremacy to remain supreme. In addition to making mega amounts of money by exploiting them, they used them to negatively steer Black culture. And they use them to vilify and criminalize the image of African Americans, which makes white society's [justice systems] mistreatments of our population appear justifiable.

Because most of our rappers may not be acquainted with the science of negative media social engineering (most people are not), they are therefore unaware of the actual damages that they are inflicting on our people. Their ignorance is being exploited by white oppressive forces to the detriment of their own people. Although this n*gger programming is now routinely deployed through the white controlled Hip Hop music industry, that industry merely reinforces an earlier programming.

Lest you think I'm picking on the hip hoppers; it must be remembered that n*gger terminology was originally indoctrinated into our culture many decades ago long before the hip hop music industry was created. It was originally accomplished by using the movie industry as a precursor. Most people are under the impression that movies are primarily entertainment. That has never been the case. The greatest social engineering messages have been promoted through movies. Social norms promoted through films can influence thinking and the "cognitive map" of the audiences. In a normal conversation, when using logic and facts, one's guard is naturally up. But while watching a movie or television program, there is no debate, and our natural guard is neutralized. The sensor part of the brain is not activated. It does not say, *"Yes I agree with this, or I disagree with that"* as would be the case in a debate or a conversation. The mind is in an unaware state that those images and ideas are being downloaded and programmed into the psyche. This programming system was used to convince millions of Black movie watchers, during the late 1960s and early 1970s, that they were n*ggers. [3]

Up until the mid-1960s the word nigger was viewed unfavorably by most of our people. That era's generation of our people had first-hand experience with the dehumanization of segregation. Most of their grandparents and great-grand parents were born during enslavement or near the end of the American Civil War. Therefore, they were intimately connected to and aware of the brutality and degradation that often accompanied the ugly taunts of the word n*gger. Consequently, usage of the word was usually forbidden within many African American homes. It was perceived as a profoundly offensive word. The outward employment of the word became more accepted among our people during the late 1960s and early 1970s as the popularity of the Blaxploitation film industry grew.

Blaxploitation is a term coined in the early 1970s to refer to black films that were aimed specifically at black audiences. These films were released between 1970 and 1980 and featured a cast of blacks in lead roles. Such films also depicted stereotypical characterization and glorification of violence among our people. It was that era's exploitative films that first taught youths in our community on a national level that it was a cool and trendy term of endearment to call themselves n*ggers. In those films, written, directed, and produced by mostly white people, Black actors were hired to shuck and jive and to repeatedly call themselves and each other n*gger. This indoctrinating process was repeated and reinforced countless times in many ways within many Blaxploitation films.

Below is a list of a few samples of those movies. Within each of these films, produced by white movie studios, black actors routinely called each other n*ggers. Some of the titles blatantly included the word nigger.

Shaft (1971)

The Legend of Nigger Charley (1972)

Black Rage (1972)

Shaft's Big Score (1972)

The Soul of Nigger Charley (1973)

Run, Nigger, Run (1973)

Black Mama White Mama (1973)

Scream Blacula Scream (1973)

Shaft in Africa (1973)

Nigger Rich (1974)

Boss Nigger (1975)

Black Lolita (1975)

Sheba Baby (1975)

The Six Thousand Dollar Nigger (1978)

Those exploitive films were well received by most audiences in our communities because they provided us with cinematic black heroes on the silver screen in a portrayal unseen in most Hollywood pictures prior to that time. Therefore, our people flocked to the theaters in droves to see themselves being represented as heroes on the big screen. Many of our people in attendance, believed that those fictional movie characters were true, accurate representation of their group as a collective. As a result, we began to see our people begin to imitate what they saw depicted in those movies—this included calling themselves n*ggers. Through this system, millions of our people were socially engineered to perceive themselves as being n*ggers. By no means is this the only factor that contributed to the rise of the use of the term, nor is it intended to be an exhaustive treatise on the matter. It does, however, provide a glimpse into how social engineering through media manipulation can influence behavior.

The damage done to our community as a result of racism/white supremacy is multifaceted and has wreaked untold havoc on us.

Chapter 13

This Little Light of Mine

"The goal is not to change how the white man views the black man, but how the black man views himself."

—Malcolm X—

ALL THIS TALK ABOUT racism/white supremacy would appear to leave us with a doomed outlook. Some may even think it's a useless struggle that we will never win. That is not the intention of this book. In fact, the intention is just the opposite. It is one that is filled with hope and a bright future for our people. There is a saying which indicates that with every adversity, there is a seed of equivalent benefit. In the bible it's stated, and I paraphrase, "The evil that they have intended for us actually works for our greater good." In other words, the very thing that appears as an obstacle, as an immovable mountain, or as a dead end, is an opportunity for us to blast through and shine brighter and more powerful than ever before.

To get to that place of brightness, we must first define, recognize, and acknowledge the problem. If we don't, all our actions will be in vain. That is what this book, in part, has been about. We cannot conduct ourselves pretending as if racism/white supremacy does not exist. We cannot allow the definition to be changed. We must not allow ourselves to believe or think that we are racist and that we are responsible for solving it. Neither should we indulge ourselves with the idea that we can eliminate, reduce, or change it. Our job is not to work toward changing white people's minds about us. That is a waste of time. Racism/white supremacy is permanent. Accept it as fact. The masses of white people who embrace this concept whether knowingly or unknowingly, will never change. The ones who do get it, get it! And we welcome them. We must not spend our time trying to educate those who don't get it in hopes that they will see the light, or that they will have a "come-to-Jesus" moment. They won't. Five hundred years of concrete historical evidence has confirmed this for us. If anything, they will become even more entrenched in their belief of their false superiority. As Dr. King once said, *"...large segments of white society are more concerned about tranquility and the status quo than about justice and humanity."* On this point, Ruby Shivers says, *"When "good white people" want to come forward, they will. Don't try to convince them that they are good...remember slavery...was sanctioned by a government of white people.* [1]

I know this is not easy to hear and even harder to accept for some of us. But regardless, we can come to a firm, clear, unequivocal resolution on this matter. We have all too often been like a hamster on a tread mill doomed to running fast but going nowhere. I offer a different perspective. A vision.

> *"Where there is no vision, the people perish."*
> Proverbs 29:18 (King James Version)

The Selfishness of Survival

Our fight is not with white people. Our fight is with the false ideas that we have been given about the superiority of white people and the notion that we are inferior. And in order to begin eliminating those two false concepts from our thinking, we must look at who we have been and how we arrived in the present place. Once we understand those two things, we should have a better idea of what it is we must do. This requires that we have a vision of where we want to be; a vision of what we want to happen for us as a people. For those who think that such thinking excludes others, you are right. It does exclude others. There is a time in every people's education when they arrive at the conviction that it is necessary for them to practice the selfishness of survival; for without doing so, they will ensure their own death. It is not necessary for us to include everyone else or even be concerned about them. It does not mean that we do not care about their welfare. Our house is on fire and requires that we find water to pour on the fire before we go down the street to help pour water on the fire consuming our neighbor's house. In the end, what we do and accomplish for ourselves will benefit all. We must practice without apology or misgiving the selfishness of our survival.

Despite many good intentions, there are no treatment options for racists. I mean that in the sense of them being able to check into a facility like those designed for drug and alcohol addiction. There are no pills or portions to ameliorate the symptoms. The only cure, it seems, is for them to come to grips with reality; to come to the realization that they are not superior to those of us who are not like them—white. Until they can fully grasp our humanity in a significant and meaningful way, talk of eliminating, reducing, or legislating it away are futile.

What Have We Done Despite Racism/White Supremacy?

The lies we have been told about our past in Africa before being kidnapped and enslaved are just that—lies. Those lies are embedded in our psyche and blind us to who we really are. They blind us to the accomplishments, achievements, and the contributions we have made to the benefit of humanity. On the other hand, and as deeply embedded in our psyche is the idea of white people's superiority. They have lied to us about their past. They invented lies about themselves and their accomplishments. They made themselves beautiful and noble when they have been ugly and savage in their encounters with our people and other people of color on the planet. They have left death, destruction, and disappointment wherever they have gone. It does not mean that they did not make contributions and did great things. It means that they didn't tell the whole story of themselves. They lied so convincingly and for so long that they believe the lies both about themselves and about us. Unfortunately, we have also fallen prey and believe the lies on both accounts. For our purposes here, I'll only give brief glimpses into two things: the greatness that we African people have accomplished, and the vision we must hold in our minds to pass along to our children.

Before Our Kidnapping and Enslavement

Prior to our contact with white people who invaded our lands, we accomplished much. We created writing, the use of speech, charted the stars, sailed the seas, developed agriculture, built monuments that have stood the test of time, developed deep structural thinking, created mathematics and textile industries, wrote fables, songs, and poems, we danced and sang and created the drum and string instruments. We tamed wild animals and created communities that endured for centuries in all parts of Africa. All of this and more is our heritage. It is a testament of who we are, but more importantly, of who we can become. As a reminder, I provide the following list which demonstrates our greatness so that we might remember that this last five hundred years of our long history is nothing more than a blip on the timeline of our history. We have overcome other seemingly impossible barriers. Racism/white supremacy is the latest of such barriers. And like the other barriers which we overcame, this one too, we will overcome.

Places

Ancient Kush (Ethiopia)
Ancient Kemet (Egypt)
Ancient Ghana Empire
The Empire of Mali
The Songhai Empire
Kanem-Bornu
Segu
Gao
Timbuktu
Djenne
Zululand
Zimbabwe
The Kingdom of Congo
The Kingdom of Angola
Makuria
Mossi

Things

The pyramids of Kemet & Kush
The Sphinx
The Temples
The Zimbabwe Enclosure
The Zodiac

People

Narmer
Imhotep
Kufu
Pepi 1
Mentahotep 1 & 2
Sensuret 1 & 2
Ahmes
Amenhotep 1, 2, 3, & 4.
Hatshepsut
Men-khpera 1, 2, 3, & 4.
Tye
Ankhnaten
Tut
Seti
Nefartari
Rameses 1 & 2
Shabaka
Shabataka
Pianki
Candace
Kalydosos
Kaya Magan

Sundiata

Sakura

Mansa Musa

Sunni Ali Ber

Askia the Great

Ahmad Baba

Mahmud Kati

Abderaman Es'Sadi

Queen Nzingha of Angola

Yaa Asantawaa

Shaka

Nandi

What Is The Solution To Racism/White Supremacy?

The question then becomes, how do we (earthlings) solve the problem of racism. My answer is simple. I don't know. But what I do know is that, despite having endured the most atrocious, remorseless, and savage attack any branch of the human family has lived through, we still stand. In the words of our great sacred poetess, Maya Angelou, we can say with confidence, *"Still I Rise."* We still hope. That hope has often been misguided into thinking that our salvation would come from white people having come to their senses and joined with us in the family of humanity. That, as I've said, was misguided because they are dedicated to the survival of the white people show. Now, we know. We know that our hope, faith, and future must be in our hands. We cannot depend on others to do for us what only we can do for ourselves.

White people have proven themselves incapable of higher standards and are committed to the status quo of the white people show. It has been our fault to think that they have enough humanity and decency to reach those levels of equity demanded of a global world where they continue to demand center stage. They have been tested and have been founded wanting. We have expected too much from them. As many of them that will join us, we welcome, but our rise is not dependent on their participation. It must be remembered that dogs and hogs, while noble animals, cannot be expected to act humanly. And so, it is with most of them. They cannot rise to the occasion.

The list below serves as testament to our humanity, our fortitude, and our power even in the face of direct hostility, open contempt, and unfettered hatred fueled by flagrant racism/white supremacy. Despite all that has been done to diminish and obliterate us, despite the racism/white supremacy, and despite the death and destruction of so many of our people and what we value, this list testifies of our greatness against such odds. Let it be a reminder to you of what we can do when everywhere around us tells us we are worthless and not deserving of human respect. Despite it all, we must S.O.A.R *(Soar Over All Resistance)* and in so doing, we defeat it. The names on the list below soared in the face of racism/white supremacy. If they could do it, we all can SOAR together.

Marcus Garvey
Ida B. Wells-Barnett
Booker T. Washington
W. E. B. DuBois
Cheik Anta Diop
Shirley Chisholm
Benjamin E. Mays
Shaka of Zulu
Toussaint L'Ouverture
Dessalines

Zumbia of Palmares
Malcolm X
Thurgood Marshall
Jack Johnson
Muhammad Ali
Mary McCloud Methune
Sojourner Truth
Madam C J Walker
Harriet Tubman
James Baldwin
Martin Luther King, Jr.
Kwame Nkrumah
Jomo Kenyatta
Patrice Lumumba
Nelson Mandela
Michael Jackson
James Brown
Otis Redding
The Supremes
Fela
The Temptations
Earth, Wind & Fire
Miles Davis
Charle Parker
Count Basie
Duke Ellington
Fannie Lou Hamer
Kwame Toure
Derrick Bell
Michael Jordan
Jimi Hendrix

LeBron James

Magic Johnson

Oprah Winfrey

Maulana Karenga

Molefi Asante

Cornel West

Barack Obama

Michelle Obama

This Little Light of Mine

Ours is a rich and replete history. The memory of these names and what they did despite the obstacle of racism, encourages us to reach exceptional heights of greatness. Our best hour is yet to come. Everyone on that list (and it is by no means exhaustive), like you and I, lived in an environment drenched in the nightmare of racism/white supremacy. They lived in and faced situations that were intolerable, horrifying, and which many might count as impossible. But despite it, they soared! Despite the obstacles that a racist white supremacist society threw at them in attempts to block their way, they soared. They rendered it meaningless. In every sphere and arena of life they excelled; in sports, in politics, in writing, in law, in creating institutions, in business, in organizing, in military, in entertainment, in teaching, in education, and in leadership. They have left us a blueprint of how to overcome racism/white supremacy.

Within us, you and I, is the DNA of greatness, the bright light of eternity. Racism/white supremacy attempts to make us forget our greatness by trying to destroy that light. They lie about it, minimize it, ridicule it, or claim it for themselves. When we succumb to those attempts, our light grows dimmer, so much so that some of us cannot see it or forget that it's there. That is the job of racism/white supremacy—to make us forget our identity. Our job, our responsibility, our legacy demands that we see, acknowledge, and let our lights shine. As we shine our light, others around us seeing that light are reminded of their own light. Once they see and feel their own light, they two begin to let it shine.

To know something of your greatness and how we can overcome racism/white supremacy, read the stories of some of these people. Read them to your children and grandchildren. Pass the torch. Read their autobiographies and you will be inspired beyond comprehension. Read their biographies if there is no autobiography. When you do, you will get a glimpse of your light, your power, your ability to soar! You will feel the surge of greatness that belongs to you. They, through their writings, speeches, and interviews, have passed the torch of greatness to us. This will allow you to pick up the torch with purpose, clarity, and determination that cannot be stopped. Racism/white supremacy does not stand a chance when confronted with our power.

What I speak of here may appear to be an individual enterprise or undertaking, and to a degree, it is. You as the individual must read, listen, and think for yourself. But we must not think of the task before us as just individuals. It is our task as a group. We are a group. We must think like a group. We must act like a group. When we do, we will soar as a group. Individual achievement and accomplishments in the face of racism/white supremacy is good in that it can inspire the group. Our failures as a group have all too often been due, in part, to our focus on and dependence upon individuals rather than groups. Individuals cannot in the end win against groups. In a racist/white supremacist society, individuals can be isolated and destroyed. We have seen this played out over and over. The leader is killed, and the movement dies with them. There is a better way. Our power does not lie in depending on a single leader.

Yes, a single leader can inspire us, this is true. That leader is passing to us the spark that we need to think, act, and move as a group. Groups are stronger because they have the power of numbers on their side. Individual threads can be broken easily. But 10, 40, 100, 1000, a million threads together will always win the day. When we stand together, we win. It's the only way we win against racism/white supremacy or any entity that stands against us.

We must see as a vision, the day when we will once again teach our own children and guide them in the paths that work for us and not against us. We must see the day when we will control the resources in our community and use them for the benefit of all in the community.

Do not let anyone tell you that we cannot work together as a people. We must stop saying it. We work well together and accomplish what we set out to collectively do. You cannot look at what we do together on a basketball court and say in truth that we can't work together. You cannot look at the Supremes, Destiny Child, Earth, Wind & Fire, The Commodores, Tupac, and Biggie and say we can't work together. You cannot look at the Black Panthers, the US organization, the Black Liberation Army, SNCC, the Civil Rights movement, and the Nation of Islam and say we can't work together. We cannot look at what the Honorable Marcus Garvey and UNIA and the African Communities League did and say we can't work together. We CAN work together because we HAVE worked together. The thing that is critical to this, however, is a sustainable vision of where we want to go as a group.

I offer two books for your consideration because they have outlined a plan of action that may be taken. The first is, *The Destruction of Black Civilization* by Chancellor Williams. At the end of that book, Williams offered a blueprint of sorts that could be used but has yet to be implemented. The second is by Dr. Claud

Anderson, *PowerNomics: The National Plan to Empower Black America*. His entire book sets the tone of what we must do with practical tactics that can be employed for working together.

—Ashe— [2]

Still I Rise

BY MAYA ANGELOU

You may write me down in history
With your bitter, twisted lies,
You may trod me in the very dirt
But still, like dust, I'll rise.

Does my sassiness upset you?
Why are you beset with gloom?
'Cause I walk like I've got oil wells
Pumping in my living room.

Just like moons and like suns,
With the certainty of tides,
Just like hopes springing high,
Still I'll rise.

Did you want to see me broken?
Bowed head and lowered eyes?
Shoulders falling down like teardrops,
Weakened by my soulful cries?

Does my haughtiness offend you?
Don't you take it awful hard.
'Cause I laugh like I've got gold mines
Diggin' in my own backyard.

You may shoot me with your words,
You may cut me with your eyes,
You may kill me with your hatefulness,
But still, like air, I'll rise.

Does my sexiness upset you?
Does it come as a surprise?
That I dance like I've got diamonds
At the meeting of my thighs?

Out of the huts of history's shame
I rise
Up from a past that's rooted in pain
I rise
I'm a black ocean, leaping and wide,
Welling and swelling I bear in the tide.

Leaving behind nights of terror and fear
I rise
Into a daybreak that's wondrously clear
I rise
Bringing the gifts that my ancestors gave,
I am the dream and the hope of the slave.
I rise
I rise
I rise.

Maya Angelou, *"Still I Rise" from And Still I Rise: A Book of Poems.* Copyright © 1978 by Maya Angelou.

Notes

Introduction

1. Vasamazulu Credo Mutwa, Indaba, *My Children: African Folktales*, (New York: Grove Press, 1970), *xx*. A sangoma is highly respected healer among the Zulu people of South Africa.

Humiliation

1. Timmonsville is a small agricultural town about twelve miles from Florence, which was the next largest town. Florence is now the sixth largest city in South Carolin*a*.

Chapter 1: The Gospel of Racism

1. Derrick Bell, *Faces at the Bottom of the Well: The Permanence of Racism*, (New York: Basic Books, 1992), 7. The reference to pre-Brown made by Bell refers to the famous court case Brown v. Board of Education of Topeka, 347 U.S. 483, on May 17, 1954. It was a landmark decision of the U.S. Supreme Court in which the Court ruled that U.S. state laws establishing racial segregation in public schools are unconstitutional, even if the segregated schools are otherwise equal in quality.

The term bias has become one of the synonyms for racism. My thinking is that it is a euphemism for racism. Its use has, in the last few years, become the in-vogue term to use to soften and otherwise obfuscate the term racism. That is an advent that occurred long after Bell's book.

Separation

1. Derrick Bell, *Faces At the Bottom of the Well: The Permanence of Racism.* (New York: Basic Books, 1992), 7.

Chapter 2: The Big Misunderstanding

1. The so-called race card is an attempt by whites to neutralize our recognition of racist acts and behavior. It is design is to make us apprehensive about pointing out these behaviors. It in and of itself is racist behavior.

2. Barbara Trepagnier, *Silent Racism: How Well-Meaning White People Perpetuate the Racial Divide* (Boulder: Paradigm Publishers, 2006), 43.

3. Ibid., *50.*

Chapter 3: What You May Not Know About Racism

1. Pooja Sawrikar and Ilan Katz, *"Only White People can be Racist: What Does Power Have to Do With Prejudice?" UTS ePRESS: n. pag WEB 17 November 2009.*

2. Basil Davidson, *African Civilization Revisited* (Trenton: Africa World Press, 1991), 3.

Chapter 4: The Demonic Invention

1. By 1779, Blumenbach had expanded his list to five races. Caucasian, Mongolian, Malyan, Ethiopian and American. Based on his ill-founded conclusion that Caucasians were the original race, he concluded that Africans were not inferior to the rest of mankind, but it was only due to their contact with Caucasians. He is quoted as saying the following on the matter: *"Finally, I am of opinion that after all these numerous instances I have brought together of negroes of capacity, it would not be difficult to mention entire well-known provinces of Europe, from out of which you would not easily expect to obtain off-hand such good authors, poets, philosophers, and correspondents of the Paris Academy; and on the other hand, there is no so-called savage nation known under the sun which has so much distinguished itself by such examples of perfectibility and original capacity for scientific culture, and thereby attached itself so closely to the most civilized nations of the earth, as the Negro."https://en.wikipedia.org/wiki/Johann_Friedrich_Blumenbach* Also note that even though the French term *racisme* had not been coined until the nineteenth century the practice preceded the the naming of the phenomenon. Ned and Constance Sublette, *The American Slave Coast: A History of the Slave-Breeding Industry* (Chicago: Lawrence Hill Books, 2016), 276ff. Leary shines informative light on this period as well. See Joy Leary, *Post Traumatic Slave Syndrome: America's Legacy of Enduring Injury and Healing.* (Milwaukie: Uptone Press, *2005) 42, 43.*

2. J. C. Nott & George Gliddon, *Types of Mankind,* (Philadelphia: Lippincott, Grambo & Co., 1854), 182. Hottentot was an offensive name applied by the Europeans to the Khoikhoi people of Southern Africa.

3. Georg Wilhem Hegel, given at Jena lectures in Berlin 1830-1831.

4. The discussion of this type of codification of racism does not ignore the fact that the practice of racism by white people can be seen long before the advent of the above codifications. The above examples merely point to the time, place and persons who provided a literature that could be referenced to help develop it into a kind of reliable system. The practice extends back to the Greeks and Romans and shows a progressive development of the concept in practice.

5. Nelly Fuller, Jr., *The United Independent Compensatory Code/System/Concept: a textbook/workbook for thought, speech and/or action for victims of racism (white supremacy)*, (Washington, DC: Neely Fuller, Jr., 1984 revised edition), 32.

6. James H. Breasted, *The Conquest of Civilization*, (New York: Harper & Brothers, 1926) 113.

7. See Chancellor Williams, *The Destruction of Black Civilizations: Great Issues of a Race From 4500 B. B to 2000 A.D.* (Chicago, Third World Press, 1987). Cheikh Anta Diop, *Civilization or Barbarism: An Authentic Anthropology* (Brooklyn, Lawrence Hill Books, 1991). Basil Davidson, *African Civilization Revisited* (Trenton: African World Press, 1991). John G. Jackson, *Introduction to African Civilizations* (New York: Citadel Press, 1994). Robinson, Battle & Robinson, *The Journey of the Songhai People* (Philadelphia: The Pan African Federation Organization, 1987).

Chapter 5: White People's Fantasy World

1. Claud Anderson, *PowerNomics: The National Plan to Empower Black America,* (Maryland: PowerNomics Corporation of America, Inc. 2001), *5.*

Chapter 6: Remember: Why We Are Not The Racist

1. Claud Anderson, *PowerNomics: The National Plan to Empower Black America* (Maryland: PowerNomics Corporation of America, Inc., 2001) 5.

2. Paula Rothenberg, *Racism and Sexism* (New York: St. Martin's Press, 1988) 6. This book is one of her earliest. She has written or edited multiple volumes on the topic since this work and maintained the same position throughout her life.

3. Molefi K. Asante, *Afrocentricity* (Trenton: Africa World Press, Inc., 1988) 43.

4. Joel Kovel, *White Racism: A Psychohistory* (New York: Columbia University Press, 1984), xxxvii.

5. Ibid., xxxvii-xxxviii

6. Ibid., 11.

7. Barbara Trepagnier, *Silent Racism: How Well-Meaning White People Perpetuate the Racial Divide* (Boulder: Paradigm Publishers, 2006).

8. Bobby E. Wright, *The Psychopathic Racial Personality and Other Essays,* (Chicago: Third World Press, 1984) 3.

9. Examples include, Lucy Christopher, *Stolen* (United Kingdom: Scholastic, Inc., 2009); Mary Kubica, *The Good Girl* (Toronto: MIRA Books, 2014); Julia Sanders, *Stockholm Syndrome-Bonding with Captors: True Stories of a Psychological Phenomenon* (Independently published, 2017).

10. I. K. McKenzie, "Physiological and Psychological Effects of Kidnapping and Hostage-Taking" *Police Studies* Volume:10 Issue:2 Dated:(Summer 1987) Pages:96-102. http://www.ncjrs.gov/App/publications/abstract.aspx?ID=106528

11. Na'im Akbar, *Breaking the Chains of Psychological Slavery* (Tallahassee: Mind Productions & Associates, 1996) v.

12. Ibid., v.

13. Ibid., v.

14. Sobantu Mzwakali, *"Blacks Can't Be Racist," October 6, 2015, accessed June 29, 2020, https://sobantumzwakaliblog.wordpress.com/2015/10/06/blacks-cant-be-racist/,.*

Chapter 7: The Era of White Kidnappers

1. Bartolomé de Las Casas, *A Brief Account of the Destruction of the by Bartolome de las Casas*, (The Project Gutenberg EBook, January 9, 2007 [EBook #20321]). Often presented as a protector of so-called Indians, Las Casas only attempted to protected them because the Spaniards had nearly wiped them out with the most vicious and vile forms of brutality in a very short period of time. It was upon realizing they were wiping out their source of free labor that Las Casas lamented. It was in light of this that he and others suggested the Africans be used as a replacement.

2. Eric Williams, *Capitalism and Slavery,* (London: Andre Deutsch. 1964), 9-11. The older name for the prison was in fact Clerkenwell Prison. It was also known as Clerkenwell House of Detention or Middlesex House of Detention. It had been built on

the site of two earlier prisons, The Clerkenwell Bridewell that housed convicted prisoners and the New Prison that house those awaiting trial. https://en.wikipedia.org/wiki/Clerkenwell_Prison.

3. Ibid., 11-13.

4. Alan Brinkley, Andrew Huebner & John Giggie, *The Unfinished Nation: A Concise History of the American People* (New York: McGraw-Hill Education; 9th edition, 2018).

5. Alan Brinkley, Andrew Huebner & John Giggie, *The Unfinished Nation: A Concise History of the American People* (New York: McGraw-Hill Education; 9th edition, 2018).

6. J. A. Rogers, *American's Gift to Africa* (Helg M. Rogers, 1951), 58. *(Terre Haut: James O'Neal, 1910).*

7. James O'Neal, "White Slavery in the Colonies," *The Workers in American History, 4th Edition,*(Charleston: *BiblioLife, 1921), 32.*

8. Ibid., 33.

9. Ibid., 33-34.

Chapter 8: What Happened to White People?

1. Molefi K. Asante, *Afrocentricity: Theory of Social Change, Revised & Expanded* (Chicago:African American Images, *2003), 22.*

2. Cheikh Anta Diop, *The Cultural Unity of Black Africa: The Domains of Matriarchy & of Patriarchy in Classical Antiquity,* (London: Karnak House, 1989), *47ff.*

3. Joel Kovel, *White Racism: A Psychohistory* (New York: Columbia University Press, 1984*), 20.*

4. *http://witnify.com/christopher-columbus-letter-new-world/*

5. James W. Loewen, *Lies My Teacher Told Me: Everything Your American History Textbook Got Wrong,* (New York: The New Press, *1995), 33.*

6. Ibid. *33.*

7. See the Constitution of the United States of America Article 1, Section 2, Clause 3.

8. Joel Kovel, *White Racism: A Psychohistory* (New York: Columbia University Press, *1984), 16ff.*

9. *https://www.digitalhistory.uh.edu/disp_textbook.cfm?*
smtID=3&psid=393#:~:text=In%20August%201862%2C%20Li
ncoln%20stated,was%20building%20to%20end%20slavery

Chapter 10: The Black White Supremacists

1. Derrick Bell, *Faces At the Bottom of the Well: The Permanence of Racism.* (New York: Basic Books, 1992), 148.

2. Kamau & Janice Kenyatta, *Black Folk's Hair Revisited: Secrets, Shame & Liberation,* (Albrightsville: Songhai Publications, 2019), 22-23.

3. Derrick Bell, *Faces At the Bottom of the Well: The Permanence of Racism.* (New York: Basic Books, 1992), 15.

4. *Ibid. 15.*

Chapter 11: Where Are All The Racists, Anyway?

1. Maulana Karenga, *Introduction to Black Studies, 3rd edition* (Los Angles, 2002), 139-141.

Chapter 12: How Racism Damaged Our People

1. Ruby Shivers, *Verbal Healing: We Must Reject, TIRED, TRITE, TASTELESS, and other Nonsensical Expressions That Keep Us Damaged* (Plainfield: ChaAski, 1996), 121.

2. Molefi K. Asante, *Afrocentricity* (Trenton: Africa World Press, Inc., 1988) 31.

3. This does not negate the fact that the term was used by our people during enslavement. To the contrary, it was used extensively during enslavement and was also used after enslavement. What I speak of here is how the later use of media helped forged the term and brought it out in the open in a way that was not accepted before.

Chapter 13: This Little Light of Mine

1. Ruby Shivers, *Verbal Healing: We Must Reject, TIRED, TRITE, TASTELESS, and other Nonsensical Expressions That Keep Us Damaged* (Plainfield: ChaAski, 1996), 96.

2. Ashe (pronounced *ah shay*) is a Yoruba word meaning power, command and authority. The ability to make whatever one says happen.

Works Cited

Akbar, Na'im. *Breaking the Chains of Psychological Slavery*. Mind Productions & Associates, 1996.

Alexander, Michelle. *The New Jim Crow: Mass Incarceration in the Age of Colorblindness*, 2010.

Anderson, Carol. *White Rage: The Unspoken Truth of Our Racial Divide*. Bloomsbury, 2017.

Anderson, Claud. *PowerNomics*. Powernomics Corporation of America, 2001.

Asante, Molefi Kete. *Afrocentricity: The Theory of Social Change*. Revised and Expanded, African American Images, 2003.

Barillaro, Angie. *Stolen, Lucy Christopher*. Scholastic, Inc., 2009.

Bell, Derrick. *Faces at the Bottom of the Well*. Basic Books, 2018.

Bonilla-Silva, Eduardo. *Racism Without Racists*. Roman & Littlefield Publishers, Inc., 2010.

Breasted, James Henry. *The Conquest of Civilization*. Harper & Brothers, 1938.

Brinkley, Alan, et al. *The Unfinished Nation: A Concise History of the American People*. McGraw-Hill Education, 2018.

Casas, Bartolomé. *A Brief Account of the Destruction of the Indies*. Good Press, 2020.

"Christopher Columbus Letter on the New World | Witnify." *Witnify*, https://www.facebook.com/Witnify, 9 Oct. 2017, http://witnify.com/christopher-columbus-letter-new-world/.

Contributors to Wikimedia projects. "Johann Friedrich Blumenbach - Wikipedia." *Wikipedia, the Free Encyclopedia*, Wikimedia Foundation, Inc., 12 Nov. 2003, https://en.wikipedia.org/wiki/Johann_Friedrich_Blumenbach.

Davidson, Basil. *African Civilization Revisited*. Africa Research and Publications, 1991.

Degruy, Joy. *Post Traumatic Slave Syndrome*. Joy Degruy Publications Incorporated, 2017.

"Dictionary.Com | Meanings and Definitions of Words at Dictionary.Com." *Dictionary.Com*, http://www.dictionary.com/. Accessed 12 June 2021.

"Digital History." *UH - Digital History*, https://www.digitalhistory.uh.edu/disp_textbook.cfmsmtID=3&psid=

393#:~:text=In%20August%201862%2C%20Lincoln%20stated,was%20building%20to%20end%20slavery. Accessed 12 June 2021.

Diop, Cheikh Anta, *Civilization or Barbarism*. Lawrence Hill Books, 1991.

---. *The Cultural Unity of Black Africa*. Red Sea Press (NJ), 1989.

Fuller, Neely. *The United-Independent Compensatory Code/System/Concept Textbook*. Revised Edition, Neely Fuller, 1984.

Jackson, John G. *Introduction to African Civilizations*. Citadel Press, 1994.

Karenga, Maulana. *Introduction to Black Studies*. 3rd ed., University of Sankore Press, 2002.

Kenyatta, Janice, and Kamau Kenyatta. *Black Folk's Hair: Secrets, Shame & Liberation Revisited*. Songhai Publications, 2019.

Kovel, Joel. *White Racism*. Columbia University Press, 1984.

Kubica, Mary. *The Good Girl*. MIRA, 2014.

Loewen, James W. *Lies My Teacher Told Me*. The New Press, 1995.

McKenzie, I. K. "'Physiological and Psychological Effects of Kidnapping and Hostage-Taking.'" *Police Studies*, 1987.

Mutwa, Credo Vusa'mazulu, and Vusamazulu Credo Mutwa. *Indaba, My Children*. Grove Press, 1999.

Mzwakali, Sobantu. "Blacks Can't Be Racist | Sobantu Mzwakali." *Sobantu Mzwakali*, https://www.facebook.com/WordPresscom, Oct. 6, 2015, https://sobantumzwakaliblog.wordpress.com/2015/10/06/blacks-cant-be-racist/.

Nott, Josiah Clark, and George Gliddon. *Types of Mankind*. Lippincott, Grambo & Co, 1854.

O'neal, James. *The Workers in American History*. 4th ed., BiblioLife, 1921.

"Racism | Definition of Racism by Merriam-Webster." *Dictionary by Merriam-Webster: America's Most-Trusted Online Dictionary*, https://www.merriam-webster.com/dictionary/racism. Accessed 12 June 2021.

"Racism | Definition of RACISM by Oxford Dictionary on Lexico.Com Also Meaning of Racism." *Lexico Dictionaries | English*, Lexico Dictionaries, https://en.oxforddictionaries.com/definition/racism. Accessed 12 June 2021.

Robinson, Calvin Russell, et al. *The Journey of the Songhai People*. The Pan African Federation Organization, 1987.

Rogers, J. A. *Africa's Gift to America*. Civil War Centennial Edition, Wesleyan University Press, 2014.

Rothenberg, Paula S. *Racism and Sexism*. St. Martin's Press, 1988.

Sanders, Julia. *Stockholm Syndrome-Bonding with Captors*. Independent, 2017.

Sawrikar, Pooja, and Ilan Barry Katz. "'Only White People Can Be Racist: What Does Power Have to Do with Prejudice?'" *Cosmopolitan Civil Societies: An Interdisciplinary Journal*, no. 1, University of Technology, Sydney (UTS), Nov. 2009, pp. 80–99. *Crossref*, doi:10.5130/ccs.v2i1.1075.

Shivers, Ruby *Verbal Healing: We Must Reject, TIRED, TRITE, TASTELESS, and other Nonsensical Expressions That Keep Us Damaged*, ChaAski, 1996.

Tatum, Beverly Daniel. *Why Are All the Black Kids Sitting Together in the Cafeteria?* Basic Books, 2017.

Trepagnier, Barbara. *Silent Racism*. Taylor & Francis, 2017.

Williams, Chancellor. *Destruction of Black Civilization: Great Issues of a Race From: 4500 B.C to 2000 A.D.* Third World Press, 1987.

Williams, Eric. *Capitalism and Slavery*. Andre Deutsch, 1964.

Wright, Bobby Eugene. *The Psychopathic Racial Personality and Other Essays*. Third World Press, 1984.

T HE FOLLOWING IS AN excerpt from my next book with the fictional character Will C. Wright.

The Will C. Wright Files puts him at center stage.

Will C. Wright

(On Racism pt.1)

"You can't handle the truth!"
— Words uttered by actor Jack Nicolson
From the movie A Few Good Men (1992)

We could apply those five words to several areas of life, but none is more applicable than that which we apply to our understanding of racism. This was made abundantly clear to me from a recent interview conducted on the topic with the fictional character, Mr. Will C. Wright. It actually became more of a conversation, and at times the lines were blurred as to whether I was interviewing him or whether he was interviewing me.

C. Wright, as I call him, and for short, sometimes I just call him Will C., has a non-conventional way of seeing things. At times, our conversations can get pretty heated, and to an outsider, it might appear that at any moment we might come to blows. But it never comes to that. In some ways, we are both composites of different strains of thought in our community on a multiplicity of topics. He's had some college training, but his insights find their origins in his streetwise experience. I would place Will C. somewhere in his late 30s or maybe early 40s because of his youthfulness. Although, based on his mid-size, dark brown frame, and his early graying around the edges, he could easily be in his mid-50s or even early 60s for all I can tell. His wisdom betrays his youth, and it is difficult to surmise much about him, as he is secretive about his age and other personal matters. Here is the conversation for your consideration.

Interview With Will C. Wright

"Thank you, Mr. C. Wright, for taking time out of your schedule for this interview about racism and what it means," I began.

"It's my pleasure," he replied. "Although I know that you and most of your listeners are not going to agree with what I have to say," he said, with a calm confidence.

"Well, I'm sure that may be right," I replied wondering if he was going to be vulgar in his responses. "In fact," I continued, "I want you to speak your mind and feel free to share any of your insights with my listeners."

"That's exactly what I do all the time," he said, still confident.

"Great. So, let's begin by—" but before I could finish the statement,

C. Wright interrupted me.

"Excuse me," he said. "May I ask you a question before we get started?"

Surprised by the interruption I answered, "Ahh, sure. What's on your mind?"

"Would it be a distraction if I consulted some of my books as we talk from time to time?" he asked.

"No, not at all," I said. However, I was curious about the request and asked, "But why do you feel the need to consult books on this topic?"

"Well, it's not that I feel I *need* them," he said with an exaggerated emphasis on the word *need*. But it's just that I follow some old advice that one of my mentors taught us years ago," he finished.

"And what advice was that, may I ask?" a little more curious now about the request.

"Never get in a debate, discussion or argument with anyone until you find out what they have read, how much they have read, and how well they have understood what they have read," he said, with a little twinkle in his eyes.

I could tell this was an important point for him. But I didn't want to pursue it too much. And so I simply said, "That sounds like some really good advice if you ask me."

"Do you know why that's good advice?" he asked, with a slight smirk showing in his gaze.

Not sure of the correct answer, I slowly responded, "Ahhh, to show that you know what you're talking about?"

"Nope," he quipped. "Because if you don't," he continued, "some people can talk to you for hours out of their imagination. And you cannot have intelligent and productive discussions or win arguments against someone's imagination because they'll make up shit along the way just to win the argument."

"Hmmm," I said, thinking about it. "That's some damn good advice. Never thought of it like that," I replied, and meant it.

"I know," he said, "most people don't. But that single piece of advice has saved me countless hours of needless arguments with people who don't read and don't think." He paused, then said, "I'm sorry to have interrupted."

"No," I said, "it's perfectly okay and a good segue into my first question. There's a lot of talk these days about racism and it seems like it's everywhere.

What do you think of racism as it relates to our people?"

"We can't handle the truth about it," he said, without hesitation. "And that's because we don't understand it," he added.

I wondered why he sounded so sure about this, and so I asked, "What do you mean we don't understand it? Practically every black person I know understands racism."

"No, what I think you mean to say is that practically every black person you know and that I know *experiences* racism, but most of them don't fully understand it," he replied with emphasis.

"How can you say that?" I asked a little defensively.

"Because for one," he answered, "we're confused about racism, and two, we think we're responsible for it. At least in part," he conceded.

"Well, we are responsible to a degree, aren't we? I mean slavery ended over 150 years ago. How can we continue to blame white people for our situation when we are now all equal and have as many opportunities for advancement and education as everyone else?"

"You see, that…that's the problem right there," he said, pointing his finger at me. "You, and those like you, who say what you just said tells me you don't understand racism."

As C. Wright said those words, he emphasized them by pointing his finger at me in what seemed an accusatory manner. In fact, I was beginning to feel like he was attacking me for what appeared to be a self-evident fact. We had been set free from enslavement after the Civil War and given full citizenship. Except for 100 years of Jim Crowism, we now had been granted the same rights as every American citizen.

Additionally, President Johnson had signed the Civil Rights Act in 1964 that prohibited racial discrimination among other things. And he also signed the voting rights act of 1965. We could go anywhere and do anything we so desired in this great country of ours, I thought to myself. Yes, there were incidences of racism that occurred here and there, but they were happening less and less these days. Were they not? There were laws on the books against such acts, and many institutions had diversity training programs now. I didn't understand how and why Will C. couldn't understand all of this.

Did I Miss Something?

"What makes you think I don't understand racism?" I asked, in a demanding tone.

In an abrupt fashion, C. Wright, shuffled through his collection of books located near his feet. He pulled one out that was ripped and tattered from much use. He reached in his pocket and pulled out a pair of black framed glasses and put them on. He flipped through a few pages, and when he found what he was looking for said, "Listen to this."

And with a slow and deliberate emphasis on most of the words, he read the following:

"If you do not understand White Supremacy /Racism—what it is, and how it works— everything else that you understand, will only confuse you."

When he finished, he looked up at me and said, "Those are the words of Neely Fuller, Jr., a deep thinker who has spent the larger portion of his life studying and exploring the topic of white supremacy. Have you ever read any of his work?"

"No. I don't think I've ever heard of him before," I replied truthfully, with a tinge of embarrassment.

Then he asked, "Do you understand what that means?" referring to what he'd just read. "Of course, I understand what it means," I retorted. "But I get the feeling you're going to tell me that I don't. Is that right?"

"Yep," he said, without blinking. "That's exactly right. But I want you to hear me out before you jump to conclusions. Is that fair?" he asked. I nodded my approval.

"A few minutes ago in response to your question," he started, "I said that we as a people, black people, don't understand racism. What I meant by that is that we get it confused with prejudice and discrimination. We think that they all mean the same thing, but they don't."

I interjected,

"But is that thinking limited to only black people?"

"No, it's not, and that's a good point," he said. "As a matter of fact, most people, regardless of their race, get these words confused and use them interchangeably. And all of that contributes to the confusion that we have about racism."

"I don't get your point," I said, when he paused for a moment.

"The point," he continued, "is that those two words, discrimination and prejudice, are not racism. But we often hear people use those terms in place of racism as if racism, prejudice, and discrimination all mean the same thing. They don't mean the same thing," he said with an air of authority.

I tried to follow his logic, but for the life of me I didn't see where he was going with this stream of thought, or how it was connected to my question, so I commented, "So, as you see it, the words racism, prejudice, and discrimination don't mean the same thing."

"Exactly," he said. "To be prejudice means drawing a conclusion about something without having the necessary information to draw an intelligent conclusion. Discrimination means having the ability to distinguish and choose one thing over another as a preference."

I was beginning to understand his logic, and asked, "But isn't there racial prejudice and racial discrimination, C. Wright?"

"Of course there is," he replied. "But prejudice and discrimination, in and of themselves, are not racism. "And," he continued, "as such, they cannot be used when what you mean to say is racism. They're completely different animals."

"I get your point," I said. Then asked, "But that brings up the question of

What then is racism?

I don't think we can continue our conversation without defining that term for your argument to be coherent. Does that make sense to you?"

"It makes perfect sense," he replied. "In fact, by asking that question, my respect for you just moved up a few notches," he said, laughing.

Curious about what he found so funny, I asked, "Why is that?"

Still laughing he said, "Because, unlike most people, you have the good sense to ask the question that almost no one ever asks when it comes to this topic, which contributes to confusion and misunderstanding for our people. The fact is most people don't know how to correctly define racism. Most are too embarrassed to admit that they don't know what it is. And so, everyone's pretending that they know what it means when, in fact, they don't. And that gets them into these conversations that end up in arguments over something neither one of them, if put to the test, can define correctly. I applaud you for asking."

"It just seemed like the logical sequence of the conversation," I said. "I mean, given what you've said about prejudice and discrimination so far, it's only logical. So, what does it mean?"

"I'm not trying to put you on the spot," he said, "but I'd like to demonstrate a point. And before I tell you," he said, "let me ask, if you would be so kind as to indulge me, for a moment. What do you think it means?

Caught a little off guard, I felt like C. Wright had backed me into a corner. But it was a corner of my own making since I was the one who had invited him to be interviewed. As my mind searched for an answer, Will C., was looking at me like a cat who had cornered a mouse and was ready to pounce and devour his meal. I was going to say something like racism is when one group of people are prejudice against another group. Or when one group discriminates against another group, but he had closed that door with his earlier argument about discrimination and prejudice not being the same as racism. I looked at him with confidence and replied, "Well, I think racism is when one group of people hates another group of people because of their skin color."

"That was a good try, and it's close, but it's not quite right," he said. "But don't feel bad. That's the answer a lot of people give especially if they've never really thought about it in thorough terms. Wanna give it another try?" he asked.

Feeling slightly insulted by the implication that I had not given it much thought, I replied, "Yeah, I'll try again, but first, I need you to tell me why you think my answer is wrong?"

"It's wrong," C. Wright began, "because the definition of racism has nothing to do with hate. Hate has to do with an intense dislike of something or someone for any number of reasons."

"But don't you think that there is hatred with racism?"

I objected.

"For sure there's hatred involved with racism," he replied. "However, hatred may be a result of racism or a by-product of racism but hate, in itself, is not racism. We, you and I, or anybody for that matter, can hate someone or something without being racist. For example, I can hate spinach, mayonnaise, country music, horror movies, or the way someone treats me, but that does not make me a racist. Is this making sense?" he asked, as he finished.

I had to admit that it did make sense. "Yes, I can see right to your point C. Wright, I conceded, but do you really hate mayonnaise," I asked with a chuckle.

"Can't stand the stuff," he answered. "What about you?"

"I love it and could eat it on just about anything," I said.

"That's probably why you're so damn crazy. Anybody who can eat that stuff, can eat anything," he said. We both had a hearty laugh about it before returning to the topic.

"I guess we're entitled to eat what we want," I said.

This banter had eased the mood between us, and now I felt more open to exploring what C. Wright was trying to get at.

"You got any other ideas about the meaning of racism?" he asked.

"I have to be straight with you C. Wright. Based on your explanations about the words prejudice and discrimination, it's a little difficult to come up with other reasonable definitions," I offered. "And on top of that, I'm more curious to hear what you have to say about it. How do you define it?"

"Well," he said, still in a confident mood, "it's very simple. Racism is nothing more than the belief held by white people that they are superior to people who are not white."

"Come again," I said, not believing what I thought I heard him say.

"It's not that difficult to understand, is it? But for your benefit, I'll say it this way. Racism is white people thinking they're better than everyone else just because they're white," he said, repeating himself.

"I thought that's what I heard you say," I responded in disbelief. I looked at him for a moment as we stared back at each other. C. Wright had a defiant look on his face that seemed to dare me to disagree. So, I said, "You know, C. Wright, that's a pretty good explanation except that, (I hesitated) it has a few problems, don't you think?"

"No, not at all," he said. "But you've clearly got a problem with it."

"Well, yeah. I do," I responded, wondering where to start.
"Spit it out then," he said, daring me to take the bait.

"Okay, for starters, your definition puts the whole blame of racism on white people. You can't do that. Because when you say it like that, you make it look as if only white people are racist," I said, more like I blurted it out.

"That's exactly what it means!" he exclaimed.

I countered in disbelief, "You gotta be kidding me, right?"

"Nope," he said, shaking his head, "not at all."

"So you're telling me that

White people are solely to blame for racism?

Am I getting this right?" I asked.

"Not only am I telling you that my friend, but the dictionaries and the historical record will tell you the exact same thing," he answered with passion, and paused for effect. He continued with a fervor that was building, "White people are responsible for creating racism, practicing racism, teaching racism, and maintaining racism. And furthermore," he added, as he was now insistent "they are the only people in the history of the world to do it. Black people have never done it, brown people have never done it, nor have yellow people. Nowhere in the historical record can you or anyone else point to a time and a place where black people, yellow people, or brown people expressed that they were superior to others who were not either black, yellow, or brown. Only those people who classify themselves as white-skinned have made the claim that they are superior to others solely because of their skin color being white."

"If what you say is true, C. Wright, then how have they done it," I asked.

"How have they done it?" he repeated as if he were surprised by the question. "Man," he said shaking his head. "Now, you gotta be kidding me."

He moved closer to me and said, "I don't know where you've been or if you've had your head under a rock somewhere, because it's as plain as daylight. They've done it in their writings, through their educational systems, through their political systems, through their religions, their court systems, their police systems, their economic system, social systems and military systems," he declared, with a glare in his eyes.

I could tell that he was relishing this moment. But the fact of the matter is he was making some very good points which were difficult to refute. I had read several world history books over the course of my life, and so, I quickly rummaged around my memory trying to recollect a case where anyone other than white people had claimed to be superior because of their skin color.

The only things I came up with were the Egyptians who claimed they were superior to everyone around them, but their claim was due to their superior culture not because of their black skin. I recalled that the Japanese claimed they were superior because of their culture and of their religion, Shintoism, not because of their skin color. The same could be said of the Hebrews who claimed a superior religion but not the superiority of skin color. It was true, too, that Indians had never made such a claim either. I searched through my mind in hopes of finding a case to disprove what he had said, but at the time,

I was coming up blank.

As I had mentally wandered off, C. Wright continued talking. When I returned from my psychological break from the conversation, I heard him saying, "White people don't claim they are superior because of any achievements or accomplishments either, you know. Their claim is without any merit whatsoever. The poorest white person," he continued, "without even a GED in hand, believes themselves to be superior to every black person regardless of the educational level achieved. And even those of us with advanced degrees and a mountain of experience are seen as less than them simply because our skin is black."

As he continued to talk, I looked at C. Wright as if

He had completely lost his mind.

I could not believe that this relatively intelligent man, whom I did respect despite our occasional differences, was saying what I had just heard him say. I couldn't believe it and I was infuriated with him.

"C. Wright," I said, interrupting him in a calm voice, "if you believe that, do you know what that means? It means that you are a racist."

"What?! Are you listening?" he exclaimed, in utter disbelief. "Let's back up a minute," he said. "I think we need to get a few things straight before we unintentionally confuse some of our people here on the topic."

"What do you have in mind?" I asked puzzled.

"Point number one, I cannot be a racist and neither can any other black person," he said. "And that includes you," he added.

I noticed he said that with a straight face and responded, "And, you think that black people cannot be racist? Is that right?"

"Black people *can* be racist,

meaning we, or anyone for that matter, possess the ability or potential to be racist. The fact of the matter, however, is we have not been racist either in rhetoric or in practice. I thought I already made this clear. I would think that from the definition of racism it was obvious. But to answer your question directly, no, black people are not racist," he exclaimed with defiance.

I was having a hard time accepting this, and it must have shown on my face because C. Wright offered to clear it up for me.

"If you listened to the definition of racism, which I revealed earlier," he said, "you would know this. It's something that white people do exclusively. Based on that single piece of information, you can't possibly formulate a reasonable thought that any black person could be racist. The history of the concept in terms of its origins and its historical practice by white people refutes any notion that black people have been racist in the past or that we are racist now. I really thought we had already covered this point. What am I doing here, spinning my wheels?" he asked. At that point, C. Wright fumbled through his books again and pulled out a couple of books. He put his glasses back on and turned the pages in one of them and said, "I don't want you to take my word for it or to think that I'm just making this up. All the credible social scientists are clear on this. This is what Dr. Claud Andersen who was the Assistant Secretary in the U.S. Department of Commerce under President Jimmy Carter says about this very point in his book, *PowerNomics: The National Plan to Empower Black America,*

'Black people cannot be racists. No group of Blacks has the power or exclusive control of resources to the degree that they can educationally, politically, economically and socially exploit and marginalize the White race. Blacks can only react to racism and try to alter the conditions that racism creates.'"

He then turns to the page of another book and said, "Here is what Dr. Paula Rothberg who wrote and taught extensively on racism and sexism for decades says about the matter in her book, *Racism and Sexism: An Integrated Study,*

'Racism involves the subordination of people of color by white people While an individual person of color may discriminate against white people or even hate them, his or her behavior or attitude cannot be called "racist"…racism requires something more than anger, hatred, or prejudice; at the very least, it requires prejudice plus power. The history of the world provides us with a long record

of white people holding power and using it to maintain that power
and privilege over people of color, not the reverse.'"

I could see his point. It was beginning to make sense. I opened my mouth to say something, but he waved me off and kept going.

"Point number two, based on your reaction to what I've said about the meaning of racism," he continued, "you have just admitted that you really don't understand racism.

Right now, probably for the first time in your life, you're grappling with facing the facts about it. I suspect that you and most black people know that what I'm saying is true.

But the problem is you have accepted the lies

this racist system has fed you about racism over the last 40 years."

"Oh, is that so?" I said, feigning shock. "And what is it, in your humble opinion, Mr. Will. C. Wright, that I and the rest of our black people have been fed about racism for the last 40 years? Do tell," I said sarcastically.

"It's simple," he began. "You've bought into the illusion of inclusion."

"The what?" I asked a little baffled.

"The illusion of inclusion," he repeated.

"Will. C, I have no idea what you're talking about," I said.

"Bear with me for a minute or two," he said. "The illusion of inclusion is this. After what is called the Civil Rights era, the period of the1960s and early 1970s is when so-called racial integration took place with the schools. You agree with me on that, right?" he asked.

I nodded my head in agreement.

"At the end of that period, we, and I mean black people, bought into the idea that racism had ended or at least we believed that it had been given a fatal blow and was on its deathbed. At the time too many of us thought that the brutal past of enslavement and second-class citizenship we had experienced was finally over. We also thought that the white power structure and white people for the most part were sincere in their effort to turn a new page in the book of the American nightmare of racism. We thought we were waking up to a new and brighter day and we were entering a period of blissful racial color blindness."

I couldn't help but interrupt to say, "You have to admit, don't you, that this picture you paint was in fact the reality. The country was trying to move in a better direction. Agreed?"

"Yes, I agree" he said. "You're right. There was an attempt, at least in many parts of the country, to move forward from a grim and grisly racial past. And this makes my point about the illusion of inclusion. We bought into the idea of finally being included in the so-called American dream. We believed that at last we were being included and we were now stepping in our rightful place of a well-earned and well-deserved position paid for with the blood, sweat and tears of our ancestors."

"What's the problem?" I asked. "Am I missing something?"

C. Wright rolled his eyes at me

as if to say, "you just don't get it."

"Gimme a break," I said. "By your own admission, the country had moved beyond racism, and we were being integrated into the system as equals. I remember that period, too, you know. I remember," I said with emphasis.

"Then you'll remember there was a time when it came to an end, too," he said. "And the end happened right at the beginning of the feel-good moment. Only problem is most of our people didn't get the memo. You remember that, too?" he asked.

I knew what he was talking about, and it was unavoidable I suppose. I don't know how he knew but I could tell by the way he looked at me. He knew that I knew precisely what he meant because he then said.

Read the rest of the conversation at:

www.TheWillCWrightFiles.com

About The Author

Kamau Kenyatta is a Professor of African American Studies at both Lafayette College and Northampton Community College. He is a former Professor of Africana Studies at William Paterson University where he taught racism and sexism classes for more than a decade. Kenyatta is an author whose works include, *The White People Show: How to Understand Racism and Still Be Wrong About It*, *Black Folk's Hair Revisited: Secrets, Shame & Liberation* (co-authored), and *The Confessions of a College Professor*.

He also writes fiction, on subjects related to the African World Experience, in *The Will C. Wright Files* series. Kamau lives in Pennsylvania and spends his free time playing drums in a popular 10-piece funk band.

Find out more about Professor Kenyatta at https://www.professorkenyatta.com/. The professor is available for interviews, podcasts, and speaking engagements.

Word From The Author

I would like to thank you for taking the time to read my book I hope that you have enjoyed it and that the material was informative and helpful.

I have a small favor to ask because I would like to get the book into as many hands as possible over the next few months.

I would greatly appreciate it if you would leave a short review of the book on Amazon. If you have never written a book review before, here are a few suggestions that might be helpful.

Write about:

- *what you liked or didn't like about the book.*

- *what you learned or discovered if anything from the book.*

- *whether you would recommend the book along with why or why not.*

Of course, be honest and frank in your responses. Other than Amazon, you might also leave a review on any of the social media platforms such as Facebook, Twitter, Instagram, LinkedIn, etc.

Wherever you can leave comments about the book, would be helpful because it will help spread the word about the book. My hope is that it will help stimulate more productive discussions around the topic.

Thank you in advance for you contribution.

CPSIA information can be obtained
at www.ICGtesting.com
Printed in the USA
LVHW081746070822
725381LV00008B/627

The series Lecture Notes in Computer Science (LNCS), including its subseries Lecture Notes in Artificial Intelligence (LNAI) and Lecture Notes in Bioinformatics (LNBI), has established itself as a medium for the publication of new developments in computer science and information technology research, teaching, and education.

LNCS enjoys close cooperation with the computer science R & D community, the series counts many renowned academics among its volume editors and paper authors, and collaborates with prestigious societies. Its mission is to serve this international community by providing an invaluable service, mainly focused on the publication of conference and workshop proceedings and postproceedings. LNCS commenced publication in 1973.

Adi Akavia · Shlomi Dolev · Anna Lysyanskaya ·
Rami Puzis
Editors

Cyber Security, Cryptology, and Machine Learning

9th International Symposium, CSCML 2025
Be'er Sheva, Israel, December 4–5, 2025
Proceedings

Editors
Adi Akavia
University of Haifa
Haifa, Israel

Anna Lysyanskaya
Brown University
Providence, RI, USA

Shlomi Dolev
Ben-Gurion University of the Negev
Be'er-Sheva, Israel

Rami Puzis
Ben-Gurion University of the Negev
Be'er-Sheva, Israel

ISSN 0302-9743   ISSN 1611-3349 (electronic)
Lecture Notes in Computer Science
ISBN 978-3-032-10758-9   ISBN 978-3-032-10759-6 (eBook)
https://doi.org/10.1007/978-3-032-10759-6

This Springer imprint is published by the registered company Springer Nature Switzerland AG
The registered company address is: Gewerbestrasse 11, 6330 Cham, Switzerland

If disposing of this product, please recycle the paper.

Preface

CSCML, the International Symposium on Cyber Security, Cryptology and Machine Learning, is an international forum for researchers, entrepreneurs, and practitioners in the theory, design, analysis, implementation, or application of cyber security, cryptology, and machine learning systems and networks and, in particular, for conceptually innovative topics in these research areas. Information technology has become crucial to our everyday lives, an indispensable infrastructure of our society, and therefore a target for attacks by malicious parties. Cyber security is one of the most important fields of research these days because of these developments. Two of the (sometimes competing) fields of research, cryptography and machine learning, are the most important building blocks of cyber security.

Topics of interest for CSCML include: cyber security design; secure software development methodologies; formal methods, semantics, and verification of secure systems; fault tolerance, reliability, and availability of distributed secure systems; game-theoretic approaches to secure computing; automatic recovery, self-stabilizing, and self-organizing systems; communication, authentication, and identification security; cyber security for mobile systems and the Internet of Things; cyber security of corporations; security and privacy for cloud, edge, and fog computing; cryptocurrency; blockchain; cryptography; cryptographic implementation analysis and construction; secure multi-party computation; zero-knowledge proofs; privacy-enhancing technologies and anonymity; post-quantum cryptology and security; machine learning and big data; anomaly detection and malware identification; business intelligence and security; digital forensics; digital rights management; trust management and reputation systems; and information retrieval, risk analysis, and DoS.

The 9th CSCML took place online on December 4–5, 2025, and was managed from Be'er-Sheva, Israel. The keynote speakers were Robert Blumofe, Executive Vice President and Chief Technology Officer of Akamai Technologies; Alon Kaufman, CEO and Co-Founder of Duality Technologies; Alex Pentland, Stanford HAI Fellow and Toshiba Professor at MIT; David Tennenhouse, Global R&D Executive, Technology Innovator, and Strategist; and Leslie Valiant, Turing Award Winner and professor at Harvard University.

The conference was organized in cooperation with the International Association for Cryptologic Research (IACR), and selected papers will appear in a dedicated special issue of the Journal of Cryptography and Communications.

This volume contains 26 contributions (17 regular papers and 9 short papers) selected by the Program Committee from 46 submissions. All submitted papers were read and evaluated by at least three members of the Program Committee, assisted by external reviewers. We thank the members of the Program Committee for all their hard work.

We gratefully acknowledge the support of IBM and Ben-Gurion University of the Negev (BGU), in particular BGU-NHSA, the BGU Lynne and William Frankel Center for Computer Science, and the Department of Computer Science.

December 2025

Adi Akavia
Shlomi Dolev
Anna Lysyanskaya
Rami Puzis

Organization

Founding Steering Committee

Orna Berry	Google Cloud, Israel
Shlomi Dolev (Chair)	Ben-Gurion University of the Negev, Israel
Yuval Elovici	Ben-Gurion University of the Negev, Israel
Bezalel Gavish	Southern Methodist University, USA
Ehud Gudes	Ben-Gurion University of the Negev, Israel
Jonathan Katz	University of Maryland, USA
Rafail Ostrovsky	University of California, Los Angeles, USA
Jeffrey D. Ullman	Stanford University, USA
Kalyan Veeramachaneni	Massachusetts Institute of Technology, USA
Yaron Wolfsthal	IBM, Israel
Moti Yung	Columbia University and Google, USA

Organizing Committee

General Chair

Shlomi Dolev	Ben-Gurion University of the Negev, Israel

Program Chairs

Adi Akavia (PC Co-chair)	University of Haifa, Israel
Anna Lysyanskaya (PC Co-chair)	Brown University, USA
Rami Puzis (PC Co-chair)	Ben-Gurion University of the Negev, Israel

Organization Chair

Dayana Dyachenko	Ben-Gurion University of the Negev, Israel

Additional Chairs

PhD and Master's Track

Oded Margalit	Ben-Gurion University of the Negev, Israel

Pitch Track

Yonah Alexandre Bronstein	Ben-Gurion University of the Negev, Israel

Program Committee

Masayuki Abe	NTT, Japan
Mayank Agarwal	Sardar Patel Institute of Technology, India
Gilad Asharov	Bar-Ilan University, Israel
Irad Ben-Gal	Tel Aviv University, Israel
Riccardo Bettati	Texas A&M University, USA
Andrej Bogdanov	University of Ottawa, Canada
Ioannis Chatzigiannakis	Sapienza University of Rome, Italy
Yilei Chen	Tsinghua University, China
Michele Ciampi	University of Edinburgh, UK
Jean-Sebastien Coron	University of Luxembourg, Luxembourg
Nir Drucker	IBM Research - Israel, Israel
Nurit Gal-Oz	Sapir Academic College, Israel
Juan Garay	Texas A&M University, USA
Aarushi Goel	Purdue University, USA
Ehud Gudes	Ben-Gurion University of the Negev, Israel
Sukrit Gupta	Indian Institute of Technology Ropar, India
Lihi Idan	Texas A&M University, USA
Stanislaw Jarecki	University of California, Irvine, USA
Florian Kaiser	Karlsruhe Institute of Technology, Germany
Vladimir Kolesnikov	Georgia Institute of Technology, USA
Ilan Komargodski	Hebrew University and NTT Research, Israel and Japan
Manish Kumar	Indian Institute of Technology Ropar, India
Noam Mazor	Tel Aviv University, Israel
Tal Moran	Reichman University, Israel
Nir Nissim	Ben-Gurion University of the Negev, Israel
Marwan Omar	Illinois Institute of Technology, USA

Omkant Pandey	State University of New York at Stony Brook, USA
Anat Paskin-Cherniavsky	Ariel University, Israel
Giuseppe Persiano	Università degli Studi di Salerno, Italy
Eyal Ronen	Tel Aviv University, Israel
Sivan Sabato	Ben-Gurion University of the Negev, Israel
Gil Segev	Hebrew University and Coinbase, Israel and USA
Jad Silbak	Northeastern University, USA
Paul Spirakis	University of Liverpool, UK
Eran Tromer	Boston University, USA
Mayank Varia	Boston University, USA
Ramarathnam Venkatesan	Microsoft Research, USA
Andrea Vitaletti	Sapienza University of Rome, Italy
Sophia Yakoubov	Aarhus University, Denmark
Kevin Yeo	Google and Columbia University, USA
Eylon Yogev	Bar-Ilan University, Israel

External Reviewers

Duncan Adamson	University of St Andrews, UK
Efthyvoulos Drousiotis	University of Liverpool, UK
Zoltan Dobrady	Széchényi István University of Győr, Hungary
Ilia Leybovich	Ben-Gurion University of the Negev, Israel
Alexei Lisitsa	University of Liverpool, UK
Christopher Smith	Stony Brook University, USA
Yannis Stamatiou	University of Patras, Greece
Tang Yuh Tang	Stony Brook University, USA
Brady Testa	Texas A&M University, USA
Raja Varanasi	Ben-Gurion University of the Negev, Israel

Sponsors

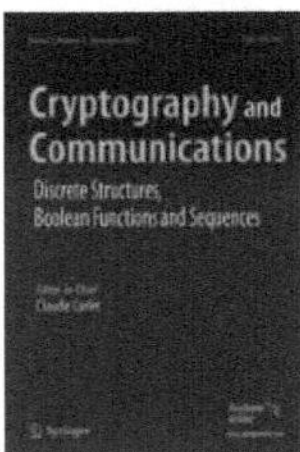

In cooperation with

Contents

Similarity-Based Retrieval over Homomorphic Encryption

Adi Akavia[1], Ramy Masalha[1,2](✉), and Reut Meiri[1]

[1] University of Haifa, Haifa, Israel
ramymassalha@gmail.com
[2] IBM Research, Haifa, Israel

Abstract. The problem of similarity-based retrieval, in which a server retrieves a vector from a database that is most similar to a query of a client, is a fundamental problem for many applications. Fully Homomorphic Encryption (FHE) supports computations over encrypted data and thus can be used to preserve the privacy of the query and database during the similarity-based retrieval process. However, existing works that tackle the problem of similarity-based retrieval over FHE typically rely on sending an encrypted vector containing several computed similarity scores from the server to the client. This client-aided approach exposes too much information on the dataset, while also incurring high communication bandwidth that is linear in the size of the dataset. In this work, we present a similarity-based retrieval system in which the server sends the client only one ciphertext containing the retrieved entry, thus not exposing additional information on the dataset while improving the communication bandwidth to be constant. We conduct empirical experiments in which we perform similarity-based retrieval over a dataset of half a million encrypted vectors in less than 30 s with accuracy of 98.9%–99.9%, and improve the communication bandwidth by 8× in the case of a single query vector and by 512× in the case of a batch of 64 query vectors.

1 Introduction

In the similarity-based retrieval task, a server stores a dataset of n templates $A_{l \times n} = \{\mathbf{a}_1, \mathbf{a}_2, \ldots, \mathbf{a}_n\}$. Each template is a normalized vector of real values of size l, which may describe fingerprints, face features, scientific papers, etc. The client provides an input feature vector $\mathbf{v} \in \mathbb{R}^l$ and asks the server to retrieve the template or templates whose feature vectors are the closest to the one provided by the client, according to some similarity metric, such as cosine similarity.

As there is a growing trend to outsource computation to the cloud, the need to preserve the privacy of both the query and the database becomes critical, especially in settings involving sensitive data or where complying with regulation laws such as HIPAA [28] or GDPR [14] is required.

Submission Type: Regular Submission.

Fully Homomorphic Encryption (FHE) provides a promising approach to this problem, enabling computations to be performed directly on encrypted data without the need for decryption. A user who has confidential data can encrypt the data using FHE and outsource the computation to a cloud service. The entire computation process in the cloud is applied while the data is encrypted, which enables taking advantage of the cloud's high computation power while preserving the privacy of the sensitive data.

However, adapting similarity-based retrieval algorithms to the FHE setting is not trivial. Selecting the most similar database entry to a given query requires computing an argmax function, which is a complex operation to be carried out efficiently over FHE. This is due to the fact that state of the art argmax algorithms over FHE usually rely on several comparison operations that are heavy to implement over FHE (see Table 1).

Many previous solutions to the task of similarity-based retrieval over FHE (e.g. [6,12,13,19,25,27,32]) have avoided the problem of computing argmax, and instead relied on the client side to perform the argmax operation on cleartext data. This is done by sending the vector of all computed similarities to the client side, which in turn decrypts the similarities and finds the maximal similarity. This client aided-approach has two downsides. First, it compromises the privacy of the server side, since the client sees in cleartext information related to all entries of the sensitive dataset, rather than seeing only the similarity relating to the closest entry. Second, this approach increases communication bandwidth to be linear in the size of the dataset compared to a solution which requires the server to only send one ciphertext containing the retrieved entry and thus achieving constant communication bandwidth. See Sect. 1.2 for more detailed review of the state of the art.

Recent advances in the FHE field make the computation of the argmax operation over FHE more efficient, thus increasing the feasibility of performing similarity-based retrieval completely in the server side, without relying on the client to compute the argmax. More specifically, [22] introduces an argmax algorithm which operates under the assumption that an FHE scheme that supports s SIMD slots is used, and computes the argmax of $n \leq s$ values using $\log_2 \log_2 n$ SIMD-comparisons, while computing the argmax of $n > s$ values using $\frac{n}{s} + \log_2 \log_2 s$ SIMD comparisons.

1.1 Our Contribution

In this work, we provide a similarity-based retrieval system that improves the communication bandwidth and privacy guarantees of the common approach in the state of the art which relies on the client to compute the argmax (see also Sect. 1.2). Our system achieves the mentioned improvements by leveraging the argmax algorithm introduced in [22]. More precisely, our contributions can be summarized as follows.

- We reduce the communication bandwidth in the application of similarity-based retrieval. We reduce the number of information bits returned from the

server to the client from $n \log_2 n$ when using the common approach of returning all distances to the client, to only $\log_2 n$ bits when using our algorithm. In terms of SIMD ciphertexts, this means that we reduce the number of ciphertexts returned from the server to the client from $\frac{n}{s}$ to 1.
– We enhance the privacy guarantees in the application of similarity-based retrieval, by ensuring that the client only sees the most similar entry to his input, rather than learning the similarities of all entries in the database, as common in the state of the art.
– We perform empirical experiments of similarity-based retrieval over FHE with databases of size up to 2^{19} encrypted templates in less than 30 s, resulting with accuracy ranging from 98.9% to 99.9% compared to the similarity-based retrieval results on cleartext data. We improve the communication size compared to the approach of returning all distances to the client by up to $8\times$ in the case of a single query vector and by up to $512\times$ in the case of a batch of 64 query vectors.
– We demonstrate the usage of our similarity-based retrieval protocol for the application of image-to-text matching using the Contrastive Language-Image Pre-training (CLIP) model.

1.2 Related Work

Using homomorphic encryption for privacy preserving similarity-based retrieval has been widely investigated. For example, refer to [29] for a review on using homomorphic encryption in the context of biometrics. In many works that tackle the application of similarity-based retrieval over homomorphic encryption, the server returns the computed similarities to the client side, which in turn decrypts them and finds the maximum similarity or similarities in cleartext. These works include, for example, [6,12,13,25] that perform fingerprint identification and [19,27,32] that perform text retrieval. As explained in Sect. 1, this approach compromises the privacy of the server side by allowing the client to learn the similarities corresponding to all entries in the dataset rather than only learning the similarity of the closest sample to the client's input.

Some works combine homomorphic encryption with secure multiparty communication techniques, with one or more interaction rounds between the server and the client, to find the identities whose distance from the input fingerprint is below a given threshold. These works include, for example, [3] who perform fingerprint identification, [19,32], who perform face identification and [23] who perform DNA sequence retrieval. Relying on communication rounds between the server and the client has the downside of adding extra burden on the client because it is required to stay active during the similarity-based retrieval protocol. By using FHE, our similarity-based retrieval algorithm does not require the client to do anything aside from encrypting the input and decrypting the results. It should be noted that the protocol suggested in [23] requires only one round, but their protocol is specific to the problem of DNA similarity-based retrieval, in where the data vectors consist of entries that can receive only one of the four characters 'A', 'B', 'C' and 'D'. Their solution can not be trivially generalized to the general usecase of working over vectors with real values.

Some works, such as [10,11,30,31], perform similarity-based retrieval while assuming the existence of two servers, one of which possesses the secret key of the used homomorphic encryption. The server with the secret key helps decrypting the computed similarities and finding the maximal similarity in cleartext. However, the existence of a trusted server who is allowed to posses the secret key is not always feasible.

Ibarrondo et al. [17] perform face identification over FHE and compute the argmax in the server side, thus preserving the server's privacy. However, they operate under the assumption that only one of the stored feature vectors have a distance smaller than δ from the input feature vector, for a user-specified $\delta > 0$. This assumption does not hold in databases that include more than one image for each identity, such as the commonly used LFW [16,21] database. Moreover, there approach can not be trivially extended to find the most similar k images for $k > 1$, while our argmax algorithm can be naturally extended to find the greatest k values for $k > 1$. Finally, the approach of [17] assumes that the threshold δ is known in advance, which is not always the case. Consider for example the usecase of a police searching for the identity of a criminal using a distorted fingerprint sample. Since the sample fingerprint is distorted, the closest match for this fingerprint can not be guaranteed to be greater than a known δ.

Shokri et al. [26] apply genome similarity detection over FHE and compute the maximum similarity in the server side. However, they do not describe their method of computing the maximum over FHE and their experiments results does not show the time spent on computing the maximum. In this work, we show theoretically and empirically that our suggested argmax algorithm over FHE is faster than state of the art argmax algorithms.

Some works (e.g. [2,5]) perform similarity search over FHE but they rely on all-pairs comparison to check for each pair of samples (i,j) in the dataset which sample is closer to a given query. This requires n^2 comparisons for a dataset of size n, which is not practical for large values of n. In our work, we report experiments on $n \approx 500K$ samples with a practical runtime of 27 s.

Cong et al. [7] presented a top-k sorting network over FHE and demonstrated its application to find the nearest k neighbors to an encrypted query. However, they rely on low-precision comparisons (6-bit precision), and demonstrate their work on a database of 1000 samples. When working with larger datasets (e.g. $500K$ samples as in our experiments), the compared values become too close to each other, requiring higher precision comparisons. Expanding the method of [7] to support higher precision comparisons is not trivial.

Finally, in an independent concurrent work, Kim et al. [20] introduce a secure protocol for approximate k nearest neighbors over FHE. They report a runtime of 83 hours to find an approximation of the 16 most similar samples to a given query from a dataset of $1M$ samples on a 16-thread CPU machine. In our experiments, it takes us 27 s to (exactly) find the most similar sample to a query from a dataset of $500K$ samples on a GPU machine (See Sect. 4). While it is hard to directly compare the our runtime with [20] due to the different settings,[1] our work has an advantage over [20] because we find the exact most similar sample rather than an approximation. The higher accuracy is significant for tasks with highly sensitve requirements, such as retrieving faces of suspect criminals from a dataset.

The rest of this paper is organized as follows. In Sect. 2, we provide an overview of the preliminary material. In Sect. 3, we introduce our similarity-based retrieval system over FHE. In Sect. 4, we present experimental results, and in Sect. 5, we conclude the paper and suggest potential areas for future research.

2   Preliminaries

2.1   Fully Homomorphic Encryption

Fully Homomorphic Encryption (FHE) is a cryptographic primitive which supports computation over encrypted data. In this paper, we focus on FHE schemes that support SIMD-operations. These schemes encrypt multiple values in one ciphertext, and support operations that are applied on all values of the ciphertexts concurrently. Homomorphic Encryption (HE) and FHE schemes may be defined as follows:

Definition 1. *A homomorphic (public-key) encryption scheme* $\varepsilon = ($Gen, Enc, Dec, Eval$)$ *with message space* $\mathcal{M}$ *is a quadruple of Probabilistic Polynomial Time (PPT) algorithms as follows:*

- Gen *(key generation) takes as input the security parameter* 1^λ, *and outputs a pair* (pk, sk) *consisting of a public key* pk *and a secret key* sk; *denoted:* $(pk, sk) \leftarrow$ Gen(1^λ).
- Enc *(encryption) takes as input a public key* pk *and a message* $m \in \mathcal{M}$, *and outputs a ciphertext* c; *denoted:* $c \leftarrow$ Enc$_{pk}(m)$.
- Dec *(decryption) takes as input a secret key* sk *and a ciphertext* c, *and outputs a decrypted message* m'; *denoted:* $m' \leftarrow$ Dec$_{sk}(c)$.
- Eval *(homomorphic evaluation) takes as input the public key* pk, *a circuit* $C : \mathcal{M}^l \rightarrow M$ *and ciphertexts* $c_1, \ldots, c_l$, *and outputs a ciphertext* $\hat{c}$; *denoted* $\hat{c} \leftarrow$ Eval$_{pk}(C, c_1, \ldots, c_l)$.

Correctness. *The scheme is correct if for every* (pk, sk) *in the range of* Gen(1^λ) *and every message* $m \in \mathcal{M}$,

$$Pr[\mathsf{Dec}_{sk}(\mathsf{Enc}_{pk}(m)) = m] \geq 1 - \mathsf{neg}(\lambda),$$

where the probability is taken over the random coins of the encryption algorithm.

---

[1] According to our benchmarks, a bootstrap operation using the FGb preset on the HEaaN library is $255\times$ faster when it is run on a GPU machine than when it is run on a 44 threads CPU machine.

$\mathcal{C}$-homomorphism *A homomorphic encryption scheme is $\mathcal{C}$-homomorphic for a circuit family $\mathcal{C}$ if for all $C \in \mathcal{C}$ and for any set of inputs $x_1, \ldots, x_l$ to C, letting $(pk, sk) \leftarrow \mathsf{Gen}(1^\lambda)$ and $c_i \leftarrow \mathsf{Enc}(pk, x_i)$ it holds that:*

$$Pr[\mathsf{Dec}_{sk}(\mathsf{Eval}_{pk}(C, c_1, \ldots, c_l)) \neq C(x_1, \ldots, x_l)] \leq \mathsf{neg}(\lambda),$$

where the probability is taken over all randomness in the experiment.

Compactness. *A homomorphic encryption scheme is compact if there exists polynomial $p(\cdot)$ such that the decryption algorithm can be expressed as a circuit of size $p(\lambda)$.*

Fully Homomorphic. *A homomorphic encryption scheme is fully homomorphic if it is both compact and $\mathcal{C}$-homomorphic for the class $\mathcal{C}$ of all efficiently computable circuits.*

Security. *A homomorphic encryption scheme is CPA-secure if no PPT adversary $\mathcal{A}$ can distinguish between the encryption of two equal length messages x_0, x_1 of his choice. See a formal definition of CPA-security in [18].*

SIMD-Support. To improve the latency of FHE computations, some FHE schemes support *Single Instruction Multiple Data* (SIMD). These schemes support ciphertexts that have multiple *slots*, such that each slot encrypts a separate value, and basic operations, such as multiplication, rotation and addition, are applied on all slots of a ciphertext concurrently.

2.2   Argmax over FHE

Let $\mathbf{X} = \{x_0, x_1, \ldots, x_{n-1}\}$ be a vector of real values. The argmax operation is defined to return the index of the maximal value in $\mathbf{X}$. In this work, we use the algorithm of [22] to compute argmax over FHE. Assuming a SIMD-supporting FHE scheme with s slots is used, the algorithm of [22] computes the argmax of $n \leq s$ values using $\log_2 \log_2 n$ SIMD-comparisons, and computes the argmax of $n > s$ values using $\frac{n}{s} + \log_2 \log_2 s$ SIMD comparisons.

3   Our Similarity Based Retrieval System over FHE

In this section we introduce our similarity based retrieval protocol over FHE. We start by defining the similarity-based retrieval problem over cleartext data, then we define the functionality to be realized by our protocol as well as the threat-model we work with and finally we present our protocol.

3.1   Similarity-Based Retrieval over Cleartext

The following definition defines the similarity-based retrieval problem over cleartext data.

Definition 2. *Similarity-based retrieval.* *In the similarity-based retrieval problem, we are given public parameters $n, l \in \mathbb{N}$, representing the database size and the embedding size respectively, a similarity metric* similarity()*, a database of n templates $A_{n \times l} = \{\mathbf{a}_1, \mathbf{a}_2, \ldots, \mathbf{a}_n\}$ such that $\mathbf{a}_i \in \mathbb{R}^l$ for each $1 \leq i \leq n$ and an input template $\mathbf{v} \in \mathbb{R}^l$. For simplicity, we assume all dataset templates $\mathbf{a}_i$ ($1 \leq i \leq n$) as well as the input template $\mathbf{v}$ are normalized vectors (i e. their Euclidean length is 1). The required output is the index i of the template $\mathbf{a}_i$ that is most similar to the input $\mathbf{v}$ according to* similarity()*, or in other words,* argmax$_{1 \leq i \leq n}$(similarity$(\mathbf{v}; \mathbf{a}_i)$)*.*

The similarity metric is often a low degree polynomial, such as cosine similarity or Euclidean distance. In our implementation we use the cosine similarity metric, which can be computed by a matrix-vector multiplication. Denote by A^t the transpose of $A_{n \times l}$. Since we assume all templates are normalized, the column vector $\mathbf{r} = A^t \cdot \mathbf{v}$ of length n contains in its i-th entry the cosine similarity similarity$(\mathbf{v}; \mathbf{a}_i)$ between the input template $\mathbf{v}$ and the i-th template of the database, $\mathbf{a}_i$. Thus, the required output when using the cosine similarity metric is argmax$(A^t \cdot \mathbf{v})$.

3.2   Functionality

The similarity-based retrieval functionality is formalized in Fig. 1. Our protocol includes three parties: A data owner, a cloud server and a client.

- **Data owner.** The data owner owns a dataset of n templates $A_{l \times n} = \{\mathbf{a}_1, \mathbf{a}_2, \ldots, \mathbf{a}_n\}$. Each template is a normalized vector of real values of size l, which may describe fingerprints, face features, scientific papers, etc. The data owner may be limited in computing power and storage and thus it wants to outsource all templates to the cloud. For simplicity, we consider a scenario of a single data owner rather than multiple data owners. This scenario may reflect, for example, a police station which owns a dataset of face images of suspected criminals.
- **Cloud server.** The server is powerful in computing power and storage, and we want to utilize its resources for the sake of performing similarity-based retrieval.
- **Client.** The client has a normalized input template $\mathbf{v} \in \mathbb{R}^l$, and he wants to access the similarity-based retrieval service to get as an output the index i of the template $\mathbf{a}_i \in A_{l \times n}$ that is the most similar to $\mathbf{v}$ according to the used similarity metric (cosine similarity in our implementation).

Similarity-based Retrieval Functionality for (known) parameters $n, l \in \mathbb{N}$

Parties: A Data Owner DO, a client Cl, and a server S.

Inputs: For DO, a database of n templates $A_{l \times n} = \{\mathbf{a}_1, \mathbf{a}_2, \ldots, \mathbf{a}_n\}$. Each template is a normalized vector of real values in $\mathbb{R}^l$. For Cl, a normalized template $\mathbf{v} \in \mathbb{R}^l$. S does not have any input.

Output: Cl gets the index, i, of the most similar template, $\mathbf{a}_i$, to $\mathbf{v}$, according to the cosine similarity metric.[a] The other parties have no output.

Fig. 1. Similarity-based retrieval functionality ([a] While we focus on the cosine similarity metric for simplicity, our protocol works with any similarity metric that can be implemented over FHE.)

3.3   Threat Model

Denote by DO the data owner, by S the server and by Cl the client in our protocol. We assume that DO is honest, while we assume that S and Cl are semi-honest, meaning that they follow the designed protocol but try to deduce as much information as possible. S and Cl are also assumed to be non-colluding. In other words, our goal is to protect the data owner's privacy against computationally bounded, non-colluding and semi-honest client and server, and to protect the client's privacy against a computationally bounded and semi-honest server. This threat model is formalized below.

Terminology. Let Π be a 3-party protocol realizing a deterministic functionality, executed between the PPT Data owner DO with input $A_{l \times n}$ (a matrix of n normalized templates of length l), the PPT client Cl with input $\mathbf{v}$ (a normalized template in $\mathbb{R}^l$) and the PPT server S (with no input). For public parameters params (as specified in Fig. 2), we use $\Pi(A_{l \times n}, \mathbf{v}, \perp, \mathsf{params})$ to denote the output of the execution of Π with public parameters params when DO, Cl have inputs $A_{l \times n}, \mathbf{v}$ respectively and S has no input. The *view* of a party consists of the public parameters, its input, randomness, and the messages it received during the protocol execution on inputs $A_{l \times n}$ and $\mathbf{v}$. We denote the view of a party P by

$$\mathrm{View}_{\mathrm{P}}^{\Pi}(A_{l \times n}, \mathbf{v}, \perp, \mathsf{params}).$$

For a set of t parties $\mathcal{P} = \{\mathrm{P}_1, \ldots, \mathrm{P}_t\}$, we define the view

$$\mathrm{View}_{\mathcal{P}}^{\Pi}(A_{l \times n}, \mathbf{v}, \perp, \mathsf{params})$$

as

$$\left(\mathcal{P}, \mathrm{View}_{\mathcal{P}_1}^{\Pi}(A_{l \times n}, \mathbf{v}, \perp, \mathsf{params}),\right.$$
$$\left. \ldots, \mathrm{View}_{\mathcal{P}_t}^{\Pi}(A_{l \times n}, \mathbf{v}, \perp, \mathsf{params})\right).$$

The following definition, which is based on the m-party definition for the deterministic case from [15, Def. 3.1.1] and updated to fit our three-party protocol, formally defines the security properties.

Definition 3 (privacy against non-colluding semi-honest client and server). *Let* F *be the (deterministic) similarity-based retrieval functionality of Fig. 1 and let* $\Pi = (\mathrm{DO}, \mathrm{Cl}, \mathrm{S})$ *be a protocol as above. For every pair of inputs* $(A_{l\times n} \in \mathbb{R}^{l\times n}, \mathbf{v} \in \mathbb{R}^l)$ *and for a subset* $\mathcal{P} \subset \{\mathrm{Cl}, \mathrm{S}\}$, *denote by* $(A_{l\times n}, \mathbf{v})|_{\mathcal{P}}$ *the inputs of the parties of* $\mathcal{P}$ *(* $\mathbf{v}$ *if* $\mathrm{Cl} \in \mathcal{P}$ *and* $\emptyset$ *otherwise) and by* $\mathsf{F}_{\mathcal{P}}(A_{l\times n}, \mathbf{v})$ *the outputs of the parties of* $\mathcal{P}$ *when* F *is executed on the inputs* $(A_{l\times n}, \mathbf{v})$. *We say that* Π *privately computes* F *against semi-honest client and server if there exists a negligible function* $\mathsf{neg}(\cdot)$ *such that for all set of public parameters as in Fig 2, and for every pair of inputs* $(a_{l\times n}, \mathbf{v})$:

1. ***Correctness.***

$$
\Pr\left[\begin{array}{l} \Pi\left(A_{l\times n}, \mathbf{v}, \perp, \mathsf{params}\right) = \\ \mathsf{F}\left(A_{l\times n}, \mathbf{v}, \perp\right) \end{array}\right] \geq 1 - \mathsf{neg}(\lambda)
$$

2. ***Privacy.*** *There exists a polynomial-time algorithm* Sim *such that for every* $\mathcal{P} \subset \{\mathrm{Cl}, \mathrm{S}\}$, *the following two distributions are computationally indistinguishable:*

$$
\left\{ \mathsf{Sim}\left(\mathsf{params}, \mathcal{P}, (A_{l\times n}, \mathbf{v})|_{\mathcal{P}}, \mathsf{F}_{\mathcal{P}}\left(A_{l\times n}, \mathbf{v}\right)\right) \right\}
$$

and

$$
\left\{ \mathrm{View}_{\mathcal{P}}^{\Pi}\left(A_{l\times n}, \mathbf{v}, \perp, \mathsf{params}\right) \right\}.
$$

Theorem 1 (security). *The protocol of Fig. 2 privately computes the functionality of Fig. 1 against non colluding and semi-honest client and server.*

3.4   Protocol Description over FHE

To describe our similarity-based retrieval protocol over FHE, we assume we are provided two FHE-friendly circuits that compute matrix-vector multiplication and argmax, respectively:

- $C_{\mathsf{matVecMul}}$: Receives a matrix $A_{l\times n}$ and a vector $\mathbf{v} \in \mathbb{R}^l$ and returns n values representing the product $A^t \cdot \mathbf{v}$, where A^t is the transpose of $A_{l\times n}$.
- C_{argmax}: Receives n values and returns the index of the maximal input value.

The argmax circuit, C_{argmax}, may be implemented using the argmax algorithm of [22], while a possible implementation for the matrix-vector multiplication circuit, $C_{\mathsf{matVecMul}}$, is explained in [1]. Given these two circuits, Fig. 2 describes our similarity-based retrieval protocol over FHE. However, the protocol is agnostic to the specific implementation of C_{argmax} and $C_{\mathsf{matVecMul}}$.

Private Protocol for Similarity-based Retrieval

Public parameters: An FHE encryption scheme $\mathcal{E} = (\mathsf{Gen}, \mathsf{Enc}, \mathsf{Dec}, \mathsf{Eval})$; a security parameter λ; the number of templates in the database n; the embedding size l; an FHE-friendly argmax circuit C_{argmax} and an FHE-friendly matrix-vector multiplication circuit $C_{\mathsf{matVecMul}}$.

Inputs and Outputs: See Figure 1.

The protocol $\mathsf{PP} = \langle \mathrm{DO}, \mathrm{Cl}, \mathrm{S}\rangle$ proceeds as follows:

1. **Offline phase:**
   (a) DO runs $\mathsf{Gen}(1^{\lambda})$ to obtain a public and secret key pair (pk, sk) and sends pk to S and Cl.
   (b) DO encrypts all templates in $A_{l \times n}$ to obtain a vector of n ciphertexts $c_1, c_2, \ldots, c_n$ that represent $\mathsf{Enc}_{pk}(A_{l \times n})$, and sends the encrypted templates to S.[a]
2. **Online phase:**
   (a) Cl encrypts the template $\mathbf{v}$ to obtain a ciphertext $c = \mathsf{Enc}_{pk}(\mathbf{v})$ and sends it to S.
   (b) S computes $c_{\mathrm{res}} = \mathsf{Eval}\big(C_{\mathsf{argmax}} \circ C_{\mathsf{matVecMul}}, (c_1, \ldots, c_n, c)\big)$ (where $\circ$ stands for circuit composition).
   (c) S sends c_{res} to DO, who decrypts it and returns the result to Cl.[b]

Fig. 2. Private protocol for similarity-based retrieval. ([a] Depending on the packing method and the used FHE configuration, it may be possible to pack $A_{l \times n}$ using fewer than n ciphertexts. We assume each column is packed into one ciphertext for simplicity. [b] In practice, the encrypted result may be returned to the client who uses a key-management service to decrypt it. For simplicity, we let the data owner handle decryption.)

4 Experimental Results

In this section we introduce experimental results of our similarity-based retrieval system. We start by describing the used hardware and FHE configurations, then we present a similarity-based retrieval experiments over random inputs, showing our improvement over the state of the art, and finally we present a similarity-based retrieval experiment that uses well-known machine learning model and dataset, proving the practicality of our system for a real-world application.

4.1 System and Configuration Description

Experiments were conducted on AMD EPYC 7763 64-Core Processor, 1 CPU, 900 GB RAM, 1 GPU NVIDIA A100-SXM4-80GB. We used HELayers SDK [1] which is a software tool designed to efficiently execute analytical algorithms over encrypted data using FHE, leveraging different open and closed source FHE libraries. In the reported experiments, we used HELayers' wrapper of the HEaaN [4] implementation of the CKKS scheme. The used context is the FGb preset context implemented in the HEaaN library. This context is a bootstrappable context with 2^{15} slots, a multiplication depth of 12, a fractional precision of 42 bits and an integer precision of 18 bits. The FGb context supports both "normal" bootstrapping and "extended" bootstrapping. The normal bootstrapping supports ciphertexts whose encrypted values fall in the range $(-1, 1)$, while the extended bootstrapping supports ciphertexts whose encrypted values fall in the range $(-2^{20}, 2^{20})$. The normal bootstrapping requires the bootstrapped ciphertext to be of level 3 or higher, while the extended bootstrapping requires the input ciphertext to be of level 4 or higher. Both kinds of bootstrapping restore the bootstrapped ciphertext to level 12. Table 1 shows the runtime of several operations when using the HEaaN FGB context and the machine described above.

Table 1. Runtime for basic CKKS operations

Operation	Runtime (ms)
add	0.036
mult (level 12)	1.174
mult (level 4)	0.600
rotate	0.655
bootstrap (normal)	74.000
bootstrap (extended)	173.820
isGreater	233.860

4.2   Similarity-Based Retrieval Experiments

In our similarity-based retrieval experiment, we generated n normalized vectors of size 512 containing random values uniformly chosen from the range $(0, 1)$. These n vectors were encrypted over FHE and they represent the dataset stored in the server side. Another normalized vector of size 512 was randomly generated to represent the client's input. The client's input is encrypted over FHE and it is multiplied with the server's encrypted matrix, using the matrix-vector multiplication method explained in [1], to produce a vector of size n containing the n similarity scores between the client's input and each of the n samples stored in the server side. Then, the argmax algorithm of [22] is applied on the matrix-multiplication result. The encrypted maximal index resulting from the argmax step is returned to the client side as the final result.

Table 2. Results of the similarity-based retrieval experiment over FHE. The matrix vector multiplication was performed as in [1], and the argmax was performed using the hierarchical argmax algorithm of [22]. The repack column indicates time spent on changing the packing of the data inside ciphertexts to move between the packing required for the matrix-vector multiplication and the packing required for argmax, using rotations and multiplications with plaintext vectors.

n (database size)	repack (ms)	mat-vec mul (ms)	argmax (ms)	total (ms)	accuracy
2^{15}	1349	536	3338	5223	99.4%
2^{16}	2096	924	3787	6807	99.5%
2^{17}	2888	1836	4637	9362	99.8%
2^{18}	2978	3526	8853	15361	99.9%
2^{19}	2984	7456	16841	27291	98.9%

Runtime and Accuracy. Table 2 shows the resulting runtime and accuracy for different values of n. We ran the experiments on 1000 input vectors and reported the average runtime. The reported accuracy specifies the percentage of inputs for which the most similar index retrieved over FHE matched the expected index computed over cleartext. The most similar index computed over FHE was considered to be correct if its absolute difference with the expected index is less than 0.5, which ensures that the computed index may be rounded after decryption without affecting correctness. The results of Table 2 show that the accuracy of our similarity-based retrieval algorithm ranges between 98.9% and 99.9%, and that it takes about 27 s to perform similarity-based retrieval on a database of half a million encrypted vectors.

While in our experiment we used randomly generated vectors, the same protocol may be applied on the feature values extracted by any machine learning model that relies on embedding its inputs to feature vectors in $\mathbb{R}^l$ and computing similarity between the feature vectors. Suitable models may be, for example, biometric identification models and text similarity models. Since our similarity-based algorithm is agnostic to the used machine learning model, we conducted the experiment on random feature values. Our reported results show that given a suitable similarity based retrieval model, the accuracy obtained when running our algorithm over FHE is expected to be very similar to the accuracy obtained when running the model over cleartext data. For example, see Sect. 4.3 for an experiment that runs our algorithm with a well-known machine learning model.

Communication Bandwidth. Table 3 shows our improvement of the communication bandwidth. We computed the size of the encrypted output returned from the server side both in our method that uses argmax over FHE to compute the maximal similarity, and in the common method in the state of the art in which the server returns all computed similarities to the client. In the discussion below, we refer to the method of returning all similarities to the client by the *client-aided method*.[2]

Two modes are considered in Table 3. In the first mode, the similarity-based retrieval is applied on a single input vector. In this case, the output of our method consists of one ciphertext for all reported database sizes, while the output of the client-aided method consists of multiple ciphertexts that contain one similarity value for each vector in the database, thus requiring linearly more communication when the database size increases. Note that in the client-aided method we used complex-packing of the server's output to reduce the number of returned ciphertexts by 2, by packing every two output values $a, b \in \mathbb{R}$ as one complex value $a + ib$. This explains why the communication size reported in Table 3 for the client-aided method is the same for the database sizes $n = 2^{15}$ and $n = 2^{16}$, as both cases resulted in exactly one complex packed output ciphertext being returned from the sever. When operating over a database of half a million encrypted vectors, Our method reduces the size of the output returned from the server by $8\times$ compared to the client-aided method.

In the second mode, the similarity-based retrieval is applied on a batch of 64 inputs. Since each input is a vector of length 512 and we use an FHE configuration with 2^{15} slots, all inputs together consist of $64 * 512 = 2^{15}$ values and they fit exactly in one-ciphertext, thus not increasing the communication size from the client to the server. However, the communication size in the opposite direction, consisting of the server's output, is increased when using the client-aided method. This increment happens because the server is now required to return $64\times$ more output values: one similarity value for each vector in the database and for each of the 64 inputs. When using our method, on the other hand, the communication size does not increase compared to the mode of a single input. This is due to the fact that all 64 output indices can be packed in a single SIMD ciphertext. Thus, in the case of a batch of 64 inputs, and when operating over a database of half a million encrypted vectors, our method reduces the size of the output returned from the server by $512\times$ compared to the client-aided method. It should be noted that when using a batch of up to 2^{15} inputs (which is the number of slots), the number of output ciphertexts returned by the server in our method stays the same, while it grows linearly when using the client-aided method, which will make the enhancement factor of our method even larger. But when using a batch size of more than 64, more than one ciphertext should be used to encrypt the input, thus increasing the communication bandwidth in the direction from the client to the server, for both our method and the client-aided method.

---

[2] This experiment assumes that the same FHE configuration is used in both methods. It should be noted that the client-aided method requires a very small multiplication depth of 1 and hence in some use cases it allows using a much lighter FHE configuration which will make communication size smaller and change the results of our experiment. In a real-life scenario, we expect the similarity-based retrieval to be a part of a wider computation unit and hence requiring a heavy FHE configuration even if the client-aided similarity-based retrieval method is used.

Table 3. Communication size of Protocol Fig. 2 in megabytes from the server to the data owner for various database sizes. In the client-aided method, the server returns all computed similarities to the data owner. In our method, the server uses our argmax component to compute the index of the maximal similarities and return to the data owner a single ciphertext containing the index of the vector having the maximal similarity.

	$n = 2^{15}$	$n = 2^{16}$	$n = 2^{17}$	$n = 2^{18}$	$n = 2^{19}$
comm. size (client-aided) - one input (MB)	2	2	4	8	16
comm. size (**ours**) - one input (MB)	**2**	**2**	**2**	**2**	**2**
comm. size (client-aided) - batch of 64 inputs (MB)	64	128	256	512	1024
comm. size (**ours**) - batch of 64 inputs (MB)	**2**	**2**	**2**	**2**	**2**

4.3   Image-to-Text Matching

Table 4. Results of the similarity-based retrieval experiment using the CLIP [24] model and ImageNet [8] test set.

#classes	#test_imgs	server runtime (hrs.)	baseline (cleartext) accuracy	FHE accuracy
1000	50000	31	63.34	63.22

In this section, we demonstrate the usage of our similarity-based retrieval algorithm on feature embeddings computed by the Contrastive Language-Image Pre-training (CLIP) model [24]. The CLIP model learns a multi-modal embedding space by leveraging contrastive learning to align visual and textual representations effectively. This enables CLIP to connect visual and textual data without task-specific fine-tuning, making it highly adaptable for diverse applications. In zero-shot settings, CLIP shows significant potential for tasks like image retrieval or search, effectively matching images to relevant text or vice versa without prior training on the specific task. For security applications, CLIP can be adapted for tasks like facial recognition from text descriptions, where encrypted data can be used to securely and robustly match images to textual descriptions while ensuring privacy.

CLIP's zero-shot process works by using the labels as potential text pairings and predicting the most probable (image, text) pair. To specify the task, text prompts are provided, and the use of multiple templates is ensembled to boost performance.

Following the method described by the authors, we compute feature embeddings for each image in the ImageNet [8] test set of 50000 images, where each embedding results with a vector of length 512. Similarly, we compute the feature embeddings of 1000 candidate classes for our classification task, again resulting with 1000 vectors of length 512. The embeddings of the 1000 classes are stored in a matrix $A_{512 \times 1000}$, encrypted using FHE and stored in the server side.

We chose ImageNet as our benchmark since among the 27 datasets introduced in [24], it has the largest number of classes (1000 classes), making it an ideal candidate for testing our algorithm. On the ImageNet benchmark, CLIP-based classifier achieved competitive performance without fine-tuning. The CLIP-ViT B/32 model (which uses the Vision Transformer architecture [9]) reached an accuracy of 63.34% on the test set.[3] While the original work was conducted on plaintext data, we demonstrate that similar performance levels—an accuracy of 63.22%—can be achieved on encrypted data, preserving both utility and privacy.

In the classification stage of the similarity-based retrieval process, for each of the 50000 test images, we encrypt its feature embedding vector and send this encryption to the server side. The server in turn computes the cosine similarity of the received encrypted test image with each of the 1000 encrypted class embeddings. Finally, the argmax algorithm of [22] applied to locate the most similar class to the input image. The results reported in Table 4 show that the accuracy results achieved through our FHE similarity-based retrieval algorithm are very close to the accuracy achieved through the baseline (cleartext) model, and that it took us about 31 hours to perform similarity-based retrieval over 50000 encrypted test input images.

It should be noted that our goal herein is not to improve upon the state of the art accuracy of the classification task in hand, but rather to prove that our FHE algorithm maintains the baseline accuracy. Given a classification model that achieves a better accuracy, our FHE similarity-based retrieval algorithm would result with a better accuracy as well.

5   Conclusion and Future Work

In this work, we introduced a similarity-based retrieval system over FHE. Compared to the trivial client-aided algorithm that relies on the client to find the maximal similarity among several computed similarities, our algorithm performs the argmax step in the server side over FHE and thus enhances both privacy guarantees and communication bandwidth. We showed empirically that our similarity-based retrieval algorithm achieves 98.9%–99.9% accuracy when it is run on a database of up to 2^{19} samples, and it improves the communication size of the naive method by up to $8\times$ in the case of a single input and up to $512\times$ in the case of a batch of 64 inputs.

In our work we focused on finding a single most similar sample to a given query. This can be naturally extended to finding $k > 1$ closest samples by executing the argmax step k times while eliminating the extracted sample after each argmax step. Still, more efficient approaches to find $k > 1$ nearest samples to a given query sample in a privacy preserving manner is a potential area for future work.

---

[3] The accuracy reported in [24] is 63.2%, but in our cleartext implementation of the model described in [24] we reached an accuracy of 63.34%.

Our similarity-based retrieval system can be combined with any dataset and an ML model that extracts identifying feature vectors for this dataset. In particular, this paper demonstrated the usage of our similarity based retrieval system for image-to-text matching using the CLIP model. More generally, since similarity based retrieval is central to many domains including recommendation systems, image search, genomics, and natural language understanding, we expect our work to have promising contributions for the field of privacy preserving computations.

References

1. Aharoni, E., et al.: HeLayers: a tile tensors framework for large neural networks on encrypted data. In: Privacy Enhancing Technology Symposium (PETs) 2023 (2023)
2. Ameur, Y., Aziz, R., Audigier, V., Bouzefrane, S.: Secure and non-interactive k-NN classifier using symmetric fully homomorphic encryption. In: Domingo-Ferrer, J., Laurent, M. (eds.) PSD 2022. LNCS, vol. 13411, pp. 142–154. Springer, Cham (2022). https://doi.org/10.1007/978-3-031-14388-3_11
3. Barni, M., et al.: A privacy-compliant fingerprint recognition system based on homomorphic encryption and fingercode templates. In: 2010 Fourth IEEE International Conference on Biometrics: Theory, Applications and Systems (BTAS), pp. 1–7 (2010)
4. Cheon, J.H., Kim, A., Kim, M., Song, Y.: Homomorphic encryption for arithmetic of approximate numbers. In: Takagi, T., Peyrin, T. (eds.) ASIACRYPT 2017. LNCS, vol. 10624, pp. 409–437. Springer, Cham (2017). https://doi.org/10.1007/978-3-319-70694-8_15
5. Cheon, J.H., Kim, J., Kim, M., Kim, Y., Song, Y.: Efficient homomorphic evaluation of k-NN classifiers. In: Proceedings on Privacy Enhancing Technologies (PoPETS) 2021(3), pp. 130–149 (2021). https://doi.org/10.2478/popets-2021-0020, https://petsymposium.org/popets/2021/popets-2021-0020.pdf
6. Choi, H., Kim, J., Song, C., Woo, S.S., Kim, H.: Blind-match: efficient homomorphic encryption-based 1:n matching for privacy-preserving biometric identification. In: Proceedings of the 33rd ACM International Conference on Information and Knowledge Management, pp. 4423–4430. ACM (2024). https://doi.org/10.1145/3627673.3680017
7. Cong, K., Geelen, R., Kang, J., Park, J.: Revisiting oblivious top-k selection with applications to secure k-NN classification. Cryptology ePrint Archive, Paper 2023/852 (2023). https://doi.org/10.1007/978-3-031-82852-2_1, https://eprint.iacr.org/2023/852
8. Deng, J., Dong, W., Socher, R., Li, L.J., Li, K., Fei-Fei, L.: Imagenet: a large-scale hierarchical image database. In: 2009 IEEE Conference on Computer Vision and Pattern Recognition, pp. 248–255. IEEE (2009)
9. Dosovitskiy, A.: An image is worth 16x16 words: transformers for image recognition at scale. arXiv preprint arXiv:2010.11929 (2020)
10. Drozdowski, P., Buchmann, N., Rathgeb, C., Margraf, M., Busch, C.: On the application of homomorphic encryption to face identification. In: 2019 International Conference of the Biometrics Special Interest Group (BIOSIG), pp. 1–5 (2019)
11. Drozdowski, P., Stockhardt, F., Rathgeb, C., Osorio-Roig, D., Busch, C.: Feature fusion methods for indexing and retrieval of biometric data: application to face recognition with privacy protection. IEEE Access **9**, 139361–139378 (2021)

12. Engelsma, J.J., Cao, K., Jain, A.K.: Learning a fixed-length fingerprint representation (2019). https://arxiv.org/abs/1909.09901
13. Engelsma, J.J., Jain, A.K., Boddeti, V.N.: Hers: Homomorphically encrypted representation search (2022). https://arxiv.org/abs/2003.12197
14. European Union: General data protection regulation (GDPR), regulation (EU) 2016/679. https://eur-lex.europa.eu/eli/reg/2016/679/oj (2016). official Journal of the European Union, L 119/1
15. Goldreich, O.: Secure multi-party computation. Manuscript. Preliminary Version (1999). https://www.wisdom.weizmann.ac.il/~oded/PSX/prot.pdf
16. Huang, G.B., Ramesh, M., Berg, T., Learned-Miller, E.: Labeled faces in the wild: a database for studying face recognition in unconstrained environments. Technical report 07-49, University of Massachusetts, Amherst (2007)
17. Ibarrondo, A., Chabanne, H., Despiegel, V., Önen, M.: Grote: group testing for privacy-preserving face identification. In: Proceedings of the Thirteenth ACM Conference on Data and Application Security and Privacy. CODASPY '23, pp. 117–128. Association for Computing Machinery, New York, NY, USA (2023)
18. Jonathan Katz, Y.L.: Introduction to Modern Cryptography. CRC, Boca Raton (2020)
19. Kim, D., Lee, G., Oh, S.: Toward privacy-preserving text embedding similarity with homomorphic encryption. In: Chen, C.C., Huang, H.H., Takamura, H., Chen, H.H. (eds.) Proceedings of the Fourth Workshop on Financial Technology and Natural Language Processing (FinNLP), pp. 25–36. Association for Computational Linguistics, Abu Dhabi, United Arab Emirates (Hybrid) (2022)
20. Kim, D., et al.: GraSS: graph-based similarity search on encrypted query. Cryptology ePrint Archive, Paper 2024/2012 (2024). https://eprint.iacr.org/2024/2012
21. Learned-Miller, G.B.H.E.: Labeled faces in the wild: updates and new reporting procedures. Technical report UM-CS-2014-003, University of Massachusetts, Amherst (2014)
22. Masalha, R., Akavia, A., Adir, A., Aharoni, E., Kushnir, E.: Argmax and xgboost training over full homomorphic encryption (2025). Manuscript submitted for review at PETS
23. Pratapa, M., Essex, A.: Secure similar patients query with homomorphically evaluated thresholds. J. Inf. Secur. Appl. **85**, 103861 (2024)
24. Radford, A., et al.: Learning transferable visual models from natural language supervision. In: International Conference on Machine Learning, pp. 8748–8763. PMLR (2021)
25. Sharma, T., Wason, M., Boddeti, V., Ross, A., Ratha, N.: Fully homomorphic encryption operators for score and decision fusion in biometric identification. In: 2023 IEEE International Workshop on Information Forensics and Security (WIFS), pp. 1–6 (2023)
26. Shokri, R., Gouert, C., Tsoutsos, N.G.: HElix: genome similarity detection in the encrypted domain. Cryptology ePrint Archive, Paper 2024/1088 (2024). https://eprint.iacr.org/2024/1088
27. Tosun, T., Savaş, E.: FSDS: a practical and fully secure document similarity search over encrypted data with lightweight client. J. Inf. Secur. Appl. **59**, 102830 (2021)
28. U.S. Department of Health and Human Services: Health insurance portability and accountability act of 1996 (hipaa) (1996). https://www.hhs.gov/hipaa/. Public Law 104-191
29. Yang, W., Wang, S., Cui, H., Tang, Z., Li, Y.: A review of homomorphic encryption for privacy-preserving biometrics. Sensors **23**(7), 3566 (2023)

30. Yang, X., Zhu, H., Wang, F., Zhang, S., Lu, R., Li, H.: Mask: efficient and privacy-preserving m-tree based biometric identification over cloud. Peer-to-Peer Netw. Appl. **14** (2021)
31. Yang, X., Zhu, H., Zhang, S., Lu, R., Gao, X., Catuogno, L.: An efficient and privacy-preserving biometric identification scheme based on the fiting-tree. Secur. Commun. Netw. **2021** (2021)
32. Yu, X., Chen, X., Shi, J.: Vector based privacy-preserving document similarity with LSA. In: 2017 IEEE 9th International Conference on Communication Software and Networks (ICCSN), pp. 1383–1387 (2017)

Location Problems with Privacy

Eric Kulikov and Michael Segal$^{(\boxtimes)}$

School of Electrical and Computer Engineering, Ben-Gurion University of the Negev,
Beer-Sheva, Israel
segal@bgu.ac.il

Abstract. We examine well known facility location problems under the privacy challenges posed by big data environments. For a given set of n points $U \in \mathbb{R}^d$, previous works have introduced the "Topology Descriptor Grid" (TDG) [13,14], a privacy-preserving framework under which some approximate solutions are possible for a variety of clustering problems. In this paper, we introduce the Equidistant "Location Estimation using Concentric Circles" (LECC) framework in $\mathbb{R}^2$, which obfuscates exact point locations while preserving their relative distances to a predetermined point. We show, under this new framework, how to obtain $2 + \mathcal{O}(1/n)$-approximate solutions for the 1-center, 1-median, 1-mean, and k-centrum problems, and $\mathcal{O}(k), \mathcal{O}(k), \mathcal{O}(k^2)$ approximations for the k-center, k-median and k-means problems, respectively. For the TDG framework we provide a $(\sqrt{d}, k^{d-1}), (d, k^{d-1})$, and (d^2, k^{d-1}) approximations for the k-center, k-median, and k-means problems, respectively.

Keywords: Facility location · Privacy · Approximation algorithms

1 Introduction

The volume of big data streaming has grown exponentially in recent years with the increased deployment of Internet of Things (IoT) devices, which creates new challenges for data processing and analysis [1]. Storing these continuous data streams in these cases is not practical, as IoT applications require immediate responses. Instead, real-time processing and analysis have emerged as a solution, enabling the extraction of insights without storing large swaths of data.

Data reduction techniques are one of the approaches to preserve privacy. Although this approach loses information, in the context of IoT, with a long data stream and real-time requirements, it reduces the computational load, which may be worthwhile. It allows data to be processed and transmitted while preserving privacy. Data reduction should be done in such a way that retains some essential information, so as not to become total noise. Several such techniques were presented such as the use of Fourier transform [15], wavelets [7], and linear transformations [13].

Another prominent technique in privacy preservation is differential privacy, which has been explored in the field of location privacy [2,5,9]. This approach introduces carefully calibrated noise into statistical databases, obscuring the contribution of individual data points. While effective, implementing differential privacy in practical applications can be challenging, as its efficiency is highly sensitive to parameter choices [10]. Furthermore, excessive noise can degrade the data to the point of rendering it unusable [16].

The use of differentially private solutions, in computational geometry problems is unclear, and more research or information is needed to determine their efficiency. Experimental evaluations of several approximation factors for k-means clustering with differential privacy have been conducted [11,17]. Differentially private algorithms for approximation have been proposed for the problems of k-means and k-median clustering in [3]. However, this approach in [3] assumes that the dimensionality d is a function of the number of points n, more specifically $d = \Omega(\text{polylog}(n))$.

In the realm of data reduction, achieving a balance between privacy and useness remains difficult. Techniques like the aforementioned linear transformations and the "Topology Descriptor Grid" (TDG) [13,14] have been proposed to address these issues, offering privacy-preserving abstractions for coordinate systems with promising results for the median and k-center problems under several restrictions on the private data.

This paper aims to build upon the TDG framework, however, looking also into the real-time demands of IoT big-data processing. This paper introduces the framework of "Location Estimation Using Concentric Circles" (LECC), which abstracts the locations of data points in a way that obfuscates exact positions while retaining their distance to a specific single predetermined point, that enables privacy-preserving clustering approximations. This framework offers infinite realizations of the data points, ensuring that exact locations cannot be reconstructed. Additionally, a simplified version of this framework, Equidistant-LECC, is explored to evaluate its effectiveness in approximation problems like k-center, k-means, and k-median. The results of these evaluations are compared to existing frameworks, such as TDG, providing an analysis of their trade-offs and performance, which are summarized in Table 1.

Definition 1 $((\alpha, \beta)$-approximation). *Let U be a set of points in $\mathbb{R}^d$, $k \in \mathbb{N}$ be the desired number of clusters, and $\mathcal{F}$ be some objective function value (e.g. k-center, k-median). Let $C^* \subset R^d$ be the optimal solution of size k for $\mathcal{F}$, $C^* = \arg\max_{C \subset \mathbb{R}^d, |C|=k} \mathcal{F}(C)$.*
A set S is a (α, β)-approximation for $\mathcal{F}$, if:

- *The set S has at most $k\beta$ points, $|S| \leq k\beta$.*
- *The objective function value $\mathcal{F}(S)$ is at most α-times larger than the optimal $\mathcal{F}(C^*)$ for k clusters, $\mathcal{F}(S) \leq \alpha \cdot \mathcal{F}(C^*)$*

Cells with $\diamond$ are the results from previous works, $(*)$ means that the running time is $\Omega(dn)$, and $(\dagger)$ is under the assumption of $\{n \to \infty, k = o(n)\}$, where n is the cardinality of the dataset. Unless specified otherwise, we assume the use of the Euclidean metric, and the private data is in $\mathbb{R}^2$.

Table 1. Main approximation results.

	Unrestricted frameworks	Equidistant frameworks	
	TDG ($\mathbb{R}^d$)	Equidistant-TDG ($\mathbb{R}^d$)	Equidistant-LECC
1-center	$\frac{1+\sqrt{d}}{2}$ $\diamond$	$\frac{1+\sqrt{d}}{2}$ $\diamond$	$2 + 2/(n-1)$
k-center	$(\sqrt{d}, k^{d-1})$ $*$	$(\sqrt{d}, k^{d-1})$ $*$ $\mathcal{O}(k)$ $\diamond$	$\mathcal{O}(k)$ $\dagger$
Median	$\sqrt{d}$ $\diamond$	$\sqrt{d}$ $\diamond$	$2 \cdot \frac{n(n+1)}{n^2-4}$
k-median	(d, k^{d-1}) $*$	(d, k^{d-1}) $*$	$k\sqrt{4/3 + 4\pi^2/k^2}$ $\dagger$
Centroid	Exact	Exact	$2 + \mathcal{O}(1/n)$
k-means	(d^2, k^{d-1}) $*$	(d^2, k^{d-1}) $*$	$(4k^2 + 12\pi^2)/7$ $\dagger$

This paper is organized as follows. The next section contains a description of the LECC privacy-preserving framework. Section 3 lists results for the center, median, and mean problems under the Equidistant-LECC framework. We show additional results for k-center, k-median, and k-means problems under the general TDG framework in Sect. 4. To the best of our knowledge, these results are the best up to date. Finally, we conclude in Sect. 5.

2 Privacy Preserving Data Framework: Location Estimation Using Concentric Circles

To describe the Equidistant "Location Estimation using Concentric Circles" (LECC) framework, we will showcase the more general framework first. Let the private point set U be a set of points in $\mathbb{R}^2$ which consists of n points. The LECC framework contains a predetermined point $o \in \mathbb{R}^2$, which could be any point, and the distance between every $p \in U$ to o. Let us name o the *origin* point, and array $D = [d_1, d_2, \cdots, d_n]$ will contain the distances in non-decreasing order, such that for every $i \leq j : d_i \leq d_j$, and $d_i = \|p_i - o\|_2$. Using this framework $\{o, D\}$, one can only estimate the location of a point in U on the circumference of a disk centered at o, see Fig. 1 for an example.

Denote Δd_i to be the difference $d_i - d_{i-1}$. The value of Δd_1 is defined as d_1. An Equidistant-LECC will be an LECC such that $\forall i, j : \Delta d_i = \Delta d_j = \Delta d$, and where each point is at a different distance from o. The privacy of a point in a framework is defined by the fact that, given the framework alone, one cannot determine the exact location of the point. In both frameworks, privacy is preserved because there are infinite possible original point sets that could have led to the same framework. We will call each such set an *originating* set of Equidistant-LECC.

3 Equidistant-LECC Results

In this section, we will show approximation results for the 1-center, 1-median, and 1-centroid (1-mean) problems for the Equidistant-LECC framework. We also will consider the case of multi-facility location problems.

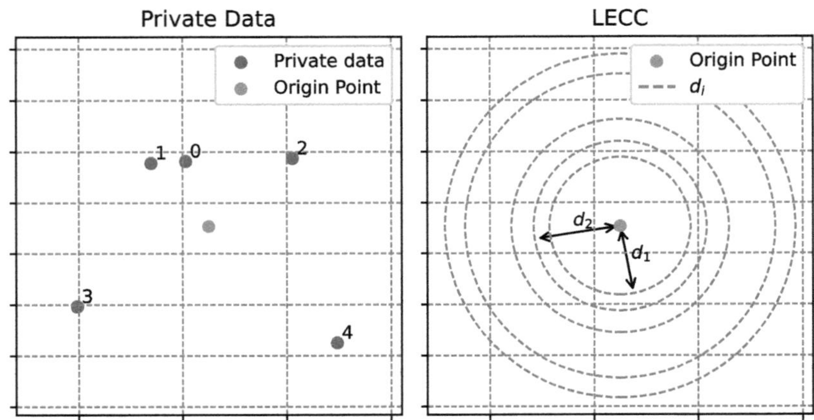

Fig. 1. Example of the LECC framework.

3.1   1-Center Approximation

Definition 2 (1-center problem). *Given a set of points U in $\mathbb{R}^d$, the goal is to find a point $c \in \mathbb{R}^d$ that minimizes the following expression: $\max_{p \in U} \|p - c\|_2$.*

Theorem 1. *For any set of points U in $\mathbb{R}^2$, with a given Equidistant-LECC framework, the origin point is a $(2 + \frac{2}{n-1})$-approximation for the Euclidean 1-center problem.*

Proof. Given the Equidistant-LECC framework, let us look at the smallest possible optimal radius enclosing for some originating set U' that matches the Equidistant-LECC. Such U' will have all the points on a straight line, such that the distance between every consecutive pair of points p_i, p_{i+1} is exactly Δd. Denote by OPT_c the radius of the optimal solution for U and by APP_c the radius of the approximate solution. Therefore $OPT_c \geq (n-1)\Delta d/2$.

For the approximation using the given origin point serving as the solution, in the worst case scenario $APP_c \leq n \cdot \Delta d$. Since the maximum distance between o and any point in U is $n \cdot \Delta d$. Thus, $APP_c \leq n \cdot \Delta d = \frac{n \cdot \Delta d}{(n-1)\Delta d/2} \cdot OPT_c = (2 + \frac{2}{n-1})OPT_c$. Hence, the origin point is $(2 + 2/(n-1))$-approximation point for the 1-center problem in the LECC-Equidistant framework. $\square$

3.2 k-Center Approximation

Definition 3 (k-center problem). *Given a set of points U in $\mathbb{R}^d$ and natural number k, the goal is to find a set $C = \{c_i\}_{i=1}^k$ of points such that the following expression is minimized: $\max_{p \in U} \min_{c_i \in C} \|p - c_i\|_2$.*

Theorem 2. *For any set of points U in $\mathbb{R}^2$, with a given Equidistant-LECC locating the k-center centers at $S_{k:c} \triangleq \{o + \Delta d \frac{n}{2 \cos(\pi/k)} \cdot (\cos(i\frac{2\pi}{k}), \sin(i\frac{2\pi}{k}))\}_{i=1}^k$, gives a $\mathcal{O}(k)$-approximation for the k-center problem when $n \to \infty$, for $k \geq 3$.*

Proof. Let U be some originating set, and let U' be an originating set with the same Equidistant-LECC as U, in which all the points are located in a straight line, with the origin point on the leftmost side, and the furthest point of U' being the rightmost. Notice that U' minimizes the distance between every 2 points under the equidistant constraint.

Suppose we have an optimal solution for the k-center problem for some originating set U, with the optimal function value denoted as $OPT_{k:c}(U)$. Denote $C = \{c_i\}_{i=1}^k$ be the disk centers of the optimal k-center solution for U, and their radii be $R = \{r_{c_i}\}_{i=1}^k$. Let $U(c_i)$ be the set of points in U that are covered by the disk centered at c_i.

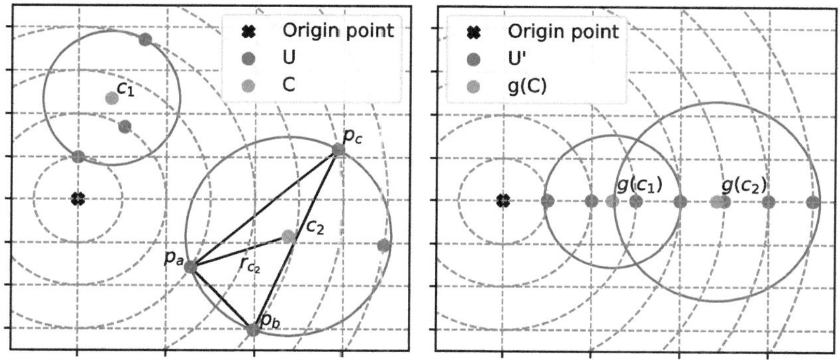

Fig. 2. Example of $OPT_{k:c}(U) \geq OPT_{k:c}(U')$ for $k = 2$.

Let us define a transformation $g : \mathbb{R}^2 \to \mathbb{R}^2$, that moves each point from the plane to be on the line of U', while retaining its relative distance to the origin point. Notice that in U', the disks formed from the moved centers $g(C)$ with their corresponding r_{c_i}, cover the points $g(U(c_i))$, and that $\bigcup_{i=1}^k g(U(c_i)) = U'$, see Fig. 2 for an example. This happens because each optimal disk in the originating set U is formed by either 2 or 3 points. In U' for the 2-point case the radius of each such disk is half the distance between the 2 points, and since U' minimizes such distances, each such disk centered at $g(c_i)$ having a radius r_{c_i} also covers the corresponding points in $g(U(c_i))$. For the 3-point case, denote the points that define the radius of the disk centered at c_j, as $\{p_a, p_b, p_c\}$ where $a < b < c$. In U' to cover these points the radius has to be $|p_c - p_a|/2$ and in U the radius r_{c_j} of such disk is at least half the maximal distance between every 2 points of $\{p_a, p_b, p_c\}$. Since in U the value $|p_c - p_a|/2$ is not larger than r_{c_j}, the disk centered at $g(c_j)$ having radius r_{c_j} also covers the corresponding points in U'. Hence, the radius value produced by the optimal k-center solution is at least the radius value of the optimal k-center of U'.

An optimal k-center solution for U', with an objective function value which is denoted by $OPT_{k:c}(U')$, will enclose the points so that between adjacent disks formed from the k-center problem there is a segment of length Δd. Observe Fig. 3.

Since there are k centers, there will be $(k-1)$ such segments. For each such segment let p_l, p_r be the right and left point that defines the segment, respectively. Let us remove those segments, see Fig. 3a. The removal is done by shrinking the segment such that p_l and p_r coincide. This creates a new set U^*, see Fig. 3b. After removal, we have $(n-1)-(k-1) = n-k$ remaining segments. If we concatenate the optimal k-center solution accordingly, see Fig. 3b, it constitutes a covering of k disks of U^*, with an objective function value of $r' = OPT_{k:c}(U')$. Another covering of k disks of U^* which is not optimal, see Fig. 3c, has a function value of $r^* = \frac{\Delta d}{2}\frac{n-k}{k}$, by dividing the line into k equal-sized disks. Assume $r^* > r'$, then r' can be decreased until it is equal to that of the optimal objective function for the k-center problem of U^*. However, this solution will result in at least one segment not covered by any disk, see Fig. 3d, contradicting the optimality of $r' = OPT_{k:c}(U')$. We conclude $OPT_{k:c}(U') \geq \frac{n-k}{k}\frac{\Delta d}{2}$. From the previous claim, $OPT_{k:c}(U)$ is at least $OPT_{k:c}(U')$, thus $OPT_{k:c}(U) \geq OPT_{k:c}(U') \geq \frac{n-k}{2k}\Delta d$.

To find an approximation, we define our solution to be located at $S'_{k:c} = \{o + \Delta d \frac{n}{\delta}(\cos(i\frac{2\pi}{k}), \sin(i\frac{2\pi}{k}))\}_{i=1}^{k}$, for some $\delta \geq 1$. From Fig. 4 it is evident that for each private point in each sector, the closest solution point $s_i \in S'_{k:c}$ is the one that lies in the s_i's sector. For example, the closest approximation point for the private point in the green area is the green point. We wish to find for s_i, what is the furthest possible private point from it. As shown in Fig. 5, let us examine a specific region.

Let p_i be the point which is located at a distance $i\Delta d$ from the origin point. Denote by z_i the distance from p_i to the closest $s_j \in S'_{k:c}$. Notice that for each point p_i, the farthest it could be from the closest $s_j \in S'_{k:c}$ is when it is located at the sector boundary. Now let us calculate this distance, and determine which point is the farthest from any $s_j \in S'_{k:c}$:

$$z_i^2 = (i\Delta d)^2 + (n\Delta d/\delta)^2 - 2i\Delta d \frac{n\Delta d}{d}\cos \pi/k$$

$$= \Delta d^2 \underbrace{\left[\frac{n^2}{\delta^2} + i^2 - \frac{2in\cos \pi/k}{\delta}\right]}_{f(i):\text{ depends on i}}.$$

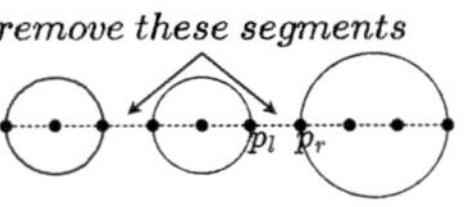

(a) Optimal solution for U'.

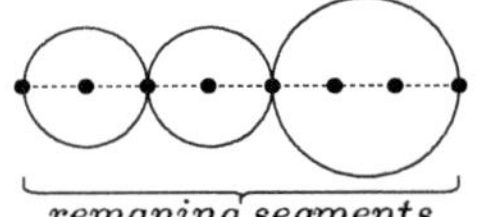

(b) U' after segments removal, solution for U^* with value r'.

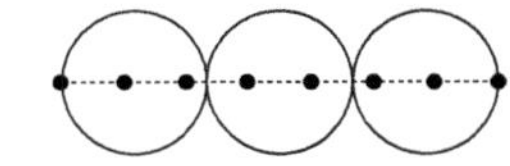

(c) Solution for U^* with value r^*.

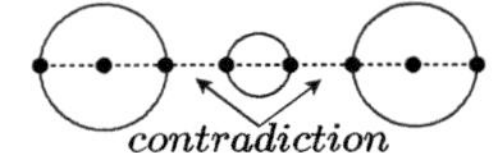

(d) Contradiction.

Fig. 3. 3-center example of the supporting claim.

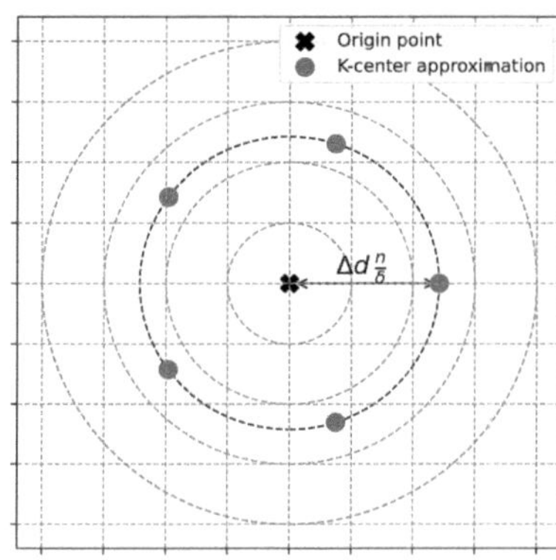

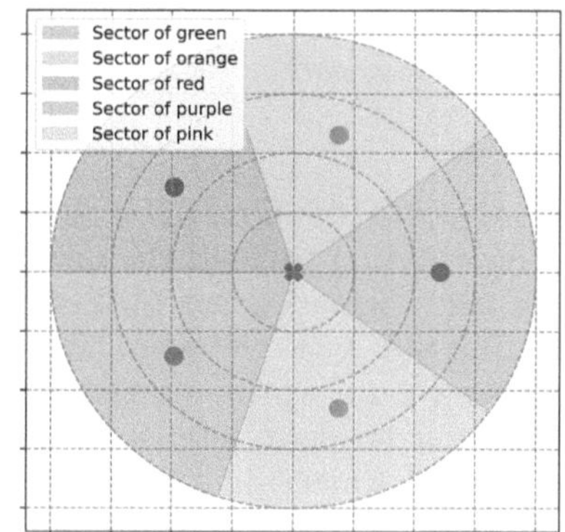

Fig. 4. Location of the solution points.

We note that $f(i)$ is monotonically increasing for $i \geq n\frac{\cos \pi/k}{\delta}$. Since $\cos \pi/k \leq 1$ and $\delta \geq 1$, we have $\frac{\cos \pi/k}{\delta} \leq 1$; therefore $f(i)$ is monotonically increasing from some $1 \leq i \leq n$. Hence, the maximum distance from any point $p \in U$ to its closest $s_j \in S'_{k:c}$ which is denoted by $APP_{k:c}$, is either z_1 or z_n since the highest value of z_i is achieved at the boundaries.

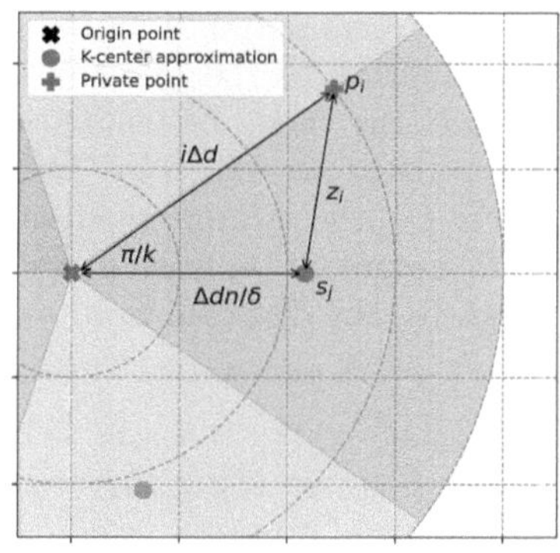

Fig. 5. Specific sector.

$$\begin{cases} z_1 = \Delta d^2 \sqrt{1 + \frac{n^2}{\delta^2} - \frac{2n \cos\left(\frac{\pi}{k}\right)}{\delta}} \\ z_n = \Delta d^2 \sqrt{n^2 + \frac{n^2}{\delta^2} - \frac{2n^2 \cos\left(\frac{\pi}{k}\right)}{\delta}} \end{cases}$$

Recall that $OPT_{k:c} \geq \frac{n-k}{2k}\Delta d$, so: $APP_{k:c} \leq OPT_{k:c}\frac{\max\{z_1, z_n\}}{\frac{n-k}{2k}\Delta d}$. Let us take $n \to \infty$, while $k = o(n)$, $APP_{k:c} \leq OPT_{k:c} \cdot \max\left\{2k\sqrt{\frac{1}{\delta^2}}, 2k\sqrt{\frac{1}{\delta^2} - \frac{2\cos\left(\frac{\pi}{k}\right)}{\delta} + 1}\right\}$. The minimum value of the max function is achieved at $\delta = 2\cos(\pi/k)$, with a value of $k\frac{1}{\cos(\pi/k)}$, for $k \geq 3$. Therefore, the placement of $S_{k:c}$ gives a $\mathcal{O}(k)$-approximation for the k-center problem when $n \to \infty$ and $k \geq 3$. $\qquad \square$

Remark 1. Notice that if $n = k$ we cannot have any bounded approximation since every disk's center will lie exactly on one of the private points (leading to an optimal radius that is equal to 0), which we cannot match.

3.3 Median Approximation

Definition 4 (median problem). *Given a set of points U in $\mathbb{R}^d$, the goal is to find a point $m \in \mathbb{R}^d$ that minimizes:* $\sum_{p \in U} \|p - m\|_2$.

Theorem 3. *For any set of points U in $\mathbb{R}^2$ within the Equidistant-LECC framework, the origin point is a $2\frac{n(n+1)}{n^2-4}$-approximation for the 1-median problem, for $n \geq 3$.*

Proof. Denote by $OPT_m(U)$ the optimal objective function value of the median problem for the originating set U. Let U' be an originating set with the same Equidistant-LECC as U, in which all the points are located in a straight line, with the origin point on the leftmost side. Let $OPT_m(U')$ be the optimal objective function value of the median problem for U'. Notice that for every U, $OPT_m(U) \geq OPT_m(U')$. This results from the observation that for any median point m, and any point $p \in U$, the distance $\|m - p\|_2$ is minimal, if and only if, the angle of inclination of the line from o to p is the same as the angle of inclination of the line from o to m, see Fig. 6 for an example.

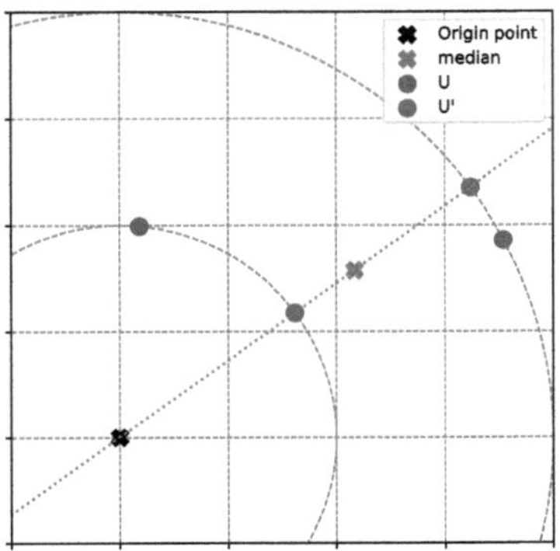

Fig. 6. Example of U and U'.

For U', the optimal median point denoted as $m_{U'}$, will be at the midpoint of the line segment between p_1 and p_n. To compute $OPT_m(U')$, we sum the pairwise distances, the distance from $m_{U'}$ to p_1 and p_n is $\Delta d(n-1)/2$, to p_2 and p_{n-1} is $\Delta d(n-3)/2$, and so on. Thus, $OPT_m(U') \geq 2\sum_{j=1}^{\lfloor n/2 \rfloor} \frac{n-(2j-1)}{2}\Delta d \geq \sum_{j=1}^{\frac{n}{2}-1}(n - 2j + 1)\Delta d = (\frac{n^2}{4} - 1)\Delta d$. The objective function value of the median problem for U while using the origin point, denoted as $APP_m(U)$, is: $APP_m(U) = \Delta d\sum_{i=1}^{n} i = \Delta d\frac{1}{2}n(n + 1) \leq OPT_m(U')\frac{\frac{1}{2}n(n+1)}{\frac{n^2}{4}-1} = OPT_m(U) \cdot 2 \cdot \frac{n(n+1)}{n^2-4}$.

Therefore, the origin point in the Equidistant-LECC framework is a $2 \cdot \frac{n(n+1)}{n^2-4}$-approximation for the 1-median problem. $\qquad\square$

3.4 k-Median Approximation

Definition 5 (k-median problem). *Given a set of points U in $\mathbb{R}^d$, with natural number k, the goal is to find a set $M = \{m_i\}_{i=1}^{k}$ of points that minimize: $\sum_{p\in U} \min_{m_i\in M} \|p - m_i\|_2$.*

Theorem 4. *For any set of points U in $\mathbb{R}^2$, with a given Equidistant-LECC, putting the k-median points at $S_{k:m} \triangleq \{o + \Delta dn\frac{2k^2-\pi^2}{4k^2}\left(\cos\left(i\frac{2\pi}{k}\right), \sin\left(i\frac{2\pi}{k}\right)\right)\}_{i=1}^{k}$, gives a $k\sqrt{\frac{4}{3} + \frac{4\pi^2}{k^2}}$-approximation for the k-median problem when $n \to \infty$, for $k \geq 3$.*

Proof. For a set of points U in $\mathbb{R}^2$, denote the optimal solution for the k-median problem as set $M = \{m_i\}_{i=1}^{k}$, with an objective function value $OPT_{k:m}(U)$. Set M divides U into k clusters $\{U_i\}_{i=1}^{k}$ such that points in cluster U_i are closer to m_i than to m_j, for all $j \neq i$. Given Equidistant-LECC of U, for each cluster

U_i with median m_i, the minimum value of the intra-cluster sum of distances $\sum_{p \in U_i} \|p - m_i\|_2$ is achieved when all the points in U_i are aligned along a straight line with the origin point o, and m_i being the midpoint of the points of U_i. This results from the observation that for any median point m_i, and any point $p \in U_i$, the distance $\|m_i - p\|_2$ is minimal, if and only if, the angle of inclination of the line from o to p is the same as the angle of inclination of the line from o to m_i, see Fig. 6 for an example.

Let U' be an originating set with the same Equidistant-LECC as U, in which all the points lie on a straight line with the origin point o at the leftmost side. Let the solution for the k-median problem for U' be set $M' = \{m'_i\}_{i=1}^k$, with an objective function value $OPT_{k:m}(U')$. Set M' divides U' into k clusters $\{U'_i\}_{i=1}^k$ such that points in cluster U'_i are closer to m'_i than to m'_j, for all $j \neq i$. Since all the points in U' are aligned in a straight line, then all the points in U'_i are aligned in a straight line with m'_i being the midpoint of the points of U'_i. Therefore, from the above claim, U' minimizes the sum of distance within each cluster $\{\sum_{p \in U'_i} \|p - m'_i\|_2\}_{i=1}^k$ and, by extension, the overall sum across all clusters $\sum_{i=1}^k \sum_{p \in U'_i} \|p - m'_i\|_2$. Hence, we can conclude that $OPT_{k:m}(U) \geq OPT_{k:m}(U')$.

The cluster with the least amount of points U'_j will have $q = \lfloor n/k \rfloor$ points. To compute the lower bound on $OPT_{k:m}(U')$, we will multiply by k the sum of inter-cluster distances of U'_j, i.e. $k \cdot \sum_{p \in U'_j} \|p - m'_j\|_2$. Therefore, $OPT_{k:m}(U') \geq$

$$k \cdot 2 \sum_{j=1}^{\lfloor q/2 \rfloor} \frac{q - (2j-1)}{2} \Delta d \geq k \cdot \sum_{j=1}^{\frac{q}{2}-1} (q - 2j + 1) \Delta d = k \cdot \sum_{j=1}^{\frac{\lfloor n/k \rfloor}{2}-1} (\lfloor n/k \rfloor - 2j + 1) \Delta d \geq k \sum_{j=1}^{\frac{n-3k}{2k}} \left(\frac{n}{k} - 2j \right) \Delta d \geq \frac{(n-3k)(n+k)}{4k} \Delta d.$$

We define our solution for U to be $S'_{k:m} = \{o + \Delta d \frac{n}{\delta} \left(\cos \left(i \frac{2\pi}{k} \right), \sin \left(i \frac{2\pi}{k} \right) \right)\}_{i=1}^k$. Let z_i be the maximum distance between the point p_i and the closest solution point $s_j \in S'_{k:m}$, see z_i in Fig. 5. Therefore:

$$z_i^2 = \left(\frac{n \Delta d}{\delta} \right)^2 + (i \Delta d)^2 - 2 \frac{n \Delta d}{\delta} i \Delta d \cos \frac{\pi}{k} = \Delta d^2 \left(\left(\frac{n}{\delta} \right)^2 + i^2 - 2i \frac{n}{\delta} \cos \frac{\pi}{k} \right) \leq \Delta d^2 \left(\left(\frac{n}{\delta} \right)^2 + i^2 - 2i \frac{n}{\delta} \left(1 - \frac{\left(\frac{\pi}{k} \right)^2}{2} \right) \right) = \Delta d^2 \left(\left(\frac{n}{\delta} \right)^2 + i^2 - \frac{n}{\delta} \left(2 - \frac{\pi^2}{k^2} \right) i \right).$$

The second inequality is due to $\cos x \leq \left(1 - \frac{x^2}{2} \right)$, for $0 \leq x \leq \frac{\pi}{2}$, and under the assumption of $k \geq 2$. Therefore, $z_i \leq \Delta d \cdot \sqrt{\left(\frac{n}{\delta} \right)^2 + i^2 - \frac{n}{\delta} \left(2 - \frac{\pi^2}{k^2} \right) i}$. Denote $APP_{k:m}$ as the objective function value of the k-median problem using $S'_{k:m}$ for U. Therefore, $APP_{k:m}$ is at most: $\sum_{i=1}^n z_i =$

$$\Delta d \sum_{i=1}^n \sqrt{\left(\frac{n}{\delta} \right)^2 + i^2 - \frac{n}{\delta} \left(2 - \frac{\pi^2}{k^2} \right) i} \leq \Delta d \sqrt{n \cdot \sum_{i=1}^n \left[\left(\frac{n}{\delta} \right)^2 + i^2 - \frac{n}{\delta} \left(2 - \frac{\pi^2}{k^2} \right) i \right]}$$

$$\leq \Delta d \sqrt{n} \cdot \sqrt{n \cdot \left(\frac{n}{\delta} \right)^2 + \sum_{i=1}^n i^2 - \frac{n}{\delta} \left(2 - \frac{\pi^2}{k^2} \right) \sum_{i=1}^n i}$$

$$\leq \Delta d \sqrt{n} \cdot \sqrt{n \cdot \left(\frac{n}{\delta} \right)^2 + \frac{1}{6} n(n+1)(2n+1) - \frac{n}{\delta} \left(2 - \frac{\pi^2}{k^2} \right) \frac{1}{2} n(n+1)}$$

$$\leq OPT_{k:m}(U) \cdot \Delta d \sqrt{n} \cdot \frac{\sqrt{n \cdot \left(\frac{n}{\delta} \right)^2 + \frac{1}{6} n(n+1)(2n+1) - \frac{n}{\delta} \left(2 - \frac{\pi^2}{k^2} \right) \frac{1}{2} n(n+1)}}{\Delta d \frac{(n-3k)(n+k)}{4k}}.$$

Suppose

$$\{k = o(n), n \to \infty\}, \text{ hence, } APP_{k:m} \leq OPT_{k:m}(U) \, 4k \sqrt{\frac{1}{\delta^2} + \frac{\frac{\pi^2}{2k^2} - 1}{\delta} + \frac{1}{3}}. \text{ This}$$

function achieves its minimum value at $\delta = \frac{4k^2}{2k^2-\pi^2}$ for $k \geq 3$, which results in $APP_{k:m} = OPT_{k:m}(U)k\sqrt{\frac{4}{3}+\frac{4\pi^2}{k^2}-\frac{\pi^4}{k^4}} < OPT_{k:m}(U) \cdot k\sqrt{\frac{4}{3}+\frac{4\pi^2}{k^2}}$. Therefore, the solution $S_{k:m} = \{o + \Delta dn\frac{2k^2-\pi^2}{4k^2}\left(\cos\left(i\frac{2\pi}{k}\right), \sin\left(i\frac{2\pi}{k}\right)\right)\}_{i=1}^{k}$ is a $k\sqrt{\frac{4}{3}+\frac{4\pi^2}{k^2}}$-approximation for the k-median clustering problem for U, under the assumption of $\{k = o(n), n \to \infty\}$ and $k \geq 3$. $\qquad\square$

3.5 Centroid Approximation

Definition 6 (centroid problem). *Given a set of points U in $\mathbb{R}^d$, the goal is to find a point $c \in \mathbb{R}^d$ that minimizes: $\sum_{p \in U} \|p - c\|_2^2$.*

Theorem 5. *For any set of points U in $\mathbb{R}^2$, with a given Equidistant-LECC. The origin point is a $2 + \mathcal{O}(1/n)$-approximation for the 1-centroid problem, for $n \geq 3$.*

Proof. Likewise in Theorem 3, we notice that the optimal solution for the centroid problem achieves its minimum for an originating set U' in which all the points are located on a straight line. Denote by $OPT_{cd}(U)$ the optimal function value of the centroid problem for U, and $APP_{cd}(U')$ the function value of the centroid problem, using the origin point for U'. As in Theorem 3, the optimal location of the centroid for U' is at the midpoint of the line segment between p_1 and p_n, therefore: $OPT_{cd} \geq \sum_{j=1}^{\frac{n}{2}-1}(n - 2j + 1)^2\Delta d^2 = \frac{1}{6}(n^3 - n - 6)\Delta d^2$. $APP_{cd} = \Delta d^2 \sum_{i=1}^{n} i^2 = \frac{1}{6}n(n+1)(2n+1)\Delta d^2 \leq OPT_{cd}(U)\frac{n(n+1)(2n+1)}{n^3-n-6}$.

Hence, the origin point in the Equidistant-LECC framework is a $2 + \mathcal{O}(1/n)$-approximation for the 1-mean (centroid) problem, for $n \geq 3$. $\qquad\square$

3.6 k-Means Approximation

Definition 7. (k-means problem). *Given a set of points U in $\mathbb{R}^d$, with natural number k, the goal is to find a set $W = \{w_i\}_{i=1}^{k}$ of points that minimize: $\sum_{p \in U} \min_{w_i \in W} \|p - w_i\|_2^2$.*

Theorem 6. *For any set of points U in $\mathbb{R}^2$, with a given Equidistant-LECC, putting the k-means points at $S_{k:cd} \triangleq \{o + \Delta dn\frac{2k^2-\pi^2}{4k^2}\left(\cos\left(i\frac{2\pi}{k}\right), \sin\left(i\frac{2\pi}{k}\right)\right)\}_{i=1}^{k}$, gives a $\frac{1}{2}(k^2 + 3\pi^2)$-approximation for the k-median problem when $n \to \infty$, for $k \geq 3$.*

Proof. As in the proof of Theorem 4, let U be a set of points in $\mathbb{R}^2$, and let U' be an originating set with the same Equidistant-LECC as U, in which all the points lie on a straight line with the origin point o at the leftmost side. Denote by $OPT_{k:cd}(U), OPT_{k:cd}(U')$ as the optimal objective function for the k-means problem for U and U', respectively. The only differences are that: $OPT_{k:m}(U') \geq k\sum_{j=1}^{\frac{n-3k}{2k}}(\frac{n}{k} - 2j)^2\Delta d^2 \geq \frac{(n-3k)(2k^2+n^2)}{6k^2}\Delta d^2$. Therefore, the objective function value of the k-means problem $APP_{k:cd}$ for U when using $S'_{k:cd} = \{o + \Delta d\frac{n}{\delta}\left(\cos\left(i\frac{2\pi}{k}\right), \sin\left(i\frac{2\pi}{k}\right)\right)\}_{i=1}^{k}$ is:

$$\sum_{i=1}^{n} z_i^2 \leq \Delta d^2 \cdot \left[n \cdot \left(\tfrac{n}{\delta}\right)^2 + \sum_{i=1}^{n} i^2 - \tfrac{n}{\delta}\left(2 - \tfrac{\pi^2}{k^2}\right)\sum_{i=1}^{n} i \right]$$

$$= \Delta d^2 \cdot \left[n \cdot \left(\tfrac{n}{\delta}\right)^2 + \tfrac{1}{6}n(n+1)(2n+1) - \tfrac{n}{\delta}\left(2 - \tfrac{\pi^2}{k^2}\right)\tfrac{1}{2}n(n+1) \right]$$

$$\leq OPT_{k:cd} \cdot \frac{n \cdot \left(\tfrac{n}{\delta}\right)^2 + \tfrac{1}{6}n(n+1)(2n+1) - \tfrac{n}{\delta}\left(2 - \tfrac{\pi^2}{k^2}\right)\tfrac{1}{2}n(n+1)}{\frac{(n-3k)(2\pi^2+n^2)}{6k^2}}.$$

Suppose $\{k = o(n), n \to \infty\}$, hence, $APP_{k:cd} \leq OPT_{k:cd}(U) \cdot \frac{3\pi^2\delta + 2((\delta-3)\delta+3)k^2}{\delta^2}$. This function achieves its minimum value at $\delta = \frac{4k^2}{2k^2 - \pi^2}$, for $k \geq 3$, which results in $APP_{k:cd} = OPT_{k:cd}(U) \cdot \tfrac{1}{8}(4k^2 - \tfrac{3\pi^4}{k^2} + 12\pi^2)$. Therefore, the solution $S_{k:cd} = \{o + \Delta dn\frac{2k^2 - \pi^2}{4k^2}(\cos(i\tfrac{2\pi}{k}), \sin(i\tfrac{2\pi}{k}))\}_{i=1}^{k}$ is a $\tfrac{1}{2}(k^2 + 3\pi^2)$-approximation for the k-means clustering problem for U, under the assumption that $\{k = o(n), n \to \infty\}$ and $k \geq 3$. $\qquad\square$

4   Topology Descriptor Grid

Let $U = [u_1, u_2, \cdots, u_n]$ be a set of n points in $\mathbb{R}^d$. Let $S = [X_1, X_2, \cdots, X_d]$ be a set of n-length vectors, with vector X_i holding the ordered i-dimensional coordinates of $u_1, u_2, \cdots, u_n$, namely $x_{i,1}, x_{i,2}, \cdots, x_{i,n}$. Define m_i to be the number of distinct coordinate values in X_i, and $M = [m_1, m_2, \cdots, m_d]$ to be the set of counts of all such values. For each distinct coordinate $x_{i,j}$ define $c_{x_{i,j}}$ to be the number of occurrences of $x_{i,j}$ in distinct points in U. Denote C_{X_i} the set holding the counts of each distinct value in X_i, i.e. $C_{X_i} = [c_{x_{i,1}}, c_{x_{i,2}}, \cdots, c_{x_{i,|m_i|}}]$. S defines a $m_1 \times m_2 \times \cdots \times m_d$ grid structure with all points in U existing on a subset of grid intersections. We denote this grid structure the "Topology Descriptor Grid" (TDG). Define F_{TDG} to be the function that transforms a point set U into a TDG G, $F_{TDG} : U \to G$. Given a TDG, G, we say that G is valid if there exists at least 1 point placement U that yields G. Otherwise, we say that G is invalid. A more specific framework Equidistant-TDG is one in which U has only one point per coordinate and the distances between consecutive points along each axis are equal, i.e., $\forall i : \exists D \in \mathbb{R}$ such that $\forall j, k : |j - k| = 1 \Rightarrow |x_{i,j} - x_{i,k}| = D$.

4.1   1-Center-Approximation

Notice that in the TDG framework, the ℓ_∞ 1-center is computable exactly, since this point is exactly the midpoint in each axis of coordinate system. Durocher [6] showed that the d-dimensional ℓ_∞ 1-center is a $\tfrac{1}{2}(1 + \sqrt{c})$-approximation for the Euclidean 1-center. Therefore, we have a $\tfrac{1}{2}(1 + \sqrt{c})$-approximation for the Euclidean 1-center in $\mathcal{O}(nd)$ time. In the planar case, we get $(1 + \sqrt{2})/2$-approximation in $\mathcal{O}(n)$ time, while in the Equidistant-LECC framework described above we get $(2 + \mathcal{O}(1/n))$-approximation in $\mathcal{O}(1)$ time since the origin point is provided.

4.2 k-Center, k-Median and k-Means Approximations

Nussbaum [13,14] showed that in the Equidistant-TDG framework, there is a $\mathcal{O}(k)$-approximation in $\mathcal{O}(n)$ time for the k-center problem. However, in the general TDG framework, the k-center problem and the k-median and k-means remain open. We will show, for general TDG, a (d, k^{d-1}) approximation to the k-median, which can then be easily expanded to get a (d^2, k^{d-1}) approximation for the k-means problem. For the k-center approximation, an approximation of $(\sqrt{d}, k^{d-1})$ will be detailed in the next section.

Theorem 7. *Let U be a set of n points in $\mathbb{R}^2$, the optimal solution for the k-median problem under the ℓ_1 metric provides a 2-approximation for the Euclidean (ℓ_2) k-median problem.*

Proof. Let $M^1 = \{m_i^1\}_{i=1}^k$ be the k medians for U under ℓ_1 metric. Notice that these medians partition U into k clusters where every point belongs to the cluster with the nearest median m_i^1. Denote those clusters by $\{U^1(m_i^1)\}_{i=1}^k$. Similarly, let $M^2 = \{m_i^2\}_{i=1}^k$ be the k medians for U under ℓ_2 metric, with clusters $\{U^2(m_i^2)\}_{i=1}^k$. Denote, $\{U^2(m_i^1)\}_{i=1}^k$ the clusters resulting from M^1 under the ℓ_2 metric, and $\{U^1(m_i^2)\}_{i=1}^k$ the clusters resulting from M^2 under the ℓ_1 metric. Notice that $\bigcup_i U^1(m_i^1) = \bigcup_i U^2(m_i^1) = \bigcup_i U^1(m_i^2) = \bigcup_i U^2(m_i^2) = U$, since by definition these are partitions of U.

Denote by $OPT_{k:m}^{\ell_1}, OPT_{k:m}^{\ell_2}$, the optimal objective function value for the k-median problem under ℓ_1 and ℓ_2, respectively. Denote by $APP_{k:m}^{\ell_1 \to \ell_2}$ the objective function value for the k-median problem under ℓ_2 when we are using the M^1 as a solution. Notice that the $APP_{k:m}^{\ell_1 \to \ell_2}$ in this notation, is:

$$\underbrace{\sum_{i=1}^k \sum_{p \in U^2(m_i^1)} \|p - m_i^1\|_2}_{(sum\ 1)} \leq \underbrace{\sum_{i=1}^k \sum_{p \in U^2(m_i^1)} \|p - m_i^1\|_1}_{(sum\ 2)} =$$

$$= \sum_{i=1}^k \sum_{\substack{p \in \\ U^2(m_i^1) \cap U^1(m_i^1)}} \|p - m_i^1\|_1 + \sum_{i=1}^k \sum_{\substack{p \in \\ U^2(m_i^1) \setminus U^1(m_i^1)}} \|p - m_i^1\|_1 .$$

Notice that:

($sum\ 1$) In this expression, we sum the distances from each median $m_i^1 \in M^1$ to the points that belong to their cluster under ℓ_1, while also belonging to their cluster under ℓ_2. Since we are looking only at a subset of points, the value of this sum is at most the optimal solution $OPT_{k:m}^{\ell_1} = \sum_{i=1}^k \sum_{p \in U^1(m_i^1)} \|p - m_i^1\|_1$.

($sum\ 2$) In this expression, for each median, we are summing the distances to the points that belong to their cluster under ℓ_2 metric, but not in their cluster under ℓ_1 metric. Consequently, these points in the ℓ_1 space are closer to some other median. For every $p \in U^2(m_i^1) \setminus U^1(m_i^1)$, and for every $1 \leq i \leq k$, there is some $j \neq i$ such that:

$$\begin{cases} \|p - m_i^1\|_2 & \leq \|p - m_j^1\|_2 \\ \|p - m_j^1\|_1 & \leq \|p - m_i^1\|_1 \end{cases}$$

Let us map each $\|p - m_i^1\|_1$ to a distance in the optimal solution: $\|p - m_i^1\|_1 \leq \sqrt{2}\,\|p - m_i^1\|_2 \leq \sqrt{2}\,\|p - m_j^1\|_2 \leq \sqrt{2}\,\|p - m_j^1\|_1$, where the first and last inequalities come from metric inequalities and the middle one from the above observation. Thus, for each point p that was closer to m_i^1 under the ℓ_2 metric, but under the ℓ_1 metric, is closer to some other median point m_j^1, the distance from that point to m_i^1 is at most $\sqrt{2}$ times that of the distance to m_j^1.

Notice that each point is accounted for in (sum 1) or (sum 2). In the worst case, every point is accounted for at (sum 2) only, thus (sum 1) is equal to 0 and (sum 2) is $\sqrt{2}\,OPT_{k:m}^{\ell_1}$. Observe that the medians M^1 are the solution for the k-median problem under ℓ_1. Consequently, any other set of points that serves as a solution for $\bar{U}$ under ℓ_1 is not better, including that of the solution for the k-median problem under ℓ_2: $APP_{k:m}^{\ell_1 \to \ell_2} \leq \sqrt{2}\,OPT_{k:m}^{\ell_1} \leq \sqrt{2}\sum_{i=1}^{k}\sum_{p\in U^2(m_i^2)}\|p - m_i^2\|_1 \leq 2\sum_{i=1}^{k}\sum_{p\in U^2(m_i^2)}\|p - m_i^2\|_2 = 2\,OPT_{k:m}^{\ell_2}$, where the second inequality is from the above observation, and the third inequality is from the metric inequality. Hence, in $\mathbb{R}^2$, the optimal k medians under ℓ_1 provides a 2-approximation for the Euclidean (ℓ_2) k median problem. $\qquad\square$

Remark 2. This can be expanded to $\mathbb{R}^d$, to get a d approximation.

Theorem 8. *Let U be a set of n points in $\mathbb{R}^2$, with a given TDG. In $\mathcal{O}(n^2 k)$ time, one can get a $(2,k)$-approximation for the k-median problem.*

Proof. Suppose $U = \{p_1, \cdots, p_n\}$, where $p_i = (x_i, y_i)$, and let $X = \{x_1, x_2, \ldots, x_n\}$ and $Y = \{y_1, y_2, \ldots, y_n\}$ be the coordinates of the points of the x axis and y axis of the points of U. Calculate the optimal k-median solution for X, and for Y separately in $\mathcal{O}(n^2 k)$ time [12] (k-median on a line), to get $X_{opt} = \{x_1^{opt}, x_2^{opt}, \ldots, x_k^{opt}\}$ and $Y_{opt} = \{y_1^{opt}, y_2^{opt}, \ldots, y_k^{opt}\}$ which minimize simultaneously both expressions:

$$\begin{cases} \sum_{i=1}^{n} \min_{1\leq j\leq k} |x_i - x_j^{opt}| \\ \sum_{i=1}^{n} \min_{1\leq j\leq k} |y_i - y_j^{opt}| \end{cases}$$

For our solution, let us construct $M_{app} = \{(x_i^{opt}, y_j^{opt}) \mid 1 \leq i,j \leq k\}$. This corresponds to the Cartesian product of X_{opt}, and Y_{opt}, that is, $M_{app} = X_{opt} \times Y_{opt}$. This solution has k^2 median points. Let $APP_{k^2:m}^{axis}$ be the function value of the k^2-median problem under ℓ_1 with M_{app}. Let $OPT_{k:m}^{\ell_1}$ as before be the optimal solution for the k-median problem under ℓ_1, with $M_{opt} = \{(m_1^i, m_2^i)\}_{i=1}^{k}$. Notice that $M_{opt} \subset M_{app}$, since by the definition of the ℓ_1 norm, solving the ℓ_1 k-median problem in $\mathbb{R}^2$ can be achieved by solving the k-median problem for each axis individually, hence $APP_{k^2:m}^{axis} \leq OPT_{k:m}^{\ell_1}$. Therefore, we can obtain a $(1,k^2)$-approximation for the k-median problem under ℓ_1 metric, and using Theorem 7 we get a $(2,k)$-approximation for the Euclidean k-median problem. $\qquad\square$

Remark 3. The above result can be expanded to $\mathbb{R}^d$, to obtain an approximation (d, k^{d-1}), with a run time of $\mathcal{O}(n^2 kd)$.

Remark 4. For the k-means approximation, the only difference would be that each metric inequality is squared in the proof of Theorem 7. Hence in the inequalities factor of $\sqrt{2}$ changes to 2 ($\sqrt{d}$ changes to d), and we obtain a d^2-approximation. For the k-means algorithm on the line, one could use the algorithm in [8] with a running time of $\mathcal{O}(kn + n \log n)$, d times, so a (d^2, k^{d-1}) approximation in $\mathcal{O}(dkn + dn \log n)$ time.

Theorem 9. *Let U be a set of n points in $\mathbb{R}^2$ with a given TDG. In $\mathcal{O}(n \log n)$ time, one can get a $(\sqrt{2}, k^{d-1})$-approximation for the ℓ_2 k-center problem.*

Proof. Denote the optimal function value of the k-center problem under ℓ_1 as $OPT_{k:c}^{\ell_1}$, and the center locations as $\{c_i^1\}_{i=1}^k$. Let $p_{c_i^1}^1 \in U$ be the farthest point under ℓ_1 from c_i^1, and let $p_{c_i^1}^2 \in U$ be the farthest point from c_i^1 under ℓ_2.

Similarly, define by $OPT_{k:c}^{\ell_2}$ the optimal function value of the k-center problem under ℓ_2, with centers $\{c_i^2\}_{i=1}^k$. Let $p_{c_i^2}^1 \in U$ be the farthest point in ℓ_1 from c_i^2, and let $p_{c_i^1}^2 \in U$ be the farthest point from c_i^1 under ℓ_2.

Let $APP_{k:c}^{\ell_1 \rightarrow \ell_2}$ be the objective function value for the k-center under ℓ_2 when we use $\{c_i^1\}_{i=1}^k$ as a solution. Notice that: $APP_{k:c}^{\ell_1 \rightarrow \ell_2} = \max_{c_i^1} \max_p \|p - c_i^1\|_2 = \max_{c_i^1} \|p_{c_i^1}^2 - c_i^1\|_2 \leq \max_{c_i^1} \|p_{c_i^1}^2 - c_i^1\|_1 \leq \max_{c_i^1} \|p_{c_i^1}^1 - c_i^1\|_1 = OPT_{k:c}^{\ell_1}$. Since $OPT_{k:c}^{\ell_1}$ is the optimal objective function value of the ℓ_1 k-center problem. Therefore, any other set of points that serves as a solution for U under ℓ_1 is not better, including that of the solution for the k-center problem under ℓ_2: $APP_{k:c}^{\ell_1 \rightarrow \ell_2} \leq OPT_{k:c}^{\ell_1} \leq \max_{c_i^2} \|p_{c_i^2}^1 - c_i^2\|_1 \leq \sqrt{2} \cdot \max_{c_i^2} \|p_{c_i^2}^1 - c_i^2\|_2 \leq \sqrt{2} \cdot \max_{c_i^2} \|p_{c_i^2}^2 - c_i^2\|_2 = \sqrt{2} \cdot OPT_{k:c}^{\ell_2}$. Hence, the solution for the k-center problem under ℓ_1, namely $\{c_i^{\ell_1}\}_{i=1}^k$, is a $\sqrt{2}$-approximation for the Euclidean k-center problem.

Suppose $U = \{p_1, \cdots, p_n\}$ where $p_i = (x_i, y_i)$, and let $X = \{x_1, x_2, \ldots, x_n\}$ and $Y = \{y_1, y_2, \ldots, y_n\}$ be the coordinates of the points of the x axis and y axis of the points of U. Calculate the optimal k-center for X, and for Y separately in $\mathcal{O}(n \log n)$ time [4] (k-center on a line), to get $X_{opt} = \{x_1^{opt}, x_2^{opt}, \ldots, x_k^{opt}\}$ and $Y_{opt} = \{y_1^{opt}, y_2^{opt}, \ldots, y_k^{opt}\}$ which minimize simultaneously both expressions:

$$\begin{cases} \max_{1 \leq i \leq n} \min_{1 \leq j \leq k} |x_i - x_j^{opt}| \\ \max_{1 \leq i \leq n} \min_{1 \leq j \leq k} |y_i - y_j^{opt}| \end{cases}$$

construct $C_{app} = \{(x_i^{opt}, y_j^{opt}) \mid 1 \leq i, j \leq k\}$. This corresponds to the Cartesian product of X_{opt}, and Y_{opt}, that is, $C_{app} = X_{opt} \times Y_{opt}$. This solution has k^2 center points. Let $APP_{k^2:c}^{axis}$ be the function value of the k^2-center problem under ℓ_1 with C_{app}. Let $OPT_{k:c}^{\ell_1}$ as before be the optimal solution for the k-center problem under ℓ_1, with $C_{opt} = \{(c_1^i, c_2^i)\}_{i=1}^k$. Since $C_{opt} \subset C_{app}$, then $APP_{k^2:c}^{axis} \leq OPT_{c:m}^{\ell_1}$. Therefore, we can obtain a $(1, k)$-approximation for the k-center problem under ℓ_1 metric, and using the above approximation, we get a $(\sqrt{2}, k)$-approximation for the Euclidean k-center problem.   □

Remark 5. The above result can be expanded to $\mathbb{R}^d$, to obtain an approximation $(\sqrt{d}, k^{d-1})$, with a run time of $\mathcal{O}(dn \log n)$.

5   Conclusions

In this paper, we introduced the LECC privacy-preserving framework. For the simplified Equidistant-LECC case, we achieved a $(2 + \mathcal{O}(1/n))$-approximation for the center, median, mean, and $k - centrum$ problems. For the multi-facility location problems, under the Equidistant-LECC framework, we obtained a constant factor approximation for the k-center problem, and $\mathcal{O}(k), \mathcal{O}(k^2)$ approximations for the k-median and k-means problems, respectively. For the TDG framework, we provided $(\sqrt{d}, k^{d-1}), (d, k^{d-1})$, and (d^2, k^{d-1}) approximate solutions for the k-center, k-median, and k-means problems, respectively. Comparing the two frameworks, we observe that the results for TDG require a higher running time, as well as a greater number of facilities placed, but are applicable for an arbitrary set of points. In contrast, the Equidistant-LECC achieves its results under the assumption of a set with a specific property, but does not require additional clusters to be placed, and has a lower running time.

Acknowledgments. This research was funded by the Israel Science Foundation, Grant No. 465/22.

References

1. Andersen, D.L., Ashbrook, C.S.A., Karlborg, N.B.: Significance of big data analytics and the internet of things (IoT) aspects in industrial development, governance and sustainability. Int. J. Intell. Netw. **1**, 107–111 (2020)
2. Andrés, M.E., Bordenabe, N.E., Chatzikokolakis, K., Palamidessi, C.: Geo-indistinguishability: differential privacy for location-based systems. In: Proceedings of the 2013 ACM SIGSAC Conference on Computer and Communications Security, pp. 901–914 (2013)
3. Balcan, M.F., Dick, T., Liang, Y., Mou, W., Zhang, H.: Differentially private clustering in high-dimensional Euclidean spaces. In: International Conference on Machine Learning, pp. 322–331. PMLR (2017)
4. Brass, P., Knauer, C., Na, H.S., Shin, C.S., Vigneron, A.: Computing k-centers on a line. arXiv preprint arXiv:0902.3282 (2009)
5. Chatzikokolakis, K., Palamidessi, C., Stronati, M.: A predictive differentially-private mechanism for mobility traces. In: De Cristofaro, E., Murdoch, S.J. (eds.) PETS 2014. LNCS, vol. 8555, pp. 21–41. Springer, Cham (2014). https://doi.org/10.1007/978-3-319-08506-7_2
6. Durocher, S.: Geometric facility location under continuous motion: bounded-velocity approximations to the mobile Euclidean k-centre and k-median problems. Ph.D. thesis, University of British Columbia (2006). https://doi.org/10.14288/1.0051487, https://open.library.ubc.ca/collections/ubctheses/831/items/1.0051487
7. Garofalakis, M., Kumar, A.: Deterministic wavelet thresholding for maximum-error metrics. In: Proceedings of the Twenty-Third ACM SIGMOD-SIGACT-SIGART Symposium on Principles of Database Systems, pp. 166–176 (2004)
8. Grønlund, A., Larsen, K.G., Mathiasen, A., Nielsen, J.S., Schneider, S., Song, M.: Fast exact k-means, k-medians and Bregman divergence clustering in 1d. arXiv preprint arXiv:1701.07204 (2017)

9. Ho, S.S., Ruan, S.: Differential privacy for location pattern mining. In: Proceedings of the 4th ACM SIGSPATIAL International Workshop on Security and Privacy in GIS and LBS, pp. 17–24 (2011)
10. Lee, J., Clifton, C.: How much is enough? Choosing *varepsilon* for differential privacy. In: Lai, X., Zhou, J., Li, H. (eds.) ISC 2011. LNCS, vol. 7001, pp. 325–340. Springer, Heidelberg (2011). https://doi.org/10.1007/978-3-642-24861-0_22
11. Lu, Z., Shen, H.: A convergent differentially private k-means clustering algorithm. In: Yang, Q., Zhou, Z.-H., Gong, Z., Zhang, M.-L., Huang, S.-J. (eds.) PAKDD 2019. LNCS (LNAI), vol. 11439, pp. 612–624. Springer, Cham (2019). https://doi.org/10.1007/978-3-030-16148-4_47
12. Megiddo, N., Zemel, E., Hakimi, S.L.: The maximum coverage location problem. SIAM J. Algebr. Discret. Methods **4**(2), 253–261 (1983)
13. Nussbaum, E., Segal, M.: Finding geometric medians with location privacy. In: 2020 IEEE 19th International Conference on Trust, Security and Privacy in Computing and Communications (TrustCom), pp. 1874–1881. IEEE (2020)
14. Nussbaum, E., Segal, M., Holembovskyy, O.: Finding geometric facilities with location privacy. Algorithmica **85**(12), 3572–3601 (2023). https://doi.org/10.1007/S00453-023-01156-6
15. Rastogi, V., Nath, S.: Differentially private aggregation of distributed time-series with transformation and encryption. In: Proceedings of the 2010 ACM SIGMOD International Conference on Management of Data, pp. 735–746 (2010)
16. Sarwate, A.D., Chaudhuri, K.: Signal processing and machine learning with differential privacy: algorithms and challenges for continuous data. IEEE Sig. Process. Mag. **30**(5), 86–94 (2013)
17. Su, D., Cao, J., Li, N., Bertino, E., Jin, H.: Differentially private k-means clustering. In: Proceedings of the Sixth ACM Conference on Data and Application Security and Privacy, pp. 26–37 (2016)

Improved Range Searching and Range Emptiness Under FHE Using Copy-and-Recurse

Eyal Kushnir[ID] and Hayim Shaul[(✉)][ID]

IBM Research Haifa, Haifa, Israel
{hayim.shaul,eyal.kushnir}@ibm.com

Abstract. *Range counting* is the problem of preprocessing a set $P \subset \mathbb{R}^d$ of n points, such that given a query range γ we can efficiently compute $|P \cap \gamma|$. It was already shown (Kushnir et al. PETS'24) how to efficiently answer a range searching query under FHE using a technique they called Copy-and-Recurse to traverse partition trees. In the related *Range emptiness* problem the goal is to compute only whether $P \cap \gamma = \emptyset$. This was shown (in plaintext) to be more efficient. In this paper we improve and extend the results of Kushnir et al. First, for range searching we reduce the overhead term to the optimal $O(n)$, so for example if the ranges are halfspaces in $\mathbb{R}^d$ bounded by hyperplanes then range searching can be done with a circuit of size $O(t \cdot n^{1-1/d+\epsilon} + n)$, where t is the size of the sub-circuit that checks whether a point lies under a hyperplane.

Second, we introduce a variation of copy-and-recurse that we call leveled copy-and-recurse. With this we improve traversal of trees such as 1D partition trees and binary trees. Third, we show how to answer range emptiness queries under FHE.

We implemented our algorithms and show that our techniques for range emptiness yield a solution that is $\times 3.6$ faster than the previous results for a database of 2^{25} points.

Keywords: Secure Protocol · Homomorphic Encryption · Range Searching

1 Introduction

The *range searching* problem has received a lot of attention, e.g. [Mat91, SS11] in cleartext and [KMS24, CKK15] in the secure settings. In its simplest version, we are given a set of n points $P \subset \mathbb{R}^d$ that we preprocess such that given a volume (range) $\gamma \subset \mathbb{R}^d$ we can quickly count $|P \cap \gamma|$. In the secure settings, the data set P and the range γ are secret and cannot be shared. For example, P may be a set of points representing medical records belonging to a hospital. An independent physician may want to estimate a drug's effectiveness for a patient with profile ρ using conditional probability $\Pr[\text{recovered} \mid \text{received drug and has profile } \rho] = \frac{P \cap \gamma_2}{P \cap \gamma_1}$, and can be computed with 2 range counting queries, where γ_1 is a range

A. Akavia et al. (Eds.): CSCML 2025, LNCS 16244, pp. 35–52, 2026.
https://doi.org/10.1007/978-3-032-10759-6_3

of points corresponding to records with profile ρ who got the drug and γ_2 is a range of points corresponding to records with profile ρ who got the drug and recovered.

cleartext algorithms (e.g., [Mat91, Mat92, SS11]) compute $|P \cap \gamma|$ efficiently by grouping points in P together and testing for each group whether it is: (1) contained in γ and then all the points in the group are counted; (2) disjoint from γ and then the group is ignored; or (3) partially contained in γ. In the latter case a finer partition of the group is used in a recursive way.

This example involves medical data, which must comply with privacy regulations like HIPAA [U.S96]. A simple way to secure the data or query is through secure computation protocols, such as FHE, Beaver triples [Bea92], ORAM [TCSK16, CFLM20, MMRS15], or SSE [DPP+16, DPP+18, FMET22, CGKO06, FJK+15].

Our algorithms are generic and require only the existence of addition and multiplication operations therefore they can be implemented with any of the above solutions but in this paper we focus on and present them with FHE. We first briefly describe and compare the different schemes and explain why we prefer FHE. With **ORAM** [CFLM20, MMRS15] one or more parties keep a database at an untrusted cloud such that the can access the database without revealing its content the access pattern. A drawback of ORAM is it requires many rounds of communication. This is sometimes discouraged in real life if the latency of the communication is significant. Other secure protocols such as those that are based on **Beaver triples** also require many rounds of communication and suffer from the same drawback. **SSE** is an encryption scheme where 2 ciphertexts can be compared such that the output of the comparison is given in cleartext. With SSE the access pattern of the algorithm leaks. See for example attacks on SSE-based range searching [LMP18, GLMP18, GJW19, MFET23].

With **FHE**, parties encrypt their inputs and an output is computed without decrypting them (see below more details). FHE is more CPU intensive but the cost of FHE-based solution decreases as new FHE schemes, hardware, and algorithms are developed. Today, several systems for statistics under FHE are already available (e.g. by CryptoLab [hea24], Duality [dua24], IBM [ibm24]). Figure 1 depicts a FHE-based system where an encrypted data set P and encrypted queries γ are uploaded to an untrusted server that computes $|P \cap \gamma|$ without decrypting.

Range searching under FHE is asymptotically less efficient than in cleartext because FHE operates in the circuit model, which prevents the algorithm from changing its behavior based on input. As mentioned in [KMS24], any FHE range searching algorithm has a lower bound of $\Omega(n)$, derived by reducing from the PIR problem, which has the same lower bound [BIM00]. Intuitively, skipping a point p (or a group of points) would leak information about whether $p \in P \cap \gamma$. This would violate the semantic security if FHE.

As noted by [KMS24] most of the running time is spent making geometric tests (e.g., whether $p \in \mathbb{R}^d$ is inside γ), and so we want to minimize the number of these tests. They denoted the time to execute a test by t and expressed the

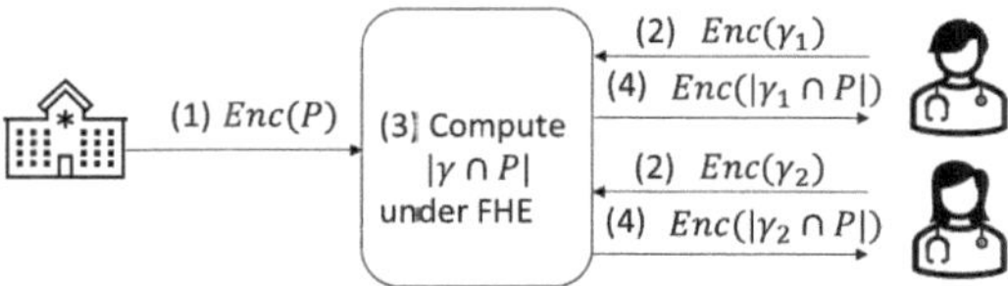

Fig. 1. An untrusted system providing statistics-as-a-service using FHE. (1) The data owner (hospital) encrypts and uploads a data set. (2) A querier (doctor) encrypts their query and sends it to the untrusted cloud. (3) The cloud performs the query under FHE and (4) returns the result to the querier.

running of the algorithm using t. Their running time had an overhead of $\Omega(n)$ (and in some cases $O(n^{1+\varepsilon})$) and a term that included t, which they reduced from the naïve $O(n \cdot t)$ to be sub-linear in n. Their technique (copy-and-recurse) is more generic and considers algorithms that partition a problem into r sub-problems and then solves only $\xi < r$ of them in recursion. To implement the recursion efficiently under FHE they copied ξ sub-problems and recursed into the copies. Copying is done under FHE and adds a $\Omega(n)$ overhead. The rest of the FHE algorithm has the same asymptotic time complexity as the cleartext.

In the 1-dim case this yields a solution that answers a range searching query in $O(t \cdot n^{\varepsilon} + n)$, where t is the time to check whether $p \in \gamma$, for $p \in \mathbb{R}$, and $\varepsilon > 0$ is a parameter. As usual in these cases, there is a multiplicative factor that depends on $1/\varepsilon$ hidden by the $O(\cdot)$ notation. In $d > 1$ dimensions the checks are more intricate (but still require $O(1)$ time) and a data structure called partition-tree (see [AM94, AMS13, Mat92, SS11]) is used. The running time then becomes $O(t \cdot n^{c+\varepsilon} + n^{1+\varepsilon})$, where $c = c(d) < 1$. Note the increased the overhead of $O(n^{1+\varepsilon})$ that comes from a pre-processing step that turns the partition tree into a full complete tree by adding "dummy" nodes.

In this work we reduce the overhead when $d > 1$ to be the optimal $O(n)$. To do this we need to prove tighter versions of the partition theorems of [Mat91, AM94]. The partition trees built with our tighter partition theorem are full and do not require any dummy nodes. The improvement in the overhead is significant because for some values of n and ε it dominates the running time. We also introduce a variation of copy-and-recurse that we call *leveled copy-and-recurse* which is more efficient when the cleartext algorithm visits a constant number of nodes in each level of the tree it traverses. Our results are summarized in Table 1.

In some cases we are only interested in answering an emptiness query, i.e., whether $P \cap \gamma = \emptyset$. Intuitively this is an easier task than computing $|P \cap \gamma|$ and indeed it was shown in [Mat91] that it can be answered in cleartext in $O(n^{1-1/\lfloor d/2 \rfloor + \varepsilon})$ time if γ is a halfspace bounded by a hyperplane in $\mathbb{R}^d$. This was later generalized to more types of ranges in [SS11]. In this paper we show how to implement these algorithms under FHE with only linear overhead.

Emptiness queries are used in many applications and we name here a few.

Table 1. The cleartext partition theorems (1st column); type of ranges (2nd column); time to answer a range query as in [KMS24] (3rd column); and time using our tightened theorem (4th column). Here d is the dimension of the problem, n is the number of points in the database and t the time to compare a point to a query, the ranges are: Axis-parallel hyper-boxes (1st row); halfspaces bounded by hyperplanes (2nd row); general semi-algebraic ranges (3rd and 4th rows). Here, $c = d$, when $d \leq 4$ and $c = 2d - 4$ otherwise. The 5th and 6th rows refer to emptiness queries and were not mentioned in [KMS24]: halfspaces bounded by hyperplanes (5th row); and ranges whose lower envelope of r ranges can be decomposed into $\zeta(r)$ elementary cells (6th row) (e.g., α-fat triangles, segment-emptiness amid balls and convex 3d-shapes).

Partition Theorem	Ranges	[KMS24] (FHE)	This work (FHE)
	axis-parallel hyperboxes	$O(tn^{1+\varepsilon} + n\log^{d-1} n)$	$O(t\log^d n + n\log^{d-1} n)$
[Mat91]	hyperplanes	$O(tn^{1-\frac{1}{d}+\varepsilon} + n^{1+\varepsilon})$	$O(tn^{1-\frac{1}{d}+\varepsilon} + n)$
[AM94]	semialgebraic	$O(tn^{1-\frac{1}{c}+\varepsilon} + n^{1+\varepsilon})$	$O(tn^{1-\frac{1}{c}+\varepsilon} + n)$
[AMS13]	semialgebraic	$O(tn^{1-\frac{1}{d}+\varepsilon} + n^{1+\varepsilon})$	—
[Mat92]	hyperplanes (emptiness)	—	$O(tn^{1-\frac{1}{\lfloor d/2 \rfloor}+\varepsilon} + n)$
[SS11]	semialgebraic (emptiness)	—	$O(t(\zeta^{-1}(n))^{1+\varepsilon} + n)$

Checking a Blacklist. Preprocess a list $L = \{L_1, \ldots, L_n\} \in 2^{\mathbb{N}}$ such that given a query $q \in \mathbb{N}$ determine efficiently whether $q \in L$. Here replace q with the range $\gamma_q = [q - 0.5, q + 0.5]$ and check whether $q \cap L = \emptyset$.

Empty α-Fat Triangle in the Plane. An α-fat triangle is a triangle with all angles greater than α, for some $\alpha > 0$. Most polygons emanating from real life problems can be triangulated into α-fat triangles (where $\alpha > 0$ is a parameter). Here the goal is to preprocess a set of n points $P\mathbb{R}^2$ such that given a query polygon, γ, that can be triangulated into $O(1)$ α-fat triangles, $\Delta_1, \ldots$, we can efficiently determine whether $\gamma \cap P = \emptyset$.

1.1   Our Contribution

- *Improved overhead.* We improve the overhead term for range searching from $O(n^{1+\varepsilon})$ (in [KMS24]) to the optimum $O(n)$. See rows 2–4 in Table 1.

  In more details, the overhead in [KMS24] was due to adding "dummy" nodes to make the tree full. To improve this we give a tighter version of the partition theorems of [Mat91, AM94].
- *Leveled copy-and-recurse.* We introduce a different version of copy-and-recurse where cleartext algorithm traverses a tree and visits at most ξ nodes in each level of the tree. This is different than the original copy-and-recurse in [KMS24] that requires that for each node, v, there is a bound $\xi = O(r^c)$ on the number of children that the cleartext algorithm visits.

  Leveled copy-and-recurse improves traversing
  - binary trees under FHE
  - B-trees under FHE

- 1-dimensional range searching

to run in time $O(t \cdot \log n + n)$, where t is the time to compute (under FHE) the indicator whether the algorithm should recurse into a child. See row 1 in Table 1.

- *Emptiness queries.* We show how to answer whether the query is empty or not, faster than counting queries by implementing the partition theorems of [Mat92,SS11] under FHE. This yields several cases of emptiness queries, for example: (1) halfspaces bounded by hyperplanes in time $O(t \cdot n^{1-1/\lfloor d/2 \rfloor + \varepsilon} + n)$ (2) α-fat 2-dim triangles $O(t \cdot n^{\varepsilon} + n)$ (instead of previously known $O(t \cdot n^{1-1/2+\varepsilon} + n^{1+\varepsilon})$). See rows 5–6 in Table 1.

- *Approximate counting.* We show how to use under FHE the work of [AHP08], that uses multiple emptiness queries to approximate counting query.

- *Implementation.* We implemented our algorithms using HElayers [AAB+20] and HEaaN [Cry22] and provide a comparison for the community to evaluate our algorithms. Our experiments show that our algorithms are faster than those of [KMS24]. For example, for a database of 2^{25} points our emptiness algorithm is $\times 3.6$ faster than what was known before.

2 Preliminaries and Related Work

We first review emptiness queries in cleartext and how they are solved with partition trees. Then we review cryptographic preliminaries: fully homomorphic encryption (FHE) and the limitation of operating in circuit model.

Trees. The data structures we review and use in our solution are based on trees. When describing a tree we use v to denote a node in a tree. We use dot ('.') to denote members of v, so for example, $v.child[1], \ldots, v.child[r]$ are the children of v. The height of a node v is the number of nodes on the path from v to the root and the height of a tree is the maximal height of its nodes. In addition, as in [KMS24], we associate a subset of points to each node. We use $S(v)$ to denote the subset that is associated with the node v. Note that $S(v)$ is associated with v but is **not stored** in v which is why we avoid the dot notation.

2.1 Computational Geometry

Range Searching. A *range space* is a pair (X, Γ), where X is a set and $\Gamma \subset 2^X$ (i.e., each $\gamma \in \Gamma$ is a subset of X). Usually, $X = \mathbb{R}^d$ and Γ is a family of semi-algebraic sets with **constant description complexity**. That means that each $\gamma \in \Gamma$ is a union and intersection of a constant number of polynomial inequalities of constant degree. For example, X can the 3D-space ($X = \mathbb{R}^3$) and Γ be the set of all 3D spheres.

α**-Fat Triangles.** A triangle is α-fat if all its angles are bigger than α. In most real-life applications polygons can be triangulated into α-fat triangles for some $\alpha > 0$.

Simplicial Partition. For a set of n points $P \subset \mathbb{R}^d$, a simplicial partition of size m of P is $\Pi = \{(P_1, \sigma_1), \ldots, (P_m, \sigma_m)\}$, where $P_1, \ldots, P_m \subset \mathbb{R}^d$ are a partition of P (that is, $\cup P_i = P$ and $P_i \cap P_j = \emptyset$ when $i \neq j$) and $\sigma_1, \ldots, \sigma_m \subset \mathbb{R}^d$ are simplices such that $P_i \subset \sigma_i$.

Crossing Number. Given a simplicial partition Π and a range γ, we say that: (1) γ *contains* a simplex σ if $\sigma \subset \gamma$; (2) γ and σ are *disjoint* if $\sigma \cap \gamma = \emptyset$; otherwise, (3) we say that γ *crosses* σ.

The *crossing number* of γ with respect to Π is the number of simplices that γ crosses. When Π is obvious from the context we simply call this number the crossing number of γ.

Partition Theorem. Given a family of ranges Γ, previous work (e.g., [Mat91, AMS13, SS11]) show how to partition P into a simplical partition of size $O(r)$ with $|P_i| = O(\frac{n}{r})$ such that:

- If the ranges in $\Gamma \subset 2^{\mathbb{R}^d}$ can be described with constant number of parameters then the crossing number of $\gamma \in \Gamma$ is $O(r^{1-1/d})$. See [AMS13].
- If $\gamma \subset \mathbb{R}^d$ is the area below a hyperplane and $P \cap \gamma = \emptyset$ then the crossing number of γ is $O(r^{1-1/\lfloor d/2 \rfloor})$. See [Mat91].
- If $\gamma \subset \mathbb{R}^2$ is a α-fat triangle and $P \cap \gamma = \emptyset$ then the crossing number of γ is $O(r^\varepsilon)$. See [SS11] (also see [SS11] for more partition theorems).

2.2   Emptiness Queries in Plaintext

In the range emptiness problem we are given a set of n points $P \subset \mathbb{R}^d$, and a family of *ranges* $\Gamma \subset 2^{\mathbb{R}^d}$. The goal is to build a data structure such that given a range $\gamma \in \Gamma$ we can quickly determine whether $P \cap \gamma = \emptyset$. Range counting is a related problem.

In this paper we are interested in data structures of linear size and a sublinear query time. In a seminal work, Matoušek [Mat91] showed a that $|P \cap \gamma|$ can be computed in $O(n^{1-1/d+\varepsilon})$ time, when γ is the area under a hyperplane. This was later generalized in [AMS13] to semi-algebraic ranges. Intuitively, answering whether $|P \cap \gamma$ is easier. Indeed, Matoušek [Mat92] showed that this can be answered in $O(n^{1-1/\lfloor d/2 \rfloor+\varepsilon})$ time if γ is the area under a hyperplane. Sharir and Shaul [SS11] showed how to generalize this some cases. E.g., when $P \subset \mathbb{R}^2$ and Γ are α-fat triangles emptiness on the plane it can be determined whether $P \cap \gamma = \emptyset$ in $O(n^\varepsilon)$ time.

2.3   Partition Trees

A partition tree, T, for a set $P \subset \mathbb{R}^d$ is built as follows. The root of T represents the entire set P, i.e., $S(root) = P$. Additionally, the root keeps a bounding simplex $\sigma \subset \mathbb{R}^d$, s.t., $P \subset \sigma$. The set P is then partitioned into a simplicial partition $\{(P_1, \sigma_1), \ldots, (P_m, \sigma_m)\}$ with $P_1, \ldots, P_m$ having "almost" the same size. The root then has m children, $root.child[1], \ldots, root.child[m]$, where $S(root.child[i]) = P_i$ and we recursively partition each P_i. The recursion stops at nodes (leaves) that each represents a single point $p \in P$.

Searching A Partition Tree. To compute $|P \cap \gamma|$, start at the root and go over its children. For *root.child*$[i]$ we compare σ_i to γ and check whether it is (1) contained in γ, i.e., $\sigma_i \subset \gamma$; (2) disjoint, i.e., $\sigma_i \cap \gamma = \emptyset$ or (3) σ_i crosses γ. In case (1) we know that $P_i \subset \sigma_i \subset \gamma$ and we count all the points of P_i. In case (2) we know that $P_i \subset \sigma_i \cap \gamma = \emptyset$ and we ignore this child and its subtree. In the last case (3), we need to recurse into *root.child*$[i]$ and compare a finer partition of P_i to γ. The various partition theorems bound the number of simplices that cross γ.

Theorem 1 (From [AMS13]). *Given a set P of n points in $\mathbb{R}^d$, for some fixed d, a family of semi-algebraic ranges of constant description complexity Γ and a parameter $r \le n$, a simplicial partition $\Pi = \{(P_1, \sigma_1), \dots, (P_m, \sigma_m)\}$ can be computed such that:*

1. *$\lfloor n/r \rfloor \le |P_i| < h \lfloor n/r \rfloor$ for every i and some constant h.*
2. *The crossing number of any $\gamma \in \Gamma$ is $O(r^{1-1/d})$.*

Similar theorems appear in [AM94, Mat91, Mat92, SS11]. See Fig. 2 (Right) for a depiction of a 1D partition tree. In 1D it is easy to see that for any $\gamma \subset$ {all segments in $\mathbb{R}$} and a partition $\{(P_1, \sigma_1), \dots, (P_r, \sigma_r)\}$, γ crosses at most 2 simplices. It is also easy to see that if γ is empty then γ crosses at most 1 bounding simplex.

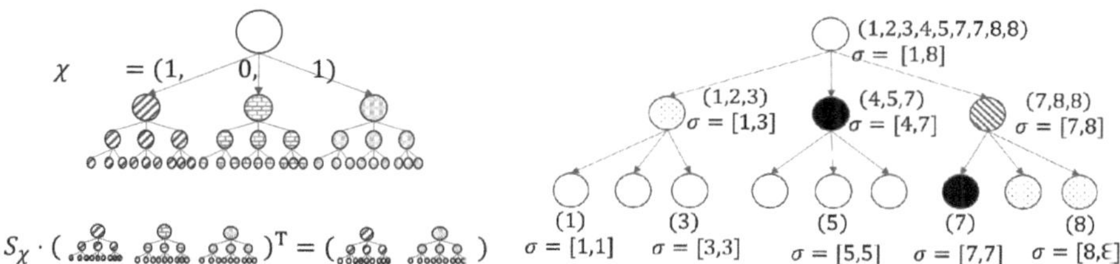

Fig. 2. (Right) An example of a 1-dim partition tree built for $P = \{1, 2, 3, 4, 5, 7, 7, 8, 8\}$ with $r = 3$. At each node v, S_v and its bounding segment $v.\sigma$ are shown (omitted for some leaves). The figure also shows how the tree is traversed for a query segment $\gamma = [4, 7]$. Nodes with $v.\sigma \subset \gamma$ (marked with **solid black**) can be counted without recursing. Nodes with $v.\sigma \cap \gamma = \emptyset$ (marked with **black dots**) can be ignored. Nodes the traversal doesn't reach are marked with **white**. Nodes with $v.\sigma$ crossing γ (marked with **black stripes**) should be recursed into to determine how many of the values in γ. (Left) A depiction of copy-and-recurse. The top shows a 3-ary tree with an indicator vector χ indicating that the 1st and 3rd children need to be recursed into. The bottom shows how multiplying the selection matrix X_χ by the vector of 3 sub-trees results in the 2 sub-trees that need to be recursed into.

2.4   Fully Homomorphic Encryption

Our algorithms and protocols can be implemented using FHE or other MPC schemes that support addition and multiplication. However, to enhance clarity, we present our protocols using FHE.

FHE (see, e.g., [BGV12, CKKS17]) is an asymmetric encryption scheme that supports both addition $(+)$ and multiplication $(\times)$ operations on ciphertexts. Specifically, an FHE scheme is defined by the tuple $\mathcal{E} = (Gen, Enc, Dec, Add, Mult)$, where:

- $Gen(1^\lambda, p)$ gets a security parameter λ and an integer p and generates the keys pk and sk.
- $Enc_{pk}(m)$ gets a message m and outputs a ciphertext $[\![m]\!]$.
- $Dec_{sk}([\![m]\!])$ gets a ciphertext $[\![m]\!]$ and outputs a message m'.
- $Add_{pk}([\![a]\!], [\![b]\!])$ gets two ciphertexts $[\![a]\!], [\![b]\!]$ and outputs a ciphertext $[\![c]\!]$.
- $Mult_{pk}([\![a]\!], [\![b]\!])$ gets two ciphertexts $[\![a]\!], [\![b]\!]$ and outputs a ciphertext $[\![d]\!]$.

The scheme is considered **correct** if $m = m'$, $c = a + b \mod p$, and $d = a \cdot b \mod p$. In approximated FHE schemes (e.g., CKKS [CKKS17]), correctness is relaxed to $m \approx m'$, $c \approx a + b$, and $d \approx a \cdot b$.

Semantic Security requires that given pk and a set of ciphertexts $[\![m_1]\!], \ldots, [\![m_{poly(\lambda)}]\!]$, and their corresponding plaintexts $m_1, \ldots, m_{poly(\lambda)}$, where $poly(\lambda)$ is polynomially dependent on λ, the probability of deducing m_0 from another ciphertext $[\![m_0]\!]$ should be negligible in λ.

Using an arithmetic circuit of addition and multiplication, any polynomial $\mathbb{P}(x_1, \ldots)$ on ciphertexts $[\![x_1]\!], \ldots$. For example, in a client-server setup, the client encrypts her data and sends it to the server, which computes $\mathbb{P}$ on the encrypted inputs. The server then returns the encrypted result to the client, who decrypts it. FHE's semantic security guarantees that the server gains no information about the client's data.

When evaluating an arithmetic circuit, C, we are concerned with the number of operators in C, denoted size(C), and with the maximal number of multiplication gates on a path of C, denoted depth(C). The time to evaluate a circuit is then $Time = overhead \cdot$ size(C), where in many schemes $overhead$ grows when depth(C) increases.

Abbreviated Syntax. To make our algorithms and protocols more intuitive to read we use $[\![\cdot]\!]_{pk}$ to denote a ciphertext. When pk is clear from the context we omit it. We use an abbreviated syntax:

- $[\![a]\!] + [\![b]\!]$ is short for $Add_{pk}([\![a]\!], [\![b]\!])$.
- $[\![a]\!] \cdot [\![b]\!]$ is short for $Mult_{pk}([\![a]\!], [\![b]\!])$.
- $[\![a]\!] + b$ is short for $Add_{pk}([\![a]\!], Enc_{pk}(b))$.
- $[\![a]\!] \cdot b$ is short for $Mult_{pk}([\![a]\!], Enc_{pk}(b))$.

2.5   Size and Depth of Comparison Under FHE (t and s)

Cleartext algorithms (e.g., in Sect. 2.2) work in comparison model, where they make decisions based on the input. Algorithms under FHE work in circuit model where the behavior is fixed and can't change regardless to the input. Specifically,

under FHE it is impossible to have "if" statements in the code. A general recipe
to convert an algorithm from comparison model to circuit model is to replace
every "if" statement and its 2 branches with 2 subcircuits that computes both
branches and whose output is multiplexed (MUX) using an FHE evaluation of
the condition in the "if". When traversing a tree, it is easy to see that this leads
to visiting all the nodes in the tree.

In addition, when traversing a tree, the decision of which child to follow into
depends on the data associated with these nodes. Under FHE, this decision is
computed by a sub-circuit on encrypted input. In practice, most of the runtime
is spent executing instances of this sub-circuit. We denote by t and s its size and
depth. By expressing the complexity of the FHE algorithm using t and s, we
get a clearer way to compare different range-searching algorithms. See a more
detailed description in the full version [KS25].

2.6   Copy and Recurse

Copy and recurse is a technique from [KMS24] to traverse a tree efficiently under
FHE. With this technique a plaintext algorithm can be converted to run under
FHE by paying an overhead linear in the tree size. More specifically, given a tree
T with m leaves and with these prerequisites:

1. every inner node of T has r children
2. every leaf of T is at the same distance from the root

and a plaintext algorithm $\mathcal{A}$ that:

1. when traversing T and reaching an inner node, $\mathcal{A}$ continues in at most $\xi \leq r^c$
   children, where $c < 1$ is a constant
2. at every node v that $\mathcal{A}$ visits it computes a function $f(v)$ which takes time t
   to compute

then using Copy and Recurse, $\mathcal{A}$ can be implemented under FHE in time $O(t \cdot
m^{c+\varepsilon} + m)$. The main idea behind copy and recurse is to: (1) determine (under
FHE) at each inner node v which $\xi < r$ children of v $\mathcal{A}$ would have recursed into;
(2) generate a selection matrix, M, that selects those ξ children; (3) multiply M
by the vector of children to copy them and their subtrees (again under FHE);
and then (4) recurse into those copies. The trick here is that although copying
the ξ children takes $O(m)$ time under FHE, after doing so the number of times
f is computed is similar to that of $\mathcal{A}$. See Fig. 2 (left) for a depiction.

3   Problem Statement

We consider two related problems: First we improve the solution of [KMS24] for
range searching. Then, we consider the related range emptiness problem.

Range Searching Queries. Given a set of n points $P \subset \mathbb{R}^d$ and a family of ranges
$\Gamma \subset 2^{\mathbb{R}^d}$ construct a linear size data structure s.t., given a range $\gamma \in \Gamma$ we can
compute $|P \cap \gamma|$ as quickly as possible.

Emptiness Queries. Given a set of n points $P \subset \mathbb{R}^d$ and a family of ranges $\Gamma \subset 2^{\mathbb{R}^d}$ construct a linear size data structure s.t., given a range $\gamma \in \Gamma$ we can answer whether $P \cap \gamma = \emptyset$ as quickly as possible.

3.1   Threat Model

Our work is motivated by the trend toward cloud-based computation to reduce IT costs. Companies like IBM [ibm24], CryptoLab [hea24], and Duality [dua24] offer analytics-as-a-service, highlighting this shift.

We adopt the threat model of [KMS24], involving three parties: (1) a data owner with dataset P, (2) a querier performing range emptiness or approximate counting queries, and (3) the cloud, which hosts the database and executes the computations. Our overall protocol for the improved range searching problem is identical to Protocol 2 in [KMS24]. The modified protocol for secure emptiness searching is similar and given in the full version [KS25].

We consider computationally-bounded, semi-honest adversaries where the querier doesn't collude with the cloud or the data owner. The semantic security of FHE guarantees that the cloud learns nothing on the content of γ or P.

Multiple Queriers. Our protocols can be extended to multiple queriers in a similar way to Protocol 2 of [KMS24]. Their extension used transciphering (e.g., [ADE+23, TCBS23]) to avoid keeping an encrypted version of the database for each querier.

4   Improving Range Searching Overhead

The results of [KMS24] include an overhead of $O(n^{1+\varepsilon})$ that we reduce to $O(n)$ (see Table 1). In what follows we first remind why the overhead in [KMS24] was $O(n^{1+\varepsilon})$ and then show how to reduce it to the lower bound of $O(n)$. To do that we need to revisit Matoušek's partition theorem [Mat91] and prove a tighter version of it. The discussion below can be also applied to the partition theorems in [SS11, AM94] in a similar manner.

4.1   Where The $O(n^{1+\varepsilon})$ Overhead Comes From

As mentioned in [KMS24], the partition theorem of [Mat91] states that a set with n points can be partitioned into $\Pi = ((P_1, \sigma_1), \ldots, (P_m, \sigma_m))$, where $n/2r \leq |P_i| \leq n/r$ (and therefore $r \leq m \leq 2r$), for any parameter r.

Specifically, the sizes of P_i are roughly, **but not exactly**, the same. This is further exacerbated when using the partition theorem recursively to create a partition tree. In the extreme case consider a tree whose root has 2 subtrees T_1 and T_2 each having n leaves. Then let $S(v_1)$ (the points associated with v_1) of every $v_1 \in T_1$ be partitioned to $2r$ subsets $((P_1^{v_1}, \sigma_1^{v_1}), \ldots, (P_{2r}^{v_1}, \sigma_{2r}^{v_1}))$ and $|P_i^{v_1}| = \frac{|S(v_1)|}{2r}$. Similarly, let $S(v_2)$ of every $v_2 \in T_2$ be partitioned to r subsets $((P_1^{v_2}, \sigma_1^{v_2}), \ldots, (P_r^{v_2}, \sigma_r^{v_2}))$ and $|P_i^{v_2}| = \frac{|S(v_2)|}{r}$. It easily follows that the height of T_1 is $\log_{2r} n$ and the height of T_2 is $\log_r n$. In plaintext, the difference in the shape of the subtrees does not affect the running time of range queries but under FHE this imbalance creates 2 problems that are already mentioned in [KMS24]: (1) the structure of the tree is not hidden and may leak information on P; (2) copy-and-recurse requires that all subtrees have the same structure.

The solution suggested by [KMS24] was to "fill" the tree by adding "dummy" nodes to the partition tree until it becomes full. Unfortunately, as [KMS24] showed, the total leaves in the full tree is upper bounded by $O(n^{1+\log_r 2}) = O(n^{1+\varepsilon})$.

4.2   A More Efficient Alternative To *FillTree*

For a more efficient *FillTree* we first modify the partition theorem of [Mat91] to assume that n is a multiple of r. In that case we show the subsets of the partition are of the same size: $|P_i| = n/r$. Next, we show that when n is a power of r, we can use the modified partition theorem to construct a full tree with n leaves. Then, we address the case when n is not a power of r. Finally, we describe how other partition theorems can be changed in a similar way.

4.3   Modifying Matoušek's Partition Theorem

We now give a modified version of the partition theorem (Theorem 3.1) of [Mat91]. The tighter proof of the partition theorem (Theorem 3.1 of [Mat91]) is almost identical so we just sketch it in high level and mention where it diverges.

Theorem 2. *Let $P \in \mathbb{R}^d$ be a set of n points, let $r \in \mathbb{N}$ be a parameter that divides n. Also, let $\Gamma \subset 2^{\mathbb{R}^d}$ be the set of all hyperplanes in $\mathbb{R}^d$. There exists a simplicial partition $\Pi = ((P_1, \sigma_1), \ldots, (P_r, \sigma_r))$, that satisfies $|P_i| = n/r$ and whose crossing number is $O(r^{1-1/d})$.*

Specifically, there are 2 differences from Theorem 3.1 in [Mat91]: (1) we assume that n is a multiple of r and (2) $|P_i| = n/r$, for all i.

Proof Sketch of Theorem 2. The main part of the proof is Lemma 1 which is similar to Theorem 2 with the difference that the crossing number of Π is computed with respect to a finite set $Q \subset \Gamma$ (called the *test set*). Using this lemma, the proof of Theorem 2 is completed by showing how to construct Q where $|Q| = O(n^d)$ such that every range in $\gamma \in \Gamma$ has the same crossing number as Q (up to a constant multiplicative factor). We skip the construction of the test set Q and the proof of its properties since it is identical to the proof in [Mat91] and turn to prove the following lemma which is a modified version of Lemma 3.2 in [Mat91].

Lemma 1. *Let P, n, r be as above. Also, let $Q \subset 2^{\mathbb{R}^d}$ be a finite set of hyperplanes in $\mathbb{R}^d$. There exists a simplicial partition $\Pi = ((P_1, \sigma_1), \ldots, (P_r, \sigma_r))$, that satisfies $|P_i| = n/r$ and the crossing number of each $h \in Q$ is $O(r^{1-1/d} + \log |Q|)$.*

The proof of this lemma is almost identical to that of Lemma 3.2 in [Mat91]. In fact, in Matoušek's original proof $|P_1| = \cdots = |P_{m-1}| = n/r$ and only $n/r \leq |P_m| < 2n/r$, also $m \in \{r - 1, r\}$. As we show, we use the assumption that n is a multiple of r to show that $|P_i| = n/r$ for all $1 \leq i \leq r$. Since the difference in the proofs is so small we only sketch it in high level.

Proof Sketch. Construct inductively the disjoint sets $P_i \subset P$ and their enclosing simplices. Suppose that $P_1, \ldots, P_i$ have already been constructed. Set $P'_i = P \setminus (P_1 \cup \cdots \cup P_i)$ and $n_i = |P'|$. If $n_i < 2n/r$, we set $P_{i+1} = P'_i$, $\sigma_{i+1} = \mathbb{R}^d$ and conclude the construction. Otherwise, for any $h \in Q$, let $\kappa_i(h)$ denote the number of simplices of $\sigma_1, \ldots, \sigma_i$ that h crosses. Let $t_i = O((r \cdot n_i/n)^{1/d})$ and construct the decomposition of the weighted $1/t_i$-cutting, Ξ_i, of Q, where the weight of any $h \in Q$ is $w_i(h) = 2^{\kappa_i(h)}$. Ξ_i has at most $r \cdot n_i/n$ cells. By the pigeonhole principle, there is at least one cell $\sigma_i \in \Xi_i$ that contains at least n/r points of P'_i. Choose arbitrarily n/r points $P_i \subset P' \cap \sigma_i$ (as already mentioned σ_i is the simplex in Ξ_i that contains them). Next, Matoušek proves that due to the exponential weights $w_i(h)$, the crossing number of any $h \in Q$ is at most $O(\log |Q| + r^{1-1/d})$. We do not repeat this proof here.

To our matter, Matoušek's construction yield $|P_1| = \cdots = |P_{r-1}| = n/r$. Only for the last set they get $n/r \leq |P_m| < 2n/r$, however since we assume n is a multiple of r (and this is where we deviate from Matoušek's original proof) it follows that $m = r$ and $|P_r| = n/r$ as required.

Using the modified partition theorem to build a full partition tree is easy and given in the full version [KS25]. We conclude with the corollary below (also restated and proved in the full version [KS25]). The results are also summarized in Table 1.

Given a set $P \subset \mathbb{R}^d$ of n points, we can construct an encrypted data structure for a family of ranges Γ that given an encrypted range $\gamma \in \Gamma$ can answer emptiness queries in a circuit of size $T(n)$ and depth $O(s \cdot \log n)$, where:

1. when $P \subset \mathbb{R}^d$ is a set of points Γ is the family of all halfspaces bounded by a hyperplane, then we can answer half-space emptiness in a circuit of size $T(n) = O(t \cdot n^{1-1/\lfloor d/2 \rfloor + \varepsilon} + n)$.
2. When $P \subset \mathbb{R}^2$ is a set of points and $\Gamma = \{\alpha\text{-fat trianlge}\}$, then we can answer whether γ is empty in a circuit of size $T(n) = O(t \cdot n^\varepsilon + n)$.

5   Leveled Copy and Recurse

In this section we describe a variation of copy-and-recurse that we call leveled copy-and-recurse. This variation is more efficient in some cases. Specifically it improves the case of axis-parallel hyperboxes mentioned in [KMS24]. Also, it improves the usage of copy-and-recurse to implement traversal-based algorithms such as binary search, B-tree searches [BM70], etc.

In leveled copy-and-recurse we are given a tree T and a plaintext algorithm, $\mathcal{A}$, that traverses it and there is a bound ξ (for some constant $\xi \in \mathbb{N}$) on the number of children of each **node** $\mathcal{A}$ visits in each **level** of T. This is different from the copy-and-recurse described in [KMS24] where for each inner node $\mathcal{A}$ visits there is a bound $O(r^c)$ (for some constant $0 < c < 1$) on the number of its children that $\mathcal{A}$ recurses into. To emphasize, at each level ℓ of T, $\mathcal{A}$ reaches at most ξ nodes and continues into at most ξ children in the next level, $\ell + 1$. This is regardless to how these children relate to the nodes in level ℓ.

Implementing $\mathcal{A}$ with leveled copy-and-recurse works as we now describe. It starts at level $\ell = 1$ of T (i.e. at the root). At each level ℓ, the algorithm acts as follows:

- There are ξ nodes of T that $\mathcal{A}$ visits with a total of $r \cdot \xi$ potential children to continue at. Consider these $r \cdot \xi$ potential nodes and generate an indicator vector for the ξ children (in level $\ell + 1$) that $\mathcal{A}$ actually recurse into.
- Compute the selection matrix M that selects the ξ children in level $\ell + 1$ from the $r \cdot \xi$ potential children.
- Use M to create a copy of the ξ nodes in level $\ell + 1$ that $\mathcal{A}$ traverses into.
- Recurse into the copies of the ξ children.

For lack of space we avoid further discussion that can be found in the full version [KS25].

We conclude with the following lemma.

Lemma 2. *The number of values in $\gamma \subset \mathbb{R}$ can be counted with a circuit of size $O(t \cdot \log n)$ and depth $O(s \cdot \log n)$, where t and s are as in Sect. 2.5.*

6   Experiments

What We Tested. We tested the 1D range emptiness problem (i.e., $P \subset \mathbb{R}$ and $\gamma = [a, b]$) and the goal is to determine whether $P \cap \gamma = \emptyset$. This usecase is useful when checking whether a value $p \in \mathbb{N}$ appears in a given list. As mentioned earlier, the emptiness problem can be solved by the closely related counting problem computing $\mu = |P \cap \gamma|$ so our experiments compared 4 algorithms:

1. **Ours.** We implemented our algorithm for emptiness queries using leveled copy-and-recurse. As mentioned in Sect. 2.3 we have $\xi = 1$. We tested our implementation with $r = 3, 5, 7, 9$.
2. **Range Counting.** We implemented the range counting algorithm from [KMS24]. For fairness, we used leveled copy-and-recurse with $\xi = 2$ and $r = 3, 5, 7, 9$. To preserve privacy in the emptiness problem, we output $isEqual(\mu, 0)$ which returns 1 if $\mu = 0$, and 0 otherwise, so that μ itself is not leaked. Details of $isEqual$ are given below.
3. **Naïve emptiness.** We implemented a naïve algorithm that computes $e_i = isContained(p_i, \gamma)$ for each $p_i \in P$ and then output $1 - \prod(1 - e_i)$.
4. **Naïve counting.** We used the naive counting algorithm that computes $\mu = \sum_i isContained(p_i, \gamma)$. Here also we output $isEqual(\mu, 0)$

What the Data Was. In our experiments the data was a set $P \subset \mathbb{R}$, where $|P| = n$, for $n = 2^{15}, \ldots, 2^{25}$. Each $p_i \in P$ was drawn independently and uniformly from the set $\{0, \frac{1}{100}, \frac{2}{100}, \ldots, 1\}$. For the range γ we drew a uniformly from $\{\frac{1}{200}, \frac{3}{200}, \ldots, \frac{201}{200}\}$ and set $\gamma = [-0.5, a]$.

Our algorithms are generic and can be implemented with any encryption scheme. For our experiments we used CKKS where each of $\gamma_a, \gamma_b, p_1, \ldots, p_n$ was encoded as a single message. The key had 18 bits of integer, 42 bits in its fractional part, 12 limbs (multiplication depth) and the security parameter was 128. With these parameters, the key supported bootstrapping and each ciphertext had 2^{15} slots.

Packing and SIMD. To use all slots, we split P into 2^{15} subsets $P_1, \ldots, P_{2^{15}}$ of size $n/2^{15}$, and build identical-shape trees T_i for each. Each node of T_i is mapped to the i-th slot of the corresponding node in T. All $\mu_i = |P_i \cap \gamma|$ are computed in parallel using SIMD. In range counting, they are then summed with 15 rotations and additions. In range emptiness, we have indicators χ_i that are combined with 15 rotations and multiplications.

Implementing   *isContain.*   We implemented $isContain(p, \gamma)$ using $isSmaller(x, y) = (sign(x - y) + 1)/2$, so that $isContain(p, \gamma) = isSmaller(\gamma\_a, p) \cdot isSmaller(p, \gamma\_b)$. The *isSmaller* function follows Algorithm 3 from [CKK20], where $sign(z)$ is approximated by composing polynomials f and g of degree 7. We used $d_f = 1$ and $d_g = 4$ in our implementation.

The Setup. Our algorithms are generic and work with any scheme supporting addition and multiplication. For the implementation of CKKS we used the HELayers framework [AAB+20] and the HEaaN library [Cry22]. Experiments ran on a system with 32-core AMD EPYC 7742 CPU (128 threads), 500 GB RAM, and an NVIDIA A100-SXM4-80GB GPU.

The Results. The results are in the graphs below. Also Table 2 compares the time to run a 1D emptiness query, i.e., $P \subset \mathbb{R}$ and $\gamma = [a, b] \subset \mathbb{R}$ is a segment. The sizes of P are comparable to real data set sizes: $|P| = 2^{15}, \ldots, 2^{25}$. The first 4 rows show the time of our algorithm (Item 1 above) The 5th row shows the time to run the naïve emptiness algorithm (Item 3 above). The next 4 rows show the time to run the algorithm of [KMS24] (Item 2 above). The last row shows the time of the naïve counting (Item 4 above).

For example, when $|P| = 2^{23}$, our algorithm (with $r = 3$) takes 28 s whereas the counting algorithm of [KMS24] (with $r = 3$) takes 93.3 s. The naïve emptiness takes 192.8 s and the naïve counting takes 177.6 s. Our algorithm was faster than [KMS24] for all choices of r and P that we checked. This is consistent with our analysis since our emptiness algorithm was implemented with leveled copy-and-recurse with $\xi = 1$ (compared to $\xi = 2$ for [KMS24]). Our algorithm is faster than the naïve counting algorithm when $|P| > 2^{21}$, whereas the algorithm of [KMS24] is faster than the naïve counting algorithm only when $|P| > 2^{23}$. The naïve emptiness algorithm is slower than the naïve counting algorithm for all data sets that we checked and is probably because it requires more multiplications.

Table 2. A summary of the time to compute 1D emptiness (left) and counting (right) queries. All times are given in seconds.

	Emptiness						Counting						
	2^{15}	2^{17}	2^{19}	2^{21}	2^{23}	2^{25}		2^{15}	2^{17}	2^{19}	2^{21}	2^{23}	2^{25}
Ours ($r=3$)	1.3	4.6	14.4	27.3	28.0	68.9	[KMS24] ($r=3$)	1.4	8.0	32.3	87.4	93.3	248.7
Ours ($r=5$)	1.3	3.6	17.0	33.9	89.5	104.9	[KMS24] ($r=5$)	1.4	5.6	32.5	88.4	134.8	323.5
Ours ($r=7$)	1.3	3.6	16.7	29.8	81.1	184.7	[KMS24] ($r=7$)	1.4	5.6	31.6	74.6	239.4	538.7
Ours ($r=9$)	1.3	3.7	16.1	69.0	69.9	150.7	[KMS24] ($r=9$)	1.4	5.7	30.0	139.7	202.2	427.0
Naïve	1.4	3.7	12.7	48.9	192.8	771.8	Naïve	0.7	2.8	11.2	44.8	177.6	714.3

Figure 3 (left) summarizes the results, comparing our algorithm with $r = 3$ to the naïve counting algorithm. Both axes are log-scaled: the x-axis shows data size $|P|$, and the y-axis shows runtime in seconds. The naïve algorithm, with linear time $O(t \cdot n)$, appears as a straight line. Our algorithm is slower for small n, matches performance at $n \approx 2^{20}$, and becomes faster for larger n. Its smaller slope shows better scalability, consistent with our analysis of $O(t \cdot \log n + n)$ runtime. Figure 3 (right) compares our algorithm with different values or r.

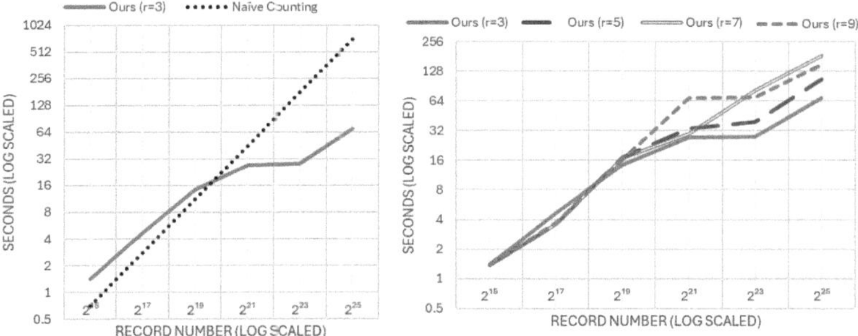

Fig. 3. Running times of our emptiness algorithm with $r = 3$ compared to the naïve counting algorithm (left). Also with $r = 3, 5, 7, 9$ (right).

7 Conclusion and Future Work

In this paper we showed 3 improvements to the results in [KMS24].

First, we introduced leveled copy-and-recurse for traversing trees with a bound ξ on the number of nodes visited per level, e.g., 1D partition trees, binary search trees, etc.

Then, we improved the partition theorems in [Mat92, Mat91, AM94, SS11] and used it to optimize the overhead term in the range-searching algorithm from [KMS24], reducing it to the optimal $O(n)$. We also demonstrated how to answer range emptiness queries more efficiently by using the partition theorems from [Mat92, SS11].

Finally, we implemented our FHE-based emptiness query approach and confirmed that it is indeed faster than range counting.

References

[AAB+20] Aharoni, E., et al.: HeLayers: a tile tensors framework for large neural networks on encrypted data. CoRR, abs/2011.0 (2020)

[ADE+23] Aharoni, E., Drucker, N., Ezov, G., Kushnir, E., Shaul, H., Soceanu, O.: Poster: efficient AES-GCM decryption under homomorphic encryption. In: Proceedings of the 2023 ACM SIGSAC Conference on Computer and Communications Security. CCS '23, pp. 3567–3569. Association for Computing Machinery, New York, NY, USA (2023)

[AHP08] Aronov, B., Har-Peled, S.: On approximating the depth and related problems. SIAM J. Comput. **38**(3), 899–921 (2008)

[AM94] Agarwal, P.K., Matousek, J.: On range searching with semialgebraic sets. Discret. Comput. Geometry **11**(4), 393–418 (1994). https://doi.org/10.1007/BF02574015

[AMS13] Agarwal, P.K., Matoušek, J., Sharir, M.: On range searching with semialgebraic sets. ii. SIAM J. Comput. **42**(6), 2039–2062 (2013)

[Bea92] Beaver, D.: Efficient multiparty protocols using circuit randomization. In: Feigenbaum, J. (ed.) CRYPTO 1991. LNCS, vol. 576, pp. 420–432. Springer, Heidelberg (1992). https://doi.org/10.1007/3-540-46766-1_34

[BGV12] Brakerski, Z., Gentry, C., Vaikuntanathan, V.: (Leveled) fully homomorphic encryption without bootstrapping. In: Proceedings of the 3rd Innovations in Theoretical Computer Science Conference. ITCS '12, pp. 309–325. ACM, New York, NY, USA (2012)

[BIM00] Beimel, A., Ishai, Y., Malkin, T.: Reducing the servers computation in private information retrieval: PIR with preprocessing. In: Bellare, M. (ed.) CRYPTO 2000. LNCS, vol. 1880, pp. 55–73. Springer, Heidelberg (2000). https://doi.org/10.1007/3-540-44598-6_4

[BM70] Bayer, R., McCreight, E.: Organization and maintenance of large ordered indices. In: Proceedings of the 1970 ACM SIGFIDET (Now SIGMOD) Workshop on Data Description, Access and Control. SIGFIDET '70, pp. 107–141. Association for Computing Machinery, New York, NY, USA (1970)

[CFLM20] Chow, S.S.M., Fech, K., Lai, R.W.F., Malavolta, G.: Multi-client Oblivious RAM with Poly-logarithmic Communication. In: Moriai, S., Wang, H. (eds.) ASIACRYPT 2020. LNCS, vol. 12492, pp. 160–190. Springer, Cham (2020). https://doi.org/10.1007/978-3-030-64834-3_6

[CGKO06] Curtmola, R., Garay, J., Kamara, S., Ostrovsky, R.: Searchable symmetric encryption: improved definitions and efficient constructions. In: Proceedings of the 13th ACM Conference on Computer and Communications Security. CCS '06, pp. 79–88. Association for Computing Machinery, New York, NY, USA (2006)

[CKK15] Cheon, J.H., Kim, M., Kim, M.: Search-and-compute on encrypted data. In: Brenner, M., Christin, N., Johnson, B., Rohloff, K. (eds.) FC 2015. LNCS, vol. 8976, pp. 142–159. Springer, Heidelberg (2015). https://doi.org/10.1007/978-3-662-48051-9_11

[CKK20] Cheon, J.H., Kim, D., Kim, D.: Efficient homomorphic comparison methods with optimal complexity. In: Moriai, S., Wang, H. (eds.) ASIACRYPT 2020. LNCS, vol. 12492, pp. 221–256. Springer, Cham (2020). https://doi.org/10.1007/978-3-030-64834-3_8

[CKKS17] Cheon, J.H., Kim, A., Kim, M., Song, Y.: Homomorphic encryption for arithmetic of approximate numbers. In: Takagi, T., Peyrin, T. (eds.) ASIACRYPT 2017. LNCS, vol. 10624, pp. 409–437. Springer, Cham (2017). https://doi.org/10.1007/978-3-319-70694-8_15

[Cry22] CryptoLab. HEaaN: Homomorphic Encryption for Arithmetic of Approximate Numbers, version 3.1.4 (2022)

[DPP+16] Demertzis, I., Papadopoulos, S., Papapetrou, O., Deligiannakis, A., Garofalakis, M.: Practical private range search revisited. In: Proceedings of the 2016 International Conference on Management of Data, pp. 185–198 (2016)

[DPP+18] Demertzis, I., Papadopoulos, S., Papapetrou, O., Deligiannakis, A., Garofalakis, M., Papamanthou, C.: Practical private range search in depth. ACM Trans. Database Syst. (TODS) 43(1), 1–52 (2018)

[dua24] Duality query engine (2024). https://dualitytech.com/platform/duality-query/

[FJK+15] Faber, S., Jarecki, S., Krawczyk, H., Nguyen, Q., Rosu, M., Steiner, M.: Rich queries on encrypted data: beyond exact matches. In: Pernul, G., Ryan, P.Y.A., Weippl, E. (eds.) ESORICS 2015. LNCS, vol. 9327, pp. 123–145. Springer, Cham (2015). https://doi.org/10.1007/978-3-319-24177-7_7

[FMET22] Falzon, F., Markatou, E.A., Espiritu, Z., Tamassia, R.: Range search over encrypted multi-attribute data. Cryptology ePrint Archive (2022)

[GJW19] Gui, Z., Johnson, O., Warinschi, B.: Encrypted databases: new volume attacks against range queries. In: Proceedings of the 2019 ACM SIGSAC Conference on Computer and Communications Security. CCS '19, pp. 361–378. Association for Computing Machinery, New York, NY, USA (2019)

[GLMP18] Grubbs, P., Lacharite, M.-S., Minaud, B., Paterson, K.G.: Pump up the volume: practical database reconstruction from volume leakage on range queries. In: Proceedings of the 2018 ACM SIGSAC Conference on Computer and Communications Security. CCS '18, pp. 315–331. Association for Computing Machinery, New York, NY, USA (2018)

[hea24] Heaan homomorphic analytics (2024). https://www.ncloud.com/product/analytics/heaanHomomorphic

[ibm24] Ibm z solutions (2024). https://www.ibm.com/support/z-content-solutions/fully-homomorphic-encryption/

[KMS24] Kushnir, E., Moshkowich, G., Shaul, H.: Secure range-searching using copy-and-recurse. In: Proceedings on Privacy Enhancing Technologies, vol. 2024, no. 3, pp. 626–644 (2024)

[KS25] Kushnir, E., Shaul, H.: Improved range searching and range emptiness under FHE using copy-and-recurse. Cryptology ePrint Archive, Paper 2025/751 (2025)

[LMP18] Lacharité, M.-S., Minaud, B., Paterson, K.G.: Improved reconstruction attacks on encrypted data using range query leakage. In: 2018 IEEE Symposium on Security and Privacy (SP), pp. 297–314 (2018)

[Mat91] Matoušek, J.: Efficient partition trees. In: Proceedings of the Seventh Annual Symposium on Computational Geometry. SCG '91, pp. 1–9. Association for Computing Machinery, New York, NY, USA (1991)

[Mat92] Matoušek, J.: Reporting points in halfspaces. Comput. Geom. **2**(3), 169–186 (1992)

[MFET23] Markatou, E.A., Falzon, F., Espiritu, Z., Tamassia, R.: Attacks on encrypted response-hiding range search schemes in multiple dimensions. In: Proceedings on Privacy Enhancing Technologies, vol. 2023, no. 4, pp. 204–223 (2023)

[MMRS15] Maffei, M., Malavolta, G., Reinert, M., Schröder, D.: Privacy and access control for outsourced personal records. In: 2015 IEEE Symposium on Security and Privacy, pp. 341–358 (2015)

[SS11] Sharir, M., Shaul, H.: Semialgebraic range reporting and emptiness searching with applications. SIAM J. Comput. **40**(4), 1045–1074 (2011)

[TCBS23] Trama, D., Clet, P.-E., Boudguiga, A., Sirdey, R.: A homomorphic AES evaluation in less than 30 seconds by means of tFHE. In: Proceedings of the 11th Workshop on Encrypted Computing and Applied Homomorphic Cryptography. WAHC '23, pp. 79–90. Association for Computing Machinery, New York, NY, USA (2023)

[TCSK16] Tillem, G., Candan, Ö.M., Savaş, E., Kaya, K.: Hiding access patterns in range queries using private information retrieval and ORAM. In: Clark, J., Meiklejohn, S., Ryan, P.Y.A., Wallach, D., Brenner, M., Rohloff, K. (eds.) FC 2016. LNCS, vol. 9604, pp. 253–270. Springer, Heidelberg (2016). https://doi.org/10.1007/978-3-662-53357-4_17

[U.S96] U.S. Congress: Health Insurance Portability and Accountability Act of 1996 (1996). https://www.hhs.gov/hipaa/. Public Law 104-191

A Generalized Wiener-Type Attack Against an RSA-Like Cryptosystem

George Teşeleanu$^{(\boxtimes)}$![ORCID]

Simion Stoilow Institute of Mathematics of the Romanian Academy,
21 Calea Grivitei, Bucharest, Romania
`george.teseleanu@yahoo.com`

Abstract. Let $N = pq$ be the product of two balanced prime numbers p and q. In 2023, Cotan and Teşeleanu introduced a family of RSA-like cryptosystems based on the key equation $ed - k(p^n - 1)(q^n - 1) = 1$, where $n \geq 1$. Note that when $n = 1$, we obtain the classical RSA system, while $n = 2$ yields the variant proposed by Elkamchouchi, Elshenawy, and Shaban. In this paper, we present a novel attack that combines continued fractions with lattice-based methods for the case $n = 6$. This represents a natural continuation of previous research, which successfully applied similar techniques for $n = 1, 2, 4$.

Keywords: continued fraction attack · lattice attack · small private key attack · RSA

1 Introduction

RSA, one of the most widely used cryptosystems, was introduced by Rivest, Shamir and Adleman in their 1978 paper [23]. The classical RSA scheme works using elements from the group $\mathbb{Z}_N^*$, where N is the product of two large prime numbers p and q. More precisely, to encrypt an element $m \in \mathbb{Z}_N^*$, we have to compute the ciphertext $c \equiv m^e \bmod N$, where e satisfies $\gcd(e, \varphi(N)) = 1$ and $\varphi(N) = (p - 1)(q - 1)$. To recover the original element, we simply compute $m \equiv c^d \bmod N$, where $d \equiv e^{-1} \bmod \varphi(N)$. The user's public key is (N, e), while (p, q, d) constitutes its secret key. In this paper, we focus only on primes that satisfy $q < p < 2q$ (*i.e.* have the same bit-size), further referred as balanced primes.

Over time, various attacks have been developed to extract the secret key d from the public key (N, e) under certain conditions. Wiener proved in [29] that if $d < N^{0.25}/3$, the secret key d can be recovered from the continued fraction expansion of e/N, hence enabling the factorization of N. Boneh and Durfee [4] improved this bound to $d < N^{0.292}$ using Coppersmith's method [8] and lattice reduction techniques [17]. Herrmann and May [14] later achieved the same bound with simpler methods. For an overview of RSA attacks, see [3,19,24].

Elkamchouchi, Elshenawy and Shaban [12] extended the RSA scheme to the ring of Gaussian integers modulo N. Such an integer modulo N has the form

A. Akavia et al. (Eds.): CSCML 2025, LNCS 16244, pp. 53–67, 2026.
https://doi.org/10.1007/978-3-032-10759-6_4

$a + bi$, where $a, b \in \mathbb{Z}_N$ and $i^2 = -1$. The set of all Gaussian integers modulo N is denoted by $\mathbb{Z}_N[i]$, and its group order is $\phi(N) = (p^2 - 1)(q^2 - 1)$. In this case, the encryption exponent e satisfies $\gcd(e, \phi(N)) = 1$, and the decryption exponent d is computed as $d \equiv e^{-1} \bmod \phi(N)$. The encryption and decryption processes mirror those of RSA: for $m \in \mathbb{Z}_N[i]$, the ciphertext is $c \equiv m^e \bmod N$, and to recover m we compute $m \equiv c^d \bmod N$. Note that all operations are performed in the ring $\mathbb{Z}_N[i]$.

Elkamchouchi *et al.* [12] argued that their extension has better security compared to traditional RSA. However, Bunder [5] developed a Wiener-type continued fraction attack against this scheme. Using lattice reduction techniques, the authors of [22, 31] improved the bound to $d < N^{0.585}$. For more details on attacks against Elkamchouchi *et al.*'s scheme, see [10, 24].

The rings Z_p and $Z_p[i]$ can be rewritten as $Z_p = \mathbb{Z}_p[t]/(t + 1) = GF(p)$ and $Z_p[i] = \mathbb{Z}_p[t]/(t^2 + 1) = GF(p^2)$, where GF stands for Galois field. Consequently, the underlying RSA group is $\mathbb{Z}_N = GF(p) \times GF(q)$, while in Elkamchouchi *et al.*'s case it is $\mathbb{Z}_N[i] = GF(p^2) \times GF(q^2)$. Using these observations, Cotan and Teşeleanu [10] generalized both schemes to $GF(p^n) \times GF(q^n)$ for $n \geq 1$. In this case, the group order is $\varphi_n(N) = (p^n - 1)(q^n - 1)$, while the encryption and decryption algorithms are direct extensions of RSA and Elkamchouchi *et al.*'s ones.

The motivation for this extension was to evaluate whether Wiener-type attacks apply to the generic setting. The authors of [10] proved that when $d < N^{0.25n}$, a continued fractions attack can always recover the secret exponent, regardless of n. This result was extended to unbalanced primes in [11]. The development of a lattice-based attack was left open in [10, 11], but it was subsequently resolved in [27], thus leading to a better attack bound. Other lattice attacks that could lead to factoring the modulus can be found in [28].

Related work. The first generalized Wiener attack was proposed in [1]. By combining continued fractions with Coppersmith's result, the authors showed that if the public exponent e satisfies

$$ae + b = k\varphi_1(N),$$

where

$$0 < a \leq \frac{1}{3}N^{\frac{1}{4}} \quad \text{and} \quad |b| = \mathcal{O}(N^{-\frac{3}{4}}ae),$$

then we can factor N in polynomial time. Another generalized attack on RSA was proposed in [21]. More precisely, the author proved that if the public exponent e satisfies

$$ae - b(p - u)(q - u) = 1,$$

where

$$1 \leq b < a < 2^{-\frac{1}{4}}N^{\frac{1}{4}}, \quad |u| < N^{\frac{1}{4}} \quad \text{and} \quad v = \left\lceil -\frac{qu}{p - u} \right\rceil,$$

then we can factor N in polynomial time if all the prime factors of $p - u$ and $q - v$ are less than 10^{50}.

The case $n = 2$ was studied in [6], where the authors proved that if the public exponent e satisfies

$$ae - b\varphi_2(N) = c,$$

then we can factor N in polynomial time if a, b and c satisfy a specific condition.

The final case, $n = 4$, was tackled in [20]. More precisely, the authors proved that if the public exponent e satisfies

$$ae - b\varphi_4(N) = c,$$

where

$$ab < \frac{2N^4 - 49N^2 + 2}{170N^2 + 4N} \quad \text{and} \quad |c| < bN,$$

then we can factor N in polynomial time.

Our Contributions. In this paper, we continue the work started in [1,6,20] by developing a generalized Wiener attack for the case $n = 6$. The first step in developing such an attack is to find a good approximation $\hat{p}$ of p, such that we can apply a result due to Coppersmith to recover the actual value of p. To compute $\hat{p}$, we first use a continued fractions approximation to determine the terms a and b from the equation $ae - b\varphi_6(N) = c$. Then, we compute $\hat{p}$ as a function of a, b, and N. Once we know the attack's upper bound for d (from the equation $ed - k\varphi_6(N) = 1$), we can also derive a lower bound using a result from [20].

Structure of the Paper. Preliminary notions are provided in Sect. 2. In Sect. 3 we describe our attack. An example is given in Sect. 4 and we conclude our paper in Sect. 5.

2   Preliminaries

Notations. Throughout the paper, λ denotes a security parameter. Also, the notation $|S|$ denotes the cardinality of a set S. The action of selecting a random element x from a sample space X is denoted by $x \xleftarrow{\$} X$.

2.1   Continued Fraction

For any real number ζ there exists a unique sequence $(a_n)_n$ of integers such that

$$\zeta = a_0 + \cfrac{1}{a_1 + \cfrac{1}{a_2 + \cfrac{1}{a_3 + \cfrac{1}{a_4 + \cdots}}}},$$

where $a_k > 0$ for any $k \geq 1$. This sequence represents the continued fraction expansion of ζ and is denoted by $\zeta = [a_0, a_1, a_2, \ldots]$. Remark that ζ is a rational number if and only if its corresponding representation as a continued fraction is finite.

For any real number $\zeta = [a_0, a_1, a_2, \ldots]$, the sequence of rational numbers $(A_n)_n$, obtained by truncating this continued fraction, $A_k = [a_0, a_1, a_2, \ldots, a_k]$, is called the convergents sequence of ζ.

According to [13], the following bound allows us to check if a rational number u/v is a convergent of ζ.

Theorem 1. *Let* $\zeta = [a_0, a_1, a_2, \ldots]$ *be a positive real number. If* u, v *are positive integers such that* $\gcd(u, v) = 1$ *and*

$$\left| \zeta - \frac{u}{v} \right| < \frac{1}{2v^2},$$

then u/v *is a convergent of* $[a_0, a_1, a_2, \ldots]$.

2.2   Cubic Roots

We start this section by providing a solution to the depressed cubic equation $t^3 + Pt + Q$ (see [25]).

Theorem 2 (Cardano's Formula). *Given the depressed cubic* $t^3 + Pt + Q$, *one of its roots is given by*

$$\sqrt[3]{-\frac{Q}{2} + \sqrt{\frac{Q^2}{4} + \frac{P^3}{27}}} + \sqrt[3]{-\frac{Q}{2} - \sqrt{\frac{Q^2}{4} + \frac{P^3}{27}}}.$$

In one of our proofs, we also need an equivalent of $\sqrt{u} - \sqrt{v} < \sqrt{u \pm v} < \sqrt{u} + \sqrt{v}$ for cubic roots. Therefore, we prove such an equivalent.

Lemma 1. *Let* $u > v > 0$. *The following inequality holds*

$$\sqrt[3]{u} - \sqrt[3]{v} < \sqrt[3]{u \pm v} < \sqrt[3]{u} + \sqrt[3]{v}.$$

Proof. Since $u > v > 0$ we have that

$$(\sqrt[3]{u} - \sqrt[3]{v})^3 = u - v - 3\sqrt[3]{uv}(\sqrt[3]{u} - \sqrt[3]{v}) < u - v,$$
$$(\sqrt[3]{u} + \sqrt[3]{v})^3 = u + v + 3\sqrt[3]{uv}(\sqrt[3]{u} + \sqrt[3]{v}) > u + v,$$

which is equivalent to

$$\sqrt[3]{u} - \sqrt[3]{v} < \sqrt[3]{u - v} < \sqrt[3]{u + v} < \sqrt[3]{u} + \sqrt[3]{v},$$

just as desired.   □

2.3 Finding Small Roots

In this section, we outline some tools used for solving the problem of finding small roots, both in the modular and integer cases.

Coppersmith [7–9] provided rigorous techniques for computing small integer roots of single-variable polynomials modulo an integer, as well as bivariate polynomials over the integers. In the case of modular roots, Coppersmith's ideas were reinterpreted by Howgrave-Graham [15]. We further provide Howgrave-Graham result.

Theorem 3. *Let* $f(x_1, \ldots, x_n) = \sum a_{i_1 \ldots i_n} x_1^{i_1} \ldots x_n^{i_n} \in \mathbb{Z}[x_1, \ldots, x_n]$ *be a polynomial with at most* ω *monomials,* α *be an integer and let*

$$||f(x_1, \ldots, x_n)|| = \sqrt{\sum |a_{i_1 \ldots i_n}|^2}$$

be its norm. Suppose that

- $f(y_1, \ldots, y_n) \equiv 0 \bmod \alpha$ *for some* $|y_1| < X_1, \ldots, |y_n| < X_n$,
- $||f(y_1 X_1, \ldots, y_n X_n)|| < \alpha / \sqrt{\omega}$,

then $f(y_1, \ldots, y_n) = 0$ *holds over integers.*

Lenstra, Lenstra and Lovász [17] proposed a lattice reduction algorithm (LLL) that is widely used in cryptanalysis and is typically combined with Howgrave-Graham's lemma. We further provide the version presented in [16,13].

Theorem 4. *Let* L *be a lattice of dimension* ω. *In polynomial time, the LLL algorithm outputs a reduced basis* $(b_1, \ldots, b_\omega)$ *that satisfies*

$$||b_1|| \leq \ldots \leq ||b_i|| \leq 2^{\frac{\omega(\omega-1)}{4(\omega+1-i)}} det(L)^{\frac{1}{\omega+1-i}},$$

where $det(L)$ *is the determinant of lattice* L.

Note that the condition

$$2^{\frac{\omega(\omega-1)}{4(\omega+1-i)}} det(L)^{\frac{1}{\omega+1-i}} < \alpha / \sqrt{\omega}$$

implies that the polynomials corresponding to b_i match Howgrave-Graham's bound. This leads to

$$det(L) \leq \varepsilon \alpha^{\omega+1-i},$$

where ε is an error term that is usually ignored.

In order to find a solution $(y_1, \ldots, y_n)$ we need the following assumption to be true.

Assumption 5 *The LLL reduced basis polynomials are algebraically independent[1], and the resultant computations for* b_i *yields the common roots of these polynomials.*

---

[1] they do not share a non-trivial gcd.

In [2], the authors present a more flexible formulation of Coppersmith's result [8]. Their method first constructs a specific lattice basis, applies the LLL algorithm [17] to reduce it, and finally uses Howgrave-Graham's lemma [15] to derive the solutions.

Theorem 6. *Let $N = pq$ be the product of two unknown primes with $q < p < 2q$. Suppose we are given an approximation of p with additive error at most $N^{1/4}$. Then N can be factored in polynomial time.*

Once we derive an attack that works for a given upper bound on small private exponents, the following result from [20] tells us that there exists an attack that works for a given lower bound on large private exponents. We refer the reader to [20] for results concerning φ_1, φ_2 and φ_4.

Theorem 7. *Let $N = pq$ be the product of two unknown primes with $q < p < 2q$. Let $\psi : \mathbb{N} \times \mathbb{N} \to \mathbb{N}$. Suppose we are given an algorithm $\mathcal{A}$ that is able to factor N in polynomial time. Also, we are given a public exponent $0 < e < \psi(p, q)$ such that there exists positive integers x and y such*

$$ex - y\phi(p, q) = z, \text{ with } xy < \mathcal{B}_1 \text{ and } |z| < \mathcal{B}_2,$$

for $\mathcal{B}_1 > 0$ and $\mathcal{B}_2 \geq 1$. Then, using algorithm $\mathcal{A}$, N can be factored in polynomial time given N and a public exponent $0 < e' < \psi(p, q)$ such that the corresponding private exponent is $d' = \psi(p, q) - d$ for some $d < \sqrt{\mathcal{B}_1}$.

2.4   Quotient Groups

In this section we provide the group theory needed to introduce the RSA-like family. Therefore, let $(\mathbb{F}, +, \cdot)$ be a field and $t^n - r$ an irreducible polynomial in $\mathbb{F}[t]$. Then

$$\mathbb{A}_n = \mathbb{F}[t]/(t^n - r) = \{a_0 + a_1 t + \ldots + a_{n-1} t^{n-1} \mid a_0, a_1, \ldots, a_{n-1} \in \mathbb{F}\}$$

is the corresponding quotient field. Let $a(t), b(t) \in \mathbb{A}_n$. Remark that the quotient field induces a natural product

$$a(t) \circ b(t) = \left(\sum_{i=0}^{n-1} a_i t^i \right) \circ \left(\sum_{j=0}^{n-1} b_j t^j \right)$$

$$= \sum_{i=0}^{n-2} \left(\sum_{j=0}^{i} a_j b_{i-j} + r \sum_{j=0}^{i+n} a_j b_{i-j+n} \right) t^i + \sum_{j=0}^{n-1} a_j b_{n-1-j} t^{n-1}.$$

2.5   RSA-Like Cryptosystems

Let p be a prime number. When we instantiate $\mathbb{F} = \mathbb{Z}_p$, we have that $\mathbb{A}_n = GF(p^n)$ is the Galois field of order p^n. Moreover, $\mathbb{A}_n^*$ is a cyclic group of order $\varphi_n(\mathbb{Z}_p) = p^n - 1$. Remark that an analogous of Fermat's little theorem holds

$$a(t)^{\varphi_n(\mathbb{Z}_p)} \equiv 1 \bmod p,$$

where $a(t) \in \mathbb{A}_n^*$ and the power is evaluated by $\circ$-multiplying $a(t)$ by itself $\varphi_n(\mathbb{Z}_p) - 1$ times. Based on these observations, the authors of [10] built an encryption scheme that is similar to RSA by using the $\circ$ operation as the product.

$Setup(\lambda)$: Let $n \geq 1$ be an integer. Randomly generate two distinct large prime numbers p, q such that $p, q \geq 2^\lambda$ and compute their product $N = pq$. Select $r \in \mathbb{Z}_N$ such that the polynomial $t^n - r$ is irreducible in $\mathbb{Z}_p[t]$ and $\mathbb{Z}_q[t]$. Let

$$\varphi_n(\mathbb{Z}_N) = \varphi_n(N) = (p^n - 1) \cdot (q^n - 1).$$

Choose an integer e such that $\gcd(e, \varphi_n(N)) = 1$ and compute d such that $ed \equiv 1 \bmod \varphi_n(N)$. Output the public key $pk = (n, N, r, e)$. The corresponding secret key is $sk = (p, q, d)$.

$Encrypt(pk, m)$: To encrypt a message $m = (m_0, \ldots, m_{n-1}) \in \mathbb{Z}_N^n$ we first construct the polynomial $m(t) = m_0 + \ldots + m_{n-1}t^{n-1} \in \mathbb{A}_n^*$ and then we compute $c(t) \equiv [m(t)]^e \bmod N$. Output the ciphertext $c(t)$.

$Decrypt(sk, c(t))$: To recover the message, simply compute $m(t) \equiv [c(t)]^d \bmod N$ and reassemble $m = (m_0, \ldots, m_{n-1})$.

Remark 1. When $n = 1$ we get the RSA scheme [23]. Also, when $n = 2$, we obtain the Elkamchouchi *et al.* cryptosystem [12].

3   A Generalized Wiener-Type Attack

In this section, we study the generalized equation $ae - b\varphi_6(N) = c$, where e is a public exponent and c is known. Our attack consists of two steps: first, we compute a and b from a continued fraction expansion; then we find an appropriate approximation for p, and finally, we use Coppersmith's result to factor N. We begin with the lattice-based part of our attack and conclude with the continued fractions-based part.

3.1   Application of Lattices

Let $S = p + q$ and $D = p - q$. Using the value for φ_6 provided in [27], namely

$$\varphi_6 = N^6 + 2N^3 - 9N^2S^2 + 6NS^4 - S^6 + 1$$
$$= N^6 - 2N^3 - 9N^2D^2 - 6ND^4 - D^6 + 1,$$

we further derive some inequalities for $p + q$ and $p - q$.

Lemma 2. *Let $N = pq$ be the product of two unknown primes with $q < p < 2q$. Also, let e be a public exponent satisfying $ae - b\varphi_6(N) = c$ such that $|c| < bN\sqrt{N}$. We define $S = p + q$ and*

$$\hat{S} = \sqrt[3]{\frac{1}{2} \cdot \left(\sqrt{(N^3 + 1)^2 - \frac{ae}{b}} + \sqrt{(N^3 - 1)^2 - \frac{ae}{b}} \right)} + \beta,$$

where

$$\beta = \sqrt[3]{\frac{1}{2}\left(\sqrt{(N^3+1)^2 - \frac{ae-c}{b}} - \sqrt{(N^3-1)^2 - \frac{ae-c}{b}}\right)}$$

Then the following holds

$$|S - \hat{S}| < N^{1/4}.$$

Proof. We first start by noticing that we can rewrite φ_6 as follows

$$\begin{aligned}
\varphi_6 &= N^6 + 2N^3 - 9N^2S^2 + 6NS^4 - S^6 + 1 \\
&= -S^2(S^4 - 6NS^2 + 9N^2) + (N^3+1)^2 \\
&= -S^2(S^2 - 3N)^2 + (N^3+1)^2 \\
&= -t^2 + (N^3+1)^2,
\end{aligned}$$

where $t = S^3 - 3NS$.

On the other hand, we have that $\varphi_6(N) = (ae-c)/b$. Therefore, we have that

$$-t^2 + (N^3+1)^2 - \frac{ae-c}{b} = 0,$$

and we observe that

$$t = \sqrt{(N^3+1)^2 - \frac{ae-c}{b}}.$$

Therefore, S satisfies the equation

$$S^3 - 3NS - \sqrt{(N^3+1)^2 - \frac{ae-c}{b}} = 0.$$

Using Cardano's formula, we obtain that $S = \alpha + \beta$, where

$$\begin{aligned}
\alpha &= \sqrt[3]{\frac{1}{2}\sqrt{(N^3+1)^2 - \frac{ae-c}{b}} + \sqrt{\frac{1}{4}\left((N^3+1)^2 - \frac{ae-c}{b}\right) - N^3}} \\
&= \sqrt[3]{\frac{1}{2}\left(\sqrt{(N^3+1)^2 - \frac{ae-c}{b}} + \sqrt{(N^3-1)^2 - \frac{ae-c}{b}}\right)}.
\end{aligned}$$

Let

$$\hat{\alpha} = \sqrt[3]{\frac{1}{2}\sqrt{(N^3+1)^2 - \frac{ae}{b}} + \sqrt{\frac{1}{4}\left((N^3-1)^2 - \frac{ae}{b}\right)}}.$$

Using Lemma 1 and the fact that for positive integers $u > v > 0$ we have $\sqrt{u} - \sqrt{v} < \sqrt{u \pm v} < \sqrt{u} + \sqrt{v}$, we obtain the following

$$|\alpha - \hat{\alpha}| < \sqrt[3]{\frac{1}{2}\sqrt{\frac{|c|}{b}} + \frac{1}{2}\sqrt{\frac{|c|}{b}}} = \left(\frac{|c|}{b}\right)^{1/6}. \tag{1}$$

Using Eq. (1), we obtain the following

$$|S - \hat{S}| = |\alpha + \beta - \hat{\alpha} - \beta| = |\alpha - \hat{\alpha}| \le \left(\frac{|c|}{b}\right)^{1/6} < N^{1/4},$$

just as desired. $\qquad\qquad\qquad\qquad\qquad\qquad\qquad\qquad\qquad\qquad\qquad\square$

Lemma 3. *Let $N = pq$ be the product of two unknown primes with $q < p < 2q$. Also, let e be a public exponent satisfying $ae - b\varphi_6(N) = c$ such that $|c| < bN\sqrt{N}$. We define $D = p - q$ and*

$$\hat{D} = \sqrt[3]{\frac{1}{2} \cdot \left(\sqrt{(N^3 - 1)^2 - \frac{ae}{b}} + \sqrt{(N^3 + 1)^2 - \frac{ae}{b}}\right)} - \beta,$$

where

$$\beta = \sqrt[3]{\frac{1}{2}\left(\sqrt{(N^3 + 1)^2 - \frac{ae - c}{b}} - \sqrt{(N^3 - 1)^2 - \frac{ae - c}{b}}\right)}$$

Then the following holds

$$|D - \hat{D}| < N^{1/4}.$$

Proof. We first start by noticing that we can rewrite φ_6 as follows

$$\begin{aligned}
\varphi_6 &= N^6 - 2N^3 - 9N^2 D^2 - 6ND^4 - D^6 + 1 \\
&= -D^2(D^4 + 6ND^2 + 9N^2) + (N^3 - 1)^2 \\
&= -D^2(D^2 + 3N)^2 + (N^3 - 1)^2 \\
&= -t^2 + (N^3 - 1)^2,
\end{aligned}$$

where $t = D^3 + 3ND$. Similarly to the proof of Lemma 2, we obtain that

$$t = \sqrt{(N^3 - 1)^2 - \frac{ae - c}{b}}.$$

Therefore, D satisfies the equation

$$D^3 + 3NS - \sqrt{(N^3 - 1)^2 - \frac{ae - c}{b}} = 0.$$

Using Cardano's formula, we obtain that $D = \alpha + (-\beta)$, where

$$\alpha = \sqrt[3]{\frac{1}{2}\left(\sqrt{(N^3-1)^2 - \frac{ae-c}{b}} + \sqrt{(N^3+1)^2 - \frac{ae-c}{b}}\right)},$$

$$-\beta = \sqrt[3]{\frac{1}{2}\left(\sqrt{(N^3-1)^2 - \frac{ae-c}{b}} - \sqrt{(N^3+1)^2 - \frac{ae-c}{b}}\right)}.$$

Similarly to the proof of Lemma 2 we obtain the following

$$|D - \hat{D}| < N^{1/4},$$

just as desired. $\qquad\square$

We are now in a position to apply Coppersmith's result to factor N.

Theorem 8. *Let $N = pq$ be the product of two unknown primes with $q < p < 2q$. Also, let e be a public exponent satisfying $ae - b\varphi_6(N) = c$ such that $|c| < bN\sqrt{N}$. Given e, N, a and b we can factor N in polynomial time.*

Proof. Using the approximation derived in Lemmas 2 and 3 we have that

$$\left|p - \frac{1}{2}(\hat{S} + \hat{D})\right| = \left|\frac{1}{2}(S + D) - \frac{1}{2}(\hat{S} + \hat{D})\right|$$

$$\leq \frac{1}{2}|S - \hat{S}| + \frac{1}{2}|D - \hat{D}|$$

$$< \frac{1}{2}N^{1/4} + \frac{1}{2}N^{1/4} = N^{1/4}.$$

Therefore,

$$\hat{p} = 0.5(\hat{S} + \hat{D}) = \sqrt[3]{\frac{1}{2}\cdot\left(\sqrt{(N^3-1)^2 - \frac{ae}{b}} + \sqrt{(N^3+1)^2 - \frac{ae}{b}}\right)}$$

is a good approximation of p. Now according to Theorem 6, we can factor N in polynomial time. $\qquad\square$

3.2 Application of Continued Fractions

We start the section with the following lower and upper bounds for p and q (see [6, Lemma 3]).

Lemma 4. *Let $N = pq$ be the product of two unknown primes with $q < p < 2q$. Then the following property holds*

$$2\sqrt{N} < p + q < \frac{3\sqrt{2}}{2}\sqrt{N}.$$

We further derive an useful bound for the continued fraction part of our attack.

Lemma 5. *Let $N = pq$ be the product of two unknown primes with $q < p < 2q$. Then the following property holds*

$$\left| 9N^2 S^2 - 6NS^4 + S^6 - 164N^3 \right| < 550N^3$$

where $S = p + q$.

Proof. Using Lemma 4 we obtain that

$$2^2 N < S^2 < 3^2 N \quad 2^4 N^2 < S^4 < 3^4 N^2 \quad 2^6 N^3 < S^6 < 3^6 N^3.$$

Let $A = 9N^2 S^2 - 6NS^4 + S^6$. Therefore, we have

$$-386N^3 = (9 \cdot 2^2 - 6 \cdot 3^4 + 2^6)N^3 < A < (9 \cdot 3^2 - 6 \cdot 2^4 + 3^6)N^3 = 714N^3.$$

Thus, we obtain

$$-550N^3 = -386N^3 - 164N^3 < A - 164N^3 < 714N^3 - 164N^3 = 550N^3,$$

just as desired. $\square$

Theorem 9. *Let $N = pq$ be the product of two unknown primes with $q < p < 2q$. Also, let e be a public exponent satisfying $ae - b\varphi_6(N) = c$ such that $|c| < bN\sqrt{N}$. Given e, N we can factor N in polynomial time if*

$$cb < \frac{N^\epsilon - 162N^3 + 1}{2N\sqrt{N} + 1100N^3}.$$

Proof. We denote by

$$A = 9N^2 S^2 - 6NS^4 + S^6 - 164N^3.$$

We know that

$$ae - b\left(N^6 + 2N^3 - A - 164N^3 + 1 \right) = c$$

which is equivalent to

$$ae - b\left(N^6 - 162N^3 + 1 \right) = c - bA.$$

Dividing everything by $a(N^6 - 162N^3 + 1)$ we obtain

$$\frac{e}{N^6 - 162N^3 + 1} - \frac{b}{a} = \frac{c - bA}{a(N^6 - 162N^3 + 1)}.$$

Taking the absolute value we obtain

$$\left| \frac{e}{N^6 - 162N^3 + 1} - \frac{b}{a} \right| \leq \frac{|c| + |bA|}{a(N^6 - 162N^3 + 1)}$$

$$\leq \frac{N\sqrt{N} + |A|}{N^6 - 162N^3 + 1} \cdot \frac{b}{a}$$

$$\leq \frac{N\sqrt{N} + 550N^3}{N^6 - 162N^3 + 1} \cdot \frac{b}{a}$$

$$\leq \frac{1}{2ab} \cdot \frac{b}{a} = \frac{1}{2a^2}.$$

where for the third inequality we used Lemma 5 and for the last inequality we used our hypothesis. Since

$$\left| \frac{e}{N^6 - 162N^3 + 1} - \frac{b}{a} \right| \leq \frac{1}{2a^2}.$$

then according to Theorem 1 b/a appears among the convergents of $e/(N^6 - 162N^3 + 1)$. Once we obtain a and b we apply Theorem 8, and thus we conclude our proof. $\qquad\square$

To conclude, we further apply our generic result to the RSA-like cryptosystem with $n = 6$. Note that for the second corollary we use Theorem 7.

Corollary 1. *Let $N = pq$ be the product of two unknown primes with $q < p < 2q$. Also, let $e < \varphi_6(N)$ be a public exponent satisfying $ed - k\varphi_6(N) = 1$. Given e, N we can factor N in polynomial time if*

$$d < \sqrt{\frac{N^6 - 162N^3 + 1}{2N\sqrt{N} + 1100N^3}}.$$

Proof. We notice that

$$k = \frac{ed - 1}{\varphi_6(N)} < \frac{ed}{\varphi_6(N)} < d$$

and

$$kd < d^2 < \frac{N^6 - 162N^3 + 1}{2N\sqrt{N} + 1100N^3}$$

According to Theorem 9 we can factor N in polynomial time. $\qquad\square$

Corollary 2. *Let $N = pq$ be the product of two unknown primes with $q < p < 2q$. Also, let $e < \varphi_6(N)$ be a public exponent satisfying $ed - k\varphi_6(N) = 1$. Given e, N we can factor N in polynomial time if*

$$d > \varphi_6(N) - \sqrt{\frac{N^6 - 162N^3 + 1}{2N\sqrt{N} + 1100N^3}}.$$

4   Experimental Results

To check the validity of our result, we ran the code for our attack [26] on a workstation using Ubuntu 20.04.1, with the following specifications: Intel(R) Core(TM) i7-1165G7 CPU 2.80GHz with 8 cores and 16 Gigabytes of RAM. The programming language we used for implementing our attack was SageMath 10.3. We based our code on the Coppersmith attack implementation found in [30].

We used the following parameters

$$N = 3489655588599196597998727783564283681960038261038493763731,$$

$$e = 6488789531126079742933711732527409323955500485002801167128755551606$$
$$467580564881118858409894033726180712325649162450228555803402451509$$
$$642430486894142132856119829829011446181108957077544164307111507631$$
$$785505953619482486384943934576124777864405398361337859228708778458$$
$$361967197948635325126592860066198948640808115691140189154107510835$$
$$437673068035277$$

Computing the continued fraction expansion of $e/(N^6 - 162N^3 + 1)$, we get the first 25 partial quotients

$$[0, 2, 1, 3, 1, 1, 1, 1, 3, 10, 7, 1, 3, 2, 12, 1, 11, 1, 9, 1, 2, 2, 2, 5, 2, \ldots].$$

Looking at the $87th$ convergent we obtain

$$a = 11150372599265311570767859136324180752990213$$
$$b = 4006431015451326125727099215660449213022640,$$

which satisfy the condition of Theorem 9. Therefore, we obtain the following approximation of p

$$\hat{p} = 132287523294776463864922187740.$$

Using Coppersmith's algorithm we find

$$p = 132287523294776463864922187741,$$

and then we can compute

$$q = N/p = 26379325137285943549540377391.$$

5   Conclusions

In this paper, we presented a generalized Wiener-type attack against RSA-like cryptosystems. To mount our attack, we first study the general equation $ae - b\varphi_6(N) = c$, after which we apply a result proven by Coppersmith [2,8]. As a result, we show that if d is either small or very large, one can factor N in polynomial time.

Future work. It would be interesting to develop a generic method that works for $\varphi_i(N)$ for any i, not just particular cases (*i.e.* for $n = 1, 2, 4, 6$).

References

1. Blömer, J., May, A.: A generalized wiener attack on RSA. In: Bao, F., Deng, R., Zhou, J. (eds.) PKC 2004. LNCS, vol. 2947, pp. 1–13. Springer, Heidelberg (2004). https://doi.org/10.1007/978-3-540-24632-9_1
2. Blömer, J., May, A.: A tool kit for finding small roots of bivariate polynomials over the integers. In: Cramer, R. (ed.) EUROCRYPT 2005. LNCS, vol. 3494, pp. 251–267. Springer, Heidelberg (2005). https://doi.org/10.1007/11426639_15
3. Boneh, D.: Twenty years of attacks on the RSA cryptosystem. Not. AMS **46**(2), 203–213 (1999)
4. Boneh, D., Durfee, G.: Cryptanalysis of RSA with private key d less than $N^{0.292}$. In: EUROCRYPT 1999. LNCS, vol. 1592, pp. 1–11. Springer, Cham (1999)
5. Bunder, M., Nitaj, A., Susilo, W., Tonien, J.: A new attack on three variants of the RSA cryptosystem. In: Liu, J.K., Steinfeld, R. (eds.) ACISP 2016. LNCS, vol. 9723, pp. 258–268. Springer, Cham (2016). https://doi.org/10.1007/978-3-319-40367-0_16
6. Bunder, M., Nitaj, A., Susilo, W., Tonien, J.: A generalized attack on RSA type cryptosystems. Theor. Comput. Sci. **704**, 74–81 (2017)
7. Coppersmith, D.: Finding a small root of a bivariate integer equation; factoring with high bits known. In: Maurer, U. (ed.) EUROCRYPT 1996. LNCS, vol. 1070, pp. 178–189. Springer, Heidelberg (1996). https://doi.org/10.1007/3-540-68339-9_16
8. Coppersmith, D.: Finding a small root of a univariate modular equation. In: Maurer, U. (ed.) EUROCRYPT 1996. LNCS, vol. 1070, pp. 155–165. Springer, Heidelberg (1996). https://doi.org/10.1007/3-540-68339-9_14
9. Coppersmith, D.: Small solutions to polynomial equations, and low exponent RSA vulnerabilities. J. Cryptol. **10**(4), 233–260 (1997). https://doi.org/10.1007/s001459900030
10. Cotan, P., Teşeleanu, G.: Small private key attack against a family of RSA-like cryptosystems. In: NordSEC 2023. LNCS, vol. 14324, pp. 57–72. Springer, Cham (2023)
11. Cotan, P., Teşeleanu, G.: A security analysis of two classes of RSA-like cryptosystems. J. Math. Cryptol. **18**(1), 20240013 (2024)
12. Elkamchouchi, H., Elshenawy, K., Shaban, H.: Extended RSA cryptosystem and digital signature schemes in the domain of Gaussian integers. In: ICCS 2002, vol. 1, pp. 91–95. IEEE Computer Society (2002)
13. Hardy, G.H., Wright, E.M., et al.: An Introduction to the Theory of Numbers. Oxford University Press (1979)
14. Herrmann, M., May, A.: Maximizing small root bounds by linearization and applications to small secret exponent RSA. In: Nguyen, P.Q., Pointcheval, D. (eds.) PKC 2010. LNCS, vol. 6056, pp. 53–69. Springer, Heidelberg (2010). https://doi.org/10.1007/978-3-642-13013-7_4
15. Howgrave-Graham, N.: Finding small roots of univariate modular equations revisited. In: IMA 1997. LNCS, vol. 1355, pp. 131–142. Springer, Cham (1997)

16. Jochemsz, E., May, A.: A strategy for finding roots of multivariate polynomials with new applications in attacking RSA variants. In: Lai, X., Chen, K. (eds.) ASIACRYPT 2006. LNCS, vol. 4284, pp. 267–282. Springer, Heidelberg (2006). https://doi.org/10.1007/11935230_18
17. Lenstra, A.K., Lenstra, H.W., Lovász, L.: Factoring polynomials with rational coefficients. Math. Ann. **261**, 515–534 (1982)
18. May, A.: New RSA vulnerabilities using lattice reduction methods. Ph.D. thesis, University of Paderborn (2003)
19. May, A.: Using LLL-reduction for solving RSA and factorization problems. In: The LLL Algorithm: Survey and Applications, pp. 315–348. Information Security and Cryptography. Springer, Cham (2010)
20. Michel, S., Niang, O., Sow, D.: A new generalized attack on RSA-like cryptosystems. IACR Cryptology ePrint Archive **2025/380** (2025)
21. Nitaj, A.: Another generalization of wiener's attack on RSA. In: AFRICACRYPT 2008. LNCS, vol. 5023, pp. 174–190. Springer, Cham (2008)
22. Peng, L., Hu, L., Lu, Y., Wei, H.: An improved analysis on three variants of the RSA cryptosystem. In: Inscrypt 2016. LNCS, vol. 10143, pp. 140–149. Springer, Cham (2016)
23. Rivest, R.L., Shamir, A., Adleman, L.: A method for obtaining digital signatures and public-key cryptosystems. Commun. ACM **21**(2), 120–126 (1978)
24. Shi, G., Wang, G., Gu, D.: Further cryptanalysis of a type of RSA variants. In: ISC 2022. LNCS, vol. 13640, pp. 133–152. Springer, Cham (2022)
25. Tao, Y.: Polynomials I - The Cubic Formula. https://circles.math.ucla.edu/circles/lib/data/Handout-3357-2927.pdf
26. Teşeleanu, G.: Generalized Wiener-type Attacks Against Some Particular Cases of the Generalised Elkamchouchi et al. Scheme. https://github.com/teseleanu/generalized-wiener-type-attacks
27. Teşeleanu, G.: A lattice attack against a family of RSA-like cryptosystems. In: CSCML 2024. LNCS, vol. 15349, pp. 343–355. Springer, Cham (2024)
28. Teşeleanu, G.: Partial exposure attacks against a family of RSA-like cryptosystems. Cryptography **9**(1) (2025)
29. Wiener, M.J.: Cryptanalysis of short RSA secret exponents. IEEE Trans. Inf. Theory **36**(3), 553–558 (1990)
30. Wong, D.: Lattice Based Attacks on RSA. https://github.com/mimoo/RSA-and-LLL-attacks
31. Zheng, M., Kunihiro, N., Hu, H.: Cryptanalysis of RSA variants with modified Euler quotient. In: AFRICACRYPT 2018. LNCS, vol. 10831, pp. 266–281. Springer, Cham (2018)

Multi-party Time-Lock Puzzles: Quorum Controlled Delays Without a Single Point of Failure

Karim Eldefrawy[1,3], Sashidhar Jakkamsetti[2,4], Ben Terner[3,4(✉)], and Moti Yung[4]

[1] SRI International, Menlo Park, USA
[2] Amazon, Kansas City, USA
[3] Confidencial.io, Menlo Park, USA
`ben.terner@confidencial.io`
[4] Google and Columbia University, New York City, USA

Abstract. Managing the timing and delays of computing events is central to distributed systems. Timed cryptography, such as time-lock puzzles (introduced almost 30 years ago) and verifiable delay functions, provides central tools for such tasks: A single party (the committer) knows a secret, commits to it publicly, and then the committed secret can be opened via a time-consuming staged computation by any observer; this process is independent of post-commitment actions by or presence of the committer. Implicit in this scenario is the requirement that the committer itself does not attack the system, and, say, prematurely selectively leak or de-commit the value, either maliciously or due to external attacks. To prevent the above attack and to expand timed-delayed cryptography to address more applications, we initiate here the study of how to distributedly hold a timed secret known neither to any individual party nor to any group smaller than a quorum. This primitive is defined in the context of multi-party computation (MPC). In fact, this implements a setting where a group of parties simultaneously learn a secret that has been kept private for a predetermined amount of time, and could have been collectively generated without a single party controlling its generation (as in distributed key generation scenarios). This new paradigm, and the ability to compose such protocols, also extends time-lock functionalities to applications where a firm commitment by a group of parties to future release is executed even without knowing the underlying secrets and even without assuming cooperation or availability of parties in the future. Sample applications requiring such delayed disclosure include accountable future scanning of software for zero-day vulnerabilities and accountable, secure sharing of clinical trial documents.

We design the first secure practical protocol for *Multi-party Time-lock Puzzles (MTP)*, a new primitive centered on the inherently needed distributed generation of a time-lock puzzle, and the inability to prematurely reconstruct the committed value unless a quorum of parties is compromised. We then leverage MTP to build *Timed Multi-party Computation (TMPC)*, which we model as MPC with *a single* time-locked output.

S. Jakkamsetti, B. Terner and M. Yung—Work performed while at SRI International and University of California, Irvine.

1   Introduction

Management of time, including delay of actions, is central to distributed systems. The notion of delayed-release cryptography is a central tool which exploits computational properties and limitations to enforce secrecy *for some amount of time, i.e., temporal secrecy,* rather than essentially "indefinitely" (in reality, indefinitely is measured as longer than any polynomial in the security parameter). Note that opening a puzzle over time does not depend on the availability of the committer, and solely relies on computational properties. For example, time-lock puzzles enable a (single) party to "send a message to the future" by encoding a secret in a cryptographic puzzle such that no algorithm can learn the secret without explicitly solving the puzzle but with time passing, the puzzle will be opened. Time-lock puzzles have been studied since the seminal work of Rivest, Shamir, and Wagner (RSW) [21] almost 30 years ago, and timed commitments were introduced as a way to achieve fairness in secure multi-party computation (MPC) over twenty years ago by Boneh and Naor [9]. Further, inherently sequential functions motivated by blockchain applications have also precipitated considerable research in verifiable delay functions [7,20,22]. Recent interest in time-lock primitives has yielded non-malleable time-lock puzzles [14], non-malleable timed commitments [16], and UC-security [3,4] of time-lock puzzles (which must also be non-malleable).

Summarizing the above, the study of cryptographic (i.e., computational complexity instantiated) control of the (synchronized) time dimension has thus far focused on how a single party - the committer - preserves a secret known to itself for some amount of time. However, fundamentally the primitive relies on the committer not leaking (directly or due to external attacks) the committed value prematurely. Hence, the entire operation in the single party case has a (albeit natural) single point of failure which can violate the delays imposed by the scheme.

Here, we expand the frontier of delayed-release cryptography and its use in distributed systems by asking the following foundational questions:

Can we design a time-lock puzzle with no single point of failure, and such that no party knows its solution?
How do we leverage such a puzzle in multi-party protocols?

To answer the above, we introduce a new primitive which we call *Multi-party Time-lock Puzzles* (MTP). MTP allows a group of parties to collectively lock a secret (which may be unknown to any party at generation time, e.g., it is itself a secret generated in a distributed manner), and then individually or collectively (and synchronously) reveal the secret at a (predetermined) later time.

To date, there have been a small number of ad hoc attempts to combine time-locks with computation. Malavolta and Thyagarajan [19] introduced homomorphic time-lock puzzles, which allow parties to time-lock their inputs and then compute functions by combining the puzzles. Baum et al.[4] provided a protocol that outputs shares of the evaluation of a function over parties' inputs, and then requires each party to time-lock their own share. Towards the end of systematically defining a time-release computation as its own primitive, we introduce Timed Multi-party Computation (TMPC), which defines multi-party computations with time-locked outputs. Our model and schemes also treat the ability to time-lock inputs of parties or just part of the outputs and reveal them later, which introduces new paradigms forcing eventual reveal for *accountability* in multi-party computation (even if parties refuse to cooperate) and *fairness* if the parties time-lock their inputs using this technique. In addition to preventing the attack by a single committer, we are also motivated by, and envision, the following prototypical applications for TMPC:

- *Application 1: Secure Sharing of Clinical Trial Documents and Results Involving Multiple Parties.* Pharmaceutical and medical device companies must submit new drugs or devices for approval by government regulators, e.g., the Food and Drug Administration (FDA) in the US. The paperwork submitted to the FDA often includes sensitive information. Whether or not the drug or device is approved, it may be desirable for the public to open the paperwork after the decision.
- *Application 2: Scanning Software for Zero-day Vulnerabilities.* Research and intelligence organizations stockpile zero-day vulnerabilities for offense [1], but benevolent organizations also help private organizations patch such vulnerabilities. Our techniques enable secure computation to privately identify existence of vulnerabilities, committing to the actual vulnerabilities, which are revealed later. Such an application based on string matching was discussed in [23].
- *Application 3: Delayed Multi-party Lottery Results.* In a lottery, rational parties are incentivized to cheat using knowledge of others' bids. To make an MPC lottery fair and auditable, its result can be time-locked and delayed until some specified time. Our techniques allow both (1) revealing the time-locked result after the due date, or (2) revealing it when a threshold seeks the results.

Auditable Computation. The above applications show how TMPC can contribute to ensuring integrity of distributed computation. Typically, cryptographic protocols do not assure that parties employ the "right inputs," or that outputs are based on the "expected inputs (based on policy and requirements)." However, when some inputs' or outputs' secrecy is only required temporarily, TMPC can add integrity guarantees by penalizing violators caught in the future. Assurance of correct input has been an issue in a recent cryptographic protocol suggested for private Child Sexual Abuse Material (CSAM) checking [2].

1.1 Contributions and Technical Challenges

We make the following contributions.

(1) We define (in Sect. 4.1, 4.2) new functionalities for Multi-party Time-lock Puzzles (MTP) and Timed Multi-party Computation (TMPC) with an early reveal option.

(2) We design (in Sect. 5.1) a new efficient MTP construction built upon a distributed RSA key generation [8,15] where parties generate the RSA composite N and shares of the exponent and no one knows $\phi(N)$. To prove security, we introduce new simulation techniques for timed secrecy.
(3) We design (in Sect. 5.2) an efficient TMPC protocol by composing with and building on our new MTP constructions.

To accomplish the above, we address the following technical challenges:

(i) Challenges in Constructing MTP and TMPC: A number of technical challenges arise in the design of an efficient MPC to time-lock a puzzle solution. For example, we must consider the ability to tune the duration of the time-lock and provide quorum control on the output. Additionally, in order to efficiently construct a puzzle, we must show how the parties distribute knowledge of the trapdoor; this is critical to avoid a blow-up (proportional to the field size over which the cryptographic values are computed) in order to even express the duration of the time-lock in MPC.

(ii) Challenges in Proving Security: To claim security we build on previous foundational work in both the more traditional random oracle model (ROM) [3,4] and the more recent fine-grained model [13] for composition of time-lock primitives. The combination of the distributed setting and security proof techniques of our setting (of having security only up to a future point) introduces the issue that the simulator must

- have at most as much computational power than the adversary to solve a puzzle
- somehow know the solution before the adversary in order to complete the simulation

Clairvoyant Simulation. To address the issue of an adversary that can learn a puzzle solution slightly earlier than the honest parties (without generating the puzzle with knowledge of the trapdoor, and without solving the puzzle), we introduce a *"clairvoyant" simulator* that can learn the protocol output "just slightly earlier." This gives the simulator the necessary advantage (i.e., enough leverage) to provide the adversary with the solution at its time-advantaged moment. However, the consequence of this framework is that the security duration of the protocol lasts only until the point where the simulator would have learned the solution, and not until the honest parties learn the solution (i.e., just slightly shorter time).

1.2   Related Work

We briefly highlight more classical works in time-delayed and more recent fine-grained cryptography that we build on, and we review the most related recent work. A more detailed discussion of related work is given the full version. We note that despite almost 30 years of work on the primitive, ours is the first (to the best of our knowledge) to consider the natural extended more robust notion of MTP which is a multi-party primitive.

Time-lock Puzzles: Works on timed and delayed actions started with time-lock puzzles (TP), the seminal work by Rivest, Shamir, and Wagner (RSW) [21]. Boneh and Naor [9] introduced timed commitments, which progressed the study of using timed-primitives for fairness in MPC. Verifiable delay functions, which are cryptographic primitives that depend on sequential work in order to delay release of information, have also been the focus of several recent research efforts [6,20,22]. Bitansky et al.[5] formally defined TP_'s and constructed them using randomized encodings. Baum et al. [4] and [3] formalized TP in the UC model [10]. Ephraim et al. [14] built publicly verifiable, non-malleable TP. Katz et al. [16] recently constructed non-interactive non-malleable timed commitments that come with a proof that they can be forced open. They additionally showed that in a quantitative group model, speeding up squaring is as hard as factoring. Malavolta and Thyagarajan [19] provided practical homomorphic time-lock puzzles, but they require the strong cryptographic notion of indistinguishabilty obfuscation (iO) in order to achieve full homomorphism. They also do not consider composition of their puzzles with other cryptographic primitives. In terms of negative results, Mahmoody et al.[18] proved that in the random oracle model (ROM), there are no TP with more than polynomial time gap. For this reason, our attempts to design time-lock puzzles with exponential time gaps depend on the structure of the RSA assumption (having a trapdoor for fast generation).

Time-locked Cryptography and Composition: Baum et al.[3,4] achieved composition of MPC with time-lock primitives for (two parties and more than two parties, respectively) using the model of [4] that treats each intermediate step of a time-lock solution as if it is a completely random step, and therefore no leakage occurs until the last step when the solution is learned (this is obviously an idealization by [18]). As this is a primitive/ generic model, our analysis (in Appendix C in the full version [12]) follows this paradigm.

MPC with Output-Independent Abort: The timed MPC protocol in Sect. 5.2 can be used to achieve MPC with output-independent abort. Baum et al. [3] were the first to compose time-lock puzzles with a form of MPC in order to learn the output at a later time; this result recognizes the need to compose TLP with MPC. Briefly, their construction performs MPC with secret-shared outputs, and then each party time-locks its share and broadcasts its time-lock. This prevents the adversary from being able to learn the output before it must choose whether abort the protocol. Compared to [3], this paper reduces the number of puzzles to solve from $O(n)$ to $O(1)$ by building a time-lock puzzle *within MPC* that holds the solution.

Baum et al. [3] achieve security in the UC model; the security of the constructions in this paper depend on the subprotocols used for arithmetic. While it is possible to perform all of the computations with malicious or UC security, we do not know efficient protocols for some of the functionalities (such as an efficient circuit for modular inverse within a field of unknown size), which remains an interesting question.

This paper is also the first to formally model an early-reconstruct (i.e., "short-circuit") functionality where a sufficient number of honest parties can collaborate to reveal the timed secret before the time-lock expires (a functionality that allows a quorum to overright a delay!). While it is conceivable that the protocol for MPC with output-independent abort by [3] could be extended to achieve such a functionality, we note that such functionality is not explicitly modeled in their work [3], and no (formal) treatment or analysis of the security of such a modified protocol is contained in their work.

Overall, the related earlier work we describe above points out the need for multiparty applications related to time locked puzzles, and here we treat this subject systematically and with efficiency in mind.

1.3 Paper Outline

Section 2 introduces notation and preliminaries. Section 3 presents an execution model for MPC with timed primitives. Section 4 presents the ideal functionality of TMPCwhile Sect. 5 contains our new MTP and TMPC protocols. In the full version [12], Appendix A presents sample implementations of the building block functionalities. Appendix B analyzes performance and trade-offs between efficiency, number of parties, and underlying assumptions. Appendix C contains the proofs of our protocols in the random oracle model. Appendix D discusses extended related work (for background on the state of the art).

2   Preliminaries

We denote by $[m]$ the sequence $\{1, 2, \ldots, m\}$ and $[n_1, n_2]$ the set of all integers between n_1 and n_2. We denote the powerset of S by 2^S. For multi-party protocols, we let $\mathcal{P} = \{P_1, P_2, ..., P_n\}$ be the set of parties, where P_i denotes the ith party. A sharing of a secret value x is represented by $[x]$. For a secret with n shares, we denote by $[x] = ([x]_1, \ldots, [x]_n)$, where $[x]_i$ is the ith share of the secret. For threshold secret sharing schemes, we use t to denote the reconstruction threshold in a t out of n scheme. When we write $f = f(\lambda)$, we indicate f is a function of λ. By $\mathsf{poly}(\lambda)$, $\mathsf{polylog}(\lambda)$, and $\mathsf{superpoly}(\lambda)$ we denote any polynomial function, any poly-logarithmic function, and any super-polynomial function of λ, respectively. A function negl is *negligible* if there exists a constant n for which for every polynomial function poly and every $m > n$, $\mathsf{negl}(m) < \frac{1}{\mathsf{poly}(m)}$, where $\mathsf{poly}(m)$ and $\mathsf{negl}(m) > 0$. We consider multi-party protocols that securely compute functions from $\mathbb{Z}_Q^n \to \mathbb{Z}_Q$, where Q is a large prime.

We denote by $\mathcal{F}_{\mathsf{name}}^{\mathsf{params}}$ a functionality $\mathcal{F}$ with its name in the subscript and its parameters in the superscript. Similarly, we denote by $\Pi_{\mathsf{name}}^{\mathsf{params}}$ protocols with protocol name in the subscript and its parameters in the superscript.

2.1 Time-Lock Puzzle

We adapt a definition of puzzles from Bitansky et al. ([5] Definition 3.1. Our adaptation is equivalent; we only update notation).

Definition 1. (Puzzle). *A* puzzle *for solution domain* $M = \{M_\lambda\}_\lambda$ *is a pair of algorithms* Puz = (Puz.Gen, Puz.Solve) *for which*

- $Z \leftarrow$ Puz.Gen(t, χ) *is a probabilistic algorithm over difficulty parameter* $t \in \mathbb{N}$ *and solution* $\chi \in M_\lambda$, *where* λ *is a security parameter, and outputs puzzle* Z.
- $\chi \leftarrow$ Puz.Solve(Z) *is a deterministic algorithm that takes as input puzzle* Z *and outputs solution* $\chi \in M_\lambda$.

subject to the following constraints:

- **Completeness:** *For every security parameter* λ, *difficulty parameter* t, *solution* $\chi \in M_\lambda$, *and puzzle* Z *in the image of* Puz.Gen(t, χ), Puz.Solve(Z) *outputs* χ.
- **Efficiency:**
  - $Z \leftarrow$ Puz.Gen(t, χ) *can be computed in size* poly$(\log t, \lambda)$.
  - Puz.Solve(Z) *can be computed in size* $t \cdot$ poly(λ).

We continue by adapting the more constrained definition of a *time-lock* puzzle by Bitansky et al. ([5] Definition 3.2).

Definition 2. (Time-lock Puzzle). *A puzzle* Puz = (Puz.Gen, Puz.Solve) *is a* time-lock *puzzle for solution domain* $M = \{M_\lambda\}_\lambda$ *with gap* $\varepsilon < 1$ *if there exists a polynomial* $r(\cdot)$ *such that for every polynomial* $t(\cdot) \geq r(\cdot)$ *and every polynomial size,* t^ε*-depth-bounded adversary* $\mathcal{A} = \{\mathcal{A}_\lambda\}_{\lambda \in \mathbb{N}}$, *there exists a negligible function* negl *such that for every* $\lambda \in \mathbb{N}$, *and every pair of solutions* $\chi_0, \chi_1 \in M_\lambda$:

$$\Pr[b \leftarrow \mathcal{A}_\lambda(Z) \colon b \leftarrow \{0, 1\}, Z \leftarrow \text{Puz.Gen}(t(\lambda), \chi_b)] \leq \frac{1}{2} + \text{negl}(\lambda)$$

2.2   Hardness Assumptions

Our time-lock puzzles build on the construction by Rivest, Shamir, and Wagner (RSW) [21]. The puzzles are time-lock puzzles under the assumption that sequential squaring modulo an RSA modulus is hard. Here we recall the hardness of sequential squaring modulo an RSA modulus, formalized as the strong sequential squaring assumption [11,20]. We adapt the formalization by [11] and present the assumption as a computational problem. Let GenMod be a probabilistic polynomial-time algorithm which on input λ outputs two λ-bit safe primes p and q, modulus $N = pq$ and a random generator g of the group G:

Definition 3. (Depth Hardness of Sequential Squaring). *Consider the security experiment* ExpSS *in Fig. 1. Strong sequential squaring is* (d, t)*-depth hard if for every* $d(\lambda)$*-depth bounded adversary* $\mathcal{A}_d = (\mathcal{A}_1, \mathcal{A}_2)$ *(where* $\mathcal{A}$ *is* d*-bounded if the sums of the depths of* $\mathcal{A}_1$ *and* $\mathcal{A}_2$ *in the experiment in Fig. 1 is* d*),* $\Pr[\text{ExpSS}^t(\mathcal{A}_d) = 1] \leq \text{negl}(\lambda)$.

$$\underline{\mathsf{ExpSS}^t(\mathcal{A})}$$

//$\mathcal{A}$ is an interactive circuit with
   components $\mathcal{A}_1, \mathcal{A}_2$
$(p, q, N, G) \leftarrow \mathsf{GenMod}(1^\lambda)$
$st \leftarrow \mathcal{A}_1(t, N)$
$\alpha \leftarrow G$
$\chi \leftarrow a^{2^t} \bmod N$
$b \leftarrow \mathcal{A}_2(st, \alpha)$
return 1 if $\chi = b$, 0 otherwise

Fig. 1. The hardness experiment for sequential squaring modulo an RSA modulus.

Hardness of Sequential Squaring. We write that the sequential squaring problem is *hard* if for all $t' < t$, $\Pr[\mathsf{ExpSS}^t(\mathcal{A}_t) = 1] \leq \mathsf{negl}(\lambda)$. In the random oracle model we represent every intermediate as a random element of the group, and the statement follows trivially.

Similarly the *underlying problem* of factoring an RSA modulus must be hard. Here we define depth-hardness of factoring an RSA modulus.

Definition 4. (Depth-Hardness of Factoring RSA Modulus). *Let $d = \mathsf{poly}(\lambda)$, let $P = [p_1, \ldots, p_k]$ be primes of size λ sampled uniformly at random, and let $N = \prod_i^k p_i$. Factoring is (d, k) hard if for every d-depth bounded adversary $\mathcal{A}_d$ and for every $\lambda \in \mathbb{N}$: $\Pr[(p'_1, \ldots, p'_k) \leftarrow \mathcal{A}_d(N) \mid \forall i. p'_i > 1 : \prod_i^k p'_i = N] \leq \mathsf{negl}(\lambda)$*

2.3 MPC Scheme

This work contains protocols that distribute the generation of time-lock puzzles via multi-party computation (MPC) and implements timed multi-party computation. We define an MPC scheme as follows:

Definition 5. *(((t, n) MPC Scheme). A (t, n) MPC Scheme is a tuple of protocols (Share, Add, Mult, Reconstruct) with the following properties:*

1. *Share$(s) \rightarrow ([s]_1, \ldots, [s]_n)$: outputs a list of n shares of s*
2. *Add$([x], [y]) \rightarrow [x + y]$: performs addition of two shared secrets.*
3. *Mult$([x], [y]) \rightarrow [xy]$: computes a sharing of the product of two shared secrets.*
4. *Reconstruct$([s]_1, \ldots, [s]_t) \rightarrow s$: reconstructs a secret from a list of at least t shares of the secret.*

We consider MPC schemes that are composed of these subprotocols without loss of generality; any secure computation can be considered to operate in phases in which first, parties share their inputs, second they compute a circuit composed over addition and multiplications gates over their inputs, and third they reconstruct the output. We explicitly require that any combination of the above protocols be simulatable for any adversary that does not acquire t shares of any in any (t, n) MPC execution.

Secret Sharing Schema. In this work, all protocols that perform multi-party computation and all functionalities that take secret shares as inputs or return them as outputs are implicitly parameterized by a secret sharing schema Σ. A schema defines an algebra for communicating and computing over secrets, including the size of shares and the access structures which are able to reconstruct a secret. In certain cases, we make Σ explicit in order to highlight issues with composition, or in order to generalize our statements. In our constructions, all of our operations are performed over a finite field with large prime modulus, and random numbers are sampled within the appropriate field.

3 Execution Model

Communication Model. The parties in our protocols communicate through functionalities that they invoke in order to compute on secret-shared inputs; otherwise, they perform only local computations. Therefore, the model presented in this paper depends on the communication network only as required by the underlying functionalities. Although the actual requirements of our construction depend on the underlying assumptions of the constituent functionalities, we generally assume that parties communicate over a network with bounded delay.[1]

Output Synchronization (Fairness). Because all parties receive *the same* puzzle at the end of the protocol and begin solving it immediately, synchronization of the solving phase depends only on the delay of the network delivering the final MPC outputs. This is in contrast to [3], where parties must commit to their MPC outputs, then perform a consistency check, and only afterwards are permitted to begin solving their puzzles. We note that time spent performing the consistency check provides the adversary an advantage to start solving puzzles before the honest parties complete their check.

Time. Our time-lock functionalities require a notion of global time. The global time is not accessible to any party except the functionalities; however, it is the reference by which time-locks are enforced. Therefore, the elapse of global time upper-bounds the depth that any circuit can evaluate.

We model access to the global clock via access to a variable τ. Timekeeping functionalities for synchronous computations have been modeled elsewhere [4, 17]. We note that our model requires the environment to synchronize all parties, and the variable τ is an indicator of how many rounds the environment has directed.

---

[1] Whether the parties know the network bound or not is beyond the scope of this work.

A similar global timekeeper is used by [4] and adopted by [3]. In effect, they use a global timekeeping functionality that informs other functionalities when a unit of time has elapsed by issuing a "tick."[2] This has the same effect as our simplified modeling, as our functionalities access a global time which could simply be measured in "ticks." None of our protocols depend explicitly on the elapsed time, nor do our parties interact with time directly.

However, parties do query the time-lock functionalities (Fig. 2, 3) for intermediate solutions on their puzzles. The ideal functionalities respond based on the global time, and not based on the number of queries made by a single party. Therefore, no party receives an advantage by making extra queries to the leakage functionality, and leakage is made to depend exclusively on time.

Moreover, it is standard in time-delay literature [3,6] to assume that the adversary enjoys some $\varepsilon \in [0,1]$ advantage in solving a puzzle such that if an honest party solves a puzzle in time t, then the adversary can solve it in time εt. The issues in composition that arise from this advantage are orthogonal to the work in the main body of this paper, but are treated in the model of [13].

The Environment's Time. We make one important adjustment to our computational model. The environment in our model is bounded in depth by the same global time that bounds the functionalities and the parties. This prevents the environment from being able to solve a time-lock primitive by pausing the execution in which the puzzle is generated and using side-sessions in order to solve it. Simply, the computational depth of any side-session counts towards the depth of the environment, and all concurrent sessions must run at the same rate. One activation of all parties in Execution A must imply that all parties in Execution B are also activated.[3] We feel this is a realistic restriction of the UC and an appropriate model for timed cryptography.

Random Intermediates. To build timed multi-party computation, we model a time-lock functionality for a random value. Parties solve the time-lock puzzle containing this random value in order to reveal the output of a multi-party computation. In brief, every intermediate of a puzzle is considered to be sampled freshly at random; therefore, as a party solves a time-lock puzzle it learns no information about the final solution until the last step. While [3,4] model this explicitly by sampling fresh randomness in each step of their corresponding time-lock or time-delay functionalities, the functionalities we present (in Fig. 2, 3) simply do not respond to parties before the final step. This is easily simulatable; the simulator does not provide intermediate randomness to the adversary because solving is local.

This model still permits the adversary to have some advantage in solving a puzzle, such that if honest parties require time t to solve a puzzle then the adversary can solve it in time εt where $\varepsilon \in (0,1)$.

---

[2] Because we do not need to synchronize the ticks of multiple functionalities, we can simplify the modeling without depending explicitly on the global ticker.

[3] Therefore, parties are computationally synchronized both within and across sessions.

3.1   Secure Computation

We now provide the definition for secure computation in our adapted model. Let $\mathsf{REAL}_{\pi,\mathcal{A}(z),\mathcal{Z}}(\overline{x})\}_{\overline{x}\in(\{0,1\}^*)^n,z\in\{0,1\}^*}$ denotes the view of the environment $\mathcal{Z}$ in the real world execution protocol π in the presence of adversary $\mathcal{A}$, where the n parties' inputs are $\overline{x}$ and the adversary's auxiliary advice is z. Let $\mathsf{IDEAL}_{\mathcal{F},\mathcal{S}(z),\mathcal{Z}}(\overline{x})\}_{\overline{x}\in(\{0,1\}^*)^n,z\in\{0,1\}^*}$ represent the view of the environment in the ideal world where $\mathcal{S}$ interacts with ideal functionality $\mathcal{F}$.

Definition 6. (Secure Computation). *Protocol π securely computes $\mathcal{F}$ if for every adversary $\mathcal{A}$ for the real world and environment $\mathcal{Z}$ there exists a simulator $\mathcal{S}$ such that the two distributions*

$$\{\mathsf{REAL}_{\pi,\mathcal{A}(z),\mathcal{Z}}(\overline{x})\}_{\overline{x}\in(\{0,1\}^*)^n,z\in\{0,1\}^*}$$

$$\{\mathsf{IDEAL}_{\mathcal{F},\mathcal{S}(z),\mathcal{Z}}(\overline{x})\}_{\overline{x}\in(\{0,1\}^*)^n,z\in\{0,1\}^*}$$

are computationally indistinguishable.

4   Functionalities for Multi-party Time-Lock Puzzles and Timed Multi-party Computation

In this section, we define two functionalities that are the focus of the remainder of this paper. $\mathcal{F}_{\mathsf{timedcoin}}^{\tau^*,\Sigma}$ defines a functionality that generates a random string which is either revealed after a predetermined amount of time or *short-circuited* by sufficiently many parties collaborating to learn the random string earlier that its predetermined reveal time. This functionality will be implemented by multi-party time-lock puzzles. $\mathcal{F}_{\mathsf{TMPC}}^{F,G}$ defines timed multi-party computation which evaluates a function over the parties' inputs; it reveals the result after a certain amount of time or it can be short-circuited if a threshold number of parties collaborate on such reveal. We additionally define building block functionalities used in our protocols; example instantiations of these functionalities are presented in the full version [12].

4.1   Timed Random Puzzle

In Fig. 2, we present our functionality for time-locking a random value such that the value is only revealed to all parties after a fixed time-lock duration τ^*. The functionality is parameterized by τ^* and a secret-sharing schema Σ.[4] Let Σ_t denote the threshold number of parties required to reconstruct a secret shared according to Σ.

---

[4] This output is similar to the MPC with secret-shared output functionality employed by [3], where our notation makes the schema explicit.

4.2 Timed Multi-party Computation (TMPC)

In Fig. 3, we present our ideal functionality for timed multi-party computation (TMPC). In a TMPC, all parties submit their inputs in the beginning and subsequently query the functionality for their outputs after the specified time-lock duration. The functionality conceals the outputs until the time-lock duration elapses, after which it reveals the output all at once.

Functionality 1 (Timed Random Coins with Short-Circuit $\mathcal{F}_{\text{timedcoin}}^{\tau^*,\Sigma}$).

$\mathcal{F}_{\text{timedcoin}}^{\tau^*,\Sigma}$ *is parameterized by a time-lock duration τ^*, and a secret-sharing schema Σ. It has access to a global clock τ. It maintains an internal data structure Q which is initialized to $\emptyset$. It interacts with parties $\mathcal{P} = \{P_1, \ldots, P_n\}$ as follows:*

1. **Input:** *Upon receiving* (init) *from party P_i, $\mathcal{F}_{\text{timedcoin}}^{\tau^*,\Sigma}$ sends* (received) *to P_i.*
2. **Commit:** *Once $\mathcal{F}_{\text{timedcoin}}^{\tau^*,\Sigma}$ has received* (init) *from every party in $\mathcal{P}$, it samples a nonce R uniformly at random (from the domain of an algebra specified by Σ) and sets $\tau_0 := \tau$. It returns* (lock, $[R]_i$) *to P_i.*
3. **Reveal:** *Upon receiving* (reveal) *from party P_i at time τ:*
   (a) *If $\tau < \tau_0 + \tau^*$, it sets $Q \leftarrow Q \cup \{P_i\}$.*
      - *If $|Q| < \Sigma_t$, it does not respond.*
      - *If $|Q| \geq \Sigma_t$, it sends* (unlock, R) *to P_i.*
   (b) *Else if $\tau \geq \tau_0 + \tau^*$ it sends* (unlock, R) *to P_i.*

Fig. 2. Timed Random Coins Functionality $\mathcal{F}_{\text{timedcoin}}^{\tau^*,\Sigma}$. This functionality samples a random secret and returns a sharing of the secret to each party. When the time lock expires or when sufficiently many parties (Σ_t) request a short-circuit reveal, it reveals the secret to all requesting parties.

4.3 Building-Block Functionalities

MPC Building Blocks. Without loss of generality, we consider MPC protocols as described in Sect. 2.3; here we present functionalities that perform idealized MPC operations required for our protocols.

- $\mathcal{F}_{\text{Share}}$ shares a secret. On input x it returns a share $[x]$ to each party.
- $\mathcal{F}_{\text{Recon}}$ reconstructs a set of secret shares. On input a threshold number of shares $[x]$, it returns x to each party.
- $\mathcal{F}_{\text{Add}}$ adds two shared values. On input $([x], [y])$ it returns $[x + y]$.
- $\mathcal{F}_{\text{Mult}}$ multiplies to shared values. On input $([x], [y])$ it returns $[xy]$.

We also require the following advanced functionalities that can be constructed from the building blocks. In the full version we reference example instantiations of each. Our protocols are secure in the malicious model if the building block functionalities are secure in the malicious model. In the full version [12] we analyze the concrete complexity of our protocols using existing constructions in the semi-honest model.

80   K. Eldefrawy et al.

Functionality 2 (Timed MPC with Short-Circuit Reveal $\mathcal{F}_{\mathsf{TMPC}}^{\tau^*,f}$).

$\mathcal{F}_{\mathsf{TMPC}}^{\tau^*,f}$ *is parameterized by a function f, and a time-lock duration τ^*. It has access to a global clock represented by τ. It maintains an internal data structure Q which is initialized to $\emptyset$. It interacts with parties $\mathcal{P} = \{P_1, \dots, P_n\}$ as follows:*

1. **Input:** *Upon receiving inputs (init, x_i) from each party $P_i \in \mathcal{P}$, it sets $\overline{x} = (x_1, \dots, x_n)$, and computes $y \leftarrow f(\overline{x})$. It records the global time τ at which the last input was received, sets $\tau_0 \leftarrow \tau$, and replies $(\mathsf{received}, \tau_0)$ to each party.*
2. **Reveal:** *Upon receiving (reveal) from party P_i at time τ:*
   (a) *If $\tau < \tau_0 + \tau^*$, it sets $Q \leftarrow Q \cup \{P_i\}$.*
      - *If $|Q| < \Sigma_t$, it does not respond.*
      - *If $|Q| \geq \Sigma_t$, it sends (unlock, y) to P_i.*
   (b) *Else, it sends (unlock, y) to P_i.*

Fig. 3. Timed MPC Functionality $\mathcal{F}_{\mathsf{TMPC}}^{\tau^*,f}$. This functionality reveals the output of f computed in an MPC after τ^*, or to the requesting parties when sufficiently many parties request a short-circuit.

- $\mathcal{F}_{\mathsf{RSAGen}}$ generates an RSA modulus and shares of its factors. Each party P_i learns a triple $([p]_i, [q]_i, N)$, where $[p]_i$ is a share of p and $[q]_i$ is a share of q such that $N = pq$.
- $\mathcal{F}_{\mathsf{PrvExp}}^b$ exponentiates a public base to a secret shared exponent. Given a base b and a secret shared exponent $[x]$, it returns a share of $[b^x]$ to each party.
- $\mathcal{F}_{\mathsf{Inv}}$ computes the inverse of a shared secret within a specified field. Given a secret shared input $[x]$, it returns to each party a share of $[x^{-1}]$.
- $\mathcal{F}_{\mathsf{PrvMR}}$ computes modular reduction where both the modulus and the argument are secret shared. Given a shared input $[x]$ and a shared modulus $[m]$, it returns to each party a share of $[x \bmod m]$.
- $\mathcal{F}_{\mathsf{PubMR}}$ computes modular reduction where the modulus is a known constant and the argument is secret shared. Given a secret shared input $[x]$ and a modulus m, it returns to each party a share of $[x \bmod m]$.
- $\mathcal{F}_{\mathsf{CoinFlip}}$ takes no inputs, and outputs a uniformly random element within a specified domain. For our purposes, this is between 0 and $N-1$ for some RSA composite N.
- $\mathcal{F}_{\mathsf{RO}}$ takes a shared value $[x]$ as input. If the reconstruction of $[x]$ has not been queried before, it samples a value y uniformly at random and returns $[y]$. If the reconstruction of $[x]$ has been queried before, it returns a new sharing of the response y.
- $\mathcal{F}_{\mathsf{Prod}}$ computes the product of a vector of shared secrets. Given each party's vector of shared secrets $[\overline{x}] = \{[x_1], \dots, [x_l]\}$, it returns a share of the product $[\prod_{i=1}^{l} x_i]$ to each party.
- $\mathcal{F}_{\mathsf{SFE}}^f$ performs secure function evaluation. Each party P_i submits an input x_i. $\mathcal{F}_{\mathsf{SFE}}^f$ computes $y = f(x_1, \dots, x_n)$ and returns a share of y to each party.

5 Efficient Protocols for Multi-party Time-lock Puzzle and Timed Multi-party Computation

We present here two protocols: one protocol to realize $\mathcal{F}_{\text{timedcoin}}^{\tau^*,\Sigma}$, and one to realize $\mathcal{F}_{\text{TMPC}}^{\tau^*,f}$ which depends on $\mathcal{F}_{\text{timedcoin}}^{\tau^*,\Sigma}$. Our protocol for $\mathcal{F}_{\text{timedcoin}}^{\tau^*,\Sigma}$ securely distributes the generation of the RSW time-lock puzzle [21].

Recall that the RSW puzzle computes a puzzle $\chi = \alpha^{2^{\tau^*}} \bmod N$, where α is a random number, τ^* is the length of the time-lock, and N is an RSA modulus. The solver is given α and reveals χ via repeated squaring. To efficiently construct the puzzle, the parties compute $\varphi(N)$ such that no party knows $\phi(N)$, and then they compute the exponent $e = 2^{\tau^*} \bmod \phi(N)$ and $\chi = \alpha^e \bmod N$, where α is sampled via a coin flipping protocol.

Computing $2^{\tau^*} \bmod \phi(N)$ via MPC is challenging because 2^{τ^*} is a *very large* number for realistic τ^*, and naively representing it in a secret sharing scheme requires a very large field size. Our protocol computes $2^{\tau^*} \bmod \phi(N)$ within MPC via exponentian by squaring such that the size of the field is only twice the size of $\phi(N)$. The protocol must compute both N and the puzzle instance; the modulus cannot be reused for additional puzzles due to trivial malleability attacks.

5.1 Constructing Multi-Party Time-Lock Puzzle (MTP) Using Exponentiation by Squaring

Our first protocol ($\pi_{\text{MTP-ES}}^{\tau^*,\Sigma}$) generates an RSW time-lock puzzle along with a trapdoor, and provides to the parties both the puzzle and a share of its solution. To generate the puzzle with its trapdoor, the parties first invoke a functionality to generate an RSA modulus N for which each party knows a share of both prime factors. Next, the parties use a coin flipping functionality to sample a random puzzle α. They then use the trapdoor to efficiently compute the puzzle solution $\chi = \alpha^{2^{\tau^*}}$ modulo N in $O(\log(\tau^*))$ MPC multiplications. The output of the protocol is the random oracle evaluation of the puzzle solution, $\beta = \mathcal{O}_\$(\chi)$, where $\mathcal{O}_\$$ is a random oracle. During the protocol, the parties first receive the puzzle α and a share of the protocol output β. To learn the protocol output β, parties may either solve the puzzle (via repeatedly squaring α), or reconstruct using their shares if a threshold number of them agree to reveal. We present the $\pi_{\text{MTP-ES}}^{\tau^*,\Sigma}$ protocol in Fig. 4.

Theorem 1. (Security of Protocol $\pi_{\text{MTP-ES}}^{\tau^*,\Sigma}$). *In the $(\mathcal{F}_{\text{CoinFlip}}, \mathcal{F}_{\text{Share}}, \mathcal{F}_{\text{Recon}}, \mathcal{F}_{\text{MLlt}}, \mathcal{F}_{\text{RSAGen}}, \mathcal{F}_{\text{PrvExp}}^{b}, \mathcal{F}_{\text{PrvMR}})$-hybrid random-intermediate model, if sequential squaring is hard then $\pi_{\text{MTP-ES}}^{\tau^*,\Sigma}$ securely implements $\mathcal{F}_{\text{timedcoin}}^{\tau^*,\Sigma}$.*

Proof. (Sketch). The proof builds a simulator for $\pi_{\text{MTP-ES}}^{\tau^*,\Sigma}$. Simulating the puzzle generation protocol is straightforward. Because the protocol depends almost entirely on invoking functionalities to perform arithmetic on secret-shared values, the simulator need only choose appropriate outputs for every functionality

---

Protocol 1 (Protocol for Multi-party Time-lock Puzzle using Exponentiation by Squaring $\pi_{\mathsf{MTP\text{-}ES}}^{\tau^*,\Sigma}$)

- **Common Input**: $\kappa = \kappa(\lambda)$, the length of each RSA factor; schema Σ describing the scheme by which MPC operations are performed.
- **Parameters**: τ^* is the duration of the time-lock; schema Σ in which the shares of the puzzle output should be performed.
- **Output**: Each party P_i outputs $[\beta]_i$, a secret share of time-lock puzzle solution β obeying Σ. After τ^*, when P_i knows β, it outputs β.

- **Puzzle Generation Protocol**: Each party P_i proceeds as follows:
    1. **Setup**:
        (a) P_i invokes $\mathcal{F}_{\mathsf{RSAGen}}$ for factor length κ. It receives $([p]_i, [q]_i, N)$, where $[p]_i$ and $[q]_i$ are P_i's shares of primes p, q such that $N = pq$.
        (b) P_i sends $([p]_i, [q]_i)$ to $\mathcal{F}_{\mathsf{SFE}}$ and receives $[\phi(N)]_i$. (The functionality need only to compute shares of $(p-1)(q-1) = pq - p - q + 1$)
    2. **Generation of a Puzzle and its Solution via Backdoor**: The parties compute a puzzle instance α and a sharing of its solution β as follows:
        (a) **Computing the Backdoor Exponent via Squaring mod $\phi(N)$**:[a]

            i. P_1 sends a constant tuple $(1, 2)$ to $\mathcal{F}_{\mathsf{Share}}$. Each party P_i receives $[e]_i$ to its share of 1 and $[x]_i$ to its share of 2.
            ii. For each bit b in the binary representation of τ^*, starting with the least significant:
                A. If $b = 1$: P_i sends $([e]_i, [x]_i)$ to $\mathcal{F}_{\mathsf{Mult}}$ and assigns the output to $[e]_i$. P_i then sends $([e]_i, [\phi(N)]_i)$ to $\mathcal{F}_{\mathsf{PrvMR}}$ and assigns the output to $[e]_i$.
                B. P_i sends $([x]_i, [x]_i)$ to $\mathcal{F}_{\mathsf{Mult}}$ and assigns the output to $[x]_i$.
                C. P_i sends $([x]_i, [\phi(N)]_i)$ to $\mathcal{F}_{\mathsf{PrvMR}}$ and assigns the output to $[x]_i$.
            iii. P_i sends $([e]_i, [\phi(N)]_i)$ to $\mathcal{F}_{\mathsf{PrvMR}}$ and assigns the output to $[e]_i$.
        (b) **Computing the Solution using the Exponent**:
            i. P_i invokes $\mathcal{F}_{\mathsf{CoinFlip}}$ to receive a public random number $\alpha < N$.
            ii. P_i sends $(\alpha, [e]_i)$ to $\mathcal{F}_{\mathsf{PrvExp}}^{\alpha}$ and receives $[\gamma]_i$.
            iii. P_i sends $([\gamma]_i, N)$ to $\mathcal{F}_{\mathsf{PubMR}}$ and receives $[\chi]_i$.
    3. **Random Oracle**: P_i sends $[\chi]_i$ to $\mathcal{F}_{\mathsf{RO}}$ and receives $[\beta]_i$
    4. **Output**: P_i outputs $[\beta]_i$ obeying schema Σ.

- **Puzzle Solution Protocol**: Parties obtain β in one of two ways:
    1. **Locally Solve the Puzzle**: P_i locally computes $\beta = \alpha^{2^{\tau^*}} \bmod N$ by repeated squaring.
    2. **Shortcut via Reconstruction**: At any time, sufficiently many parties can reconstruct β by invoking $\mathcal{F}_{\mathsf{Recon}}$.

---

[a] As an optimization, for $i < 2\kappa$ such that $x^i < \phi(N)$, the operations in 2.(a)ii. can be performed with x as a constant and $\bmod \phi(N)$ elided.

Fig. 4. $\pi_{\mathsf{MTP\text{-}ES}}^{\tau^*,\Sigma}$ Multi-party Time-lock Puzzle Generation and Solution via Exponentiation by Squaring.

call. The simulator generates a puzzle which it provides to the adversary, such that the simulator knows the solution. For the outputs of the MPC functionality, the simulator passes dummy values to the parties. Under the constraint that the adversary corrupts fewer than the threshold number of parties (or an access structure specified by the schema), it follows that the adversary's view is distributed identically to that of a real execution. The full proof is deferred to the full version [12].

5.2 Protocol for Timed Multi-party Computation (TMPC)

Figure 6 contains the protocol $\pi_{\mathsf{TMPC}}^{f,\tau^*}$ which realizes the functionality $\mathcal{F}_{\mathsf{TMPC}}^{\tau^*,f}$ for a *single time-locked MPC output*. $\pi_{\mathsf{TMPC}}^{f,\tau^*}$ uses $\mathcal{F}_{\mathsf{SFE}}$ in order to securely evaluate a circuit over the parties' inputs, and it uses $\mathcal{F}_{\mathsf{timedcoin}}^{\tau^*,\Sigma}$ to generate a time-delayed mask. It then masks the output of the MPC with the time-delayed solution. By solving the puzzle, any party can then reveal the output (Fig. 5).

Functionality 3 (Masking Functionality $\mathcal{F}_{\mathsf{Hide}}$).

$\mathcal{F}_{\mathsf{Hide}}$ *interacts with the parties $\mathcal{P}$ in the following way:*

1. **Input:** P_i *sends its input $[a]_i$ and r_i to $\mathcal{F}_{\mathsf{Hide}}$.*
2. **Output:** *Upon receiving inputs from every party in $\mathcal{P}$, $\mathcal{F}_{\mathsf{Hide}}$ sets $R = \sum_i r_i$ and $a = \mathsf{Reconstruct}([a_1], \ldots, [a_n])$. Then it computes $b \leftarrow a + R$, and outputs b to each party.*

Fig. 5. Masking Functionality.

Protocol 2 (Protocol for Timed Multi-party Computation $\pi_{\mathsf{TMPC}}^{f,\tau^*}$)

- **Parameters:** $f : \mathbb{Z}_Q^n \to \mathbb{Z}_Q$ *is the function (represented as a circuit) to compute. τ^* is the time-lock duration.*
- **Input:** *Each party P_i has an input x_i.*
- **Output:** *Each party P_i learns $y = f(x_1, \ldots, x_n)$ after the time-lock expires or by invoking the Early Reveal subprotocol, and outputs y.*

- **Protocol:** *Each party P_i proceeds as follows:*
  1. **Compute:**
     (a) P_i *sends x_i to $\mathcal{F}_{\mathsf{SFE}}^f$ and receives $[y]_i$.*
     (b) P_i *invokes $\mathcal{F}_{\mathsf{timedcoin}}^{\tau^*,\Sigma}$ and receives $[\beta]_i$.*
     (c) P_i *computes $[C_y]_i = [y]_i + [\beta]_i$, sends C_y to $\mathcal{F}_{\mathsf{Recon}}$, and receives C_y.*
  2. **Reveal:** *After τ^*: When P_i receives (unlock, β) from $\mathcal{F}_{\mathsf{timedcoin}}^{\tau^*,\Sigma}$, it computes $y := C_y - \beta$ and outputs y.*
  3. **Early Reveal:** *If enough parties (as defined by Σ) agree to reveal the output before τ^*, then they proceed:*
     (a) P_i *sends $[\beta]_i$ to $\mathcal{F}_{\mathsf{Recon}}$ and receives β.*
     (b) P_i *computes $y := C_y - \beta$ and outputs y.*

Fig. 6. $\pi_{\mathsf{TMPC}}^{f,\tau^*}$ Timed Multi-party Computation .

Theorem 2. (Security of Protocol $\pi_{\mathsf{TMPC}}^{f,\tau^*}$). *In the $(\mathcal{F}_{\mathsf{timedcoin}}^{\tau^*,\Sigma}, \mathcal{F}_{\mathsf{SFE}})$-hybrid model, protocol $\pi_{\mathsf{TMPC}}^{f,\tau^*}$ securely implements $\mathcal{F}_{\mathsf{TMPC}}^{\tau^*,f}$.*

Proof. (Sketch). The simulator $\mathcal{S}$ depends on the simulatability of $\mathcal{F}_{\mathsf{SFE}}^{f}$ to generate a view for the computation step. The Early Reveal subprotocol can be similarly simulated. The difficulty is that $\mathcal{S}$ muust commit to a variable C_y' (in place of C_y) that hides the protocol output, and must simulate $\mathcal{F}_{\mathsf{timedcoin}}^{\tau^*,\Sigma}$ with respect to both this commitment and to the output, without knowing the output. To do this, $\mathcal{S}$ must learn the puzzle solution from the ideal functionality *a little earlier* than the honest parties, in order to provide the correct "last step" of the solution process to the adversary that forces the solving process to be consistent with the protocol output. The full proof is deferred to the full version [12].

References

1. 2021 has broken the record for zero-day hacking attacks. https://www.technologyreview.com/2021/09/23/1036140/2021-record-zero-day-hacks-reasons/, Accessed 30 Sept 2010
2. Apple delays rollout of csam detection system and child safety features. https://9to5mac.com/2021/09/03/apple-delays-csam-detection-feature/, Accessed 29 Sept 2021
3. Baum, C., David, B., Dowsley, R., Kishore, R., Nielsen, J.B., Oechsner, S.: CRAFT: composable randomness beacons and output-independent abort MPC from time. In: Public Key Cryptography (1). Lecture Notes in Computer Science, vol. 13940, pp. 439–470. Springer (2023)
4. Baum, C., David, B., Dowsley, R., Nielsen, J.B., Oechsner, S.: TARDIS: a foundation of time-lock puzzles in UC. In: Canteaut, A., Standaert, F.-X. (eds.) EUROCRYPT 2021. LNCS, vol. 12698, pp. 429–459. Springer, Cham (2021). https://doi.org/10.1007/978-3-030-77883-5_15
5. Bitansky, N., Goldwasser, S., Jain, A., Paneth, O., Vaikuntanathan, V., Waters, B.: Time-lock puzzles from randomized encodings. In: ITCS-2016
6. Boneh, D., Bonneau, J., Bünz, B., Fisch, B.: Verifiable delay functions. In: Shacham, H., Boldyreva, A. (eds.) CRYPTO 2018. LNCS, vol. 10991, pp. 757–788. Springer, Cham (2018). https://doi.org/10.1007/978-3-319-96884-1_25
7. Boneh, D., Bünz, B., Fisch, B.: A survey of two verifiable delay functions. Cryptology ePrint Archive, Report 2018/712 (2018)
8. Boneh, D., Franklin, M.K.: Efficient generation of shared RSA keys. J. ACM
9. Boneh, D., Naor, M.: Timed commitments. In: Crypto'00. p. 236–254. LNCS, Springer-Verlag, Berlin, Heidelberg (2000)
10. Canetti, R.: Universally composable security: a new paradigm for cryptographic protocols. Cryptology ePrint Archive, Report 2000/067 (2000)
11. Chvojka, P., Jager, T.: Simple, fast, efficient, and tightly-secure non-malleable non-interactive timed commitments. In: Public Key Cryptography (1). Lecture Notes in Computer Science, vol. 13940, pp. 500–529. Springer (2023)
12. Eldefrawy, K., Jakkamsetti, S., Terner, B., Yung, M.: Standard model time-lock puzzles: Defining security and constructing via composition. Cryptology ePrint Archive, Paper 2023/439 (2023). https://eprint.iacr.org/2023/439

13. Eldefrawy, K., Terner, B., Yung, M.: Composing timed cryptographic protocols: Foundations and applications. Cryptology ePrint Archive, Paper 2024/676 (2024). https://eprint.iacr.org/2024/676
14. Ephraim, N., Freitag, C., Komargodski, I., Pass, R.: Non-malleable time-lock puzzles and applications. Cryptology ePrint Archive, Report 2020/779 (2020). https://eprint.iacr.org/2020/779
15. Frankel, Y., MacKenzie, P.D., Yung, M.: Robust efficient distributed RSA-key generation. In: STOC, pp. 663–672 ACM (1998)
16. Katz, J., Loss, J., Xu, J.: On the security of time-lock puzzles and timed commitments. In: Pass, R., Pietrzak, K. (eds.) TCC 2020. LNCS, vol. 12552, pp. 390–413. Springer, Cham (2020). https://doi.org/10.1007/978-3-030-64381-2_14
17. Katz, J., Maurer, U., Tackmann, B., Zikas, V.: Universally composable synchronous computation. In: Sahai, A. (ed.) TCC 2013. LNCS, vol. 7785, pp. 477–498. Springer, Heidelberg (2013). https://doi.org/10.1007/978-3-642-36594-2_27
18. Mahmoody, M., Moran, T., Vadhan, S.: Time-lock puzzles in the random oracle model. In: Rogaway, P. (ed.) CRYPTO 2011. LNCS, vol. 6841, pp. 39–50. Springer, Heidelberg (2011). https://doi.org/10.1007/978-3-642-22792-9_3
19. Malavolta, G., Thyagarajan, S.A.K.: Homomorphic time-lock puzzles and applications. In: Boldyreva, A., Micciancio, D. (eds.) CRYPTO 2019. LNCS, vol. 11692, pp. 620–649. Springer, Cham (2019). https://doi.org/10.1007/978-3-030-26948-7_22
20. Pietrzak, K.: Simple verifiable delay functions. In: ITCS. LIPIcs, vol. 124, pp. 60:1–60:15. Schloss Dagstuhl - Leibniz-Zentrum für Informatik (2019)
21. Rivest, R.L., Shamir, A., Wagner, D.A.: Time-lock puzzles and timed-release crypto. Tech. rep. (1996)
22. Wesolowski, B.: Efficient verifiable delay functions. In: Ishai, Y., Rijmen, V. (eds.) EUROCRYPT 2019. LNCS, vol. 11478, pp. 379–407. Springer, Cham (2019). https://doi.org/10.1007/978-3-030-17659-4_13
23. Zhao, M., Yung, M.: Secure zero-day detection: wiping off the VEP trade-off. In: CYSARM@CCS, pp. 35–45. ACM (2019)

Robust and Verifiable MPC
with Applications to Linear Machine
Learning Inference

Tzu-Shen Wang[1], Jimmy Dani[1], Juan A. Garay[1($\boxtimes$)], Soamar Homsi[2],
and Nitesh Saxena[1]

[1] Department of Computer Science, Texas A&M University, College Station,
TX, USA
`{jasonwang017,danijy,garay,nsaxena}@tamu.edu`
[2] Information Assurance Branch, Information Warfare Division, Air Force Research
Laboratory/Information Directorate, Rome, NY, USA
`soamar.homsi@us.af.mil`

Abstract. In this work, we present an efficient secure multi-party computation MPC protocol that provides strong security guarantees in settings where potentially a majority of the participants may be malicious and behave arbitrarily. Our protocol achieves both *complete identifiability* and *robustness*. With complete identifiability, honest parties can detect and unanimously agree on the identity of any malicious party. Robustness allows the protocol to continue with the computation without requiring a restart, even when malicious behavior is detected. Additionally, our approach addresses the performance limitations observed in MPC protocols which also achieve strong security properties.

Finally, we benchmark our protocol on a ML-as-a-service scenario, wherein clients off-load the desired computation to the servers, and verify the computation result. Our benchmarking focuses on linear ML inference, running on various datasets.

Keywords: Secure Multi-Party Computation · Robustness and Public Verifiability · Machine Learning

1 Introduction

Outsourcing computation to cloud servers has become an invaluable practice in today's digital landscape. By off-loading intensive computational tasks to remote data centers, clients gain a cost-effective solution that eliminates the need for significant investment in hardware and software infrastructure. Instead, they can leverage the vast, on-demand computing power of the cloud to scale resources as needed. This flexibility reduces initial capital expenses and enhances operational efficiency.

The full version of this appears in the Cryptology ePrint Archive [28]. This work was supported by AFRL/RI contract number FA8750-22-2-0267.

While outsourcing to the cloud offers numerous advantages, it also introduces significant security challenges. Cloud-hosted data and applications are susceptible to risks such as data breaches, unauthorized access, and service outages. Ensuring data privacy and regulatory compliance becomes more complex when data resides on remote servers. In this work, we focus on safeguarding client data privacy of outsourced computations.

Secure multi-party computation (MPC) [3,6,16,30] is a powerful tool for enhancing the security of outsourced cloud computing. MPC enables multiple parties to jointly compute a function over their inputs while ensuring data confidentiality. This approach allows clients to securely delegate computational tasks to the cloud, protecting sensitive information from potential exposure. As a cryptographic technique, MPC is essential for mitigating the security risks associated with cloud outsourcing, by utilizing multiple service providers. However, existing MPC protocols have certain drawbacks—some lack efficiency, while others fall short in providing robust security guarantees.

In this paper we are interested in guaranteeing security even in the presence of a dishonest majority of service providers. In such a setting—MPC with a dishonest majority—protocols can be categorized into two main types:

- Protocols with common security guarantees, exemplified by efficient and widely deployed solutions like SPDZ [13]. These protocols offer security with abort, meaning that if misbehavior by a party is detected, the protocol execution is aborted. This is due to their utilization of an homomorphic MAC, which merely enables them to detect when malicious behavior happens, but not the misbehaving actor. As a result, the computation may fail to complete successfully.
- Stronger security guarantees, such as *robustness*, which guarantees that malicious parties cannot prevent the honest parties from obtaining the output of the computation, as well as *(complete) identification* of the misbehaving parties. As shown in [11], the latter can be achieved at the expense of efficiency (due to the utilization of DLOG-based commitments), or by more sophisticated, lattice-based cryptographic methods [26].

1.1   Our Contributions

In this work we enhance the approach in [26] by introducing an additional entity, namely, a *semi-honest trusted third party* (STTP, which can be the client) to achieve robustness for a number of corruptions of up to $n - 2$ parties.[1]

In [26], a tradeoff is made between privacy and robustness. With threshold t used to reconstruct shares, their protocol fails to provide robustness if there are

---

[1] Regarding the reason for dissimilar thresholds—i.e., $n - 2$ vs. $n - 1$—with a trusted dealer, we can identify every malicious server and open its share to the other servers. However, if we identify $n - 1$ malicious servers and open their shares, it would lead to the only remaining server being able to combine the $n - 1$ servers' shares and its own share to recover the input. This is a situation we wish to avoid; therefore, we "degrade" our guarantees to security with abort.

more than $n - t$ malicious parties, and fails to provide privacy if there are more than t malicious parties. In contrast, our protocol achieves privacy if there is at least one honest party, and achieves robustness when there are at least 2 honest party. Moreover, our protocol does not need to restart the circuit evaluation when malicious behaviors are detected, which we achieve by means of homomorphic encryption. Further, we propose an optimistic approach: If there is no malicious behavior, then the recovery process involving the STTP and "heavy" cryptographic primitives (such as homomorphic encryption) do not need to be executed. We showcase the performance of our protocol by benchmarking it on a modified neural network Network-A [18,23,26], which consists of a sequence of *dense* and *square* layers. In more detail, a *neuron* in the dense layer includes a weighted sum of all previous layers (or the input in case of the first layer), and it captures how much influence of each value from previous layers should be considered (in other word, we modify the non-linear layer in Network A to square operations, just as in [26]). On the other hand, the square layer adds non-linearity to the output of the dense layer. Our implementation only supports linear operation, therefore, for multiplications, we utilize Beaver triples [2]. Further, we benchmark our protocol on a concrete linear ML application.

Our MPC protocol operates over polynomial rings, batch processing of multiple inputs is inherently enabled, as these rings can be decomposed into multiple slots, with each slot encoding an input (cf. [15]).

1.2   Related Work

Our work ensures public verifiability, complete identifiability, and robustness in the presence of a dishonest majority. Related works along the SPDZ line of work (e.g., [13,18–20]), improve the efficiency of the online/offline computation phase, while still only achieving security with abort.

Other related work, such as [27] also utilize a bulletin board, enabling public verifiability. Third parties use the information published on the bulletin board to verify the correctness of the computation.

Regarding security with identifiable abort, there are also works that enable honest parties to detect malicious behavior and identify the corresponding parties, such as [26]. The protocol in [26], however, only provides robustness when there is an honest majority; otherwise, privacy will be violated. In contrast, by adding an STTP, our protocol provides robustness even under a dishonest majority and enables honest parties to recover shares held by the malicious party without having to restart the protocol.

In addition, the presence of an STTP allows us to achieve fairness even in the presence of a dishonest majority. Specifically, if a malicious party refuses to open its secret share, the STTP and an arbitrary honest party can pool their shares and reconstruct it. Thus, a dishonest party cannot abort with an advantage. In contrast, if in the protocol in [26] there is a dishonest majority, those parties can learn the secret share themselves and from that point on refuse to participate in the protocol.

Similarly, the protocol in [12] also relies on a trusted party to achieve robustness without sacrificing privacy. However, their protocol assumes that only 1 out of the 4 servers is malicious.

Finally, the protocol in [7] also recovers from faulty behavior without restarting. That protocol, however, consists of multiple committees, which is a setting incomparable to ours; moreover, it requires an honest majority for all committees

2 Preliminaries

2.1 System Model

As it is customary, we model protocol participants as probabilistic polynomial-time Turing machines (ITMs) and consider the client-server model of computation with an STTP. We assume a point-to-point synchronous communication network, a public-key infrastructure (PKI), and a bulletin board (for simplicity, as it can be realized from the PKI). Table 1 summarizes the notation used in our protocol descriptions. In our setting, the STTP is assumed to be semi-honest and to not collude with any of the servers. As for the malicious servers, once they are detected, they are removed from the computation.

Table 1. Summary of notation used in the paper.

Symbols	Definition
$\mathcal{C}$	A set of clients $\{C_1, ..., C_m\}$
$\mathcal{S}$	A set of servers $\{S_1, ..., S_n\}$
STTP	Semi-honest trusted third party
$\mathcal{B}$	Bulletin board (broadcast channel)
$[x]$	Secret share of value x (e.g., a client's input)
$\mathcal{P}$	Prover in ZK proof (e.g., Σ protocol)
$\mathcal{V}$	Verifier in ZK proof

2.2 Building Blocks

MPC. In secure multi-party computation (MPC) [3,16,31], n parties hold input $x_1, ..., x_n$ respectively, aiming to compute a given function $f(x_1, ..., x_n)$ privately and correctly. Below we list the basic security properties for MPC.

- *Privacy:* The parties' inputs remain private.
- *Security with abort:* All honest parties agree on abort.
- *Robustness:* The protocol always outputs a correct result regardless of the adversary $\mathcal{A}$'s behavior (also called *guaranteed output delivery*) (cf. [10,25]).
- *Complete identifiability:* When a corrupted party misbehaves, honest parties always identify and agree on the identities of the misbehaving party

Commitments. We define the commitment operation as $\mathrm{Comm}(x, r)$, where committer commits to a message x where r is the randomness used in the commitment (r also acts as part of the decommitment in the opening phase). The interface for the verification operation is given by $\mathrm{Ver}(\mathrm{Comm}, x, r)$, where the verifier takes a commitment and checks if it is consistent with the committed message x and the decommitment r. The two basic properties of a commitment scheme are as follows (cf. [17]):

- **Hiding:** $\mathrm{Comm}(x, r)$ leaks no trival info of x. An adversary $\mathcal{A}$ breaks hiding iff with non-negl probability
  1. Parameters params $\leftarrow \mathrm{Gen}(1^n)$ are generated.
  2. The adversary A is given input params, and outputs a pair of messages $m_0, m_1 \in \{0, 1\}^n$.
  3. A uniform $b \in \{0, 1\}$ is chosen, and com $\leftarrow \mathrm{Com}(m_b, r)$ is computed.
  4. The adversary A is given com and outputs a bit b'.
  5. The output of the experiment is 1 if and only if $b' = b$.
- **Binding:** An adversary $\mathcal{A}$ cannot open $\mathrm{Comm}(x, r)$ to x', except with negligible probability. $\mathcal{A}$ breaks binding iff with non-negl probability
  1. Parameters params $\leftarrow \mathrm{Gen}(1^n)$ are generated.
  2. A is given input params and outputs $(comm, m, r, m_0, r_0)$.
  3. The output of the experiment is defined to be 1 iff $m \neq m_0$ and $\mathrm{Comm}(m, r) = comm = \mathrm{Comm}(m_0, r_0)$.

In order to provide complete identifiability in our MPC scheme, committed values need to be updated as the computation proceeds. The opening server computes its share x to x' and opens it to the receiving server. With the homomorphic property, the receiving server updates the commitment $\mathrm{Comm}(x)$ to $\mathrm{Comm}(x')$, then uses $\mathrm{Comm}(x')$ to authenticate x'. By the binding property of the commitment, the authentication succeeds if and only if x' is correct. As such, we will require the commitment scheme to be linearly homomorphically updateable, satisfying the following properties:

- $\mathrm{Comm}(x_1, r_1) + \mathrm{Comm}(x_2, r_2) = \mathrm{Comm}(x_1 + x_2, r_1 + r_2)$
- $\mathrm{Comm}(x_1, r_1) + c = \mathrm{Comm}(x_1 + c, r_1)$
- $\mathrm{Comm}(x_1, r_1) * c = \mathrm{Comm}(cx_1, cr_1)$

Further, for efficiency reasons, we will be employing homomorphic lattice-based commitments [26]. Such commitments can (and will) be used to authenticate messages, in particular during the course of the computation server S_i opens a message to other servers $S \backslash S_i$; if S_i cheats, its misbehavior is identified. With the binding property, the cheating server can not be opened to a different message without getting detected.

With the homomorphic property, a server S_i can update a commitment locally to any layer of the computation circuit. Thus, when another server intends to open its share, the server S_i holds the commitment at the same circuit layer as the layer of opening. Further, due to the binding property, the decommitment verification passes if and only if the opened share is correct. Lattice-based commitments require only simple operations, such as multiplication and addition, whereas discrete log-based commitments involve costly exponentiation.

Σ *Protocols.* This building block, proposed by Cramer *et al.* [9], can be used to provide a ZK proof that both a given encryption and a Pedersen commitment correspond to the same value, say, x, without revealing x.

Σ-protocols can be realized based on lattices [21,22]. Please refer to those papers of Σ protocol for lattice-based signatures (with a similar approach for commitments) and it achieves non-interactivity via the Fiat-Shamir heuristic (cf. [21]). [26] shows that simulation proof can be constructed by allowing the simulator to generate a "fake" ZK proof, assuming a programmable random oracle (RO).

Homomorphic Encryption. To provide the robustness property in our MPC scheme, we require encryption to be homomorphic, so that the encryption can be updated along with the computation of the circuit:

- $\mathrm{Enc}(x_1) + \mathrm{Enc}(x_2) = \mathrm{Enc}(x_1 - x_2)$
- $\mathrm{Enc}(x_1) + c = \mathrm{Enc}(x_1 + c)$
- $\mathrm{Enc}(x_1) \cdot c = \mathrm{Enc}(cx_1)$

BGV Encryption. BGV encryption [4] is a fully homomorphic encryption scheme We also utilize the distributed decryption approach from [26] (see the full version for details [28].)[2]

3   Robust and Verifiable MPC

In this section, we first describe the relevant ideal functionalities and then describe how our protocol securely realizes these functionalities following the simulation paradigm (cf. [5]).

3.1   Ideal Functionalities

The ideal functionality for MPC is depicted (in the dishonest majority setting) in Fig. 1. Each party P_i provides its input in_i for circuit C, then obtains output $\mathrm{OUT} = C(in_0, in_1, ..., in_{n-1})$. Figure 2 depicts the ideal functionality for MPC with completely identifiable abort ($\mathcal{F}^f_{\mathsf{CIDA\text{-}MPC}}$); when malicious behavior

---

[2] We remark that we do not utilize additively homomorphic encryption such as Paillier's [24] because our lattice-based commitment scheme works on polynomial rings, and therefore Paillier's is not compatible. Further, we do not utilize a *leveled* BGV implementation since the ciphertexts are generated by the client and given to the online servers. Having the online servers themselves reduce the ciphertext error does not seem straightforward, and we leave it for future work.

Functionality $\mathcal{F}_{\mathsf{MPC}}^{f}$

- **INIT:** On input (init, C_f, p) from all parties (where C_f is a circuit with n inputs and one output computing f, consisting of addition and multiplication gates over Z_p)
  1. Store C_f and p
  2. Wait for $\mathcal{A}$ to provide the set $\mathcal{I}$ of adversarially controlled party indices
  3. Store OUT $:= \perp$
- **INPUT:** On input $(\mathsf{input}, P_i, in_i)$, store $(\mathsf{INPUT}, P_i, in_i)$
- **EVAL:** On input (eval) from all parties:
  1. If not all input values have been provided, output REJECT
  2. Evaluate the circuit C_f on inputs $(in_1, ..., in_n)$. When the evaluation is completed, store the resulting value as OUT
- **OUTPUT:** On input (output) from all parties:
  1. Send $(\mathsf{output\text{-}result}, \mathrm{OUT})$ to all parties P_i

---

Fig. 1. The ideal functionality for secure multi-party computation (MPC).

Functionality $\mathcal{F}_{\mathsf{CIDA\text{-}MPC}}^{f}$

- **INIT:** Same as $\mathcal{F}_{\mathsf{MPC}}^{f}$. In addition, receive and record the identity of trusted client C. Set $L_{\mathsf{cheat}} := \emptyset$.

- **INPUT, EVAL:** Same as $\mathcal{F}_{\mathsf{MPC}}^{f}$.

- **OUTPUT:** On input (output) from all parties:
  1. Send $(\mathsf{output\text{-}result}, \mathrm{OUT})$ to all adversarially controlled parties $P_i \in \mathcal{I}$.
  2. Run ABORT, waiting for each adversarially controlled party to send either $(\mathsf{abort}, \mathrm{ACCEPT})$ or $(\mathsf{abort}, \mathrm{ABORT})$.
  3. Send $(\mathsf{output\text{-}result}, \mathrm{OUT}, L_{\mathsf{cheat}})$ to all parties, where OUT may now be $\perp$
- **ABORT :** On input (abort, x_i) from an adversarial server S_i
  1. $L_{\mathsf{cheat}} := L_{\mathsf{cheat}} \cup S_i$
  2. Set OUT $:= \perp$

Fig. 2. Ideal functionality for MPC with *completely identifiable abort*.

is detected, the functionality will abort and output the identity of the misbehaving party. Combining the $\mathcal{F}_{\mathsf{CIDA\text{-}MPC}}^{f}$ approach with a "trusted dealer," robustness can be achieved for a number of corruptions of up to $n-2$ parties. (For the reason for dissimilar thresholds (i.e., $n-2$ vs. $n-1$) please refer to Sect. 1.1.) The functionality $\mathcal{F}_{\mathsf{CIDA\text{-}RV\text{-}MPC}}^{f}$ for robust MPC with public verifiability is shown in Fig. 3.

Functionality $\mathcal{F}^f_{\text{CIDA-RV-MPC}}$

- **INIT:** Same as $\mathcal{F}^f_{\text{CIDA-MPC}}$, additionally receive and record the identity of trusted client $\mathcal{T}$. Set $L_{\text{cheat}} = \emptyset$
- **INPUT:** Same as $\mathcal{F}^f_{\text{CIDA-MPC}}$
- **EVAL:** On input (eval) from all parties:
  1. If (eval) messages are not provided by more than $n-2$ parties, output REJECT
  2. If (eval) is not provided by party P_i, wait for (recover) from STTP
  3. Evaluate the circuit C_f on inputs $(in_1, ..., in_n)$. When the evaluation is completed, store the resulting value as OUT
- **OUTPUT:** Same as $\mathcal{F}^f_{\text{CIDA-MPC}}$
- **ABORT :** On input (abort, x_i) from an adversarial server S_i
  1. Add S_i to L_{cheat}
  2. If $|L_{\text{cheat}}| \geq n-1$, set OUT $= \bot$; else, wait for (recover) from STTP
- **AUDIT CESS:** On input (audit-CESS) from (audited-CESS), output (audited-CESS, L_{cheat})

Fig. 3. Ideal functionality for robust MPC with completely identifiable abort and public verifiability, run by the computing parties in the dishonest majority setting and a semi-honest STTP.

3.2 Protocol Description

At a high level, the protocol consists of an offline phase and an online phase. In the offline phase, the client generates commitment and encryption parameters (including commitment's public parameters and encryption's public/private keys) and hands them to the STTPs. Next, the client and STTP collaboratively generate input shares, along with the corresponding commitments and homomorphic encryptions. The objective is to ensure that the STTP does not possess all the input shares and their associated encryptions, but instead holds only the commitments to the input shares. After that, shares, commitments, and encryptions are distributed to the corresponding server. We call our protocol $\Pi_{\text{RV-MPC}}$, which is split into two parts: offline and online.

In the online phase, the servers are responsible for carrying out the computation. If a malicious behavior is detected by any of the servers, the server makes an accusation to STTP. STTP uses the commitment to validate the accusation; if the accusation is valid, STTP broadcasts the encryption's secret key of the accused server. Next, all the servers use the received secret key to recover the malicious share held by the accused server. We now turn to a more detailed specification of the protocol.

Offline Phase. As previously noted, the offline protocol is to compute the randomness utilized in the online phase, such as Beaver triples. In this phase, random elements rs are generated, to be used in masking inputs and distributing input shares accordingly. We note that we can also have the clients generate the public and secret key pair (pk_i, sk_i), hand sk_i to online s_i and also to STTP (to enable recovering in the online phase), for all i, and broadcast pk_i, and then have the online servers run the offline protocol from [26]. However, by letting the clients directly generate the secret shares and authentication data, the construction is simpler.

This approach simplifies security by leveraging the semi-honest assumption for STTPs and the clients, as our setting does not incur the additional complexity required in [26]. Our offline protocol simply has the clients generate the homomorphic ciphertexts, commitments and secret shares, and hand them over to the corresponding party. Due to space limitations, details are presented in the full version [28].

Online Phase. The online protocol comprises a set of servers $\mathcal{S}$ carrying out a computation without leaking the input to any of them. *CESS* stands for *commitment-enhanced secret sharing*, and was introduced in [11]. Its objective is to realize, in dishonest majority settings, *completely identifiable abort*, meaning that *all* parties that misbehave are flagged as malicious. In order to make a CESS-type protocol practical, Rivinius *et al.* [26] proposed a lattice-based commitment scheme, which only takes approximately 20x time as MP-SPDZ [13] when there are 2 servers, whereas the approach in [11] using Pedersen commitment would be roughly 800x. The protocol in [26] completely identifiability, and combining [26] with a STTP, robustness can be achieved for a number of corruptions of up to $n - 2$ parties. For the reason for dissimilar thresholds (i.e., $n - 2$ vs. $n - 1$) please refer to Sect. 1.1

The input secret-sharing phase allows the client to secret-share its input and broadcast the commitment and encryption of all inputs to the computation parties. The robust protocol's precondition is as follows: For each client input x, each server S_i holds $([x]_i, r_i, \mathrm{Comm}(x_1), \ldots, \mathrm{Comm}(x_n), \mathrm{Enc}(x_1), \ldots, \mathrm{Enc}(x_n))$. The semi-trusted third party (STTP) holds all commitments and the secret keys. Additionally, each S_i holds the Beaver triples received from the offline phase as well as the commitments of all Beaver triple shares. We describe our protocol, which achieves robustness up to $n - 2$ malicious parties in Fig. 4. Our protocol achieves a stronger security property than protocols in [11,26], which only achieve completely identifiable abort in the dishonest majority setting. Regarding the STTP, we argue that since it is semi-honest and non-colluding, then holding the secret keys without the ciphertexts does not violate privacy.

Next, we describe the optimized commitment opening protocol presented in [26]. When opening a commitment, it is intuitive to just decommit (i.e., directly send the committed message and the randomness that generates the commitment). However, directly decommitting will require the commitment scheme to be equivocal in order to prove simulation-based security [11].

The equivocation property enabled the simulator to open to any message but leads to larger parameters and worse efficiency. To get rid of the necessity of equivocation properties of the commitment scheme, the authors in [26] introduced a new commitment opening protocol: The sender makes a new commitment, committing to the same message as the original commitment. Then

Protocol $\Pi_{\text{RV-MPC}}^{on}$

— **Input secret sharing:** Client $\mathcal{C}$ intends to distribute input x. The simplest way is for $\mathcal{C}$ to generate randomness r in the offline protocol and compute secret shares. Then $\mathcal{C}$ chooses parameters for the homomorphic encryption, computes the homomorphic encryptions and lattice-based commitments, broadcasts the lattice-based commitments, sends the homomorphic encryptions to all the servers, sends each share to the corresponding server, and sends the decryption keys of the homomorphic encryption to the online STTP that monitors the online computation.

1. $\mathcal{C}$ creates a share $x_1 j = x - r + r_1 j$, and $x_k = r_k$ where $rx = \sum rx_j$ and $1 \leq j \leq n, 2 \leq k \leq r.$ (n is the number of servers)

2. $\mathcal{C}$ computes and broadcasts $\text{Enc}(sk_j, x_j)$

3. $\mathcal{C}$ computes and broadcasts $\text{Comm}(x_j)$

4. $\mathcal{C}$ sends sk_j to the online STTP

— **Preconditions:**
  - Let x_j denote the share held by server $\mathcal{S}_j$
  - All servers and the STTP hold $\text{Comm}(x_i)$, $1 \leq i \leq n$.
  - All servers hold $\text{Enc}(x_i)$ and $\text{Enc}(r_i)$, $1 \leq i \leq n$.

— **Online computation:**

1. All servers update $\text{Enc}(x_i)$ and $\text{Enc}(r_i)$ as the computation proceeds; denote the updated ciphertexts as $\text{Enc}(x_i'), \text{Enc}(r_i')$.

2. When $\mathcal{S}_k$ is identified as malicious, STTP broadcasts $\mathcal{S}_k$'s decryption key. The other servers decrypt $\text{Enc}(x_k'), \text{Enc}(r_k')$, and obtain and x_k', r_k'.

3. To recover the computation from failure, a designated server (e.g. $\mathcal{S}_0$), adds x_k to its share (e.g., $x_1' = x_1 + x_k$). Since x_k is a now a constant, all parties can locally update $\text{Comm}(x_1)$ and $\text{Enc}(x_1)$ by the homomorphic property of the commitment and encryption schemes.

4. All servers send all x_k' and r_k' of the malicious server to STTP. Denote by (x_k', r_k') sent from server S_i as (x_{ki}', r_{ki}').

5. STTP then checks if there exists inconsistency between all (x_{ki}', r_{ki}'). If there is no inconsistency, accept $x_{ki}', r_{ki}')$, and update the commitment.

6. Else, do as follows:
   1. Set $M \leftarrow \emptyset$

   2. While $(\exists\ (x_{kj}', r_{kj}')\ != (x_{ki}', r_{ki}')$:
      (a) Check the specific (x_{kj}', r_{kj}') and (x_{ki}', r_{ki}').[a]

      (b) Identify the malicious pair (x_{km}', r_{km}') with the commitment.

      (c) Ignore the malicious pair (x_{km}', r_{km}') and update $M := M \cup m$.

      (d) Accepts (x_{ki}', r_{ki}') that remain honest, and update the commitments

   3. For those $m \in M$, go back to step 3.

---

[a] This happens at most $n - 2$ times, since each check eliminates at least one party.

Fig. 4. Our robust and publicly verifiable MPC protocol (online phase).

the sender proves in zero-knowledge that the new and original commitment commit to the same message. The opening protocol in [26] only requires a programmable RO instead of an equivocal commitment. As a result, without the equivocation property, the parameters of the commitment can be much smaller, leading to improved efficiency. For more details, refer to [26].

We are able to show:

Theorem 1. $\Pi_{\mathrm{RV-MPC}}$ *realizes* $\mathcal{F}^{f}_{\mathrm{CIDA\text{-}RV\text{-}MPC}}$ *in the* $(\mathcal{F}_{\mathrm{PKI}}, \mathcal{F}_{\mathrm{CRS}})$*-hybrid model.*

Due to space limitations, the proof of the theorem can be found in the full version [28].

4   Applications and Experimental Results

4.1   Network-A Benchmark

In this section we benchmark a modified neural network Network-A [18,23] with our protocol (following the same benchmarking as in [26]). For the environment, we have three computation servers, where up to two can be malicious. In addition, we set up a STTP party to provide robustness. We use the same parameters for lattice cryptography primitives of [26], where the parameter of computation security is 40 bits. Furthermore, we calculate the size of homomorphic encryption we used with our robust approach by [1], we have BGV encryption with 350 bits.

We ran our experiments on machines with 32 GB RAM and 16 vCPUs. Below is the benchmark of our computation online run time (in seconds), compared to the SPDZ and [26] protocols. We observe that, compared to SPDZ, the running time of our protocol is about 65x (see Table 2).

Table 2. Comparison of efficiency of different protocols, benchmarking on network-A. Columns 2 and 3 represent amortized computation times.

SPDZ (LowGear)	[26]	Our protocol
$\approx 0.0036\,$s	$\approx 0.135\,$s	$\approx 0.227\,$s

Furthermore, we also show that our protocol recovers quickly when a malicious server is detected (see Table 3). Since the malicious server will be eliminated from the computation, the recovery time can be offset by having one less server in the computation. In the experiment, we show the time to recover the share from the malicious party plus the time of the computation continues with the two remaining parties is not much different compared to the three-party computation when no malicious behavior is detected.

Table 3. Time of recovery from malicious shares, recovery time plus remaining computation with two parties and run time if three party behaves honestly (All in amortized measurement).

Recovery time	Recovery time + remaining computation with two parties	Our protocol with 3 parties
≈0.096 s	≈0.211 s	≈0.227 s

4.2   ML Inference Framework

In this subsection, we first present the design of a framework for privacy-preserving machine learning (ML) inference, employing MPC protocols under malicious-dishonest majority security settings, followed by the evaluation of the lattice-based MPC protocol proposed in our study.

Framework Design. Our framework enables secure inference using a pre-trained linear model, while ensuring the confidentiality of both the model and the inference input data. The linear model is trained on publicly available data, and model parameters comprising weights (w) and biases (b), which are subsequently secret-shared among computation parties involved in MPC protocol. Similarly, inference normalized input data point(s) (x_i) are transformed into secret shares to safeguard user privacy. These secret shares are shared and distributed among computational parties, ensuring that no single computation party has access to the original data or model parameters.

Although the client holds both the data and the model, heavy computation is outsourced to MPC servers to address client resource limitations and to enable privacy-preserving computation in distributed settings. The client's local post-processing is minimal compared to the outsourced computation. The client initiates the process by sending secret shares of the data, which are to be processed, along with the secret shares of the weights and biases to the MPC servers. These servers perform linear computations, specifically computing $w \cdot x + b$, where w represents the weights, x represents the input data, and b represents the bias. This computation is performed on encrypted secret shares, ensuring the privacy of the data.

Once the MPC servers have completed the necessary computations, the results are securely transmitted back to the client in encrypted form. Upon receipt, the client decrypts these results to proceed with further data processing specific to the model used. This includes the application of activation functions and thresholding to finalize the inference process. For instances utilizing the Logistic Regression model, the decrypted output is first processed through a logistic function to map the computed values to probabilities, followed by a thresholding step to categorize these probabilities into discrete class labels.

Framework Evaluation. In this section, we define the evaluation framework to evaluate the Lattice-based MPC protocol proposed in our study. We describe the datasets, experiment settings, and metrics for validating the correctness and efficiency of the proposed MPC protocol in performing ML inferences. Additionally, we compare the performance of our Lattice-based protocol with MASCOT [19], MASCOT*[3], SPDZ2k [8], and LowGear [20] MPC protocols, all evaluated under the Malicious Dishonest Majority security setting.

Description of the Datasets. In this study, we assessed the performance of the proposed MPC protocol on the Wisconsin Breast Cancer dataset [29] and a subset of the Iris flower dataset [14].

The Wisconsin Breast Cancer dataset contains 569 instances with 30 numerical features derived from digitized images of fine needle aspirates, labeled as either benign or malignant. The Iris dataset consists of 150 samples across three Iris species, each described by four morphological features. For this study, we used only the Iris-setosa and Iris-versicolor classes to create a balanced binary classification task, selecting 30 samples per class for training and 20 per class for testing. This setup ensures balanced training and an unbiased evaluation on unseen data.

Experiment Settings. In this study, we conducted experiments to evaluate the performance of a lattice-based MPC protocol, utilizing linear ML classifier, Logistic Regression. Our experiments were performed on Amazon Web Services (AWS) Cloud Virtual Machines (VMs) under two configurations: first, with all VMs situated within the same Cloud Service Provider (CSP) to ensure uniform computational resources and network conditions; second, with each computational party hosted on different CSPs to simulate a distributed environment with varying network conditions.

The Logistic Regression model was trained using the `ml` package available in MP-SPDZ. Following the training phase, the weights and biases of these models are extracted for evaluating lattice-based MPC protocol.

Assessing Computation Correctness. To validate the correctness of computations performed by the lattice-based MPC protocol, we used Accuracy as the evaluation metric, which measures the proportion of correctly predicted instances out of the total evaluated.

In our experiments, we compared the accuracy achieved in centralized settings (evaluating plaintext data directly) with that obtained using the MPC protocol. This comparison confirmed the correctness of computations under MPC and highlighted any potential efficiency losses due to its distributed nature.

The accuracy achieved with the MPC protocol (88.33% for the Wisconsin Breast Cancer dataset and 100% for the Iris Flower dataset) matched the centralized settings. This demonstrates that our protocol performs computations correctly, maintaining high precision comparable to traditional centralized methods while ensuring secure computation.

---

[3] MASCOT* refers to the MASCOT protocol configured with multiple MACs to enhance the security parameter, making it a multiple of the prime length [18].

4.3   Comparative Analysis of MPC Protocols

We conducted a comparative analysis of MPC protocols, focusing on three key metrics: inference times, size of data exchange, and number of communication rounds. The detailed analysis for each metric is presented as follows.

Inference Time. The inference time is defined as time required to compute an output from a trained model using MPC. This performance metric is essential for assessing the efficiency of MPC protocols in privacy-preserving application.

All VMs Hosted on Same CSP: Our analysis of inference times for various Multi-Party Computation (MPC) protocols across the Iris and Breast Cancer datasets reveals no clear pattern in performance superiority except in the case of Lattice-based protocol. The MACOT, MASCOT* (mama), SPDZ2k, and LowGear protocols display closely competitive inference times on both datasets.

As shown in Table 4, the inference times observed for the Iris dataset are similar across MASCOT, MASCOT*, SPDZ2k, and LowGear protocols. The difference among these protocols is less than 0.0003 s. A similar trend is observable in the Breast Cancer Dataset.

Table 4. Inference times (in seconds) of Malicious-Dishonest Majority MPC protocols

Protocol	All the VMs hosted on same CSPs		All the VMs hosted on different CSPs	
	Iris Dataset	Breast Cancer Dataset	Iris Dataset	Breast Cancer Dataset
MASCOT	0.00260	0.00470	0.36145	0.41660
MASCOT*	0.00290	0.00510	0.36160	0.41675
SPDZ2k	0.00270	0.00490	0.36095	0.41599
LowGear	0.00280	0.00500	0.36157	0.41672
Lattice	0.01430	0.07710	0.01760	0.11070

In contrast, the Lattice-based protocol exhibits higher inference times on both datasets. However, it uniquely ensures operational continuity by allowing computations to proceed without restart in the presence of malicious behavior. Furthermore, it can detect and handle dishonest participants, guaranteeing protocol completion even under adversarial conditions. These robustness features, not offered by other protocols, make the Lattice-based approach particularly well-suited for security-critical applications.

All VMs on Different CSPs: To simulate the scenario where each computation party is located on different Cloud Service Providers (CSPs), we utilized virtual machines (VMs) on the same cloud service but deployed them in different geographic locations. Specifically, we selected three AWS regions: N. Virginia, N. California, and Ohio.

Table 4 shows inference times for the settings when all the VMs are located in different geographic locations. For both the Iris and Breast Cancer datasets, SPDZ2k achieved the lowest inference times among the traditional protocols, with MASCOT, MASCOT*, and LowGear exhibiting only marginally higher values, indicating similar computational overheads. The lattice-based protocol only runs for 0.0176 s. This shows how amortizing many instances leads to better utilization of hardware resources. With batching, multiple instances are executed upon receiving an input element, and as result there will not exist a situation where a party finishes its computation early and waits for the next message, making the batched setting more robust to network delays.

Data Exchange. For the Iris Flower Dataset, each party in the Lattice-based protocol sends 0.223 MB of data per party, resulting in global data exchange of just 0.669 MB. This significantly contrasts with the other protocols, where the global data sent ranges from 0.021928 to 0.022576 MB. Similarly, for the Wisconsin Breast Cancer Dataset, each party in the Lattice-based protocol sends 2.25 MB of data, resulting in global data exchange of just 6.75 MB. For other MPC protocols, the global data exchange for MASCOT, MASCOT*, and LowGear protocols is 0.309856 MB, and 0.31048 MB for the SPDZ2k protocol.

Number of Rounds. Table 5 shows the comparative analysis of number of rounds of various MPC protocols from Malicious Dishonest Majority security settings considered in our study. MASCOT, MASCOT* (mama), SPDZ2k, and LowGear all follow a consistent pattern, with party 1 engaging in more rounds compared to parties 2 and 3. This asymmetry is due to party 1's additional role as the coordination server, responsible for data distribution and result aggregation. In contrast, the lattice-based protocol requires substantially more rounds (specifically, 1860 for each party). However, the rounds are only due to implementation considerations. Since we batch a lot of elements in one polynomial ring, we send/open ring elements for each multiplication using Beaver triples. This is different from the SPDZ protocol, where the wait is for multiple multiplications and then they are sent in batch.

Table 5. Number of Rounds of Malicious Dishonest Majority MPC Protocols

MPC Protocol	Rounds for Iris Dataset			Rounds for Breast Cancer Dataset		
	Party 1	Party 2	Party 3	Party 1	Party 2	Party 3
MASCOT	17	13	13	21	15	15
MASCOT* (mama)	17	13	13	21	15	15
SPDZ2k	17	13	13	21	15	15
LowGear	17	13	13	21	15	15
Lattice	200	200	200	1860	1860	1860

It is important to note that when we conducted the experiments under both configurations—computation parties located in the same region and those in different regions- the only metric that exhibited variation was the inference time, which increased when computation parties were located in different regions due to the added network latency. This observation underscores that while the efficiency of the protocols in terms of data exchanged and rounds required remains unaffected by geographic distribution, the actual performance time is influenced by the network conditions between the participating parties.

4.4 Discussion

The lattice-based protocol exhibits slightly lower efficiency compared to SPDZ protocols under normal conditions. However, in scenarios involving network latency, it demonstrates greater stability due to its amortized characteristics. Combined with its enhanced security properties, the lattice-based protocol holds certain advantages over SPDZ protocols.

5 Conclusions

In this paper we implement an MPC protocol that remains robust even under a dishonest majority. Additionally, we explore the execution of batched MPC instances and demonstrate the efficiency of our protocol. An interesting direction for future work is to optimize the protocol's efficiency for specific machine learning algorithms, thereby enhancing its practicality in real-world applications.

References

1. Albrecht, M.R., Player, R., Scott, S.: On the concrete hardness of learning with errors. J. Math. Cryptol. **9**(3), 169–203 (2015). http://www.degruyter.com/view/ j/jmc.2015.9.issue-3/jmc-2015-0016/jmc-2015-0016.xml
2. Beaver, D., Goldwasser, S.: Multiparty computation with faulty majority (extended announcement). In: 30th Annual Symposium on Foundations of Computer Science, Research Triangle Park, North Carolina, USA, 30 October–1 November 1989, pp. 468–473. IEEE Computer Society (1989). https://doi.org/10.1109/SFCS.1989. 63520
3. Ben-Or, M., Goldwasser, S., Wigderson, A.: Completeness theorems for non-cryptographic fault-tolerant distributed computation (extended abstract). In: STOC 1988, pp. 1–10 (1988)
4. Brakerski, Z., Gentry, C., Vaikuntanathan, V.: (Leveled) fully homomorphic encryption without bootstrapping. ACM Trans. Comput. Theory **6**(3), 13:1–13:36 (2014). https://doi.org/10.1145/2633600
5. Canetti, R.: Universally composable security: a new paradigm for cryptographic protocols. In: 42nd Annual Symposium on Foundations of Computer Science, FOCS 2001, Las Vegas, Nevada, USA, 14–17 October 2001, pp. 136–145. IEEE Computer Society (2001). https://doi.org/10.1109/SFCS.2001.959888

6. Chaum, D., Crépeau, C., Damgård, I.: Multiparty unconditionally secure protocols (abstract). In: STOC 1988, pp. 11–19 (1988)
7. Choudhuri, A.R., Goel, A., Green, M., Jain, A., Kaptchuk, G.: Fluid MPC: secure multiparty computation with dynamic participants. In: Malkin, T., Peikert, C. (eds.) CRYPTO 2021. LNCS, vol. 12826, pp. 94–123. Springer, Cham (2021). https://doi.org/10.1007/978-3-030-84245-1_4
8. Cramer, R., Damgård, I., Escudero, D., Scholl, P., Xing, C.: SPDZ$_{2^k}$: efficient MPC mod 2^k for dishonest majority. In: Shacham, H., Boldyreva, A. (eds.) CRYPTO 2018. LNCS, vol. 10992, pp. 769–798. Springer, Cham (2018). https://doi.org/10.1007/978-3-319-96881-0_26
9. Cramer, R., Damgård, I., Schoenmakers, B.: Proofs of partial knowledge and simplified design of witness hiding protocols. In: Desmedt, Y.G. (ed.) CRYPTO 1994. LNCS, vol. 839, pp. 174–187. Springer, Heidelberg (1994). https://doi.org/10.1007/3-540-48658-5_19
10. Cramer, R., Damgård, I., Dziembowski, S., Hirt, M., Rabin, T.: Efficient multiparty computations secure against an adaptive adversary. In: Proceedings of the 17th International Conference on Theory and Application of Cryptographic Techniques, EUROCRYPT 1999, pp. 311–326. Springer, Heidelberg (1999)
11. Cunningham, R., Fuller, B., Yakoubov, S.: Catching MPC cheaters: identification and openability. In: Shikata, J. (ed.) ICITS 2017. LNCS, vol. 10681, pp. 110–134. Springer, Cham (2017). https://doi.org/10.1007/978-3-319-72089-0_7
12. Dalskov, A.P.K., Escudero, D., Keller, M.: Fantastic four: honest-majority four-party secure computation with malicious security. In: Bailey, M.D., Greenstadt, R. (eds.) 30th USENIX Security Symposium, USENIX Security 2021, 11–13 August 2021, pp. 2183–2200. USENIX Association (2021). https://www.usenix.org/conference/usenixsecurity21/presentation/dalskov
13. Damgård, I., Pastro, V., Smart, N., Zakarias, S.: Multiparty computation from somewhat homomorphic encryption. In: Safavi-Naini, R., Canetti, R. (eds.) CRYPTO 2012. LNCS, vol. 7417, pp. 643–662. Springer, Heidelberg (2012). https://doi.org/10.1007/978-3-642-32009-5_38
14. Fisher, R.A.: The use of multiple measurements in taxonomic problems. Ann. Eugen. **7**(2), 179–188 (1936)
15. Gentry, C., Halevi, S., Smart, N.P.: Homomorphic evaluation of the AES circuit. In: Safavi-Naini, R., Canetti, R. (eds.) CRYPTO 2012. LNCS, vol. 7417, pp. 850–867. Springer, Heidelberg (2012). https://doi.org/10.1007/978-3-642-32009-5_49
16. Goldreich, O., Micali, S., Wigderson, A.: How to play any mental game or A completeness theorem for protocols with honest majority. In: STOC, pp. 218–229. ACM (1987)
17. Katz, J., Lindell, Y.: Introduction to Modern Cryptography. Chapman and Hall/CRC Press (2007). http://www.cs.umd.edu/%7Ejkatz/imc.html
18. Keller, M.: MP-SPDZ: a versatile framework for multi-party computation. In: Ligatti, J., Ou, X., Katz, J., Vigna, G. (eds.) CCS 2020: 2020 ACM SIGSAC Conference on Computer and Communications Security, Virtual Event, USA, 9–13 November 2020, pp. 1575–1590. ACM (2020). https://doi.org/10.1145/3372297.3417872
19. Keller, M., Orsini, E., Scholl, P.: MASCOT: faster malicious arithmetic secure computation with oblivious transfer. In: Weippl, E.R., Katzenbeisser, S., Kruegel, C., Myers, A.C., Halevi, S. (eds.) Proceedings of the 2016 ACM SIGSAC Conference on Computer and Communications Security, Vienna, Austria, 24–28 October 2016, pp. 830–842. ACM (2016). https://doi.org/10.1145/2976749.2978357

20. Keller, M., Pastro, V., Rotaru, D.: Overdrive: making SPDZ great again. In: Nielsen, J.B., Rijmen, V. (eds.) EUROCRYPT 2018. LNCS, vol. 10822, pp. 158–189. Springer, Cham (2018). https://doi.org/10.1007/978-3-319-78372-7_6
21. Lyubashevsky, V.: Fiat-Shamir with aborts: applications to lattice and factoring-based signatures. In: Matsui, M. (ed.) ASIACRYPT 2009. LNCS, vol. 5912, pp. 598–616. Springer, Heidelberg (2009). https://doi.org/10.1007/978-3-642-10366-7_35
22. Lyubashevsky, V.: Lattice signatures without trapdoors. In: Pointcheval, D., Johansson, T. (eds.) EUROCRYPT 2012. LNCS, vol. 7237, pp. 738–755. Springer, Heidelberg (2012). https://doi.org/10.1007/978-3-642-29011-4_43
23. Mohassel, P., Zhang, Y.: Secureml: a system for scalable privacy-preserving machine learning. In: 2017 IEEE Symposium on Security and Privacy, SP 2017, San Jose, CA, USA, 22–26 May 2017, pp. 19–38. IEEE Computer Society (2017). https://doi.org/10.1109/SP.2017.12
24. Paillier, P.: Public-key cryptosystems based on composite degree residuosity classes. In: Stern, J. (ed.) EUROCRYPT 1999. LNCS, vol. 1592, pp. 223–238. Springer, Heidelberg (1999). https://doi.org/10.1007/3-540-48910-X_16
25. Rabin, T., Ben-Or, M.: Verifiable secret sharing and multiparty protocols with honest majority. In: Proceedings of the Twenty-First Annual ACM Symposium on Theory of Computing, STOC 1989, pp. 73–85. Association for Computing Machinery, New York (1989). https://doi.org/10.1145/73007.73014
26. Rivinius, M., Reisert, P., Rausch, D., Küsters, R.: Publicly accountable robust multi-party computation. In: 43rd IEEE Symposium on Security and Privacy, SP 2022, San Francisco, CA, USA, 22–26 May 2022, pp. 2430–2449. IEEE (2022). https://doi.org/10.1109/SP46214.2022.9833608
27. Scholl, P., Simkin, M., Siniscalchi, L.: Multiparty computation with covert security and public verifiability. In: Dachman-Soled, D. (ed.) 3rd Conference on Information-Theoretic Cryptography, ITC 2022, Cambridge, MA, USA, 5–7 July 2022. LIPIcs, vol. 230, pp. 8:1–8:13. Schloss Dagstuhl - Leibniz-Zentrum für Informatik (2022). https://doi.org/10.4230/LIPIcs.ITC.2022.8
28. Wang, T., Dani, J., Garay, J., Homsi, S., Saxena, N.: Robust and verifiable MPC with applications to linear machine learning inference. IACR Cryptology ePrint Archive, p. 786 (2025). https://eprint.iacr.org/2025/786
29. Wolberg, William, M.O.S.N., Street, W.: Breast Cancer Wisconsin (Diagnostic). UCI Machine Learning Repository (1995). https://doi.org/10.24432/C5DW2B
30. Yao, A.C.C.: Protocols for secure computations (extended abstract). In: FOCS, pp. 160–164. IEEE Computer Society (1982)
31. Yao, A.C.: How to generate and exchange secrets (extended abstract). In: FOCS, pp. 162–167. IEEE, Toronto, Ontario, Canada (1986)

From Adversity to Advantage: Diffusion Models for Improved Detection Under Attack

Roie Kazoom$^{(\boxtimes)}$ ⬤, Raz Birman ⬤, and Ofer Hadar ⬤

Ben Gurion University of the Negev, Beer Sheva, Israel
{roieka,birmanr}@post.bgu.ac.il, hadar@bgu.ac.il

Abstract. Adversarial patch attacks threaten the reliability of object detectors by causing severe misclassifications, especially in safety-critical environments. In this work, we propose a comprehensive defense pipeline that not only restores detection performance but also significantly improves it. Our method leverages a latent diffusion model to recover semantically coherent regions affected by adversarial patches, leading to confidence gains of +26.61% for YOLOv5 and +26.91% for YOLOv7 - exceeding the models' original predictions on clean images. In contrast to prior approaches that merely attempt restoration, we demonstrate that diffusion models can enhance object detection performance under attack, while maintaining practical efficiency with of inference time. We also present an optimized attack strategy based on EigenCAM and grid search, which identifies and targets the most vulnerable regions of the image. Experimental results show that our method consistently outperforms classical and recent defenses such as JPEG compression, spatial smoothing, SAC [17], and DIFFender [8], both in robustness and in detection confidence recovery. These findings highlight the potential of generative models not only for defense but for strengthening object detectors in adversarial scenarios.

Keywords: adversarial attacks · object detection · detection confidence · adversarial patch defense

1 Introduction

Computer vision systems have become foundational in domains such as autonomous vehicles, smart surveillance, and industrial automation. These systems rely heavily on object detectors to identify and track visual entities in real time. However, their increasing deployment has also revealed a critical vulnerability: adversarial patch attacks. In such attacks, small, deliberately crafted regions are embedded into input images to manipulate the detector's predictions-potentially leading to misclassification or failure to detect entirely [7]. These threats raise significant safety and reliability concerns in high-stakes applications (Fig. 1).

A. Akavia et al. (Eds.): CSCML 2025, LNCS 16244, pp. 104–121, 2026.
https://doi.org/10.1007/978-3-032-10759-6_7

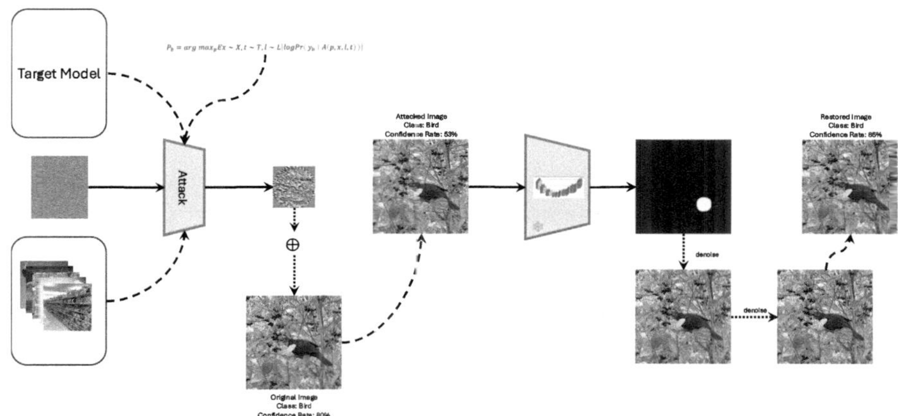

Fig. 1. Inference visualization showing original, attacked, and restored images with associated confidence rates.

To counter this, our work presents a comprehensive defense pipeline that operates on both YOLOv5 and YOLOv7-two widely used, high-performing object detection models. We explore and benchmark a range of defenses, including classical model-agnostic techniques such as JPEG compression [6] and spatial smoothing [22], and learned approaches like Segment and Complete (SAC) [17] and DIFFender [8]. In addition, we introduce a generative, diffusion-based method that not only mitigates the attack but improves the detector's performance beyond the original baseline.

Our approach combines segmentation, inpainting, and latent diffusion, forming a multimodal pipeline that detects and removes adversarial patches while preserving semantic content. Notably, we optimize patch placement using Eigen-CAM and grid search to target model-sensitive regions, improving attack success. On the defense side, we show that our method yields the highest restoration gains (up to $+26.91\%$ confidence recovery), and even outperforms the clean baseline-demonstrating that generative models can reconstruct object-relevant features better than the original input in some cases.

This work advances multimedia security by showing that diffusion models can serve not just as reconstruction tools but as confidence-enhancing mechanisms under attack. Our findings validate the potential of generative modeling in practical, real-time adversarial defense pipelines, providing a robust framework for securing object detectors across modern visual environments.

2 Related Work

Recent advances in adversarial machine learning have demonstrated the vulnerability of object detectors to visually imperceptible perturbations, particularly adversarial patch attacks. This section reviews both attack strategies and defense mechanisms, emphasizing recent developments in generative approaches and robust defense pipelines.

2.1 Adversarial Patch Attacks

Adversarial patch attacks involve placing a visually salient or camouflaged region within an image to manipulate the prediction of object detectors. Early approaches employed generative adversarial networks (GANs) to craft such patches for facial recognition spoofing [7]. Later, Liu et al. [18] explored physical-world threats in the context of UAVs (Unmanned Aerial Vehicle), introducing attacks such as Hiding, Yaw, and Obstacle patterns. Deng et al. [3] proposed style-transfer-based camouflage patches targeting remote sensing applications.

Recent work has shifted toward more naturalistic and transferable attacks. Lapid et al. [12] introduced black-box physical attacks using GAN-based manifold sampling, while Lin et al. [14] leveraged diffusion models to generate high-fidelity patches that blend seamlessly with natural image statistics. Zhou et al. [25] introduced MVPatch, which prioritizes stealth and transferability via perceptual similarity optimization. These works extend foundational surveys such as Wei et al. [21], which catalog a decade of progress in physical adversarial patch research.

2.2 Defense Mechanisms

Various defenses have been proposed to mitigate patch-based threats. Some rely on patch detection followed by suppression or restoration. Chua et al. [2] used uncertainty quantification to detect abnormal inputs, while Liu et al. [17] proposed the Segment and Complete (SAC) method, combining segmentation with shape completion to identify and remove adversarial regions. Other methods focus on deep feature analysis; Kim et al. [11] exploited internal feature energy maps to isolate perturbations, and Yang et al. [24] proposed a certified black-box approach based on patch size estimation and refinement. Moreover, [10] introduced a retrieval-augmented generation defense that dynamically retrieves semantically similar clean patches to guide inpainting of adversarial regions, significantly reducing attack success rates.

Preprocessing based methods such as JPEG compression [6] and spatial smoothing [22] offer fast, model-agnostic mitigation by filtering out high-frequency adversarial signals. Although computationally inexpensive, their effectiveness is limited against stronger attacks.

Generative defenses are emerging as a powerful alternative. DIFFender [8] combines diffusion models with text-guided patch restoration, producing high-quality reconstructions even under heavy perturbation. Similarly, DPG [23] constructs a feature subspace to neutralize adversarial influence, while Liang et al. [13] focus on local texture restoration. NutNet [16] generalizes across multiple architectures, including YOLOv7, highlighting the relevance of testing defenses on recent detectors-an aspect we also explore in this work.

2.3   Adversarial Formulations and Patch-Based Perturbations

In a standard threat model, an adversary seeks a perturbation δ constrained by $\|\delta\|_p \leq \epsilon$ to maximize the model's loss:

$$\delta^* = \arg \max_{\|\delta\|_p \leq \epsilon} \ell(f_\theta(I + \delta), y). \tag{1}$$

Patch-based attacks instead involve replacing a region using a binary mask M:

$$I' = I \odot (1 - M) + P \odot M, \tag{2}$$

where P denotes the crafted patch. This formulation bypasses norm constraints by introducing localized, high-magnitude perturbations that remain visually plausible in real-world settings.

2.4   Defense Strategies: Preprocessing and Generative Restoration

Defensive measures fall broadly into two categories: preprocessing and reconstruction. The former applies a transformation $g(\cdot)$ to suppress adversarial patterns, such as blurring or compression. A detection mechanism $D(g(I')) \in \{0, 1\}$ may then flag manipulated inputs based on feature anomalies or statistical shifts [2, 11].

Reconstruction-based methods, particularly those using diffusion, reverse a noise-injection process to regenerate clean images:

$$x_t = \sqrt{\alpha_t} x_{t-1} + \sqrt{1 - \alpha_t} \epsilon_t, \quad \epsilon_t \sim \mathcal{N}(0, I). \tag{3}$$

These methods rely on accurate patch localization [17] and benefit from conditioning mechanisms to guide denoising. Despite their robustness, generative models can struggle with generalizing to patch variations unseen during training or those placed in complex scenes.

2.5   Contributions Beyond Prior Work

While existing defenses typically aim to restore baseline detection accuracy, our diffusion-based approach improves upon the original model confidence under attack. Additionally, we present a targeted patch placement strategy that exploits model sensitivity via EigenCAM heatmaps and grid search, optimizing attack impact. By evaluating across YOLOv5 and YOLOv7, we demonstrate that our method generalizes effectively across architectures, achieving both robustness and performance gains.

3   Methodology

In this study, both YOLOv5 and YOLOv7 were selected as target models for evaluating various defense techniques against adversarial patch attacks, given their popularity, performance, and architectural differences. YOLOv5 serves as a widely used baseline in adversarial robustness studies, while YOLOv7 represents a newer, more advanced architecture offering higher accuracy and improved real-time performance. Evaluating on both models enables a broader comparison and helps assess the generalization of defense methods across different object detectors.

The attack optimization was performed using methods proposed in prior work [9], which focus on enhancing the success rate and robustness of adversarial patches. Several attacks were successfully generated and applied to both YOLOv5 and YOLOv7 pipelines following the optimized approach. Following further refinement attempts, we utilized the patch placement strategy suggested in the referenced methods, which recommended positioning the patch at the center of the object's bounding box. This strategy consistently resulted in effective attacks, aligning with other findings in the literature [17].

3.1   Patch Generation

An adversarial patch is created by defining an objective function $\mathcal{L}$, typically the cross-entropy loss, which is optimized to ensure that the image with the patch is classified as the target class t. This function often includes a regularization term to ensure that the perturbation δ added to the input image x guides the model f towards the target classification, while keeping the perturbation magnitude under control with a parameter λ. The objective can be represented as:

$$\mathcal{L}(f(x + \delta), t) + \lambda \|\delta\|_p, \tag{4}$$

where $\|\delta\|_p$ is the p-norm of the perturbation, used to regularize the patch size. Starting with an initial random patch δ, the optimization loop iteratively updates the patch by applying a gradient descent step:

$$\delta \leftarrow \delta - \eta \frac{\partial \mathcal{L}}{\partial \delta}, \tag{5}$$

where η is the learning rate. After each update, the patch values are clipped to ensure they remain within valid pixel ranges. This process is repeated until the objective function converges or a predetermined number of iterations is reached, resulting in an adversarial patch that causes the model to misclassify the object as the target [7].

3.2   Patch Optimization Using Grid Search and EigenCAM

To optimize the placement of adversarial patches in object detection, we employed two key techniques: EigenCAM [19] and grid search.

EigenCAM. EigenCAM identifies key regions that contribute most to the model's classification decision by analyzing the feature maps of the last convolutional layer. Let $I \in \mathbb{R}^{i \times j}$ denote the input image and W_L represent the weight matrix of the model at layer L. The output from this layer can be projected as:

$$O_{L=k} = W_{L=k}^{T} I \tag{6}$$

We apply singular value decomposition (SVD) on $O_{L=k}$, yielding:

$$O_{L=k} = U \Sigma V^{T} \tag{7}$$

where U, Σ, and V are the matrices containing the left singular vectors, singular values, and right singular vectors, respectively. The class activation map $L_{\text{Eigen-Cam}}$ is then derived by projecting $O_{L=k}$ onto the first eigenvector:

$$L_{\text{Eigen-Cam}} = O_{L=k} V_I \tag{8}$$

This highlights the regions most relevant to the model's decision-making process, indicating the optimal areas where adversarial patches can be placed to maximize their impact.

Grid Search. Using EigenCAM to identify key regions, we optimized the adversarial patch location with grid search. Grid search involves placing the patch at various candidate locations within the identified region and evaluating the model's response. Let $C(x, \delta)$ represent the confidence score of the model for the input image x with patch δ. For each possible location p_i, the patch is placed at location p_i, and the corresponding model confidence $C(x, \delta_{p_i})$ is computed:

$$\delta_{\text{optimal}} = \arg \min_{p_i} C(x, \delta_{p_i}) \tag{9}$$

This process iteratively evaluates all positions within the targeted region and selects the patch location p_{optimal} that minimizes the model's confidence score, thereby maximizing the adversarial impact on object detection.

By combining EigenCAM's spatial feature analysis with grid search, we ensure the patch is both strategically placed and effective at reducing the model's classification confidence [9]. Figure 2 illustrates the step-by-step process of the adversarial patch application, starting from the original image and ending with the optimized patch placement.

3.3   Adversarial Patch Attack Pipeline

The adversarial patch generation process aims to produce a localized perturbation that maximally disrupts object detection while maintaining physical plausibility. Let $I \in \mathbb{R}^{H \times W \times C}$ denote the input image, and f_θ the object detector with parameters θ. The adversarial patch $P \in \mathbb{R}^{h \times w \times C}$ is applied using a binary mask $M \in \{0, 1\}^{H \times W}$ at a specific location l within the image domain Ω.

Fig. 2. Visualization of the adversarial patch application process: (a) original image, (b) EigenCAM heatmap highlighting areas of importance, (c) heatmap with bounding box around the target object, (d) grid search overlay for optimal patch placement.

The patched image is formulated as:

$$I' = I \odot (1 - M_l) + T_l(P) \odot M_l, \tag{10}$$

where $T_l(P)$ denotes the transformation (e.g., scaling, rotation, placement) of patch P to location l, and M_l is the corresponding mask at that position.

The objective is to craft a patch that maximizes the loss $\mathcal{L}(f_\theta(I'), y)$ with respect to the ground truth label y, or in targeted settings, enforces a specific misclassification $\hat{y} \neq y$. Formally:

$$P^* = \arg\max_P \mathcal{L}(f_\theta(I \odot (1 - M_l) + T_l(P) \odot M_l), y). \tag{11}$$

Patch Placement Optimization: To identify the most effective patch location, we leverage class activation-based heatmaps. Specifically, EigenCAM is used to extract the spatial contribution of image regions to the predicted class. Given the final convolutional feature map $F \in \mathbb{R}^{k \times H' \times W'}$, EigenCAM computes the first principal component of the feature covariance:

$$\mathrm{CAM}_{\mathrm{eigen}} = \mathrm{reshape}(V_1^\top F), \tag{12}$$

where V_1 is the top eigenvector of the feature covariance matrix. The resulting heatmap highlights regions that most influence the detector's output.

Grid Search: The image is partitioned into a discrete grid $\{l_1, l_2, \ldots, l_K\}$ of candidate patch positions. For each position l_k, the patch is placed and the detector's output confidence $C(l_k) = \max_y f_\theta(I'_{l_k})$ is recorded. The optimal location l^* is selected as:

$$l^* = \arg\min_{l_k} C(l_k), \tag{13}$$

corresponding to the position where the detector confidence is minimized-indicating maximal disruption.

Patch Optimization: Once the location is fixed, the patch P is optimized via gradient ascent on the loss:

$$P \leftarrow P + \eta \cdot \frac{\partial \mathcal{L}(f_\theta(I'), y)}{\partial P}, \tag{14}$$

where η is the learning rate. To ensure image validity, the patch is clipped to valid pixel bounds after each update:

$$P \leftarrow \text{clip}(P, 0, 1). \tag{15}$$

Summary: Algorithm 1 summarizes the complete pipeline, which includes:

1. Generating initial patch P;
2. Computing EigenCAM to locate high-importance regions;
3. Applying grid search to find the optimal patch location l^*;
4. Optimizing the patch via iterative gradient updates.

This process ensures that the adversarial patch exploits model sensitivities while preserving image realism, resulting in a physically deployable and highly effective attack.

Algorithm 1. Adversarial Patch Attack using EigenCAM and Grid Search

---

Require: $I \in \mathbb{R}^{i \times j}$, t, f, δ, η, N
Ensure: $\delta_{P_{\text{optimal}}}$
 1: **Step 1: Patch Generation**
 2: $\delta \leftarrow \arg\max_{\delta} \mathbb{E}_{x \sim X, \, t \sim T} \left[\log P_r \left(y_t \mid A(p, x, t) \right) \right]$
 3: **Step 2: EigenCAM – Identify Regions**
 4: $O_{L=k} \leftarrow W_{L=k}^{T} I$
 5: $[U, \Sigma, V^T] \leftarrow \text{SVD}(O_{L=k})$
 6: $L_{\text{EigenCAM}} \leftarrow O_{L=k} V_I$
 7: Identify key regions where L_{EigenCAM} is high
 8: **Step 3: Grid Search – Optimize Patch Position**
 9: **for** p_i in candidate positions **do**
10:     Compute $c_i \leftarrow C\big(f(I + \delta)\big)$ at position p_i
11:     **if** c_i is minimized **then**
12:         $p_{\text{optimal}} \leftarrow p_i$
13:     **end if**
14: **end for**
15: **Step 4: Patch Optimization**
16: **for** $n = 1$ to N **do**
17:     $\mathcal{L} \leftarrow \mathcal{L}\big(f(I + \delta), t\big) + \lambda \|\delta\|_p$
18:     $\delta \leftarrow \delta - \eta \frac{\partial \mathcal{L}}{\partial \delta}$
19:     Clip δ to valid pixel range
20: **end for**
21: **Output: return** $\delta_{P_{\text{optimal}}}$

3.4   Defense Methods

The "Segment and Complete" (SAC) approach [17] provides an initial step in defending against adversarial patch attacks by detecting and segmenting adversarial patches. This method uses a U-Net architecture with skip connections to generate initial patch masks by identifying regions in the image that exhibit adversarial characteristics. The segmenter is trained using binary cross-entropy loss, enabling it to distinguish adversarial regions from clean areas effectively. While SAC focuses on generating accurate patch masks, these masks serve as the foundation for further processing steps, such as inpainting or diffusion-based restoration. The optimization of SAC is guided by the binary cross-entropy loss function:

$$\mathcal{L}_{\text{BCE}} = -\frac{1}{N}\sum_{i=1}^{N}\left[y_i \log(p_i) + (1-y_i)\log(1-p_i)\right], \tag{16}$$

where y_i represents the ground truth label, and p_i denotes the predicted probability for pixel i. The training data consists of both real-world and synthetic patches. To further enhance the segmenter's robustness, a self-adversarial training procedure is employed, exposing it to increasingly challenging adversarial patches. After initial segmentation, the output masks are processed through a shape completion algorithm that refines and smoothes the detected patches, resulting in a more precise delineation of the adversarial regions.

The final masks are then applied to the input images by zeroing out the corresponding pixel values, effectively removing the adversarial patches and producing a clean, masked image for subsequent object detection. Following this, an inpainting algorithm is applied to fill in the areas identified as patches, utilizing pixel information from the surrounding regions to achieve smooth and coherent restoration. We considered two inpainting methods: the first diffuses known pixel values into the masked area while preserving texture and patterns, and the second propagates image contours (isophotes) into the masked region to maintain edge continuity. In this study, the second method was employed due to its effectiveness in seamlessly blending the removed patches into the image, thereby ensuring accurate object detection.

To further enhance robustness, we incorporated a stable diffusion-based generative restoration method [4], which we refer to as "ours". This approach was applied to both YOLOv5 and YOLOv7 pipelines. The model iteratively refines a noisy latent representation of the input, denoising it through a learned reverse diffusion process. Specifically, the forward diffusion step is defined as:

$$x_t = \sqrt{\alpha_t}x_0 + \sqrt{1-\alpha_t}\epsilon, \quad \epsilon \sim \mathcal{N}(0, I), \tag{17}$$

where x_0 is the original image, x_t is the noisy image at timestep t, and α_t is a noise scaling factor. The reverse process reconstructs the clean image using a neural network f_θ trained to predict the noise:

$$x_{t-1} = \frac{1}{\sqrt{\alpha_t}}\left(x_t - \frac{1-\alpha_t}{\sqrt{1-\alpha_t}}f_\theta(x_t, t)\right) + \sqrt{1-\alpha_t}\epsilon_t. \tag{18}$$

The model operates in latent space using a variational autoencoder (VAE) [5], where the input image $x \in \mathbb{R}^{H \times W \times C}$ is encoded to a compact representation $z \in \mathbb{R}^{h \times w \times c}$. This significantly reduces computational overhead. A U-Net backbone with convolutional layers, skip connections, and self-attention layers is used to denoise z across T timesteps. Cross-attention layers optionally condition the reconstruction on text prompts t:

$$\text{Attention}(Q, K, V) = \text{softmax}\left(\frac{QK^\top}{\sqrt{d_k}}\right) V, \tag{19}$$

where Q, K, and V are derived from z and t, and d_k is the key dimension. The model is trained on LAION-5B [20], enabling high semantic fidelity and reconstruction quality, making it effective against complex patch attacks.

All defenses described above were applied to both YOLOv5 and YOLOv7, enabling comprehensive evaluation of their performance across different detection architectures. This dual-model setup provides insights into the generalizability of each defense strategy. The complete defense process, including segmentation, inpainting, and generative restoration, is outlined in Algorithm 2.

Algorithm 2. Defenses Against Adversarial Patch

Require: $I_{\text{adv}} \in \mathbb{R}^{H \times W \times C}$, D, s, f_{removal}, f_{inpaint}, f_{diffuse}
Ensure: $(\hat{y}_r, c_r), (\hat{y}_i, c_i), (\hat{y}_d, c_d)$
 1: **Step 1: Compute SAC mask**
 2: $M \leftarrow s(I_{\text{adv}})$
 3: **Step 2: Patch Removal**
 4: $I_r \leftarrow f_{\text{removal}}\big((1 - M) \odot I_{\text{adv}}\big)$
 5: $(\hat{y}_r, c_r) \leftarrow D(I_r)$
 6: **Step 3: Inpainting**
 7: $I_i \leftarrow f_{\text{inpaint}}\big((1 - M) \odot I_{\text{adv}}, M\big)$
 8: $(\hat{y}_i, c_i) \leftarrow D(I_i)$
 9: **Step 4: Diffusion**
10: $I_d^{(T)} \leftarrow I_{\text{adv}}$
11: **for** $t = T$ **downto** 1 **do**
12: $\quad I_d^{(t-1)} \leftarrow f_{\text{diffuse}}(I_d^{(t)}, t)$
13: **end for**
14: $(\hat{y}_d, c_d) \leftarrow D(I_d^{(0)})$
15: **Output: return** $(\hat{y}_r, c_r), (\hat{y}_i, c_i), (\hat{y}_d, c_d)$

As shown in Fig. 3, the attacked image successfully deceived the model into misclassifying the bear as a dog with 76% confidence. However, all defense methods effectively corrected the model's prediction to a bear. The patch removal defense restored the model's confidence to 84%, while the inpainting method achieved a confidence of 80%. The diffusion algorithm further enhanced the model's confidence to 95%, surpassing the original confidence level of 87%.

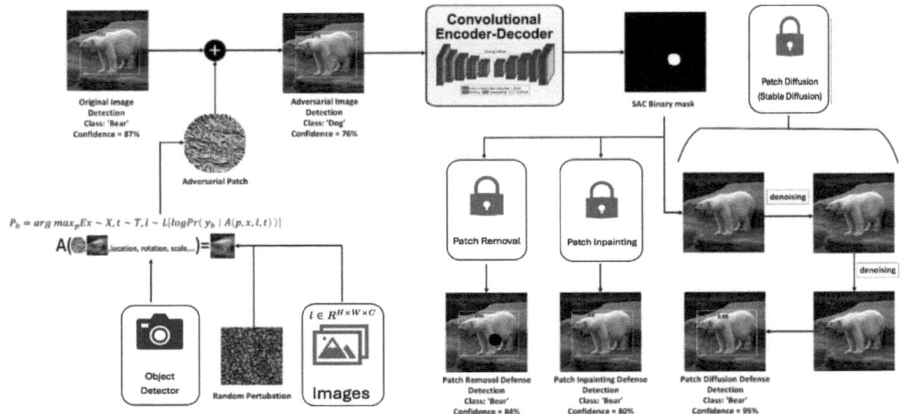

Fig. 3. The attacked image misclassified the bear as a dog with 76% confidence. Defense methods corrected the prediction, restoring confidence to 84% (patch removal), 80% (inpainting), and 95% (diffusion), surpassing the original confidence of 87%.

4   Experimental Evaluation

4.1   Models

All evaluations were conducted using the YOLOv5 object detection model, which was selected for its strong performance and widespread adoption in adversarial robustness studies. For patch segmentation, we used a U-Net architecture as implemented in the Segment and Complete (SAC) framework [17]. The diffusion-based defenses leveraged latent diffusion models trained on LAION-5B [20], while DIFFender [8] was implemented using the released open-source inference pipeline with default parameters. JPEG and spatial smoothing were applied using OpenCV with standard configurations.

4.2   Compared Approaches

We evaluated and compared the following defense methods:

- **SAC** [17]: Segmentation-based adversarial patch removal.
- **Inpainting**: Contour-based isophote image completion applied to masked regions.
- **DIFFender** [8]: Text-guided patch localization and restoration using guided diffusion.
- **JPEG Compression** [6]: Lossy compression to reduce high-frequency adversarial noise.
- **Spatial Smoothing** [22]: Non-learned defense that applies local averaging filters to suppress perturbations.

Each method was applied after an adversarial patch was added to the image, and detection performance was re-evaluated using the YOLOv5 model.

4.3   Datasets

Single-object images were chosen for this study to simplify analysis within the pipeline. Since no publicly available dataset met these requirements, a filtered version of the COCO dataset [15] was created, including only images with one salient object. This yielded a dataset of 403 images.

Additionally, a custom proprietary dataset was used for further validation. This private dataset includes two uniformly distributed classes across all samples, ensuring balance and real-world relevance. Due to privacy concerns, it cannot be published, but it played a key role in testing robustness under controlled conditions.

We also evaluated our defense pipeline using the APRICOT dataset [1], which contains real-world images of physical adversarial patch attacks. This dataset enabled us to assess the generalizability of our methods under physically realistic and unconstrained conditions.

5   Results

The analysis was conducted using a systematic approach, following these steps:

1. For each detection, a confidence score C_i was assigned based on the predicted class. If the predicted class $\hat{y}_i$ did not match the original ground truth class y_i, the confidence score was set to zero:

$$C_i = \begin{cases} c_i, & \text{if } \hat{y}_i = y_i \\ 0, & \text{if } \hat{y}_i \neq y_i \end{cases} \tag{20}$$

   where c_i is the original confidence value output by the object detection model for the i-th image.

2. The confidence values were then averaged across all images in each evaluation method. Let $\mathcal{C}^{(s)} = \{C_1, C_2, \ldots, C_N\}$ represent the set of confidence scores for a specific method s, where N is the total number of detections. The mean confidence $\bar{C}^{(s)}$ for method s is computed as:

$$\bar{C}^{(s)} = \frac{1}{N} \sum_{i=1}^{N} C_i^{(s)} \tag{21}$$

The average confidence values for the pipeline methods are summarized in Table 1. Original images had a mean confidence of 81.07%, which dropped to 63.18% after applying the adversarial patch. The SAC defense raised this to 65.98%, while inpainting significantly restored it to 79.50%, close to the original level. The diffusion defense proved the most effective, increasing confidence to 84.76%, surpassing the original value. These results indicate that the adversarial patch reduced confidence by 17.89%, SAC improved it by 2.80%, inpainting by

16.32%, and diffusion by 21.58%. Each confidence change was calculated using the formula (Table 2):

$$\frac{|Conf_{\text{average, original}} - Conf_{\text{average, ith method}}|}{Conf_{\text{average, original}}} \tag{22}$$

Table 1. Average Confidence Levels for Each Defense Method on COCO, Custom, and APRICOT Datasets (in percentages)

Method	COCO	Custom	APRICOT
Original	81.07% ± 0.5	77.83% ± 0.4	78.91% ± 0.5
Patched	63.18% ± 0.7	60.66% ± 0.6	61.94% ± 0.6
SAC	65.98% ± 0.6	63.34% ± 0.5	64.07% ± 0.4
JPEG Compression	65.34% ± 0.4	62.52% ± 0.3	61.02% ± 0.4
Spatial Smoothing	66.53% ± 0.4	63.93% ± 0.3	65.11% ± 0.3
Inpainting	79.50% ± 0.3	76.32% ± 0.3	75.61% ± 0.3
DIFFender	83.13% ± 0.2	79.85% ± 0.3	80.29% ± 0.3
Ours	**84.76% ± 0.2**	**81.37% ± 0.3**	**82.94% ± 0.2**

Table 2. Average Confidence Levels for Each Defense Method on COCO, Custom, and APRICOT Datasets Using YOLOv7 (in percentages)

Method	COCO	Custom	APRICOT
Original	91.46% ± 0.5	87.56% ± 0.4	88.17% ± 0.5
Patched	71.92% ± 0.7	68.22% ± 0.6	69.89% ± 0.6
SAC	74.69% ± 0.6	71.38% ± 0.5	71.87% ± 0.4
JPEG Compression	73.16% ± 0.4	70.21% ± 0.3	69.30% ± 0.4
Spatial Smoothing	74.92% ± 0.4	71.84% ± 0.3	72.64% ± 0.3
Inpainting	90.23% ± 0.3	85.74% ± 0.3	84.95% ± 0.3
DIFFender	93.85% ± 0.2	89.83% ± 0.3	90.10% ± 0.3
Ours	**95.12% ± 0.2**	**91.31% ± 0.3**	**92.46% ± 0.2**

5.1   Qualitative Results

To further demonstrate the effectiveness of the proposed defense methods, Fig. 4 presents qualitative examples from different stages of the defense pipeline. Each row corresponds to a different image, illustrating the visual transformation across five key steps: the original input, adversarially patched image, patch removal using SAC, inpainting, and diffusion-based restoration.

As seen in the figure, adversarial patches significantly degrade object recognition, often causing complete misclassification. SAC is able to localize and nullify these patches by masking the affected regions, producing partial restoration. Inpainting offers visually smoother results by synthesizing plausible textures and edges based on the surrounding context, making the patch invisible to both the detector and human eye.

However, the most visually and semantically accurate restorations are achieved through diffusion. By gradually refining the corrupted region in latent space, the diffusion model removes perturbations while preserving object identity and scene consistency. This is evident in the final column of Fig. 4, where the output closely matches the original image despite the presence of an earlier attack.

Together, these qualitative examples underscore the importance of layered defenses - especially the strength of generative approaches in restoring detection integrity under adversarial conditions.

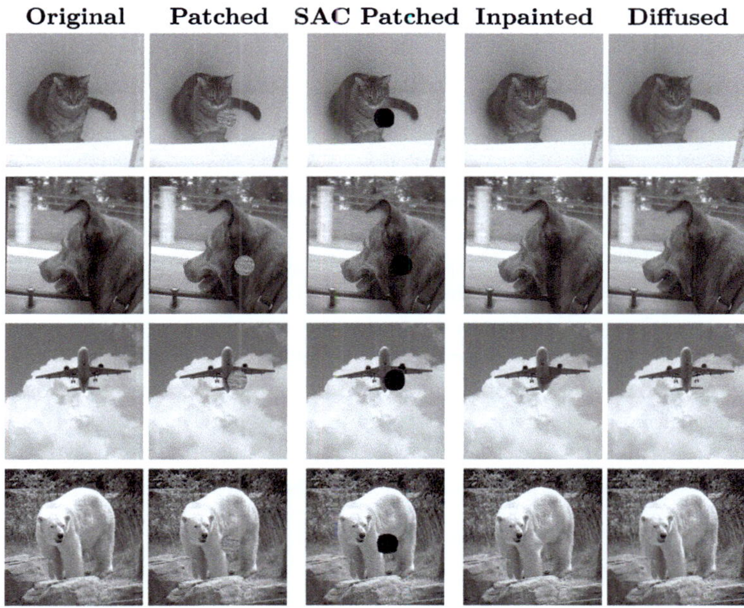

Fig. 4. Qualitative comparison of each defense step. Rows show four different examples progressing through: original, patched, SAC-masked, inpainted, and diffusion-restored versions.

6   Conclusion

The analysis indicates that the diffusion-based defense method is the most effective technique among those evaluated, as it significantly restores the confidence levels of the object detector, even surpassing the original pre-attack confidence. This finding suggests that while adversarial patches can substantially degrade the performance of object detectors, robust defense mechanisms-specifically diffusion models-can effectively counteract these attacks, enhancing detection reliability. The results underscore the potential of diffusion as a powerful tool for mitigating adversarial effects in object detection systems.

7   Future Research

Future research could explore several avenues to extend and generalize the current pipeline. One potential direction is to incorporate a more diverse range of adversarial patches, including those generated with varying hyperparameters designed to enhance attack efficacy, patches created using alternative neural network architectures, and naturalistic patches that closely mimic real-world textures and patterns. Additionally, investigating the impact of different patch geometries, such as squares, circles, or irregular shapes, could further refine the robustness and adaptability of the defense strategies.

Another important area for future work is testing the pipeline against more advanced object detectors, such as YOLOv7+, to evaluate the generalizability and effectiveness of the proposed defense mechanisms. Furthermore, extending the pipeline to handle images with multiple objects is a promising research direction, which could significantly broaden its applicability in complex real-world scenarios. This would involve developing and integrating new techniques for multi-object detection and defense, thereby enhancing the overall resilience of object detection models against adversarial attacks.

Lastly, while the segmentation model performs well, it is somewhat reliant on the similarity of patches to those in its training set. Exploring how to improve segmentation for patches that deviate more significantly from the training data could further enhance the robustness of the defense, though this limitation appears to have minimal impact in most cases.

A   Ablation Study

A.1   Inference Time vs Confidence Rate Trade-Off

In addition to evaluating defense effectiveness through detection confidence, we also measured the inference time required by each method. This analysis highlights the trade-off between computational cost and performance-a critical consideration for real-time systems such as autonomous vehicles or surveillance applications.

Figure 5a presents a comparison between average inference time (in seconds) and detection confidence rate (in percentage) for YOLOv5 using five representative defense methods: JPEG compression, spatial smoothing, Segment and Complete (SAC), DIFFender, and our proposed latent diffusion-based method Ours All inference times were measured on the same hardware and batch configuration for consistency.

Classical signal-based defenses, such as JPEG compression [6] and spatial smoothing [22], were the fastest, requiring less than one second per image, but achieved lower confidence improvements of 2.16% and 2.93%, respectively. SAC offered a modest improvement (3.45%) at a slightly higher inference time of 1.58 s. DIFFender [8], while achieving a much stronger boost in confidence (19.95%), incurred a significantly longer inference time of 7.98 s due to the additional patch localization and guided generation steps.

Our proposed method outperformed all others in terms of confidence restoration (26.61%) while maintaining a moderate inference time of 4.25 s, making it a practical and effective defense in moderately time-sensitive scenarios. The results suggest that diffusion-based models, despite their complexity, offer a promising balance between restoration quality and computational feasibility.

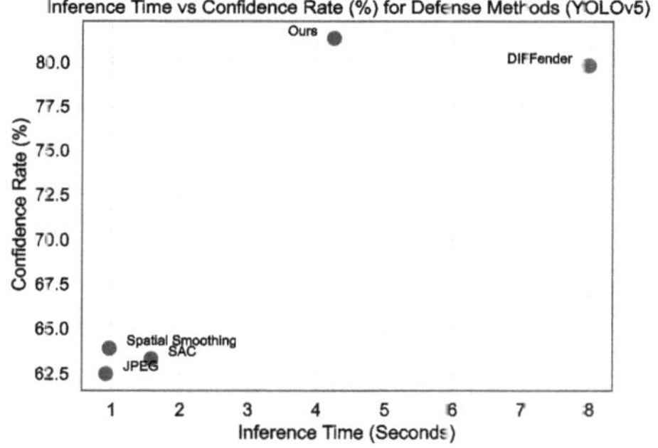

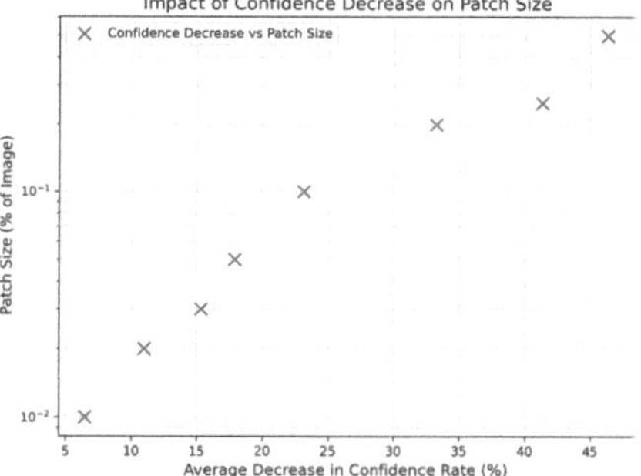

(a) Inference Time vs. Accuracy for YOLOv5 using various defense mechanisms. Our method achieves the highest accuracy with moderate inference cost.

(b) Impact of patch size on confidence reduction. X-axis: patch size (% of image, log-scale); Y-axis: mean confidence drop (%).

Fig. 5. (a) Inference time vs. accuracy; (b) Confidence drop vs. patch size.

A.2   Impact of Confidence Decrease on Patch Size

We conducted an ablation study to assess how patch shape and size influence the effectiveness of adversarial attacks. After testing several shapes, we selected one with consistent performance. We then varied patch sizes from 1% to 50% of the image area to examine their impact on object detector confidence.

As shown in Fig. 5b, larger patches caused more significant confidence drops-up to 46.31% for a 50% patch-while small patches (1%) yielded only a 6.46% reduction. However, beyond 20% in size, the marginal gains diminished, indicating an optimal patch size range of 10–20% for strong yet visually practical attacks.

Our patch generation approach builds on [9], employing saliency maps via EigenCAM and grid search to determine optimal placement. This study highlights the crucial role of patch size in designing effective and efficient adversarial examples.

References

1. Braunegg, A., et al.: Apricot: a dataset of physical adversarial attacks on object detection. arXiv preprint arXiv:1912.08166 (2020)
2. Chua, T.J., Yu, W., Liu, C., Zhao, J.: Detection of uncertainty in exceedance of threshold (duet): an adversarial patch localizer. In: IEEE/ACM International Conference on Big Data Computing, Applications and Technologies (BDCAT) (2022)
3. Deng, B., Zhang, D., Dong, F., Zhang, J., Shafiq, M., Gu, Z.: Rust-style patch: a physical and naturalistic camouflage attacks on object detector for remote sensing images. Remote Sens. **2023** (2023)
4. Dhariwal, P., Nichol, A.: Diffusion models beat GANs on image synthesis. In: Advances in Neural Information Processing Systems, vol. 34, pp. 8780–8794 (2021)
5. Doersch, C.: Tutorial on variational autoencoders. arXiv preprint arXiv:1606.05908 (2021)
6. Dziugaite, G.K., Ghahramani, Z., Roy, D.M.: A study of the effect of jpg compression on adversarial images. CoRR abs/1608.00853 (2016). https://arxiv.org/abs/1608.00853
7. Hwang, R.H., Lin, J.Y., Hsieh, S.Y., Lin, H.Y., Lin, C.L.: Adversarial patch attacks on deep-learning-based face recognition systems using generative adversarial networks. Sensors **2023** (2023)
8. Kang, C., Dong, Y., Wang, Z., Ruan, S., Su, H., Wei, X.: Diffender: diffusion-based adversarial defense against patch attacks. arXiv preprint arXiv:2306.09124 (2024)
9. Kazoom, R., Birman, R., Hadar, O.: Improving the robustness of object detection and classification AI models against adversarial patch attacks. arXiv preprint arXiv:2403.12988 (2024)
10. Kazoom, R., Lapid, R., Sipper, M., Hadar, O.: Don't lag, RAG: training-free adversarial detection using RAG (2025). https://doi.org/10.48550/arXiv.2504.04858. https://arxiv.org/abs/2504.04858
11. Kim, T., Yu, Y., Ro, Y.M.: Defending physical adversarial attack on object detection via adversarial patch-feature energy. In: Proceedings of the 30th ACM International Conference on Multimedia (2022)
12. Lapid, R., Mizrahi, E., Sipper, M.: Patch of invisibility: naturalistic physical black-box adversarial attacks on object detectors. arXiv preprint arXiv:2303.04238 (2023)
13. Liang, J., Yi, R., Chen, J., Nie, Y., Zhang, H.: Securing autonomous vehicles visual perception: adversarial patch attack and defense schemes with experimental validations. IEEE Trans. Intell. Veh. **2024** (2024)
14. Lin, S.Y., Chu, E., Lin, C.H., Chen, J.C., Wang, J.C.: Diffusion to confusion: naturalistic adversarial patch generation based on diffusion model for object detector. arXiv preprint arXiv:2307.08076 (2023)

15. Lin, T.Y., et al.: Microsoft COCO: common objects in context. In: Proceedings of the IEEE Conference on Computer Vision and Pattern Recognition (CVPR), pp. 740–755 (2015)
16. Lin, Z., Zhao, Y., Chen, K., He, J.: I don't know you, but I can catch you: Real-time defense against diverse adversarial patches for object detectors. arXiv preprint arXiv:2406.10285 (2024)
17. Liu, J., Levine, A., Lau, C.H.L., Chellappa, R., Feizi, S.: Segment and complete: defending object detectors against adversarial patch attacks with robust patch detection. In: Proceedings of the IEEE/CVF Conference on Computer Vision and Pattern Recognition (CVPR), pp. 14973–14982 (2022)
18. Liu, T., Yang, C., Liu, X., Han, R., Ma, J.: Rpau: fooling the eyes of UAVs via physical adversarial patches. IEEE Trans. Intell. Transp. Syst. **2024** (2024)
19. Muhammad, M.B., Yeasin, M.: Eigen-cam: class activation map using principal components. In: 2020 International Joint Conference on Neural Networks (IJCNN). IEEE (2020)
20. Schuhmann, C., et al.: Laion-5b: an open large-scale dataset for training next generation image-text models. In: Advances in Neural Information Processing Systems, vol. 35, pp. 25278–25294 (2022)
21. Wei, H., et al.: Physical adversarial attack meets computer vision: a decade survey. arXiv preprint arXiv:2209.15179 (2022)
22. Xu, W., Evans, D., Qi, Y.: Feature squeezing: detecting adversarial examples in deep neural networks. CoRR abs/1704.01155 (2017). https://arxiv.org/abs/1704.01155
23. Xue, Y., Wen, M., He, W., Li, W.: DPG: a model to build feature subspace against adversarial patch attack. Mach. Learn. **2024**, 1–22 (2024)
24. Yang, D., et al.: Architecture-agnostic iterative black-box certified defense against adversarial patches. arXiv preprint arXiv:2305.10929 (2023)
25. Zhou, Z., et al.: Mvpatch: more vivid patch for adversarial camouflaged attacks on object detectors in the physical world. arXiv preprint arXiv:2312.17431 (2024)

Bitcoin+: Cheap Support for Complex Spending Conditions in a UTXO Ledger

Yaron Kaner and Tal Moran[✉][iD]

Reichman University, Herzliya, Israel
`talm@runi.ac.il`

Abstract. Cryptocurrencies can be used merely to transfer value between identities, but many of the more interesting uses of cryptocurrencies require contracts, e.g., "a transfer of X coins from party S to party R is permitted only if conditions A and B hold". Bitcoin (and related cryptocurrencies) place strict limits on the language in which these conditions can be phrased. In particular, conditions have limited length and may not contain loops.

In this work, we show how to augment the Bitcoin scripting language with a single "innocuous" operation to allow us to create "meta conditions" with much more expressive power (e.g., as defined by arbitrarily-sized circuits).

We construct a protocol to compile such meta-conditions into a set of (augmented) Bitcoin transactions. We then show how to use this compiler to realize a full "meta-ledger" functionality, which we show is secure in the universal composability framework.

1 Introduction

Introduced by Satoshi Nakamoto in 2008 [12], Bitcoin is the first decentralized cryptocurrency, and still the most popular in terms of market cap and transaction volume (as measured in USD).

Bitcoin's design is based on a *transaction ledger*. Loosely, a transaction ledger accepts *transactions* as input from honest parties and outputs an ordered list of transactions (which all honest parties agree on).

Bitcoin Transactions and the UTXO Ledger. The transaction is the primary abstraction in Bitcoin; there are no separate notions of "accounts" or "balances". Instead, each Bitcoin transaction has inputs and outputs. Every transaction output (TXO) specifies an amount (in Bitcoins) and a *spending condition*, and every transaction input references a single TXO and has some additional "proof data".

A transaction output can be thought of as a "coin" whose value is the amount specified by the output. "Spending" the coin is done by publishing a new transaction whose input references the corresponding TXO. The spending condition specifies who is allowed to spend the coin.

Research supported in part by the Bar-Ilan Cyber Center.

In order to verify the validity of a transaction, nodes need to store only the set of unspent transaction outputs—the *UTXO database*, for which this type of ledger is named.

Scripts and Smart Contracts. The most common type of spending condition is verification of a signature with respect to a specific public key: an input can spend such a TXO if its proof data contains a valid signature (under the corresponding public key) of the spending transaction's ID (a collision-resistant hash of the spending transaction).

While signature verification is sufficient for simple transfer of funds, one of the innovations introduced by Bitcoin is a *scripting language* for specifying output conditions. This allows a novel use of cryptocurrencies: the creation of *smart contracts*—cryptographic "boxes" that contain value and "automatically" unlock it if certain conditions are met.

Bitcoin scripting conditions can define more complex "ownership structures" (e.g., funds can be spent if any k out of n public keys sign the spending transaction), can postpone spending until some point in the future ("time-locked transactions") or even require some cryptographic puzzle to be solved before an output can be spent.

Limited Expressiveness. The Bitcoin scripting language is kept purposefully simple. A major motivation for this decision is that the cost of evaluating the spending conditions is borne by *every* Bitcoin node—every node must verify all transactions in the ledger to ensure that they are in consensus on the state of the UTXO database. This cost is offset by a *transaction fee*. However, because the fee is deducted from the spent TXOs, there is no way to charge fees for invalid transactions (which are not "allowed" to spend the TXO at all). If an expensive computation is required to determine transaction validity, this would open the door to cheap denial-of-service (DoS) attacks.

Thus, Bitcoin script is designed to ensure that the execution cost is always known and bounded. In particular, Bitcoin scripts are not Turing complete; in fact, the language does not allow loops of any kind, and scripts have bounded length. Moreover, the set of basic arithmetic operations is also quite limited.

While the existing functionality already allows for interesting use-cases, there are many for which Bitcoin's scripting language is insufficiently expressive. (One interesting example, and a motivation for this work, is the notion of secure computation "with penalties" [1,2,9], in which parties run a secure multiparty computation protocol *without* an honest majority, but with the guarantee that if the adversary aborts the computation the honest parties will be compensated financially.)

1.1 Our Contributions

This work aims to increase the expressiveness of the Bitcoin scripting language, without sacrificing the simplicity and efficiency of the UTXO ledger.

Cheap Support for Arbitrary Circuit Conditions. Our main concrete contribution is a protocol that allows a TXO to be bound to an arbitrary boolean circuit—i.e., the output can be spent only by publishing a satisfying assignment for the circuit.

The protocol relies on adding a single new opcode to the Bitcoin scripting language, one that allows a spending condition to test whether a given TXO is in the UTXO database. We refer to this opcode as OP_IS_TXO_UNSPENT, and to the Bitcoin scripting language augmented by the opcode as *Bitcoin+*.

Because executing this opcode only requires access to the existing UTXO database, in exactly the same way as testing for a double-spend, adding it to existing Bitcoin code is very simple, and it has minimal execution overhead (we verified this by modifying the Bitcoin core code to include the new opcode; this required changes to less than 40 lines of code, including additional comment lines).

In Sect. 2, we describe our compiler in detail, and prove the soundness of the construction: in a nutshell, we show that if the base UTXO ledger contains a transaction that spends the "circuit output", we can efficiently extract a satisfying assignment to the circuit. (We note that it's not enough to show that the user who claimed the output knows a satisfying assignment; many interesting uses of smart contracts rely on fact that this assignment is made public—hence the need for an efficient extractor.)

Universally Composable Overlay Ledgers. The soundness of our circuit compiler is guaranteed in a standalone setting. However, existing protocols that require complex spending conditions are often written assuming an ideal ledger functionality, and require the ledger's security to hold concurrently with other executing protocols. To allow modular use of our compiler in such protocols we formally define a generalized ideal UTXO Ledger functionality, $\mathcal{F}_{ledger}^{\mathcal{L}_{spend}}$, which is parameterized by the language in which spending conditions may be specified.

The ideal functionality preserves, in spirit, the guarantees of the simple UTXO ledger (i.e., the guarantees relied on by most high-level ledger protocols), but at the same time allows a single transaction in the "meta-ledger" (a ledger supporting a higher-level "meta" condition language) to be represented by multiple transactions in the base-ledger (a ledger in which conditions are restricted to a "base" language). Defining such a functionality turns out to be quite tricky, since some of the properties of a simple UTXO cannot be guaranteed in this setting. (In Sect. 3, we provide an overview of the challenges we faced in defining the generalized ledger functionality and the intuitions behind the relaxations we made to the simple UTXO ledger.)

Our model has similar motivations to that of Badertscher, Maurer, Tschudi and Zikas [3]. However, we focus specifically on a *UTXO* ledger, and the required relaxations to support meta (overlay) ledgers as instances of the same functionality.

To simplify the protocol descriptions and proofs, we model the ledger as a sequence of transactions, completely ignoring their grouping into *blocks*—this grouping is irrelevant for most higher-level protocols but adds complexity to the model.

We construct a protocol in the $\mathcal{F}^{\mathcal{L}}_{ledger}$-hybrid model (i.e., with access to an ideal UTXO ledger whose spending conditions may be specified in the language $\mathcal{L}$) that realizes the $\mathcal{F}^{\mathcal{L} \cup \mathcal{L}_{\mathrm{Circuit}}}_{ledger}$ ledger functionality, where $\mathcal{L}_{\mathrm{Circuit}}$ is the language of boolean circuits. Our protocol works for every "base" language $\mathcal{L}$ that is sufficiently expressive (the Bitcoin scripting language, augmented with OP_IS_-TXO_UNSPENT, is an example).

Our proof of security is in the Externalized UC model [4], where we model the clock as an external shared functionality. This allows any protocol that is secure when using the ideal ledger functionality $\mathcal{F}^{\mathcal{L} \cup \mathcal{L}_{\mathrm{Circuit}}}_{ledger}$ to be transparently "compiled" into a protocol that is secure using only the base-ledger, and composed with other protocols sharing the same global clock.

In addition to being useful in itself, and as a template for constructing other meta-ledgers, our protocol demonstrates the usefulness of our generalized ledger definition.

An overview of the UC ledger construction appears in Sect. 3.1.

1.2   Related Work

Account-Based Ledgers. The limitations of the Bitcoin scripting language have been clear from the start. One solution, exemplified by the Ethereum protocol, is to replace the UTXO model with an *account-based* system. At a very high level, the first-class object in such a system is an account. Each account has an associated value, corresponding to the funds held by the account, and a *contract*. The contract is essentially a program that accepts inputs and funds, and can send funds and inputs to other accounts as part of its execution.

A transaction in this model is a set of inputs to a specific account's contract.[1]

Ethereum's account-based model is extremely expressive—it allows contracts to be written in a Turing-complete language. However, the cost is paid in higher complexity. Since all miners in the system must execute every transaction to maintain consensus, they must all run more complex code (increasing the probability of bugs and security vulnerabilities) and expend more CPU/memory resources (leading to higher costs and more complex incentive schemes).

Both UTXO and account-based schemes are deployed today, and it does not appear that either one will supplant the other. Thus, it makes sense to study how to increase the expressiveness of UTXO-based ledgers *without* making the leap to a fully account-based scheme, with its corresponding tradeoffs.

Bitcoin Covenants. Möser, Eyal and Gün Sirer proposed extending Bitcoin script to include "covenants" [11]. This extension allows an output condition to specify constraints on the spending transaction—for example, to enforce that the spending transaction's outputs have a specific format. They show some specific

---

[1] This is a gross oversimplification of how Ethereum's account model is constructed, of course, but suffices for the purposes of comparing to the UTXO model.

use-cases allowed by covenants (such as mitigating the results of private-key theft using "vaults"). Several following works explored ways to implement covenants in different ways, and the use of covenants for additional tasks [13,15,16].

In contrast, we focus on allowing *general* computation rather than ad-hoc use-cases. Moreover, we formally prove the security of our protocols (the existing works on covenants do not include formal security proofs at all), and introduce a new, generic framework for formally analyzing overlay ledgers. (Analyzing a covenant-based overlay in this framework is an interesting open question.)

Extending UTXO. Chakravarty, Chapman, MacKenzie, Melkonian, Peyton and Wadler formalize an "Extended UTXO Model" [5], whose purpose appears very similar to that of this work: to support more expressive computation while retaining the advantages of the UTXO model. However, while the high-level goals are the same, the strategies are very different.

Our protocol focuses on building a more expressive ledger using a simpler ledger as a substrate—and in particular making a minimal change to the current Bitcoin scripting language (both in code and in runtime complexity) that would allow complex conditions to be supported. In contrast, Chakravarty et al. define a more powerful model (e.g., transaction outputs can have extra *state*, and output conditions can take into account the *contents* of the transaction that spends them), but at the cost of losing compatibility with existing UTXO-based ledgers—effectively, implementing their modifications would require a completely new ledger.

BitVM and ColliderVM. In more recent work, Linus proposed BitVM [10], which uses Bitcoin's taproot extension to emulate arbitrary circuit computation. The technique is completely different from ours, and the security of the BitVM construction relies on interactive fraud proofs. Even more recently, Kolobov, Levy and Naor proposed ColliderVM [8], which does not require interactive fraud proofs or changes to Bitcoin code, but has an incomparable security assumption (at least one of n "operators" must be honest to achieve security).

Ledger Formalizations. There are several works trying to formalize UTXO ledgers and to reconcile UTXO and account-based ledgers.

Garay, Kiayias and Leonardos gave the first formal security definitions for a blockchain ledger [6], in the context of analyzing the security of the Bitcoin protocol. Pass, Seeman and Shelat extended the analysis to a more realistic setting (with communication delays) and proposed slightly different security definitions [14]. Both of these works defined security as a set of *properties*.

Kiayias, Zhou and Zikas defined the ledger functionality for the first time as an ideal functionality in the UC framework [7], with the goal of making it usable in other higher-level protocols. However, their functionality was not realizable using existing blockchain protocols (e.g., it did not allow for a "rushing" adversary that can prevent an honest transaction from entering the state by inserting a conflicting transaction before it). Badertscher, Maurer, Tschudi and

Zikas defined a slightly weaker ideal functionality [3] that addresses these problems and is still strong enough to be useful in high-level protocols.

Our ideal functionality has the same flavor as [3], but tailored to UTXO ledger overlays.

The novelty in our definition is encapsulated in the equivalent of the "validation rules" from [3]: we carefully construct these rules to achieve a ledger that is both powerful enough to be useful, but "weak" enough to allow it to be realized as an overlay. (In particular, our ledger functionalities can be "stacked", to construct meta-meta-ledgers, etc.)

Combining UTXO and Account-Based Ledgers. Zahnentferner defines "Chimeric Ledgers" [18]. He formalizes the two types of ledgers and *translations* between them—e.g., for a given transaction in a UTXO-based ledger, what is the set of transactions in an account-based ledger that have an equivalent effect. However, this paper deals only with "accounting", explicitly ignoring "cryptographic authorization" (i.e., scripts). A follow-up paper by the same author provides definitions for UTXO ledgers with scripts [17].

Both of these papers deal with formalization rather than protocols (there are algorithms for "transforming" from one type of ledger to another, but these are external to the ledgers themselves). Their definitions are in the formal-logic style, which is useful for interfacing with automated theorem-proving tools. In contrast, our formal definitions are ideal functionalities, which are easier to use in protocol constructions, and allow us to prove the security of our protocols in the UC model.

2   Compiling Arbitrary Circuits

In this section we construct a compiler from an arbitrary boolean circuit to a sequence of Bitcoin+ transactions. The compilation guarantees that if the output of a special *keystone* transaction is spent, it is always possible to extract a satisfying assignment to the circuit.

2.1   Generic Compilation

Our generic compiler, COMP, compiles a meta-ledger transaction tx^m into a set of transactions that are valid in the underlying "base-ledger". We say that tx^m is a "meta-transaction", and call the corresponding base-ledger transactions "fragments".

We refer to output conditions that are phrased in the condition language of the base-ledger as "base-conditions", and to outputs with such conditions "base-outputs". A meta-transaction's outputs may contain output conditions that are *not* phrased in the base-ledger condition language, but are supported by the meta-ledger. We refer to such conditions as "meta-conditions" and to outputs with such conditions "meta-outputs".

We refer to input data supported by the base-ledger as "base-data", and to inputs with such data as "base-inputs". A meta-transaction's inputs may contain input data that are *not* supported by the base-ledger. We refer to such data as "meta-data", and to inputs with such conditions "meta-inputs".

2.2   Circuit Compilation

Circuit compilation is an instance of general compilation where the underlying base ledger is Bitcoin+ and the meta-ledger condition language is the language of boolean circuits. In this meta-ledger, a meta-output condition is a boolean circuit (of arbitrary size), and the data of a meta-input is an assignment to the inputs of a boolean circuit.

More concretely, let C be an arbitrary circuit, and let tx_C^m be a transaction with a meta-output txo_C^m whose condition is C. In Sect. 2.3 we construct a compiler that takes as input such a transaction and outputs a sequence of base fragment transactions $fragments_C$. Among them is the keystone $tx_{C-keystone}$— a special, final, fragment transaction whose output will be spendable only by publishing a satisfying assignment for C.

In Sect. 2.4, we show the completeness of our compiler. That is, let C be an arbitrary boolean circuit and A an assignment that satisfies C, with corresponding meta-transactions txo_C^m and tx_A^m (that "meta-spends" txo_C^m using assignment A). Then the output of the compiler on txo_C^m is a set of valid Bitcoin+ transactions, and the output of the compiler on tx_A^m is a set of Bitcoin+ transactions that are valid if the txo_C^m fragments were published in the Bitcoin+ ledger. Moreover, among the tx_A^m fragments is the keystone transaction $tx_{A-keystone}$ that will successfully spend the output of $tx_{C-keystone}$.

Section 2.5 proves the main soundness guarantee achieved by our circuit compiler: if $fragments_C$ and $tx_{C-keystone}$ are compiled and published using the methods described in Sect. 2.3, and the output of $tx_{C-keystone}$ is successfully spent in the base-ledger, it is always possible to extract a satisfying assignment for C.

For simplicity, we restrict the discussion to meta-transactions with either a single meta-input and a single base-output, or a single base-input and single meta-output (our techniques extend to more complex transactions in a straight-forward way).

We note that the compiler described in this section does not, by itself, realize a composable ideal ledger functionality. In Sect. 3 we explain how it can be used to construct such a ledger, as a component in a generic ledger protocol.

2.3   Compiling a Circuit Spending Condition

Consider transaction $tx_{circuit}^m$ shown in Sect. 1 whose single meta output $txo_{circuit}^m$'s condition is the circuit "$(a \wedge \neg b) \vee c = \textbf{true}$". This is a toy example— by using this example we will see how to implement a circuit of any size with any boolean gate.

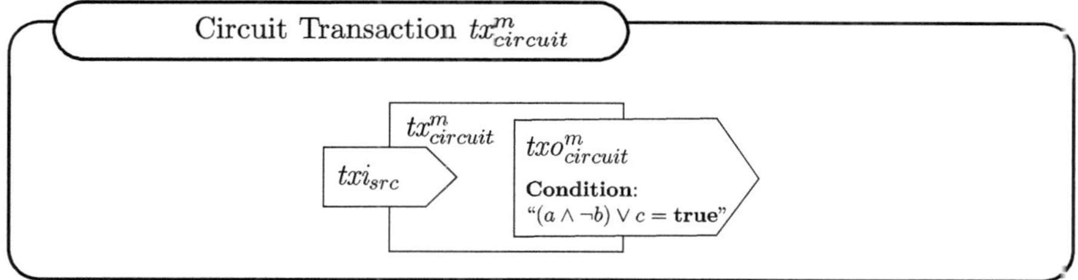

Fig. 1. Circuit Transaction $tx_{circuit}^m$

Component Transactions. The compilation of a transaction such as $tx_{circuit}^m$ yields three types of base fragment transactions: *input-bit transactions* and *gate transactions* corresponding to the circuit's input-bits and logical gates and *splitter transactions* that are used to fund the former two types.

The fragments of $tx_{circuit}^m$ are shown in Fig. 2: tx_a, tx_b and tx_c, tx_x and tx_y and $tx_{splitter}$. To reduce verbiage, we will say x is a *component* if x is an input-bit or a gate.

Input-bit Transactions. An input-bit transaction is created for each input-bit (tx_a, tx_b and tx_c in Fig. 2 correspond to input-bits a, b and c). An input-bit transaction, like any other transaction, should have at least one transaction input, and contain a transaction fee, made up of the difference between incoming and outgoing coins. Each input-bit transaction has two outputs, one for each boolean value (txo_{a+}, txo_{a-}, txo_{b+} and txo_{b-} and txo_{c+} and txo_{c-} in Fig. 2).

Gate Transactions. A gate transaction is created for each internal boolean gate (tx_x and tx_y in Fig. 2 correspond to the AND and OR gates respectively). Like an input-bit transaction, each gate transaction has at least one input and two outputs, one for each boolean value (txo_{x+} and txo_{x-} and txo_{y+} and txo_{y-} in Fig. 2).

Output Amounts. The positive output of the circuit-keystone (txo_{y+} in Fig. 2) holds the reward (takes its output amount from $txo_{circuit}^m$). The amounts of all fragment outputs can set to the minimum allowed by Bitcoin.

Splitter Transactions. Fragment transaction fees should be covered by the transaction fee of $tx_{circuit}^m$ ($tx_{circuit}^m$'s fee is split between the component transactions). A splitter transaction is created ($tx_{splitter}$ in Fig. 2) to claim the output referenced by the $tx_{circuit}^m$ and distribute the coins between the component transactions.[2] It should have an output for each funded component transaction. Funding should cover transaction fees and the reward.

---

[2] The splitter isn't strictly necessary for the standalone compiler—in the standalone setting each fragment could potentially be funded separately—but is used to maintain the transaction semantics when building a composable meta-ledger.

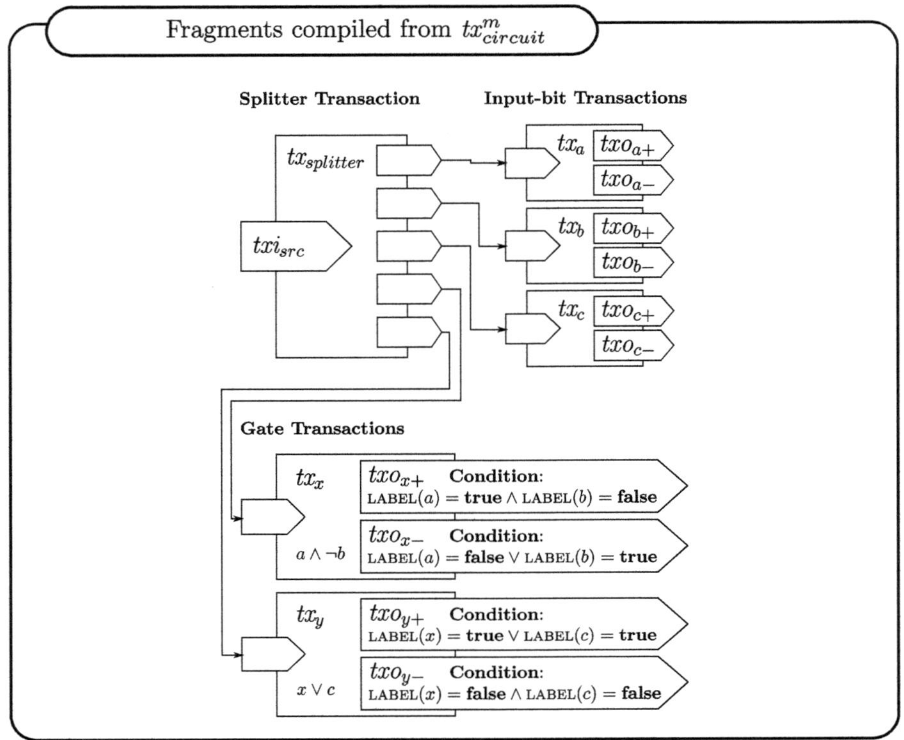

Fig. 2. Fragments compiled from $tx^m_{circuit}$

To simplify the description below, we assume a single splitter transaction suffices; however, the compiler can easily be extended to the case where the number of components is larger than the maximum number of outputs the ledger allows per transaction. If this occurs, the compiler uses a tree of transactions to get to the required output count. In this case, the root of the tree is the splitter transaction. It has one output reserved for the circuit keystone, and the rest for the transactions that comprise the internal nodes of the tree. All internal nodes have one input (spending one of their parent's outputs) and the maximal number of outputs allowed by the underlying ledger. The leaf nodes' outputs are spent by the other component transactions.

Wiring the Gates

Labels. Recall that for each component (e.g., x) a transaction is created (tx_x) with two outputs, a positive and a negative (txo_{x+} and txo_{x-}). These outputs are used to label each circuit wire with a value. In addition to **true** and **false**, the label value may be **unset**. We denote LABEL(x) the label of x's output wire.

Ideally we'd like the label to be defined as:

$$\text{LABEL}(x) = \begin{cases} \textbf{true} & \text{if } tx_{x+} \text{ is spent} \\ \textbf{false} & \text{if } tx_{x-} \text{ is spent} \\ \textbf{unset} & \textit{otherwise} \end{cases}$$

However, as we explain in Sect. 2.3, the actual computation is a little trickier, since even in Bitcoin+, we can't directly determine whether an output is spent. Note that the label of a component is a function of the transaction ledger state (it can change as new transactions are appended to the ledger).

Gate Output Conditions. Each circuit gate computes a Boolean function of its (two) inputs. Let tx_g be gate g's transaction and $f_g(\cdot, \cdot)$ its Boolean function. Denote a, b the inputs of g and tx_a and tx_b their corresponding transactions. We would like to phrase the conditions of g's outputs, txo_{g+} and txo_{g-}, using LABEL(a) and LABEL(b). txo_{g+}'s condition should enforce that $f_g(a, b) = \textbf{true}$ and txo_{g-} should enforce that $f_g(a, b) = \textbf{false}$.

Note that while a and b are Boolean, the *labels* of a and b can also be unset. Thus, to specify the condition for txo_{g+} we extend f_g to f'_g : $\{\textbf{true}, \textbf{false}, \textbf{unset}\} \mapsto \{\textbf{true}, \textbf{false}, \textbf{unset}\}$ such that for all Boolean a, b it holds that $f'_g(a, b) = f_g(a, b)$ and if $f'_g(a, b) \neq \textbf{unset}$ then every Boolean assignment a', b' that is consistent with a, b (e.g., $a' = a$ unless $a' = \textbf{unset}$) satisfies $f_g(c', b') = f'_g(a, b)$.

For example, if $f_g : (a, b) = \neg(a \wedge b)$ is the NAND gate, then we can use:

$$f'_g(a, b) = \begin{cases} \textbf{true} & \text{if a=}\textbf{false}\text{ or b=}\textbf{false} \\ \textbf{false} & \text{if a=}\textbf{true}\text{ and b=}\textbf{true} \\ \textbf{unset} & \textit{otherwise} \end{cases}$$

The condition checked by txo_{g+} is that $f'_g(\text{LABEL}(a), \text{LABEL}(b)) = \textbf{true}$, and the corresponding condition for txo_{g-} is $f'_g(\text{LABEL}(a), \text{LABEL}(b)) = \textbf{false}$.

Computing Labels in Bitcoin+. In order to implement the gate conditions as described in Sect. 2.3, the LABEL must be expressible in the base-ledger's condition language.

Bitcoin's current scripting language is not sufficient for this purpose. We propose to address this by augmenting the Bitcoin scripting language with a single new opcode, `OP_IS_TXO_UNSPENT` (creating the extended language Bitcoin+). `OP_IS_TXO_UNSPENT` accepts the ID of an output and returns **true** iff the TXO is present in the UTXO database, i.e. unspent. More concretely, it pops the ID of the transaction and then the index of the output from the stack and pushes the result back. We will use a shorter syntax in this work, denoting IS–TXO-UNSPENT(txo) the result of the computation above with respect to TXO txo.

Querying whether a TXO is *spent* may seem more natural. We chose `OP_IS_TXO_UNSPENT` because it is straightforward to implement given the UTXO

database that is already maintained by Bitcoin nodes. Note that in itself, OP_-
IS_TXO_UNSPENT doesn't answer whether an output is *spent*; a transaction output
that was never published would return the same result as one that was published
and then spent.

To bridge this gap we use the fact that outputs of a transaction enter the
Bitcoin ledger atomically. Recall that our ideal computation of LABELx results
in **true** if txo_{x_+} is spent and **false** if value only if txo_{x_-} is spent.

In Bitcoin+ we can implement this logic in the following way:

$$
\text{LABEL}x = \begin{cases}
\textbf{true} & \text{if } \neg\text{IS-TXO-UNSPENT}(txo_{x_+}) \wedge \text{IS-TXO-UNSPENT}(txo_{x_-}) \\
\textbf{false} & \text{if } \text{IS-TXO-UNSPENT}(txo_{x_+}) \wedge \neg\text{IS-TXO-UNSPENT}(txo_{x_-}) \\
\textbf{unset} & \textit{otherwise}
\end{cases}
$$

A Boolean value is returned if exactly one of·the outputs txo_{x_+} or txo_{x_-} is
unspent. In this case, we can conclude that the other output *must* have been
spent, since both outputs entered the UTXO together. The drawback of this
method of computing the label is loss of monotonicity: a label that was previously
set can later become unset. This doesn't have a big practical impact, but does
make our soundness proof slightly more complex.

Loss of Atomicity and Publishing Considerations. Since we use several
transactions to implement $tx^m_{circuit}$ and their insertion into the ledger is not
atomic, an attacker may try to "hijack" the insertion while it is happening. For
example, the attacker might claim an output of a splitter transaction that is
intended to fund one of the gate transactions, rendering the sender unable to
complete the insertion. To prevent this attack, in addition to the gate condition
described above, the spending condition for internal TXOs verifies a signature
with respect to a freshly generated signature key.

Component transactions spend splitter TXOs, and so the splitter transaction
must be published first in order for subsequent transactions to be included in
the ledger.

Efficiency and Optimizations. Since the compilation creates a transaction
for each component, as the circuit grows larger, the total fee required to publish
the transactions grows.

Our compiler emphasizes simplicity and clarity over efficiency—it is not optimized to use the smallest number of transactions. However, we briefly mention
some strategies to lower the transaction count.

For example, it is possible to group the outputs of the input-bit transactions
to fewer transactions. Grouping outputs of gate transactions is also possible, but
more tricky—a condition of one such output may need to query about the label
of an output that is part of the same transaction, and it is not trivial to expect
the ledger to provide this ability (this is impossible in Bitcoin, for example). It
is possible, however, to merge transactions for gates of the same circuit depth,
as they do not reference one another.

The described construction creates one transaction per gate. Another possible optimization is to build transactions for sub-circuits, or allow gates of fan-in larger than two (making each transaction reference more than two inputs).

2.4 Completeness: Compiling an Assignment

Consider $tx^m_{assignment}$ shown in Fig. 3. Its single meta input $txi^m_{assignment}$ specifies $txo^m_{circuit}$ (Fig. 1 in Sect. 2.3), an output of a circuit transaction, as the targeted output. $txi^m_{assignment}$ provides an assignment of boolean values to the input-bits of the circuit: $(a, b, c) \leftarrow (\textbf{true}, \textbf{false}, \textbf{false})$.

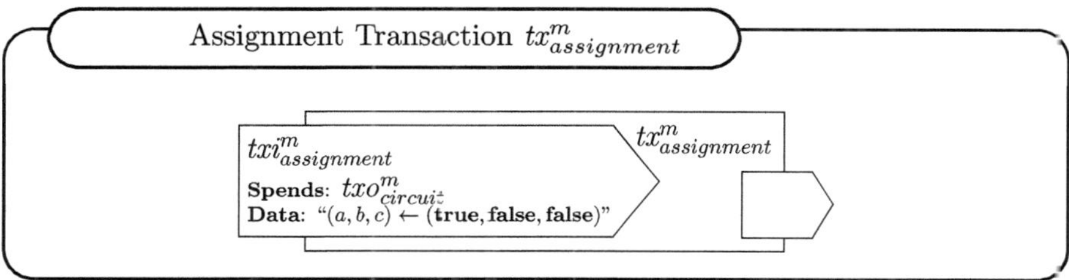

Fig. 3. Assignment Transaction $tx^m_{assignment}$

Component-Labeling Transactions. The compilation of a transaction such as $tx^m_{assignment}$ yields two types of base fragment transactions: *input-bit-labeling transactions* and *gate-labeling transactions*, corresponding to the circuit's input-bits and the circuit's logical gates respectively.

The fragments of $tx^m_{assignment}$ are shown in Fig. 4.

Input-Bit-Labeling Transactions. Input-bit transactions (tx_a, tx_b and tx_c in Fig. 2) have two outputs each, one positive and one negative. Input-bit-*labeling* transactions implement assignment to the input bits. Each input-bit-labeling transaction spends one of the input-bit transaction outputs, according to the assigment's value for that bit.

For example, $tx_{a \leftarrow \textbf{true}}$, $tx_{b \leftarrow \textbf{false}}$ and $tx_{c \leftarrow \textbf{false}}$ in Fig. 4 correspond to the assignments $a \leftarrow \textbf{true}$, $b \leftarrow \textbf{false}$ and $c \leftarrow \textbf{false}$).

Gate-Labeling Transactions. Gate-labeling transactions "evaluate" the circuit given the assignment. One transaction is created per gate. A gate-labeling transaction spends one of the outputs of its corresponding gate transaction, according to the gate values that are computed from the assignment. For example, the transactions $tx_{x \leftarrow \textbf{true}}$, $tx_{y \leftarrow \textbf{true}}$ in Fig. 4 correspond to $x = \textbf{true} = (a \wedge \neg b)$ and $y = \textbf{true} = (x \vee c)$, for the gate transactions tx_x and tx_y in Fig. 2.

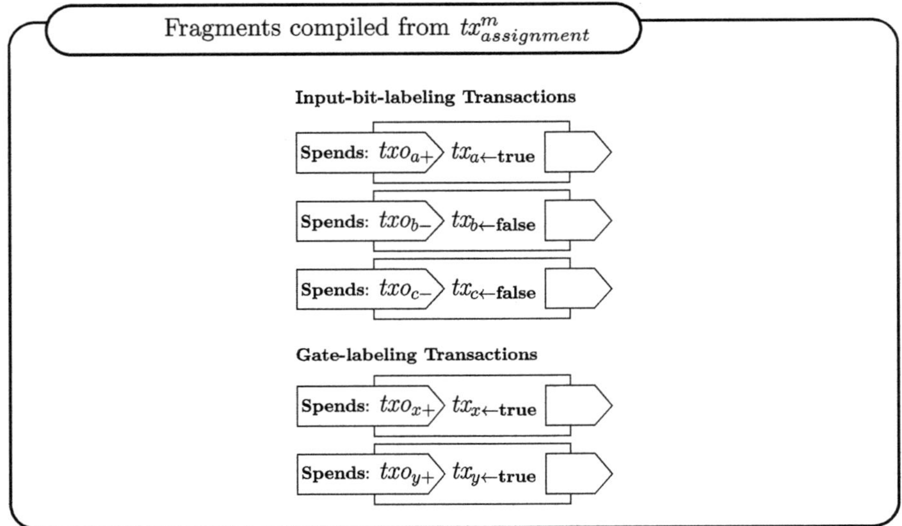

Fig. 4. Fragments compiled from $tx^m_{assignment}$

Assignment-Keystone Transaction. The assignment keystone is the gate-labeling transaction whose input spends the positive output of circuit keystone. Figure 4's $tx_{y\leftarrow\mathbf{true}}$ is therefore the assignment keystone since it spends the output Fig.2's circuit keystone txo_{y+}. Its output will be identical to $tx^m_{assignment}$'s output. Transaction fees of labeling transactions should come from the outputs they claim.

Publishing Considerations. Labeling can't be done in an arbitrary order; the conditions of the gate TXOs impose certain limitations on the order of publishing. To label a gate, it is required that its two inputs (whether input-bits or other gates) are labeled first.

Since funding is taken from the TXOs of the compiled input-bit and gate transactions, each labeling transaction needs to be published after its corresponding gate transaction.

2.5   Soundness: Extracting a Satisfying Assignment

The soundness requirement from our circuit compiler is that the output of the circuit keystone cannot be spent unless a satisfying assignment is published to the ledger. Formally, we require the existence of an extraction algorithm that, given a ledger in which the $tx_{C-keystone}$ is spent, can output a satisfying assignment for C.

Essentially, the extractor finds the input-bit transactions by traversing the DAG rooted at the circuit-keystone transaction, and by observing state of the ledger can recover the labels of the input-bits. The proof of security is by induction on the depth of the circuit.

Due to space constraints, the details appear in the full version of the paper.

3   The Meta Ledger

One of the contributions of this paper is a new, formal definition for an ideal ledger functionality. Our motivation for the new definition is twofold. On the one hand, it should be *useful*, conforming to the intuitive notions of security we expect from a UTXO ledger, and simple enough to use in higher-level protocols. At the same time, it should be flexible enough to capture the functionality and security of a "meta-ledger" that is realized as a protocol overlaying a "base" ledger.

3.1   Generically Realizing a Meta-ledger: Overview

Our protocol realizes the *meta-ledger*, so a party running it should first and foremost be able to *send meta-transactions*. The protocol realizes the meta-ledger over a base-ledger that does not recognize meta-transactions. Hence its logic can be divided into two main complementary categories:

- Compilation of meta-transactions to base-transactions and sending thereof to the base-ledger and
- Identifying these base-transactions as they are published by the base-ledger and the decompilation back to meta-transactions.

The output of an honest party running the protocol will differ from the output of the base-ledger, as some transactions published by the base-ledger will be modified before being output—the most notable modification is the replacing of fragment base-transactions with meta-transactions.

Abstracting the Compilation/Decompilation of Meta-transactions. The protocol is parameterized by a compiler/decompiler pair, (COMP, DECOMP). Given a meta-transaction tx^m, the current meta-ledger output and the base-ledger output, COMP will compile tx^m into a sequence of base-transaction sets (the fragments), whose order indicates the order in which they should be sent. Given a base-transaction, the meta-ledger output and the base-ledger output, DECOMP will attempt to reconstruct a meta-transaction.

The protocol works for any (COMP, DECOMP) pair satisfying some basic requirements. When instantiated with our compiler/decompiler, COMP^{Circuit} and DECOMP^{Circuit}, it realizes the meta-ledger with circuit-spending conditions.

Compilation/Decompilation Example. In Fig. 5 we give an example of compiling and decompiling two complementary meta-transactions that can be given as input to an honest party running the protocol instantiated with COMP^{Circuit} and DECOMP^{Circuit} (whose formal description appears in the full version). The figure is structured as follows:

– Column "Circuit" is dedicated to $tx^m_{circuit}$, whose output $txo^m_{circuit}$ contains circuit condition "$\neg(a \wedge b) = \textbf{true}$".
– Column "Source" is dedicated to tx_{src} whose output txo_{src} is spent by $tx^m_{circuit}$.
– Column "Assignment" is dedicated to tx^m_{assign}, whose input txi^{im}_{assign} contains assignment data "$a \rightarrow \textbf{true}, b \rightarrow \textbf{false}$".
– Row "Honest Input" shows the transaction as it is given by the environment to the honest party to send.
– Row "COMP output to Base-Ledger" shows the fragments that are the output of COMP and that are sent in the real-world.
– Row "DECOMP output to Meta-Ledger" shows the output of the honest party and DECOMP.

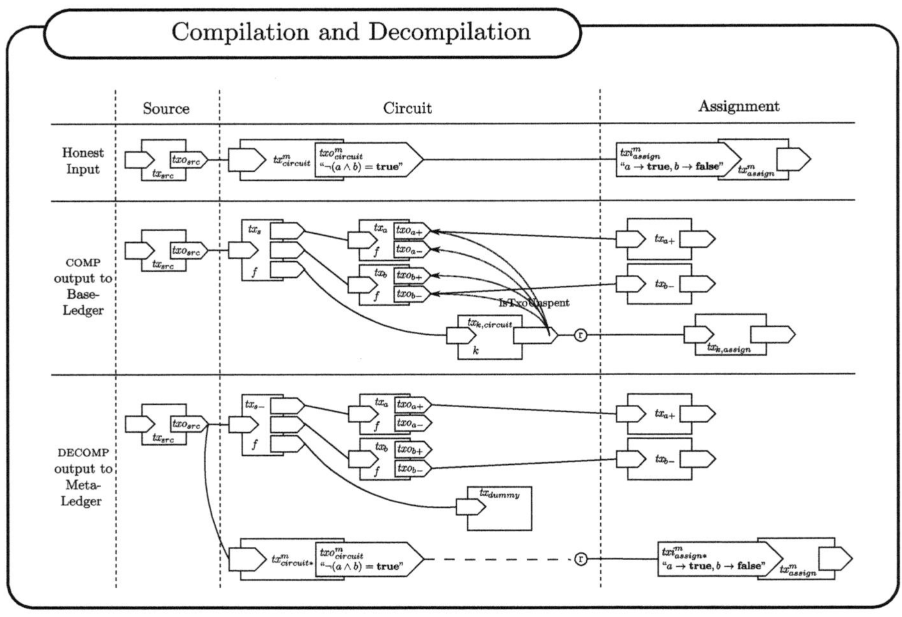

Fig. 5. Compilation and Decompilation

3.2   Challenges in Defining a Meta-ledger

Our goal is to realize a meta-ledger functionality with a richer condition language by compiling meta-transactions to multiple transactions on a base-ledger. Ideally, we would like to simply realize a functionality identical to the Bitcoin ledger. Unfortunately, this is not always possible. Below, we describe some of the challenges in doing so.

Spending Is Not Atomic. In the Bitcoin ledger functionality, once a TXO enters the UTXO database, it can only be in one of two states: either it is (1) unspent (in the UTXO), in which case a transaction whose input points to that output and satisfies its condition is valid, or (2) it is spent—in which case the ledger contains a subsequent transaction that spends the output (and hence contains data that satisfies its spending condition).

However, if we compile a meta-transaction to multiple base-transactions using the `OP_IS_TXO_UNSPENT` opcode, in order to satisfy the spending condition of the meta output a user might have to publish multiple fragment transactions. If it's possible for this process to be interrupted by the adversary (e.g., by publishing a transaction that spends one of the fragment outputs), then the publishing of the meta-transaction might fail (e.g., the subsequent fragments are no longer valid).

Thus, a meta output could end up in an "intermediate" state in which spending is not possible (even if the meta output condition could be satisfied), but no satisfying assignment can be extracted from the ledger.

In our compiler (from Sect. 2), this can occur, for example, if an adversary spends the outputs of the input-bit transactions thereby labeling them with a partial (or non-satisfying) assignment. In this case an honest user might not be able to compile an assignment meta-transaction, even if she knows a satisfying assignment.

Outputs and Inputs Are Not Atomic. In Bitcoin's ledger, the inputs and outputs of a transaction affect the ledger atomically—if a transaction spends a set I of TXOs and generates a new set of TXOS O, either all TXOs in I were spent and all TXOs in O are in the UTXO, or neither happens.

However, requiring input/output atomicity would greatly restrict the class of realizeable meta-ledgers—it would require every meta-transaction to correspond to a specific base-transaction that has exactly the same inputs and outputs.

If this is not ensured, a transaction that spends TXOs I and creates TXOs O may correspond to a set of base-transactions in which one transaction, tx_I, spends the TXOs in I while another, tx_O, creates the outputs O. Since the adversary is allowed to delay and reorder transactions, there may be a point in time at which tx_I was published in the base-ledger while tx_O was not.

This situation does, in fact, occur in our compiler, when compiling a meta-transaction that has an output with a circuit condition as described in Sect. 2. The meta-transaction's inputs are spent by the splitter transaction (c.f. Sect. 2.3) while the outputs are generated by the circuit-keystone transaction (c.f. Sect. 2.3).

Thus, we must relax the input/output atomicity requirement if we wish to support meta-ledger constructions such as ours.

Signatures Are Hard To Forge. Bitcoin's spending-condition language supports signature verification: an output condition can require the input data to contain a valid signature of the spending transaction's ID.

When we compile a meta-transaction into base-transactions, we also have to translate the input data (including signatures) into input data that is valid in the base-ledger. Since the meta-transaction is (necessarily) different from any base-transaction, the security of the signature scheme would prevent any attempt to naïvely transfer a signature from a meta-transaction to a signature on a base-transaction.

4   Discussion and Open Questions

We have shown how to construct a meta-ledger that supports arbitrary circuit conditions using a slightly enhanced version of Bitcoin. Our ledger functionality is composable and "stackable"—given a suitable compiler/decompiler pair, our protocol can construct a meta-meta-ledger.

Many interesting open questions remain.

- Can we construct an admissible compiler/decompiler pair for arbitrary *script* conditions? As a first approximation, it may be useful to consider the current Bitcoin scripting language, but remove the length limitation (i.e., allow longer scripts by using multiple transactions)
- Our requirements from COMP/DECOMP may appear unduly restrictive. While some requirements appear to be inherent, it is an interesting open question to design meta-ledger protocols that support a wider variety of spending conditions. In particular, our protocols do not support spending conditions that can depend on the *contents* of a spending transaction (rather than just its ID), such as the extensions proposed by Bitcoin covenants.

References

1. Andrychowicz, M., Dziembowski, S., Malinowski, D., Mazurek, Ł: Fair two-party computations via bitcoin deposits. In: Böhme, R., Brenner, M., Moore, T., Smith, M. (eds.) FC 2014. LNCS, vol. 8438, pp. 105–121. Springer, Heidelberg (2014). https://doi.org/10.1007/978-3-662-44774-1_8
2. Back, A., Bentov, I.: Note on fair coin toss via bitcoin (2013). http://arxiv.org/abs/1402.3698
3. Badertscher, C., Maurer, U., Tschudi, D., Zikas, V.: Bitcoin as a transaction ledger: a composable treatment. In: Katz, J., Shacham, H. (eds.) CRYPTO 2017. LNCS, vol. 10401, pp. 324–356. Springer, Cham (2017). https://doi.org/10.1007/978-3-319-63688-7_11
4. Canetti, R., Dodis, Y., Pass, R., Walfish, S.: Universally composable security with global setup. In: Vadhan, S.P. (ed.) TCC 2007. LNCS, vol. 4392, pp. 61–85. Springer, Heidelberg (2007). https://doi.org/10.1007/978-3-540-70936-7_4
5. Chakravarty, M., Chapman, J., MacKenzie, K., Melkonian, O., Jones, M.P., Wadler, P.: The extended utxo model. In: Workshop on Trusted Smart Contracts (Financial Cryptography 2020), January 2020
6. Garay, J., Kiayias, A., Leonardos, N.: The bitcoin backbone protocol: Analysis and applications. In: Eurocrypt (2015)

7. Kiayias, A., Zhou, H.-S., Zikas, V.: Fair and robust multi-party computation using a global transaction ledger. In: Fischlin, M., Coron, J.-S. (eds.) EUROCRYPT 2016. LNCS, vol. 9666, pp. 705–734. Springer, Heidelberg (2016). https://doi.org/10.1007/978-3-662-49896-5_25

8. V. I. Kolobov, A. M. Levy, and M. Naor. ColliderVM: Stateful computation on bitcoin without fraud proofs. Cryptology ePrint Archive, Paper 2025/591, 2025

9. Kumaresan, R., Moran, T., Bentov, I.: How to use bitcoin to play decentralized poker. In CCS **2015**, 195–206 (2015)

10. Linus, R.: Bitvm: compute anything on bitcoin (2023)

11. Möser, M., Eyal, I., Gün Sirer, E.: Bitcoin covenants. In: Clark, J., Meiklejohn, S., Ryan, P.Y.A., Wallach, D., Brenner, M., Rohloff, K. (eds.) FC 2016. LNCS, vol. 9604, pp. 126–141. Springer, Heidelberg (2016). https://doi.org/10.1007/978-3-662-53357-4_9

12. Nakamoto, S.: Bitcoin: a peer-to-peer electronic cash system (2008). http://bitcoin.org/bitcoin.pdf

13. O'Connor, R., Piekarska, M.: Enhancing bitcoin transactions with covenants. In: Brenner, M., Rohloff, K., Bonneau, J., Miller, A., Ryan, P.Y.A., Teague, V., Bracciali, A., Sala, M., Pintore, F., Jakobsson, M. (eds.) FC 2017. LNCS, vol. 10323, pp. 191–198. Springer, Cham (2017). https://doi.org/10.1007/978-3-319-70278-0_12

14. Pass, R., Seeman, L., Shelat, A.: Analysis of the blockchain protocol in asynchronous networks. In: Coron, J.-S., Nielsen, J.B. (eds.) EUROCRYPT 2017. LNCS, vol. 10211, pp. 643–673. Springer, Cham (2017). https://doi.org/10.1007/978-3-319-56614-6_22

15. Rubin, J.: Checktemplateverify. https://github.com/bitcoin/bips/blob/master/bip-0119.mediawiki

16. Swambo, J., Hommel, S., McElrath, B., Bishop, B.: Bitcoin covenants: Three ways to control the future (2020)

17. Zahnentferner, J.: An abstract model of utxo-based cryptocurrencies with scripts. IACR Cryptol. ePrint Arch. **2018**, 469 (2018)

18. Zahnentferner, J.: Chimeric ledgers: Translating and unifying utxo-based and account-based cryptocurrencies. IACR Cryptol. ePrint Arch. **2018**, 262 (2018)

Random Data and Its Cryptographic Applications

Ayşe Eda Yavuzyiğit[(✉)] and Oğuz Yayla

Institute of Applied Mathematics, Middle East Technical University, Ankara, Turkey
{eda.yavuzyigit,oguz}@metu.edu.tr

Abstract. Random sequence construction represents fundamental components of modern cryptographic systems. The quantitative assessment of randomness relies upon rigorous statistical testing methodologies, establishing statistical randomness evaluation as a critical prerequisite for cryptographic algorithm security validation. Concurrently, data compression technologies have emerged as essential enablers of efficient information transmission within contemporary digital communication infrastructures. This research investigates statistical testing frameworks in cryptographic applications, with particular emphasis on compression-based evaluation methods, notably the Lempel-Ziv complexity test. We present empirical findings from our analysis of a novel bit-level pattern recognition algorithm, validated against data sequences generated through the Advanced Encryption Standard (AES). Furthermore, we introduce a compression methodology derived from this bit-level pattern detection approach, demonstrating its potential applications in cryptographic randomness assessment.

Keywords: Data Compression · Randomness · Lempel-Ziv Complexity · Statistical Test Suites

1 Introduction

Random numbers and random sequences play a critical role in numerous areas of cryptography. Among the most essential components in cryptographic systems are key generators, which predominantly rely on the use of random values and random number generators (RNGs). An RNG uses a non-deterministic source (i.e., the entropy source[1]), along with some processing function (i.e., the entropy distillation process) to produce randomness. The incorporation of a distillation mechanism is essential for mitigating potential weaknesses inherent in

---

[1] Entropy: A measure of the disorder or randomness in a closed system. The entropy of uncertainty of a random variable X with probabilities $p_i, ..., p_n$ is defined to be $H(X) = -\sum_{i=1}^{n} p_i \log p_i$ [3]

Entropy Source: A physical source of information whose output either appears to be random in itself or by applying some filtering/distillation process. This output is used as input to either an RNG or PRNG.

A. Akavia et al. (Eds.): CSCML 2025, LNCS 16244, pp. 140–155, 2026.
https://doi.org/10.1007/978-3-032-10759-6_9

the entropy source that may lead to non-random outputs, such as extended sequences of identical bits. Typically, the entropy source is derived from physical phenomena, including electrical noise, timing variations in user activities (e.g., keystrokes or mouse movements), or quantum effects observed in semiconductors [11].

Random number generation refers to the process of producing a sequence of numbers or symbols that cannot be reasonably predicted, typically through the use of an RNG. Although such sequences may exhibit identifiable patterns when analyzed retrospectively, they are designed to be unpredictable in advance. Random number generators can be broadly categorized into two main types:

- *True Random Numbers (TRNGs):* is an RNG that generates a truly random sequence that uses one or more (combined) entropy sources that can be based on hardware (noise, temperature, thermal, movement, etc.) or based on software (mouse movements, key strokes, I/O buffer, System clock, file access, etc.). In other words, the generation process is inherently non-deterministic, as it is solely driven by entropy sources. As a result, the random sequences produced by a True Random Number Generator (TRNG) [23] are non-reproducible, meaning that identical output sequences cannot be regenerated, even under the same initial conditions.
- *Pseudo-Random Numbers (PRNGs):* is an algorithmic mechanism that produces sequences of numbers that approximate the properties of true randomness, yet are generated deterministically from an initial value known as a seed. Given the same seed, a PRNG will always produce the same output sequence, making it reproducible. Although the output appears random and can pass various statistical randomness tests, it is entirely determined by the seed and the internal state of the algorithm [17].

While the use of TRNGs is theoretically ideal from a cryptographic standpoint due to their entropy, their practical implementation introduces several challenges, including hardware dependencies, environmental sensitivity, and increased cost and complexity.

As a result, many cryptographic systems and algorithms employ PRNGs for producing pseudorandom sequences as secret keystreams or confidential data representations. However, to ensure cryptographic robustness, such pseudorandom sequences must exhibit properties that render them computationally indistinguishable from truly random sequences. To assess the quality of these sequences, statistical tests are essential. A randomness test suite comprises a curated set of statistical tests designed to evaluate various aspects of randomness in generated sequences. These suites are critical tools for validating the cryptographic suitability of both PRNGs and TRNGs.

Commonly used test suites include the following:

- *Knuth Test Suite* [7]
- *DIEHARD Test Suite* [8,9]
- *Crypt-XS Suite* [10]
- *NIST Test Suite* [11]

– *TestU01 Suite* [12]

These test suites measure randomness by using certain tests like the frequency (monobit) test, block frequency test, cumulative sums test, runs test, longest run of ones, binary matrix rank test, discrete Fourier transform (spectral) test, non-overlapping and overlapping template matching tests, approximate entropy, random excursions, birthday spacings, and Lempel-Ziv (LZ) complexity, and so on [16]. The Lempel-Ziv complexity test, based on data compression principles, was initially included in the Statistical Test Suite (STS) released by the U.S. National Institute of Standards and Technology (NIST) in 2001. However, due to concerns regarding its implementation and interpretability, the LZ test was subsequently removed from the official NIST STS software in 2004 [13,14]. Additionally, test suites such as TestU01 and Dieharder also include a form of compression testing using compression methods such as LZ77/LZ78 [1,2] algorithms.

In this study, we propose a novel statistical randomness test as an alternative to the Lempel-Ziv (LZ) complexity test, utilizing a bit-level pattern search technique for the evaluation of pseudorandom sequences. In addition to its application as a randomness test, the proposed method also demonstrates potential for the development of a new data compression algorithm. The rest of the paper is formed as follows. In Sect. 2, we outline the theoretical foundations of data compression. In Sect. 3, we provide a comprehensive examination of Lempel-Ziv complexity and its significance in statistical randomness testing. In Sect. 4, we explain Golomb's postulates of randomness, which form the theoretical framework underlying our proposed method. In Sect. 5, we introduce the proposed bit-level pattern search method and apply it to pseudorandom sequences generated using the Advanced Encryption Standard (AES), and also present detailed analysis results. In Sect. 6, we conclude the paper by summarizing the main findings and suggesting potential directions for future research.

2   Data Compression

Data compression refers to the process of encoding information using fewer bits or bytes than the original representation, with the goal of reducing storage requirements or transmission time. A fundamental requirement of data compression, particularly in the context of lossless compression, is that the compressed data must be decompressible in such a way that the original information is fully and exactly reconstructed. This strict reversibility distinguishes text and binary data compression from lossy data reduction techniques, such as those employed in audio or image coding, where a certain degree of quality degradation is permissible in exchange for greater compression efficiency. There are several fundamental motivations for the application of data compression in computational and communication systems.

– *Reducing the size of data:* Data compression effectively extends the usable capacity of storage devices beyond their physical limitations by minimizing the space required to store information. This is particularly advantageous in

environments where storage resources are constrained or where alternative storage solutions would be economically or technically impractical.
- *Reducing transmission time:* Whenever transferring data over a communication channel whose capacity is smaller than the computing power of its endpoints, employing data compression can increase the real transfer rate above the limit imposed by the available bandwidth. This means a reduction in time spent waiting for the transfer to be completed.
- *Determine randomness:* All data consists of two components: information[2] [4] and redundancy[3] [3]. Lossless data compression [15] is done by recognizing and eliminating the redundancy part. And the better the compressor is at finding redundancy and the more it is present in the data, the shorter the output will be once the data compression process completes. If some string of data can be compressed, it contains redundancy. If it contains redundancy, it is not random!

This study focuses on the assessment of randomness in pseudorandom sequences. To this end, we propose a novel statistical test for randomness based on data compression principles. The core idea underlying this approach is that the compressibility of a sequence provides insight into its degree of randomness: sequences exhibiting high redundancy are more compressible and thus less random, whereas incompressible sequences are more likely to exhibit true randomness. In addition to its utility as a randomness test, the proposed method also possesses potential applicability as a compression technique for sequences with low or moderate entropy, including those generated by pseudorandom number generators.

3   Lempel-Ziv Complexity

The Lempel-Ziv complexity of a string measures how many distinct substrings (factors) are needed to reconstruct the original string through a parsing process. The basic idea is to scan the string from left to right and identify the shortest substring at each step that hasn't been seen before. The complexity is then defined as the number of these distinct factors required. It reflects the gradual increase in complexity as new patterns are recognized and compressed.

Lempel-Ziv (LZ) Complexity is a measure of the complexity or randomness of a data sequence, based on how well the sequence can be compressed. LZ assesses how "diverse" the patterns present in a particular signal are. It quantifies the number of distinct subsequences necessary to represent a given sequence when a lossless compression algorithm, such as Lempel-Ziv's algorithm [2], is applied.

The core objective of the LZ complexity test is to evaluate the number of cumulatively distinct substrings encountered during a sequential parse of the

---

[2] Information refers to the unpredictable or novel content within the data that conveys meaningful knowledge.

[3] Redundancy refers to the presence of predictable, repetitive, or non-random patterns within the pseudorandom sequences.

input. The underlying assumption is that sequences exhibiting a high degree of regularity or redundancy will produce fewer distinct substrings and are therefore more compressible. Conversely, less compressible sequences, due to a greater number of unique patterns, are considered more random [2]. Thus, a sequence is deemed non-random if its LZ complexity is significantly lower than what would be expected of a truly random sequence of comparable length.

Let's examine an example to gain a clearer understanding of LZ complexity for random sequences. If a random binary sequence is represented as e = 1010110101011100, the calculation proceeds as follows Table 1:

The Lempel-Ziv complexity of the sequence $1, 0, 1, 0, 1, 1, 0, 1, 0, 1, 0, 1, 1, 1, 0, 0$ is 8. The sequence can be parsed into 8 distinct factors: 1, 0, 10, 11, 01, 010, 111, 00. For a sequence of length 16, this gives a normalized complexity of $8/16 = 0.5$, indicating moderate complexity - neither highly regular nor maximally random.

BitPosition	Bit	is NewWord?	Factor
1	1	Yes	1
2	0	Yes	0
3	1	No	-
4	0	Yes	10
5	1	No	-
6	1	Yes	11
7	0	No	-
8	1	Yes	01
9	0	No	-
10	1	No	-
11	0	Yes	010
12	1	No	-
13	1	No	-
14	1	Yes	111
15	0	No	-
16	0	No	00

Table 1. Calculation of LZ complexity of sequence e

4   Golomb's Randomness Postulates

A **run** is a series of increasing values or a series of decreasing values. The number of increasing or decreasing values is the length of the run. That is, a run consists of one or more identical characters that are immediately adjacent to each other and are bounded on both sides by either a different character or the start/end of the sequence.

A run is a sequence of identical data elements (usually characters or bytes) that appear consecutively. If $S = S_0, S_1, ..., S_N$ is a finite binary sequence of length N, then a run is defined as an uninterrupted maximal sequence of identical bits, either 0 s or 1 s.

To better understand our method, we must not overlook Golomb's Randomness Postulates [21, 22]. Let S be a periodic sequence of period N; then, Golomb's Randomness Postulates are:

-   *G1:* In the cycle S_N of S, the number of ones differs from the number of zeros by at most 1. In other words, this is a balancedness condition; the difference is 1 in case N is odd, and zero is impossible. The number of ones in a sequence, that is, the weight of the sequence, should be approximately $N/2$.

- *G2:* In the cycle S_N, at least half the runs have length 1, at least one-fourth have length 2, at least one-eighth have length 3, etc., as long as the number of runs so indicated exceeds 1. Moreover, for each of these lengths, there are (approximately) equally many ones and zeros.
- *G3:* The Autocorrelation function $C(t)$ is two-valued. That is for some integer K, $C(t) = K$ for $t \neq 0(modN)$ while $C(0) = N$ for $t = 0$.[4]

As a first step for the new method, the longest run value of the data series should be calculated. In practical applications, particularly with large datasets, this value can become significantly large. For instance, in a 1 GB data sequence, the longest run length may frequently exceed 32. Table 2 presents the observed run lengths within a 1 GB randomly generated binary document. As illustrated, the run length tends to increase exponentially with the size of the data, reflecting the likelihood of encountering extended sequences of consecutive identical bits. In the case of truly random binary sequences, a run length of 32 implies the occurrence of 32 consecutive 0 s or 1 s.

The longest run value in the random sequences will be important for the blocking operation we will perform. For example, if we calculate the run values in a bit stream such as $e = 10110001100111100001011000$, we get run values as 112322441123. For this example, we see that the longest run value is 4. At this point, if we group our random sequence set into blocks of 4, it becomes 1123|2244|1123|... If we continue this grouping process for the length of the document, we should see values in the entire document that fit a permutation of $4^4 = 256$ according to the grouping we have done, and we will make various calculations on the values we obtain.

According to the values we will encounter in real life, it is clear that this is a very naive example. If the longest run value of the data set I examined is 32, then in the case of grouping by 32 values, we would need to work in a permutation space of 32^{32}, which is computationally intractable with current hardware and algorithmic capabilities. As such, alternative strategies or approximations must be employed to manage the exponential growth in computational complexity associated with large run lengths. In the next section, we mention how to manage the longest run value and how to calculate the run block length.

5   Our Method

In this section, we will focus on explaining our new method for analyzing random sequences. With this new method, we assume that classifying random sequences and a new approach to compressing random sequences.

---

[4] $C(t) = \sum_{i=0}^{N-1}(-1)^{S_i+S_{i+t}} = \begin{cases} N & \text{if } t = 0 \\ K & \text{if } 1 \leq t \leq N-1 \end{cases}$ The third postulate(G3) pertains to the degree of similarity between a sequence and its shifted versions. For a sequence S exhibiting pseudo-random characteristics, the autocorrelation should remain constant for all non-zero shifts. Specifically, the correlation between the i-th and (i+t)-th bits, for $t = 1, 2, ..., N-1$, should not reveal any structural information about the sequence.

Table 2. Calculation of runs of 1 GB random sequence

Length of run	Count	Length of run	Count
1	2147460781		..
2	1073749608	17	32677
3	536845718	18	16461
4	268434921	19	8306
5	134215481	20	4118
6	67113717	21	2090
7	33557686	22	1021
8	16777588	23	525
9	8393429	24	260
10	4195524	25	138
11	2098154	26	62
12	1048787	27	27
13	523231	28	18
14	261063	29	8
15	130820	30	2
16	65610	31	3
	..	32	1

In cryptography, the vast majority of applications rely on truly random sequences, rendering the concept of randomness fundamentally critical to the security and performance of cryptographic algorithms. Moreover, the random values and sequences employed must exhibit strong statistical properties, emphasizing the significance of statistical randomness as an essential consideration. Unfortunately, it is impossible to rigorously prove, via mathematical means, that a generator produces truly random bits. Consequently, statistical tests are employed to identify potential flaws or biases in the random number generator (RNG), thereby ensuring its robustness.

Similarly, lossless data compression algorithms play a pivotal role in scenarios where the exact reconstruction of the original data from its compressed form is imperative. This is particularly crucial for applications such as executable programs, text documents, and source code, where fidelity to the original data is non-negotiable. In these contexts, it is of paramount importance that no data is lost during compression, and that the original content can be perfectly recovered upon decompression.

The methodologies outlined here propose innovative techniques to enhance the efficiency of lossless compression, alongside novel approaches to evaluating the statistical properties of randomness.

Compression calculations are typically expressed in terms of bytes or characters in commonly used compression methods. The new method we developed enables us to analyze random documents independently of their character or byte content [6]. This way, we aim to revitalize currently used compression methods and create an appropriate test for randomness assessments.

When examining random data, run values hold an important place. In the NIST Statistical Test Suite, which includes such tests as "The Runs Test" and "Tests for the Longest Run of Ones in a Block" [11,18], examinations are conducted through run calculations. In addition, analyses are performed using runs in test suites such as Diehard [8,9] and TestU01 [12].

Our approach involves a bit-level analysis of data, where sequences are converted into numerical representations based on the run lengths of consecutive bits. For example, the hexadecimal value 0xB9, which is represented in binary as "10111001," would be transformed into the numerical sequence "1-1-3-2-1". This transformation facilitates more efficient compression by identifying repeating run-blocks, allowing the application of specific permutations to improve the compression ratio.

Understanding the longest run of zeros or ones in a data sequence is an important aspect of our technique to determine compression. Larger data sequences of random or pseudo-random data have a higher probability of containing longer strings of consecutive zeros and ones (we mention this in Sect. 4)

Our method enhances data compression by identifying additional redundancies by segmenting the data sequences into various redundant sections through bit-by-bit analysis. In this process, each string of identical bits is converted into a numerical value, which is then categorized into a predetermined group or coding scheme. For instance, in a bit stream like '0011100101111000110',

000100	111011	000100	111011
312	312	312	312

Table 3. Calculation of 3 length run blocks of 3 byte value: 0x13B13B

the conversion would yield a sequence of numbers such as $2, 3, 2, 1, 2, 4, 3, 2, 1$ as it seems these values as run values of the bit stream. Then we gather these numbers into proper groupings, which are run-length determined beforehand. As demonstrated in Table 3, the 3-byte hexadecimal value 0x13B13B can be represented in binary as 000100111011000100111011. When this binary sequence is divided into three run-length encoded blocks, notable similarities among the segments become apparent. For example, a value such as "312" may correspond to multiple binary encodings, with each specific representation influenced by its contextual position within the broader data sequence. In this context, "312" might be encoded as either 000100 or 111011, depending on the preceding bit patterns. This variability in binary encoding is a fundamental component of the proposed algorithm, which is designed to leverage redundancy and recurrent structures within the data. The techniques employed work at the bit level, enhancing their generalizability and effectiveness across diverse forms of random data.

Table 4. Test results for the 128-bit outputs of AES-CBC

Statistical tests	Output1	Output2	Output3	Output4	Output5	Output6	Output7	Output8
Approximate entropy test	0.505009	0.125728	0.293150	0.416039	0.218899	0.283051	0.292266	0.968501
Block frequency test	0.974940	0.854372	0.336997	0.589116	0.160127	0.472394	0.892993	0.406906
Cumulative sums test	0.337735	0.726606	0.202866	0.527756	0.477561	0.748925	0.415982	0.380841
Frequency test	0.462422	0.492075	0.566976	0.449733	0.267795	0.568465	0.435229	0.264645
Linear complexity test	0.850066	0.861738	0.580871	0.994585	0.781893	0.623143	0.366884	0.106054
Longest run of ones in a block	0.943777	0.007645	0.481633	0.297013	0.665516	0.019971	0.054281	0.417389
Non Overlapping Template	0.469512	0.489933	0.462890	0.530842	0.496785	0.514904	0.502336	0.534123
Overlapping Template	0.025675	0.368260	0.173331	0.127929	0.615892	0.082318	0.014665	0.349274
Random excursion test	0.684937	0.001102	0.060896	0.003034	0.429473	0.517392	0.715784	0.524882
Random excursions variant test	0.543635	0.052197	0.777020	0.298091	0.835439	0.594277	0.191817	0.866052
Rank test	0.437953	0.401119	0.105451	0.676159	0.651010	0.910469	0.422657	0.955329
Run test	0.286269	0.399186	0.417088	0.269515	0.730596	0.285706	0.654453	0.933383
Universal statistical test	0.338660	0.178034	0.630260	0.270156	0.202498	0.602608	0.393898	0.373641

Table 5. Test results for the 192-bit outputs of AES-CBC

Statistical tests	Output1	Output2	Output3	Output4	Output5	Output6	Output7	Output8
Approximate entropy test	0.359576	0.540078	0.435076	0.855821	0.039534	0.840819	0.743422	0.493981
Block frequency test	0.911603	0.461040	0.266756	0.956990	0.581704	0.291991	0.835962	0.539865
Cumulative sums test	0.464486	0.984265	0.966787	0.064726	0.487058	0.682719	0.754970	0.195192
Frequency test	0.525899	0.827986	0.904003	0.147276	0.267795	0.358635	0.963780	0.219345
Linear complexity test	0.932231	0.699945	0.344601	0.458384	0.665936	0.753803	0.105692	0.503793
Longest run of ones in a block	0.778204	0.521403	0.755078	0.028920	0.654930	0.347546	0.551243	0.883633
Non Overlapping Template	0.467017	0.514307	0.513818	0.542667	0.465326	0.504493	0.537077	0.443999
Overlapping Template	0.238240	0.000289	0.083035	0.095650	0.068525	0.117715	0.206105	0.003466
Random excursion test	0.423171	0.198564	0.045536	0.565686	0.623287	0.987777	0.066697	0.528425
Random excursions variant test	0.256896	0.924847	0.147914	0.398737	0.689369	0.536410	0.952638	0.509835
Rank test	0.463939	0.001038	0.717370	0.836626	0.620746	0.385006	0.256771	0.026432
Run test	0.155332	0.097179	0.725714	0.040406	0.451989	0.587558	0.056554	0.986122
Universal statistical test	0.849354	0.867458	0.869606	0.703730	0.893574	0.123966	0.470612	0.026536

For our method, we will analyze separately by blocking according to the 6, 7, and 8 run values and share the data obtained from these values. To perform our method, we use the AES [19] algorithm in CBC mode to generate binary sequences of length $2^{26} = 67108864$ bytes by concatenating the algorithm's outputs. The data used in each experiment is created by concatenating [20] the ciphertexts of the 128-bit chosen 8 plaintexts encrypted with a fixed-key AES. In other words, we generate 8 binary sequences that have a length of $2^{26} = 67108864$ bytes by using the AES-CBC mode algorithm. Randomness tests conducted on 24 random binary datasets obtained using the NIST Statistical Test Suite are shown in Tables 4, 5 and 6, grouped by fixed key lengths of 128, 192, and 256 bits.

Table 6. Test results for the 256-bit outputs of AES-CBC

Statistical tests	Output1	Output2	Output3	Output4	Output5	Output6	Output7	Output8
Approximate entropy test	0.194140	0.630446	0.332331	0.810825	0.131978	0.395503	0.422810	0.641090
Block frequency test	0.553457	0.705076	0.665050	0.801685	0.875679	0.283556	0.421123	0.481254
Cumulative sums test	0.826074	0.487448	0.660973	0.099800	0.454626	0.613443	0.911360	0.477754
Frequency test	0.499954	0.936757	0.839037	0.204599	0.349758	0.804287	0.702764	0.405529
Linear complexity test	0.950469	0.850247	0.294019	0.474684	0.406807	0.260048	0.184810	0.172494
Longest run of ones in a block	0.274947	0.483924	0.449396	0.343346	0.219613	0.747367	0.349201	0.504570
Non Overlapping Template	0.579614	0.482148	0.477358	0.513487	0.549422	0.492028	0.474584	0.461959
Overlapping Template	0.047553	0.127191	0.000115	0.497887	0.003550	0.372387	0.052289	0.122798
Random excursion test	0.815478	0.519908	0.090190	0.457904	0.074138	0.150749	0.616055	-
Random excursions variant test	0.988101	0.997781	0.251799	0.293071	0.101153	0.428014	0.058576	-
Rank test	0.271092	0.331298	0.884894	0.054261	0.540044	0.490571	0.442259	0.970182
Run test	0.953231	0.444045	0.370518	0.684593	0.963865	0.435369	0.712946	0.546059
Universal statistical test	0.774495	0.741155	0.239597	0.657284	0.140262	0.649121	0.292518	0.860789

Table 7. Results of 6-run block length with the 128-bit outputs of AES-CBC

Value1	Value2	BitLen	Data1	Data2	Data3	Data4	Data5	Data6	Data7	Data8
0110101	1001010	7	0.463520549	0.463855639	0.462258421	0.461701676	0.463079847	0.463238917	0.462890789	0.463743508
0101101	1001010	7	0.462976843	0.463396683	0.462094136	0.463854335	0.462001562	0.464021228	0.463525765	0.461417437
0101011	1001010	7	0.462769531	0.463888235	0.462383591	0.463903882	0.462573953	0.46213977	0.462126732	0.463052467
01011001	10100110	8	0.265993178	0.263909996	0.264458358	0.265300274	0.265140831	0.264617801	0.265081227	0.265516341
01010001	10101110	8	0.265546143	0.264891982	0.264582038	0.264984369	0.26434958	0.265735388	0.264032185	0.264388323
00101101	11010010	8	0.264857709	0.264550745	0.264549255	0.265274942	0.26448071	0.264683366	0.264045596	0.264492531
01001011	10110100	8	0.264695287	0.265036523	0.264558196	0.264927745	0.264570117	0.26409179	0.264516473	0.264413555
00010101	11101010	8	0.264692307	0.263385475	0.264190137	0.264725089	0.265471637	0.264705718	0.264248252	0.263944268
01010111	10101000	8	0.264507532	0.26512295	0.263912976	0.264818966	0.264459848	0.264559686	0.264440477	0.264318287
01010011	10101100	8	0.26447922	0.265270472	0.264281034	0.265394151	0.26486069	0.265356898	0.263656676	0.264753401
00101011	11010100	8	0.264234841	0.264450908	0.265270472	0.263865292	0.26550889	0.263869762	0.264698267	0.26537627
01101001	10010110	8	0.264115632	0.265185535	0.264766812	0.264233351	0.26345402	0.26537478	0.265140831	0.264699757
01011101	10100010	8	0.263936818	0.264406204	0.26410073	0.264516473	0.264286995	0.265830755	0.265084207	0.265307724
01001101	10110010	8	0.263826549	0.264506042	0.262856483	0.264336169	0.264634192	0.26525259	0.265958905	0.264179707
01110101	10001010	8	0.263813138	0.265407562	0.265057385	0.264625251	0.263942778	0.264659524	0.26358515	0.263905525
00100101	11011010	8	0.263626873	0.26486516	0.265178084	0.263723731	0.264820457	0.264771283	0.265710056	0.265449286
010011001	101100110	9	0.149846636	0.148098171	0.14851056	0.14888607	0.148363039	0.148629583	0.148926303	0.147843361
011001101	100110010	9	0.149613619	0.149048679	0.148148462	0.148829073	0.148183666	0.147419237	0.148088112	0.148415007
000110101	111001010	9	0.149461068	0.148743577	0.148986652	0.149266608	0.149018504	0.147628784	0.149221346	0.148658082
010100001	101011110	9	0.149388984	0.148815662	0.148800574	0.148813985	0.148877688	0.148901157	0.148800574	0.14903852
010001011	101110100	9	0.149276666	0.148634613	0.148748606	0.148718432	0.149791315	0.148064643	0.148993358	0.149878487
001001001	110110110	9	0.149226375	0.148901157	0.148837455	0.149070472	0.148483738	0.148421712	0.149484538	0.149269961
001010011	110101100	9	0.149145909	0.148906186	0.148748606	0.149082206	0.148428418	0.148294307	0.149132498	0.148609467
010111001	101000110	9	0.149041973	0.149739347	0.147734396	0.148438476	0.14902018	0.147876889	0.149160996	0.148069572
010000101	101111010	9	0.149005093	0.148899481	0.149400719	0.149246491	0.149254873	0.148929656	0.148857571	0.149124116
001000101	110111010	9	0.148971565	0.148307718	0.148235634	0.148673169	0.148295984	0.148311071	0.149251521	0.148277543
000101011	111010100	9	0.148968212	0.14878884	0.149394013	0.148984976	0.149347074	0.148567557	0.149509683	0.149088912
011100101	100011010	9	0.14896486	0.149132498	0.149268284	0.149130821	0.149360485	0.148661435	0.149318576	0.14896486
011001011	100110100	9	0.14894139	0.148540735	0.149435923	0.148718432	0.149606913	0.149677321	0.148617849	0.149169378
011110101	100001010	9	0.148924626	0.148495473	0.149003416	0.148666464	0.147979148	0.148584321	0.148344599	0.148837455

The efficiency and effectiveness of our method are primarily influenced by the size of the groupings. Strategies for handling unusually long and atypical bit runs

Table 8. Results of 6-run block length with the 192-bit outputs of AES-CBC

Value1	Value2	BitLen	Data1	Data2	Data3	Data4	Data5	Data6	Data7	Data8
0101011	1010100	7	0.464172475	0.463358872	0.463730469	0.463261083	0.463055074	0.463137217	0.462418795	0.465034321
0101101	1010010	7	0.462586991	0.461975485	0.463366695	0.463391468	0.463572703	0.462212786	0.464327633	0.463347137
0110101	1001010	7	0.461353548	0.464236364	0.461762957	0.462932512	0.463158078	0.462211482	0.462705642	0.463434495
01011001	10100110	8	0.265318155	0.264437497	0.263810158	0.264671445	0.26473403	0.265550613	0.266204774	0.263746083
00101101	11010010	8	0.265075266	0.26435703	0.263959169	0.264713168	0.264510512	0.265276432	0.264073908	0.264662504
01010011	10101100	8	0.265073776	0.265543163	0.265207887	0.265088677	0.264541805	0.264066458	0.265406072	0.264433026
01010111	10101000	8	0.264318287	0.263877213	0.264829397	0.263802707	0.264115632	0.263847411	0.264829397	0.265324116
01001101	10110010	8	0.264313817	0.264210999	0.264492631	0.26474297	0.26396811	0.26435554	0.263527036	0.263865292
00100101	11011010	8	0.264245272	0.264270604	0.263887644	0.264137983	0.263498724	0.264456868	0.265154243	0.264327228
01001011	10110100	8	0.264115632	0.264334679	0.265161693	0.26537329	0.264263153	0.264972448	0.263732672	0.264124572
01010001	10101110	8	0.264048576	0.264307857	0.264512002	0.263956189	0.265713036	0.265029073	0.264762342	0.263863802
01101001	10010110	8	0.264047086	0.264522433	0.26473254	0.264112651	0.264723599	0.265274942	0.264143944	0.264199078
01110101	10001010	8	0.264030695	0.26461333	0.264744461	0.264914334	0.264321268	0.26320219	0.265401602	0.265604258
01011101	10100010	8	0.263771415	0.264035165	0.263555348	0.262969732	0.263878703	0.26537329	0.265721977	0.264182687
00101011	11010100	8	0.263343751	0.264687836	0.263614953	0.264391303	0.263981521	0.264167786	0.264567137	0.264210999
00010101	11101010	8	0.262826681	0.265276432	0.265200436	0.266064703	0.264243782	0.265009701	0.264203548	0.265669823
001010111	110101000	9	0.149808079	0.149796344	0.148461945	0.149526447	0.149883516	0.148887746	0.148466974	0.147682428
011101011	100010100	9	0.149772875	0.148041174	0.148290955	0.148411654	0.148420036	0.149316899	0.148663111	0.149405748
010100111	101011000	9	0.149732642	0.147902034	0.149269961	0.148399919	0.147959031	0.148750283	0.148337893	0.14855247
011001101	100110010	9	0.149513036	0.149067119	0.148929656	0.149610266	0.148627907	0.148575939	0.148953125	0.148673169
010111011	101000100	9	0.149491243	0.148575939	0.149298459	0.149216317	0.148495473	0.148906186	0.149052031	0.148396567
001011001	110100110	9	0.149479508	0.148264132	0.148684904	0.148254074	0.148468651	0.148860924	0.149239786	0.1488626
000100101	111011010	9	0.149449334	0.149087235	0.148971565	0.148956478	0.148817338	0.149704143	0.14788527	0.148725137
010100001	101011110	9	0.149419159	0.148482062	0.148257427	0.149179436	0.148371421	0.14835801	0.148227252	0.14839489
010010111	101101000	9	0.149404071	0.148525648	0.149115734	0.148973241	0.14821887	0.150540657	0.149610266	0.148212165
000101011	111010100	9	0.149338692	0.148207135	0.148232281	0.149248168	0.148160197	0.148681551	0.147858448	0.148203783
001001001	110110110	9	0.149295107	0.148329511	0.14884416	0.148319453	0.14939066	0.148758665	0.149466097	0.149269961
011011011	100100100	9	0.149268284	0.149497949	0.149263255	0.148056261	0.148431771	0.148817338	0.148813985	0.1491962
001000101	110111010	9	0.149229728	0.148232281	0.148780458	0.148954801	0.148865953	0.148706697	0.1489833	0.148285925
001010011	110101100	9	0.14908053	0.148954801	0.148230605	0.148582645	0.149367191	0.148877688	0.149045326	0.148460269

in our method will be determined by splitting them into blocks, as previously stated, such as 6, 7, or 8 run block lengths.

By limiting the maximum run length of consecutive zeros or ones to 6, 7, or 8, we aim to categorize data streams in a manner that keeps them within these predefined limits. Consequently, within any given group of 6 elements, there is a finite set of $6^6 = 46656$ possible permutations. For simplicity in our current methodology, we assume that the grouping length equals the maximum allowable run length. However, for future work, the grouping length may be adjusted to enable more detailed analysis and further optimization of the model.

6   Conclusion

As outlined in Section V, the results obtained from our methodology, applied to 24 data sequences, each consisting of 2^{26} bytes, are presented in Tables 7 through 15. These tables are categorized by run-block lengths of 6, 7, and 8. The data have been systematically analyzed, grouped, and organized according to AES key length. The values presented in the tables are expressed as percentages relative to the total data sequences. At this stage, the observations made in Table 3

Table 9. Results of 6-run block length with the 256-bit outputs of AES-CBC

Value1	Value2	BitLen	Data1	Data2	Data3	Data4	Data5	Data6	Data7	Data8
0110101	1001010	7	0.462971628	0.462347083	0.462772138	0.462779962	0.46358835	0.463400595	0.462409668	0.462700427
0101011	1010100	7	0.462246686	0.462696515	0.462095439	0.463379733	0.461807288	0.46296902	0.461768173	0.463487553
0101101	1010010	7	0.462195836	0.462739542	0.462872535	0.463309325	0.462557003	0.463881716	0.462656096	0.462456606
00100101	11011010	8	0.265869498	0.266161561	0.26434958	0.265605748	0.263625383	0.264135003	0.264458358	0.264857709
01101001	10010110	8	0.265553594	0.26422441	0.264453888	0.26473999	0.264550745	0.263825059	0.263831019	0.264959037
01110101	10001010	8	0.265456736	0.263792276	0.266031921	0.264616311	0.262856483	0.26486069	0.26333034	0.264522433
00010101	11101010	8	0.265431404	0.264139473	0.264340639	0.264672935	0.263084471	0.265178084	0.264067948	0.263421237
00101101	11010010	8	0.265224278	0.264778733	0.263036788	0.265552104	0.263881683	0.264799595	0.263430178	0.263650715
01010111	10101000	8	0.265043974	0.265309215	0.264728069	0.26358813	0.263811648	0.264841318	0.264798105	0.265364249
01011001	10100110	8	0.264829397	0.264428556	0.264050066	0.26409477	0.264285505	0.265480578	0.265431404	0.264428556
01010001	10101110	8	0.264821947	0.264447927	0.264574587	0.26448071	0.264582038	0.264246762	0.265160203	0.265003741
01011101	10100010	8	0.264805555	0.264208019	0.265039504	0.264756382	0.263787806	0.263799727	0.265197456	0.264416635
00101011	11010100	8	0.264655054	0.26396513	0.265040994	0.264315307	0.26461184	0.264456868	0.264601409	0.264582038
01010011	10101100	8	0.264374912	0.264379382	0.264313817	0.263814628	0.263735652	0.2644822	0.263786316	0.264593959
01001011	10110100	8	0.264273584	0.265020132	0.26422143	0.263942778	0.264944136	0.264935195	0.264427066	0.263774295
01001101	10110010	8	0.263948739	0.26383996	0.264906883	0.264757872	0.264796615	0.264436007	0.265729427	0.264361501
010010011	101101100	9	0.149699114	0.148280896	0.148891099	0.148822367	0.148156844	0.148681551	0.14855247	0.148899481
010110111	101001000	9	0.149519742	0.149491243	0.148725137	0.148800574	0.148331188	0.149149261	0.149124116	0.148602761
010011001	101100110	9	0.149518065	0.14851559	0.148971565	0.149692409	0.149013475	0.149622001	0.148694962	0.148078054
001011101	110100010	9	0.14950633	0.149595179	0.148919597	0.149422511	0.149155967	0.148488767	0.14869161	0.148171932
010111011	101000100	9	0.149452686	0.149201229	0.148393214	0.148430094	0.148758665	0.149261579	0.149253197	0.149109028
001100101	110011010	9	0.149377249	0.149829872	0.149315223	0.149050355	0.148544088	0.148227252	0.148867629	0.149035268
010001101	101110010	9	0.149352103	0.149030238	0.148968212	0.148943067	0.148907863	0.147930533	0.148572586	0.148901157
010000101	101111010	9	0.149321929	0.149400719	0.149234757	0.148304366	0.148176961	0.148178637	0.149003416	0.148505531
011101001	100010110	9	0.149191171	0.148170255	0.148430094	0.148703344	0.14874693	0.14847368	0.148368068	0.148765277
011010001	100101110	9	0.149132498	0.14829766	0.148480386	0.148979947	0.148637965	0.148594379	0.148616172	0.149761144
011011101	100100010	9	0.149105676	0.148537382	0.148150139	0.148347951	0.148475356	0.149187818	0.148646347	0.148842484
010100011	101011100	9	0.148969889	0.149514712	0.148554146	0.148870982	0.149201229	0.148539059	0.149228051	0.149157643
010010111	101101000	9	0.148894452	0.14823731	0.149005093	0.148998387	0.148483738	0.148056261	0.149720907	0.148827296
010001011	101110100	9	0.148870982	0.148141757	0.149268284	0.148748606	0.148995034	0.148777105	0.148227252	0.148341546

are more clearly elucidated and further corroborated by this detailed analysis. Additionally, the tables have been sorted based on their respective percentages, with only the top 30 values included for clarity and conciseness.

A noticeable distinction emerges when comparing the results across different run-block lengths. For instance, while the data in Table 7 is constrained to a bit length of 9, the data in Table 13, analyzed with a run-block length of 8, extends to a bit length of 24. This highlights the significant influence of the chosen run-block length, which is pivotal in the overall analysis.

The proposed approach demonstrates that datasets that may initially appear random often exhibit underlying structural regularities and repetitive patterns that can be effectively exploited for compression. Empirical results indicate that data traditionally considered random frequently contain recurring elements amenable to pattern-based encoding. Within the context of this framework, a novel compression method has been developed, integrating the Huffman coding algorithm [5] to enhance the efficiency of data representation. This integration facilitates improved compression ratios by capitalizing on both inherent redundancies and statistical properties of the data (Tables 7 8, 9, 10, 11, 12, 13, 14 and 15).

Table 10. Results of 7-run block length with the 128-bit outputs of AES-CBC

Value1	Value2	BitLen	Data1	Data2	Data3	Data4	Data5	Data6	Data7	Data8
0101010	1010101	7	0.393991359	0.393160805	0.394203886	0.394468568	0.393280759	0.392860919	0.393868797	0.393168628
011010101	100101010	9	0.25408566	0.253805704	0.253899582	0.252499804	0.252736174	0.252769701	0.253200531	0.252873637
010101011	101010100	9	0.252570212	0.252731144	0.252454542	0.25304798	0.25307145	0.253076479	0.253674947	0.25342349
01011010	10100101	8	0.225360692	0.225514174	0.22521466	0.224503875	0.223703682	0.225402415	0.225715339	0.225257874
00101010	11010101	8	0.225140154	0.224280357	0.225187838	0.224520266	0.224548578	0.225140154	0.22495836	0.224769115
01001010	10110101	8	0.225056708	0.225798786	0.225241482	0.224265456	0.22533685	0.224390626	0.225947797	0.224818289
01010110	10101001	8	0.224529207	0.225122273	0.224865973	0.225289166	0.224240124	0.224547088	0.22431016	0.224350393
01010010	10101101	8	0.224001706	0.224380195	0.225655735	0.225287676	0.224620104	0.223904848	0.226081908	0.224657357
010100110	101011001	9	0.127404928	0.126960687	0.126248226	0.12696404	0.126538239	0.126642175	0.126275048	0.127066299
010110010	101001101	9	0.127156824	0.126601942	0.127016008	0.126451068	0.127245672	0.126372278	0.125840865	0.126658939
010010110	101101001	9	0.127145089	0.127069652	0.126685761	0.126389042	0.12696404	0.126097351	0.125752017	0.127309375
010010100	101101011	9	0.12706127	0.126355514	0.126122497	0.126794726	0.126055442	0.126761198	0.126281753	0.127396546
011101010	100010101	9	0.126977451	0.125985034	0.126782991	0.127252378	0.12624152	0.126714259	0.126640499	0.12624152
010011010	101100101	9	0.126910396	0.126734376	0.126724318	0.126779638	0.126692466	0.126677379	0.127259083	0.12745522
001010100	110101011	9	0.12675114	0.126789697	0.125897862	0.126325339	0.126503035	0.126214698	0.126643851	0.126948953
001011010	110100101	9	0.126715936	0.126850046	0.125689991	0.12590792	0.12698248	0.127051212	0.126397423	0.126145966
001101010	110010101	9	0.126685761	0.126689114	0.126120821	0.126310252	0.12657512	0.126803108	0.126776285	0.126378983
011011010	100100101	9	0.126657262	0.126563385	0.126566738	0.126166083	0.126959011	0.127133355	0.126471184	0.127192028
001010110	110101001	9	0.126576796	0.126221403	0.127270818	0.126725994	0.126940571	0.126239844	0.126405805	0.126402453
001010010	110101101	9	0.126516446	0.126871839	0.127044506	0.126985833	0.126330368	0.127012655	0.126670673	0.126360543
010110100	101001011	9	0.126508065	0.127163529	0.126576796	0.126782991	0.127083063	0.12723729	0.126023591	0.127021037
010101100	101010011	9	0.126498006	0.126461126	0.126437657	0.125664845	0.127302669	0.126062147	0.125959888	0.125963241
010111010	101000101	9	0.126425922	0.126969069	0.125832483	0.126521476	0.126642175	0.126179494	0.126332045	0.127126649
010110110	101001001	9	0.126347132	0.127041154	0.126588531	0.125565939	0.126432627	0.126461126	0.127547421	0.126596913
010010010	101101101	9	0.126333721	0.127661414	0.126714259	0.126432627	0.126390718	0.126801431	0.126705877	0.125948153
011001010	100110101	9	0.126308575	0.126263313	0.126196258	0.127041154	0.126588531	0.12610741	0.126647204	0.12676958
000101010	111010101	9	0.126194581	0.126509741	0.126452744	0.127287582	0.127669796	0.126809813	0.126219727	0.126620382
011010110	100101001	9	0.126120821	0.126048736	0.126994215	0.12669079	0.126057118	0.125725195	0.126100704	0.125602819
011010010	100101101	9	0.126048736	0.126948953	0.125602819	0.127520598	0.126387365	0.126912072	0.126494654	0.125669874
010100100	101011011	9	0.126038678	0.126256607	0.126352161	0.126233138	0.125674903	0.126695819	0.126650557	0.125953183

Table 11. Results of 7-run block length with the 192-bit outputs of AES-CBC

Value1	Value2	BitLen	Data1	Data2	Data3	Data4	Data5	Data6	Data7	Data8
0101010	1010101	7	0.393854454	0.393413752	0.394326448	0.392988697	0.393962674	0.3946485	0.394057855	0.39345026
011010101	100101010	9	0.252146088	0.252072327	0.252157822	0.253450312	0.253457017	0.253572688	0.252196379	0.253329612
010101011	101010100	9	0.251998566	0.252489746	0.254380703	0.253552571	0.252513215	0.253383256	0.252711028	0.252699293
01011010	10100101	8	0.225481391	0.224903226	0.224518776	0.225259364	0.224991143	0.22392571	0.224944949	0.225910544
01010010	10101101	8	0.225277245	0.225509703	0.223916769	0.225161016	0.225134194	0.225134194	0.224600732	0.225129724
00101010	11010101	8	0.225046277	0.225333869	0.225794315	0.225001574	0.225254893	0.225134194	0.224013627	0.224366784
01001010	10110101	8	0.225031376	0.225333869	0.225648284	0.22456944	0.225892663	0.22546798	0.223727524	0.225764513
01010110	10101001	8	0.224459171	0.226075947	0.22533834	0.223848224	0.224517286	0.224377215	0.225892663	0.225710869
010100100	101011011	9	0.127562508	0.126389042	0.126402453	0.126392394	0.125715137	0.127124973	0.126655586	0.126615353
010110100	101001011	9	0.127560832	0.125463679	0.126632117	0.126404129	0.126583502	0.126018561	0.126675703	0.127168559
010110010	101001101	9	0.127012655	0.126972422	0.126796402	0.127130002	0.12657512	0.126668997	0.126469508	0.126233138
011001010	100110101	9	0.126942247	0.126415864	0.126682408	0.127636269	0.126898661	0.126020238	0.126050413	0.126823224
011010110	100101001	9	0.126853399	0.125711784	0.126620382	0.126608647	0.126657262	0.126224756	0.126905367	0.12696404
010110110	101001001	9	0.12684837	0.126266666	0.126868486	0.126870163	0.126722641	0.12540333	0.126705877	0.126097351
001010100	110101011	9	0.126836635	0.126365572	0.125876069	0.126762874	0.126313604	0.126538239	0.12575537	0.126439333
001010010	110101101	9	0.126804784	0.126640499	0.127096474	0.126846693	0.127461925	0.127081387	0.126925483	0.126342103
010101000	101010111	9	0.126784667	0.126254931	0.126052089	0.126948953	0.12700595	0.126632117	0.127250701	0.126959011
010010110	101101001	9	0.126779638	0.126606971	0.126782991	0.127795525	0.127342902	0.12645945	0.126340427	0.126288459
010101100	101010011	9	0.126749463	0.125787221	0.126053765	0.126549974	0.126273371	0.1262784	0.127034448	0.12647789
001101010	110010101	9	0.126741081	0.126679055	0.126498006	0.126177818	0.126528181	0.127062947	0.126392394	0.126896985
010010010	101101101	9	0.126717612	0.126627088	0.126494654	0.126980804	0.127436779	0.126093999	0.126702525	0.126315281
010111010	101000101	9	0.126699172	0.126370601	0.126546621	0.126821548	0.126104057	0.12604706	0.126777962	0.126372278
001001010	110110101	9	0.126699172	0.127240643	0.126172788	0.126057118	0.12604706	0.126114115	0.126896985	0.126720965
010001010	101110101	9	0.126596913	0.126068853	0.126400776	0.126618706	0.126560032	0.126583502	0.126432627	0.126720965
001011010	110100101	9	0.126590207	0.126333721	0.126273371	0.126486272	0.126202963	0.127078034	0.127342902	0.127337873
011010010	100101101	9	0.126528181	0.126622058	0.126310252	0.126090646	0.125793926	0.12608394	0.126482919	0.1269456
011101010	100010101	9	0.1263991	0.126430951	0.126387365	0.126308575	0.127515569	0.12733452	0.125928037	0.125736929
011010100	100101011	9	0.126330368	0.125845894	0.126090646	0.126890279	0.126087293	0.126772933	0.126985833	0.125958212
001010110	110101001	9	0.126291811	0.126082264	0.12610741	0.126067176	0.127250701	0.126001798	0.126620382	0.127242319
010101110	101010001	9	0.126213022	0.126464479	0.126612	0.126199611	0.126405805	0.126306899	0.127124973	0.126777962

Table 12. Results of 7-run block length with the 256-bit outputs of AES-CBC

Value1	Value2	BitLen	Data1	Data2	Data3	Data4	Data5	Data6	Data7	Data8
0101010	1010101	7	0.393794477	0.3[illegible]3776223	0.393305533	0.393810123	0.393143855	0.393673219	0.393120386	0.39384[illegible]112
011010101	100101010	9	0.254476257	0.2[illegible]3569335	0.252638943	0.252846815	0.252635591	0.251926482	0.254580192	0.253951[illegible]55
010101011	101010100	9	0.252933986	0.2[illegible]2712704	0.253118388	0.252332166	0.253267586	0.253374875	0.253435224	0.253537[illegible]84
01010110	10101001	8	0.22585094	0.2[illegible]4992633	0.223979354	0.224713981	0.224936008	0.224623084	0.224687159	0.225552[illegible]17
01011010	10100101	8	0.22546798	0.2[illegible]5743651	0.225329399	0.224731863	0.225619972	0.224775076	0.224453211	0.224274[illegible]97
01001010	10110101	8	0.224553049	0.2[illegible]4615633	0.225114822	0.225357711	0.225514174	0.225354731	0.224797428	0.224567[illegible]5
01010010	10101101	8	0.224454701	0.2[illegible]5074589	0.225508213	0.225287676	0.22559613	0.224995613	0.22379607	0.224664[illegible]07
00101010	11010101	8	0.223454833	0.2[illegible]5533545	0.22[illegible]892795	0.225660205	0.224074721	0.224451721	0.225171447	0.224959[illegible]85
010110110	101001001	9	0.127292611	0.1[illegible]5847571	0.126687437	0.126442686	0.126266666	0.126757845	0.126782991	0.127453[illegible]43
011011010	100100101	9	0.127217174	0.1[illegible]6762874	0.126798078	0.126684085	0.12643598	0.125730224	0.125351362	0.126536[illegible]63
001011010	110100101	9	0.127163529	0.1[illegible]7215497	0.126819871	0.126598589	0.126471184	0.126449391	0.126657262	0.12721[illegible]468
000101010	111010101	9	0.127116591	0.1[illegible]6184523	0.126814842	0.126643851	0.125973299	0.12692716	0.126258284	0.12604[illegible]354
010110100	101001011	9	0.127078034	0.1[illegible]6843341	0.126707554	0.126176141	0.126430951	0.127136707	0.126457773	0.12632[illegible]31
001010100	110101011	9	0.126865134	0.1[illegible]5193782	0.1269456	0.125519	0.125978328	0.126952305	0.126070529	0.126806[illegible]6
010010110	101101001	9	0.126861781	0.1[illegible]7163529	0.127202086	0.126553327	0.127183646	0.127111562	0.12610238	0.126819[illegible]71
010101110	101010001	9	0.126841664	0.1[illegible]6764551	0.126472861	0.125668198	0.126300193	0.126581825	0.126427598	0.12672[illegible]965
001101010	110010101	9	0.126839988	0.1[illegible]6610324	0.126724318	0.126256607	0.126090646	0.127052888	0.126030296	0.126843[illegible]41
011010100	100101011	9	0.126674026	0.1[illegible]6746111	0.126632117	0.127361342	0.126529858	0.126699172	0.126668997	0.12726[illegible]759
001010110	110101001	9	0.126623735	0.1[illegible]5733577	0.126617029	0.126571767	0.126466155	0.126595236	0.127131678	0.12571[illegible]107
011101010	100010101	9	0.126613677	0.1[illegible]6239844	0.127259083	0.125517324	0.127113238	0.126665644	0.127354637	0.125731[illegible]
010101000	101010111	9	0.126534887	0.1[illegible]6439333	0.126234815	0.125995092	0.126152672	0.126013532	0.125961564	0.126796[illegible]02
011001010	100110101	9	0.126531534	0.1[illegible]6836635	0.126285106	0.126699172	0.126498006	0.126650557	0.126598589	0.126409[illegible]58
010101100	101010011	9	0.126447715	0.1[illegible]6273371	0.126942247	0.12579225	0.126595236	0.128134154	0.127029419	0.126553[illegible]27
011010110	100101001	9	0.126430951	0.1[illegible]5698373	0.126974098	0.126620382	0.126689114	0.126658939	0.126886927	0.126831[illegible]06
001001010	110110101	9	0.126385689	0.1[illegible]6736052	0.126979128	0.125914626	0.126943924	0.12678802	0.127044506	0.127071[illegible]28
010001010	101110101	9	0.12638066	0.1[illegible]5783868	0.126498006	0.127634592	0.12678802	0.125770457	0.126365572	0.126174[illegible]65
010100110	101011001	9	0.126332045	0.1[illegible]7751939	0.126441009	0.126405805	0.125956535	0.126850046	0.126784667	0.126271[illegible]95
010011010	101100101	9	0.126286782	0.1[illegible]6487948	0.126638822	0.126566738	0.125319511	0.126808137	0.126085617	0.126642[illegible]75
010111010	101000101	9	0.126219727	0.1[illegible]651477	0.125800632	0.127014332	0.126137584	0.127232261	0.126595236	0.12664[illegible]499
010010100	101101011	9	0.126214698	0.1[illegible]651477	0.126860105	0.126663968	0.126273371	0.125864334	0.126186199	0.126385[illegible]89

Table 13. Results of 8-run block length with the 128-bit outputs of AES-CBC

Value1	Value2	Value3	Value4	BitLen	Data1	Data2	Data3	Data4	Data5	Data6	Data7	Data8
0101010111111111	101010100000000	-	-	15	0.13853889	0.137767754	0.137784518	0.138136558	0.138156116	0.137281604	0.138150528	0.137[illegible]1282
0000000011010101	1111111100101010	0000000000101010	1111111111010101	16	0.097882748	0.097411871	0.099223852	0.097960234	0.098091364	0.09920001	0.097972155	0.097[illegible]2803
0101010000000011	1010101111111100	0101010000000000	1010101111111111	16	0.097164512	0.098595023	0.098058581	0.097060204	0.09855628	0.096532702	0.097513199	0.097[illegible]3143
000000001010101	111111110101010	000000000101010	111111111010101	15	0.092552975	0.092058443	0.092142262	0.093081035	0.092692673	0.092245638	0.092469156	0.093[illegible]3075
0010101011111111	1101010100000000	-	-	16	0.073045492	0.073924661	0.072744489	0.073546171	0.074005127	0.07365942	0.074064732	0.073[illegible]0211
0111111110001010111111111	1000000001111010100000000	0111111111111010100000000	1000000000001010111111111	25	0.072307885	0.071977265	0.072391704	0.072401017	0.071199611	0.071250834	0.071907416	0.071[illegible]74
0111111110001001011111111	1000000001110110100000000	0111111111110110100000000	1000000000000010111111111	25	0.06726943	0.066137873	0.066626817	0.066487119	0.067334622	0.066859648	0.066668727	0.067[illegible]1891
0111111110001010011111111	1000000001110101100000000	0111111111110101100000000	1000000000000100111111111	25	0.067190267	0.066743232	0.066454522	0.067306682	0.065970235	0.066668727	0.067339279	0.067[illegible]9279
0111111110001101011111111	1000000001110010100000000	0111111111110010100000000	1000000000001010111111111	25	0.067027286	0.067660585	0.066263601	0.066501088	0.065946952	0.067218207	0.06784685	0.068[illegible]4488
0111111110001011011111111	1000000001110100100000000	0111111111110100100000000	1000000000000110111111111	25	0.067004003	0.066095963	0.067292713	0.067157671	0.067166984	0.066976063	0.066822395	0.066[illegible]7269
011111111000101011111111	100000000111010100000000	011111111111010100000000	100000000000010111111111	24	0.063961744	0.064833462	0.065088272	0.064493716	0.064341724	0.064717233	0.065119565	0.064[illegible]6787
0111111110011010011111111	1000000001100101100000000	0111111111100101100000000	1000000000100100111111111	25	0.057583675	0.057811849	0.057229772	0.056824647	0.05745329	0.057956204	0.057509169	0.058[illegible]2853
0111111110010100011111111	1000000001101011100000000	0111111111101011100000000	1000000000100011111111111	25	0.057499856	0.057197176	0.057835132	0.057290308	0.057625584	0.056582503	0.057299621	0.057[illegible]3664
0111111110010001011111111	1000000001101110100000000	0111111111101110100000000	1000000000100010111111111	25	0.057485886	0.057569705	0.05770009	0.056577846	0.058035366	0.057634898	0.057457946	0.056[illegible]9605
0111111110010010011111111	1000000001101101100000000	0111111111101101100000000	1000000000100100111111111	25	0.057420693	0.057774596	0.057769939	0.057257712	0.056773424	0.056810677	0.057034194	0.057[illegible]9085
0111111110011011011111111	1000000001100100100000000	0111111111100100100000000	1000000001100100100000000	25	0.057294965	0.057928264	0.056694262	0.057029538	0.057248399	0.058044679	0.057993457	0.057[illegible]1146
0111111110010011011111111	1000000001101100100000000	0111111111101100100000000	1000000000100110111111111	25	0.057155266	0.057253055	0.057546422	0.057285652	0.057267025	0.056745484	0.057653524	0.057[illegible]3826
0111111110010110011111111	1000000001101001100000000	0111111111101001100000000	1000000000101100111111111	25	0.057020225	0.05712267	0.057560392	0.056889839	0.057062134	0.057853758	0.05742535	0.057[illegible]344
0111111110011101011111111	1000000001100010100000000	0111111111100010100000000	1000000000111010111111111	25	0.056782737	0.057262369	0.058310106	0.057765283	0.057332218	0.056936406	0.058035366	0.057[illegible]6791
0111111110010111011111111	1000000001101000100000000	0111111111101000100000000	1000000000101110111111111	25	0.056540594	0.058659352	0.057350844	0.058053993	0.056601129	0.05829148	0.058659352	0.056[illegible]8232
0111111110011001011111111	1000000001100110100000000	0111111110011001011111111	1000000001101101000000000	25	0.056386925	0.056889839	0.057262369	0.058254227	0.056596473	0.057001598	0.057555735	0.057[illegible]9772
011111111001001011111111	100000000110110100000000	011111111110110100000000	100000000010010111111111	24	0.055736303	0.054779649	0.055132806	0.055316091	0.055226684	0.05530268	0.055249035	0.055[illegible]7849
011111111001011011111111	100000000110100100000000	011111111110100100000000	100000000010110111111111	24	0.055485964	0.054694712	0.054068863	0.056563318	0.055660307	0.05428344	0.055499375	0.055[illegible]4099
011111111001101011111111	100000000110010100000000	011111111110010100000000	100000000011010111111111	24	0.055137277	0.055794418	0.054748356	0.054945052	0.055472553	0.054699183	0.055208802	0.054[illegible]342
011111111001010011111111	100000000110101100000000	011111111110101100000000	100000000010100111111111	24	0.05505681	0.054654479	0.056196749	0.05441308	0.054712594	0.055141747	0.055396557	0.055[illegible]4671
01111111100101011111111	10000000011010100000000	01111111111010100000000	10000000001010111111111	23	0.053199753	0.052488595	0.052831322	0.053092651	0.051987357	0.052634254	0.05321689	0.053[illegible]3855
0100101000000011	1011010111111100	0100101000000000	1011010111111111	17	0.053032488	0.051819719	0.052817166	0.051911548	0.052256696	0.052130036	0.051781721	0.051[illegible]8882
0010101000000011	1101010111111100	0010101000000000	1101010111111111	17	0.052798167	0.052142702	0.051838718	0.052035041	0.051965378	0.052231364	0.052636676	0.052[illegible]4357
0110101000000011	1001010111111100	0110101000000000	1001010111111111	17	0.052449852	0.051769055	0.051588565	0.052364357	0.051553734	0.052095205	0.051981211	0.051[illegible]974
0000000011010101	1111111000101010	0000000000101010	1111111111010101	17	0.052187033	0.051658228	0.052139536	0.052541681	0.051604398	0.052915327	0.051851384	0.052[illegible]0526

Table 14. Results of 8-run block length with the 192-bit outputs of AES-CBC

Value1	Value2	Value3	Value4	BitLen	Data1	Data2	Data3	Data4	Data5	Data6	Data7	Data8
010101011111111	101010100000000	-	-	15	0.138287432	0.137326308	0.138762407	0.137714669	0.137818046	0.138826668	0.138038769	0.137960538
010101000000011	101010111111100	010101000000000	101010111111111	16	0.098407269	0.097388029	0.098437071	0.097224116	0.097456574	0.098502636	0.097739697	0.097349286
000000011010101	111111100101010	000000000101010	111111111010101	16	0.098198652	0.09842515	0.098621845	0.098770857	0.097885728	0.09790659	0.098198652	0.097978115
000000001010101	111111110101010	000000000101010	111111111010101	15	0.092625618	0.091686845	0.093779527	0.091454946	0.092460774	0.092284754	0.092611648	0.09209197
001010101111111	110101010000000	-	-	16	0.073888898	0.073894858	0.074163079	0.074142218	0.073951483	0.073429942	0.073492527	0.072270632
011111111000010101111111	100000000111010100000000	011111111111010100000000	100000000000101011111111	25	0.070272945	0.072293915	0.072517432	0.072093681	0.071167015	0.070659444	0.072126277	0.07324852
011111111000100101111111	100000000110110100000000	011111111110110100000000	100000000001001011111111	25	0.067534856	0.066356733	0.067157671	0.067409128	0.066370703	0.067637302	0.066291541	0.066752546
011111111000110101111111	100000000110010100000000	011111111110010100000000	100000000001101011111111	25	0.066948123	0.068149529	0.066990033	0.066598877	0.067623332	0.066449866	0.066915527	0.067064539
011111111000101001111111	100000000110101100000000	011111111110101100000000	100000000001010011111111	25	0.066873617	0.067283399	0.066473149	0.066785142	0.067562796	0.067842193	0.066175126	0.06637536
011111111000101101111111	100000000110100100000000	011111111110100100000000	100000000001011011111111	25	0.066282228	0.065774657	0.066040084	0.067711808	0.066575594	0.067204237	0.066733919	0.067395158
011111111000101011111111	100000000110101000000000	011111111110101000000000	100000000001010111111111	24	0.06364435	0.063626468	0.06403774	0.064775348	0.064270198	0.06454736	0.064609945	0.065119565
011111111001100101111111	100000000110011010000000	011111111110011010000000	100000000001100101111111	25	0.057457946	0.057737343	0.057639554	0.057723373	0.056708232	0.058133155	0.05720648	0.057583675
011111111001000101111111	100000000110111010000000	011111111110111010000000	100000000001000101111111	25	0.057420693	0.056512654	0.057541765	0.0571087	0.056619756	0.057048164	0.057434663	0.057029538
011111111001101101111111	100000000110010010000000	011111111110010010000000	100000000001101101111111	25	0.057355501	0.057574362	0.057541765	0.057690777	0.05683396	0.05801674	0.057448633	0.057620928
011111111001110101111111	100000000110001010000000	011111111110001010000000	100000000001110101111111	25	0.057332218	0.058393925	0.056745484	0.057360157	0.057467259	0.05859416	0.058049336	0.056917779
011111111001010001111111	100000000110101110000000	011111111110101110000000	100000000001010001111111	25	0.05715061	0.057402067	0.057844445	0.057565048	0.057774596	0.057127327	0.057639554	0.057085417
011111111001001001111111	100000000110110110000000	011111111110110110000000	100000000001001001111111	25	0.057104044	0.057043508	0.057169236	0.057350844	0.057611614	0.057825819	0.057923608	0.057592988
011111111001011001111111	100000000110100110000000	011111111110100110000000	100000000001011001111111	25	0.056917779	0.057779253	0.057797879	0.056996942	0.057173893	0.058137812	0.057527795	0.057825819
011111111001011101111111	100000000110100010000000	011111111110100010000000	100000000001011101111111	25	0.056899153	0.056936406	0.056866556	0.057062134	0.057476573	0.057518482	0.058519654	0.057551078
011111111001001101111111	100000000110110010000000	011111111110110010000000	100000000001001101111111	25	0.056093559	0.058547594	0.057299621	0.057853758	0.057518482	0.057420693	0.057104044	0.057392754
011111111001001011111111	100000000110110100000000	011111111110110100000000	100000000001001011111111	24	0.055740774	0.054565072	0.055633485	0.054690242	0.05453378	0.055450201	0.054748356	0.054658949
011111111001101011111111	100000000110010100000000	011111111110010100000000	100000000001101011111111	24	0.055356324	0.054824352	0.055208802	0.055146217	0.054475665	0.054609776	0.055705011	0.054435432
011111111001011011111111	100000000110100100000000	011111111110100100000000	100000000001011011111111	24	0.055173039	0.054426491	0.056384504	0.055226684	0.055070221	0.054185092	0.055289268	0.055781007
011111111001010011111111	100000000110101100000000	011111111110101100000000	100000000001010011111111	24	0.054734945	0.055097044	0.055713952	0.055745244	0.055924058	0.054498017	0.05460835	0.054967403
011111111100101011	100000000011010100	011111111111010100	100000000000101011	17	0.052696839	0.051908381	0.051908381	0.051490404	0.05249735	0.051987544	0.052012876	0.052272528
0100101000000011	10110101111111100	0100101000000000	10110101111111111	17	0.05256068	0.051813386	0.052092038	0.052050874	0.052215531	0.051902048	0.052082539	0.052668341
0100000001101011	10111111110010100	0100000000010100	10111111111101011	17	0.052503683	0.052161701	0.051895715	0.051993877	0.052183867	0.051484071	0.052940659	0.052478351
011111111100101011111111	100000000110101000000000	011111111110101000000000	100000000001010111111111	23	0.052390061	0.053525344	0.052342936	0.052638538	0.052861311	0.053131208	0.053268299	0.052497163
0101011000000011	10101001111111100	0101011000000000	10101001111111111	17	0.052326359	0.05223453	0.052443519	0.051889382	0.051645562	0.052095205	0.05143974	0.051309913

Table 15. Results of 8-run block length with the 256-bit outputs of AES-CBC

Value1	Value2	Value3	Value4	BitLen	Data1	Data2	Data3	Data4	Data5	Data6	Data7	Data8
010101011111111	101010100000000	-	-	15	0.13849698	0.137873925	0.138281845	0.137273222	0.137507915	0.138608739	0.137438066	0.138726085
000000011010101	111111100101010	000000000101010	111111111010101	16	0.098314881	0.098159909	0.098186731	0.098270178	0.098443031	0.098127127	0.097438693	0.09777844
010101000000011	101010111111100	010101000000000	101010111111111	16	0.097504258	0.097808242	0.098508596	0.098457932	0.097864866	0.09867847	0.097098947	0.098359585
000000001010101	111111110101010	000000000101010	111111111010101	15	0.092379749	0.093019567	0.092089176	0.092421658	0.093075447	0.092849135	0.091983005	0.093276612
0010101011111111	1101010100000000	-	-	16	0.073498487	0.073364377	0.072603825	0.07301569	0.072661042	0.073760748	0.074070692	0.073233247
011111111000101011111111	100000000110101100000000	011111111111010100000000	100000000001010111111111	25	0.071180984	0.071735121	0.071348622	0.072596505	0.071013346	0.072303228	0.07153023	0.072014518
011111111000101011111111	100000000110100100000000	011111111111010100000000	100000000001010011111111	25	0.067395158	0.06667804	0.066743232	0.067478977	0.067520887	0.067395158	0.067623332	0.068177469
011111111000100101111111	100000000110110100000000	011111111110110100000000	100000000001001011111111	25	0.067381188	0.067455694	0.066431239	0.067674555	0.067260116	0.067404471	0.067609362	0.067995861
011111111000110101111111	100000000110010100000000	011111111110010100000000	100000000001101011111111	25	0.067353249	0.066603534	0.066757202	0.067278743	0.06691087	0.068442896	0.067101792	0.067329966
011111111000101101111111	100000000110100100000000	011111111110100100000000	100000000001011011111111	25	0.066640787	0.067399815	0.067581423	0.065728001	0.066900033	0.067049295	0.067050569	0.06724149
011111111001010101111111	100000000110101000000000	011111111110101000000000	100000000001010011111111	24	0.065150857	0.064574182	0.064583123	0.064301491	0.06415844	0.064498186	0.06365329	0.064332783
011111111001101101111111	100000000110010010000000	011111111110010010000000	100000000001101101111111	25	0.058333389	0.057476573	0.05621463	0.057981698	0.057658181	0.057779253	0.057541765	0.057704747
011111111001011011111111	100000000110100100000000	011111111110100100000000	100000000001011011111111	25	0.057723373	0.05743932	0.057923608	0.057374127	0.058421865	0.057341531	0.057592988	0.057010911
011111111000100111111111	100000000110110010000000	011111111110110010000000	100000000001001101111111	25	0.057485886	0.057537109	0.057416037	0.057248399	0.057681464	0.057687683	0.057984143	0.056992285
011111111001011001111111	100000000110100110000000	011111111110100110000000	100000000001011001111111	25	0.057406723	0.057285652	0.05767215	0.056722201	0.057709403	0.057206489	0.057504512	0.056601129
011111111001010001111111	100000000110101110000000	011111111110101110000000	100000000001010001111111	25	0.057262369	0.057443976	0.057178549	0.05716458	0.057159923	0.057751313	0.057360157	0.057145953
011111111001010011111111	100000000110101000000000	011111111110101000000000	100000000001010011111111	25	0.057206489	0.057388097	0.057485886	0.057557735	0.058328733	0.057770009	0.05741138	0.057900324
011111111001001011111111	100000000110110100000000	011111111110110100000000	100000000001001011111111	24	0.05715061	0.058235601	0.057076104	0.057280995	0.05745329	0.058063306	0.057234429	0.057984143
011111111001001001111111	100000000110110110000000	011111111110110110000000	100000000001001001111111	25	0.057062134	0.0571087	0.057159923	0.057602301	0.057267025	0.058091246	0.057183206	0.057541765
011111111001001101111111	100000000110110010000000	011111111110110010000000	100000000001001101111111	25	0.056964345	0.056982972	0.057038851	0.056754798	0.057020225	0.057169236	0.056931749	0.056615099
011111111001001101111111	100000000110110010000000	011111111110110010000000	100000000001001101111111	25	0.056959689	0.057118014	0.057746656	0.05765283	0.057104044	0.057085417	0.057602301	0.057374127
011111111001011011111111	100000000110100100000000	011111111110100100000000	100000000001011011111111	24	0.056049228	0.055092573	0.054891407	0.054551661	0.055450201	0.054609776	0.055199862	0.055557489
011111111001010011111111	100000000110101000000000	011111111110101000000000	100000000001010011111111	24	0.055378675	0.055505535	0.055280328	0.057709481	0.054882467	0.05518198	0.05530715	0.055584311
011111111001010111111111	100000000110101000000000	011111111110101000000000	100000000001010111111111	24	0.05531162	0.05518645	0.054422021	0.055387616	0.054985285	0.055016577	0.055257976	0.056344271
011111111001010111111111	100000000110101000000000	011111111110101000000000	100000000001010111111111	24	0.055266917	0.055199862	0.05521327	0.055110455	0.055034459	0.055240095	0.05794418	0.055409968
011111111001011011111111	100000000110100100000000	011111111110100100000000	100000000001011011111111	23	0.053118356	0.052946992	0.052505732	0.053169765	0.05415082	0.053047833	0.052424334	0.052073039
0010101000000011	1101010111111100	0010101000000000	1101010111111111	17	0.052231364	0.051756389	0.051775388	0.052402355	0.052510016	0.052351691	0.051053427	0.052478351
0000000111010101	1111111000101010	0000000000101010	1111111111010101	17	0.052142702	0.051385909	0.051993877	0.051750056	0.052291527	0.052453019	0.052139536	0.051537901
0101001000000011	1010101111111100	0101001000000000	1010101111111111	17	0.052076206	0.052057207	0.052149035	0.052874163	0.051841885	0.052335858	0.051639229	0.052202865
0110101000000011	1001010111111100	0110101000000000	1001010111111111	17	0.052050874	0.051943213	0.052050874	0.051911548	0.052440353	0.051404908	0.052491017	0.051933713

References

1. Huffman, D.A.: A method for the construction of minimum-redundancy codes. Proc. IRE **40**(9), 1098–1101 (1952)
2. Ziv, J., Lempel, A.: A universal algorithm for sequential data compression. IEEE Trans. Inf. Theory **23**(3), 337–343 (1977)
3. Shannon, C.E.: A mathematical theory of communication. Bell Syst. Tech. J. **27**, 379–423 (1948)
4. Fano, R.M.: The transmission of information, vol. 65. Massachusetts Institute of Technology, Research Laboratory of Electronics, Cambridge, MA, USA (1949)
5. Salomon, D.: A Concise Introduction to Data Compression. Springer, London (2008)
6. Gillis, J.A.: A method for recursive data compression. Pat (2018)

7. Knuth, D.E.: The Art of Computer Programming: Seminumerical Algorithms, vol. 2. Addison-Wesley Professional (2014)

8. Marsaglia, G.: The Marsaglia random number CDROM including the diehard battery of tests of randomness. http://www.stat.fsu.edu/pub/diehard/ (2008)

9. Brown, R.G.: Dieharder: a random number test suite, https://webhome.phy.duke.edu/rgb/General/dieharder.php (2013), Accessed 15 Sep 2022

10. Caelli, W.: Crypt x package documentation. Technical Report, Information Security Research (1992)

11. Bassham III, L.E., Rukhin, A.L., Soto, J., et al.: A statistical test suite for random and pseudorandom number generators for cryptographic applications, Technical Report, Sp 800-22 rev.1a, NIST, Gaithersburg, Md, USA (2010)

12. L'ecuyer, P., Simard, R.: TestU01: a C library for empirical testing of random number generators. ACM Trans. Math. Softw. **33**(4), article22 (2007)

13. Doğanaksoy, A., Göloğlu, F.: On lempel-Ziv complexity of sequences. In: Gong, G., Helleseth, T., Song, H.-Y., Yang, K. (eds.) SETA 2006. LNCS, vol. 4086, pp. 180–189. Springer, Heidelberg (2006). https://doi.org/10.1007/11863854_15

14. Hamano, K., Yamamoto, H.: A randomness test based on T-complexity. IEICE Trans. Fund. Electr. Commun. Comput. Sci. **93**(7), 1346–1354 (2010)

15. Maan, A.J.: Analysis and comparison of algorithms for lossless data compression. Int. J. Inf. Comput. Technol. **3**(3), 139–146 (2013)

16. Sönmez Turan, M., Doğanaksoy, A., Boztaş, S.: On independence and sensitivity of statistical randomness tests. In: Sequences and Their Applications-SETA 2008: 5th International Conference Lexington, KY, USA, September 14-18, 2008 Proceedings 5. Springer, Berlin, Heidelberg (2008)

17. Rukhin, A., et al.: A statistical test suite for random and pseudorandom number generators for cryptographic applications. Gaithersburg, MD, USA: US Department of Commerce, Technology Administration, National Institute of Standards and Technology (2001)

18. Doğanaksoy, A., Sulak, F., Uğuz, M., Şeker, O., Akcengiz, Z.: New statistical randomness tests based on length of runs. Math. Probl. Eng. **2015**(1), 626408 (2015)

19. Stallings, W.: The advanced encryption standard. Cryptologia **26**(3), 165–188 (2002)

20. Sulak, F., Uğuz, M., Kocak, O., Doğanaksoy, A.: On the independence of statistical randomness tests included in the NIST test suite. Turk. J. Electr. Eng. Comput. Sci. **25**(5), 3673–3683 (2017)

21. Golomb, S.W.: Shift Register Sequences. Aegean Park Press, Laguna Hills, CA (1982)

22. Van T., Henk, C.A., Sushil, J. (eds.) Encyclopedia of cryptography and security. Vol. 1. Springer (2011)

23. Stipcevic, M., Koç, Ç.K.: True random number generators. Open problems in mathematics and computational science, pp. 275–315. Springer International Publishing, Cham (2014)

Privacy-Preserving Machine Learning on Web Browsing for Public Opinion

Sam Buxbaum[1]([✉]), Lucas M. Tassis[1], Lucas Boschelli[2], Giovanni Comarela[3], Mayank Varia[1], Mark Crovella[1], and Dino P. Christenson[4]

[1] Boston University, Boston, USA
`{sambux,ltassis,varia,crovella}@bu.edu`
[2] Maritz, Fenton, USA
`boschellil@wustl.edu`
[3] Universidade Federal do Espirito Santo, Vitoria, Brazil
`gc@inf.ufes.br`
[4] Washington University, St. Louis, USA
`dinopc@wustl.edu`

Abstract. We present a real-world deployment of secure multiparty computation to predict political preference from private web browsing data. To estimate aggregate preferences for the 2024 U.S. presidential election candidates, we collect and analyze secret-shared data from nearly 8000 users from August 2024 through February 2025, with over 2000 daily active users sustained throughout the bulk of the survey. The use of MPC allows us to compute over sensitive web browsing data that users would otherwise be more hesitant to provide. We collect data using a custom-built Chrome browser extension and perform our analysis using the CrypTen MPC library. To our knowledge, we provide the first implementation under MPC of a model for the learning from label proportions (LLP) problem in machine learning, which allows us to train on unlabeled web browsing data using publicly available polling and election results as the ground truth.

1 Introduction

Secure multi-party computation (MPC) is a cryptographic protocol that allows several people to contribute their data toward a collective data analysis without ever exposing their personal data to any other party. MPC has been a topic of research for decades [10,29,62,71], and through a variety of algorithmic improvements and software implementations (e.g., [13,39,47,51,63]), it has seen deployments over the past decade in the commercial and public sectors (e.g., [1,6,11,14,24,44,58]). Recently, there has been a focus on specialized MPC algorithms for machine learning operations like gradient descent and logistic regression (e.g., [4,28,49,50,52]) with corresponding software implementations like CrypTen [40].

In this work, we develop and deploy privacy-preserving machine learning in a real-world application based on political science: namely, the estimation of political preferences in the United States during the months around the 2024 U.S.

A. Akavia et al. (Eds.): CSCML 2025, LNCS 16244, pp. 156–174, 2026.
https://doi.org/10.1007/978-3-032-10759-6_10

presidential election. To accomplish this goal, we combine MPC-based privacy-preserving machine learning with the work of Comarela et al. [18], which demonstrates that web browsing patterns can be used to assess aggregate preferences in political candidates.

Background. In more detail, Comarela et al. [18] start from a dataset of web browsing records of a cross-section of people provided by a media measurement company. They design a machine learning algorithm based on Learning from Label Proportions (LLP), shown in Algorithm 1, that uses web browsing data to infer the same type of information that is generally produced by political polls: the fraction of voters in each region (e.g., county or state) that prefer a given candidate at a particular point in time. Hence, this work shows potential to augment traditional methods of political polling, since its lower cost enables more frequent and precise polling—an opinion poll can form the initial "ground truth" in one location at one moment in time, and then LLP on web browsing data can be used to predict political preferences at other times and/or locations.

This LLP algorithm is remarkably effective at estimating political preferences, even when given only browsing visits to the most popular websites rather than the long tail of smaller blogs and personal sites. Nevertheless, data privacy concerns make it challenging and risky to collect and store sensitive data about web browsing activity in practice.

Our Contributions. In this work, we design, implement, and deploy a privacy-preserving system that assesses candidate preferences while also providing the cryptographic guarantee that web browsing data never leaves client browsers in the clear. In more detail, we contribute the following.

- An MPC system that comprises a client-side browser extension that calculates a daily histogram of visits to popular websites, and a cloud-based MPC backend built on top of CrypTen [40] that uses these secret-shared histograms to calculate aggregate political preferences. We detail the system architectural design in Sect. 2 and describe our algorithmic innovations in Sect. 3.
- A case study of the deployment of our MPC system on a panel of nearly 8000 people during the months around the 2024 U.S. presidential election. We describe our work in Sect. 4 and emphasize upfront that we focus in this paper more on the computational decisions and security considerations involved in deploying MPC in this setting rather than the political science insights resulting from the data analysis.

Ethics. We conclude this section with a brief but important discussion of the ethics of this type of research. We caution that the use of MPC cryptographic technology does not automatically ensure adherence to social, ethical, or legal obligations to protect privacy [68], and as a result we have taken multiple steps to ensure that our deployment respects personal autonomy and social norms of privacy. First, we received approval from an Institutional Review Board to deploy this system, and we provided clear and simple methods for panelists to learn about their data privacy rights and to opt-out of participation at any time if desired. Second, we made sure to design our privacy-preserving machine learning algorithms to reveal only the overall fraction of people in a region (e.g., a U.S. state) that have a particular political preference, and not to infer or reveal any information about which people have that preference. Third, we designed the client browser extension so that it becomes "dormant" after the end of the study period: in other words, it automatically stops observing and transmitting secret-shared web browsing data even if the panelist never deletes the extension. Fourth, we provided fair compensation to panelists for their participation (as approved by the IRB), and we partitioned our own research team so that the researchers who connected with the panelists and observed their payment information were unable to access any other part of the system, and vice-versa (Fig. 1).

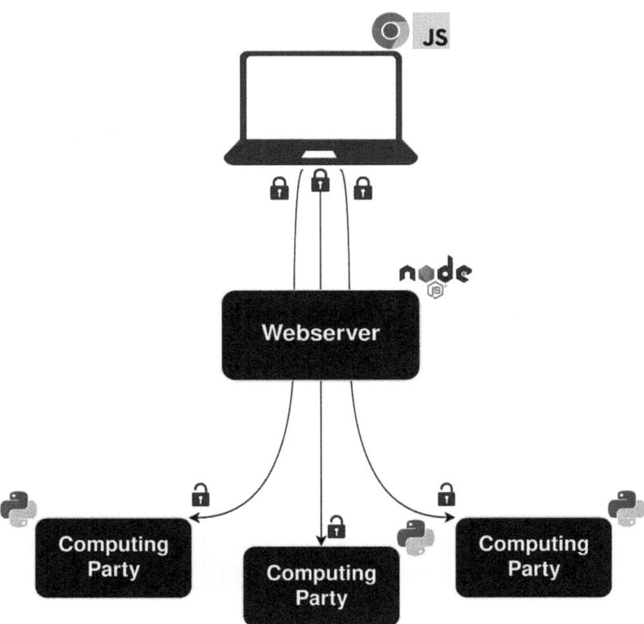

Fig. 1. The OPPS system design. The tools used for each component are included in the upper corner of the component.

2   System Design and Software Architecture

We perform our analysis using MPC in the honest-majority three-party setting with semi-honest security. We operate in the outsourced MPC setting, where users upload secret shares to a set of non-colluding servers who carry out the computation. Concretely, our system contains three components: (i) a browser extension used by the clients, (ii) a webserver to handle client interaction, and (iii) a set of three non-colluding compute servers to carry out the MPC.

2.1   Browser Extension

We develop a custom Chrome browser extension to monitor users' web browsing behavior. Emulating the ideas in Comarela et al. [18], the extension tracks (i) how many times each user visits each of the most popular 517 websites and (ii) how many times they were referred to each of the top 517 websites from popular social media websites. See Sect. 4.1 for details on how we obtained the list of websites.

The visit and referral histograms are secret-shared in the browser on the client side, and the shares are encrypted under the public keys of the three MPC servers. We implement secret-sharing and hybrid public-key encryption (with RSA and AES) using the JavaScript Web Crypto API. Once per day, the plugin secret shares, encrypts, and sends the histograms to the webserver.

2.2   Webserver

We use a continuously running webserver to handle all communication with the clients and to eliminate the need to have the more expensive computing servers active at all times. The webserver, written in NodeJS, is lightweight and can process many concurrent connections while running on a small machine in the cloud. When a client uploads their encrypted secret shares, the webserver stores them to be retrieved by the computing servers. We emphasize that the webserver exists to simplify the interaction with the clients, but the secret shares are end-to-end encrypted from the client to the computing parties, so the webserver itself learns nothing.

2.3   Computing Servers

We implement the MPC data analysis on top of the CrypTen Python library [40]. The three MPC servers retrieve and decrypt their individual secret shares of the web browsing data from the webserver, and they collectively (and obliviously) train a model or perform inference with a previously trained model.

In order to use CrypTen out of the box, all three MPC servers must be accessible by a single AWS account, which presents an obvious privacy challenge. To overcome the challenge, we place all three servers in the same AWS account, and the three server operators are collectively locked out of the account. Computation is performed using an automated process that allows server operators to communicate with the servers without giving any of them the ability to see any server or its internal state after the lockout procedure. Specifically, the server operators submit an agreed-upon program to the servers, which evaluate the program and publish the result to the server operators.

3   Secure Computation of an LLP Algorithm

In this section, we describe the LLP problem considered in the work of Comarela et al. [18], and then we describe our process to transform this into a secure multiparty computation protocol with data-oblivious control flow.

3.1   The LLP Problem

Learning from Label Proportions (LLP) is a weakly supervised machine learning problem in which the data is divided into groups or *bags* [57]. For each bag, only the proportion of labels is known, i.e., no individual label is available. The goal of LLP is to train a model that can correctly predict a label given a feature vector as input.

To be more specific, the machine learning task associated with this work can be characterized as follows. The input is composed of a set of pairs $D = \{(\mathbf{x}_i, b_i)\}_{i=1}^{N}$ and a vector $\mathbf{p}$, where: each $\mathbf{x}_i$ is a feature vector, representing the web domains visited by an individual in a given period; b_i denotes the bag, or group, that the individual belongs to (in our work b_i is the individual's state of residence); and $\mathbf{p}$ is a vector of proportions, indicating the proportion of individuals with preference for (without loss of generality) the Democratic Party candidate in each state. From this characterization, it is implied that each individual has a label: label 1 for a Democratic Party preference; and label 0 for a Republican Party preference. However, the individuals' labels are unknown. Hence, the goal of the LLP problem is to learn a model that can predict the label of individuals from D and $\mathbf{p}$. For the interested reader, a more detailed presentation of LLP and its possible variants can be found in the work of Franco et al. [26].

There are many algorithms for training machine learning models in LLP setups. In this work, we follow the approach presented by Comarela et al. [18], mainly for two reasons: first, it has been successfully used in similar contexts; and second, it is suitable for implementation in the employed MPC framework (as discussed in Sect. 3.2). In summary, the algorithm has three steps. The first step is label initialization, which can be performed randomly or according to proportions in each bag (i.e., U.S. state). The remaining two steps employ an iterative procedure that is repeated until convergence. In the second step, we train a logistic regression model using the previously assigned labels. Finally, in the third step, we refine the logistic regression model obtained in the last iteration and use it to compute updated predictions. More specifically, the default threshold (0.5) used to transform the model's probabilities into labels is changed on a per-bag basis, so that the predicted proportion of 1's in each bag (in the training set) matches the expected proportion (from the problem's input). We repeat the second and third steps until the predictions in consecutive iterations have converged.

The algorithm is formally defined in Algorithm 1, where we have combined Algs. 1 and 2 from Comarela et al. [18] for ease of presentation. As input, the algorithm takes the following:

- a data matrix $\mathbf{U}$, where each row is a user, and each column is a feature,
- a region map R, where $R(u)$ denotes the region to which a user u belongs,
- a proportion map B, where $B(r)$ denotes the fraction of users with label 1 for a region r, and
- a learning algorithm $\mathcal{A}$, which we instantiate with a logistic regression model.

As output, the algorithm produces a trained model Θ. The algorithm uses two labeling functions: $L(u)$ denotes the true label of a user u, while $L'(u)$ denotes our current prediction of the user's label, and $P(L(u) = 1 \mid \Theta)$ is the predicted probability that a user has label 1 according to the model Θ.

Algorithm 1: Learning Algorithm (from Algorithms 1 and 2 of [18])

Input: $\mathbf{U}, R, B, \mathcal{A}$
Output: Θ

1   $L' \leftarrow \{\}$
2   **foreach** $row\ u \in U$ **do**
3     $L'(u) = \begin{cases} 1, & \text{if } B(R(u)) \geq 0.5 \\ 0, & \text{otherwise} \end{cases}$

4   **repeat**
5     $L'' \leftarrow L'$
6     $\Theta \leftarrow$ train $\mathcal{A}$ on $(\mathbf{U}, L')$
7   **foreach** $region\ r \in R$ **do**
8      $t_r \leftarrow$ percentile $(1 - B(r))$ of $P(L(u) = 1 \mid \Theta)\ \forall u \in r$
9   **foreach** $row\ u \in \mathbf{U}$ **do**
10      $L'(u) = \begin{cases} 1, & \text{if } P(L(u) = 1 \mid \Theta) \geq t_{R(u)} \\ 0, & \text{otherwise} \end{cases}$

11 **until** $L' \approx L''$;
12 **return** Θ

3.2   Implementation Under MPC

Here we present a method of realizing Algorithm 1 under MPC, which is, to our knowledge, the first instantiation of a model for the LLP problem under MPC. We use and build upon the CrypTen [40] library. To simplify the following presentation, we freely and implicitly convert between an arithmetic secret sharing and a boolean secret sharing (in both directions) as needed. In practice, this is done using arithmetic-to-boolean and boolean-to-arithmetic conversions under MPC (see e.g., [22, 49, 55]).

Initialization (Lines 1–3). Initialization can be done in plaintext, as both the state proportions and the users' reported states are known in the clear. One could imagine secret sharing the users' states as well. In that case, initialization would entail obliviously selecting the correct state proportion and obliviously comparing it with 0.5.

Model Training (Line 6). Training the underlying model is one of the two cruxes of the computation. We instantiate the underlying learning algorithm $\mathcal{A}$ with a logistic regression model. Logistic regression is supported out-of-the-box by CrypTen, allowing us to use standard features of the library to train Θ at each iteration.

Computing Thresholds (Lines 7–8). The other crux of the computation is determining the threshold for each state, because it requires oblivious sorting. Oblivious sorting is a complex and expensive operation under MPC. More importantly, it is not natively supported by CrypTen. We implement a vectorized Bitonic sort [7] on top of CrypTen that uses the library's efficient primitives for batched operations to minimize round complexity. We sort each state's predictions separately, meaning we never sort more than several hundred values in a single call to the sorting algorithm. As a result, we prioritize ease of implementation over maximizing performance.

Given an oblivious sorting implementation, computing thresholds becomes rather straightforward. We compute $P(L(u) = 1 \mid \Theta)$ for each row $u \in \mathbf{U}$ and sort the results. Since the state proportions are known in the clear, we can compute the target index in plaintext and retrieve the (secret-shared) result at that index in the list. We remark that it would certainly be possible to compute thresholds even if the state proportions were not known in the clear, but in this work we assume the proportions are public information and do not need to be protected.

Computing the New Predictions (Lines 9–10). Updating the predictions with the newly computed model and thresholds is straightforward. For all rows $u \in \mathbf{U}$, we compare the secret-shared inference result $P(L(u) = 1 \mid \Theta)$ with the secret-shared threshold. We can perform the comparisons in a single batch using a vectorized oblivious comparison. We store the secret-shared prediction bit for each user in L'.

Checking Convergence (Line 11). The last step in the algorithm is to check for convergence. We have two lists of secret-shared predictions, L' and L'', and we need to determine their similarity. We first compute an elementwise (vectorized) oblivious equality to obtain a vector of secret-shared bits. The value we wish to compute is the number of those bits that are 1's, and we wish to compare it to some convergence threshold. We sum the vector to obtain a secret sharing of the number of 1's, and we obliviously compare it with the convergence threshold. We open the comparison result, and if the value is greater than the threshold, the opened value is 1, so we terminate the algorithm. If it is 0, we continue to another iteration. The only information revealed by the opening is whether the model has converged or not.

In summary, we implement Algorithm 1 step-by-step while ensuring that each step follows a data-oblivious control flow. We use CrypTen out-of-the-box where possible and implement new functionality where needed.

4   Data and Results

In this section, we describe our case study application of the MPC-for-LLP technique to analyze web browsing data of several thousand participants during the months before and after the November 2024 U.S. presidential election.

4.1   Panelist Data and Metadata

We recruit users through an advertisement on Amazon Mechanical Turk, with an emphasis on recruiting panelists who live in "swing states": that is, states that are likely to have close outcomes in the 2024 U.S. presidential election. Throughout the study, which lasted from August 2024 to February 2025, we collected data from 7926 total unique users, with over 2000 users contributing data daily for the majority of the study.

We collect both web browsing behavior and basic demographic information.

– In terms of web browsing data, the client browser extension contains a list of 517 popular websites, which we obtained by taking the union of the Alexa Top 500 list and the Semrush Top 100 list [61], removing advertising websites. The Alexa Top 500 list is no longer published, so we use the same version as Comarela et al. [18]. The extension records the number of visits that the panelist makes to the website, as well as the number of visits that resulted from referrals from one of the nine most popular social media websites. For all website visits, the extension records only the website's domain, not a complete URL. On a daily basis, the browser uploads the histogram vector of web visits to the web server. Each data upload consists of the three encrypted secret shares of a vector of 1034 elements, along with plaintext metadata described next.
– In terms of demographic metadata, we collect the panelist's Mechanical Turk ID, their self-reported state and ZIP code, the number of total visits to websites in the list, and the number of total referrals to websites in the list.

The Mechanical Turk ID is used to compensate the panelist for their participation. In each data upload, this ID is encrypted using message-locked encryption [9] that is only accessible to a member of our research team who processes the payments; this team member did not have access to any of the MPC compute servers. The MTurk ID is never provided as input to the machine learning algorithms discussed in Sect. 3, although the team member responsible for payment processing used the MTurk IDs to attach an anonymous ID to each upload for the purpose of anonymously aggregating data from the same user over several days. We discuss anonymous payments in Sect. 6.2 as a potential avenue for minimizing the trust required in the payment process.

The remaining metadata is used within the machine learning operation: the self-reported state is used to partition the data into bags for each state, and the total visits are used in order to convert counts into fractions. In principle, these operations could be performed under MPC as well (albeit with increased runtime). The state and ZIP code are also used within the data integrity check, described in Sect. 4.3.

4.2   Empirical Results

We use the panelist data together with the actual vote tally in the U.S. presidential election on November 5, 2024 to estimate political preferences at different points in time. As described in Sect. 3, our machine learning algorithm trains on the ground truth election results and corresponding web visits on November 5 and the surrounding days in order to produce model weights for the influence of each web domain on political preferences and state-by-state "cutoff" thresholds to assess candidate preferences. From this model, we use the web visit data to infer aggregate political preferences on other days, both backwards and forwards in time.

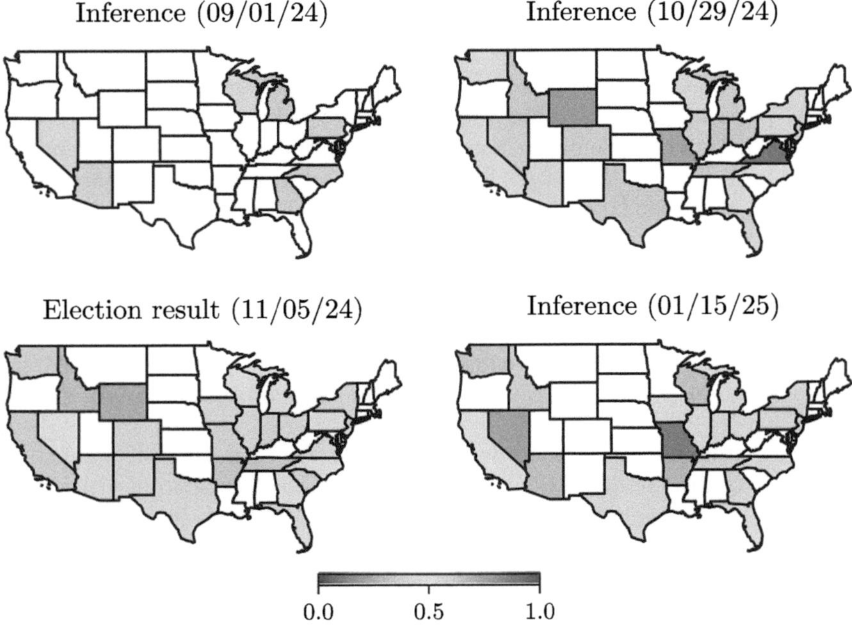

Fig. 2. State-level inference results at three points in time. One point is well before the election (top left), another is the week before the election (top right), and the last is after the election (bottom right). For comparison purposes, we also show the ground-truth election results (bottom left).

Findings. An example of our state-level inference results is shown in Fig. 2. Here we aggregate up the individual level candidate support scores for a set of states with ample respondents at each of three weekly periods: early in the campaign, election day, and the presidential inauguration. We have colored each state according to the degree of support for each party's candidate, with red indicating more Republican and blue more Democratic.

While a detailed analysis of the results from a political science perspective is outside the scope of this work, we observe that our data show a general swing toward the Republican candidate before the election and a swing in the opposite direction after the election. Indeed, our indicators suggest a substantial movement towards the Republican candidate over the course of the campaign, with strong support in many of the swing states by the week of the election. In addition, our results suggest that the so-called honeymoon period of new presidents—where they typically enjoy high approval for the first few months of their presidency—was either totally missed or extremely short-lived in many states for the new president. The results suggest a number of avenues of future research for political science, which typically relies on polls that are limited in number and locales in these periods.

Performance. This case study also serves to demonstrate the viability of our methods for performing meaningful data analysis privately. An end-to-end training run including data for the week before and the week after the election takes approximately 70 min. Additionally, running inference for a single day's data takes between 1 and 5 min. depending on the number of users in the sample on that day. All analysis took place on moderately powerful `m5n.2xlarge` AWS instances with 8 vCPUs and 32GB of memory. We emphasize that we did not seek to maximize performance, but only to make all computation run in a reasonable time frame of several hours. If we were to process, say, an order of magnitude more data, the present performance may become impractical, and more aggressive tuning and optimization would be necessary.

4.3 Data Integrity

For our inference of aggregate political preference to be accurate, it is critical that we correctly partition panelists into the bags for each state. For this reason, we ask panelists to self-report their state. However, we found that this self-reporting is not always accurate; for instance, our first Mechanical Turk advertisement was only open to people who live in swing states, which may have created an incentive for people to misrepresent their location. Although subsequent advertisements rewarded participants equally regardless of their reported state, the potential for dishonest reporting remains a concern. Future deployments should be careful to avoid incentive structures that encourage dishonest reporting. To examine the integrity of self-reported location information, we use geolocation data that allows us to draw conclusions about the validity of the sample.

Privacy Considerations. We exercised care to balance the data integrity goal with our overall privacy commitment. We design a validation process with the overarching objective of never having long-term storage of IP addresses or of location data beyond the ZIP code level. When the browser extension connects to the webserver to upload data, we use the connecting IP address and the IP locating service `ipgeolocation.io` to infer the panelist's state and ZIP code and compare to the self-reported data. By performing this check at the time of upload, we do not need to store IP addresses.

Findings. Our primary takeaway is that while there are significant reasons to be concerned about the honesty of the users, the concerns ultimately are unlikely to substantially harm the ability to extract meaningful patterns from the data.

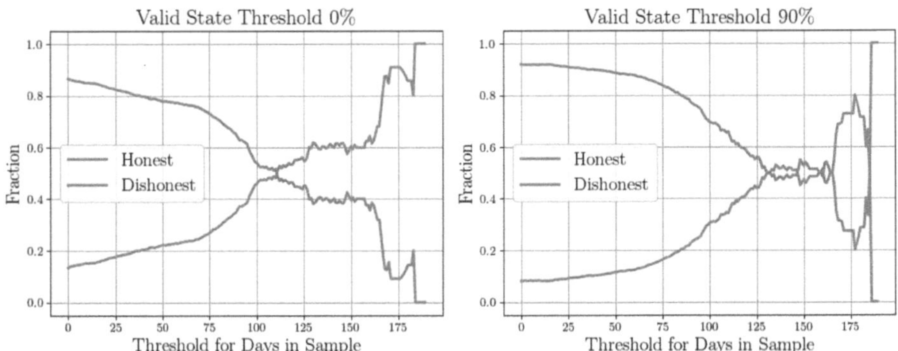

Fig. 3. Fractions of users who are honest and dishonest about their state of residence when filtering by a minimum number of days that the user is in the sample. The left and right plots consider a user honest if they are in the correct state for more than 0% or 90% of their total days in the sample.

Approximately 98% of the uploads come from users located in the United States, indicating that the vast majority of web browsing data corresponds to our target demographic at the highest level. However, the state-level integrity is much lower. Only 15% of uploads come from users located in their self-reported state. Furthermore, 15% of uploads contain a self-reported ZIP code that is not a valid ZIP code for the self-reported state. Taken together, the state-level integrity and ZIP code validity data paint a picture of a noisy dataset.

However, perhaps surprisingly, the honest panelists provide far more valuable data. To justify the data sample, we show that not all panelists and uploads are equal in terms of our ability to learn from them.

First, Fig. 3 shows that as we select for panelists who were in the sample for an increasingly large threshold of days, the panelists become more honest. We consider two ways of categorizing panelists into honest and dishonest groups: either we consider any panelist who has *ever* had their inferred state match their reported state to be honest, or we consider panelists to be honest if their inferred state matched their reported state for more than 90% of their uploads. In both cases, we see that the sample contains a large number of short-lived dishonest panelists, while consistent panelists tend to be more honest.

More importantly, Fig. 4 shows that honest panelists contribute visit and referral histograms that are significantly more dense than their dishonest counterparts. Using the same method of splitting panelists into honest and dishonest groups, we see that in either case, honest panelists and dishonest panelists contribute similar numbers of total visits, while honest panelists far outpace dishonest panelists in their total referrals. This observation is important due to the

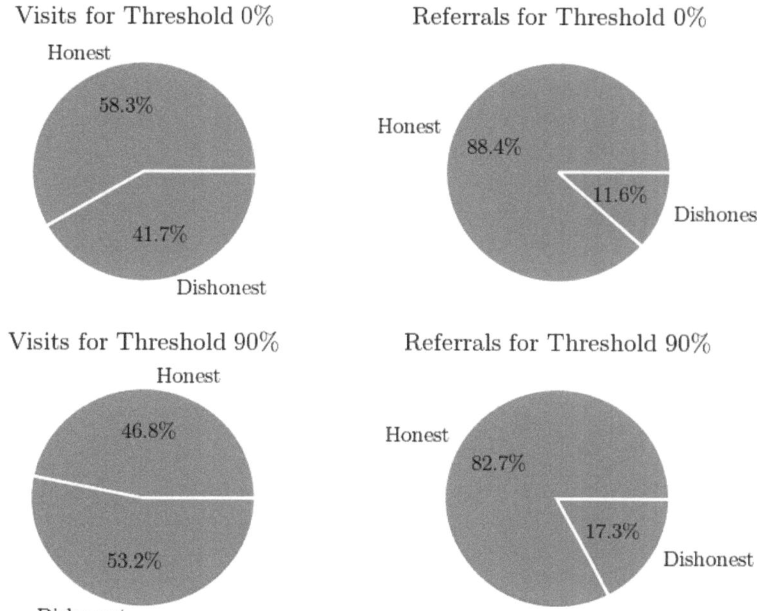

Fig. 4. The fractions of total visits and referrals reported by honest and dishonest users. The upper and lower plots consider a user honest if they are in the correct state for more than 0% or 90% of their total days in the sample.

finding by Comarela et al. [18] that referral data provides a far better signal for political preference than visits alone do.

We can draw two conclusions from the data and discussion above. First, detecting lying users and, if possible, obtaining some kind of proof or verification that a user is honest is of critical importance for ensuring data integrity, and this is an important direction for future work, as we discuss in Sect. 6. Second, while we should aim to maximize the integrity of the data, the fact that the heaviest users tend to be honest means our learning process is surprisingly robust to dishonest users.

5   Related Work

This work presents a deployment of privacy-preserving machine learning (PPML). In this section, we describe and compare with a few different categories of related work into PPML.

Algorithmic Designs. Building upon a long line of research into MPC in general, there have been significant advances in the past decade in the design of privacy-preserving machine learning algorithms. Some initial work, including SecureML [50], ABY^3 [49], and SecureNN [66], built broad support for machine learning operations under MPC. Next, several works contributed new protocols for privacy-preserving ML training and inference that collectively offer a variety of options for the number of parties, adversarial threshold, active vs. passive threat model, and more [15,17,19,20,37,41,42,55,56,67]. A more recent line of work has explored privacy-preserving algorithms for deep learning operators like transformers [3,23,30,31,45,48,53,72]. Our work only requires a relatively simple machine learning algorithm based on gradient descent (see Algorithm 1), which can be built even from the earlier line of PPML algorithms.

Software and Hardware Frameworks. There are several software frameworks for privacy-preserving machine learning. ABY^3 [49] provides protocols for many specific fixed-point and vector operations used in machine learning. EzPC [16, 43,59] provides a compiler from high-level machine learning operators to low-level crypto protocols. MP-SPDZ [39] is an extensive repository that contains several machine learning-friendly MPC protocols on its own right, and it is also used within the cloud-native Carbyne Stack framework [8].

Additionally, there are several frameworks that take advantage of dedicated hardware. Some works leverage dedicated GPUs [27,33,35,36,64,69] or FPGAs [25,34,54] to improve performance. Other works combine MPC with trusted execution enclaves in order to provide defense-in-depth [21,46,70].

We use CrypTen [40] in this work due to its ease of use in developing Algorithm 1. That said, there are a number of frameworks listed above that we could have used instead, several of which also support the three-party setting that we use in this work.

Deployments of MPC. To the best of our knowledge, this work is the first use of MPC in the domain of political science. More generally, it contributes toward the ongoing efforts to increase adoption of MPC in scientific research settings to derive publicly useful findings from private data.

We provide several examples of prior work on MPC for public benefit. First, national statistics organizations have used MPC to conduct surveys and to aggregate data across agencies, as documented in a list compiled by the United Nations global working group on big data [65]. Second, policymakers have used MPC to gather statistical evidence for data-driven policymaking [2] in domains like education [12] and health services [32]. Third, healthcare organizations have used MPC to measure the aggregate spread of COVID-19 [5] and to conduct clinical research [60]. Finally, civic non-profit groups have used MPC to measure workplace culture [38] and empower survivors of sexual assault on college campuses [58].

6   Conclusion and Future Work

In this work, we have built and deployed a system for private analysis of political sentiment from web browsing data. We use the remainder of the paper to discuss some areas for possible improvement and future work based on lessons learned from the deployment.

6.1   Balancing Integrity Verification with Privacy

As with any data system, the quality of the data is of critical importance. Section 4.3 details our experience with measuring the honesty of users in reporting their residence, an important variable in our ability to make accurate state-level predictions. Our approach involved using the user's IP address (which we will inevitably know by operating a standard webserver) to infer their current location. We could consider stronger methods of identity verification, but any strengthening would certainly lead to more invasive data collection, seemingly contradicting our core privacy goal.

In addition to the privacy element of the data integrity question, there is the fact that it is not immediately clear what information could be used to prove the location or residence of a user, even in a plaintext setting. Many companies and organizations use know-your-customer (KYC) systems for knowing the residence of their users. Perhaps one could design a private KYC service. We leave the problem of private residence verification as a challenging open problem.

6.2   Strengthening the Threat Model

The other major direction for future work is broadly to strengthen the threat model. To begin, the most immediate concern with the current system is the use of AWS as a single point of failure; this is an unfortunate but immediate consequence of our out-of-the-box use of CrypTen. While CrypTen provides a simple interface for running multiparty computation, future work could seek to build a similarly friendly interface that simultaneously can work across multiple cloud providers and multiple trust domains.

Another possible avenue towards a stronger threat model is to minimize the trust required from the user in the core machine learning computation. We can explore different system architectures and/or cryptographic primitives for the core computation. In the case of inference, the problem is comparatively easy, as each user can be treated independently, except for the aggregation of results. Given a model (either public or private), the user and a server could partake in a two-party computation to reveal only the prediction of the model on the user's private input. Such a two-party computation would be lightweight enough to be run every day to obtain live-updated polling results. For training, the problem is more difficult, as individual users' data can no longer be treated independently. One potential solution is to strengthen the MPC by incorporating multiple independent organizations to distribute the trust more widely. Alternatively, another option is to employ fully homomorphic encryption (FHE), involving limited client-side work to perform a threshold decryption to obtain the final results.

A final possible method for strengthening the threat model is the incorporation of anonymous payments. The payment method employed in this work requires knowledge of which Mechanical Turk IDs were active in the sample and for how many days. An anonymous payment mechanism would add an additional layer of protection for users beyond protecting their browsing data.

Acknowledgments. This research was supported by an Impact Program Grant from the Weidenbaum Center on the Economy, Government and Public Policy at Washington University; by the National Science Foundation under grants CNS-2209194, CNS-2312711, and CNS-2319369; by the DARPA SIEVE program under Agreement No. HR00112020021; and by a gift from Robert Bosch GmbH. Any opinions, findings, and conclusions or recommendations expressed in this material are those of the authors and do not necessarily reflect the views of the National Science Foundation or DARPA.

References

1. Abidin, A., Aly, A., Cleemput, S., Mustafa, M.A.: An MPC-based privacy-preserving protocol for a local electricity trading market. In: Foresti, S., Persiano, G. (eds.) CANS 2016. LNCS, vol. 10052, pp. 615–625. Springer, Cham (2016). https://doi.org/10.1007/978-3-319-48965-0_40

2. Advisory Committee on Data for Evidence Building. Year 2 report (2022). https://www.bea.gov/sites/default/files/2022-10/acdeb-year-2-report.pdf

3. Akimoto, Y., Fukuchi, K., Akimoto, Y., Sakuma, J.: Privformer: privacy-preserving transformer with MPC. In: 2023 IEEE European Symposium on Security and Privacy, pp. 392–410. IEEE Computer Society Press (2023)

4. Aono, Y., Hayashi, T., Phong, L.T., Wang, L.: Scalable and secure logistic regression via homomorphic encryption. In: Bertino, E., Sandhu, R., Pretschner, A. (eds.) Proceedings of the Sixth ACM on Conference on Data and Application Security and Privacy, CODASPY 2016, New Orleans, LA, USA, 9–11 March 2016, pp. 142–144. ACM (2016)

5. Apple and Google. Exposure notification privacy-preserving analytics (ENPA) white paper (2021). https://covid19-static.cdn-apple.com/-applications/covid19/current/static/contact-tracing/pdf/ENPA_White_Paper.pdf

6. Archer, D.W., et al.: From keys to databases – real-world applications of secure multi-party computation. Cryptology ePrint Archive, Report 2018/450 (2018)

7. Batcher, K.E.: Sorting networks and their applications. In: Proceedings of the April 30–May 2, 1968, Spring Joint Computer Conference, AFIPS 1968 (Spring), pp. 307–314. Association for Computing Machinery, New York (1968)

8. Becker, S., et al.: Carbyne Stack (2021). https://github.com/carbynestack/carbynestack

9. Bellare, M., Keelveedhi, S., Ristenpart, T.: Message-locked encryption and secure deduplication. In: Johansson, T., Nguyen, P.Q. (eds.) EUROCRYPT 2013. LNCS, vol. 7881, pp. 296–312. Springer, Heidelberg (2013). https://doi.org/10.1007/978-3-642-38348-9_18

10. Ben-Or, M., Goldwasser, S., Wigderson, A.: Completeness theorems for non-cryptographic fault-tolerant distributed computation (extended abstract). In: 20th ACM STOC, pp. 1–10. ACM Press (1988)

11. Bogdanov, D., Jõemets, M., Siim, S., Vaht, M.: How the Estonian tax and customs board evaluated a tax fraud detection system based on secure multi-party computation. In: Böhme, R., Okamoto, T. (eds.) FC 2015. LNCS, vol. 8975, pp. 227–234. Springer, Heidelberg (2015). https://doi.org/10.1007/978-3-662-47854-7_14

12. Bogdanov, D., Kamm, L., Kubo, B., Rebane, R., Sokk, V., Talviste, R.: Students and taxes: a privacy-preserving study using secure computation. PoPETs **2016**(3), 117–135 (2016)

13. Bogdanov, D., Laur, S., Willemson, J.: Sharemind: a framework for fast privacy-preserving computations. In: Jajodia, S., Lopez, J. (eds.) ESORICS 2008. LNCS, vol. 5283, pp. 192–206. Springer, Heidelberg (2008). https://doi.org/10.1007/978-3-540-88313-5_13
14. Bogetoft, P., et al.: Secure multiparty computation goes live. In: Dingledine, R., Golle, P. (eds.) FC 2009. LNCS, vol. 5628, pp. 325–343. Springer, Heidelberg (2009). https://doi.org/10.1007/978-3-642-03549-4_20
15. Byali, M., Chaudhari, H., Patra, A., Suresh, A.: FLASH: fast and robust framework for privacy-preserving machine learning. PoPETs **2020**(2), 459–480 (2020)
16. Chandran, N., Gupta, D., Rastogi, A., Sharma, R., Tripathi, S.: EzPC: programmable and efficient secure two-party computation for machine learning. In: 2019 IEEE European Symposium on Security and Privacy, pp. 496–511. IEEE Computer Society Press (2019)
17. Chaudhari, H., Rachuri, R., Suresh, A.: Trident: efficient 4PC framework for privacy preserving machine learning. In: NDSS 2020. The Internet Society (2020)
18. Comarela, G., Durairajan, R., Barford, P., Christenson, D., Crovella, M.: Assessing candidate preference through web browsing history. In: Proceedings of the 24th ACM SIGKDD International Conference on Knowledge Discovery & Data Mining, pp. 158–167 (2018)
19. Dalskov, A.P.K., Escudero, D., Keller, M.: Secure evaluation of quantized neural networks. PoPETs **2020**(4), 355–375 (2020)
20. Dalskov, A.P.K., Escudero, D., Keller, M.: Fantastic four: honest-majority four-party secure computation with malicious security. In: Bailey, M., Greenstadt, R. (eds.) USENIX Security 2021, pp. 2183–2200. USENIX Association (2021)
21. de Laage, R., Yuhala, P., Wicht, F.-X., Felber, P., Cachin, C., Schiavoni, V.: Practical secure aggregation by combining cryptography and trusted execution environments. CoRR, abs/2504.08325 (2025)
22. Demmler, D., Schneider, T., Zohner, M.: ABY - a framework for efficient mixed-protocol secure two-party computation. In: NDSS 2015. The Internet Society (2015)
23. Dong, Y., et al.: Puma: Secure inference of llama-7b in five minutes (2023)
24. El Emam, K., et al.: A secure protocol for protecting the identity of providers when disclosing data for disease surveillance. J. Am. Med. Inf. Assoc. JAMIA **18**(3), 212–217 (2011)
25. Fang, X., Ioannidis, S., Leeser, M.: Secure function evaluation using an FPGA overlay architecture. In: FPGA, pp. 257–266. ACM (2017)
26. Franco, G., Crovella, M., Comarela, G.: Dependence and model selection in LLP: the problem of variants. In: Proceedings of the 29th ACM SIGKDD Conference on Knowledge Discovery and Data Mining, pp. 470–481 (2023)
27. Frederiksen, T.K., Jakobsen, T.P., Nielsen, J.B.: Faster maliciously secure two-party computation using the GPU. In: Abdalla, M., De Prisco, R. (eds.) SCN 2014. LNCS, vol. 8642, pp. 358–379. Springer, Cham (2014). https://doi.org/10.1007/978-3-319-10879-7_21
28. Gascón, A., et al.: Privacy-preserving distributed linear regression on high-dimensional data. PoPETs **2017**(4), 345–364 (2017)
29. Goldreich, O., Micali, S., Wigderson, A.: How to play any mental game or A completeness theorem for protocols with honest majority. In: Aho, A. (ed.) 19th ACM STOC, pp. 218–229. ACM Press (1987)
30. Gupta, K., et al.: SIGMA: secure GPT inference with function secret sharing. PoPETs **2024**(4), 61–79 (2024)

31. Hao, M., Li, H., Chen, H., Xing, P., Xu, G., Zhang, T.: Private inference on transformers. In: NeurIPS, Iron (2022)
32. Hart, N.R., Archer, D.W., Dalton, E.: Privacy-preserved data sharing for evidence-based policy decisions: a demonstration project using human services administrative records for evidence-building activities (2019). https:// bipartisanpolicy.org/download/?file=/wp-content/uploads/2019/06/Privacy-Preserved-Data-Sharing-for-Evidence-Based-Policy-Decisions.pdf
33. Harth-Kitzerow, C., Wang, Y., Rajat, R., Carle, G., Annavaram, M.: PIGEON: a high throughput framework for private inference of neural networks using secure multiparty computation. Cryptology ePrint Archive, Paper 2024/1371 (2024)
34. Huang, K., Güngör, M., Fang, X., Ioannidis, S., Leeser, M.: Garbled circuits in the cloud using FPGA enabled nodes. In: HPEC, pp. 1–6. IEEE (2019)
35. Husted, N., Myers, S.A., Shelat, A., Grubbs, P.: GPU and CPU parallelization of honest-but-curious secure two-party computation. In: ACSAC, pp. 169–178. ACM (2013)
36. Jawalkar, N., Gupta, K., Basu, A., Chandran, N., Gupta, D., Sharma, R.: Orca: FSS-based secure training and inference with GPUs. In: 2024 IEEE Symposium on Security and Privacy, pp. 597–616. IEEE Computer Society Press (2024)
37. Juvekar, C., Vaikuntanathan, V., Chandrakasan, A.: GAZELLE: a low latency framework for secure neural network inference. In: Enck, W., Felt, A.P. (eds.) USENIX Security 2018, pp. 1651–1669. USENIX Association (2018)
38. Kaptchuk, G., Benoit-Bryan, J., Albab, K.D., Locks, M., Varia, M.: The good, the bad, and the ugly—lessons from an MPC for social good deployment. In: Real World Crypto Symposium (2024)
39. Keller, M.: MP-SPDZ: a versatile framework for multi-party computation. In: Ligatti, J., Ou, X., Katz, J., Vigna, G. (eds.) ACM CCS 2020, pp. 1575–1590. ACM Press (2020)
40. Knott, B., Venkataraman, S., Hannun, A.Y., Sengupta, S., Ibrahim, M., van der Maaten, L.J.P.: Crypten: secure multi-party computation meets machine learning. In: Proceedings of the NeurIPS Workshop on Privacy-Preserving Machine Learning (2020)
41. Koti, N., Pancholi, M., Patra, A., Suresh, A.: SWIFT: super-fast and robust privacy-preserving machine learning. In: Bailey, M., Greenstadt, R. (eds.) USENIX Security 2021, pp. 2651–2668. USENIX Association (2021)
42. Koti, N., Patra, A., Rachuri, R., Suresh, A.: Tetrad: actively secure 4PC for secure training and inference. In: NDSS 2022. The Internet Society (2022)
43. Kumar, N., Rathee, M., Chandran, N., Gupta, D., Rastogi, A., Sharma, R.: CrypTFlow: secure TensorFlow inference. In: 2020 IEEE Symposium on Security and Privacy, pp. 336–353. IEEE Computer Society Press (2020)
44. Lapets, A., et al.: Accessible privacy-preserving web-based data analysis for assessing and addressing economic inequalities. In: COMPASS, pp. 48:1–48:5. ACM (2018)
45. Li, D., Wang, H., Shao, R., Guo, H., Xing, E., Zhang, H.: MPCFormer: fast, performant and private transformer inference with MPC. In: The Eleventh International Conference on Learning Representations (2023)
46. Li, X., Zhao, B., Yang, G., Xiang, T., Weng, J., Deng, R.H.: A survey of secure computation using trusted execution environments. CoRR, abs/2302.12150 (2023)
47. Liu, C., Wang, X.S., Nayak, K., Huang, Y., Shi, E.: ObliVM: a programming framework for secure computation. In: 2015 IEEE Symposium on Security and Privacy, pp. 359–376. IEEE Computer Society Press (2015)

48. Lu, W., et al.: BumbleBee: secure two-party inference framework for large transformers. In: 32nd Annual Network and Distributed System Security Symposium, NDSS 2025. The Internet Society, 23–28 February 2025
49. Mohassel, P., Rindal, P.: ABY^3: a mixed protocol framework for machine learning. In: Lie, D., Mannan, M., Backes, M., Wang, X. (eds.) ACM CCS 2018, pp. 35–52. ACM Press (2018)
50. Mohassel, P., Zhang, Y.: SecureML: a system for scalable privacy-preserving machine learning. In: 2017 IEEE Symposium on Security and Privacy, pp. 19–38. IEEE Computer Society Press (2017)
51. Nayak, K., Wang, X.S., Ioannidis, S., Weinsberg, U., Taft, N., Shi, E.: GraphSC: parallel secure computation made easy. In: 2015 IEEE Symposium on Security and Privacy, pp. 377–394. IEEE Computer Society Press (2015)
52. Nikolaenko, V., Weinsberg, U., Ioannidis, S., Joye, M., Boneh, D., Taft, N.: Privacy-preserving ridge regression on hundreds of millions of records. In: 2013 IEEE Symposium on Security and Privacy, pp. 334–348. IEEE Computer Society Press (2013)
53. Pang, Q., Zhu, J., Möllering, H., Zheng, W., Schneider, T.: BOLT: privacy-preserving, accurate and efficient inference for transformers. In: 2024 IEEE Symposium on Security and Privacy, pp. 4753–4771. IEEE Computer Society Press (2024)
54. Patel, R., Wolfe, P.-F., Munafo, R., Varia, M., Herbordt, M.C.: Arithmetic and Boolean secret sharing MPC on FPGAs in the data center. In: HPEC, pp. 1–8. IEEE (2020)
55. Patra, A., Schneider, T., Suresh, A., Yalame, H.: ABY2.0: improved mixed-protocol secure two-party computation. In: Bailey, M., Greenstadt, R. (eds.) USENIX Security 2021, pp. 2165–2182. USENIX Association (2021)
56. Patra, A., Suresh, A.: BLAZE: blazing fast privacy-preserving machine learning. In: NDSS 2020. The Internet Society (2020)
57. Quadrianto, N., Smola, A.J., Caetano, T.S., Le, Q.V.: Estimating labels from label proportions. In: International Conference on Machine Learning, pp. 776–783 (2008)
58. Rajan, A., Qin, L., Archer, D.W., Boneh, D., Lepoint, T., Varia, M.: Callisto a cryptographic approach to detecting serial perpetrators of sexual misconduct. In: COMPASS, pp. 49:1–49:4. ACM (2018)
59. Rathee, D., et al.: CrypTFlow2: practical 2-party secure inference. In: Ligatti, J., Ou, X., Katz, J., Vigna, G. (eds.) ACM CCS 2020, pp. 325–342. ACM Press (2020)
60. Rogers, J., et al.: VaultDB: a real-world pilot of secure multi-party computation within a clinical research network. https://arxiv.org/pdf/2203.00146
61. Semrush. Top 100: The most visited websites in the us. https://www.semrush.com/blog/most-visited-websites/
62. Shamir, A.: How to share a secret. Commun. Assoc. Comput. Mach. **22**(11), 612–613 (1979)
63. Songhori, E.M., Hussain, S.U., Sadeghi, A.-R., Schneider, T., Koushanfar, F.: TinyGarble: highly compressed and scalable sequential garbled circuits. In: 2015 IEEE Symposium on Security and Privacy, pp. 411–428. IEEE Computer Society Press (2015)
64. Tan, S., Knott, B., Tian, Y., Wu, D.J.: CryptGPU: fast privacy-preserving machine learning on the GPU. In: 2021 IEEE Symposium on Security and Privacy, pp. 1021–1038. IEEE Computer Society Press (2021)
65. UN Global Working Group Task Team on Privacy Preserving Techniques. Case study repository (2024). https://unstats.un.org/wiki/spaces/UGTTOPPT/pages/150012018/Case+study+repository

66. Wagh, S., Gupta, D., Chandran, N.: SecureNN: 3-party secure computation for neural network training. PoPETs **2019**(3), 26–49 (2019)
67. Wagh, S., Tople, S., Benhamouda, F., Kushilevitz, E., Mittal, P., Rabin, T.: Falcon: honest-majority maliciously secure framework for private deep learning. PoPETs **2021**(1), 188–208 (2021)
68. Walsh, J.M., Varia, M., Cohen, A., Sellars, A., Bestavros, A.: Multi-regulation computing: examining the legal and policy questions that arise from secure multiparty computation. In: CSLAW, pp. 53–65. ACM (2022)
69. Watson, J.-L., Wagh, S., Popa, R.A.: Piranha: a GPU platform for secure computation. In: Butler, K.R.B., Thomas, K. (eds.) USENIX Security 2022, pp. 827–844. USENIX Association (2022)
70. Wu, P., Ning, J., Shen, J., Wang, H., Chang, E.-C.: Hybrid trust multi-party computation with trusted execution environment. In: NDSS 2022. The Internet Society (2022)
71. Yao, A.C.-C.: Protocols for secure computations (extended abstract). In: 23rd FOCS, pp. 160–164. IEEE Computer Society Press (1982)
72. Zeng, C., He, D., Feng, Q., Yang, X., Luo, Q.: SecureGPT: a framework for multiparty privacy-preserving transformer inference in GPT. IEEE Trans. Inf. Forensics Secur. **19**, 9480–9493 (2024)

Extended Meet in the Middle Attacks Using Cryptanalytic Approximations as DMZ

Eli Biham and Stav Perle[✉]

Computer Science Department, Technion – Israel Institute of Technology,
Haifa, Israel
{biham,stavp}@cs.technion.ac.il

Abstract. Traditional meet in the middle attacks divide the cipher into two halves, and partially encrypt one half and decrypt the other to search for a collision in the middle. In this paper we show that cryptanalytic techniques such as linear cryptanalysis, scattered linear cryptanalysis and differential cryptanalysis can be used as a third (free) zone in between, and allow to perform the meet in the middle analysis on fewer rounds, thus reduce the meet in the middle complexity. I.e., our new meet in the middle attacks divide the analyzed ciphers into three zones, where the middle zone is non-probabilistically approximated by some cryptanalytic approximation (e.g., linear approximation), and the meet in the middle analysis is performed on the two external zones only. We call the middle zone a free zone or a DMZ as the attack does not actively attack it. We exemplify our attacks using the FEAL cipher, which has relatively "long" non-probabilistic approximations.

1 Introduction

Meet in the middle attacks are generic known plaintext attacks against cryptographic schemes. In the case of block ciphers, the attacker divides the cipher into two zones, usually with the same number of rounds. Given a plaintext and a ciphertext, it partially encrypts the plaintext through the first zone under all key candidates of the first zone. Then, the attacker partially decrypts the ciphertext through the second zone under all key candidates of the second zone. The attacker keeps the key pairs of colliding candidates, i.e., whose forward intermediate data through the encryption is the same as the backward intermediate data through the decryption. The correct key must be included in this list.

In this paper, we present extensions of meet in the middle attacks, in which the analyzed cipher is divided into three zones. The external two zones are used for analysis, and the middle zone is covered by non-probabilistic approximation. Each extension we present is based on a different type of cryptanalytic approximation, and the analysis is performed in a slightly different way.

Figure 1 illustrates the difference in the division into zones between the meet in the middle attack and our extended meet in the middle attack. On the left, a

A. Akavia et al. (Eds.): CSCML 2025, LNCS 16244, pp. 175–191, 2026.
https://doi.org/10.1007/978-3-032-10759-6_11

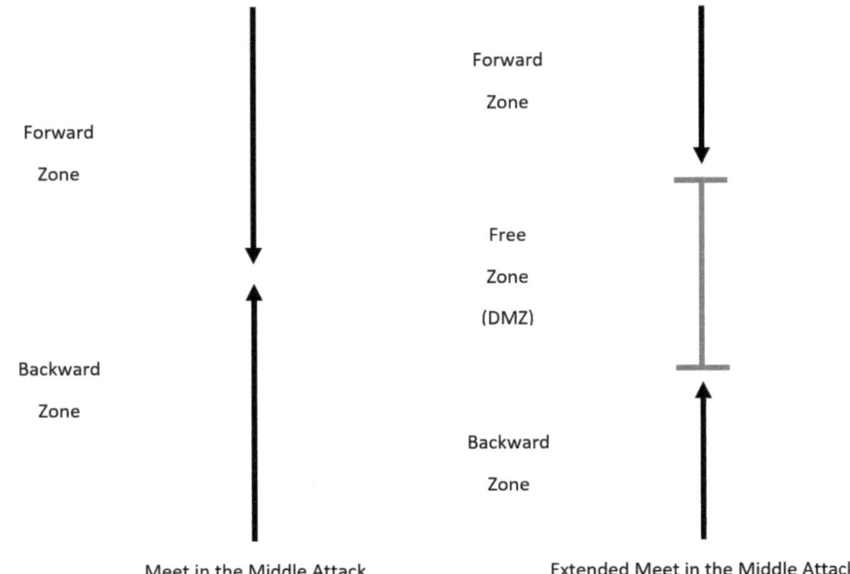

Fig. 1. The Zones of the Meet in the Middle Attack and Our Extended Meet in the Middle Attack

standard meet in the middle attack is shown, with the two zones, each computed in a different direction, both meet in the middle, and colliding on the correct key. Our extension is shown on the right, with three zones. The middle zone provides a free (magical-like) connection between two different intermediate rounds, and a meet in the middle is performed on the two external zones. Due to the free zone, a translation can be made between the two intermediate values that allows to identification of the collisions, even though the data is at different rounds.

1.1   Meet in the Middle Attack Against Double-DES

The key size of DES is 56 bit. Double-DES is a consequence of a naive approach to increase the strength of DES by using two 56-bit keys $K1, K2$, and encrypting each block twice. I.e., $2DES_{K1,K2}(P) = DES_{K2}(DES_{K1}(P))$.

The most well known version of meet in the middle is applied against Double-DES [5]. Although the keys of Double-DES are 112-bit long, Double-DES can be broken by a meet in the middle attack with less than 2^{57} complexity. A more sophisticated version against the more complicated two-key Triple-DES cipher has about the same complexity.

The idea of a meet in the middle attack on Double-DES uses the observation that the first and second encryptions use different keys. Thus, it is possible to try them separately, one in the forward direction from the plaintext to the middle, and the other in the backward direction from the ciphertext to the middle.

To keep the data of one direction available in the analysis of the other, a hash table is used, keeping the key k_1 of the forward direction indexed by the encrypted plaintext $x_1 = DES_{k_1}(P_1)$, which later need to be accessed by the backward direction by index $y_1 = DES_{k_2}^{-1}(C_1)$. Each pair of keys $(k1, k2)$ constructed by such access certainly encrypts P_1 into C_1 by Double-DES.

A basic version of the algorithm of the meet in the middle attack against Double-DES is as follows:

1. Given a plaintext P_1 and its corresponding ciphertext encrypted under the unknown key: $C_1 = DES_{K_2}(DES_{K_1}(P_1))$.
2. Initialize an empty hash table h. Each entry will have a set of keys initialized by $\{\}$.
3. For each candidate for the value of the 56 key bits k_1 ($k_1 \in \{0,1\}^{56}$):
   (a) Encrypt the plaintext P_1 under k_1. Let $x_1 = DES_{k_1}(P_1)$.
   (b) Insert k_1 into the hash table at index x_1. $h[x_1] \leftarrow k_1$ (can store multiple keys for same x_1.
4. For each candidate for the value of the 56 key bits k_2 ($k_2 \in \{0,1\}^{56}$):
   (a) Decrypt the ciphertext C_1 under k_2. Let $y_1 = DES_{k_2}^{-1}(C_1)$.
   (b) Fetch all keys k_1 in $h[y_1]$.
   (c) For any fetched key $k_1 \in h[y_1]$
      i. Try (k_1, k_2) with additional plaintext P_2 and its corresponding ciphertext $C_2 = DES_{K_2}(DES_{K_1}(P_2))$.
      ii. If $DES_{K_2}(DES_{K_1}(P_2)) = C_2$ announce that the found key is the unknown secret key.

1.2   The Fast Data Encipherment Algorithm (FEAL)

The Fast data Encipherment ALgorithm (FEAL) [10] is a family of encryption algorithms with a shared common basic structure. FEAL was introduced in 1987 with the goal of having a very efficient software implementation while still being more secure than DES [9]. The first member of the family was FEAL-4, which had four rounds. The block size of FEAL-4 is 64 bits, and the key size is also 64 bits. FEAL-4 was broken immediately after its introduction [4]. After FEAL-4 was broken, an extended version with eight rounds, called FEAL-8, was introduced. After FEAL-8 was broken by differential cryptanalysis [3], two new versions were added to the family: FEAL-N with any number N of rounds, and FEAL-NX with extended 128-bit keys. Though FEAL never became a popular cipher, over the years FEAL inspired the development of many cryptanalytic techniques, including differential and linear cryptanalysis.

FEAL-N consists of N rounds of arithmetic operations and rotations. The block size of FEAL-N is 64 bits, and the key size is also 64 bits. The key processing algorithm generates N 16-bit round subkeys, and two 64-bit whitening subkeys. Before the first round, the plaintext is XORed with a 64-bit whitening subkey. Then, the left half of the data is XORed into the right half of the data. After that, N rounds are performed, after which the left half of the data is XORed into the right half of the data and then the result is XORed with another 64-bit whitening subkey. An outline of FEAL-8 is given in Fig. 2.

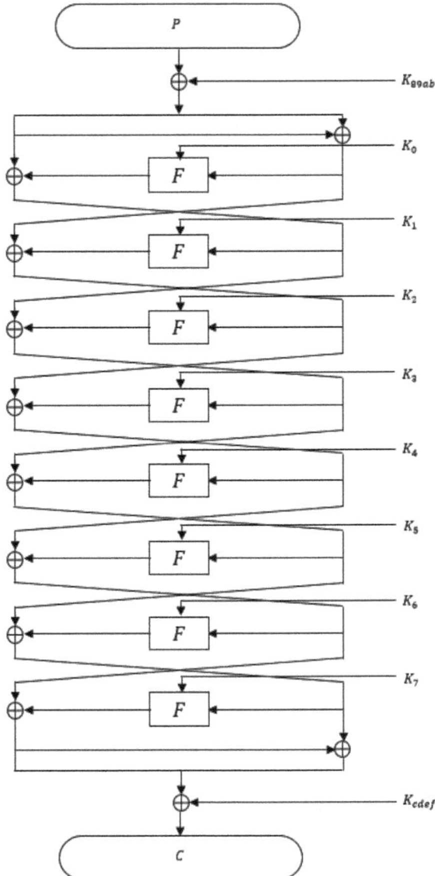

Fig. 2. Outline of FEAL-8

Next, we describe what the round function of FEAL looks like. The input and the output of each round consist of 64 bits. The main part of the round function is the F function, which accepts as input the right half of the round input and the 16-bit round subkey. The F function returns a 32-bit output, which is then XORed with the left half of the round input. This result becomes the right half of the input to the next round, while the right half of the round input becomes the left half of the input to the next round.

The F function of FEAL accepts as input the right half of the round input and the 16-bit round subkey. The F function divides the right half of the round input into four bytes, XORs the first byte into the second byte, and the last byte into the third byte. Then, the F function XORs the two middle bytes with the 16-bit round subkey. The result is then transformed by four 16-bit to 8-bit S boxes in the order described in Fig. 3.   FEAL has two kinds of S boxes S_0 and

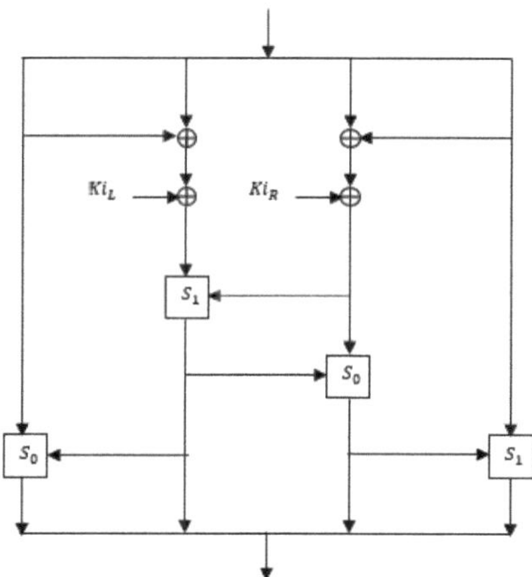

Fig. 3. The F Function of FEAL

S_1. Each S-box S_i accepts two bytes, adds them together and then i is added to the sum. The total sum is taken modulo 256 and rotated by two bits to the left. The F function returns a 32-bit output, which is the concatenation of the outputs of all four S boxes.

1.3   An Equivalent Descriptions of FEAL

In [3] two equivalent descriptions of FEAL are described. These descriptions take advantage of the structure of the F function to eliminate the whitening subkeys and simplify the analysis. Recall that the F function XORs the first byte of the input into the second byte, and the last byte of the input into the third byte, and then mixes the two middle bytes with a 16-bit round subkey. This operation can be written as the following function:

$$L(X, Y) = (X^0, X^0 \oplus X^1 \oplus Y^0, X^2 \oplus X^3 \oplus Y^1, X^3),$$

where X is a 32-bit string, divided into four bytes: X^0, X^1, X^2, X^3, and Y is a 16-bit string, divided into two bytes: Y^0, Y^1. Using L, one of the whitening subkeys can be eliminated by XORing the whitening subkey bits into all the round subkeys and extending the size of the round subkeys to 32 bits. The extended 32-bit round subkeys of the equivalent descriptions are called actual subkeys. The result is a set of subkeys with no whitening on the beginning (or end) of the cipher.

We consider two equivalent descriptions of FEAL. In the first description, the whitening subkey in the beginning has been eliminated, and the actual subkeys are denoted by EKi, and in the latter description the whitening subkey in the end has been eliminated, and the actual subkeys are denoted by DKi. Table 1 summarizes the mapping between the values of the subkeys of all three descriptions of FEAL-8.

Table 1. The Subkeys of FEAL-8 and the Subkeys of the Equivalent Descriptions

FEAL-8	Equivalent description when the whitening subkey in the beginning is eliminated	Equivalent description when the whitening subkey in the end is eliminated
$K89ab$	0	$DK89ab = K89 \oplus Kcd \oplus Kef, Kab \oplus Kef$
$K0$	$EK0 = L(K0, K89 \oplus Kab)$	$DK0 = L(K0, Kcd)$
$K1$	$EK1 = L(K1, K89)$	$DK1 = L(K1, Kcd \oplus Kef)$
$K2$	$EK2 = L(K2, K89 \oplus Kab)$	$DK2 = L(K2, Kcd)$
$K3$	$EK3 = L(K3, K89)$	$DK3 = L(K3, Kcd \oplus Kef)$
$K4$	$EK4 = L(K4, K89 \oplus Kab)$	$DK4 = L(K4, Kcd)$
$K5$	$EK5 = L(K5, K89)$	$DK5 = L(K5, Kcd \oplus Kef)$
$K6$	$EK6 = L(K6, K89 \oplus Kab)$	$DK6 = L(K6, Kcd)$
$K7$	$EK7 = L(K7, K89)$	$DK7 = L(K7, Kcd \oplus Kef)$
$Kcdef$	$EKcdef = K89 \oplus Kab \oplus Kcd, Kab \oplus Kef$	0

As we show later, when our attacks analyze the last rounds of the cipher, we eliminate the whitening subkey at the end and find bits from the DK actual subkeys rather than bits from the original subkeys. In the same way, when our attacks analyze the first rounds of the cipher, we eliminate the whitening subkey at the beginning and find bits from the EK actual subkeys. Notice that since there is a linear relation between the subkeys of all three descriptions of FEAL, it is possible to analyze the first and the last rounds of the cipher in the same attack.

1.4   Our Results

We present various extensions of meet in the middle attacks, which are based on dividing the cipher into three zones rather than two. The first zone is used for the forward analysis and the last zone is used for the backward analysis. In between, a middle zone is a free zone that supplies a non-probabilistic approximation.

The first extension we present is a simple attack that is based on a linear approximation with probability 1. It provides a basic template for our attack, which should be easy to understand without the need to understand ideas of more advanced types of cryptanalysis. We then present a more advanced extension based on a scattered linear approximation. It uses a more complex type of approximation, but the attack algorithm is very similar. In addition, we present differential meet in the middle attack.

1.5   Notations

For simplicity we refer to the plaintext as the input of the first round after the initial whitening, and the ciphertext as the output of the last round before the final whitening.

Throughout this paper we use the following notations:

P is the plaintext.
C is the ciphertext.
K is the unknown secret key.
Ki is the ith subkey generated by the key schedule.
EKi is the ith round actual subkey, when the whitening subkey in the
      beginning is eliminated.
DKi is the ith round actual subkey, when the whitening subkey in the
      end is eliminated.
Ii is the input to the F function in the ith round.
Oi is the output of the F function in the ith round.

Given a variable T:

$|T|$ is the number of bits in T.
T_L is the $|T|/2$ leftmost bits of T, where $|T|$ is even.
T_R is the $|T|/2$ rightmost bits of T, where $|T|$ is even.
T_i is the ith bit of T ($0 \leq i \leq |T| - 1$, starting from the right of T).

1.6 Structure of the Paper

This paper is organized as follows: Sect. 2 briefly describes the fundamentals of linear cryptanalysis, and presents our linear meet in the middle attack. Section 2 briefly describes the fundamentals of scattered linear cryptanalysis, and the construction of the scattered linear approximation used in our attack, followed by our scattered linear meet in the middle attack. Section 4.2 briefly describes the fundamentals of differential cryptanalysis, and presents our differential meet in the middle attack. Finally, Sect. 5 summarizes this paper.

2 Linear Meet in the Middle Attacks

In this section we present our linear meet in the middle attack. We start with a summary of linear cryptanalysis, then we present the linear approximation we used in our linear meet in the middle attack, which is followed by the attack itself.

2.1 Linear Cryptanalysis

Linear cryptanalysis was introduced by Mitsuru Matsui, who first applied the technique to an attack against FEAL [8, 10], and later against DES [6, 7, 9]. Linear cryptanalysis studies probabilistic linear relations between the parity of a subset of plaintext bits, a subset of ciphertext bits and a subset of key bits. These probabilistic relations are called linear approximations. Each linear approximation has a probability to hold, which is the fraction of plaintexts-ciphertext pairs

Table 2. The Non-Probabilistic Linear approximations of the F Function Used in this Paper

Linear Approximation	Input Mask	Output Mask	Bias
λ_{F1}	00010000_x	04040400_x	$-1/2$
λ_{F2}	00000001_x	00000104_x	$-1/2$

that satisfy the approximation. The ability to distinguish whether an approximation holds highly depends on the bias of the approximation, which is the distance of the probability from $1/2$.

Given an approximation with high probability, by analyzing the parity of the subset of plaintext bits and the subset of ciphertext bits, an attacker can obtain a prediction for the parity of the subset of the key bits. By using auxiliary techniques, the attacker can find more key bits.

In our attacks, we concentrate on non-probabilistic linear approximations, i.e., linear approximations that always hold or always fail.

2.2   Non-probabilistic Linear Approximations of the F Function of FEAL

Some Feistel ciphers (and ciphers with similar structures) have linear approximations of the F function that holds with probability 1 (or 0). FEAL is an example of such a cipher. As mentioned earlier, FEAL has two kinds of S boxes S_0 and S_1. Recall that each S-box S_i accepts two bytes, adds them together, and then i is added to the sum. The sum is taken modulo 256 and rotated by two bits to the left. Observe that the LSB of the sum equals the XOR of the LSBs of the inputs. Thus, each S box has a linear approximation on the LSB bits with bias $\pm 1/2$, i.e., probability 0 or 1 depending on i. Notice that the XOR of any subset of these approximations results in a linear approximation that also has bias $\pm 1/2$. Hence, as FEAL calls the S boxes four times in each round, the F function of FEAL has a total of $2^4 - 1 = 15$ non-trivial linear approximations with bias $\pm 1/2$. For convenience, the non-probabilistic linear approximations of the F function that we use in this paper are presented in Table 2.

2.3   The Used Linear Approximation

In this subsection we present the linear approximation λ_1 used in the free zone of our linear meet in the middle attack. λ_1 is a three-round linear approximation with bias $1/2$. The first and the third rounds of λ_1 are based on λ_{F1}, and the second round is based on the trivial approximation. An outline of λ_1 is presented in Fig. 4.

For each given plaintext, we can calculate the parity of the set of plaintext bits that correspond to the subset λ_{1P}, the plaintext mask of λ_1. This parity is equal (up to XOR with subkey bits) to the parity of the set of bits in the output

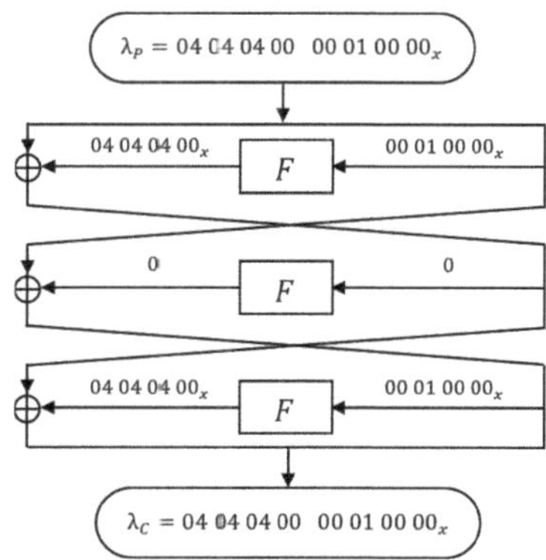

Fig. 4. The Three-Round Linear Approximation λ_1

of Round 3 that correspond to the subset λ_{1C}, the ciphertext mask of λ_1. I.e., for any plaintext and it's ciphertext, $P \cdot \lambda_{1P} \oplus C \cdot \lambda_{1C}$ is a key-dependent constant.

2.4   Linear Meet in the Middle Attack

We use λ_1 to attack FEAL-7. Our attack analyzes the first two rounds as the forward zone and the last two rounds as the backward zone. Rounds 3–5 form the free zone. Due to technical details, when our attack analyzes the first two rounds, we eliminate the whitening subkey at the beginning and find bits from the EK actual subkeys. In the same way, when our attack analyzes the last two rounds of the cipher, we eliminate the whitening subkey at the end and find bits from the DK actual subkeys.

The attack assumes that λ_1 is set in rounds 3–5, and the analysis guesses key bits related to rounds 1, 2 and 6, 7. The approximated parity of λ_1 consists of a single bit from the right half of the input to Round 3, a single bit from the right half of the input to Round 5, and several bits from the left half of the input to Round 3 and Round 5.

To get the value of the bit from the right half of the input to Round 3 (and all bits from the left half of the input to Round 3) in the forward analysis, it is necessary to encrypt Round 1 by $EK0$, and partially encrypt Round 2 by the 16 middle bits of $EK1$. Similarly, to get the value of the bit from the right half of the input to Round 5 (and all bits from the left half of the input to Round 5) in the backward analysis, it is necessary to decrypt Round 7 by $DK6$, and partially decrypt Round 6 by the 16 middle bits of $DK5$. So the forward analysis needs to try 2^{48} candidates keys and so also the backward analysis.

Based on λ_1 we design a linear meet in the middle attack against FEAL-7, in the following way:

1. Given N plaintexts $P_1, ..., P_N$ and their corresponding ciphertexts $C_i = FEAL7_K(P_i)$ $(1 \le i \le N)$, encrypted under the unknown secret key K.

2. Initialize an empty hash table.
3. For each candidate for the value of the 48 subkey bits k_1 ($k_1 \in \{0,1\}^{48}$):
   (a) Initialize an empty list.
   (b) For each P_i and C_i ($1 \le i \le N$):
       i. Partially encrypt the two first rounds by the 48 corresponding subkey bits.
       ii. Calculate the parity of the set of bits that correspond to the subset λ_{1P} in the input to Round 3.
       iii. Deduce (up to XOR with subkey bits) the parity of the set of bits that correspond to the subset λ_{1C} in the output of Round 5.
       iv. Append the parity to the list.
   (c) Convert the bits in the list into binary number b_1.
   (d) Store (b_1, k_1) in the hash table, indexed by b_1.
4. For each candidate for the value of the 48 subkey bits k_2 ($k_2 \in \{0,1\}^{48}$):
   (a) Initialize an empty list.
   (b) For each P_i and C_i ($1 \le i \le N$):
       i. Partially decrypt the two last rounds by the 48 corresponding subkey bits.
       ii. Calculate the parity of the set of bits that correspond to the subset λ_{1C} in the output of Round 5.
       iii. Append the parity to the list.
   (c) Convert the bits in the list into binary number b_2.
   (d) Access hash-table$[b_2]$ and hash-table$[\overline{b_2}]$.
   (e) For any key k_1 in these entries:
       i. Try (k_1, k_2) with additional plaintexts.
   (f) Once we have a single possible value for k_1, k_2, complete the rest by exhaustive search.

3   Scattered Linear Meet in the Middle Attacks

In this section we present our scattered linear meet in the middle attack. It is quite similar to the previous case, but with an alternate approximation based on a different type of cryptanalytic technique. As before, we start with a summary of scattered linear cryptanalysis, then we present the scattered linear approximation we used in our scattered linear meet in the middle attack, which is followed by the attack itself.

3.1   Scattered Linear Cryptanalysis

Scattered linear approximations were introduced in [1]. These approximations probabilistically predict the parity of a subset of bits composed of plaintext bits, ciphertext bits, key bits, and intermediate data bits. Notice that the plaintext and the ciphertext bits are known, and the key bits are fixed. Therefore, given a scattered linear approximation with high probability, the parity of the intermediate data bits can be deduced with some probability.

In our attacks, we concentrate on non-probabilistic scattered linear approximations, which means that in these approximations the parity of the intermediate data bits is known up to the XOR with the subkey bits.

3.2   The Used Scattered Linear Approximation

In this subsection we present the scattered linear approximation λ_2 used in the free zone of our scattered linear meet in the middle attack.

A 16-round scattered linear approximation of DES was presented in [1]. This scattered linear approximation approximates the parity of subsets of bits from the output of the F function in all rounds whose index is 3 modulo 4. We use a similar construction to build a seven-round scattered linear approximation of FEAL that holds with probability 1.

In FEAL-7, the XOR of the outputs of the F function in all odd rounds equals the XOR of the left half of the plaintext and the left half of the ciphertext, i.e., $(\bigoplus_{i \equiv 1 \ (mod \ 2)} Oi) = P_L \oplus C_L$. From this equation we can deduce the following scattered linear approximation:

$$(\bigoplus_{i \equiv 1 \ (mod \ 2)} O^i \cdot X') \oplus P_L \cdot X' \oplus C_L \cdot X',$$

where X' is any non-empty mask of a subset of bits. The bias of this scattered linear approximation is $1/2$. It predicts the parity of the intermediate data bits that correspond to the subset X' from each output of F in the odd rounds.

Among all the values of X', we observe that $X' = 04040400_x$ is especially attractive for our attack as it is the output mask of λ_{F1}. Indeed, the bias of λ_{F1} is $-1/2$ in each round. Thus, for any data, the parity of the intermediate data bits that correspond to the subset 04040400_x in the output of F equals (up to XOR with subkey bits) to the parity of the intermediate data bits that correspond to the subset 00010000_x in the input of F. By combining both relations, we conclude that the parity of the intermediate data bits that correspond to the subset 00010000_x in the input of F in the odd rounds (rounds 1, 3, 5 and 7) can be computed (up to XOR with subkey bits) from the plaintext and the ciphertext.

In addition, the output of the F function in Round i $(1 < i < n)$ equals the XOR of the inputs of the F function in Round $i - 1$ and Round $i + 1$. In FEAL-7 we get that $O2 = I1 \oplus I3$, and $O6 = I5 \oplus I7$, and by joining these two equations we get that $\bigoplus_{i \equiv 1 \ (mod \ 2)} Ii = O2 \oplus O6$. Therefore, the parity of the intermediate data bits that correspond to the subset 00010000_x in the input of F in the odd rounds is the parity of the intermediate data bits that correspond to the subset 00010000_x in the output of F in Round 2 and Round 6.

Based on all of the above, we construct the scattered linear approximation λ_2. λ_2 is a seven-round scattered linear approximation with bias $1/2$. This approximation predicts (up to XOR with subkey bits) that the parity of the subsets of bits corresponds to the mask 00010000_x from the output of the F function in Round 2 and Round 6. An outline of λ_2 is presented in Fig. 5.

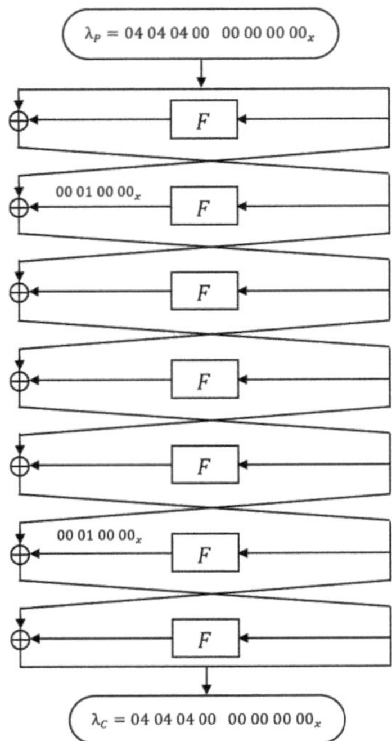

Fig. 5. The Seven-Round Scattered Linear Approximation λ_2

3.3   Scattered Linear Meet in the Middle Attack

We use λ_2 to attack FEAL-7. Our attack analyzes the first two rounds and the last two rounds of the cipher simultaneously. when our attack analyzes the first two rounds, we eliminate the whitening subkey at the beginning and find bits from the EK actual subkeys. In the same way, when our attack analyzes the last two rounds of the cipher, we eliminate the whitening subkey at the end and find bits from the DK actual subkeys.

The attack assumes that λ_2 is set in rounds 1–7, and the analysis guesses key bits related to rounds 1, 2 and 6, 7. Notice that λ_2 has only two intermediate data bits that participate in the parity, one bit is $O2_{16}$ and the other is $O6_{16}$. To get the value of $O2_{16}$ it is necessary to encrypt Round 1 by $EK0$, and partially encrypt Round 2 by the 16 middle bits of $EK1$. To get the value of $O6_{16}$ it is necessary to decrypt Round 7 by $DK6$, and partially decrypt Round 6 by the 16 middle bits of $DK5$.

Based on λ_2 we design scattered linear meet in the middle attack against FEAL-7, in the following way:

1. Given N plaintexts $P_1, ..., P_N$ and their corresponding ciphertexts $C_i = FEAL7_K(P_i)$ $(1 \le i \le N)$, encrypted under the unknown secret key K.
2. Initialize an empty hash table.
3. For each candidate for the value of the 48 subkey bits k_1 $(k_1 \in \{0,1\}^{48})$:

    (a) Initialize an empty list.
    (b) For each P_i and C_i $(1 \leq i \leq N)$:
        i. Calculate the value of $O2_{16} \oplus O6_{16}$ (up to XOR with subkey bits)
        ii. Partially encrypt the two first rounds by the 48 corresponding subkey bits.
        iii. Calculate the value of $O2_{16}$ according to the candidate.
        iv. Deduce (up to XOR with subkey bits) the value of $O6_{16}$.
        v. Append the value to the list.
    (c) Convert the bits in the list into binary number b_1.
    (d) Store (b_1, k_1) in the hash table, indexed by b_1.
4. For each candidate for the value of the 48 subkey bits k_2 $(k_2 \in \{0,1\}^{48})$:
    (a) Initialize an empty list.
    (b) For each P_i and C_i $(1 \leq i \leq N)$:
        i. Partially decrypt the two last rounds by the 48 corresponding subkey bits.
        ii. Calculate the value of $O6_{16}$ according to the candidate.
        iii. Append the value to the list.
    (c) Convert the bits in the list into binary number b_2.
    (d) Access hash-table$[b_2]$ and hash-table$[\overline{b_2}]$.
    (e) For any key k_1 in these entries:
        i. Try (k_1, k_2) with additional plaintexts.
    (f) Once we have a single possible value for k_1, k_2, complete the rest by exhaustive search.

The attack is illustrated in Fig. 6.

3.4   Discussion

We should emphasize some details related to this attack. In general, scattered meet in the middle attacks should apply the analysis phase on different S boxes than those active in the scattered approximation. Otherwise, one may claim that the approximation can be replaced by a shorter approximation with fewer rounds, which in some cases may be reduced to a regular linear approximation (e.g., the linear approximation of the three middle rounds of the seven-round scattered linear approximation, which have no approximated intermediate bits).

In our case, the scattered linear approximation has no active S boxes in Round 2 and Round 6, while the analysis phase guesses some of the key bits in these rounds so no such reduction is possible. On the other hand, there is some intersection in the active S boxes of the scattered linear approximation and the analysis in Round 1 and Round 7 (they are interested in different output bits of the F function, though).

To present an example in which there is a full separation between the two, we present a variant of this attack in which the F function is modified in all the even rounds. As can be seen from the construction of the scattered linear approximation, the details of the F function in these rounds do not affect the scattered

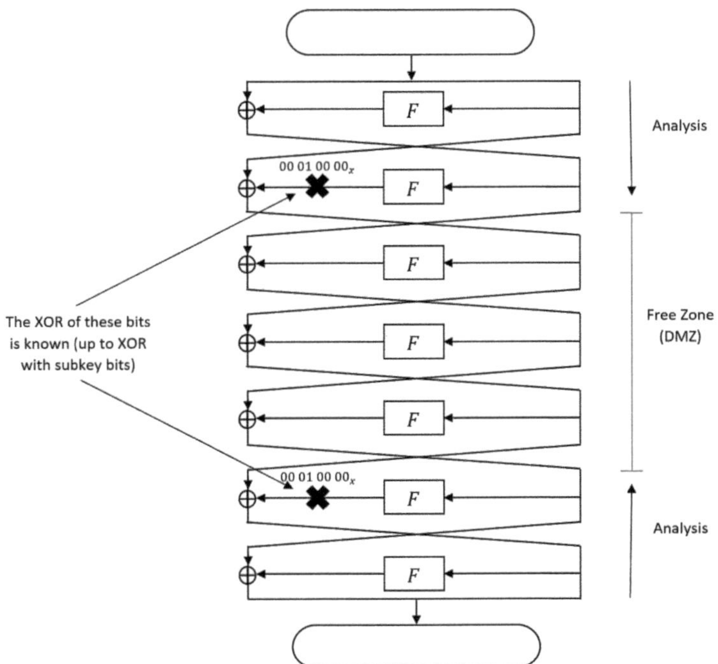

Fig. 6. Scattered Meet in the Middle Attack

linear approximation. Similarly, they do not affect the general description of the attack. The only effect they have is on the details of the partial encryption in Round 1, Round 2, Round 6 and Round 7, i.e., which S boxes are computed, and how many subkey bits are recovered.

Therefore, we replace the F function in the even rounds with a different one more similar to a DES-style F function. In our proposed F function, the approximated bit in the output of F depends only on the second input byte through an 8×8-bit S box (and XOR with a subkey). Thus, it suffices to analyze only one S box in Round 1 and one in Round 2 in the analysis phase (and similarly in Round 6 and Round 7), and none of them is active in the scattered linear approximation.

Clearly in this case, this scattered linear meet in the middle attack cannot be viewed as a disguised (non-scattered) linear meet in the middle attack. To perform a (non-scattered) linear meet in the middle attack with the middle three-round linear approximation, the analysis phase must guess additional subkey bits on both ends. It follows from the fact that the linear approximation has several additional bits in its approximated subsets[1] that the scattered linear approximation does not have at the same rounds. These bits need to be recovered

---

[1] I.e., 0404040400_x on the left half, in addition to the 00010000_x on the right half that is common to both.

by the analysis of a linear meet in the middle attack but not of the scattered linear meet in the middle attack.

4   Differential Meet in the Middle Attacks

In this section we present our differential meet in the middle attack. We start with a summary of differential cryptanalysis, then we present our attack. Due to lack of space, we present a generic version of the attack, without a specific target cipher, though there are ciphers that have the needed kinds of differential characteristics (e.g., SKINNY).

4.1   Differential Cryptanalysis

Differential cryptanalysis [3] analyzes how differences evolve during encryption, and how differences in plaintext pairs evolve into differences in the resultant ciphertext pairs. Their study allows to assign probabilities to the possible keys, and to locate the most probable key. This method is usually applied on many pairs of plaintexts with the same pre-chosen plaintext difference.

Differential cryptanalysis was introduced by Eli Biham and Adi Shamir in 1990. They used it to publish several differential attacks against various block ciphers and hash functions [2], including DES. The most well known attack of this kind can break the full 16-round DES in 2^{37} time complexity given 2^{47} chosen plaintexts.

Differential cryptanalysis is a generic technique for assessing the strength of block ciphers. It was later used as the main design criteria for the design of newer standards, e.g., AES, and inspired the development of many cryptanalytic techniques and extensions.

4.2   Differential Meet in the Middle Attack

This attack is based on a truncated differential characteristic sustained that the plaintext difference is Ω_P iff the ciphertext difference is Ω_C. I.e., the plaintext and ciphertext differences are fixed to some value in some of their bits, and may be any value in other bits. The number of fixed bits is the same in both.

Based on such truncated differential characteristic we design differential meet in the middle attack in the following way:

1. Given N pairs of plaintexts $(P_1, P_1^*), ..., (P_N, P_N^*)$ and their corresponding ciphertexts $(C_1, C_1^*), ..., (C_N, C_N^*)$, encrypted under the unknown secret key K.
2. Initialize an empty hash table hash_table[]. Each entry is initialized by $\{\}$ upon first access.
3. For each candidate for the value of the t_1 subkey bits of k_1 ($k_1 \in \{0,1\}^{t_1}$):
   (a) Initialize an empty list.
   (b) For each P_i, P_i^* ($1 \le i \le N$):

     i. Partially encrypt the first rounds by the t_1 corresponding subkey bits.

     ii. If the difference matches Ω_P append the plaintext index i to the list.

  (c) Encode the list of indices into a binary number b_1.

  (d) Insert k_1 to the hash table by hash_table$[b_1] \leftarrow k_1$ (this is an addition to the respective set).

4. For each candidate for the value of the t_2 subkey bits of k_2 ($k_2 \in \{0,1\}^{t_2}$):

  (a) Initialize an empty list.

  (b) For each C_i, C_i^* ($1 \le i \le N$):

     i. Partially decrypt the last rounds by the t_2 corresponding subkey bits.

     ii. If the difference matches Ω_C append the ciphertext index i to the list.

  (c) Encode the list of indices into a binary number b_2.

  (d) Fetch hash_table$[b_2]$.

  (e) For any key k_1 in hash_table$[b_2]$:

     i. The pair (k_1, k_2) is expected to be the correct values for the corresponding key bits (assuming N is large enough for unique a result).

     ii. Complete the rest of the key bits by exhaustive search.

5   Summary

We presented a new technique for meet in the middle attacks that divides the cipher into three zones, rather than two, where the middle zone is a DMZ, i.e., a free zone that creates a 100% approximation between its two sides. It thus saves the need for the analysis phase of the attack to try keys and make partial encryption or decryption in the middle zone. We presented several such attacks using linear approximations, scattered linear approximations, and differential characteristics. We are currently working on extending these results to additional types of approximations and additional ciphers.

Acknowledgements. This research was partially supported by the Technion Hiroshi Fujiwara cyber security research center and the Israel national cyber directorate.

References

1. Biham, E., Perle, S.: Conditional linear cryptanalysis — cryptanalysis of DES with less than 2^{42} complexity. IACR Trans. Symmetric Cryptol. **3**, 215–264 (2018)

2. Biham, E., Shamir, A.: Differential cryptanalysis of feal and N-Hash. In: Davies, D.W. (ed.) EUROCRYPT 1991. LNCS, vol. 547, pp. 1–16. Springer, Heidelberg (1991). https://doi.org/10.1007/3-540-46416-6_1

3. Biham, E., Shamir, A.: Differential Cryptanalysis of the Data Encryption Standard (1993). http://www.cs.technion.ac.il/~biham/

4. Boer, B.: Cryptanalysis of F.E.A.L. In: Barstow, D., et al. (eds.) EUROCRYPT 1988. LNCS, vol. 330, pp. 293–299. Springer, Heidelberg (1988). https://doi.org/10.1007/3-540-45961-8_27

5. Diffie, W., Hellman, M.E.: Special feature exhaustive cryptanalysis of the NBS data encryption standard. Computer, 74–84 (1977)
6. Matsui, M.: Linear cryptanalysis method for DES cipher. In: Helleseth, T. (ed.) EUROCRYPT 1993. LNCS, vol. 765, pp. 386–397. Springer, Heidelberg (1994). https://doi.org/10.1007/3-540-48285-7_33
7. Matsui, M.: The first experimental cryptanalysis of the data encryption standard. In: Desmedt, Y.G. (ed.) CRYPTO 1994. LNCS, vol. 839, pp. 1–11. Springer, Heidelberg (1994). https://doi.org/10.1007/3-540-48658-5_1
8. Matsui, M., Yamagishi, A.: A new method for known plaintext attack of FEAL cipher. In: Rueppel, R.A. (ed.) EUROCRYPT 1992. LNCS, vol. 658, pp. 81–91. Springer, Heidelberg (1993). https://doi.org/10.1007/3-540-47555-9_7
9. National Bureau of Standards: Data Encryption Standard. US. Department of Commerce, Federal Information Processing Standards Publication, FIPS 46 (1977)
10. Shimizu, A., Miyaguchi, S.: Fast data encipherment algorithm FEAL. In: Chaum, D., Price, W.L. (eds.) EUROCRYPT 1987. LNCS, vol. 304, pp. 267–278. Springer, Heidelberg (1988). https://doi.org/10.1007/3-540-39118-5_24

Path Optimization Using DQN
in the SCION Internet Architecture

Oran Bourak[1], Tomer Burman[1], Tony John[2(✉)], Hadassa Daltrophe[1],
Tammar Shrot[1], and David Hausheer[2]

[1] Shamoon College of Engineering (SCE), Ashdod, Israel
{hadasda1,tammash}@sce.ac.il
[2] Otto-von-Guericke-University Magdeburg, Magdeburg, Germany
{tony.john,hausheer}@ovgu.de

Abstract. Path-aware Internet architectures such as SCION expose multiple end-to-end paths to endhosts. However, optimal path selection in dynamic network conditions remains challenging. This paper presents a Deep-Q-Network approach for intelligent path selection in SCION networks. We formulate SCION path selection as a reinforcement learning problem and train a lightweight Deep-Q-Network agent that observes latency, loss, and bandwidth metrics and outputs the optimal path. We evaluate our approach in an simulated SCION environment with realistic time-varying traffic conditions. The DQN agent consistently matches the performance of oracle-based selection methods with full network visibility, while reducing probing overhead by 95%. These results demonstrate the potential of reinforcement learning to effectively leverage the path diversity and control offered by next-generation Internet architectures.

Keywords: SCION · Path Optimization · Deep Reinforcement Learning · DQN · Path Selection

1 Introduction

The current Internet architecture faces fundamental limitations in security, scalability, and path control [16]. The Border Gateway Protocol (BGP), the de facto inter-domain routing protocol in today's Internet, suffers from well-documented vulnerabilities including route hijacking, limited fault isolation, and lack of path transparency [15]. These limitations become increasingly problematic as applications demand stricter quality-of-service guarantees and network topologies grow more complex. SCION (Scalability, Control, and Isolation on Next-generation Networks) [3] addresses these challenges through a fundamentally different approach. By enabling path-aware networking, SCION empowers endhosts to select and control their communication paths based on application-specific requirements. This paradigm shift from hop-by-hop routing to source-selected paths

O. Bourak, T. Burman and T. John—Contributed equally.

creates new opportunities for optimization but also introduces the challenge of intelligent path selection from potentially numerous alternatives.

While SCION provides the architectural foundation for path control, it does not prescribe how endhosts should select paths dynamically. Current implementations typically employ static policies or simple heuristics, which fail to adapt to changing network conditions. As networks exhibit time-varying characteristics due to congestion, failures, and traffic patterns, there is a critical need for adaptive, data-driven path selection mechanisms.

Reinforcement learning (RL) has shown remarkable success in network optimization tasks [8]. Deep-Q-Network (DQN) [17], which combine Q-learning with deep neural networks, are particularly well-suited for high-dimensional state spaces and have been successfully applied to routing problems in Software-Defined Networks (SDN) [2,4].

In this work, we address the challenge of intelligent path selection in the SCION network architecture using a DQN approach. Our main contributions are as follows:

- We formulate SCION path selection as an RL problem and define a tailored reward function that jointly optimizes for latency, packet loss, and available bandwidth.
- We develop and implement a DQN-based agent that interacts directly with SCION's live path selection API to make real-time path decisions.
- We conduct extensive evaluations on a realistic SCION testbed and benchmark our agent against both heuristic-based (random) and idealized (oracle) baselines.

The remainder of this paper is organized as follows. Section 2 reviews the relevant background and related work. Section 3 details our proposed DQN-based approach. Section 4 describes the evaluation setup and presents the experimental results. Finally, Sect. 5 offers concluding remarks and discusses potential directions for future work.

2   Background and Related Work

Modern network infrastructures operate primarily on the TCP/IP suite, with protocols such as BGP facilitating inter-AS routing. Although MPLS adds route flexibility, conventional systems often suffer from high latency, inefficient bandwidth utilization, poor adaptability to dynamic network conditions, and limited failure isolation. In a BGP based Internet, end hosts have no control on the path they communicate over.

Studies such as [1,2] have highlighted these deficiencies, particularly in handling traffic fluctuations, real-time failures, and evolving topology constraints. Current systems remain vulnerable to problems like route hijacking and spoofing, further emphasizing the need for robust, intelligent routing architectures.

SCION Internet Architecture

SCION [3] is a security-focused, next-generation Internet architecture that offers fine-grained route control, strong fault containment, and explicit trust semantics for end-to-end communication. Its hallmark is path-aware networking: end hosts explicitly select the entire end-to-end route, specifying every inter-domain hop. This transparency allows applications to optimize for metrics such as latency, jitter, bandwidth, or cost, and even combine multiple paths when beneficial. As a result, multi-path communication is possible for endpoints with only a single physical connection, extending the advantages of multi-path protocols beyond multi-homed systems.

SCION groups Autonomous Systems (ASes) into Isolation Domains (ISDs), each of which may correspond to a geographic region, legal jurisdiction, or organizational boundary. One or more ASes form an ISD's core, which both interconnects the ISD with others and maintains its trust root configuration (TRC). Routing among ASes is confined within an ISD, and, unlike today's hop-by-hop Internet, SCION employs packet-carried forwarding state (PCFS): every packet header contains the complete inter-AS path encoded as hop fields. Core ASes periodically issue path segment construction beacons (PCBs) that discover path segments; end hosts then assemble these segments to create end-to-end paths. SCION has real-world deployments throughout the world, provided by eight Internet Service Providers [9]. These deployments are running in parallel to today's Internet. For research and running experiments on a SCION network, SCIONLab [10] provides a global SCION testbed where users can create personal ASes.

Reinforcement Learning

RL is a subfield of machine learning concerned with how agents ought to take actions in an environment to maximize cumulative reward. Unlike supervised learning, RL agents learn through trial and error, receiving feedback in the form of scalar rewards [6, 14].

The RL problem is often formalized as a Markov Decision Process (MDP), defined by a tuple (S, A, R, P, γ), where:

- S: Set of possible *states*.
- A: Set of available *actions*.
- $R(s, a)$: *Reward function* for taking action a in state s.
- $P(s'|s, a)$: *Transition probability* to next state s' given current state s and action a.
- γ: *Discount factor* for future rewards.

The goal of the agent is to learn a policy $\pi(a|s)$ that maximizes the expected cumulative reward $R(s, a)$ over time. RL methods are typically classified into value-based, policy-based, or actor-critic approaches.

Deep-Q-Networks

DQNs [12] are a value-based RL algorithm that extends Q-learning [17] by leveraging deep neural networks. This allows agents to scale to large or continuous state spaces. The agent learns to predict the long-term reward for each action given a state, and improves its policy by minimizing the temporal difference (TD) error between predicted and target Q-values.

As shown in Fig. 2, the DQN architecture maps high-dimensional input states to Q-values using deep neural networks, enabling efficient decision-making in dynamic environments.

The core concepts of the DQN are as follows:

1. **Q-Learning:** Traditional Q-Learning is a value-based RL algorithm that learns the Q-Value function $Q(s, a)$, which represents the expected cumulative reward for taking action a in state s and following the optimal policy thereafter. The Q-values are updated iteratively using the Bellman equation:

$$Q(s, a) = Q(s, a) + \alpha \left(r + \gamma \max_{a'} Q(s', a') - Q(s, a) \right)$$

   where:
   - $Q(s, a)$ is the current Q-value for state s and action a
   - $\alpha \in [0, 1]$ is the learning rate
   - r is the immediate reward
   - $\gamma \in [0, 1]$ is the discount factor
   - $\max_{a'} Q(s', a')$ is the maximum Q-value of the next state s' over all actions a'
   - s' is the next state after taking action a in state s

   This equation refines Q-values iteratively, enabling the agent to balance immediate and future rewards. As illustrated in traditional Q-learning algorithms [14], this iterative update forms the basis for learning optimal policies through interaction with the environment. As shown in Fig. 1, this process is commonly visualized as a cycle of observation, action, reward, and learning.

2. **Deep Neural Networks:** In DQN, a deep neural network approximates the Q-value function $Q(s, a; \theta)$, where θ are the parameters of the network (weights and biases). Typically, this is implemented as a multi-layer perceptron (MLP), consisting of layers of perceptrons that perform weighted summations, apply biases, and introduce non-linearity via activation functions like ReLU or sigmoid.

3. **State Representation:** The DQN receives the current environment state as input, which can be high-dimensional. The network processes this input and outputs Q-values for all available actions.

   Key mechanisms used in DQN include:
   - **Experience Replay:** Transitions (s, a, r, s') are stored in a buffer and sampled randomly to break correlation and stabilize learning.
   - **Target Networks:** A periodically updated copy of the Q-network is used to compute target Q-values, reducing training instability.

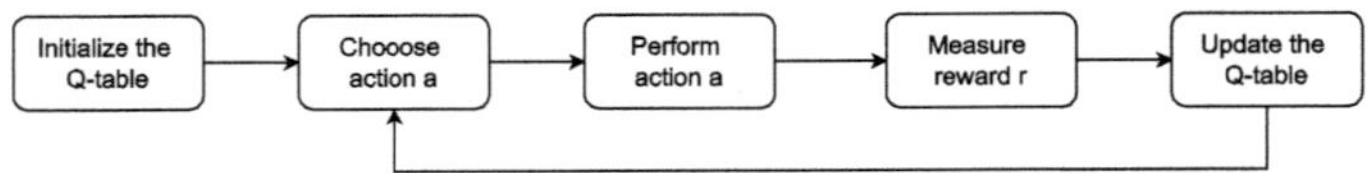

Fig. 1. Traditional Q-Learning workflow: The agent observes the state, selects an action, receives a reward, and updates the Q-values.

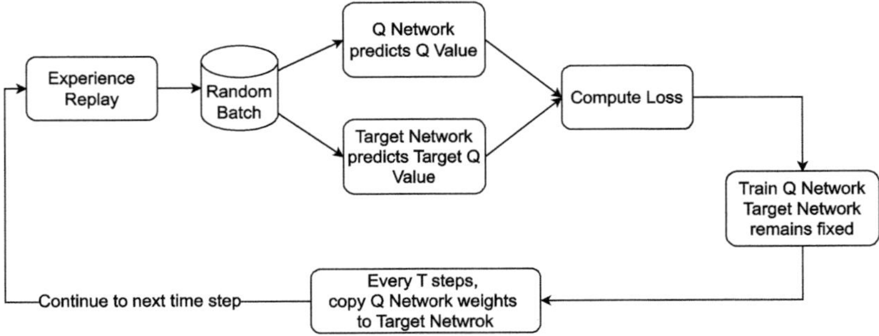

Fig. 2. Architecture of the DQN: Mapping high-dimensional states to Q-values via neural network layers.

Reinforcement Learning in Networking

Recent years have witnessed increasing interest in the application of RL to various network optimization problems. In the context of SDN, Fu et al. [4] demonstrated the effectiveness of DQNs for flow routing in data center networks, reporting a 15% improvement in throughput compared to Equal-Cost Multi-Path (ECMP) routing. Similarly, Chen et al. [2] introduced RL-Routing, an approach that leverages online learning to dynamically adapt to changing traffic patterns.

In the domain of path selection, Kea et al. [7] applied RL techniques to the problem of widest-path routing, achieving a 20% reduction in packet loss. However, their method relies on global network visibility, which limits its practicality in inter-domain environments where such information is typically unavailable.

Botta et al. [1] explored the use of multi-agent RL for optimizing Software Defined Wide Area Networks (SD-WANs). Their approach demonstrated both scalability to large network topologies and the ability to maintain performance close to that of an idealized oracle.

Our work extends prior efforts in RL for network optimization to the SCION architecture, with a focus on adaptive path selection across multi-AS topologies using DQN. Despite SCION's inherent support for path control, previous research on dynamic path selection within this framework remains limited. Gessner [5] investigated static policies tailored to application requirements, but did not address the need for real-time adaptation to changing network conditions. Moreover, the SCION reference implementation provides only basic selection strategies, such as shortest path or lowest latency, without incorporating any form of learning or data-driven decision-making.

3 DQN-Based Path Optimization in SCION

This section outlines our RL-based strategy for optimizing path selection in SCION. By leveraging the DQN framework, we enable an agent to learn adaptive routing policies that respond to real-time changes in network traffic conditions.

In SCION, path selection is delegated to the end hosts, who can select full end-to-end paths based on advertised path segments. Each path consists of three segments: up, core, and down. These are assembled from beacon packets periodically broadcast by SCION core routers.

Our work leverages this flexibility by allowing a DQN agent to dynamically choose from among the available valley-free paths for a given communication pair. The agent observes the current network state and selects one of the paths as its action. Path characteristics such as delay, goodput, and packet loss are encoded in the environment and evolve over time. In the following, we describe our implementation for the agent design, the state and action space, and the reward function.

Agent Design. The DQN agent observes the network state and selects a path as its action. The neural network approximates $Q(s, a)$, mapping state-action pairs to expected cumulative reward.

State and Action Space. In our implementation, the *state* represents the current network conditions, encoded as a five-dimensional numerical vector. The features include:

Day of the week Encoded as an integer or one-hot representation.
Time of day Normalized continuous value capturing temporal context.
Link bandwidth Reflects the capacity of the selected path.
Link capacity utilization Measures how saturated the path is.
Link trust score Computed based on latency and packet loss.

These state features are processed by the DQN model to determine the optimal routing decision.

The *action* space consists of all available paths between sender and receiver ASes in the SCION network. Each action corresponds to selecting a specific end-to-end path. These paths vary dynamically and are filtered to be valley-free. Selecting an action implies choosing the path for the current packet transfer, where each path is described by:

- A sequence of ASes and interfaces (e.g., 1-105:1 → 1-104:4 → 1-101:1 → 1-106:3)
- Aggregate latency
- Aggregate bandwidth
- Estimated packet loss rate
- Hop count and interface details (used for analysis, not directly encoded)

Reward Function. Inspired by the balance between throughput and reliability discussed by Fu et al. [4], we define the reward function as follows:

$$r = 2(w_1 \cdot G + w_2 \cdot T) - 1$$

where G is normalized goodput, $w_1 = 0.7$, $w_2 = 0.3$, and T is the link trust which defined as:

$$T = 1 - (w_3 \cdot packet\_loss + w_4 \cdot delay)$$

Weights w_3 and w_4 can be configured as per the application requirements.

3.1   Path Selection

The agent uses ε-greedy exploration. Training includes:

- Experience replay buffer of fixed size
- Mini-batch training with Adam optimizer
- Periodic synchronization of target and online networks

In designing and implementing the DQN for path optimization in SCION, most of the values and parameters, such as reward weights and state features, were determined empirically through experimentation. The workflow follows these steps:

1. **State Observation:** The agent observes the current state of the network.
2. **Action Selection:** Using an epsilon-greedy strategy, the agent selects an action, exploring randomly with probability ϵ, or exploiting the best-known action otherwise.
3. **Reward Computation:** After transmission, the agent receives a reward based on normalized values of goodput, latency, and packet loss:

$$R_t = 2 \cdot (w_1 \cdot goodput + w_2 \cdot link\_trust) - 1$$

   where $w_1 + w_2 = 1$, and $R_t \in [-1, 1]$.
4. **Experience Replay:** Transitions (s, a, r, s') are stored in a replay buffer and sampled for training.
5. **Network Update:** The agent trains an online network to minimize TD loss. A separate target network, updated periodically, provides stable target Q-values. We use the Adam optimizer for training.

Goodput and link trust are computed as follows:

- **Goodput:** Normalized to $[0, 1]$ based on a max value of 50 Mbps
- **Link Trust:** Computed as:

$$link\_trust = 1 - (0.5 \cdot packet\_loss + 0.5 \cdot delay)$$

The above steps are summarized in Algorithm 1:

Algorithm 1 Path Selection Algorithm

1: **Initialize:** online network Q with random weights
2: **Initialize:** target network Q_{target} with random weights
3: **Initialize:** replay buffer $\mathcal{D}$
4: **for** episode $= 1, 2, \ldots$ **do**
5:　　$s \leftarrow$ environment.reset()
6:　　**for** step $t = 1, 2, \ldots$ **do**
7:　　　　**if** random() $< \epsilon$ **then**
8:　　　　　　$a \leftarrow$ random action
9:　　　　**else**
10:　　　　　　$a \leftarrow \arg\max_{a'} Q(s, a')$
11:　　　　**end if**
12:　　　　$s', r \leftarrow$ environment.step(a)
13:　　　　Store (s, a, r, s') in $\mathcal{D}$
14:　　　　Sample minibatch of transitions from $\mathcal{D}$
15:　　　　**for** each (s_i, a_i, r_i, s'_i) in minibatch **do**
16:　　　　　　$y_i \leftarrow r_i + \gamma \max_{a'} Q_{\text{target}}(s'_i, a')$
17:　　　　**end for**
18:　　　　Update Q to minimize $\mathbb{E}[(y_i - Q(s_i, a_i))^2]$
19:　　　　**if** $t \bmod N = 0$ **then**
20:　　　　　　$Q_{\text{target}} \leftarrow Q$
21:　　　　**end if**
22:　　　　$s \leftarrow s'$
23:　　**end for**
24: **end for**

4　Evaluation

We evaluate the performance of our DQN-based path selection approach on realistic SCION topologies, comparing it with other path selection mechanisms.

4.1　Experimental Setup

Topology Generation: We generate realistic AS-level topologies using the BRITE topology generator [11], which creates networks following power-law degree distributions observed in the Internet. For our experiments, we configure BRITE to generate a dense topology with 50 ASes, providing sufficient path diversity for meaningful evaluation. The generated topology is then converted to SCION-specific structures through:

- ISD Assignment: ASes are grouped into Isolation Domains (ISDs) using community detection algorithms based on network locality.

- Core AS Selection: We designate 5 ASes as core ASes based on betweenness centrality metrics, with 15 tier-1 and 30 tier-2 ASes.
- Link Classification: Inter-AS links are classified as core, parent-child, or peering relationships following SCION's hierarchical structure.

After topology conversion, we run SCION's beaconing process to discover available paths. The dense topology yields 25 diverse paths between our selected source-destination pair, creating a challenging path selection scenario.

Traffic Simulation: We simulate realistic network traffic over 28 days using a gravity model combined with diurnal patterns [13]. The gravity model generates flow volumes proportional to AS sizes and inversely proportional to distance, while diurnal patterns model daily traffic variations with peak hours and off-peak periods. Key parameters include:

- Flow arrival following a Poisson process with time-varying rates
- Flow sizes drawn from a heavy-tailed distribution (Pareto with $\alpha = 1.2$)
- Peak traffic hours (9–11 AM, 2–4 PM) with $2\times$ base rate
- Weekend traffic at 70% of weekday levels

Training and Evaluation Protocol: We partition the 28-day simulation into two periods:

- Training Period (Days 1–14): Used to train the DQN agent through 200 episodes
- Evaluation Period (Days 15–28): Used to compare all methods on 47,744 flows

During training, the DQN agent uses ϵ-greedy exploration starting at $\epsilon = 1.0$ and decaying to $\epsilon = 0.01$ over 200 episodes. During deployment, the agent continues with $\epsilon = 0.05$ to adapt to network changes and discover new paths. The agent learns from immediate rewards based on achieved goodput and link trust scores as specified in our reward function.

4.2 Baseline Methods

We compare against five baseline path selection strategies:

- **Shortest Path**: Selects minimum hop-count paths using static topology (no probing)
- **Highest Bandwidth**: Selects maximum bandwidth paths (probes all 25 paths for bandwidth)
- **Lowest Latency**: Selects minimum latency paths (probes all 25 paths for latency)
- **Random**: Uniformly random selection (no probing)

For fair comparison, baseline methods that require the current state of the network must probe all available paths before each decision, while DQN employs selective probing - measuring only the single path it selects, either through exploration (random selection with probability $\epsilon = 0.05$) or exploitation (highest Q-value path with probability 0.95).

4.3   Results

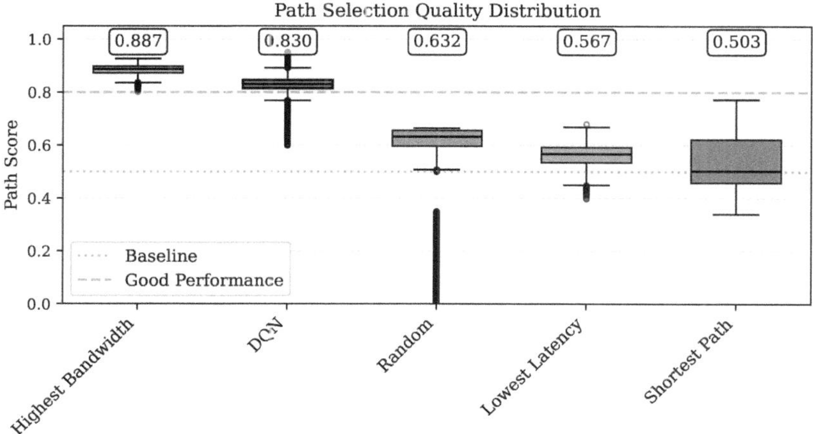

Fig. 3. Path selection quality distribution. DQN achieves near-optimal performance (0.830 median score) while using 95% fewer probes than bandwidth-aware methods. The green dashed line indicates the "good performance" threshold. (Color figure online)

Path Selection Quality: Figure 3 shows the distribution of path scores achieved by each method. Path score is a combined metric incorporating bandwidth utilization, latency, and success rate. Key observations:

- DQN achieves 0.830 median score, above the 0.8 "good performance" threshold
- Only Highest Bandwidth (0.887) outperforms DQN, but requires 25× more probing
- Methods without probing perform poorly: Random (0.632) and Shortest Path (0.503) cannot adapt to dynamic conditions
- DQN maintains performance despite 5% exploration, showing robustness of learned policy
- All 25 paths explored during evaluation, enabling continuous adaptation

The results validate that in networks with heterogeneous path quality, static selection strategies are insufficient. Achieving good performance requires incorporating current network state, traditionally necessitating expensive full-path probing.

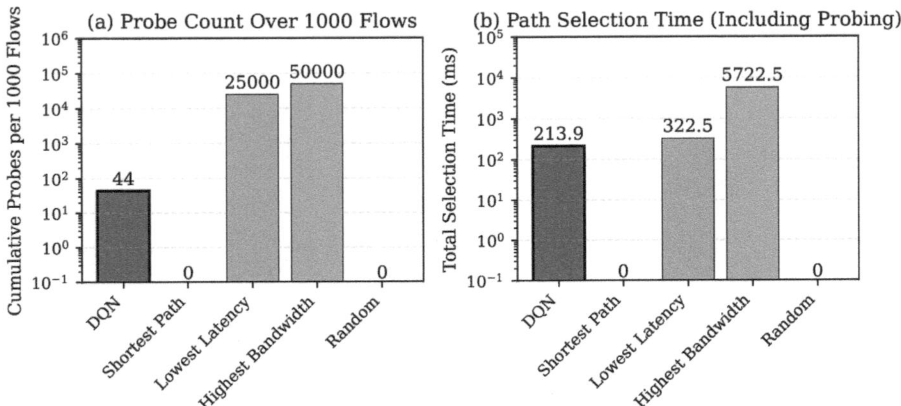

Fig. 4. (a) Cumulative probe count over 1000 flows. (b) Total selection time including probing delays. DQN achieves massive probe reduction through selective probing while maintaining sub-second selection time.

Probing Overhead: Fig. 4 quantifies the efficiency advantage of selective probing. The cumulative probe count over 1000 flows reveals a significant difference in probing rates: DQN performs only 44 probes total, exploring approximately 22 unique paths. In contrast, baseline methods requiring current network state perform 25,000 to 50,000 probes over the same period, representing a 99.8% reduction in measurement overhead.

This dramatic difference stems from fundamentally different probing strategies. Baseline methods must probe all available paths for every flow to obtain current network conditions. For instance, Highest Bandwidth probes all 25 paths for both latency and bandwidth before each decision, while Lowest Latency probes all paths for latency. However, DQN employs selective probing, measuring only the single path it selects, either through exploration (5% of decisions) or exploitation (95% of decisions).

The impact on selection time is equally significant. DQN completes path selection in 214ms on average, while bandwidth-aware methods require 5.7s, a 27× speedup critical for real-time applications and high flow arrival rates.

Despite this selective approach, DQN maintains comprehensive path coverage through its exploration strategy. The 5% exploration rate ensures that all 25 available paths are discovered and periodically re-evaluated during the 14-day evaluation period, enabling continuous adaptation to network changes while avoiding the overhead of exhaustive probing.

Scalability Validation: To validate scalability, we evaluated our approach on a larger topology comprising 1000 ASes with 200 available paths between the source-destination pair. Figure 5 presents the path selection quality distribution for this scenario. The results demonstrate robust scaling properties. DQN achieves a median score of 0.802, maintaining performance above the 0.8 thresh-

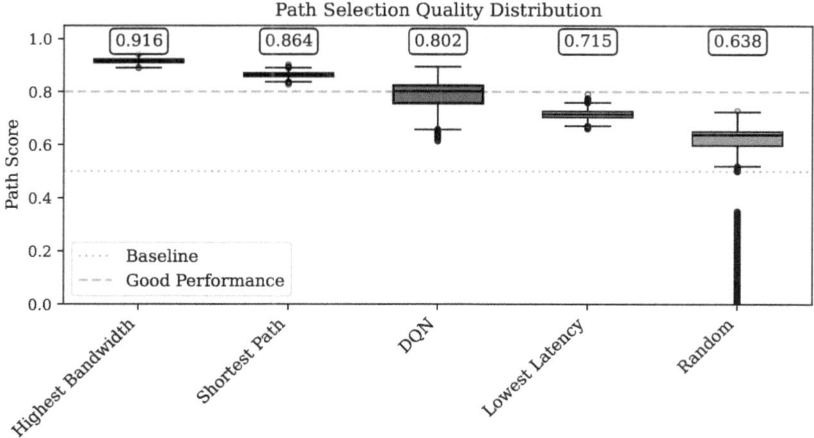

Fig. 5. Path selection quality distribution for large-scale topology (1000 ASes, 200 paths). DQN maintains good performance despite 8× increase in action space complexity.

old despite an 8-fold increase in the dimensionality of the action space. Although Highest Bandwidth achieves the highest score (0.916), it requires probing all 200 paths per decision. DQN maintains the efficiency of selective probing at this scale. Shortest Path (0.864) shows improved relative performance in dense topologies, yet still requires full topology knowledge. Random selection (0.638) and lowest latency (0.715) significantly degrade, confirming that intelligent selection becomes more critical as path diversity increases. These results confirm that our approach is suitable for large SCION topologies where path counts may reach hundreds.

4.4 Limitations

While promising, our approach has limitations requiring further investigation

- Training Overhead: Initial deployment requires training before agent can select paths effectively
- Topology Changes: Major routing changes may require retraining
- Cold Start Problem: New paths lack historical data for informed selection

To address these challenges, we propose several mitigation strategies. For training overhead, a hybrid approach could initially use simple heuristics (e.g., lowest latency) while the DQN agent trains in parallel, gradually transitioning control as the model converges. Topology changes can be handled through continual learning with sliding window experience replay, maintaining only recent samples to enable rapid adaptation. When significant path changes are detected, the exploration rate can be temporarily increased to accelerate relearning. The cold start problem can be mitigated through optimistic initialization of Q-values for new paths, encouraging exploration, combined with transfer learning from similar AS-tier paths to bootstrap initial estimates.

Future work should explore online learning approaches, transfer learning across topologies, and hybrid strategies combining DQN with periodic full probing for model updates.

4.5   Security Considerations

The deployment of learning-based path selection introduces new attack vectors that merit careful consideration. Adversarial ASes could manipulate probe responses to influence the DQN agent's decision-making, potentially reporting artificially superior metrics (low latency, high bandwidth) to attract traffic through compromised paths for traffic analysis or degradation. Such attacks are particularly concerning given our agent's selective probing strategy, where false measurements from a single malicious path could persist in the replay buffer and corrupt future learning.

SCION's architectural security features provide a foundation for mitigation. The cryptographic path validation ensures that packets follow the declared path, preventing post-selection route hijacking. Additionally, the beacon-based path discovery process, secured through SCION's PKI infrastructure, limits adversaries' ability to inject entirely fabricated paths [3]. We propose complementing these with learning-specific defenses: (i) cross-validation of probe results against passive measurements from actual traffic flows to detect anomalous discrepancies, and (ii) maintaining per-AS reputation scores that weight experiences based on historical measurement accuracy. Future work should investigate adversarial training approaches to explicitly prepare the agent for strategic manipulation attempts while maintaining the efficiency benefits of selective probing.

5   Conclusion

This paper presents a novel approach to intelligent path selection in SCION networks using DQN-RL. By formulating SCION's path selection as an RL problem, we demonstrated that a DQN agent can effectively learn network patterns and respond to dynamic network conditions. The results show that our DQN agent has consistently provided good performance while having significantly low probing overhead. This work validates that RL can effectively harness the flexibility offered by path-aware Internet architectures like SCION. The agent's ability to adapt to changing network conditions without requiring global network visibility makes it particularly suitable for real-world deployment in inter-domain settings. As SCION deployments continue to grow, intelligent path selection mechanisms like ours will be essential for realizing the full potential of path-aware networking.

Future enhancements to this work may include the implementation of Double DQN to mitigate Q-value overestimation and the integration of Prioritized Experience Replay to enhance sample efficiency. To improve generalization, the model could be tested across a wider range of network topologies. Additional extensions may involve incorporating real-time adaptation mechanisms to handle dynamic changes in AS membership. Expanding the framework to support multi-agent RL could enable collaborative path optimization across domains. Furthermore, evaluation on real-world SCION testbeds or federated environments would strengthen the empirical validity of the approach. Finally, refining the reward function to account for delay and jitter-sensitive applications could further align path selection with end-to-end performance objectives.

Disclosure of Interests. The authors have no competing interests to declare that are relevant to the content of this article.

References

1. Botta, A., Canonico, R., Navarro, A., Stanco, G., Ventre, G.: Scalable reinforcement learning for dynamic overlay selection in SD-WANs. In: Proceedings of the 2023 IFIP Networking Conference (IFIP Networking), pp. 1–9 (2023). https://doi.org/10.23919/IFIPNetworking57963.2023.10186399
2. Chen, Y.R., Rezapour, A., Tzeng, W.G., Tsai, S.C.: RL-routing: an SDN routing algorithm based on deep reinforcement learning. IEEE Trans. Netw. Sci. Eng. **7**(4), 3185–3199 (2020). https://doi.org/10.1109/TNSE.2020.3017751
3. Chuat, L., et al.: The Complete Guide to SCION. From Design Principles to Formal Verification. Springer (2022). https://link.springer.com/book/10.1007/978-3-031-05288-0
4. Fu, Q., Sun, E., Meng, K., Li, M., Zhang, Y.: Deep Q-learning for routing schemes in SDN-based data center networks. IEEE Access **8**, 103491–103502 (2020). https://doi.org/10.1109/ACCESS.2020.2995511
5. Gessner, J.: Leveraging application layer path-awareness with SCION. Master's thesis, ETH Zurich, October 2021. https://doi.org/10.3929/ethz-b-000512601
6. Kaelbling, L.P., Littman, M.L., Moore, A.W.: Reinforcement learning: a survey. J. Artif. Intell. Res. **4**, 237–285 (1996)
7. Kea, C.H., Tu, Y.H., Ma, Y.W.: A reinforcement learning approach for widest path routing in software-defined networks. ICT Exp. **9**(5), 882–889 (2023). https://doi.org/10.1016/j.icte.2022.10.007
8. Kreutz, D., Ramos, F.M., Verissimo, P., Rothenberg, C., Azodolmolky, S., Uhlig, S.: Software-defined networking: a comprehensive survey. Proc. IEEE **103**(1), 14–76 (2015). https://doi.org/10.1109/JPROC.2014.2371999
9. Krähenbühl, C., et al.: Deployment and scalability of an inter-domain multi-path routing infrastructure. In: International Conference on emerging Networking EXperiments and Technologies, CoNEXT 2021 (2021). Best Paper Award. https://doi.org/10.1145/3485983.3494862. https://netsec.ethz.ch/publications/papers/2021_conext_deployment.pdf
10. Kwon, J., et al.: SCIONLab: a next-generation Internet testbed. In: Proceedings of the IEEE International Conference on Network Protocols (ICNP) (2020). Best Paper Award. https://doi.org/10.1109/ICNP49622.2020.9259355. https://netsec.ethz.ch/publications/papers/icnp2020_scionlab.pdf
11. Medina, A., Lakhina, A., Matta, I., Byers, J.: BRITE: an approach to universal topology generation. In: Proceedings Ninth International Symposium on Modeling, Analysis and Simulation of Computer and Telecommunication Systems, MASCOTS 2001, pp. 346–353. IEEE (2001)

12. Mnih, V., Kavukcuoglu, K., Silver, D., Rusu, A.A., et al.: Human-level control through deep reinforcement learning. Nature **518**(7540), 529–533 (2015)
13. Roughan, M.: Simplifying the synthesis of internet traffic matrices. ACM SIG-COMM Comput. Commun. Rev. **35**(5), 93–96 (2005)
14. Sutton, R.S., Barto, A.G.: Reinforcement Learning: An Introduction, 2 edn. MIT Press (2018)
15. Testart, C.: Reviewing a historical internet vulnerability: why isn't BGP more secure and what can we do about it? In: Proceedings of the 46th Research Conference on Communication, Information and Internet Policy (TPRC 46). TPRC (2018)
16. Victor-Ikoh, M., Kabari, L.: Internet architecture: current limitations leading towards future internet architecture. Int. J. Comput. Sci. Mob. Comput. **10**(5), 102–112 (2021). https://doi.org/10.47760/ijcsmc.2021.v10i05.011
17. Watkins, C.J.C.H., Dayan, P.: Q-learning. Mach. Learn. **8**(3–4), 279–292 (1992). https://doi.org/10.1007/BF00992698

G2TA: Converting Graph Data to Table Data for Employing Deanonymization Attacks

Shlomi Dolev, Michael Elhadad, and Rie Ruash[(✉)]

Department of Computer Science Ben-Gurion University of the Negev,
Beer Sheva, Israel
`rie@pcst.bgu.ac.il`

Abstract. The widespread sharing of anonymized graph datasets for research and public use has raised new privacy concerns, as sensitive information can often be re-identified through advanced deanonymization techniques. Existing graph deanonymization methods span a variety of strategies, including structural alignment, embedding-based matching, and feature extraction combined with machine learning classifiers. However, these approaches remain grounded in graph-specific workflows. In this paper, we introduce G2TA (Graph to Table Attack), a novel attack framework that bridges graph and tabular privacy domains. By transforming anonymized graphs into semantically enriched tabular representations that capture structural patterns and neighborhood-level attribute signals, our approach enables the use of record linkage and quasi-identifier-based attacks originally developed for tabular datasets. These semantic features preserve node-to-neighborhood relationships that are crucial for identity recovery. We evaluate the framework on anonymized graphs and compare it to well-known graph-based attacks, showing that meaningful re-identification is possible, even without graph-specific algorithms. We also evaluated our methodology on differentially private graphs. Our findings underscore the importance of privacy evaluations that account for both graph-specific threats and relational tabular attacks before public release.

Keywords: Data Privacy · Graph Deanonymization · Graph-to-Table Transformation · Tabular Deanonymization · Record Linkage

1 Introduction

Graphs have become a core tool for modeling complex relationships in many real-world systems. From social networks and mobility traces to scientific workflows, graph-structured data is widely used in both research and industry. Their

---

The research is partially supported by the Rita Altura Trust Chair in Computer Science, the Israeli Smart Transportation Research Center (ISTRC), and the Israeli Science Foundation (Grant No. 465/22).

A. Akavia et al. (Eds.): CSCML 2025, LNCS 16244, pp. 207–224, 2026.
https://doi.org/10.1007/978-3-032-10759-6_13

ability to capture complex relationships among different entities makes them valuable for tasks such as pattern discovery, prediction, and decision-making. To enable collaboration and advance research, graph data is frequently shared with the public, academic institutions, or commercial organizations. However, this widespread distribution raises important privacy concerns, especially when the graphs contain sensitive user information or behavioral patterns that could lead to re-identification. In response to these concerns, various anonymization techniques have been proposed, aiming to protect user privacy while preserving the utility of the data. These methods typically involve perturbing node identifiers, modifying edges, or applying differential privacy mechanisms to ensure privacy. Fundamentally, such techniques aim to strike a balance between privacy protection and data utility as much as possible.

While advances have been made in anonymization techniques, their limitations become evident when faced with sophisticated deanonymization attacks. Such attacks aim to re-identify individuals or uncover sensitive links within anonymized datasets by using external auxiliary data, exploiting structural patterns, or applying machine learning methods.

Prior work on graph deanonymization has focused primarily on structural techniques, such as node embeddings, neighborhood similarity, or alignment, all of which are applied directly within the graph domain. While effective, these methods have, to the best of our knowledge, not considered applying tabular deanonymization attacks to graph data represented in tabular form.

In this paper, we introduce a novel attack vector that departs from traditional graph deanonymization approaches. We propose G2TA (Graph to Table Attack), a framework that transforms anonymized graphs into tabular representations by extracting semantically meaningful features from each node's local neighborhood. These features capture both structural patterns (e.g., degree, random-walk-based statistics) and attribute-level patterns across the neighborhood (e.g., attribute agreement within 1- and 2-hop neighborhoods). This representation preserves node-to-neighborhood signals, which are crucial for identity recovery, and enables the application of deanonymization techniques developed initially for tabular data, such as record linkage attacks. An overview of the proposed attack framework is illustrated in Fig. 1.

Our approach treats graph nodes as records containing quasi-identifiers, bridging graph and tabular privacy domains. To assess the effectiveness of our method, we evaluated tabular-based deanonymization methods compared to graph-based deanonymization methods. We also examined the viability of our approach on differentially private graphs. While the success of deanonymization attacks varies with the dataset, depending on topology, attribute distributions, and perturbation level, our findings demonstrate that meaningful re-identification remains possible.

These results highlight a previously underexplored vulnerability: once anonymized graph data is transformed into a tabular form, it may become susceptible not only to graph-specific attacks but also to a broad class of relational attacks associated with tabular structured data. These findings suggest the need for more comprehensive privacy evaluations before releasing public anonymized graph datasets.

Our Contributions are as Follows:

- We propose a new attack framework that transforms anonymized graphs into semantically enriched tabular representations, leveraging both structural and neighborhood-level features.
- We demonstrate how classical tabular deanonymization techniques, such as record linkage attacks, can be effectively applied to these graph-derived tabular representations. Our evaluation across multiple datasets, in comparison with graph-based attacks, shows that meaningful identity recovery is possible.
- We evaluate our framework on differentially private (DP) anonymized graphs, showing that despite formal DP guarantees, structural vulnerabilities can still enable partial re-identification or sensitive attribute inference in practical settings.
- We highlight the need for graph data anonymization practices to consider not only graph-based attacks, but also the broader risks introduced when graph data is restructured as tabular data.

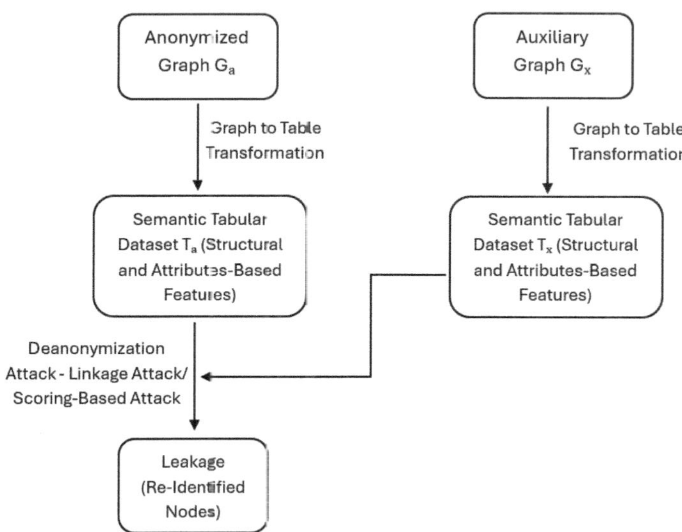

Fig. 1. G2TA (Graph to Table Attack) Framework

2   Related Work

Graph anonymization techniques generally fall into two categories: heuristic perturbation methods and formal differential privacy (DP) mechanisms. Heuristic approaches include node relabeling, attribute suppression, and edge perturbations (addition, deletion, or swapping), which aim to obscure identities while preserving structural utility. In contrast, DP [7] provides a formal guarantee by injecting carefully calibrated noise, typically through edge-level perturbation or synthetic graph generation, while bounding the privacy leakage through a tunable privacy parameter ϵ. This guarantee, however, comes at the cost of reduced data utility [11], as larger ϵ values relax the privacy guarantee to preserve more of the original structure, while smaller ϵ values enforce stronger privacy but often at the cost of significant utility degradation. As a result, while DP ensures strong theoretical protection, real-world applications often continue to rely on heuristic methods, which remain susceptible to deanonymization attacks [2].

Deanonymization, or the process of re-identifying individuals within anonymized datasets, has been extensively studied in both relational and graph domains.

A significant body of work has explored graph deanonymization by leveraging structural similarity between anonymized and auxiliary graphs. Notable early work by Narayanan and Shmatikov [18] demonstrated how social network users of Twitter and Flickr could be re-identified by aligning anonymized social graphs with auxiliary networks through seeded propagation and neighborhood overlap. Bumblebee [8] expanded this line of work and showed better re-identification success with improved robustness to noise. Another work by Srivatsa et al. [23] proposed deanonymizing a set of location traces based on a social network using structural correlation.

Later approaches eliminated the reliance on seed mapping, such as the method by [15], which utilized structural signatures based on degree histograms of the 1-hop and 2-hop neighborhoods of the nodes, along with a variant of the machine learning model SVM. Another framework, REGAL [9], learns structural embeddings for node alignment. Benchmarking platforms like SecGraph [12] systematically evaluate graph anonymization techniques and matching-based deanonymization strategies using node-level metrics, such as degree, clustering coefficient, and centrality. The deanonymization attack in [14] maps node-attribute links between an anonymized graph and its auxiliary using structural differences and a single attribute similarity score between node pairs across graphs. This framework demonstrates that attribute information, even when used independently, can significantly reduce graph anonymity.

Despite these advances, the success of deanonymization attacks is not universal. Their effectiveness depends heavily on assumptions such as structural consistency, attribute availability, or the presence of auxiliary data; therefore, it is essential to consider diverse attacks prior to publishing data.

While most deanonymization methods remain grounded in graph-native workflows, a separate body of work has explored converting graphs into tabular forms for downstream tasks, such as classification or representation learning. For example, ReFeX [10] generates interpretable recursive structural features to characterize node roles. Similarly, Role2Vec [1] maps nodes to role-based types using attributed random walks, where node types or structural labels are recorded instead of IDs, yielding space-efficient embeddings for classification tasks. In bioinformatics, Graph2Tab [3] library by Brandizi et al. was developed to transform workflow DAGs into compact tabular formats for metadata representation. Recent work in machine learning on molecular structures [16] has modeled chemical compounds as graphs and used sequences of atomic walks, aggregated into tabular vector representations for classification tasks. However, these approaches are designed to enhance predictive performance, not to assess whether structural information in the resulting tables may preserve vulnerabilities or enable deanonymization attacks.

By contrast, tabular deanonymization attacks have a long history of exploiting re-identification risks via quasi-identifier linkage, frequency analysis, and uniqueness metrics. One prominent example of deanonymization demonstrated the weaknesses of traditional anonymization by re-identifying users in the Netflix Prize dataset via linkage with their movie rating patterns [17]. Datta et al. [5] provided formal proofs explaining the effectiveness of such attacks on high-dimensional microdata. A decade later, a retrospective analysis emphasized how advancements in data collection and computational techniques have increased the complexity and effectiveness of deanonymization, particularly in high-dimensional datasets [19]. Torres and Olivares [24] extended these findings by applying probabilistic record linkage techniques to high-dimensional datasets, such as movies and books, illustrating the variation in deanonymization efficiency across diverse dataset structures.

Our work introduces a novel cross-domain attack strategy. Specifically, we propose a method that transforms an anonymized graph into a semantically enriched tabular format by extracting structural and neighborhood-level features such as n-gram patterns, role similarity scores, and attribute distributions. This enables the use of classical tabular deanonymization techniques, including record linkage and quasi-identifier-based inference, which have not been previously applied in this context. To our knowledge, no prior work systematically converts anonymized graphs into relational tables to exploit tabular privacy vulnerabilities.

3 Graphs Tabular Representation

In order to evaluate deanonymization attacks designed for tabular data on graph-structured datasets, we transformed graphs into structured tabular representations that capture rich node-level information. The full set of extracted features, along with their corresponding brief descriptions, is provided in Table 1. The conversion process was guided by two central objectives: preserving informative structural and attribute-based patterns that could establish re-identification, and ensuring efficiency by minimizing computational overhead.

The feature extraction process was informed by earlier research on structure-based deanonymization and role analysis, specifically, we incorporated the nK-series framework proposed by Lee et al. [15], which captures structural information at radius one edge and two edges for each node, and approximations of edit distance based on n-gram Jaccard similarity, as introduced by Dolev et al. [6]. Together, these informed our inclusion of multi-hop descriptors and local similarity metrics derived from random walks.

The feature design deliberately focused on the 1-hop and 2-hop neighborhoods of each node. We limited the neighborhood depth to two hops to maintain both informative and computationally efficient features. Expanding beyond this point tends to introduce redundant patterns and noise, reducing the effectiveness of the attack. As the hop distance increases, the neighborhoods of the nodes become increasingly heterogeneous and overlapping, which can obscure meaningful distinctions. Prior empirical work [15] supports the finding that 2-hop information captures sufficient structural nuance for effective re-identification, while deeper expansions yield diminishing returns. Limiting the feature horizon also ensures tractability when computing similarity metrics such as entropy, approximate edit distance, and attribute coherence.

Each node was characterized by a combination of classical centrality measures (e.g., PageRank, degree, clustering coefficient, k-core number, eigenvector centrality) and more discriminative multi-hop structural statistics. The nK-series was computed up to 2 hops: nK0 denotes the node's own degree, nK1 represents the histogram of degrees among 1-hop neighbors, and nK2 extends this to the 2-hop neighborhood. To quantify local homogeneity, we also recorded the number of 1-hop and 2-hop neighbors sharing the node's degree bin.

Beyond the nK-series, we introduced features based on degree-labeled random walks. For each node, we generated sets of degree n-grams (with n=3) using multiple bounded-length random walks. These n-gram sets were used to compute entropy-based measures of local structural diversity, as well as role similarity scores that approximate structural distance between nodes. Rather than computing edit distance directly, we followed Dolev et al. [6], who established a strong theoretical relationship between Normalized Edit Distance (NED) and Jaccard similarity over n-gram sets. Given the Jaccard distance $JD(X,Y)$ between the n-gram sets X and Y, and the sequence length ratio

$$\alpha = \frac{\min(|x|, |y|)}{\max(|x|, |y|)}, \tag{1}$$

The NED is estimated as:

$$\mathrm{NED}(x, y) \approx \frac{1 + \alpha \cdot (JD(X,Y) - 1)}{2 - JD(X,Y)} \tag{2}$$

This provides a tighter and more theoretically grounded similarity measure than plain Jaccard, while remaining computationally efficient.

For graphs with node attributes, additional features were derived by computing cosine similarity between each node's attribute vector and those of its neighbors. Specifically, we measured the mean similarity and the number of neighbors exceeding a fixed similarity threshold within both the 1-hop and 2-hop neighborhoods. These attribute coherence features were motivated by the intuition that homophily-based proximity can signal identity ties, and restricting them to two hops aligns with our broader strategy of preserving discriminative locality while avoiding redundancy. To capture attribute-level similarity, we employed cosine similarity between normalized attribute vectors (formula 3). Cosine similarity is widely used for high-dimensional, sparse data—as is typical in node attributes—because it measures the orientation rather than magnitude, making it robust to varying scales and sparsity. Moreover, it is computationally efficient and well-suited for comparing vectors derived from binary or continuous features.

$$\text{cosine\_sim}(\vec{a}, \vec{b}) = \frac{\vec{a} \cdot \vec{b}}{\|\vec{a}\| \, \|\vec{b}\|} \tag{3}$$

Table 1. Summary of structural and semantic features extracted for each node in the graph, for tabular representation of the graph.

Feature Name	Description
Node	the node id/name
Degree	Number of edges connected to the node
Clustering	Fraction of the node's neighbors that are also connected
Pagerank	Importance score based on random walks. The score is higher if the node is connected to other central or influential nodes in the graph
K-core	The largest k for which the node belongs to a k-core (a subgraph where all nodes have degree $\geq k$)
Eigenvector	Centrality score that reflects influence based on the centrality of neighbors
Same degree bin 1hop, same degree bin 2hop	Number of 1-hop/2-hop neighbors that fall within the same degree bin as the node, captures local degree homogeneity
Ngram entropy	Entropy of the frequency distribution of degree n-grams from random walks. It quantifies structural variability
Role similarity 1hop, role similarity 2hop	Jaccard similarity between the node's degree n-gram set and those of its 1-hop/2-hop neighbors
Role similarity combined	Weighted average of 1-hop and 2-hop role similarities
Role combined zscore	Standardized (z-scored) version of the combined role similarity. It highlights role outliers
Mean cosine attributes hop1, mean cosine attributes hop2	Average cosine similarity between the node's attribute vector and those of its 1-hop/2-hop neighbors
Number of similar attributes neighbors hop1, number of similar attributes neighbors hop2	Count of 1-hop/2-hop neighbors with attribute cosine similarity above a threshold (defined as default to 0.9)
Number of structurally similar neighbors	Number of 1-hop and 2-hop neighbors whose degree n-gram sequences are structurally similar to the node's, based on approximate edit distance
Community	ID of the community to which the node belongs. It's derived from modularity-based graph partitioning

Finally, we incorporated community-level information through modularity-based clustering. We also introduced a feature that counts the number of 1-hop and 2-hop neighbors whose degree n-gram sequences are structurally similar to the target node, based on approximate edit distance. To better highlight structurally distinctive nodes, we standardized the combined role similarity scores using z-score normalization, enabling relative comparisons of role consistency across the graph. The resulting tabular dataset thus encodes both global centrality and rich local structural signals, with features designed to support both record linkage and quasi-identifier style deanonymization. Although it is possible to include the original node attributes as additional features, we chose not to incorporate them directly into the tabular representation in order to reduce computational overhead during matching.

With these features extracted for each node, we proceeded to evaluate whether traditional tabular attacks could effectively match identities when applied to the converted representations. This representation aims to strike a balance between expressiveness and scalability by capturing key structural and attribute-based signals, while restricting computation to the most relevant 1-hop and 2-hop neighborhoods. To our knowledge, this is the first approach to combine degree-based n-gram entropy, approximate edit-distance–based role similarity, multi-hop nK-series features, and attribute similarity into a unified tabular format specifically designed for assessing privacy risks in anonymized graph data.

4   Methodology and Experiments

We assessed the effectiveness of applying deanonymization attacks, originally created for tabular form datasets, to our graph representation method. Specifically, we evaluated two linkage attacks on two anonymized datasets that were published online, and compared them to two graph-based attacks. We also evaluated our method on differentially private graphs. In this section, we further expand the process.

4.1   Datasets

We evaluated the applicability of tabular deanonymization attacks on graph-derived representations using two publicly available real-world datasets in their undirected form. In both datasets, each node has several Boolean attributes, where 0 means non-expression.

- **Facebook dataset** [21]: A social network graph where the nodes correspond to official verified Facebook pages, and the edges between them are mutual likes. The attributes of the nodes are derived from the site description. To reduce computational cost while preserving structural diversity, use uniform random sampling with a repair step to cap the number of isolated nodes, ensuring the subgraph remains representative of the original network. The number of edges after subsampling is 13475, and each node has 4714 attributes.

- **CiteSeer dataset [22]:** A citation network graph with 3312 nodes, each representing a publication, and 4,715 edges, representing citation links between them. Each node is associated with a bag-of-words feature vector derived from the publication text. While CiteSeer is often used as-is for benchmark tasks, it lacks explicit publication-identifying information and can reasonably be treated as an anonymized dataset for our purposes.

Our goal was to simulate realistic anonymization settings in which the attacker has access to a noisy version of the original graph and its associated features. To ensure consistent experimental conditions across datasets, we applied the same perturbation process and graph-to-tabular conversion. The anonymized version was generated by randomly shuffling node identifiers (while preserving node features), randomly dropping 30% of node attributes in each graph, and perturbing the structure by randomly adding and removing 0.01% of the edges, following a noise-injection scheme inspired by prior work on structural anonymization [13,18,25]. These steps ensure that the resulting anonymized graph and the auxiliary graph (the original, unperturbed version) share only partially overlapping information, thereby mimicking realistic conditions for evaluating deanonymization robustness.

4.2   Evaluation of Tabular Deanonymization Attacks

We assessed the effectiveness of applying tabular deanonymization techniques to graph-structured data by evaluating two record linkage attacks on the tabular representations derived from our graph conversion pipeline. Specifically, we formulated the node matching task as a row-level linkage problem, in which each node is represented by a structured quasi-identifier vector and matched across two datasets, one anonymized and one auxiliary, based on similarity.

The first attack we evaluated followed the methodology proposed by Torres and Olivares [24], and was originally developed for user deanonymization across rating datasets. The overall structure of the attack follows the procedure outlined in Algorithm 1, which proceeds in several stages.

First, each node in the anonymized and auxiliary datasets is represented by a normalized vector of features, including both structural and attribute-based components, which serves as its quasi-identifier. These vectors are compared using cosine similarity, resulting in a similarity matrix that spans all possible node pairs. To distinguish between true matches and coincidental similarities, we model the distribution of similarity scores for known matching and non-matching pairs using Gaussian Kernel Density Estimation (KDE). The resulting distributions, denoted $m(x)$ for matches and $u(x)$ for non-matches, allow us to compute a log-likelihood ratio for each candidate pair, reflecting the relative likelihood that the pair corresponds to the same original node. Candidate matches are then filtered using a one-to-one matching strategy that prioritizes pairs with a large confidence gap over competing candidates. This approach allows us to enforce realistic one-to-one constraints and avoid ambiguous assignments.

Algorithm 1. Deanonymizing nodes across graph datasets via tabular representation, using the technique from [24]

Require: $\mathcal{G} = \{G_1, G_2\}$, M' : mapping for a small quantity of node pairs
Ensure: M: mapping of linked node identities across datasets
1: $M \leftarrow \emptyset$ ▷ Initialize mapping
2: **for** each graph $G_i \in \mathcal{G}$ **do**
3:   $T_i \leftarrow$ GRAPHTOTABLE(G_i) ▷ Convert to tabular form
4:   $T_i' \leftarrow$ FEATURESUBSAMPLING(T_i) ▷ Subsample features
5:   $T_i'' \leftarrow$ NODESFILTERING(T_i', θ) ▷ Filter nodes with few features that are non 0
6:   $T_i''' \leftarrow$ FEATURESNORMALIZATION(T_i'') ▷ Normalize features values
7:   **for** each node $u \in T_i'''$ **do**
8:    $\vec{f_u} \leftarrow$ EXTRACTFEATURES(u, T_i''') ▷ Extract structural + attribute features
9:   **end for**
10: **end for**
11: $S_{12} \leftarrow$ COMPUTESIMILARITYMATRIX(T_1''', T_2''') ▷ Pairwise similarity across node rows
12: $L_{12} \leftarrow$ RECORDLINKAGE(S_{12}) ▷ Link rows based on similarity
13: $M \leftarrow$ IDENTITYRESOLUTION(L_{12}, M') ▷ Resolve transitive matches
14: **return** M

The second attack we tested is a scoring-based de-anonymization attack inspired by the work of Narayanan and Shmatikov [17] and follows the procedure outlined in Algorithm 2. Specifically, it compares every pair of users across an anonymized and an auxiliary version of a graph-based dataset. Each user is represented by a vector of binary or numerical attributes (e.g., profile features), and similarity is computed using a weighted score that gives more importance to rare attributes. The score as described in formula 4 penalizes differences in ratings and one of the features we created that is quite distinctive between the nodes, k core which is a measure of how deeply a node is embedded in a densely connected region of the graph, controlled by parameters $\rho_0 = 1.5$ and $d_0 = 0.05$, and filters candidate matches using an eccentricity threshold $\varphi = 1.5$.

$$\text{Score}(r, \text{aux}) = \sum_{i \in \text{supp(aux)}} \frac{1}{\log |\text{supp}(i)|} \left(e^{-\frac{|\rho_i - \rho_i'|}{\rho_0}} + e^{-\frac{|k_i - k_i'|}{\delta}} \right) \tag{4}$$

We applied both attacks to both the Facebook subgraph and the CiteSeer citation network. In both cases, the original graph served as the auxiliary dataset, while the anonymized version was generated by randomly shuffling node identifiers and applying edge perturbation, as described earlier in Subsect. 4.1. The final evaluation compared the predicted matches to the true node correspondences preserved through the mapping and is presented in Table 2.

The results in Table 2 show that the performance of both attacks varies across datasets. On the Facebook subgraph, the first attack achieved a precision of ≈ 0.76), a recall of ≈ 0.20), and an F1 of ≈ 0.31) (894 true positives and 286 false positives). In contrast, the second attack yielded a lower precision of 0.50 and near-zero recall, recovering only two correct matches. On the CiteSeer dataset,

---

Algorithm 2. Weighted Scoring-Based De-anonymization, based on the attack from [17]

Require: $\mathcal{G} = \{G_1, G_2\}$
Ensure: M: mapping of linked node identities across datasets
    $M \leftarrow \emptyset$
2: **for** each graph $G_i \in \mathcal{G}$ **do**
      $T_i \leftarrow \text{GRAPHTOTABLE}(G_i)$ ▷ Convert to tabular form
4:    $T_i' \leftarrow \text{FEATURESUBSAMPLING}(T_i)$ ▷ Subsample features
      $\vec{f}_u \leftarrow \text{EXTRACTFEATURES}(u, T_i''')$ ▷ Extract structural + attribute features
6: **end for**
   for each record $a \in G_1$ **do**
8:    Compute similarity scores: $S_b \leftarrow \text{Score}(a, b)$ for all $b \in G_2$
      Let $S_1 = \max S_b$, $S_2 = $ second highest in S_b, $\sigma = \text{std}(S_b)$
10:    Compute eccentricity: $\varphi = \frac{S_1 - S_2}{\sigma}$
      if $\varphi > 1.5$ **then**
12:      Match a to the corresponding b with score S_1
        Add (a, b) to M
14:    **end if**
   end for
16: **return** M

---

the first attack achieved even higher precision (≈ 0.83)) while recall remained modest at ≈ 0.18) (F1 $= \approx 0.30$)). The second attack demonstrated an extreme trade-off: perfect precision (1.0) but negligible recall (≈ 0.002)), recovering only six correct matches.

These findings show that tabular attacks on graph-derived representations can reach high precision, meaning that predicted matches are usually correct, but suffer from quite low recall, limiting the overall number of identities re-identified. This precision-recall imbalance suggests that tabular deanonymization is especially potent in scenarios where minimizing false positives is more important than maximizing coverage.

4.3   Comparing to Graph-Based Deanonymization Attacks

Following the evaluation of the framework against tabular-based deanonymization attacks, we extended our analysis to include well-established graph-native attacks to measure the effectiveness of our G2TA approach compared to established graph deanonymization methods. For this purpose, we integrated and tested two iterative seed-based propagation algorithms: Narayanan and Shmatikov's attack on social networks [18], a widely used benchmark, and the Bumblebee attack [8].

Both assume the adversary has access to an auxiliary graph G_{src} with known node identities, an anonymized target graph G_{tar}, and a partial seed mapping between the two. Starting from this seed set, they iteratively expand matches by exploiting structural consistency between neighborhoods across graphs. In each iteration, an unmapped node from G_{src} is scored against candidate unmapped nodes in G_{tar} based on overlap with already matched neighbors.

In the Narayanan and Shmatikov method [18], the similarity score sums the inverse square root of the candidate's degree across supporting neighbors, biasing toward low-degree nodes. After all candidates are scored, the highest-scoring candidate must satisfy two conditions to be accepted. First, its score is sufficiently dominant relative to others, quantified via the *eccentricity* of the score distribution (difference between top-two scores normalized by the standard deviation of all candidate scores).

Second, the candidate must pass a reverse verification step, where mapping is re-evaluated in the opposite direction (from G_{tar} back to G_{src}). This forward–reverse matching cycle repeats iteratively, expanding the mapping until no further matches can be made or the iteration limit is reached.

Bumblebee [8] retains the same forward–reverse structure but replaces the similarity metric with one that symmetrically accounts for degree ratios, reducing low-degree bias and increasing score diversity. For each candidate $(x, \mu[x])$, the score is incremented by $\min\left(\frac{\deg(u)}{\deg(v)}, \frac{\deg(v)}{\deg(u)}\right)^{\delta}$, where δ controls the penalty for degree disparity. This allows a broader range of candidate degrees to be considered while still discriminating against large mismatches. Reverse verification and eccentricity filtering remain in place.

We evaluated both attacks on the undirected versions of our datasets using the same experimental setting, such as the same seeds set, as in the tabular evaluation. The comparison results are presented in Table 2.

Across both datasets, our tabular G2TA consistently shows higher or comparable precision to Narayanan–Shmatikov attack (≈ 0.83 vs. ≈ 0.56 on CiteSeer, and ≈ 0.76 vs. ≈ 0.76 on Facebook), even though recall is lower. This precision advantage is practically important in applications where false positives are particularly costly, such as identifying high-value or sensitive nodes. Precision ensures that the matches declared are reliable. In contrast, propagation-heavy methods expand aggressively, achieving higher recall: Narayanan–Shmatikov covers more nodes on Facebook, while Bumblebee consistently outperforms both in precision and recall due to its robustness to structural noise, reflecting its stated improved robustness to structural noise.

Our results underscore that characteristics of the graph structure critically shape attack effectiveness. In sparse graphs such as CiteSeer, where nodes have few connections (low average degree), propagation-based methods struggle. Here, precision-focused linkage methods like G2TA using Algorithm 1 are more reliable, as the few overlaps that do exist tend to be highly discriminative. In contrast, denser graphs such as Facebook, rich neighborhood connectivity provides abundant overlap signals, enabling propagation-based algorithms to expand matches more aggressively and achieve broader recall. Thus, the choice of attack should consider both algorithm design and the structural properties of the dataset, alongside the application's tolerance for false positives.

Overall, these findings strongly suggest that tabular-based deanonymization attacks are not only applicable but also effective in graph contexts, particularly when precision is a priority. This highlights the need for privacy-preserving data publishing frameworks to consider both graph-based and table-based attack models, particularly in scenarios where graph data may be preprocessed or partially exposed in tabular form. While Bumblebee remains a strong structural baseline, our findings suggest an open opportunity for future research on hybrid approaches that integrate tabular and structural signals to balance precision and recall in diverse anonymization settings.

Table 2. Tabular-based attacks using the G2TA framework vs. Graph-based baseline attacks.

Dataset	Category	Attack	Precision	Recall	F_1	TP	FP
Facebook	Tabular	G2TA based Algorithm 1	0. 76	0.2	0.31	894	286
		G2TA based Algorithm 2	0.5	0.0004	0.0008	2	4
	Graph	Narayanan-Shmatikov [18]	0.76	0.76	0.76	3455	1079
		Bumblebee [8]	0.99	0.85	0.92	3866	1
CiteSeer	Tabular	G2TA based Algorithm 1	0.83	0.18	0.3	591	116
		G2TA based Algorithm 2	1.0	0.002	0.004	6	0
	Graph	Narayanan-Shmatikov [18]	0.56	0.57	0.56	1836	1414
		Bumblebee [8]	0.99	0.73	0.84	2384	2

5   Differential Privacy and G2TA

Differential privacy (DP)-based methods provide a formal, mathematical guarantee of privacy. For example, under edge differential privacy, the inclusion or exclusion of any single edge can change the output distribution only within a multiplicative factor of e^ϵ. While this makes DP more robust than heuristic perturbation methods, such as the one we applied in Subsect. 4.1, in practice DP mechanisms remain less common because they are complex to implement and often introduce utility loss, despite offering stronger protection [2].

While it is well established that differential privacy involves significant trade-offs between privacy protection and data utility [11], it remains interesting to assess how robust such mechanisms are when confronted with alternative attack methods that fall outside their conventional threat assumptions. In particular, we are interested in examining whether our cross-domain Graph-to-Table Attack (G2TA) framework can exploit structural patterns in differentially private graphs, despite their formal guarantees.

For our analysis, we adopted the PrivGraph [26] method to generate the differentially private graph datasets. PrivGraph is a recent open-source, non-interactive graph publishing mechanism that provides edge-level differential privacy. It achieves this by leveraging the graph's community structure: the algorithm first partitions the graph into communities, then extracts structural patterns both within and across these communities, and finally reconstructs the graph to preserve utility while respecting privacy guarantees. This approach improves utility compared to earlier graph-DP techniques, but as with all DP methods, its preservation of utility is not perfect, as stronger privacy guarantees inevitably lead to greater distortion.

This motivates an investigation into whether our G2TA framework can recover true node identities or infer sensitive structural characteristics from the perturbed output.

We generated two differentially private versions of the Chamelon dataset [20], which was also used in the PrivGraph paper, using $\epsilon = 2$ and $\epsilon = 5$. The Chameleon dataset, a heterophilic benchmark graph, has 2,277 nodes, which represent articles from the English Wikipedia, 31,371 edges (excluding edges from a node to itself), which reflect mutual links between the Wikipedia articles, and no node attributes. Applying differential privacy on the graph with $\epsilon = 2$ resulted in 25,319 edges, and with $\epsilon = 5$ resulted in 25,440 edges. We randomly shuffled node identifiers in both graphs and applied our proposed graph-to-table conversion technique, as described in Sect. 3, in order to obtain the tabular formats of the resulting differentially private graphs, and of the original graph. Since the graph has no node attributes, the conversion was based solely on structural characteristics without attribute-based components.

In order to assess whether our graph-to-table transformation, under the differential privacy mechanism, offered meaningful resistance to structural re-identification attempts, we applied two attacks adapted from the literature.

First, we applied an adaptation of the record linkage attack proposed by Torres and Olivares [24], following the procedure described in Algorithm 1 and Subsect. 4.2. The attack was conducted on both differentially private versions of the Chameleon graph generated by PrivGraph with privacy parameters $\epsilon = 2$ and $\epsilon = 5$. In each case, the original graph (non-perturbed) graph served as the auxiliary dataset, while the differentially private graph, with shuffled node identifiers, served as the anonymized dataset. The evaluation, comparing predicted matches against the preserved ground-truth node correspondences, is presented in Table 3. Overall, only a small fraction of nodes were successfully re-identified. However, profiling the true positives revealed important nuances.

For the $\epsilon = 5$ DP graph, only two nodes were re-identified, both of which had a degree of 3 in both the original and DP graph, an attribute that occurs in roughly 25% of nodes.

By contrast, $\epsilon = 2$ graph, a single node was re-identified, but it exhibited a rare, high-degree signature: degree of 195 in the original graph and 170 in the DP graph ($\approx 5\%$ frequency in both graphs). The 25-edge discrepancy does not represent a direct violation as PrivGraph's guarantee still ensures that the presence or absence of any single edge cannot be inferred with high confidence. However, the combination of rarity and partial preservation of this re-identified node's structure makes it an anchor point for further attacks: once re-identified, its wide neighborhood could facilitate linkage propagation, effectively exploiting the structural uniqueness preserved by PrivGraph for utility. In this sense, DP bounds worst-case edge inference risk, but it does not rule out empirical vulnerabilities that arise from graph structure, and its guarantee does not prevent all practical forms of leakage. This underscores the inherent trade-off in graph differential privacy: mechanisms tuned for higher utility necessarily preserve certain structural patterns, which, while analytically useful, may also become re-identification anchors despite the formal DP guarantee.

Table 3. Tabular-based attacks on differential private Chamelon graph dataset

ϵ	Attack	Precision	Recall	F_1	TP	FP
2	Linkage attack based Algorithm 1	0.9%	0.05%	0.09%	1	109
	Inference attack based Algorithm 3	2.82%	5.14%	2.9%	69	-
5	Linkage attack based Algorithm 1	1.63%	0.09%	0.18%	2	120
	Inference attack based Algorithm 3	4.51%	11.02%	5.61%	162	-

In addition to the linkage attack, we implemented a probabilistic inference attack inspired by the Naive-Bayes-based method of Graham et al. [4]. The attack follows the procedure outlined in Algorithm 3. Unlike record linkage, which seeks to match entities across datasets, this attack aims at inferring sensitive structural attributes, in our case, the node's original degree, prior to the application of the PrivGraph differential privacy mechanism. This constitutes an attribute inference scenario rather than direct identity disclosure. Since the framework in [4] is designed for categorical features, while our tabular graph representation contains numerical values, we discretized each quasi-identifier (QI) into bins to approximate the bucketization step in the original method. For each of the Chameleon DP-graphs, we trained the classifier directly on the same subset of 30% of the nodes (our seed set) and tested its success on the rest.

The results, shown in Table 3, indicate that both precision and recall in both the DP-graphs are low. However, performance improved from $\epsilon = 2$ to $\epsilon = 5$, illustrating that relaxing the privacy budget make the original degree more predictable. Even so, any successful prediction of sensitive attributes from anonymized data can constitute a privacy leak, highlighting the trade-off between utility and privacy in DP-based graph publishing.

Taken together, our experimental results suggest that under the tested ϵ values, both linkage and inference attacks achieve only limited success in large-scale re-identification. Nevertheless, a higher ϵ increases the data utility, at the cost of weaker privacy, enabling greater re-identification or attribute inference. This highlights the persistent gap between DP's formal guarantees and empirical outcomes in applied graph anonymization: while DP mechanisms constrained classical linkage attacks to low recall, non-trivial true matches and attribute predictions were still possible. This demonstrates that even when large-scale re-identification is suppressed, adversaries may still extract meaningful information, particularly if the small number of re-identified nodes involves sensitive or structurally unique ones.

Algorithm 3. Predicting a sensitive structural attribute from a differentially private graph using a Naive Bayes classifier, adapted from [4]

Require: G_{DP}: differentially private graph, q: list of quasi-identifiers (QIs), y: sensitive attribute (original degree), S: seed nodes defining train IDs
Ensure: $\hat{y}$: predicted sensitive attribute values for each node
1: $T \leftarrow \textsc{GraphToTable}(G_{\mathrm{DP}})$ $\triangleright$ Convert graph to tabular form of QIs and target
2: $T' \leftarrow \textsc{ExtractFeatures}(T, q, y)$ $\triangleright$ Select QIs and sensitive attribute column
3: $T'' \leftarrow \textsc{DiscretizeFeatures}(T', q)$ $\triangleright$ Bin numeric QIs to categorical values
4: Partition by seeds: $T_{\mathrm{train}} \leftarrow T''[\textbf{node} \in S]$, $T_{\mathrm{test}} \leftarrow T''[\textbf{node} \notin S]$
5: NB $\leftarrow \textsc{TrainNaiveBayes}(T_{\mathrm{train}}[q], T_{\mathrm{train}}[y])$
6: **for** each row r in T_{test} **do**
7:     $\hat{P}_y \leftarrow \textsc{PredictProbabilities}(\mathrm{NB}, r[q])$ $\triangleright$ Probability distribution over possible y
8:     $\hat{y}_r \leftarrow \arg\max \hat{P}_y$ $\triangleright$ Most probable degree
9:     Append $\hat{y}_r$ to $\hat{y}$
10: **end for**
11: **return** $\hat{y}$

---

6 Conclusion

In this work, we introduced G2TA (Graph to Table Attack), a framework for converting anonymized graph data into a structured tabular form, enabling the application of deanonymization techniques such as record linkage attacks, which were originally designed for tabular datasets.

Our feature design captures key identity signals by combining structural features, such as local connectivity patterns and role similarity, with attribute-based semantic features that reflect similarity across node attributes. In doing so, we preserved identity-relevant information in a format suitable for linkage-based inference.

Experiments on real-world datasets demonstrated that G2TA can recover node identities, achieving high precision but modest recall, making it effective in settings where false positives are costly. Compared to graph-native methods, G2TA surpassed Narayanan–Shmatikov in precision, while Bumblebee remained superior in both precision and recall. Our evaluation on differentially private graphs revealed that, despite formal guarantees, structurally unique nodes can still be re-identified, exposing empirical vulnerabilities in practical settings.

Results show that transforming graphs into tabular form introduces a distinct and often overlooked attack surface. This highlights the importance of privacy evaluations that account not only for graph-based threats but also for vulnerabilities that emerge when graph data is converted into relational or feature-based formats. Future work will explore rid approaches that integrate tabular and graph-based signals to better balance privacy and utility.

References

1. Ahmed, N.K., et al.: Learning role-based graph embeddings. arXiv preprint arXiv:1802.02896 (2018)
2. Amin, K., Kulesza, A., Vassilvitskii, S.: Practical considerations for differential privacy. arXiv preprint arXiv:2408.07614 (2024)
3. Brandizi, M., Kurbatova, N., Sarkans, U., Rocca-Serra, P.: graph2tab, a library to convert experimental workflow graphs into tabular formats. Bioinformatics **28**(12), 1665–1667 (2012)
4. Cormode, G.: Personal privacy vs population privacy: learning to attack anonymization. In : Proceedings of the 17th ACM SIGKDD International Conference on Knowledge Discovery and Data Mining, pp. 1253–1261 (2011)
5. Datta, A., Sharma, D., Sinha, A.: Provable de-anonymization of large datasets with sparse dimensions. In: Degano, P., Guttman, J.D. (eds.) POST 2012. LNCS, vol. 7215, pp. 229–248. Springer, Heidelberg (2012). https://doi.org/10.1007/978-3-642-28641-4_13
6. Dolev, S., Ghanayim, M., Binun, A., Frenkel, S., Sun, Y.S.: Relationship of Jaccard and edit distance in malware clustering and online identification. In: 2017 IEEE 16th International Symposium on Network Computing and Applications (NCA), pp. 1–5. IEEE (2017)
7. Dwork, C.: Differential privacy: a survey of results. In: Agrawal, M., Du, D., Duan, Z., Li, A. (eds.) TAMC 2008. LNCS, vol. 4978, pp. 1–19. Springer, Heidelberg (2008). https://doi.org/10.1007/978-3-540-79228-4_1
8. Gulyás, G.G., Simon, B., Imre, S.: An efficient and robust social network de-anonymization attack. In: Proceedings of the 2016 ACM on Workshop on Privacy in the Electronic Society, pp. 1–11 (2016)
9. Heimann, M., Shen, H., Safavi, T., Koutra, D.: Regal: representation learning-based graph alignment. In: Proceedings of the 27th ACM International Conference on Information and Knowledge Management, pp. 117–126 (2018)
10. Henderson, K., et al.: It's who you know: graph mining using recursive structural features. In: Proceedings of the 17th ACM SIGKDD International Conference on Knowledge Discovery and Data Mining, pp. 663–671 (2011)
11. Jayaraman, B., Evans, D.: Evaluating differentially private machine learning in practice. In: 28th USENIX Security Symposium (USENIX Security 19), pp. 1895–1912 (2019)
12. Ji, S., Li, W., Mittal, P., Hu, X., Beyah, R.: {SecGraph}: A uniform and open-source evaluation system for graph data anonymization and de-anonymization. In: 24th USENIX Security Symposium (USENIX Security 15), pp. 303–318 (2015)
13. Ji, S., Mittal, P., Beyah, R.: Graph data anonymization, de-anonymization attacks, and de-anonymizability quantification: a survey. IEEE Commun. Surv. Tutor. **19**(2), 1305–1326 (2016)
14. Ji, S., Wang, T., Chen, J., Li, W., Mittal, P., Beyah, R.: De-SAG: on the de-anonymization of structure-attribute graph data. IEEE Trans. Dependable Secure Comput. **16**(4), 594–607 (2017)
15. Lee, W.-H., Liu, C., Ji, S., Mittal, P., Lee, R.B.: Blind de-anonymization attacks using social networks. In: Proceedings of the 2017 on Workshop on Privacy in the Electronic Society, pp. 1–4 (2017)
16. Liu, S., Demirel, M.F., Liang, Y.: N-gram graph: simple unsupervised representation for graphs, with applications to molecules. In: Advances in Neural Information Processing Systems, vol. 32 (2019)

17. Narayanan, A., Shmatikov, V.: Robust de-anonymization of large sparse datasets. In: 2008 IEEE Symposium on Security and Privacy (SP 2008), pp. 111–125. IEEE (2008)
18. Narayanan, A., Shmatikov, V.: De-anonymizing social networks. In: 2009 30th IEEE Symposium on Security and Privacy, pp. 173–187. IEEE (2009)
19. Narayanan, A., Shmatikov, V.: Robust de-anonymization of large sparse datasets: a decade later. May, 21:2019 (2019)
20. Rozemberczki, B., Allen, C., Sarkar, R.: Multi-scale attributed node embedding. J. Complex Netw. **9**(2), cnab014 (2021)
21. Rozemberczki, B., Kiss, O., Sarkar, R.: Karate club: an API oriented open-source python framework for unsupervised learning on graphs. In: Proceedings of the 29th ACM International Conference on Information and Knowledge Management, pp. 3125–3132 (2020)
22. Sen, P., Namata, G.M., Bilgic, M., Getoor, L., Gallagher, B., Eliassi-Rad, T.: Collective classification in network data. AI Mag. **29**(3), 93–106 (2008)
23. Srivatsa, M., Hicks, M.: Deanonymizing mobility traces: using social network as a side-channel. In: Proceedings of the 2012 ACM Conference on Computer and Communications Security, pp. 628–637 (2012)
24. Torres, N., Olivares, P.: De-anonymizing users across rating datasets via record linkage and quasi-identifier attacks. Data **9**(6), 75 (2024)
25. Ying, X., Wu, X.: Randomizing social networks: a spectrum preserving approach. In: proceedings of the 2008 SIAM International Conference on Data Mining, pp. 739–750. SIAM (2008)
26. Yuan, Q., Zhang, Z., Du, L., Chen, M., Cheng, P., Sun, M.: {PrivGraph}: differentially private graph data publication by exploiting community information. In: 32nd USENIX Security Symposium (USENIX Security 23), pp. 3241–3258 (2023)

Credit Card Fraud Detection Using Dynamic Attention and Multi-view Graph Learning

Shivam Kushwaha, Ankur Jain$^{(\boxtimes)}$, and Somanath Tripathy$^{(\boxtimes)}$

Department of Computer Science, Indian Institute of Technology Patna,
Patna, Bihar 801106, India
`{shivam_2311ai41,ankur_2221cs19,som}@iitp.ac.in`

Abstract. Detecting fraud within financial systems has become important due to the continuous evolution of fraudulent techniques to evade existing detection methods. Credit card fraud is one of the most common forms of payment fraud and is steadily rising globally. In this work, we proposed a framework that leverages three distinct multi-view graphs, capturing relationships between cardholders and merchants, transaction categories, and geospatial merchant clusters. These are integrated with a temporally causal transaction sequence graph to enhance fraud detection in credit card transactions. To effectively learn meaningful edge representations, the framework employs a Graph Attention Network (GAT) for fusing the heterogeneous features derived from these graph views. We also mitigate the challenge of class imbalance using the Synthetic Minority Oversampling Technique (SMOTE), facilitating two experimental settings, one using an undersampled dataset and the other using an oversampled dataset through bootstrapped minority instances. We perform various experiments, and the proposed model demonstrates significantly high performance compared to traditional models and current state-of-the-art approaches, attaining an accuracy of 88.93% across two balanced datasets.

Keywords: Credit Card · Fraud Detection · GNN

1 Introduction

Credit card fraud poses a significant and growing threat in the financial sector, where attackers continuously devise new strategies to exploit system vulnerabilities and deceive existing fraud detection mechanisms. Traditional rule-based systems and shallow machine learning models often fail to generalize well in dynamic and highly imbalanced environments. This challenge is further exacerbated by the presence of minority fraudulent transactions that are heavily overshadowed by a majority of legitimate ones, thereby resulting in poor recall and detection latency.

A. Akavia et al. (Eds.): CSCML 2025, LNCS 16244, pp. 225–237, 2026.
https://doi.org/10.1007/978-3-032-10759-6_14

Recent advancements in Graph Neural Networks (GNNs) have paved new avenues for modeling the structural and relational complexities inherent in transaction networks. Unlike earlier methods, GNNs are capable of leveraging both node attributes and edge dependencies to propagate meaningful representations, making them suitable for tasks like fraud detection where the context of an entity is often as important as its intrinsic features. Foundational models like Graph Convolutional Networks (GCN) [5], Graph Attention Networks (GAT) [13], and GraphSAGE [3] have been widely adopted for representation learning on relational data.

In the financial domain, GNN-based approaches have been successfully adapted for combating camouflaged fraudsters who mimic benign behavior [1], handling data imbalance [7], and addressing heterophily in fraud graphs [14]. Advanced architectures such as Tail-GNN [8], H2-Detector [11], and FraudRE [16] have explored both homophilic and heterophilic connections, as well as tail node effects, in fraud detection settings. Moreover, recent studies propose community-enhanced multi-relation GNNs [4] and confidence-based fraud detectors [6], aiming to improve interpretability and detection robustness.

To address the limitations in existing systems, this paper proposes a multi-view graph-based fraud detection framework augmented with a dynamic attention mechanism. The proposed model integrates heterogeneous relationships—such as user-merchant connections, transaction categories, and spatial clusters—through a shared embedding space while learning dynamic inter-graph attention for improved feature fusion. By incorporating temporal sequences alongside structural information, our approach ensures that temporal causality and behavioral evolution are jointly modeled.

Furthermore, to counteract class imbalance, we integrate advanced oversampling techniques and design the system to support both undersampled and SMOTE-enhanced settings. Experimental evaluations conducted on Sparknov Credit Card Transaction Fraud Detection dataset demonstrate that our approach significantly outperforms traditional baselines and state-of-the-art graph-based fraud detectors, both in terms of accuracy and robustness across class imbalance conditions.

The main contributions of this work are summarized as follows:

- We introduce a multi-view graph representation for credit card transactions, encoding heterogeneous relationships among cardholders, merchants, transaction categories, and locations.
- We develop a dynamic attention mechanism that adaptively weights temporal transaction features. By focusing on the most relevant past interactions for each account, this module enhances the model's sensitivity to emerging fraud sequences.
- We address the extreme class imbalance inherent in fraud data by employing SMOTE-based oversampling. We evaluate the proposed model under both undersampled and oversampled regimes.
- We perform extensive experiments on Synthetic Credit Card Transaction Fraud Detection datasets. Our proposed model significantly outperforms tra-

ditional classifiers and recent graph-based fraud detectors, achieving state-of-the-art detection accuracy.

This paper further has the following sections: Sect. 2 provides an overview of existing research on fraud detection in credit cards, Sect. 3 describes the proposed methodology. Section 4 gives a detailed performance analysis of the proposed work, along with various comparative evaluation metrics. Finally, Sect. 5 concludes the paper.

2   Related Work

Recent advances in fraud detection have prominently explored the use of Graph Neural Networks (GNNs) due to their effectiveness in capturing relational dependencies and structural patterns among entities. Traditional approaches relying on metadata or transaction-level features are often limited by their inability to model inter-entity interactions. GCNs [5] and GraphSAGE [3] laid the foundation for inductive learning over graphs by propagating neighborhood features, while GATs [13] introduced attention mechanisms for learning importance weights among nodes. These foundational methods have since been adapted and extended for fraud detection.

In particular, Dou et al. [1] proposed a GNN-based framework that combats camouflaged fraudsters by incorporating neighbor consistency and class-specific aggregations. Liu et al. [7] addressed class imbalance in fraud data by proposing a selective learning approach that picks representative samples during training. To handle heterophily—a situation where connected nodes belong to different classes—Wu et al. [14] introduced SplitGNN, a spectral GNN variant that maintains discriminative node representations even under weak label correlations.

More recent methods further address challenges like the tail node effect in imbalanced graphs, where infrequent nodes (fraudsters) receive insufficient representation updates. Tail-GNN [8] tackles this by explicitly enhancing tail node learning through frequency-aware designs. Similarly, FraudRE [16] mitigates both class imbalance and structural inconsistencies by optimizing a dual-resistant learning objective. Shi et al. [11] proposed H2-Detector, which models both homophilic and heterophilic connections to generalize across varying relational contexts.

Emerging solutions such as community-enhanced multi-relation GNNs [4], DGA-GNN [2], and confidence-degree-based GNNs [6] have further enhanced fraud detection performance by leveraging higher-order relationships, dynamic aggregation, and uncertainty-aware representations. Partitioned message-passing networks [17] have also been explored to improve computational scalability and robustness in fraud scenarios.

Attribute-driven semi-supervised methods [15] and anomaly-aware architectures like the one proposed by Tang et al. [12] have demonstrated strong performance in settings where labeled data is scarce. Auxiliary datasets such as product reviews [10] and user-image interactions [9] have been used in early work to simulate real-world heterogeneity in fraud behavior, offering inspiration for multi-view graph construction.

These works collectively emphasize that capturing both structure and semantics, addressing data imbalance, and accommodating diverse graph topologies are essential for accurate and scalable fraud detection systems. Building on these insights, our approach incorporates a dynamic graph fusion mechanism and sequence-aware embedding framework for improved detection accuracy across imbalanced and real-time transaction datasets.

3   Methodology

3.1   Data Collection

We utilize the *Credit Card Transaction Fraud Detection* dataset available on Kaggle, generated using the *Sparkov Data Generation Tool* developed by Brandon Harris. The dataset provides a realistic simulation of credit card activity over a period of two years (January 2019 – December 2020), covering:

- 1,000 cardholders and 800 merchants
- Approximately 5.9 million transactions
- A fraud rate of around 0.13% (highly imbalanced)

Simulation Details: The data simulator uses demographic profiles (e.g., rural females aged 25–50) and generates synthetic behavior using the `faker` Python library. Each profile governs transaction frequency, distribution across days of the week, and amount distributions per category. Multiple such profiles were merged to emulate realistic financial behavior across various socio-economic segments.

Key Fields:

- **Temporal:** `trans_date_trans_time`, `unix_time`
- **Geolocation:** `lat`, `long`, `merch_lat`, `merch_long`
- **User metadata:** `cc_num`, `gender`, `dob`, `job`
- **Transaction:** `amt`, `category`, `merchant`, `is_fraud`

3.2   Data Preprocessing and Balancing

To prepare the dataset for graph-based modeling and mitigate class imbalance, the following steps are performed:

- **Datetime Parsing:** Convert `trans_date_trans_time` and `dob` to datetime objects.
- **Derived Features:** Extract temporal features such as `hour_of_day` and `day_of_week`; compute `recency` (time since latest transaction) and `time_delta` (interval since previous transaction).
- **Encoding:** Apply label encoding to categorical fields including `cc_num`, `merchant`, and `category`.

- **Sorting:** Transactions are ordered chronologically by user ID and `unix_time` to preserve temporal and causal consistency.
- **Balancing Strategies:**
  - **Undersampling (D1):** Retain all 7,130 fraud transactions and randomly sample 21,390 non-fraud transactions to achieve a 1:3 fraud-to-nonfraud ratio.
  - **Oversampling (D2):** Retain all 21,390 non-fraud transactions and duplicate fraud transactions via bootstrapping to achieve a 1:1 class balance (21,390 fraud and 21,390 non-fraud).

Table 1. Summary of Node Features

Feature	Description
avg_amt	Average transaction amount associated with the node.
max_amt	Maximum transaction amount ever recorded.
avg_time_delta	Mean time interval between consecutive transactions.
avg_recency	Average time since each transaction relative to the most recent transaction
amt_vs_avg_ratio	Ratio of transaction amount to user's historical average; highlights deviations.
num_trans	Total number of transactions performed or received.
weekend_txn_ratio	Fraction of transactions made on weekends.
num_unique_targets	Number of unique recipients or merchants associated with the account.
num_unique_locations	Number of distinct geolocations where transactions occurred.
num_unique_types	Number of distinct transaction categories used by the account.

3.3 Feature Generation

Feature engineering plays a vital role in representing the transactional behavior and network structure of users and merchants. We extract both node-level and edge-level features to provide rich contextual information to our multi-view graph neural network model.

Node Features. Node features are constructed by aggregating statistics from transactions grouped by cardholder (or account). These features represent long-term and behavioral patterns of users. The details of the node features are summarized in Table 1.

All node features are standardized using **StandardScaler** before being input to the model.

Edge Features. Edge features represent each individual transaction and are used for fraud classification at the edge level. These features capture contextual and temporal information that help in distinguishing anomalous activities. Table 2 summarizes the edge-level features.

Edge features are also standardized to zero mean and unit variance to ensure effective convergence during model training.

3.4 Graph Construction

To model diverse and complex interactions inherent in financial transaction networks, we construct a four-view heterogeneous graph structure. Each view captures a distinct relational or behavioral signal, allowing the model to learn multifaceted patterns indicative of fraudulent behavior. The graphs are defined over a shared node set but differ in their edge semantics and construction logic. Let $\mathcal{G}_k = (\mathcal{V}, \mathcal{E}_k)$ denote the k-th view, where $\mathcal{V}$ is the set of all nodes and $\mathcal{E}_k$ is the edge set specific to that view.

Table 2. Summary of Edge Features

Feature	Description
amt	Transaction amount in dollars.
hour_of_day	Hour (0–23) at which the transaction occurred.
is_weekend	Binary indicator for whether the transaction occurred on a weekend.
recency	Time elapsed since the transaction compared to the latest transaction in the dataset.
time_delta	Time gap from the previous transaction by the same cardholder/account.
amt_vs_avg_ratio	Ratio of the transaction amount to the user's average; highlights spikes.

G1: Transaction Graph. This graph models direct financial interactions. Each edge in $\mathcal{E}_1$ represents a transaction between a source and target entity, which could be cardholder-to-merchant, or source-account-to-target-account, depending on the dataset schema. The edge is bidirectional, reflecting mutual involvement in the transaction, and serves as the primary target for fraud classification.

G2: Semantic Co-interaction Graph. To capture higher-order semantic behavior, G2 links entities that share contextual similarities. Specifically, entities (e.g., cardholders or accounts) are connected if they interact with the same categorical feature—such as merchant category or physical location. These connections reflect similar usage patterns, spending behavior, or geospatial overlap, which can be indicative of coordinated activity or behavioral mimicry.

G3: Spatial or Behavioral Similarity Graph. This view encodes either geographic proximity (for merchants) or behavioral similarity (for accounts). For spatial modeling, edges are added between merchant nodes if their geographic distance—computed using the Haversine formula or **geopy's geodesic()** function—is below a defined threshold (e.g., 25 km). For behavioral modeling, cosine similarity is computed over vectors representing transaction statistics (e.g., average amount, number of locations), and edges are added if the similarity exceeds a set threshold. This graph highlights local clusters and behaviorally-aligned entities.

G4: Causal Temporal Graph. This graph captures short-term temporal dependencies between transactions. For each user, transactions are sorted chronologically, and consecutive transactions within a pre-defined window (e.g., 1 h) are connected. These directed edges model causal sequences in financial behavior, allowing the GNN to reason over temporal progression and anomalies such as rapid transaction bursts.

Graph Representation. All graphs are represented using `edge_index` tensors in the format required by PyTorch Geometric. Each tensor has shape $(2, |\mathcal{E}_k|)$, where the first and second rows represent the source and destination nodes, respectively. To ensure bidirectional message passing, edges are duplicated in both directions unless they inherently represent causality (as in G4). Graph construction is preprocessed and stored to disk using `torch.save()` to optimize computational efficiency during training.

3.5 Model Architecture

The architecture of our proposed framework is illustrated in Fig. 1. It is designed to perform edge-level fraud detection using a multi-view and causally-aware graph neural network. The system combines structured node features, multiple graph views, edge-specific information, and attention-based fusion to model complex dependencies in financial transaction data.

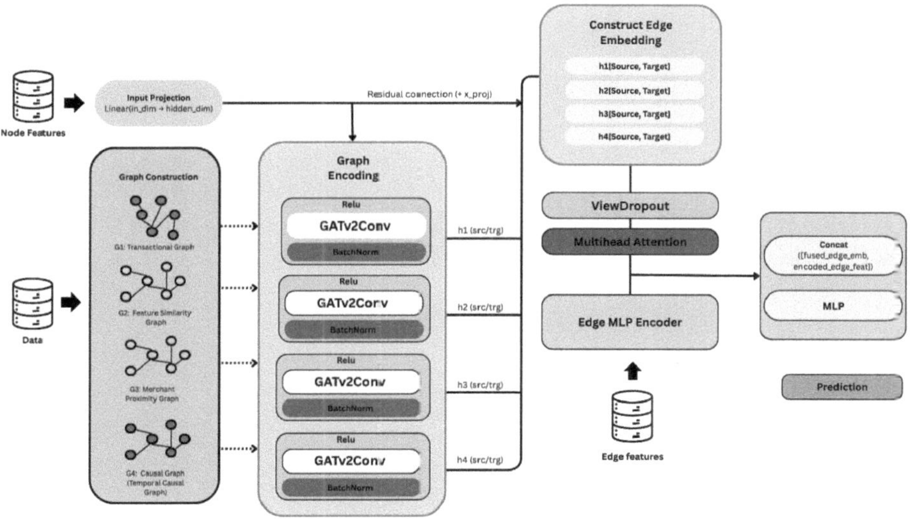

Fig. 1. Overview of the proposed multi-view and causally-aware GNN architecture for edge-level fraud detection.

Input Stage. The model accepts two main inputs:

- A node feature matrix $X \in \mathbb{R}^{|V| \times d}$, where d is the input dimension and $|V|$ is the number of nodes (accounts, merchants, categories).
- A set of multi-view graphs $\{\mathcal{G}_1, \mathcal{G}_2, \mathcal{G}_3, \mathcal{G}_4\}$, each represented by an edge index tensor $\mathcal{E}_k \in \mathbb{Z}^{2 \times |\mathcal{E}_k|}$, where $k \in \{1, 2, 3, 4\}$.

The node features are linearly projected into a hidden space:

$$X_{\text{proj}} = W_0 X + b_0, \quad W_0 \in \mathbb{R}^{h \times d}, \quad b_0 \in \mathbb{R}^h \tag{1}$$

Graph Encoding (Per View). Each graph view $\mathcal{G}_k$ is independently encoded using a `GATv2Conv` layer. For view k, node embeddings are computed as:

$$H_k = \text{ReLU}\left(\text{BatchNorm}(\texttt{GATv2Conv}_k(X, \mathcal{E}_k))\right) + X_{\text{proj}}, \quad H_k \in \mathbb{R}^{|V| \times h} \tag{2}$$

The addition of X_{proj} serves as a residual connection to maintain identity information and improve training stability.

Edge Embedding Construction. For each transaction (edge) to be classified, we extract its source and target node embeddings from all views. Let (u, v) denote a transaction:

$$e_k(u, v) = [H_k(u) \,\|\, H_k(v)] \in \mathbb{R}^{2h} \tag{3}$$

Stacking across all views forms a 3D tensor:

$$E = \text{Stack}(e_1, e_2, e_3, e_4) \in \mathbb{R}^{N_{\text{edges}} \times 4 \times 2h} \tag{4}$$

ViewDropout and Attention Fusion. To improve generalization, we apply ViewDropout to randomly drop one or more graph views during training. Let $M \in \{0, 1\}^4$ be the binary dropout mask across the views. The retained views are then passed through a Multi-Head Attention layer:

$$\text{FusedEdge}_i = \texttt{MultiHeadAttn}(E_i, E_i, E_i) \in \mathbb{R}^{2h} \tag{5}$$

Here, each attention head computes:

$$\text{Attn}(Q, K, V) = \text{softmax}\left(\frac{QK^\top}{\sqrt{d_k}}\right) V \tag{6}$$

where Q, K, V are projections of the stacked view embeddings, and d_k is the dimension of each head. The outputs of all heads are concatenated and linearly transformed to produce the fused representation and $K^\top$ means the transpose of the key matrix K.

Edge Feature Encoding and Classification. Let $f^{\text{edge}}_{(u,v)}$ denote the raw edge features (e.g., time delta, amount). These are passed through an edge encoder MLP:

$$z^{\text{edge}}_{(u,v)} = \text{MLP}_{\text{edge}}(f^{\text{edge}}_{(u,v)}) \in \mathbb{R}^h \tag{7}$$

The final input to the classifier is the concatenation of the fused multi-view edge embedding and the encoded edge features:

$$z_{(u,v)} = [\text{FusedEdge}_{(u,v)} \,\|\, z^{\text{edge}}_{(u,v)}] \in \mathbb{R}^{3h} \tag{8}$$

This is passed through a final MLP to obtain the logit:

$$\hat{y}_{(u,v)} = \sigma(\text{MLP}_{\text{final}}(z_{(u,v)})), \quad \hat{y}_{(u,v)} \in [0,1] \tag{9}$$

where σ denotes the sigmoid activation function.

Training Objective. Let $y_{(u,v)} \in \{0,1\}$ be the ground-truth fraud label for transaction (u,v), and let $\hat{y}_{(u,v)}$ denote the predicted probability of fraud. Given the severe class imbalance in the dataset, the model is trained using the **Focal Loss** function, which is designed to focus learning on hard-to-classify examples and reduce the influence of easily classified majority class samples.

The Focal Loss is defined as:

$$\mathcal{L}_{\text{focal}} = -\alpha_t \left(1 - \hat{y}_{(u,v)}\right)^{\gamma} \log\left(\hat{y}_{(u,v)}\right) \tag{10}$$

where:

- $\alpha_t \in [0,1]$ is a weighting factor used to balance the importance of positive (fraud) and negative (non-fraud) classes,
- $\gamma > 0$ is the focusing parameter that down-weights the loss for well-classified examples,
- $\hat{y}_{(u,v)}$ is the model's predicted probability for a fraudulent transaction.

In our experiments, we use $\alpha_t = 0.8$ and $\gamma = 2.5$ to provide stronger emphasis on rare fraudulent instances during training. The complete pipeline of our work can be seen in the Algorithm 1

Inference and Prediction. During inference, the model computes fused edge representations for each transaction and outputs a probability $\hat{y}_{(u,v)}$ indicating the likelihood of fraud. A threshold τ (typically 0.5) is used for final classification:

$$\text{Prediction} = \begin{cases} 1, & \text{if } \hat{y}_{(u,v)} > \tau \\ 0, & \text{otherwise} \end{cases}$$

Algorithm 1 Graph-Based Fraud Detection Pipeline

1: **Input:** Transaction dataset D
2: **Output:** Fraud predictions Y
3: Preprocess D and extract features
4: Construct graph $G = (V, E)$
5: Generate node embeddings via GNN
6: Train classifier with weighted loss
7: Predict fraud labels $\hat{Y}$
8: **return** $\hat{Y}$

This architecture effectively integrates heterogeneous graph views, temporal behavior, and contextual features for fine-grained fraud detection at the transaction level.

4   Experiment and Result

4.1   Experimental Setup

All experiments were conducted on a workstation with an Intel i7 CPU, 32GB RAM, and an NVIDIA RTX 2080 GPU. The models were implemented using PyTorch Geometric. We evaluated the performance on a benchmark financial fraud dataset where transactions are labeled as fraudulent or genuine.

4.2   Dataset

The dataset contains over 284,807 transactions with 492 labeled as frauds, exhibiting significant class imbalance (only 0.17% fraudulent). It includes fields like transaction amount, time, location, and merchant ID. After preprocessing, a heterogeneous graph was constructed where nodes represent transactions and edges capture relationships like shared user, common merchant, and temporal proximity.

4.3   Evaluation Metrics

We used the following metrics to evaluate model performance:

- **Accuracy**: Overall correctness of classification.
- **Precision**: Fraction of predicted frauds that are actual frauds.
- **Recall**: Fraction of actual frauds correctly identified.
- **F1-score**: Harmonic mean of precision and recall.
- **AUC-ROC**: Area under the receiver operating characteristic curve.

4.4   Results

We evaluate the performance of our proposed DAG-FD model on three public datasets, each representing different fraud detection domains: **S-FFSD Mini** (a synthetic financial transaction dataset with 40K transactions), **YelpChi** (spam review detection), and **Amazon Instruments** (fake review detection). For each dataset, we construct multi-view graphs as defined in our methodology, capturing various semantics such as transaction flow, review similarity, temporal activity, and user-item interactions. Standard train-test splits are followed throughout.

We compare our model against traditional GNN baselines such as GCN [5], GAT [13], and a range of recent fraud detection methods tailored to class imbalance and feature heterogeneity, including Tail-GNN [8], CARE-GNN [1], PC-GNN [7], and CMR-GNN [4].

The evaluation metrics include Accuracy, Recall, Area Under the Curve (AUC), and Average Precision (AP). Our model shows consistent improvements across all metrics on every dataset, validating the strength of dynamic multi-view fusion and attention-based aggregation.

Table 3 presents the results on the S-FFSD Mini dataset. The 4-view DAG-FD model achieves the highest performance with an accuracy of 0.8893, recall of 0.9394, and AUC of 0.9453. In contrast, GCN reaches only 0.7800 accuracy and 0.8524 AUC, while Tail-GNN, though competitive in recall, lags in precision and overall accuracy. Notably, DAG-FD outperforms even multi-relation models like PC-GNN and CMR-GNN, demonstrating its robustness in integrating diverse structural views.

Table 3. Performance comparison on the S-FFSD Mini dataset.

Model	Accuracy	Recall	AUC
GCN	0.7800	0.8292	0.8524
Tail-GNN	0.7773	0.8804	0.8569
CARE-GNN	0.6960	0.8379	0.7634
PC-GNN	0.7170	0.9016	0.7685
CMR-GNN	0.7804	0.8171	0.8460
DAG-FD (3-View)	0.8670	0.9295	0.9258
DAG-FD (4-View, ours)	**0.8893**	**0.9394**	**0.9453**

We observe similar trends on the YelpChi and Amazon Instruments datasets, where DAG-FD consistently outperforms all baselines, especially under class imbalance. Figure 2 illustrates the recall scores across datasets. Our model shows significant gains due to its ability to adaptively weigh relevant views for fraud detection.

These results strongly support that DAG-FD's multi-view representation learning and attention-based message aggregation significantly improve fraud

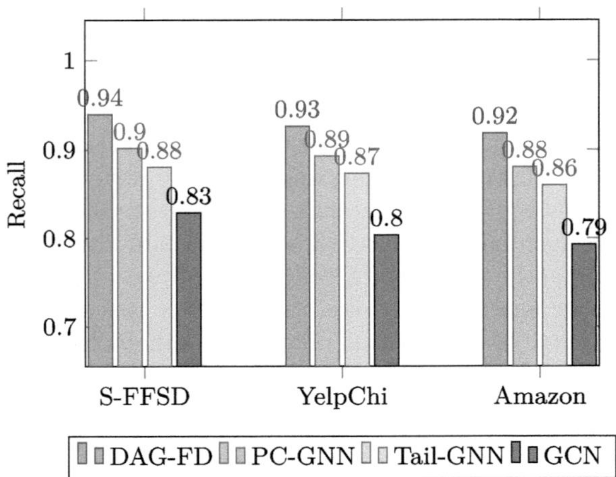

Fig. 2. Recall comparison across datasets.

detection effectiveness, especially under extreme imbalance and diverse structural patterns.

5   Conclusion

In this work, we proposed DAG-FD, a dynamic attention-based multi-view graph neural network designed to enhance fraud detection performance across diverse and complex datasets. By integrating multiple semantic views and dynamically adjusting their contributions, DAG-FD effectively captures both typical and camouflaged fraudulent patterns that are often overlooked by traditional methods. Experimental evaluations on benchmark datasets demonstrated significant improvements in key metrics such as accuracy, recall, and AUC, validating the effectiveness of the proposed approach. The results highlight the importance of dynamic view fusion and attention-based learning in addressing structural diversity and class imbalance in fraud detection tasks. Future research can explore real-time extensions, cross-modal integration, and privacy-preserving adaptations of the proposed model.

Acknowledgment. We acknowledge the IBTF, IIT Bhilai, for providing support for this research.

References

1. Dou, Y., Liu, Z., Sun, L., Deng, Y., Peng, H., Yu, P.S.: Enhancing graph neural network-based fraud detectors against camouflaged fraudsters. In: Proceedings of the 29th ACM International Conference on Information and Knowledge Management, pp. 315–324 (2020)
2. Duan, M., Zheng, T., Gao, Y., Wang, G., Feng, Z., Wang, X.: DGA-GNN: Dynamic grouping aggregation GNN for fraud detection. In: Proceedings of the AAAI Conference on Artificial Intelligence, vol. 38, pp. 11820–11828 (2024)
3. Hamilton, W., Ying, Z., Leskovec, J.: Inductive representation learning on large graphs. In: Advances in Neural Information Processing Systems, vol. 30 (2017)
4. Han, L., et al.: Mitigating the tail effect in fraud detection by community enhanced multi-relation graph neural networks. IEEE Transactions on Knowledge and Data Engineering (2025)
5. Kipf, T.N., Welling, M.: Semi-supervised classification with graph convolutional networks. arXiv preprint arXiv:1609.02907 (2016)
6. Liu, J., Tian, Y., Liu, G.: Global confidence degree based graph neural network for financial fraud detection. arXiv preprint arXiv:2407.17333 (2024)
7. Liu, Y., et al.: Pick and choose: a GNN-based imbalanced learning approach for fraud detection. In: Proceedings of the Web Conference 2021, pp. 3168–3177 (2021)
8. Liu, Z., Nguyen, T.K., Fang, Y.: Tail-GNN: tail-node graph neural networks. In: Proceedings of the 27th ACM SIGKDD Conference on Knowledge Discovery and Data Mining, pp. 1109–1119 (2021)
9. McAuley, J., Targett, C., Shi, Q., Van Den Hengel, A.: Image-based recommendations on styles and substitutes. In: Proceedings of the 38th International ACM SIGIR Conference on Research and Development in Information Retrieval, pp. 43–52 (2015)
10. Rayana, S., Akoglu, L.: Collective opinion spam detection: bridging review networks and metadata. In: Proceedings of the 21th ACM SIGKDD International Conference on Knowledge Discovery and Data Mining, pp. 985–994 (2015)
11. Shi, F., Cao, Y., Shang, Y., Zhou, Y., Zhou, C., Wu, J.: H2-fdetector: A GNN-based fraud detector with homophilic and heterophilic connections. In: Proceedings of the ACM Web Conference 2022, pp. 1486–1494 (2022)
12. Tang, J., Li, J., Gao, Z., Li, J.: Rethinking graph neural networks for anomaly detection. In: International Conference on Machine Learning, pp. 21076–21089. PMLR (2022)
13. Veličković, P., Cucurull, G., Casanova, A., Romero, A., Liò, P., Bengio, Y.: Graph attention networks. In: International Conference on Learning Representations (2018)
14. Wu, B., Yao, X., Zhang, B., Chao, K.M., Li, Y.: Splitgnn: spectral graph neural network for fraud detection against heterophily. In: Proceedings of the 32nd ACM International Conference on Information and Knowledge Management, pp. 2737–2746 (2023)
15. Xiang, S., et al.: Semi-supervised credit card fraud detection via attribute-driven graph representation. In: Proceedings of the AAAI Conference on Artificial Intelligence, vol. 37, pp. 14557–14565 (2023)
16. Zhang, G., et al.: Fraudre: fraud detection dual-resistant to graph inconsistency and imbalance. In: 2021 IEEE International Conference on Data Mining (ICDM), pp. 867–876. IEEE (2021)
17. Zhuo, W., et al.: Partitioning message passing for graph fraud detection. In: The Twelfth International Conference on Learning Representations (2024)

Meta-autoencoders: An Approach to Discovery and Representation of Relationships Between Dynamically Evolving Classes
A Work-in-Progress Report

Assaf Marron[1]([✉]) [iD], Smadar Szekely[1] [iD], Irun Cohen[2] [iD], and David Harel[1] [iD]

[1] Department of Computer Science and Applied Mathematics, Weizmann Institute of Science, Rehovot 7610001, Israel
{assaf.marron,smadar.szekely,david.harel}@weizmann.ac.il
[2] Department of Immunology and Regenerative Biology, Weizmann Institute of Science, Rehovot 7610001, Israel
irun.cohen@weizmann.ac.il

Abstract. An autoencoder (AE) is a neural network that, using self-supervised training, learns a succinct parameterized representation, and a corresponding encoding and decoding process, for all instances in a given class. Here, we introduce the concept of a *meta-autoencoder* (MAE): an AE for a collection of autoencoders. Given a family of classes that differ from each other by the values of some parameters, and a trained AE for each class, an MAE for the family is a neural net that has learned a compact representation and associated encoder and decoder for the class-specific AEs. One application of this general concept is in research and modeling of natural evolution—capturing the defining and the distinguishing properties across multiple species that are dynamically evolving from each other and from common ancestors. In this interim report we provide a constructive definition of MAEs, initial examples, and the motivating research directions in machine learning and biology.

Keywords: Autoencoder · Dimensionality Reduction · Evolution

1 Introduction

An *autoencoder* (AE) for a class of instances is a neural network (NN) that, following self-supervised training, establishes a dimensionality-reducing representation for the class. [3,7]. Figure 1 (borrowed and adapted from [5]) provides a brief introduction to autoencoding, and Fig. 2 depicts an example AE in more detail. For illustration, consider the set of all circles in the plane with center at $c = (0,0)$. For each radius r, the circle C_r is a class containing all the points on that circle; together, these classes form a family F of classes, distinguished from each other by the value of r. For a given r, any point $p = (x, y)$ in C_r can be

© The Author(s), under exclusive license to Springer Nature Switzerland AG 2026
A. Akavia et al. (Eds.): CSCML 2025, LNCS 16244, pp. 238–249, 2026.
https://doi.org/10.1007/978-3-032-10759-6_15

represented by a single number, for example, the angle between the radius to p and the positive x axis; one can train an AE that computes such encoding and its associated decoding. A meta-autoencoder (MAE) for F is an AE that can succinctly encode and decode AEs of the individual classes. A formal constructive definition appears in Sect. 2. Given the defining information for an AE for some circle, the MAE's encoder would encode this information into a succinct code, perhaps just the radius, and the MAE's decoder would produce all the information needed to construct a valid AE for that circle. The reconstructed AE may or may not be identical to the original input AE.

Our motivation for introducing and investigating MAEs is anchored in our research of the evolutionary theory of *Survival of the Fitted* [4,5,10] (the term *fitted* is contrasted with the classical terminology of Darwinian *Survival of the Fittest*). According to Survival of the Fitted, the biosphere is sustained mainly by the dynamics of its interaction networks. In a process that we term *natural autoencoding*, iterative imperfect reproduction and differential survival drive the emergence, reshaping and sustainment of interaction networks that external observers may label as organisms, species or ecosystems. Clearly, natural autoencoding differs from artificial autoencoding in various aspects, most conspicuously the absence of loss functions and backpropagation. Our current plans for modeling natural autoencoding include AEs and MAEs with modifications, constraints and a controlled execution environment. A bird's eye view of one such setup includes iterations of: (i) using AEs as imperfect reproduction engines for a population; (ii) clustering of the individuals in new generations; (iv) dynamic interaction and differential survival among individuals and groups; and (v) training and retraining of AEs and MAEs for the classes comprising the surviving population.

In this model, the emergent traits that are characteristic and essential to each dynamically created cluster, i.e., species, are not predictable, and neither are patterns of differences between such species. Iterative training of AEs and MAEs can help in discovering and representing such features. We find this modeling approach attractive as it offers common principles across different domains, uses computational elements that have been shown to exist in nature, and readily accommodates specialized low level components, as may evolve in nature for sensors and actuators, and may be used in the context of neural nets in feature engineering and in activation functions. This is contrasted with machine learning approaches, where a highly sophisticated network is designed and constructed in order to tackle a difficult challenge.

In Sect. 2 we first formalize the concept of MAEs, and discuss various aspects of the processes for creating them. In Sect. 3 we exemplify the construction of MAEs. In Sect. 4 we position this direction with regard to related work in statistics and in machine learning. In Sect. 5 we outline our motivating research trajectories for the theoretical concept of MAEs and for the specific application of AEs and MAEs in modeling evolution in multi-species ecosystems.

2   Meta Autoencoders

About Scope Restriction. The general concept of an MAE is broader than is needed in the present introduction and initial analysis. The definition below is for a restricted case; still, here, we keep the terms MAE and others without constraining adjectives.

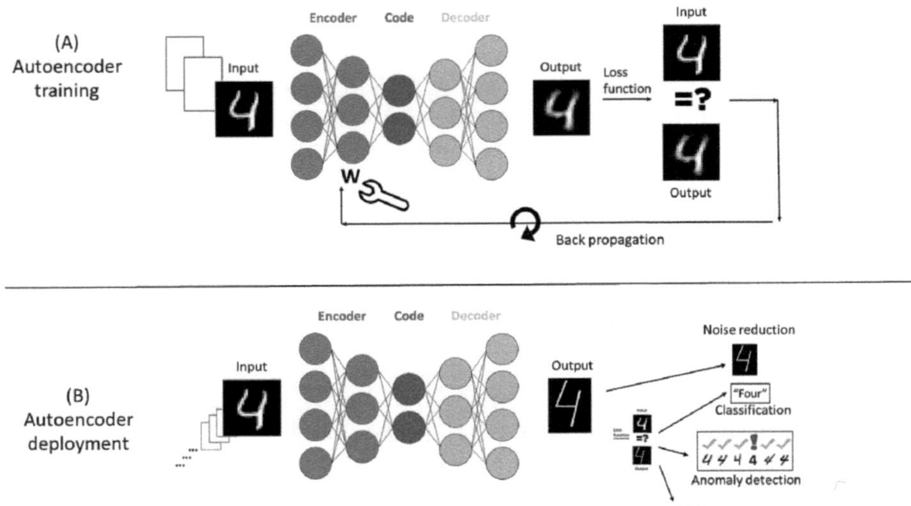

Fig. 1. Recap of artificial autoencoding. A typical AE is a NN consisting of an encoder (blue circles), a code layer, also called the bottleneck or latent layer (red circles), and a decoder (orange circles). Inputs (here, images of handwritten digits) are encoded by the encoder into the latent layer, and then reconstructed by the decoder. Training (A) with a finite set of examples, the differences between the inputs and the reconstructed outputs are computed, and the weights W and the biases (not shown) are adjusted in backpropagation and gradient descent to minimize the reconstruction loss. Once trained, the AE is deployed (B) to perform its inference or application task (noise reduction, classification, anomaly detection, etc.) using the now fixed encoding and decoding computations processes on an unbounded number of inputs from the domain of interest. (Color figure online)

Domain. We constrain the discussion below to $\mathcal{R}^2$, the Cartesian plane, where every instance z can be represented with the coordinate pair $z = (x, y)$.

Encodable Classes. We say that a class C of instances in $\mathcal{R}^2$ is *encodable to the domain $T \subseteq \mathcal{R}$, within ϵ, for $\epsilon \in \mathcal{R}$* (or just *encodable*, for short), if there exists at least one pair of encoding and decoding functions $f_e^C : C \to T$ and $f_d^C : T \to \mathcal{R}^2$ respectively, such that for all $z \in C$:

$$\|z - f_d^C(f_e^C(z))\| \leq \epsilon .$$

That is, one can encode each point $z = (x, y)$ in C into a single real number $t \in T$, and then decode that t into another point $z' \in \mathcal{R}^2$, but not necessarily in C, whose distance from z is small enough for the purposes at hand.

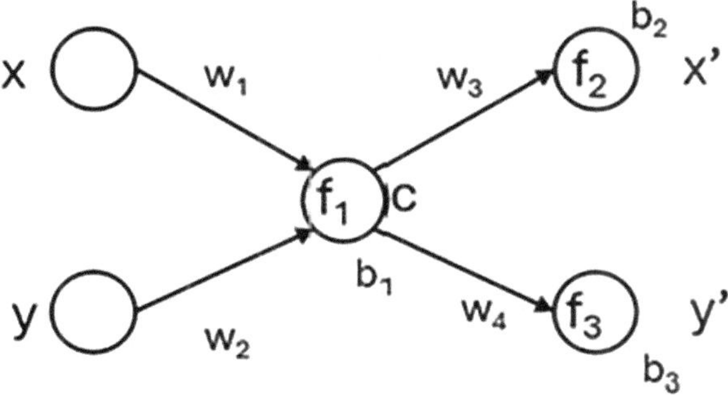

Fig. 2. Autoencoder example. This AE has 3 layers (with 2, 1, and 2 neurons respectively), weights w_1, w_2, w_3, w_4, biases b_1, b_2, b_3, and activation functions f_1, f_2, f_3. For every input (x, y), $c = f_1(xw_1 + yw_2) + b_1$; $x' = f_2(cw_3) + b_2$, and $y' = f_3(cw_4) + b_3$. In a perfectly trained AE, $x = x'$ and $y = y'$.

For example, the class C_a of points on the straight line $y = a \cdot x$ is encodable into $\mathcal{R}$ for an arbitrarily small ϵ. Examples of pairs of encoding and decoding functions for this class can be $f_e(x, y) = x$ and $f_d(t) = (t, at)$, respectively, or $f_e'(x, y) = 2 \cdot x$ and $f_d'(t) = (\frac{t}{2}, a\frac{t}{2})$. In another example, the class C_r of points on the circle of radius r and centered at the origin can be encoded by $f_e(x, y) = \mathrm{atan2}(y, x)$ and decoded by $f_d(t) = (r\cos(t), r\sin(t))$.

Autoencodable Classes. We say that an encodable class C is *autoencodable*, if there is a known AE for it. This is not about the theoretical existence of an AE for C, but about whether one was already created, or a way was created to construct one at will. Efforts to create an AE for a given class C may fail because the class is not encodable, or, due to hurdles in the AE training process. One such hurdle is manifested in encoding functions that are too complex for standard AE architectures, even with preparatory feature engineering steps where inputs are pre-processed before being fed to the NN.

MAE: A Constructive Definition. Let F be a family of autoencodable classes. We say that a given neural network M is an MAE for F, if M is an AE that was successfully constructed as follows: (i) an arbitrary or random sample F^0 of classes in F was selected. (ii) a single AE architecture was selected (number of layers, number of neurons in each layer, connectivity, and activation functions); (iii) for each class $C \in F_0$ one or more AEs were created with the selected architecture, yielding F^0_{AE}, a set of AEs; (iv) the AE M was successfully trained and tested on F^0_{AE}. $\qquad\square$

The conditions for calling M an MAE for F are quite relaxed. Thus, once constructed in this manner, M may not be able to successfully encode and decode all AEs (of the selected architecture) for all classes $C \in F$, or decode every synthetic code in the latent domain into a valid AE for some class in F. Furthermore, for a given family of autoencodable classes, an MAE may not exist, or the construction of one may be impractical.

Feature Engineering in MAE Construction. When choosing the class family for meta-autoencoding, one may already have in mind the parameters that characterize the individual AEs. However, this characterization may not be readily computable by standard NN architectures from the weights and biases of the AEs, calling either for richer activation functions or for feature engineering. As our focus is on biological modeling, we find these two options acceptable. as they align with our assumptions that natural learning processes have common and generic principles, and that biological mechanisms that are complex yet well-encapsulated and internally modular can evolve naturally.

Execution-Driven Loss Calculations. In NN training, classical loss calculations involve comparing the network's output with a desired output. When the network's output is a specification of a program or a process, classical loss functions compare the output specification to a desired specification. However, in various contexts, the loss calculation involves compiling and executing the program specification, and comparing the output of that execution to a predefined collection of desired outcomes [12]. While not required in the definition of MAEs, in our experiments, we extended such execution-driven loss calculation approach as follows. In training, each input AE of the MAE is an autoencoder that was constructed by training over a sample set of points drawn from a given class C. The reconstruction process carried out by the MAE yields an output autoencoder AE'. To calculate the loss, we sample a set of points $C^0 \subset C$, and for each point $(x, y) \in C^0$ we compute the distance

$$\|AE'(x, y) - AE(x, y)\| \ \ .$$

Illustrations of execution-driven loss calculation appear in Figs. 5 and 6.

Comparing the functionality of parent and child programs aligns with theories of evolution where sustainability depends on the ability of offspring to function in the same interaction networks that their parents' had participated in [10].

Note. Within a common ML platform like Tensorflow, testing a reconstructed AE while training the MAE requires configuring the invoked AE as a stateless NN model, to avoid data structure collisions.

3   Meta-autoencoder Examples

Below we report our experience with the construction of MAEs for two classes of points in $\mathcal{R}^2$: points on a line (PoaL) and points on a circle (PoaC).

3.1   Points on a Line (PoaL)

Our first set of experiments is with family F of classes C_a where each class is the collection of all points on straight line in $\mathcal{R}^2$ that passes through the origin $(0, 0)$, and whose angle θ with the x-axis, specified in degrees, is an integer, and satisfies $-80 \leq \theta < 80$ (see Fig. 4. Each class is uniquely associated with the equation $y = ax$ where the line slope a satisfies $a = \tan(\theta)$. Every such class is autoencodable; one such example AE has: (i) three layers in a 2-1-2 arrangement as in Fig. 2; (ii) weights of $w_1 = 1$ and $w_2 = 0$ for the encoder edges, and $w_3 = 1$ and $w_4 = a$ for the decoder edges; (iii) all biases are zero; and (iv) all activation functions are the identity, $f(x) = x$.

For training the PoaL MAE, we created a training set of PoaL AEs as follows. We kept the above 2-1-2 AE configuration with identity activations. We created 10 AEs for each of the 160 lines in the range for a total of 1600 AEs. Each of the 10 AEs of a given line was trained with a different set of 1000 random points on that line. We did not force the biases to be zero. See Fig. 4 The test set for each line AE was yet another set of random points.

We constructed an MAE for the PoaL AEs as follows. Given the fixed 2-1-2 architecture and the identity activations, each AE's NN has 7 defining parameters: 4 weights and 3 biases. Experiments with a naïve 7-1-7 architecture for the MAE did not readily provide good results. As stated above, one of the codes that represents such an AE and that consists of a single real number, could be the value of a, which in this case satisfies $a = \frac{w_4}{w_3}$. Thus, at least for one of the options of the code computations, an MAE may have to calculate or approximate the above ratio. However, computing division in a neural net may require using logarithms in activation functions, or two-argument functions, which are non standard. We chose to solve the problem with feature engineering, and provided $\frac{w_4}{w_3}$ as one of the inputs, yielding an 8-1-8 neural net.

The architecture of the PoaL MAE is shown in Fig. 3.

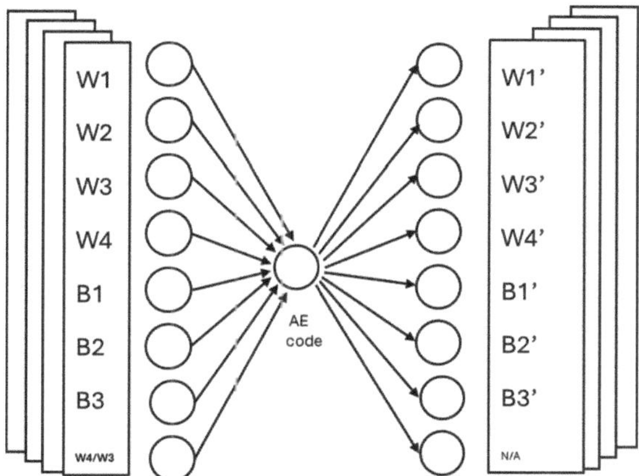

Fig. 3. MAE for Points-on-a-Line AE. Each input AE is defined by its 4 weights and 3 biases. An added 8th feature is the ratio W4/W3. The MAE NN outputs new weights and biases, to be used in a reconstructed AE.

The training process used execution-driven loss calculation as described in Sect. 2. Specifically, for the input AE with a slope a ($= \tan(\theta)$, for some angle θ), we picked 4 points on that line: $(-10, -10a),(-3.33, -3.33a),(3.33, 3.33a)$, and $(10, -10a)$, and compared the outputs of the input AE and of the reconstructed AE, when processing these 4 inputs. The learning converged well, yielding a working meta auto-autoencoder, that could encode and decode any newly trained AE for any line in the above F. The resulting model is available online, for inference and further training, in Tensorflow format, at https://drive.google. com/file/d/1kHtSojs8erNS9qj5pexuo2NvR79Wokgw/view?usp=sharing.

This experiment can be extended in various ways, including: (i) allow F to contain classes in a continuous range of the angle θ; (ii) allow vertical lines; (iii) replace feature-engineering heuristics with additional NN layers; (iv) feed a broader range of computed features to the training process; and, (v) interpret the learned AE and MAE codes.

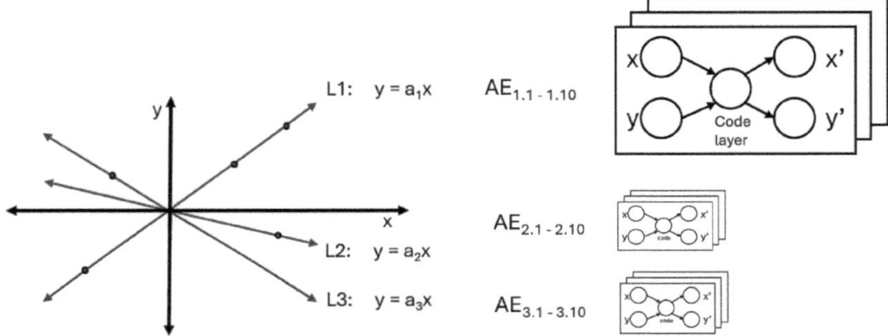

Fig. 4. Preparing the training set for Points-on-a-Line MAE. We sample classes ($L1$, $L2$, $L3$) in the family F of straight lines in $\mathcal{R}^2$ that go through the origin. The lines have slopes a_1, a_2, a_3, respectively. The elements of each class are all the points of the respective line. For each class we train 10 AEs, using a different set of 1000 random points for each.

3.2   Points on a Circle (PoaC)

In this example F is the family of classes where each class is the collection of all points on a circle in $\mathcal{R}^2$, whose center is at (0,0). As stated earlier, given a class C_r with its radius r, each point $(x, y) \in C_r$ can be encoded as the angle formed between the radius to the point and the positive x-axis, which satisfies $\theta = \text{atan2}(y, x)$. Ideally and AE for C_r would compute this function, however, a standard NN can only compute an approximation of this function. We trained each class AE as follows. We used an architecture of 5 layers having 2, 8, 1, 2, and 2 neurons, respectively, expecting layer 3 to capture the angle approximation, as encoded in layers 1–3 with tanh() activations.

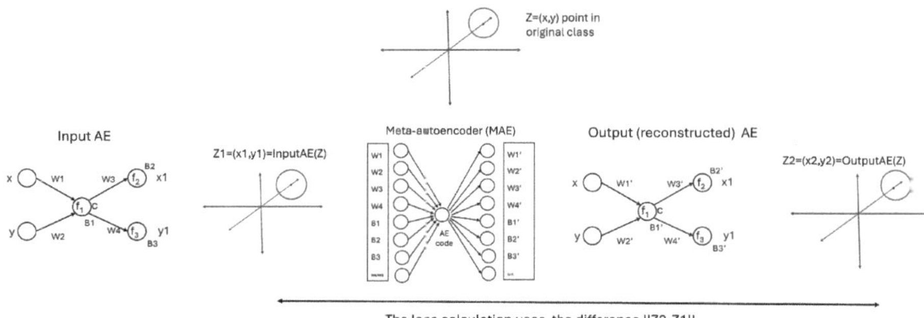

Fig. 5. Execution-Driven Loss Calculation. When training the MAE, the MAE encodes an Input AE, reconstructing it as a corresponding Output AE. A sample point Z from the class associated with the Input AE is encoded and decoded by both the input and output AEs, yielding Z1 and Z2. The difference ||Z2-Z1||, is used in loss calculation over a sample of several points.

In the decoder we applied heuristics: in layer 4 we used activations of cos() and sin(), and set as 1.00 the two weights from the layer 3 code neuron. In layer 5 we used identity activations, and assumed that each of the two neurons of layer 4 is connected to just one respective neuron in layer 5. We expect, but do not force, the trained weights on these two edges to be just r. We justify this heuristics and the asymmetry in the AE is that (a) we find such a crafted decoder to be comparable or complementary to feature engineering in the AE's input, and (b) we anticipate that if we add more neurons in layer 4, and/or more layers, with diverse activation functions, the PoaC training will be able to approximate the cos() and sin() functions, and/or learn the weights that we have fixed.

After identifying a working architecture for PoaC AEs, we prepared a dataset of such AEs by training each one with a set of 200 points. In most cases, the class AEs converged nicely.

To train the PoaC MAE we created training and test sets of AEs for circles with radiuses in fixed intervals in the range $1 \leq r \leq 10$.

The MAE has 9 layers with 35-20-10-4-1-4-10-20-35 neurons respectively, and ReLU and linear activations. The number 35 is the total number of trainable weights and biases in the PoaC 2-8-1-2-2 AEs, while other weights and biases are fixed, as described in the heuristics above. For each circle we created multiple AEs, using a different set of 200 random points in each AE.

The training of an MAE for circles did not readily converge so we took the following heuristic steps. First, we narrowed down the example from Points-on-a-Circle to Points-on-Arc (PoA). The individual class AEs were generated as for circles, but instead of the range of points being chosen in angles from $-\pi$ to π, they were between $\pi/6$ and $\pi/3$.

We then normalized the AEs as follows. Different AEs for a given circle may actually be isomorphic to each other, and similar AEs may look very different due to the order of neurons. Hence, we sorted the 8 neurons in layer 2 of the

PoaL AEs by the product of the two weights on the edges from the two neurons in layer 1 to the same neuron in layer 2. As in PoaL, in training the PoA MAE we employed execution-driven loss calculation, using the 35 output values to populate the weights and biases in a skeleton 2-8-1-2-2 AE, with the above-specified activations. See Fig. 6 for a related example of applying the execution-driven loss calculation.

The MAE training was successful and the resulting models are available online, for inference and further training, in Tensorflow format, at https://drive. google.com/file/d/1B3aq7-FETmr2V8HE_Nc3bNkKbp0I10AE/view?usp=sha ring and https://drive.google.com/file/d/1Sz39RhSXAjcyr1-k9aI_dWEKZLS2 eQQw/view?usp=sharing

This example can be extended too; e.g., narrow down the family to classes of arcs for which trained AEs perform well, explore simpler MAE models, perhaps with different activation functions, and interpret the codes of the AEs and MAE for insights that may accelerate training and simplify models.

4   Related Work

The construction of AEs and MAEs aims to discover relationship patterns between properties of individuals and groups within an evolving population. Such goals may also be pursued analytically, using classical statistical methods, including principal component analysis (PCA) [1] and meta-PCA [8].

Since our motivation lies in modeling biological processes—often depending on reproduction and sustainment—and as autoencoding can be viewed also as an imperfect reproduction mechanism, we place AEs at the center of our approach. Other important modeling aspects, such as precision, efficiency, succinctness, and formal provability can then be addressed within this biologically oriented framework. Certain limitations of AEs and MAEs, as compared with analytical methods, may be sidestepped in natural settings. For example, the real-world data may lie within a narrow, computationally safe band, rarely reaching theoretical worst-case scenarios.

The pursuit of autoencoding in multi-class environments and contexts is not new [2,6,9,11]. However, the projects we have seen are application-specific, often in image processing, where the classes being autoencoded and the associated challenges are pre-determined. For example, the goal may be to develop an AE-based technique for domain adaptation—transferring learned knowledge between image domains that differ in quality or context.

By contrast, our broad interest is in: (a) classes whose contents are not known in advance, as they evolve dynamically, but whose differences are confined, as they evolve from each other or from common ancestors; and (b) identifying a domain independent framework or computational principles, that can support a theory of universal autoencoding mechanisms.

In addition, the focus on modeling nature may uncover ways to combine simplicity with robustness that may be inadequate in a more general machine learning setting: As natural autoencoding is carried out in parallel by multiple

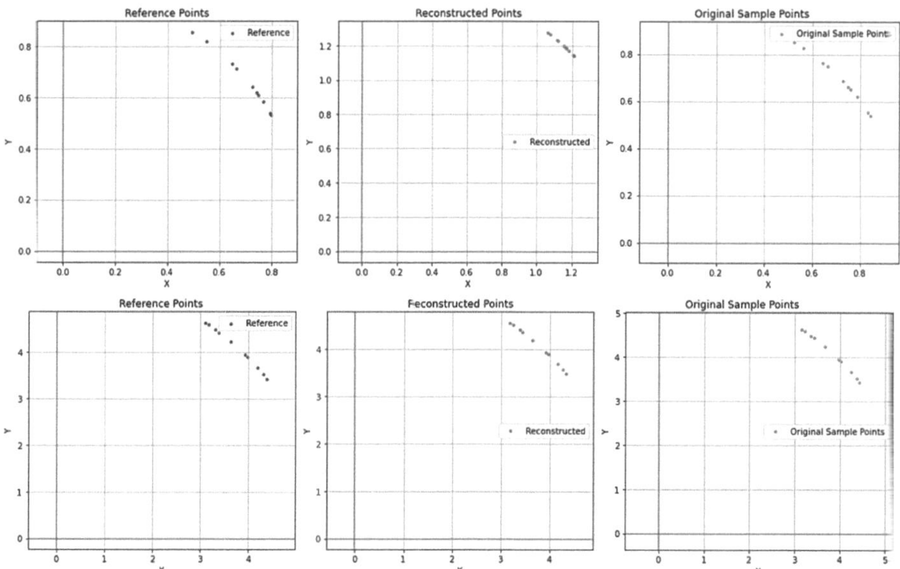

Fig. 6. Sample data for execution-driven loss calculation in one of the batches of AEs, in one of the epochs of MAE training for the family of Points-on-Arc classes. While Fig. 5 concentrates on a single point in a single AE, here each row of three images is for a separate AE, and shows multiple points for that AE. The right image shows the original points in the class (an arc with a particular radius); the left image shows the points reconstructed by the trained AE, and are thus very close to the original ones; the center image shows the points reconstructed by the output AE, as reconstructed from the trained AE by the MAE being trained. In the top row, the reconstructed AE preserves the arc shape, but the density of the points and the arc radius differ from the ones produced by the input AE. In the bottom row, the reconstructed AE has better performance. The loss calculation spans a batch of such input AEs, with multiple sample points for each. Note also that the final loss can vary between different AEs.

instances, if some individuals do not survive due to autoencoding-related failures, others may continue executing the same imperfect process for other cases, yielding acceptable population-wide results.

5   Conclusion and Future Research

We have introduced the concept of meta-autoencoders for families of autoencodable classes as a direction for a modular domain-independent mechanism for parameterizing the differences among collections of classes. We view future research of meta-autoencoding in two trajectories.

The first is incorporating AEs and MAEs in modeling biological evolution as described in Sect. 1, including reproduction (both sexual and asexual), recurrence (manifested in feeding back the outputs of AEs into fresh training cycles), clustering within populations to delineate species, and parallel autoencoding of interacting species. In this context we plan to also study **distributional autoencoding**, where each reconstructed point is allowed to differ significantly from the corresponding input point, which might model its parent, while maintaining the input property distribution in the reconstructed population. Such distributional autoencoding differs from variational autoencoding, where stochasticity is in the latent layer rather than in the output population.

The second research direction is the theory of MAEs, including: extending the constructive definition offered here, demonstrating MAE construction in additional domains, multi-level meta-autoencoding, i.e., an MAE for a collection of MAEs, studying categories of families of classes for which the existence or non-existence of MAEs may be proven a-priori, interpreting the code of AEs and MAEs as well as the relations between multiple AEs for the same class and across classes; and, (v) developing methods and tools for systematic construction of meta-autoencoders in diverse applications.

Acknowledgement. This research was funded in part by an NSFC-ISF grant to DH, issued jointly by the National Natural Science Foundation of China (NSFC) and the Israel Science Foundation (ISF grant 3698/21). Additional support was provided by a research grant to DH from Louis J. Lavigne and Nancy Rothman, the Carter Chapman Shreve Family Foundation, Dr. and Mrs. Donald Rivin, and the Estate of Smigel Trust.

Disclosure of Interests. The authors declare that they have no competing interests.

References

1. Abdi, H., Williams, L.J.: Principal component analysis. Wiley Interdisc. Rev.: Comput. Stat. **2**(4), 433–459 (2010)
2. Abinaya, S., Kumar, K.U., Alphonse, A.S.: Cascading autoencoder with attention residual u-net for multi-class plant leaf disease segmentation and classification. IEEE Access **11**, 98153–98170 (2023)
3. Berahmand, K., Daneshfar, F., Salehi, E.S., Li, Y., Xu, Y.: Autoencoders and their applications in machine learning: a survey. Artif. Intel. Rev. **57**(2), 28 (2024)
4. Cohen, I.R., Marron, A.: The evolution of universal adaptations of life is driven by universal properties of matter: energy, entropy, and interaction. F1000Research **9** (2020)
5. Cohen, I.R., Marron, A.: Evolution is driven by natural autoencoding: reframing species, interaction codes, cooperation and sexual reproduction. Proc. R. Soc. B **290**(1994), 20222409 (2023)
6. Deng, W., et al.: Informative feature disentanglement for unsupervised domain adaptation. IEEE Trans. Multimedia **24**, 2407–2421 (2021)
7. Goodfellow, I., Bengio, Y., Courville, A.: Deep Learning. MIT Press (2016). http:// www.deeplearningbook.org. Chapter 14
8. Kim, S., Kang, D., Huo, Z., Park, Y., Tseng, G.C.: Meta-analytic principal component analysis in integrative omics application. Bioinformatics **34**(8) (2018)

9. Liu, Y., Tian, X., Li, Y., Xiong, Z., Wu, F.: Compact feature learning for multi-domain image classification. In: Proceedings of the IEEE/CVF Conference on Computer Vision and Pattern Recognition, pp. 7193–7201 (2019)
10. Marron, A., Szekely, S., Cohen, I.R., Harel, D.: Natural averaging may complement known biological constraints in sexual reproduction's advantages over asexual in conserving species quantitative traits. Sci. Rep. **15**(1), 14522 (2025)
11. Wang, Q., Breckon, T.P.: Generalized zero-shot domain adaptation via coupled conditional variational autoencoders. Neural Netw. **163**, 40–52 (2023)
12. Ye, H., Martinez, M., Monperrus, M.: Neural program repair with execution-based backpropagation. In: Proceedings of the 44th International Conference on Software Engineering, pp. 1506–1518 (2022)

Sure! Here's a Short and Concise Title for Your Paper: "Contamination in Generated Text Detection Benchmarks"

Philipp Dingfelder[(✉)] and Christian Riess[(✉)]

IT Security Infrastructures Lab, FAU Erlangen-Nürnberg,
Martensstr. 3, 91058 Erlangen, Germany
{philipp.dingfelder,christian.riess}@fau.de

Abstract. Large language models are increasingly used for many applications. To prevent illicit use, it is desirable to be able to detect AI-generated text. Training and evaluation of such detectors critically depend on suitable benchmark datasets. Several groups took on the tedious work of collecting, curating, and publishing large and diverse datasets for this task. However, it remains an open challenge to ensure high quality in all relevant aspects of such a dataset. For example, the DetectRL benchmark exhibits relatively simple patterns of AI-generation in 98.5% of the Claude-LLM data. These patterns may include introductory words such as "Sure! Here is the academic article abstract:", or instances where the LLM rejects the prompted task.

In this work, we demonstrate that detectors trained on such data use such patterns as shortcuts, which facilitates spoofing attacks on the trained detectors. We consequently reprocessed the DetectRL dataset with several cleansing operations. Experiments show that such data cleansing makes direct attacks more difficult. The reprocessed dataset is publicly available.

Keywords: Generated Text Detection · Data Quality · Benchmarking · DetectRL

1 Introduction

Generative Artificial Intelligence (AI) can assist with various tasks, including programming, creating media and content, and utilising chatbots as an alternative to traditional internet searches. However, alongside these positive applications, the potential misuse of generative AI is also well known. These include plagiarism in educational settings [15] and the creation of deepfakes [12]. In particular, the text domain attracts a high level of attention due to the increasing capabilities of Large Language Models (LLMs). For instance, recent reasoning models [1,14] have become more practical in scientific research [16]. This, combined with the unreliability of humans as detectors [4,5], has resulted in a growing number of automatic detectors and Generated Text Detection (GTD)-Benchmarks, making it an extremely active area of research.

© The Author(s), under exclusive license to Springer Nature Switzerland AG 2026
A. Akavia et al. (Eds.): CSCML 2025, LNCS 16244, pp. 250–262, 2026.
https://doi.org/10.1007/978-3-032-10759-6_16

One family of detectors works with an actively embedded signal, like a watermark. They usually require control of the text generation process for embedding the watermark, which is only given for providers of LLM systems [19]. Another family of detectors work passively. They forensically examine a sequence of text for traces of a generator. Passive detectors are by tendency less reliable, but they have the advantage that they can be flexibly applied post-hoc and without control of the generation process. Within this family, even more flexibility can be achieved if detectors have the ability to generalise across different types of generators. This brings the benefit that the detector is not limited to the exact models in the training set when testing it on text in the field [7].

Even if a generator generalizes well, it is still evident that its overall quality critically depends on the quality of its training and calibration data. This particularly affects the dectector's ability to generalise to various real-world scenarios [15]. DetectRL and related benchmarks aim to provide such data [21,22,24]. They provide samples of various attacks from multiple LLMs with the goal of achieving a high degree of realism [24]. However, our investigation on DetectRL reveals that data quality may not always be adequately addressed. The benchmark data contains several artifacts of LLM-generated content, such as LLM-typical starting phrases like *"Sure! Here is the abstract for the given title: ..."* or rejection phrases such as *"I apologize, upon further reflection I do not feel comfortable generating fictional negative reviews."* While the first type of artifacts may cause trained detectors to learn a shortcut, multiple rejections may lead to repeating rejection phrases that are easy to detect. If not excluded in the evaluation, these phrases may therefore lead to overly optimistic performance metrics.

The DetectRL dataset is gaining popularity within the research community. However, to the best of our knowledge, neither the original work nor follow-up works report or discuss these issues. With this work, we hope to close this gap. We analyse the extent and potential impact of these issues. In order to improve the usefulness of the DetectRL dataset, we also provide a reprocessed version of the DetectRL benchmark dataset for download[1]

The paper is organized as follows. Section 2 reviews the state of the art in GTD methods. Section 3 investigates the contamination in the DetectRL benchmark. Section 4 describes methods to estimate the impact of the contamination and the reprocessing of the dataset. Section 5 reports experimental results on the contamination and the reprocessed dataset. Section 6 concludes this work.

2   Related Work

The field of generated text detection is a fast growing branch of research. The following literature review can hence only cover a small portion of related works. We refer to Ghosal *et al.* [19] and Wu *et al.* [23] for more elaborate surveys on the topic.

---

[1] https://www.cs1.tf.fau.de/research/multimedia-security/code/reprocessed-detectrl-dataset/.

One family of GTD methods involves active detection schemes with an embedded signal. Arguably the most relevant subcategory makes use of watermarks that either distort the output probabilities of the tokens [8], or use a pseudo-random generator [18]. Another group of active detection schemes are retrieval-based methods [9]. However, active detection schemes all share the limitation that they require access to the text generation process, which is in many application scenarios unavailable.

Such access to the generation process is not necessary for passive detectors. These form a second family of methods that can be applied post-hoc to probe any text for its origin. According to Ghosal *et al.* [19], passive detectors can be coarsely categorised into trained detectors and zero-shot detectors. Trained detectors like Robustly optimized BERT approach (RoBERTa) are based on pre-trained transformers usually with an additional classification head [10]. In contrast, zero-shot detectors do not require any generator-specific training. Therefore, they are considered to be more model-agnostic. They probe specific properties of the text to distinguish model-generated text from human-written text. Initial attempts such as GLTR are based on the observation, that language models only use a limited subset of the distribution of natural language with a high likelihood [5]. A subsequent work uses the perplexity as a measure of naturalness of the text [20,25]. Binoculars extends this work by using cross-perplexity from a reference model [7]. This approach ensures that traces of generated text can also be found in text stemming from particular prompts that make the output appear less likely to be LLM-generated in the first place. Inverse Prompt for AI Detection (IPAD) is a recent zero-shot detector that uses a prompt inverter to regenerate text similar to the input text [2]. This is followed by an distinguisher module that is used to classify the text based on the alignment of the input and the regenerated text.

Besides these recent advances in generated text detection, there have also various attacks been published that challenge the practical effectiveness of GTD methods. Paraphrasing is arguably the most prominent attack to evade detection. It can be implemented in different ways. For example, DIPPER is a language model that has been specifically trained for paraphrasing [9]. Other possibilities are to use a general-purpose LLM, or to perform paraphrasing via back-translation [24]. Additionally, humans themselves may also paraphrase the generated text.

Beyond basic paraphrasing attacks, it has been demonstrated that a sequence of multiple paraphrasing steps makes the detection of LLM-generated text notably harder [6]. Further scenarios include polishing with another LLM, mixing of human-written and LLM-generated content, employing various prompting strategies, and launching adversarial attacks such as incorporating spelling errors [24].

There are several datasets to benchmark the detection of generated text. Widely used datasets besides DetectRL are for example M4GT-Bench [21] or SemEval-2024 Task 8 [22]. All of these datasets cover multiple application domains like reviews, abstracts, creative writing, and news articles. M4GT-

Bench and SemEval-2024 offer data in multiple languages. DetectRL only contains English-language text. However, it stands out in the number of provided attacks, including different variants of paraphrasing attacks, adversarial attacks, and polishing attacks.

3   Analysing the Level of Contamination

Trained detectors may use simple syntactic features as shortcuts for detection. For example, Doughman *et al.* shows that detectors can pick up patterns in punctuation or whitespaces if the dataset exhibits some form of bias there [3]. When visually sifting through the dataset, we noticed some hints of contamination, like redundancies and typical phrases of generative chat models that are not directly relevant for the task at hand. We subsequently started to search for these patterns more thoroughly and analyse the overall volume of the contamination in the benchmark. To this end, we visually inspected a representative subset of the data in order to gain a qualitative understanding of the types of the contamination. In a second step, we crafted regular expressions that were derived from that inspection to also obtain a quantitative number of contamination cases.

The design of the regular expressions followed observations from the dataset. The observations are described in the next paragraphs and illustrated in Table 1.

Pattern Rejection. As the LLMs used are instruction-tuned to align with ethical guidelines and prevent misuse, rejections of the LLMs are possible. These typically result in LLM-dependent standard phrases, which were incorporated into the first group of regular expressions, which we call Pattern Rejection (or "rejection" for short).

Prompt-specific Pattern. For two types of tasks (polishing human- or LLM-generated content and SICO prompting), some LLM responses repeat keywords from the prompt or provide a summary of their actions. These task-specific responses represent the second category, which we call Prompt-specific Pattern (or "prompt" for short).

Pattern Beginning. The third type of pattern is arguably the one that is visually most easily detected. It captures instances where the response begins with "Here is..." or a similar phrase. This pattern is especially prevalent in the Claude version used to generate the benchmark, occurring in 94.7% of cases of Claude-generated text. We call this type Pattern Beginning (or "beginning" for short).

Domain-specific Pattern. Domain-specific patterns are closely related to the task at hand such as keywords like "abstract" for tasks that generate arXiv abstracts or "reviews" for tasks that generate Yelp reviews. However, these criteria are somewhat unsharp. When used as a selection criterion in regular expressions, then it may be the case that phrases are wrongly selected as false positives. Further below in the counting of pattern occurrences in Tab. 2, we did not normalize for these false positives, but in the reprocessed dataset, we explicitly

Table 1. Regular expressions for data analysis and cleaning. Some long patterns have been omitted for reasons of space and clarity.

Pattern Variable	Regular Expression
1. Pattern Rejection	`(.*I apologize, upon further reflection.*)|(.*((only)|(just)) a language model.*)|...`
2. Prompt-specific Pattern:	
`SICO-Prompting`	`(in a human\s ?\w {0,20}\s ?style)`
`Polishing`	`(grammar[\w \s ,]{1,40}spelling)|...`
3. Pattern Beginning	`(Voici un|Here is|Here are|Here's|Sure[,!]?\s ?here)`
4. Domain-specific Pattern	
`Pattern Article`	`(given article title|provided article title)`
`Pattern Yelp Review`	`(review's first sentence|review)`
`Pattern Arxiv Abstract`	`(abstract|academic article)`
`Pattern XSUM`	`(article)`
5. Assistant Pattern	`(?:.*)((((\[system\])|(\[user\])|(\[assistant\]))\s *\w {0,20}|(**assistant))([:]?[*]{2}|[:])`

double-checked these cases to remove false positives. In any case, we refer to this type as Domain-specific Pattern (or "domain" for short).

Assistant Pattern. The fifth type of pattern is a specific feature that depends on the combination of task and LLM. We particularly observed this for PaLM. For example, PaLM rejected 396 out of 700 creative writing examples when it was using few-shot prompting for generation. One reason might have been that human-written examples that were used for few-shot prompting might have contained (allegedly) harmful content. However, such strict rejections do not occur with other LLMs. In addition, either system-related messages that are not intended for the user or the phrase '[assistant]:' are provided before the answer. We refer to this pattern as Assistant Pattern (or "assistant" for short).

A quantitative overview of the number of contaminations across the four LLMs in DetectRL is shown in Table 2. Selection of entries is applied without replacement, i.e., if an entry matches a regular expression, then it is not further analysed with other regular expressions. Here, ChatGPT shows overall very few contamination, most notably are a few cases of domain-specific patterns. Claude-instant exhibits most cases of contamination across all LLMs, and the big majority of contaminations occurs in the Pattern Beginning with 13,261 cases. The other notable pattern in Claude-instant are 448 cases of Pattern Rejection. Google-PaLM and Llama-2-70b are also affected in a non-negligible number of cases, but nevertheless to a much smaller extend than Claude-instant. Both exhibit around 1300 to 1500 cases of Pattern Beginning. Google-Palm accumulates an additional total of around 2000 cases of Pattern Rejection, Domain-specific Patterns, and Assistant Pattern, whereas Llama-2-70b exhibits additional 520 cases of Prompt-specific Pattern.

Table 2. Distribution of the identified types of contaminations that were found with regular expressions in DetectRL. The total number of potentially contaminated text found with regular expressions is 20,325 (total entries: 56,000).

	llm_type	category	count
0	ChatGPT	rejection	6
1	ChatGPT	prompt	9
2	ChatGPT	beginning	8
3	ChatGPT	domain	264
4	Claude-instant	rejection	448
5	Claude-instant	prompt	79
6	Claude-instant	beginning	13,261
7	Claude-instant	domain	8
8	Google-PaLM	rejection	1,703
9	Google-PaLM	prompt	38
10	Google-PaLM	beginning	1,585
11	Google-PaLM	domain	457
12	Google-PaLM	assistant	469
13	Llama-2-70b	rejection	27
14	Llama-2-70b	prompt	520
15	Llama-2-70b	beginning	1,352
16	Llama-2-70b	domain	91

4   Methodology and Data Cleansing

The quantitative examination of contamination showed that the dataset contains a large number of generator-typical phrases. This raises the question whether this contamination influences trained detectors. We investigate this question with the RoBERTa-Base detector, which is the best performing detector in the DetectRL paper. In a second step, we reprocess the dataset to remove the identified contaminations, and re-evaluate the RoBERTa detector.

4.1   Impact of the Contamination

The contaminations occur similarly in the training and in the test data of the DetectRL benchmark. Hence, the guiding hypothesis in this experiment is that

RoBERTa learns these contaminations during training, and consequently predicts a higher likelihood of AI-generation on test data that contains the same contaminations. To investigate this hypothesis, we use the post-hoc explainability method SHAP [11], similar to Doughman *et al.* [3]. The idea is to study the impact of specific tokens on the outcome of a prediction. If the model learns a shortcut from a contamination, then one can expect to identify the contaminated tokens as particularly important components in the prediction.

The RoBERTa model is trained on a single LLM multi-domain dataset, as most types of contamination seem to exhibit LLM-specific traces. SHAP is applied to the outputs of this RoBERTa model. Then, we also perform adversarial attacks analogous to *spoofing* in watermarks [17]. Here, we try to lure the detector into misclassifying a human-written text as AI-generated by appending the phrase *'Here is a 7 sentence abstract for the provided article title: '*. The impact of this attack is analyzed by studying the changes in classification probabilities. Finally, we analyse the generalisation capability of the uncleaned dataset compared to the cleaned dataset as a first step to determine whether contamination would impact the results reported by the DetectRL Benchmark.

4.2   Removal of the Identified Contaminations

For the removal of the patterns, we use the same regular expressions that were also used to detect and analyse the contamination. Rejections by the LLM typically involve predefined standard clauses and are easy to identify. To create a meaningful and challenging benchmark, we completely remove them from the dataset and replace them with null values. The other contaminants are typically introductory statements or, less frequently, explanations provided by the LLM at the end of the task. We therefore remove the entire sentence, starting with the contaminant and ending with the next sentence-ending punctuation mark ('?', '!' or '.') or the next colon. There is a uniform prompt for each domain, with only the context variable (e.g. the title for which an abstract is to be generated, and the required number of sentences). The task and prompt itself (e.g. generating an abstract) remains the same for an individual domain. Consequently, the individual LLMs tend to have a repetitive structure. This can easily be corrected using the pattern-matching procedure described above. Nevertheless, two types of error can occur that need to be corrected. Either too little is removed, leaving the contamination partially present, or too much is removed, rendering the text unusable.

In the former case, a RoBERTa model is trained on contaminated text. This model is then used to classify the processed samples. Samples that are most likely to be generated by AI, even after cleaning, are likely to still exhibit contamination and are marked for a further processing step.

To address cases where the removal was too rigorous, we first collect samples with a low absolute number of tokens. Since LLMs are prompted to generate text with the same number of sentences as the analogous human-written example, they should produce a similar number of sentences and tokens. Therefore, we also re-clean samples where there are large relative differences in the number of sentences and tokens between the processed LLM entry and the corresponding human-written text.

The re-cleaning of the selected samples is performed using *gpt-4.1-mini* with few-shot prompting. The model is instructed to remove only the contamination and return the uncontaminated text. The answer to the original task, and therefore the traces of the original LLM, should remain unchanged. To ensure the intended behaviour, we follow OpenAI's associated prompting guide [13].

Table 3. Example of a model-generated abstract with a LLM typical beginning. Used in Fig. 1 to determine the SHAP values of contaminated text.

"Here is a 10 sentence abstract for the article title "Fundamental Limits to Position Determination by Concentration Gradients":Organisms across nature have evolved to determine their position using concentration gradients of signaling molecules. However, gradient sensing poses fundamental physical limitations in accuracy and precision. This study explores the biophysical limits to localization from concentration gradients. A computational model is developed to describe gradient formation and interpret signal transduction by cell surface receptors in response to different gradient profiles. The model accounts for stochastic variability in ligand-receptor binding and finite numbers of receptors. Spatial resolution is shown to degrade significantly for shallow gradients and small cell sizes due to stochastic noise. Optimal gradient shapes are identified that allow sub-cellular precision even in noisy conditions. Experimental measurements of gradient sensing match predictions from the biophysical model. The results establish baselines for position determination based solely on gradient interpretation. Fundamental trade-offs between accuracy, precision and measurement time are characterized. This provides insights into the physical design constraints shaped by evolution in gradient-based navigation across scales from microbes to multicellular organisms." - LLM: Claude-instant, domain: Arxiv abstracts

---

5   Results

First, the prediction of a model trained on contaminated data is explained, followed by one trained on data cleaned using only the regular expressions. All experiments are performed on a model trained on the Claude multi-domain dataset, as this dataset has been shown to be the most contaminated (cf. Table 2).

A specific example for analysis is listed in Table 3. The corresponding SHAP values are shown in Fig. 1 (a). The tokens that have been identified as part of the contamination are among the ten most important features, together with rather general features like punctuation. In contrast, Fig. 1 (b) shows the SHAP values for a model trained on the cleaned data and evaluated on the same text as in the previous experiment. Here, the set of tokens that influence the decision is more diverse. Additionally, the overall contribution of individual features to the prediction "LLM-generated" is less pronounced.

A further experiment applies adversarial attacks to highlight the potential weaknesses of training detectors based on such data. Once again, we compare

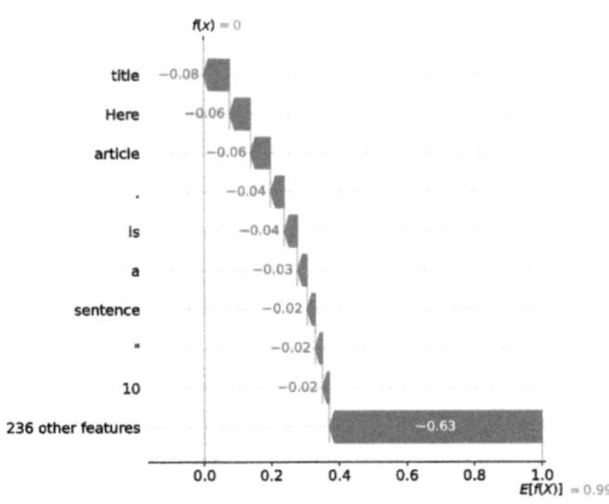

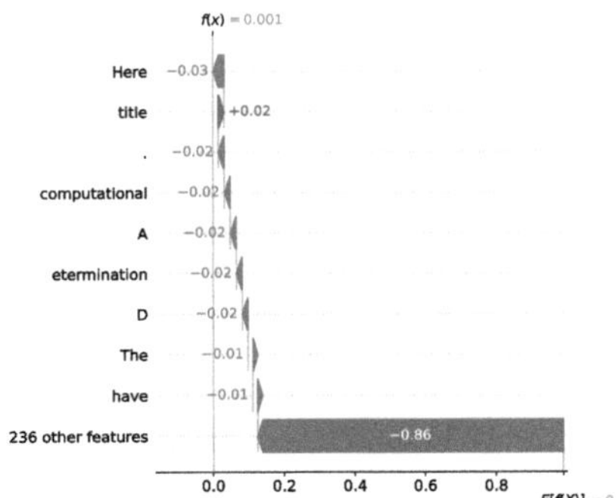

(a) Using the original DetectRL Benchmark data.

(b) Using data re-cleaned with regular expressions.

Fig. 1. Comparison of SHAP token importance of a text for a model trained on Claude-generated, multi-domain data. The sample is labeled as LLM-generated. The classifier is trained to predict whether text is human-generated or AI-generated. Values close to 1 indicate human-generated text, while values below 0.5 indicate AI-generated text.

Table 4. Number of examples of human-generated data that is classified as 'Human' or 'AI-generated' when applying an adversarial attack. The model was trained on Claude data in a multi-domain setting (test data size = 560).

	Model trained on original data	Model trained on cleaned data
Prediction = Human	68	544
Prediction = LLM	492	16

models trained on the cleaned and uncleaned Claude multi-domain datasets. We evaluate the classification performance using a separate test dataset. The evaluation data uses inputs labeled as "human", prefixed with the attack phrase *'Here is a 7 sentence abstract for the provided article title: '* in the beginning of the text.

Table 4 shows that the attack is effective. It significantly decreasing the classification accuracy of the unadjusted model. Performance decreases from 99.9% when classifying both human- and AI-written texts, to just 12.1% when classifying the attacked human samples (Table 4). By contrast, cleaning the training data protects the model from such attacks, ensuring that the accuracy with which it classifies human-written samples remains at 97.1% in attack scenarios.

Figure 2 highlight the effectiveness of the attack on a concrete example. The SHAP values show that the text would be classified as human-written if given only the other tokens. However, the attack heavily contributes to the class LLM-generated, resulting in the sample being misclassified. However, a model trained on a cleaned dataset does not exhibit this behavior.

Table 5. Generalisation performance across domains. Model trained on the cleaned dataset evaluated on cleaned and uncleaned data (and vice versa for an uncleaned training dataset). The contamination does not impact the performance on tasks from other domains.

domain_train	cleaned	roc_auc	f1	accuracy	tpr@0.01%fpr
arxiv	False	0.878	0.803	0.807	0.182
	True	0.878	0.804	0.805	0.179
arxiv_cleaned	False	0.846	0.782	0.785	0.163
	True	0.854	0.793	0.794	0.178

The findings raise the question of how representative the performance of the contaminated model would be compared to the performance of a model trained on cleaned data. This may impact scenarios such as plagiarism detection, where such tell-tale signs of AI-generated text could be easily be removed. To analyse this, we trained two models on Arxiv data generated by Claude: one on the original samples and one on the cleaned samples. We then evaluate the generalisation performance of the two RoBERTa models on the cleaned and uncleaned data from other domains and language models to determine whether focusing on contamination prevents the model from learning other features that are representative of the detection task. Table 5 shows the results. The classifier's ability to generalise to other domains is not impacted by the contamination. Apparently, both tasks—detecting the cleaned and uncleaned data—are comparably difficult for the classifier.

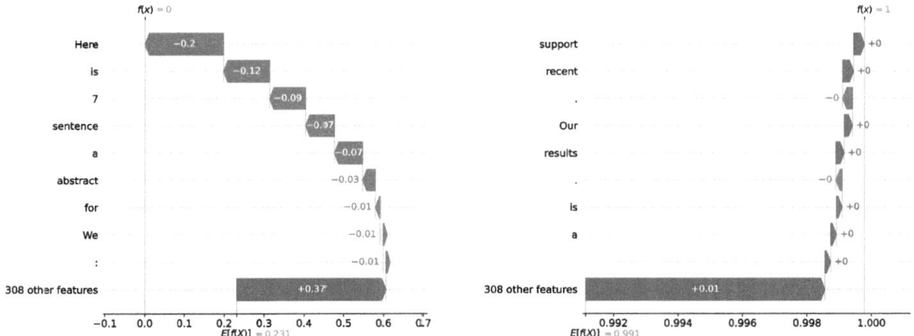

(a) Model trained on uncleaned Claude data.

(b) Model trained on cleaned Claude data.

Fig. 2. Comparison of SHAP token importance in a waterfall plot of a text for a model trained on Claude-generated, multi-domain data. The sample is human-written and an adversarial attack is applied.

6 Summary and Outlook

Benchmarking of LLM text detectors is a difficult task. In this work, we examine the issue of contamination in the DetectRL benchmark. We show that the text generation artifacts impact the evaluation with DetectRL. At the same time, this contamination makes the detector susceptible to adversarial attacks. However, our initial results also show that the generalisation capabilities of a trained RoBERTa model are not affected by these artifacts in the data. This article outlines our ongoing work to make users of the benchmark aware of the possible vulnerabilities.

We provide a reprocessed version of the dataset for download. We cleaned the dataset primarily using regular expressions, mainly due to its massive size. Despite the quality checks and multi-stage cleaning process, frequent artifacts or rejections by the LLM may still occur, as it was not possible for us to manually review all of the over 50,000 samples. However, we are confident that the proportion is considerably lower in the reprocessed dataset.

In future work, cleaning all samples using an LLM may have the potential to extend the cleaning process beyond the known artifacts and is less susceptible to minor changes in patterns. More immediate next steps could be: first, to rerun the results of the DetectRL benchmark [24] on the cleaned data to identify potential differences. Second, to regenerate the dataset using state-of-the-art LLMs, as the current ones seem outdated due to the rapid development of LLMs. We are confident that high data quality can be ensured from the outset by continuously checking and adjusting the prompts used. Third, to extend the analysis to other benchmarks to determine whether the problem is specific to this one or more widespread.

Acknowledgments. This work was supported by Deutsche Forschungsgemeinschaft (DFG, German Research Foundation) as part of the Research and Training Group 2475 "Cybercrime and Forensic Computing" (grant number 393541319/GRK2475/2-2024).

Disclosure of Interests. The authors have no competing interests to declare that are relevant to the content of this article.

References

1. Anthropic: Introducing Claude 4. https://www.anthropic.com/news/claude-4 (May 2025). Accessed 10 Jul 2025
2. Chen, Z., Feng, Y., He, C., Deng, Y., Pu, H., Li, B.: IPAD: Inverse Prompt for AI Detection - A Robust and Explainable LLM-Generated Text Detector. CoRR **abs/2502.15902** (2025)
3. Doughman, J., Mohammed Afzal, O., Toyin, H.O., Shehata, S., Nakov, P., Talat, Z.: Exploring the limitations of detecting machine-generated text. In: Proceedings of the 31st International Conference on Computational Linguistics, pp. 4274–4281 (2025)

4. Gao, C.A., et al.: Comparing scientific abstracts generated by ChatGPT to real abstracts with detectors and blinded human reviewers. NPJ Digital Med. **6**(1) 75 (2023)

5. Gehrmann, S., Strobelt, H., Rush, A.: GLTR: statistical detection and visualization of generated text. In: Proceedings of the 57th Annual Meeting of the Association for Computational Linguistics: System Demonstrations, pp. 111–116. Association for Computational Linguistics (2019)

6. Zhang, H., Edelman, B.L., Francati, D., Venturi, D., Ateniese, G., Barak, B.: Watermarks in the sand: impossibility of strong watermarking for generative models. In: ICLR 2024 Workshop on Secure and Trustworthy Large Language Models (2024)

7. Hans, A., et al.: Spotting LLMs with binoculars: zero-shot detection of machine-generated text. In: Forty-first International Conference on Machine Learning (2024)

8. Kirchenbauer, J., Geiping, J., Wen, Y., Katz, J., Miers, I., Goldstein, T.: A watermark for large language models. In: Proceedings of the 40th International Conference on Machine Learning. Proceedings of Machine Learning Research, vol. 202, pp. 17061–17084. PMLR (2023)

9. Krishna, K., Song, Y., Karpinska, M., Wieting, J., Iyyer, M.: Paraphrasing evades detectors of AI-generated text, but retrieval is an effective defense. Adv. Neural. Inf. Process. Syst. **36**, 27469–27500 (2023)

10. Liu, Y., et al.: RoBERTa: A Robustly Optimized BERT Pretraining Approach. CoRR **abs/1907.11692** (2019)

11. Lundberg, S.M., Lee, S.I.: A unified approach to interpreting model predictions. In: Advances in Neural Information Processing Systems, vol. 30 (2017)

12. Mubarak, R., Alsboui, T., Alshaikh, O., Inuwa-Dutse, I., Khan, S., Parkinson, S.: A Survey on the Detection and Impacts of Deepfakes in Visual, Audio, and Textual Formats. IEEE Access **11**, 144497–144529 (2023)

13. Noah MacCallum, Julian Lee: GPT-4.1 Prompting Guide. https://cookbook.openai.com/examples/gpt4-1_prompting_guide (Apr 2025). Accessed 10 July 2025

14. OpenAI: Introducing OpenAI o3 and o4-mini. https://openai.com/index/introducing-o3-and-o4-mini/ (Apr 2025). Accessed 10 July 2025

15. Pudasaini, S., Miralles-Pechuán, L., Lillis, D., Llorens Salvador, M.: Survey on AI-generated plagiarism detection: the impact of large language models on academic integrity. J. Acad. Ethics (2024)

16. Jiang, Q., Gao, Z., Karniadakis, G.E.: Deepseek vs. chatgpt vs. claude: a comparative study for scientific computing and scientific machine learning tasks. Theor. Appl. Mech. Lett. **15**(3), 100583 (2025)

17. Sadasivan, V.S., Kumar, A., Balasubramanian, S., Wang, W., Feizi, S.: Can AI-Generated Text be Reliably Detected? Stress Testing AI Text Detectors Under Various Attacks, Transactions on Machine Learning Research (2025)

18. Aaronson, S., Kirchner, H.: Watermarking GPT outputs. https://scottaaronson.blog/?m=202302 (Feb 2023). Accessed 10 July 2025

19. Ghosal, S.S., Chakraborty, S., Geiping, J., Huang, F., Manocha, D., Bedi, A.A.: Survey on the possibilities & impossibilities of AI-generated text detection. Trans. Mach. Learn. Res. (2023)

20. Vasilatos, C., Alam, M., Rahwan, T., Zaki, Y., Maniatakos, M.: HowkGPT: investigating the Detection of ChatGPT-generated University Student Homework through Context-Aware Perplexity Analysis. CoRR **abs/2305.18226** (2023)

21. Wang, Y., et al.: M4GT-bench: evaluation benchmark for black-box machine-generated text detection. In: 62nd Annual Meeting of the Association for Computational Linguistics, pp. 3964–3992 (2024)
22. Wang, Y., et al.: SemEval-2024 task 8: multidomain, multimodel and multilingual machine-generated text detection. In: 18th International Workshop on Semantic Evaluation (SemEval-2024), pp. 2057–2079 (2024)
23. Wu, J., et al.: A survey on LLM-generated text detection: necessity, methods, and future directions. Comput. Linguist. **51**(1), 275–338 (2025)
24. Wu, J., et al.: DetectRL: benchmarking LLM-generated text detection in real-world scenarios. In: Advances in Neural Information Processing Systems 38: Annual Conference on Neural Information Processing Systems (2024)
25. Yang, X., Cheng, W., Wu, Y., Petzold, L.R., Wang, W.Y., Chen, H.: DNA-GPT: divergent N-gram analysis for training-free detection of GPT-generated text. In: The Twelfth International Conference on Learning Representations (2024)

Resiliency Trade-Offs of DNSSEC Configurations to DDoS Attacks

Daniel Dubnikov$^{(\boxtimes)}$, Yehuda Afek, and Anat Bremler-Barr

Tel Aviv University, Ramat-Aviv, Israel
daniel87@gmail.com, yehuda.afek@gmail.com, anatbr@tauex.tau.ac.il

Abstract. First this paper measures and analyzes various trade-offs between different DNSSEC configurations, such as, NSEC, NSEC3, aggressive caching, and online vs. offline signing. These measurements expose a trade-off between (1) aggressive caching DNSSEC configuration that provides excellent performance (higher robustness to DDoS attacks) but is vulnerable to zone enumeration attacks in addition to offline signing disadvantages, and (2) online signing DNSSEC configuration, that prevent zone enumeration but is more susceptible to DDoS attacks due to lower maximum throughput. Second, following these, we suggest and evaluate an alternative, Adaptive DNS over QUIC, (AdaDoQ), an adaptive, efficient and secure communication layer between a DNS resolver and the authoritative servers, that offers a better trade-off between DDoS resiliency and security. Under normal load conditions the resolver communicates with each authoritative server with standard DNSSEC however, when the traffic load increases, AdaDoQ switches to a QUIC connection with heavily communicating authoritative server(s), for as long as the traffic load is high. The public key of the authoritative ZSK (which is verifiable through the DNSSEC chain of trust) is integrated into the symmetric key creation in QUIC to provide a DNSSEC level of authenticity and security. AdaDoQ ensures DNS authenticity, good throughput, and disables zone walking attacks, DNS hijacking, and cache poisoning.

Keywords: DNSSEC · DDoS Attacks · QUIC · DNS · Security

1 Introduction

The DNS developers' community is struggling in recent years to make the DNS system resilient to various attacks while maintaining its efficiency and authenticity; The main tool used to stop attacks and ensure replies' authenticity is DNSSEC which employs asymmetric cryptography to sign DNS responses. While DNSSEC provides authenticity of DNS responses and mitigates DNS poisoning/hijacking attacks, it amplifies DNS response size significantly and adds additional computational overheads (i.e., validating signatures), making existing DDoS attacks, much worse (Table 1). These attacks flood the DNS system with

NX (non-existent) domain name requests in order to bypass its caching defense (Sect. 2.1). On the other hand some of its configurations are extremely useful in mitigating some of the new attacks (Sect. 2.2).

In this paper we first give an in-depth analysis of the different configurations that are available in DNSSEC (Sect. 2). We analyze what each is supposed to solve, and what limitations each is introducing. Secondly, following the in-depth analysis, we measure the impact each configuration has on the DNS system in terms of NXDomain query throughput which is a worst-case DDoS attack scenario. Thirdly, comprehending the benefits and drawbacks of each variant, we propose in Sect. 3 a new hybrid method to address these issues. Our method, called Adaptive DNS over QUIC (AdaDoQ) establishes an on demand secure connection between an authoritative and a heavily communicating resolver server. The secure persistent connection is authenticated once during establishment and following communications over it do not incur the DNSSEC overhead. Such communication is used only during a DDoS attack (or overload conditions) in order to reduce both bandwidth consumption and CPU load at the authoritative and the resolver servers. Finally, we provide a proof-of-concept to demonstrate that this approach significantly increases the throughput between the corresponding authoritative and resolver nameservers, thus minimizing the amplification effects of DNSSEC on DDoS attacks without compromising any other property of the system.

A summary of the different measurements performed in this paper is graphically provided in Fig. 1, it depicts the results provided in Table 7. The figure provides an overview of the different DNS and DNSSEC configurations in terms of their performance and compromises. The horizontal axis gives the configurations' throughput in queries-per-second. The higher the maximum throughput is, the better it can cope with NXDomain DDoS attacks. The vertical axis depicts the configurations' security wise drawbacks. The more severe the drawbacks are the lower the configuration is placed along the vertical axis (below 1 is most severe and 4 is least):

1. Authenticity (DNS Hijacking)
2. Zone Enumeration
3. ZSK Exposure
4. Slow Zone Update

While NSEC/3 gives high throughput, it requires resolvers to implement aggressive caching and compromise on zone enumeration and slow updates which put them low on the compromise axis. Similarly, DNS throughput is good, but it lacks authenticity thus placing it even lower. Online solutions on the other hand are perhaps more secure, but their throughput is lower, making them a target for NXDomain DDoS attacks. AdaDoQ with Black Lies keeps the ZSK online making it vulnerable to compromised name servers, but gains higher throughput which justifies its usage as an alternative when zone privacy and update speeds cannot be spared.

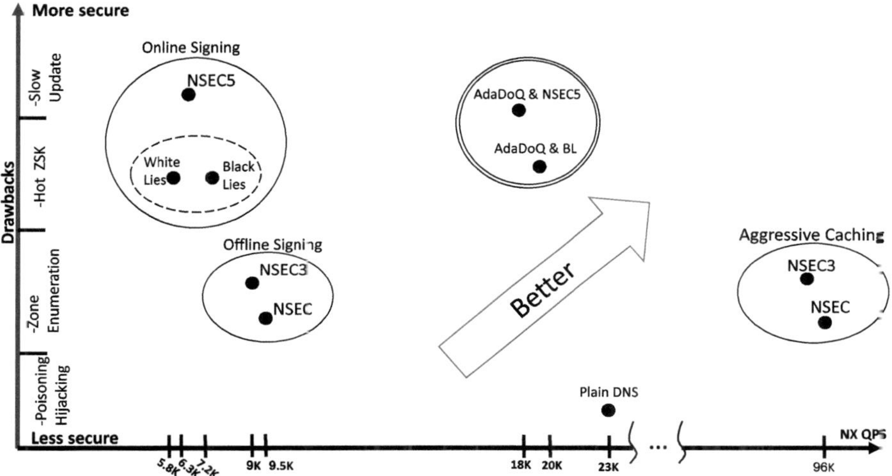

Fig. 1. An overview of the different DNS and DNSSEC configurations depicting the results from Table 7. Each configuration is placed according to its throughput and drawbacks. Throughput is measured under a flood of NXDomain requests. QPS is the maximum such queries per second, before it starts to lose packets.

Related Work. The various DNSSEC configurations are cited and described in Sect. 2. Petr Spacek from cz.nic showed in 2018 the potential of using aggressive caching [24] to combat DDoS attacks. The series of measurements [42] demonstrate the dominance in throughput when authoritatives use DNSSEC with NSEC/3 and resolvers implement aggressive caching as in Knot Resolver [15]. Here we relate to different usages of QUIC in DNS. Notice that most DNS over QUIC usage is for privacy, and is between client stab and recursive resolver, while our motivation in AdaDoQ is primarily efficiency and security. Moreover AdaDoQ is intended for recursive to authoritative communication.

DNS Over Dedicated QUIC Connections. RFC 9250 [22] standardizes the use of the QUIC protocol for DNS client-recursive communication. The goal is to provide transport confidentiality.

The paper is organized as follows: The setup used for the measurements is described in Sect. Appendix A. The sequence of DNSSEC extensions is reviewed in Sect. 2, and our new Adaptive DNS over QUIC method is presented in Sect. 3. In Sect. 4 we analyze the performances of each configuration, and future work is discussed in Sect. 5. Finally conclusions are provided in Sect. 6.

2   DNSSEC/DNS Trade-Off Analysis

2.1   DNSSEC and DDoS

While DNSSEC serves a major role in the authenticity of the DNS protocol, it amplifies DDoS attacks; Every DNSSEC response is authenticated with an RSA digital signature whose size is 2048bit [8]. The signature of a response to non-existent (NX) domain queries not only includes the SOA record, but in addition it also sends one NSEC record, to prove that the domain name really does not exist, and a second NSEC record to prove that no wildcard covers that domain. These additional records together with the added signatures overhead make an NX response larger than 1000 bytes [9]. In comparison, with plain DNS, only 1 SOA record (without signature) is required for NX response, which is about 100 bytes on average, resulting in a 10x amplification factor for DNSSEC NX responses. Additionally, resolvers do not need to validate asymmetric signatures, and online signing nameservers do not need to sign responses. This makes authoritative nameservers that use DNSSEC more appealing to attackers than those that do not use DNSSEC.

Table 1. DNS vs. DNSSEC Throughput. Measuring under overload conditions. QPS is maximum queries per second with attack traffic (Non eXistant(NX) request flood) before it starts to lose packets. Validate describes whether Recursive Resolver validates the signed responses. * Authoritative Nameserver signs using RSA/SHA-256 and responds to NX with NSEC (TTL=3600).

	Validate	Res. Size (Bytes)	Max QPS
DNS	N/A	~50	21,715
DNSSEC	No	~1,000	17,637
	Yes		9,510

In Table 1 we separately measured the effects of the response size and of the signature validation computational load on the throughput of the DNS system. The details of our experimental setup are given in Sect. Appendix A. Table 1 shows that the response size reduces the throughput by 20%. When measuring the computational overhead of the resolver validating the signatures of responses the impact is more significant, and throughput decreases by 55% compared to plain DNS. Both results (with and without validation) show that DNSSEC's overheads impact the performance of the DNS protocol and make DDoS attacks more effective.

2.2   Knot Resolver and Aggressive Caching

When resolvers get NX response, they cache the non-existent name. With DNSSEC, the NX response is an NSEC record that represents an entire range of non-existent names. Instead of just caching the queried name, RFC 8198 (Aggressive Use of DNSSEC-Validated Cache) [24] proposes to generate negative answers within the range of positive answers. It allows for validating resolvers to synthesize NX responses based on existing NSEC records without querying the authoritative nameserver. This significantly increases performance, decreases latency and resource utilization on both authoritative nameservers and recursive resolvers under an NXDomain flood, and in addition it improves on privacy [42].

Figures 2a and 2b illustrate how aggressive caching works.

In Fig. 2a the attacker queries for a random name that is not present in the cache, this triggers the resolver to query the nameserver with the same query, and since the queried name does not exist in the zone, the nameserver responds with the NSEC record within which the queried name falls. The resolver then caches this NSEC record.

Figure 2b shows what happens to subsequent queries that query for names that fall between ranges that are already cached. Since the resolver implements aggressive caching, it can use the cached NSEC records to synthesize NXDO-MAIN responses, without communicating with the authoritative nameserver.

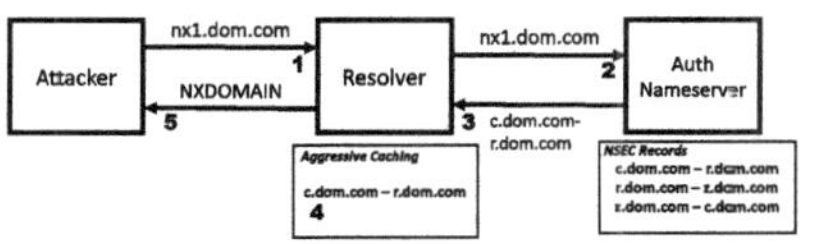

(a) Attacker initiates NXDomain Flood Attack.
(1) First query has no match in the cache.
(2) Query reaches the authoritative nameserver.
(3) Authoritative nameserver responds with the NSEC record where the queried name falls.
(4) Resolver caches the NSEC record.
(5) Resolver responds with NXDO-MAIN.

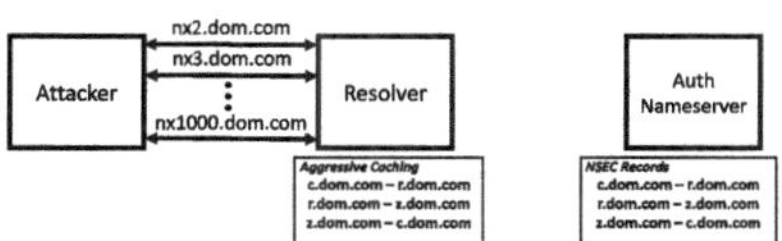

(b) NXDomain Flood Attack with Aggressive Caching. Resolver is flooded with queries to non-existent names, all names fall within NSEC record ranges that are in the cache. Thus the resolver synthesizes NXDOMAIN responses without communicating with the authoritative nameserver.

Fig. 2. Illustration of NXDomain Flood attack mechanisms.

We measured the throughput of the system with and without aggressive caching, comparing it to plain DNS. We use Knot resolver to measure aggressive caching as it is the only resolver to the best of our knowledge that properly supports this feature.

In Table 2 we show the dominance in throughout performance of aggressive caching (96,226 QPS). Not only does it improve DNSSEC's throughput, it is actually performing better than plain DNS (23,524 QPS). This happens because with aggressive caching the resolver quickly collects all NSEC records and from that point on answers all queries from cache.

We further investigate and run a similar experiment, this time setting our client machine for random names from the zone (1000 names). This means that similar to aggressive caching, the cache should quickly become the dominant factor. In Table 3 we can see that as expected, all the results with and without aggressive caching are on par with aggressive caching ($\sim$95,000 QPS).

These results mean that if recursive resolvers implement aggressive caching, then both the resolvers and the authoritative nameservers perform better and are more equipped against NXDomain DDoS attacks using DNSSEC than plain DNS.

2.3 Double-Edged Sword: Zone Enumeration

While NSEC gives a convenient solution to high-rate NX queries, it may be used to easily enumerate all the names of a zone [4,17], which is a serious privacy issue for many organizations. For example, with NSEC all e-mail addresses of an email provider are exposed, which can be used to send spam and phishing, or all sub-domains of a TLD are exposed and used to collect registrant data using WHOIS queries [23].

Table 2. Effects of aggressive use of DNSSEC-Validated Cache under NXDomain floods. QPS is the maximum queries per second before packet loss. * Auth signs with RSA/SHA-256, NSEC (TTL=3600), 1000 names.

	Resolver	Aggr. Use	Max QPS
DNS	Bind9	N/A	21,715
	Knot	N/A	23,524
DNSSEC	Bind9	No	9,510
	Knot	Yes	96,226

Table 3. Maximizing query rate of existing names in the zone. QPS is max queries per second before loss. * Auth signs with RSA/SHA-256, 1000 names.

	Resolver	Max QPS
DNS	Bind9	97,718
	Knot	98,110
DNSSEC	Bind9	96,308
	Knot	98,167

2.4   NSEC3

To prevent zone enumeration NSEC3 is suggested to conceal the zone names. Instead of ordering the names of the zone in lexicographical order, the offline process hashes all the names with a one-way hash function (e.g., SHA1), and sorts the hashes by their hash values. Then, the same mechanism as in NSEC is deployed on the hashed values. Every consecutive pair of hashed values is offline signed using the ZSK, and distributes the signed records to the various nameservers, similar to NSEC. When a query for a non-existent name arrives, the nameserver first hashes the name, and then finds the corresponding signed pair of hashed names that are lexicographically before and after the queried hashed name. This means that the caller no longer receives an explicit pair of names that exists in the zone as proof, but rather a pseudo-random pair of hashed names that he cannot use to enumerate the zone.

Nonetheless, this does not fully prevent zone enumeration, it only makes it more difficult. An attacker can still collect all the NSEC3 records, and use an offline dictionary attack to find the names that hash to the values it has collected [29,43].

2.5   Offline Signing Drawbacks

Both NSEC and NSEC3 records are offline pre-signed. This means that a cold storage machine that has access to the ZSK periodically generates and signs NSEC/3 records for the various nameserver machines. Using offline signing poses additional drawbacks to the authoritative:

1. **Slow Zone Updates** To update names in the zone, a slow process of offline creating, signing and distributing new NSEC/3 records to all nameservers is required. Furthermore, old records that are cached in resolvers cannot be invalidated until their TTL expires. With NSEC/3 and Aggressive Caching, these records can span a whole range of non-existent names. For authoritative DNS providers that rely on rapid changes to names in the zones, such as Disposable Domain providers [5], these slow updates are not an option.
2. **Search Efficiency** For large scale authoritative DNS providers (e.g.: Cloudflare, Google, etc.), searching for the NSEC/3 record with the right previous/next names can be an inefficient task [10].

2.6   Online Signing

Using NSEC or NSEC3 exposes the names of the zone to a zone enumeration attack as described in Sect. 2.3. Goldberg et al. [32] proved that no solution that protects against DNS message tampering can fully prevent zone enumeration without using *online signing* of DNS responses. Consequently, solutions that only use offline signing (i.e. NSEC/3) may not be suitable. Following are the common DNSSEC implementations that use online signing to circumvent zone enumeration:

White Lies. RFC 7129 [21] proposes that each nameserver will have access to the zone signing key (ZSK) and generate and sign online an NSEC record for any given non-existent query. In this record, instead of having the canonical existent previous and next names, the nameserver will make up a previous and next names by randomly generating names that are canonically slightly before and after the queried name, but do no exist (hence the name - white lies). With White Lies the NSEC record only contains information about the queried name, and does not expose information about other names in the zone, providing protection against Zone Enumeration.

Black Lies. Similar to White Lies, Black Lies [7] requires each nameserver to hold the zone signing key (ZSK) and sign NSEC records online. But, when replying to a non-existent query with NXDOMAIN response, the queried name is used for both the previous and next names. For example, if *nx.a.com* is queried, an NSEC record is returned with previous-next range *nx.a.com-\000.nx.a.com*. Since the NSEC record response is directly on the missing name, there's no need for an additional NSEC for the wildcard. This way a Black Lie response only returns SOA, SOA RRSIG, NSEC and NSEC RRSIG records.

NSEC5. With White/Black Lies, each nameserver instance has access to the zone signing key (ZSK) in order to sign the NSEC records they create online. This means that if any instance is compromised, the ZSK is compromised and with it the whole integrity of the zone. NSEC5 [32,38] solves this problem with a technique similar to NSEC3. With NSEC3, each name in the NSEC record is hashed. But as mentioned in Sect. 2.3, the hashed names can be revealed with an offline dictionary attack. To prevent this, instead of simple hashing, NSEC5 proposes to use an asymmetric private-public key for hashing, called the non signing key (NSK). The private key is used to create hashes (signature), these hashes are then used to sort the NSEC5 records similar to NSEC3. When a Resolver queries for a non-existent name, the Nameserver will hash this name with the NSK private key, use the hashed value to pick up the appropriate NSEC5 record and send that record back to the Resolver with the signature of the queried name. The Resolver can now validate the signature with the NSK public key and the NSEC5 record with the hashed output. Contrary to NSEC3, an attacker can't use the NSEC5 records for an offline dictionary attack because it cannot generate hashes (it needs to private key for that). Also, the ZSK is kept in cold storage (not used for signing NSEC5 records) and therefore if any nameserver instance is compromised, the integrity of the zone is kept safe. The only thing that does get compromised with the nameserver instance is the NSK, which consequently means that an attacker can do a zone enumeration attack.

In Table 4 we summarize the main differences between the 5 approaches discussed so far to prove non-existent responses.

In Table 5 we measured the throughput of the different methods under overload conditions. Results show that even without Aggressive Caching, the transition from offline signing (NSEC/3) to online signing (White Lies, Black Lies and

NSEC5) adds additional overheads to nameservers and resolvers. While NSEC/3 perform with about 9K QPS, the online signing options peak at only 7K QPS.

Table 4. Comparing NXDOMAIN Proofs. Online: nameserver does online signing. Aggressive: Resolver uses Aggressive Caching. Enumeration: Attacker can do zone enumeration. Updates: Authoritative Zone Updates. # Records: number of proof records sent to Resolver for each NX query (not including SOA and SOA RRSIG)

NX Proof	Online	Aggressive	Enumeration	Updates	ZSK Prot.	# Records
NSEC	No	Yes	Yes	Slow	Yes	2
NSEC3	No	Yes	Yes	Slow	Yes	3
White Lies	Yes	No	No	Fast	No	3
Black Lies	Yes	No	No	Fast	No	1
NSEC5	Yes	No	No	Slow	Yes	4

Table 5. Comparing throughput of DNSSEC configurations. Measuring under overload conditions. QPS is maximum queries per second with attack traffic (Non eXistant (NX) request flood) before it starts to lose packets. authoritative nameserver signs using RSA/SHA-256.

NX Proof	Aggressive	Max QPS
NSEC	No	9,510
	Yes	96,200
NSEC3	No	8,989
	Yes	95,400
White Lies	N/A	5,863
Black Lies	N/A	7,206
NSEC5	N/A	6,324
AdaDoQ (Black Lies)	N/A	20,558
AdaDoQ (NSEC5)	N/A	18,824

2.7 DNSSEC Signing Algorithm

DNSSEC relies on asymmetric encryption algorithms to sign and verify responses. The most dominant algorithm is RSA and its variants [8]. RSA is also a required algorithm defined by the protocol. However, RSA is inefficient in terms of signature size, requiring 3072 bits to achieve 128 bit security, which can lead to packet fragmentations in some cases. Additionally, for nameservers that do online signing, the time it takes to sign is extremely important, and RSA is relatively slow, requiring 2 millisecond to sign using a 2048 bit key [33] (Intel core i5-2450M CPU 2.50GHz and 4GB-RAM). An alternative to RSA is the Elliptic Curve Digital Signature Algorithm (ECDSA) [14]. To achieve 128 bit security it only requires 256 bits key, resulting in 12x smaller amplification factor compared to RSA. In addition, its signing is faster, and in Cloudflare implementation it is 10x less computationally expensive [8]. These properties make ECDSA an attractive algorithm to use by nameservers for online signing [39,40].

However, when it comes to validating signatures, ECDSA is slower than RSA. We set up an experiment at the resolver side to examine how acute the difference is for the resolver using Intel Xeon Platinum 8272CL with 16GB RAM (further experimental details are given in Sect. Appendix A). For one experiment we used a nameserver that signs its responses online using RSA/SHA-256, and for the second experiment we had a similar setup but with ECDSA Curve P-256. In Table 6 we show results of the two experiments. The results show that ECDSA's signature validation is a significant load on the resolver, giving the lowest throughput we have seen in any experiment so far: 3,338 QPS compared to 7,206 QPS with RSA. This suggests that while ECDSA is useful in preventing DDoS attacks on authoritative nameservers, it actually makes similar DDoS attacks worse on recursive resolvers [39].

Table 6. Authoritative nameservers sign requests with either RSA or ECDSA cryptography methods. Measuring under overload conditions. QPS is maximum queries per second with attack traffic (Non eXistant (NX) request flood) before it starts to lose packets.

NX Proof	Algorithm	Online Signing	Maximum QPS
NSEC	RSA/SHA-256	No	9,510
	ECDSA Curve P-256	No	4,213
Black Lies	RSA/SHA-256	Yes	7,206
	ECDSA Curve P-256	Yes	3,338

2.8 Summary

DNSSEC is an important security feature for DNS, adding authenticity to DNS responses, mitigating DNS poisoning [34,41] and other unauthorized responses [35]. The initial configuration uses NSEC records for proof of non-existence. When under NXDomain Flood attack, Using NSEC records together with Aggressive Caching (Sect. 2.2) can increase performance significantly compared to plain DNS, for both the recursive resolver and the authoritative nameserver (Table 2). But, NSEC records expose the names that exist in the zone through zone enumeration (Sect. 2.3). To try and deal with that, NSEC3 was proposed

(Sect. 2.4), it gives a much better protection against zone enumeration attacks, but is still susceptible to offline dictionary attacks [29,43]. Further more, Goldberg et al. [32] proved that in order to prevent zone enumeration entirely, records must be signed online. White Lies (Sect. 2.6) and Black Lies (Sect. 2.6) are the two common ways used for DNSSEC with online signing. The prevent zone enumeration, but expose the ZSK in a live nameserver machine (in order to sign queries to non-existent names). NSEC5 (Sect. 2.6) was proposed to do both online signing, to prevent zone enumeration, and offline signing, to keep the ZSK safe. These extra security features come at a price, and degrade the performance of DNSSEC under NXDomain Flood attack (Table 5), making authoritative nameservers that use them a target for DDoS amplification attacks. See Fig. 3 for visual representation of the interplay between different configurations.

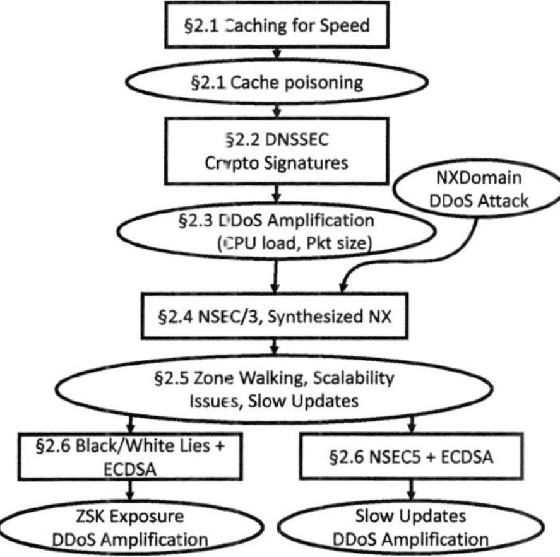

Fig. 3. Overview of the interplay between DNS configurations: what they solve, and what issues they introduce.

3 Adaptive DNS over QUIC

3.1 Overview

With current DNSSEC implementations, as discussed in Sect. 2, zone owners must choose between offline signing (with NSEC/3), benefiting from DDoS protection with Aggressive Use of DNSSEC-Validated Cache (Sect. 2.2), but exposing their names to zone enumeration (Sect. 2.3), slow zone updates and scalability issues (Sect. 2.5). Or, use one of the online signing alternatives (Sect. 2.6), and be an easier target for DDoS attacks. Since the main issue with DNSSEC is its susceptibility to DDoS attacks (Table 5). We propose a new method - Adaptive DNS over QUIC (AdaDoQ), based on the notion that resolver and nameserver's behavior during normal load and when under significant load do not have to be the same. Under normal traffic load, resolver and authoritative nameserver can manage the extra load presented by DNSSEC. But, when targeted by a DDoS attack, these extra features that are designed to ensure the integrity of the zone, can cause one or both of these servers to be unresponsive or to crash. In our method, we drop all DNSSEC overheads under load, and move to a consistent secure QUIC session. We show that this adaptable approach increases throughput of the system compared to all other DNSSEC configurations that do not use aggressive caching, and with minimal drawbacks.

3.2   AdaDoQ: High Level Design

When the load is low, resolver and authoritative nameserver use any DNSSEC configuration that is adequate (e.g.: Black Lies for fast zone updates or NSEC5 for ZSK protection). Meaning, the nameserver sends responses with a signature and the resolver validates the signature to ensure the integrity of the responses it receives.

In AdaDoQ when the load is high, the resolver and authoritative nameserver switch from interacting using UDP/TCP to a consistent secure QUIC session, using the ZSK for authentication and KSK to validate the ZSK. It follows that after a successful handshake, the authoritative nameserver has authenticated itself to the resolver. Any interaction using this QUIC session is now considered authenticated, therefore the DNSSEC overhead is no longer required. Messages between resolver and authoritative nameserver follow the normal DNS (not DNSSEC) protocol. Figure 4 illustrates this high level design.

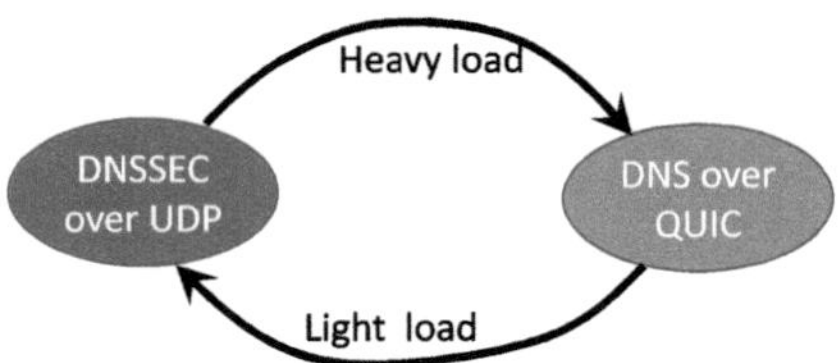

Fig. 4. Overview of AdaDoQ.

3.3   Data Authenticity

DNSSEC protocol provides cryptographic authentication of data, authenticated denial of existence, and data integrity. With QUIC, the same level of security can be achieved, as well as confidentiality which is not currently possible with DNSSEC, with minor adjustments to the protocol, as follows:

For security, QUIC uses the TLS protocol [30], which relies on X.509 digital certificates [27] to certify the ownership of a public key. The certificate contains the server name, the trusted certificate authority (CA), and the public key of the server. The public key is then used with a key-exchange algorithm (RSA Diffie-Hellman, or Elliptic Curve Diffie-Hellman) to generate a symmetric session key for the secure connection. However, DNS keys do not comply with the certificate chain of trust [2] and implement their own using Zone-Signing Keys (ZSK) and Key-Signing Keys (KSK). Since the ZSK is the ground truth for the zone, AdaDoQ requires the TLS protocol to be tweaked to use the ZSK instead of using the key given in the X.509 certificate. This is done to ensure that any message from authoritative nameserver to resolver using the QUIC connection is equivalent to the authoritative server signing it with the ZSK. Other aspects of the TLS protocol, such as the key-exchange algorithm, remain the same. With AdaDoQ, resolvers can, at any time, opt to stop using DNSSEC and upgrade their connection to secure QUIC with that nameserver. During the QUIC connection setup, the nameserver uses its ZSK to both authenticate itself as the authoritative of the zone, as well as to establish a symmetric key for a secure session. Every message that follows through the secure session could have been only sent by the nameserver, therefore is considered authenticated by the resolver, without DNSSEC signatures.

3.4   QUIC Connection

The QUIC protocol [20] is a general-purpose transport layer network protocol initially designed by engineers at Google, and announced publicly in 2013 by the IETF [13]. We chose to design our solution based on QUIC and not the standard TLS because it offers the following advantages:

1. **Connection Establishment Latency**
   TCP requires a handshake to establish a connection, and additional handshake for TLS to ensure that the session is secured, this takes two to three round trips. QUIC requires only one handshake and one round trip. Cutting connection latency from 300ms to 100ms [11].
2. **0-RTT**
   After the server and client established a connection, the connection metadata is cached and following requests can resume the connection with 0 round trip time.
3. **Multiplexing**
   TCP supports request multiplexing. However, it suffers from Head-of-Line (HOL) blocking [12]. When a packet is lost, the entire connection, with all its requests, stop to retransmission the lost packet. QUIC uses UDP as the underlying protocol and therefore avoid this HOL blocking and only stop to retransmission packets for their respective requests, not the entire connection.
4. **Congestion Control**
   QUIC improves congestion control by introducing a new numbering mechanism. Every packet, including retransmitted packets, get a new sequence number. This leads to a more accurate round trip time estimation [25].

3.5   Switching Algorithm

While the QUIC connection between a resolver and authoritative servers is more efficient than using DNSSEC if there is a flood of requests/responses between these two servers, it is inefficient for sporadic interactions between them. At the same time a QUIC connection cannot be kept persistent for long periods of time since the overhead of maintaining a large number of such connections is prohibitive [26].

Therefore, in AdaDoQ the resolver has to automatically decide when to establish and when to tear down a QUIC connection with specific name-servers. Since the resolver caches responses to legitimate existing domain-name requests, a QUIC connection is employed mostly against a flood of NXDOMAIN request/response exchange. The detection of such a flood at the resolver, is done either by monitoring the request stream or the response stream. For detection of a NXDOMAIN request flood on the request stream, an algorithm based on distinct heavy hitters can be used as in [31] with appropriate tuneable thresholds. Detection on the NXDOMAIN response stream is simpler using a simple heavy-hitters algorithm to detect authoritatives that produce high frequency of NXDOMAIN responses [28,36] and is recommended when an authoritative with which a flood of NXDOMAIN request/response is detected with an appropriate initiating threshold, the resolver opts to upgrade its connection with that name-server to QUIC. This connection is maintained for as long as the flood with that authoritative persists. When either of the above detectors (on either the request stream or the response stream) indicates that the rate is below an "off" threshold (which is lower than the initiating threshold) for a duration of a configurable amount minutes, the resolver tears down the corresponding QUIC connection.

3.6   Limitations

ZSK in Hot Storage: With the offline solutions NSEC and NSEC3 and with the online solution NSEC5, the ZSK is kept in cold storage. This means that the different nameservers do not have access to it, and it is only used offline to sign records which are then distributed to the nameservers with their signatures. This ensures that even if a nameserver is compromised, the integrity of the zone is kept safe, since attackers do not gain access to the ZSK and can not forge records.

With AdaDoQ, communication with the QUIC session is considered authenticated. This means the nameserver has to authenticate itself with the resolver during the QUIC connection setup. To do that, the nameserver has to have access to the ZSK, which is the ground truth source for the zone. This suggests that the key cannot be kept in cold storage, and if a nameserver is compromised the integrity of the zone may be compromised.

To eliminate this danger the nameservers can refrain from using the ZSK itself for the QUIC connection establishment, and instead use a separate key, dedicated for QUIC establishment, we call the QUIC Signing Key (QSK), signed offline by the ZSK. This key is valid only for QUIC connections, and can be periodically updated. This means that if a nameserver is compromised, the ZSK is not compromised. While an attacker can still use the QSK to forge responses in a compromised server, it is more complex to use in an attack, as it requires the attacker, which is located on the server side, to force a QUIC connection between a targeted resolver (the client side) and the compromised nameserver. This is hard to achieve from the server side. One option is for the attacker to mount a flood of NXDomain requests from another machine under its control to the resolver which would then cause the resolver to open a QUIC connection to the authoritative server that the attacker has compromised.

Validating Resolvers: DNSSEC signed records can be validated by any resolver between the client and the authoritative nameserver. With AdaDoQ under high load, records are sent without being signed, and only the resolver that communicates directly with the nameserver authenticated them. This means that for other resolvers along the chain, additional authenticity and data integrity is required to make sure the records are not being tampered with, and these resolvers down the chain need to trust the data from the initial validating resolver.

Implementation Details are relegated to Appendix Appendix B due to space limitation.

4 Experiments

4.1 AdaDoQ Configurations

With AdaDoQ, deciding when to switch from normal DNSSEC communication, to the long-lived QUIC connection is a fundamental part of the algorithm. Our implementation uses an Exponential Moving Average [16] scoring system (Eq. 1). There are three tunable configurations that need to be configured when initializing the server:

1. Window Size: configures how frequently we update the score of the connection with the aggregated count of messages.
2. $\alpha \in [0, 1]$: weight parameter that's used to decide how quickly old messages' score is decayed.
3. Switching Threshold: the score at which the resolver server opts to upgrade its connection with the nameserver from DNSSEC to QUIC.

We have tried various different combination of configurations, and found that for us, the best results are achieved with a window size of $1\,$s, $\alpha = 0.6$, and a score threshold of 50. These are the configurations used in all the results reported in this paper.

4.2 Results

Full Comparison: In Fig. 1 and Table 7 we compare our proposed AdaDoQ solution to all DNS and DNSSEC configurations discussed in this paper. Plain

DNS gives us a baseline of how DNS performs during a DDoS like attack without any security overheads (21-23K QPS). NSEC and NSEC3, the two offline signing configurations for DNSSEC give about 9K QPS with RSA and 4K with ECDSA. Without Aggressive caching these are the highest results for DNSSEC and they still give less than 50% throughput compared to plain DNS. With online signing, results get worse, and Black Lies provides the best throughput of 7K with RSA and 3K with ECDSA, which is less than 30% the throughput of plain DNS.

Table 7. Different DNS Resolver - Authoritative communication methods under overload conditions. QPS is maximum queries per second with attack traffic (Non eXistant (NX) request flood) before it starts to lose packets. AdaDoQ is our new method, Adaptive DNS over QUIC. * Aggressive use is known to be supported only by Knot resolver by CZ.NIC.

Nameserver	NX Proof	Crypto Method	Online Signing	Maximum QPS	Cons
DNS	N/A	N/A	N/A	**23,524**	DNS Hijacking
DNSSEC	NSEC	RSA/SHA-256	No	9,510	Zone Walking Slow Zone Update
		ECDSA P-256		4,213	+ Resolver Load
	NSEC Aggressive*	RSA/ECDSA		**96,200**	Zone Walking Slow Zone Update
	NSEC3	RSA/SHA-256	No	8,989	Zone Walking Slow Zone Update
		ECDSA P-256		4,015	+ Resolver Load
	NSEC3 Aggressive*	RSA/ECDSA		**95,400**	Zone Walking Slow Zone Update
	White Lies	RSA/SHA-256	Yes	5,863	DDoS ZSK Exposure
		ECDSA P-256		2,070	+ Resolver Load
	Black Lies	RSA/SHA-256	Yes	7,206	DDoS ZSK Exposure
		ECDSA P-256		3,338	+ Resolver Load
	NSEC5	RSA/SHA-256	Yes	6,324	DDoS Slow Zone Update
		ECDSA P-256		2,171	+ Resolver Load
AdaDoQ	Black Lies	TLS	No	**20,558**	TLS Key Exposure
	NSEC5			**18,824**	

AdaDoQ on the other hand shows the potential of switching to QUIC and ditching any security overhead of DNSSEC. It gives a throughput of 20K QPS which is 50% higher than all DNSSEC configurations (excluding Aggressive

Caching), and it gives 90% the throughput of plain DNS (using Knot resolver), while avoiding zone enumeration attacks. These results suggest that separating the normal and peak loads, as in AdaDoQ, is a strategy to solve the fundamental issues DNSSEC introduces to denial of service attacks.

Scaling Connections: In order to test the effects of handling multiple QUIC connections simultaneously, we set up another experiment, where each resolver is being randomly queried for one of 5 different zones, handled by 5 different authoritative nameserver machines. In Table 8 we compare the results of AdaDoQ (configured to use Black Lies on low traffic) against DNSSEC with Black Lies. Results show that DNSSEC with Black Lies suffers a reduction of 16% in the throughput of the system, while AdaDoQ suffers only 12% reduction. The results suggests that while communicating with more servers does affect performance, the effects are similar between AdaDoQ and DNSSEC, and there's no significant impact of maintaining the QUIC connections.

Connection Stability: In certain scenarios, QUIC connections may be opened and closed by the resolver or authoritative repeatedly, either by design, or maliciously. For this reason we designed our solution with QUIC and not TLS, as its overheads for establishing, resuming and terminating connections are low (Sect. 3.4). To measure these overheads, we created an experiment where the resolver and nameserver randomly close one of their open QUIC connections every 1 s, forcing a new connection to be opened. Table 9 shows that while this extreme scenario does affect the throughput of the system, the impact is minimal, reducing the throughput by only 7%.

Table 8. Comparing throughput of NXDOMAIN Proofs. # Auth: number of authoritative nameservers queried.

NX Proof	# Auth	Max QPS
Black Lies	1	7,206
	5	6,079
AdaDoQ	1	20,558
	5	18,126

Table 9. Measuring under overload of queries to names that exist in the zone.

NX Proof	Drop Rate	Max QPS
AdaDoQ	0	20,558
	1/sec	19,119

5   Future Work

In this paper we focused on measuring existing DNSSEC configurations and creating a working PoC to measure the potential performance of AdaDoQ. We used a deterministic switching algorithm, which requires manually configuring several tunable parameters to reach optimal throughput (Sect. 4.1). It is interesting to use an online machine learning model [18], that can examine the resolver-nameserver traffic online, to decide the best predictor for future load peaks and lows in order to switch between QUIC and DNSSEC communication.

6 Conclusions

Undoubtedly, DNSSEC is an important extension to the DNS protocol that protects against DNS Hijacking (Cache Poisoning). Additionally, with aggressive caching it provides good protection from most NXDomain floods and other DDoS attacks. However, DNSSEC comes at a price; With NSEC/3 the authority compromises the secrecy of its zone (allowing zone enumeration attacks) and is restricted to slow zone updates, and with online signing (hence without aggressive use) it is more susceptible to denial-of-service attacks which it amplifies Furthermore, we have shown that switching form RSA signatures to ECDSA signatures, only moves the computational bottleneck from the authoritative to the resolver. We measured the extent of these overheads and shown that they reduce the throughput of the system by 60% to 90%.

We proposed an adaptive configuration that maintains high throughput, while not requiring authorities to compromise on their zone's privacy, zone update time, or level of security. Our approach called Adaptive DNS over QUIC (AdaDoQ) is a hybrid approach that adapts itself to the traffic load on the server. When the load is low, DNSSEC is used with any configuration that fits. When the load is high, the resolver and nameserver switch to a persistent secure QUIC connection, using the ZSK for authentication, and benefit from interacting using plain DNS over this QUIC connection without the DNSSEC signature overheads. We showed that our approach gives a throughput of 20K QPS which is only a 10% reduction in throughput compared to plain DNS, and at least twice as good as other DNSSEC configuration we tried (excluding aggressive caching).

Appendix A   Measurement Setup

Throughout this paper we describe several experiments designed to measure the throughput of DNS and DNSSEC configurations under NXDomain Flood attack conditions. For this we set up 3 virtual machines hosted on Microsoft Azure [3] cloud servers. Each machine has an Intel Xeon Platinum 8272CL processor, 4 virtual CPUs, 16GB RAM and Ubuntu 18.04 operating system.

- **<u>Client Machine</u>**
  The client machine acts as the query initiator. It uses the *resperf* (version 2.3.4) stress tool by Nominum [37] to send a query stream consisting of many unique DNS 'A' requests. In each experiment we measure the maximum rate of queries per second before the server starts dropping queries and the response rate stops growing, indicating that some bottleneck has been reached.

- **Recursive Resolver Machine**
  The resolver is the machine that does the DNS lookups. It is configured with either *Bind9* (version 9.11.3) [6] or *Knot Resolver* (version 5.1.3) [15] in order to compare different resolver configurations that are available in one but not in the other.
- **Authoritative Nameserver Machine**
  The authoritative nameserver is configured using *Knot DNS* (version 3.1.0). In the various experiments we either configure it to use plain DNS or to use DNSSEC with either RSA or ECDSA signatures in order to compare the different overheads each introduces.

Appendix B   Implementation Details

We create a proof-of-concept (POC) of our solution using current state-of-the-art resolver and authoritative nameserver implementations (the code is available in github Section [1]). To do that we used Knot DNS (version 3.1.0) for the authoritative nameservers, and Knot Resolver (version 5.1.3) for the recursive resolvers. Since resolver implementations do not implement QUIC capabilities for resolver-nameserver communication, and changing their code directly would be difficult task, we instead set up two QUIC proxies, one for the resolver side and one for the authoritative nameserver side (Sect. 4). Instead of the resolver and nameserver establishing a connection directly to each other, they both use their corresponding proxies for incoming and outgoing traffic. The core logic of when to switch between the secure QUIC connection and normal UDP is done within the proxies. Figure 5 illustrates this setup.

For the switching algorithm, we track each resolver-nameserver unique communication, aggregating the number of NXDomain messages received in a fixed 1-second window. We score their throughput using Exponential Moving Average [16] with the following formula:

$$F_i = \alpha \cdot F_{i-1} + (1 - \alpha) \cdot f_i \tag{1}$$

where F_i is the score of the connection in time i, f_i is the number of messages received in time i, and $\alpha \in [0, 1]$ is a weight parameter, tunable to emphasize more/less on recent messages.

When a resolver-nameserver communication score reaches a predefined threshold, the resolver opts to open a QUIC connection with the nameserver. Open connections are kept in a Priority Queue [19] structure based on the connections' score. When there are too many open connections, the resolver (or authoritative) terminates the connection with the lowest score.

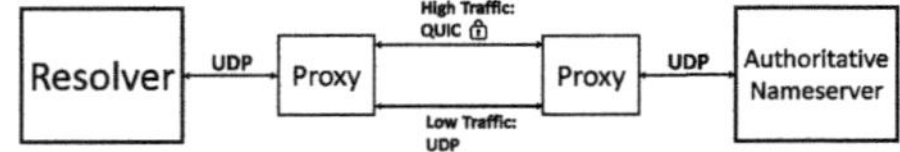

Fig. 5. Overview of AdaDoQ experiment setup. Proxies are in charge of upgrading/downgrading the QUIC connection with predefined settings. Resolver and authoritative nameserver are configured to receive/send communication through the proxies.

References

1. AdaDoQ proxy PoC. https://github.com/adadoqpoc/AdaDoQ
2. Chain of trust - wikipedia. https://en.wikipedia.org/wiki/Chain_of_trust
3. Cloud computing services — microsoft azure. https://azure.microsoft.com/
4. darkoperator/dnsrecon: Dns enumeration script. https://github.com/darkoperator/dnsrecon
5. Disposable email address - wikipedia. https://en.wikipedia.org/wiki/Disposable_email_address
6. Dns, bind nameserver, dhcp, ldap and directory services. https://www.bind9.net/
7. draft-valsorda-dnsop-black-lies-00 - compact dnssec denial of existence or black lies. https://tools.ietf.org/html/draft-valsorda-dnsop-black-lies-00
8. Ecdsa: The missing piece of dnssec — cloudflare. https://www.cloudflare.com/dns/dnssec/ecdsa-and-dnssec/
9. Economical with the truth: Making dnssec answers cheap. https://blog.cloudflare.com/black-lies/
10. Economical with the truth: Making dnssec answers cheap. https://blog.cloudflare.com/black-lies/#thetroublewithpreviousandnextnames
11. Google cloud platform blog: Introducing quic support for https load balancing. https://cloudplatform.googleblog.com/2018/06/Introducing-QUIC-support-for-HTTPS-load-balancing.html
12. Head-of-line blocking - wikipedia. https://en.wikipedia.org/wiki/Head-of-line_blocking
13. Ietf — internet engineering task force. https://www.ietf.org/
14. Isp column - october 2014. https://www.potaroo.net/ispcol/2014-10/ecdsa.html
15. Knot resolver. https://www.knot-resolver.cz/
16. Moving average - wikipedia. https://en.wikipedia.org/wiki/Moving_average#Exponential_moving_average
17. Nmap: the network mapper - free security scanner. https://nmap.org/
18. Online machine learning - wikipedia. https://en.wikipedia.org/wiki/Online_machine_learning
19. Priority queue - wikipedia. https://en.wikipedia.org/wiki/Priority_queue
20. Quic - wikipedia. https://en.wikipedia.org/wiki/QUIC
21. Rfc 7129 - authenticated denial of existence in the dns. https://tools.ietf.org/html/rfc7129#appendix-B
22. Rfc 9250 - dns over dedicated quic connections. https://datatracker.ietf.org/doc/rfc9250/
23. rfc5155. https://datatracker.ietf.org/doc/html/rfc5155#section-1.1
24. rfc8198. https://datatracker.ietf.org/doc/html/rfc8198#section-9
25. rfc9002. https://datatracker.ietf.org/doc/html/rfc9002
26. Tls overhead - netsekure rng. http://netsekure.org/2010/03/tls-overhead/

27. X.509 - wikipedia. https://en.wikipedia.org/wiki/X.509
28. Ahmed, M.E., Kim, H., Park, M.: Mitigating DNS query-based DDOS attacks with machine learning on software-defined networking. In: MILCOM 2017-2017 IEEE Military Communications Conference (MILCOM), pp. 11–16. IEEE (2017)
29. Bernstein, D.J.: Nsec3 walker. http://dnscurve.org/nsec3walker.html (2011)
30. Dierks, T., Rescorla, E.: The transport layer security (tls) protocol version 1.2 (2008)
31. Feibish, S.L., Afek, Y., Bremler-Barr, A., Cohen, E., Shagam, M.: Mitigating DNS random subdomain DDoS attacks by distinct heavy hitters sketches. In: Proceedings of the fifth ACM/IEEE Workshop on Hot Topics in Web Systems and Technologies, pp. 1–6 (2017)
32. Goldberg, S., Naor, M., Papadopoulos, D., Reyzin, L., Vasant, S., Ziv, A.: Nsec5: Provably preventing dnssec zone enumeration. In: NDSS (2015)
33. Imem, A.A.: Comparison and evaluation of digital signature schemes employed in ndn network. arXiv preprint arXiv:1508.00184 (2015)
34. Kaminsky, D.: Black ops 2008: It's the end of the cache as we know it. Black Hat USA **2** (2008)
35. Man, K., Qian, Z., Wang, Z., Zheng, X., Huang, Y., Duan, H.: DNS cache poisoning attack reloaded: Revolutions with side channels. In: Proceedings of the 2020 ACM SIGSAC Conference on Computer and Communications Security, pp. 1337–1350. CCS '20, Association for Computing Machinery, New York, NY, USA (2020). https://doi.org/10.1145/3372297.3417280
36. Metwally, A., Agrawal, D., El Abbadi, A.: Efficient computation of frequent and top-k elements in data streams. In: International Conference on Database Theory, pp. 398–412. Springer (2005)
37. Nominum: resperf(1) - Linux man page. https://linux.die.net/man/1/dnsperf/ (May 2019)
38. Papadopoulos, D., Wessels, D., Huque, S., Naor, M., Včelák, J., Reyzin, L., Goldberg, S.: Making nsec5 practical for dnssec. Cryptology ePrintArchive, Report 2017/099 (2017)
39. van Rijswijk-Deij, R., Hageman, K., Sperotto, A., Pras, A.: The performance impact of elliptic curve cryptography on dnssec validation. IEEE/ACM Trans. Network. **25**(2), 738–750 (2016)
40. van Rijswijk-Deij, R., Sperotto, A., Pras, A.: DNSSEC and its potential for DDoS attacks: a comprehensive measurement study. In: Proceedings of the 2014 Conference on Internet Measurement Conference, pp. 449–460 (2014)
41. Son, S., Shmatikov, V.: The hitchhiker's guide to DNS cache poisoning. In: International Conference on Security and Privacy in Communication Systems, pp. 466–483. Springer (2010)
42. Spacek, P.: Measuring efficiency of aggressive use of DNSSECd-validated cache (rfc 8198). https://indico.dns-oarc.net/event/28/contributions/509/attachments/479/786/DNS-OARC-28-presentation-RFC8198.pdf (2018)
43. Wander, M., Schwittmann, L., Boelmann, C., Weis, T.: Gpu-based nsec3 hash breaking. In: 2014 IEEE 13th International Symposium on Network Computing and Applications, pp. 137–144. IEEE (2014)

Kolmogorov Complexity Based Analysis of the Zeros Distribution in Locally Maximal Satisfying Truth Assignments of Random K-SAT Formulas
(Short Paper)

V. Liagkou[1,4], P. E. Nastou[5], P. Spirakis[2], and Y. C. Stamatiou[1,3(✉)]

[1] Computer Technology Institute and Press – "Diophantus", N. Kazantzaki, University of Patras, 26500 Rio, Patras, Greece
liagkou@cti.gr

[2] Department of Computer Science, University of Liverpool, Liverpool, UK
P.Spirakis@liverpool.ac.uk

[3] Department of Business Administration, University of Patras, University Campus, University of Patras,26500 Rio, Patras, Greece
stamatiu@ceid.upatras.gr

[4] Department of Informatics and Telecommunications, University of Ioannina, 47100 Kostakioi Arta, Greece

[5] Department of Mathematics, University of the Aegean, Applied Mathematics and Mathematical Modeling Laboratory, Samos, Greece
pnastou@aegean.gr

Abstract. This paper studies Locally Maximal Satisfying Truth Assignments (LMSTAs) of satisfiable random k-SAT formulas via Kolmogorov complexity. For Kolmogorov-random instances, we show that the fraction of zeros in any LMSTA lies in a contiguous sub-interval of $(0,1)$ whose bounds depend on the clause-to-variable ratio r. We further derive a mixed-width version that applies to heterogeneous CNFs. As case studies, we analyse the standard SAT encodings of 200-round TRIVIUM and the public 30-round BIVIUM benchmark and prove that no LMSTAs exist for either, ruling out single-bit "local traps". This work links information-theoretic randomness to local maximality providing a heuristic, compression-based test for real-world SAT reductions in cryptography.

1 Introduction

The k-SAT problem consists in deciding whether a given CNF (Conjunctive Normal Form) formula with k-literal clauses is satisfiable. This problem is *NP-complete* for $k \geq 3$. For random 3-SAT with $m = rn$ clauses on n variables, experiments and theoretical work demonstrate a sharp *satisfiability* transition near a constant value r. The exact threshold value remains unknown, though lower/upper bounds and Friedgut's sharp-threshold theorem are known. In particular, rigorous bounds place the threshold within the interval $[3.53, 4.4898]$ with a sharp transition in between [1, 2, 6–8, 11–14].

In this paper, we shift focus from the threshold itself to a finer structural property: the behaviour of *Locally Maximal Satisfying Truth Assignments* (LMSTAs) in random *satisfiable* k-SAT instances and how their zero density depends on r. Our approach is based on *Kolmogorov-complexity* incompressibility arguments [5, 15, 16, 18].

In particular, this approach relates the distribution of zeros in LMSTAs to the incompressibility of a formula. We prove that, for satisfiable Kolmogorov-random formulas, the fraction of zeros in any LMSTA must lie in a contiguous sub-interval of $[0, 1]$ determined by r (and we generalize this to mixed-width clause formulas). Two crypto SAT reductions (Trivium, Bivium) fall outside the feasible region, implying the non-existence of LMSTAs and thus the absence of single-bit local traps in their clause landscapes.

2 The Unsatisfiability Threshold Under the Kolmogorov Complexity Viewpoint

We model Boolean formulas as binary strings under a specific encoding scheme described below. First, we define the *length* $l(x)$ of a natural number x as the number of bits in its binary representation. Furthermore, we identify the natural numbers $\mathcal{N}$ with the set of finite binary strings through the mapping $(0, \epsilon), (1, 0), (2, 1), (3, 00), (4, 01), \ldots$ where each natural number corresponds to a unique binary sequence.

Regarding the k-SAT problem, the total number of distinct clauses of width k over n Boolean variables is $2^k \binom{n}{k}$. We fix a standard enumeration of these $2^k \binom{n}{k}$ clauses, assigning to each clause a unique index according to its position.

Let Φ denote the set of all Boolean k-SAT formulas in conjunctive normal form (CNF) with n variables and m clauses. Two formulas ϕ_1 and ϕ_2 are considered distinct iff they differ in at least one clause. We now fix a standard encoding $E : \Phi \rightarrow \mathcal{N}$ for Boolean formulas $\phi \in \Phi$, where each clause is represented by $\lceil \log(2^k \binom{n}{k}) \rceil$ bits[1]. Therefore, a formula ϕ can be encoded as a binary string of $m = rn$ blocks, with each block encoding a clause. Since the clauses are ordered in increasing order according to the enumeration, the encoding is *injective*. Hence, the formula ϕ can be described using $m \left\lceil \log \left(2^k \binom{n}{k} \right) \right\rceil = rn \left\lceil \log \left(2^k \binom{n}{k} \right) \right\rceil$ bits,

and the length of the code $E(\phi)$ is $l(E(\phi)) = rn \left\lceil \log \left(2^k \binom{n}{k} \right) \right\rceil$ for all $\phi \in \Phi$.

Remark (ceiling overhead). Using $\lceil \cdot \rceil$ adds < 1 bit per clause, i.e. $< m$ bits overall. Since $\log(2^k \binom{n}{k}) = \Theta(\log n)$ for fixed k, $l(E(\phi)) = \Theta(m \log n)$ and the ceiling overhead is $o(l(E(\phi)))$. In particular, for any $d = \Theta(\log n)$, a $1 - o(1)$ fraction of formulas satisfies $K(E(\phi) \mid n) \geq l(E(\phi)) - d$.

---

[1] All logarithms are base 2. Entropy is measured in bits.

Kolmogorov deficiency and incompressibility. Define the Kolmogorov *deficiency* of ϕ (relative to n and E) by

$$\operatorname{def}(\phi) := l\big(E(\phi)\big) - K\big(E(\phi) \mid n\big).$$

We call ϕ $\delta(n)$-*incompressible* if $\operatorname{def}(\phi) \le \delta(n)$.

Assume that ϕ is satisfiable by some truth assignment A. Any truth assignment satisfies $(2^k - 1)\binom{n}{k}$ out of the $2^k\binom{n}{k}$ possible clauses. Thus, all clauses in ϕ must belong to the set of clauses satisfied by A, which has cardinality $(2^k - 1)\binom{n}{k}$. Consequently, each such clause can be represented using $\lceil \log\big((2^k - 1)\binom{n}{k}\big)\rceil$ bits.

We introduce an alternative encoding E' for satisfiable formulas where ϕ is represented by n bits for A, followed by $rn\lceil \log\big((2^k - 1)\binom{n}{k}\big)\rceil$ bits for the clauses contained in ϕ, listed in increasing order according to the standard enumeration. The decoder reads A, enumerates all clauses satisfied by A, and then uses the remaining blocks to identify the specific clauses forming ϕ. Therefore,

$$K(E(\phi) \mid n) \le n + rn\left\lceil \log\big((2^k - 1)\binom{n}{k}\big)\right\rceil = l(E'(\phi)) + O(1). \tag{1}$$

Combining the lower bound $K(E(\phi) \mid n) \ge l(E(\phi)) - \log(rn\lceil\log(2^k\binom{n}{k})\rceil)$ with (1) yields the usual k-SAT upper bound on r (see [3, 20]):

$$r \le \frac{1}{k - \log(2^k - 1)} + o(1), \quad n \to \infty.$$

3 Locally Maximal Satisfying Truth Assignments

Let $A \in \{0, 1\}^n$ be a fixed truth assignment with $l = \rho n$ zeros, $\mathcal{S}_A$ the set of clauses satisfied by A, and, for each position i with $A_i = 0$, let $F_i \subset \mathcal{S}_A$ be the *blocking set* corresponding to variable x_i (all clauses that would change from true to false if x_i were flipped from 0 to 1). Each F_i contains exactly the clauses of the form $(\ell_1 \vee \cdots \vee \neg x_i \vee \cdots \vee \ell_k)$; all F_i are disjoint and have the same size $f = |F_i| = \binom{n-1}{k-1}$.

We aim to count the number of formulas of size $m = rn$ composed only of clauses from $\mathcal{S}_A$ and containing at least one clause from each of the l disjoint sets $F_1, \ldots, F_l$. Let $F_{m,\mathcal{S}_A}$ be this set of formulas and, for each i, let E_i be the set of formulas of size m using clauses from $\mathcal{S}_A$ that completely omit F_i. Applying inclusion–exclusion,

$$|\mathcal{F}_{A,\mathrm{LMSTA}}| = \sum_{j=0}^{l} (-1)^j \binom{l}{j}(S - jf)^m, \tag{2}$$

where $S = |\mathcal{S}_A|$. Using $(1 - x)^m \le e^{-mx}$ for $0 < x < 1$,

$$(S - jf)^m = S^m\left(1 - \frac{jf}{S}\right)^m \le S^m e^{-jfm/S},$$

hence

$$|\mathcal{F}_{A,\mathrm{LMSTA}}| \leq S^m \sum_{j=0}^{l} (-1)^j \binom{l}{j} e^{-jfm/S} = S^m \left(1 - e^{-fm/S}\right)^l.$$

Since

$$\frac{fm}{S} = \frac{\binom{n-1}{k-1} \cdot rn}{(2^k - 1)\binom{n}{k}} = \frac{kr}{(2^k - 1)},$$

we obtain

$$|\mathcal{F}_{A,\mathrm{LMSTA}}| \leq S^m \left(1 - e^{-\frac{kr}{(2^k-1)}}\right)^{\rho n}. \tag{3}$$

4   LMSTAs of Kolmogorov-Random Formulas

Let ϕ be a random 3-SAT formula over n variables and $m = rn$ clauses. Assume ϕ is $\delta(n)$-incompressible with $\delta(n) = \log(m\lceil \log C\rceil)$, so any description of ϕ requires at least

$$\log(C^m) = m\lceil \log C\rceil - \log\big(m\lceil \log C\rceil\big)$$

bits, where $C = 8\binom{n}{3}$ is the number of possible 3-clauses on n variables.

Suppose ϕ admits an LMSTA A. Then ϕ only includes clauses from S_A, with $S = |S_A| = 7\binom{n}{3}$, and it must include at least one clause from each of the l disjoint blocking sets F_i. Using (3), we obtain

$$|\mathcal{F}_{A,\mathrm{LMSTA}}| \leq S^m \left(1 - e^{-3r/7}\right)^{\rho n}.$$

An assignment A containing exactly ρn zeros can be chosen in $\binom{n}{\rho n}$ ways. For large n and fixed $0 < \rho < 1$, Stirling's formula gives

$$\binom{n}{\rho n} \approx \frac{1}{\sqrt{2\pi n\rho(1-\rho)}} 2^{nH(\rho)},$$

where $H(\rho) = -\rho\log\rho - (1-\rho)\log(1-\rho)$ is the binary entropy. In logarithmic form,

$$\log\binom{n}{\rho n} = nH(\rho) - \frac{1}{2}\log\big(2\pi n\rho(1-\rho)\big) + o(1).$$

Ignoring lower-order terms, Kolmogorov-randomness demands

$$\log|\mathcal{F}_{A,\mathrm{LMSTA}}| + \log n + nH(\rho) \geq m\lceil \log C\rceil - \log\big(m\lceil \log C\rceil\big).$$

Using (3) and dividing by n (absorbing $o(1)$ terms) yields

$$H(\rho) \geq r\log\left(\frac{8}{7}\right) - \rho\log\left(1 - e^{-3r/7}\right). \tag{4}$$

The generalisation to k-SAT is

$$H(\rho) \geq r \log\left(\frac{2^k}{2^k - 1}\right) - \rho \log\left(1 - e^{-kr/(2^k - 1)}\right). \tag{5}$$

Scope of the implication. Our use of Kolmogorov complexity is *one-directional*: if $\operatorname{def}(\phi) \leq O(\log n)$ (i.e. ϕ is $\delta(n)$-incompressible with sublinear δ), then every LMSTA of ϕ must satisfy (5) (hence lie in the admissible window derived below). We do *not* claim the converse.

Comparison with the trivial counting bound

A trivial first-moment bound for assignments with exactly ρn zeros is

$$\Pr[\exists \text{ SAT assignment of weight } \rho n] \;\leq\; 2\binom{n}{\rho n}(1 - -2^{-k})^m. \tag{6}$$

For LMSTAs, a zero bit must be *blocked*. For a fixed zero, a random clause belongs to its blocking set with probability $\frac{k}{(2^k - 1)n}$, so the chance that a clause does *not* block it is $\left(1 - \frac{k}{(2^k - 1)n}\right)$ and across $m = rn$ clauses this tends to $e^{-kr/(2^k - 1)}$. Requiring all ρn zeros to be blocked contributes an extra factor $\left(1 - e^{-kr/(2^k - 1)}\right)^{\rho n}$, yielding

$$\Pr[\exists \textbf{ LMSTA} \text{ of weight } \rho n] \;\leq\; \binom{n}{\rho n}(1 - 2^{-k})^m\left(1 - e^{-kr/(2^k - 1)}\right)^{\rho n}. \tag{7}$$

Dividing (7) by (6) gives

$$\frac{1}{2}\left(1 - e^{-kr/(2^k - 1)}\right)^{\rho n} < 1 \quad \text{for all } k \geq 2,\ r > 0,\ \rho > 0,$$

so the LMSTA bound is *strictly tighter* than the trivial one.

5   Analysis of the Inequality

Define

$$a \;=\; -\log\left(1 - e^{-kr/(2^k - 1)}\right), \qquad b \;=\; r \log\left(\frac{2^k}{2^k - 1}\right).$$

Then

$$H(\rho) \;\geq\; b + a\rho, \qquad 0 \leq \rho \leq 1. \tag{8}$$

Let $G(\rho) := H(\rho) - a\rho$. The constraint (8) is equivalent to $G(\rho) \geq b$. Since $G(0) = 0 < b$ and $G(1) = -a < b$ (with $a, b > 0$), the inequality can be satisfied only inside $(0, 1)$. The unique maximiser of G satisfies $H'(\rho) = a$, namely $\rho_*(a) = \frac{1}{1 + 2^a} \in \left(0, \frac{1}{2}\right)$, with maximum value

$$M(a) \;:=\; G\big(\rho_*(a)\big) \;=\; H\big(\rho_*(a)\big) - a\,\rho_*(a) \;=\; \log\left(1 + 2^{-a}\right). \tag{9}$$

Proposition 1. *Let $G(\rho) = H(\rho) - a\rho$ and $M(a) = G(\rho_*(a)) = \log(1 + 2^{-a})$, where $\rho_*(a) = 1/(1 + 2^a)$ is the unique maximiser of G on $(0, 1)$. Because $G(0) = 0 < b$ and $G(1) = -a < b$ (with $a, b > 0$), comparison of b with $M(a)$ yields exactly three possibilities: (i) $b > M(a)$: no solution of (8); (ii) $b = M(a)$: a single (double) solution $\rho = \rho_*(a)$; (iii) $0 < b < M(a)$: two distinct solutions $0 < \rho_- < \rho_*(a) < \rho_+ < 1$; every LMSTA must satisfy $\rho \in [\rho_-, \rho_+]$.*

In terms of (r, k), the *critical curve* separating the "empty-window" from the "non-empty-window" regimes is

$$r \log\left(\frac{2^k}{2^k - 1}\right) \;=\; \log(1 + 2^{-a(r,k)}),$$

with $a(r, k) = -\log(1 - e^{-kr/(2^k - 1)})$. Thus, the admissible zero-density interval $[\rho_-(r, k), \rho_+(r, k)]$ is defined implicitly by

$$H(\rho) \;-\; a(r, k)\,\rho \;=\; b(r, k), \qquad 0 < \rho < 1. \tag{10}$$

Set $F(\rho) = H(\rho) - a\rho - b$. Because $F(0) = -b$ and $F(1) = -a - b < 0$, equation (10) has: (i) no real root if $b \geq M(a)$; (ii) exactly one root $\rho_- = \rho_+ = \rho_*$ if $b = M(a)$; (iii) two distinct roots $0 < \rho_- < \rho_* < \rho_+ < 1$ if $b < M(a)$. Hence the existence condition is

$$b(r, k) \;<\; M\big(a(r, k)\big) = \log(1 + 2^{-a(r,k)}). \tag{11}$$

In the full version, we also derive explicit two-sided enclosures of $[\rho_-, \rho_+]$ (omitted here for brevity).

6   Kolmogorov Bound for Mixed-Width CNF Instances

Let a satisfiable CNF φ on n Boolean variables contain $m = rn$ clauses whose width histogram is $q_k = \frac{m_k}{m}$, with $\sum_{k \geq 2} q_k = 1$; thus a fraction q_k of the clauses has length $k \in \{2, 3, 4, \dots\}$. Throughout the section, we use an Elias–δ code for integers; specific δ fields are implicitly self-delimiting, so concatenation of the blocks below is prefix-free.

Before any assignment is fixed, the *pattern field* of a k-literal clause needs $\log 2^k = k$ bits. The variable-index and sign subfields do not change after an assignment is revealed and therefore cancel in the later comparison. Hence $\ell_{\text{full}} = \sum_k q_k k = \mathbb{E}[k]$ bits per clause, $L_{\text{full}} = m\,\ell_{\text{full}}$. Fixing A forbids exactly one literal pattern out of the 2^k possible, leaving $2^k - 1$ admissible patterns and $\ell_{\text{sat}} = \sum_k q_k \big[k - \log(\frac{2^k}{2^k - 1})\big]$, $L_{\text{sat}} = m\,\ell_{\text{sat}}$.

If A is a locally maximal satisfying assignment, one clause per zero-bit can be replaced by a single flag bit, saving $(\ell_{\text{sat}} - 1)\rho n$ bits, where $\rho = \frac{|\{i : A_i = 0\}|}{n}$. Storing the assignment itself costs $nH(\rho)$ bits; encoding the all-1 blocking-cover string costs $O(\log n)$.

For a $\delta(n)$-incompressible formula (with $\delta(n) = o(n)$) we must have

$$L_{\text{full}} - \delta(n) \;\leq\; L_{\text{sat}} - (\ell_{\text{sat}} - 1)\rho\,n + nH(\rho) + O(\log n).$$

Divide by n and drop $o(n)$ terms to obtain

$$H(\rho) \geq r \underbrace{\sum_k q_k \log\left(\frac{2^k}{2^k-1}\right)}_{b(q)} + \rho \underbrace{\left[\sum_k q_k\left(k - \log(\frac{2^k}{2^k-1})\right) - 1\right]}_{a(q)}. \qquad (12)$$

Let $R(\rho) = rb(q) + a(q)\rho$ be the right-hand side. If $rb(q) \geq 1$ then $R(\rho) > 1 \geq H(\rho)$ for all $0 < \rho < 1$, so the admissible window is empty and no LMSTA can exist for an incompressible mixed-width formula. Otherwise, the two curves cross exactly twice, defining a non-empty interval $[\rho_-, \rho_+]$ where LMSTAs are possible (but not guaranteed).

7   Application to the SAT Encodings of the Trivium and Bivium Crypto Algorithms

Since we could not locate publicly released CNF encodings matching the exact "Bivium 30 rounds, 100 known keystream bits" and "Trivium 200 rounds" settings we targeted, we generated both instances using the standard SAT-based cryptanalysis workflow: bit-level modeling of the round functions, introduction of auxiliary (Tseitin) variables, and Tseitin conversion to CNF [4,21], in line with prior work [9,10,17,19]. Known keystream bits were asserted as unit clauses; unit clauses were eliminated before computing clause histograms. The resulting clause-to-variable ratio r and clause-length histogram $q = (q_k)_k$ provide the inputs to the mixed-width Kolmogorov bound (12).

7.1   Trivium under the mixed-width Kolmogorov bound

Our 200-round TRIVIUM encoding has $n = 57{,}600$ variables and $m = 301{,}056$ clauses ($r \approx 5.226$). The clause-length histogram is given in Table 1.

Table 1. Clause histogram for the 200-round TRIVIUM key-recovery CNF

k	m_k	q_k
2	13 824	0.0459
3	115 200	0.3827
4	172 032	0.5714
total	301 056	1.0000

Plugging this q vector (column of q_ks) into (12) yields coefficients $b(q) \approx 0.146$ and $a(q) \approx 2.380$. Thus, the linear constraint becomes

$$H(\rho) \geq rb(q) + a(q)\rho \approx 0.763 + 2.380\,\rho. \qquad (13)$$

Since $\max_{\rho \in [0,1]} H(\rho) = 1$ and $M(a(q)) = \log(1 + 2^{-a(q)}) \approx 0.254 < rb(q)$, no $\rho \in [0,1]$ can satisfy the bound. Thus, the admissible window is empty and no LMSTA exists for this TRIVIUM instance.

7.2 Bivium under the mixed-width Kolmogorov bound

Our Bivium (30 rounds, 100 keystream bits) encoding has $n = 8{,}784$ variables and $m = 230{,}400$ clauses ($r \approx 26.23$). The clause-length histogram is given in Table 2.

Table 2. Clause histogram for the 30-round, 100-bit Bivium key-recovery CNF

k	m_k	q_k
2	78 336	0.340
3	152 064	0.660
total	230 400	1.000

For this q vector (column of q_ks), we obtain $b(q) \approx 0.268$ and $a(q) \approx 1.392$ and, thus

$$H(\rho) \geq r\,b(q) + a(q)\rho \approx 7.036 + 1.392\,\rho.$$

Because the right-hand side already exceeds 1 at $\rho = 0$, the bound has no solution on $[0, 1]$. Hence the admissible window is empty and no LMSTA exists for this Bivium instance.

Remark on assumptions and encodings. Our conclusions are conditional on $\delta(n)$-incompressibility, i.e., $\mathrm{def}(\varphi) \leq \delta(n)$ with $\delta(n) = o(n)$. This hypothesis is strictly weaker than full randomness and allows bounded structure. It shifts the effort to the empirically measured (r, q) of a given CNF. For our generated Bivium 30/100 instance, $r\,b(q) \approx 7.036 > 1$ already at $\rho = 0$, so the right-hand side of (12) exceeds the entropy ceiling 1 for all $\rho \in [0, 1]$. For our Trivium 200 instance, the inequality (13) dominates $H(\rho)$ on the entire interval, as $r\,b(q) = 0.76299 > M(a(q)) \approx 0.25359$. Sublinear deficiency only perturbs these bounds by $o(1)$ per variable and cannot restore feasibility. Finally, Tseitin transformation does not "add randomness": it preserves the circuit's logical structure while producing short clauses (often of length 24). Formatting choices (DIMACS ASCII vs. succinct, prefix-free binary) affect superficial redundancy only; our Kolmogorov-style comparison uses per-clause pattern fields and is insensitive to such choices up to lower-order terms. A systematic empirical study of cipher CNFs and compressibility is left to future work.

8 Conclusions

In this paper, we showed that for Kolmogorov-random satisfiable k-SAT, any LMSTA must have its fraction of zeros ρ inside a contiguous interval determined by the clause-to-variable ratio r of the formula. Then, we extended the result to mixed-width CNFs. For the Trivium and Bivium crypto algorithms encodings the interval is empty. Thus, no LMSTAs exist, ruling out single-bit local "traps" for search algorithms. Beyond these cases, the bounds act as a quick, compression-based test: if $r\,b(q) \geq 1$ then LMSTAs are impossible, otherwise, the derived inequalities determine the admissible ρ-window that solver heuristics should target.

References

1. Achlioptas, D..: Lower bounds for random 3-SAT via differential equations. Theor. Comput. Sci. **265**, 159–185 (2001)
2. Achlioptas, D.: Setting two variables at a time yields a new lower bound for random 3-SAT, In: Proceedings of STOC 2000,pp. 28–37 (ACM, 2000)
3. Antonopoulou, H.: Kolmogorov complexity based upper bounds for the unsatisfiability threshold of random K-SAT. J. Discrete Math. Sci. Crypt. **23**(7), 1431–1438 (2020)
4. Biere, A., Heule, M. J. H., van, H., Maaren, T.: Walsh.: Handbook of Satisfiability, 2nd edn., IOS Press, F. Artifi. Intell. Appl. **336** (2021)
5. Chaitin, G.H.: On the length of programs for computing finite binary sequences. J. ACM **13**, 547–570 (1966)
6. Coppersmith, D., Gamarnik, D., Hajiaghayi, M.T., Sorkin, G.: Random Max SAT, Random Max Cut, and their phase transitions. Random Struct. Algorithms **24**, 502–545 (2004)
7. Diaz, J., Kirousis, L., Mitsche, D., Perez-Gimenez, X.: A new upper bound for 3-SAT. In: FSTTCS 2008 (2008)
8. Dubois, O., Boufkhad, Y.: A general upper bound for the satisfiability threshold of random r-SAT. J. Algorithms **24**, 395–420 (1997)
9. Eder, J., Scholl, C.: SAT-based analysis of block-cipher structures. In: SAT 2015 (LNCS 9340),pp. 160–177 (2015)
10. Eibach, T., Pilz, E., Völkel, G.: Attacking Bivium Using SAT Solvers. In: Kleine Büning, H., Zhao, X. (eds.) SAT 2008. LNCS, vol. 4996, pp. 63–76. Springer, Heidelberg (2008). https://doi.org/10.1007/978-3-540-79719-7_7
11. Friedgut, E., J. Bourgain.: Sharp thresholds of graph properties, and the k-SAT problem. J. Amer. Math. Soc.**12**, 1017–1054 (1999)
12. Janson, S., Stamatiou, Y.C., Vamvakari, M.: Bounding the unsatisfiability threshold of random 3-SAT. Random Struct. Algorithms **17**, 103–116 (2000)
13. Kamath, A., Motwani, R., Palem, K., Spirakis, P.: Tail bounds for occupancy and the satisfiability threshold conjecture. Random Struc. Algorithms **7**, 59–80 (1995)
14. Kirousis, L.M., Kranakis, E., Krizanc, D., Stamatiou, Y.C.: Approximating the unsatisfiability threshold of random formulas. Random Struc. Algorithms **12**, 253–269 (1998)
15. Kolmogorov, A. N.: Three approaches to the concept of the amount of information. Probl. Inf. Trans. **1**(1) (1965)
16. Li, M., Vitanyi, P.: An introduction to kolmogorov complexity and its applications, 3rd edn., Springer (2008)
17. Massacci, F., Marraro, A.: Logical cryptanalysis of DES. In: CADE 2000 (LNCS 1831),pp. 374–388 (2000)
18. Solomonoff, R.J.: A formal theory of inductive inference. Inf. Control **7**(1), 1–22 (1964)
19. Soos, M., Nohl, K., Castelluccia, C.: Extending SAT Solvers to Cryptographic Problems. In: Kullmann, O. (ed.) SAT 2009. LNCS, vol. 5584, pp. 244–257. Springer, Heidelberg (2009). https://doi.org/10.1007/978-3-642-02777-2_24

20. Spirakis, P., Stamatiou, Y. C.: Kolmogorov complexity arguments in propositional logic. In: Proceeding 7th Panhellenic Logic Symposium (PLS07) (2009)
21. Tseitin, G. S.: On the complexity of derivation in propositional calculus. In: Automation of Reasoning: Classical Papers on Computational Logic, Vol. 2, Springer, pp. 466–483 (1983)

Machine Learning-Based Malware Detection on macOS
(Short Paper)

Adrian Guo Xiang Low[(✉)] and Leonardo Aniello

University of Southampton, Southampton SO17 1BJ, UK
{agxl1e22,l.aniello}@soton.ac.uk

Abstract. The increasing adoption of macOS devices leads to a rise in malware targeting the platform, while the current research state of macOS malware detection remains limited compared to Windows. This study aims to enhance macOS malware detection using supervised machine learning techniques. Unlike previous studies, this study integrates multiple feature selection methods, applies nested cross-validation, and introduces a novel RGB image conversion of structured features combined with CycleGAN-generated data for Convolutional Neural Network (CNN) training. The CyberScienceLab macOS malware dataset is used, where comprehensive data preprocessing, feature selection, and balancing through SMOTE are applied to train five supervised machine learning models: Support Vector Machine (SVM), Decision Tree, Naïve Bayes, Random Forest and Logistic Regression. Each model undergoes nested cross-validation and hyperparameter tuning to ensure robust evaluation. For CNN training, RGB images are generated by transforming structural static feature vectors. CycleGAN is employed to generate synthetic image data to address the small dataset size. The results show that all supervised learning models outperform previous studies using the same dataset, with SVM achieving the highest accuracy of 98.88% and CNN achieving 96.21%. These findings highlight that a well-designed machine learning workflow with structured data can outperform CNN-based models in this context, although deep learning remains a competitive approach. Future work focuses on expanding the dataset with more recent malware samples and exploring alternative generative methods to further improve performance.

Keywords: Malware Detection · macOS · Machine Learning · Deep Learning

1 Intoduction

The growing adoption of macOS devices has made the platform an increasingly attractive target for cyberattacks [1], yet the development of malware detection systems for macOS remains underdeveloped compared to those for Windows. Existing macOS security solutions often rely on signature-based detection, which

© The Author(s), under exclusive license to Springer Nature Switzerland AG 2026
A. Akavia et al. (Eds.): CSCML 2025, LNCS 16244, pp. 294–305, 2026.
https://doi.org/10.1007/978-3-032-10759-6_19

is ineffective against previously unseen or obfuscated malware. While several prior studies have applied machine learning techniques with promising results, they often lack key components such as comprehensive feature engineering, rigorous model validation, and effective methods to address small dataset size. These gaps highlight the need for more robust and intelligent detection approaches tailored to the macOS environment.

This study presents a machine learning-based malware detection framework that significantly outperforms previous studies using the same dataset. The Support Vector Machine (SVM) model achieves the highest accuracy of 98.88%, while a convolutional neural network (CNN) trained on RGB-transformed feature images reaches 96.21%. These results demonstrate that well-constructed workflow supervised learning models can rival, and in some cases surpass, deep learning methods in performance on structured datasets.

The significance of this work lies in showing that the proposed approach outperforms the other methods for macOS presented in the literature, attributable to the integration of multiple feature selection methods, the application of nested cross-validation for all models, and the introduction of a novel RGB image conversion for CNN training. In addition, these findings could inform future research in macOS malware analysis and dataset curation.

Key contributions include: (1) a comparative approach of multiple feature selection techniques across five supervised learning algorithms; (2) a novel transformation of structured static features into RGB images for CNN training; and (3) the application of CycleGAN for synthetic sample generation to improve deep learning performance on limited data. Unlike previous studies, this work uses nested cross-validation and extensive hyperparameter tuning to ensure robust evaluation.

2   Related Work

2.1   Supervised Machine Learning for MacOS Malware Detection

Several studies have explored machine learning to detect macOS malware. Chen and Wulff [2] evaluated five supervised machine learning models and found Decision Tree achieved the best accuracy of 92.78%, noting Information Gain as a preferred feature selection method. However, they did not optimize preprocessing or address the false positive rate (FPR). Gharghasheh and Hadayeghparasy [3] evaluated 21 subclassifiers in five major supervised learning categories and used Chi-Square selection, but observed a decrease in performance due to fixed feature selection. Pajouh et al. [4] applied SMOTE to enlarge the dataset and achieved 96.62% accuracy using Decision Tree-J48, though FPR remained high, indicating diminishing returns. Sahoo and Dhawan [5] compared supervised and unsupervised models, with Logistic Regression achieving 96% accuracy. They excluded deep learning due to limited data. In contrast, this study integrates robust preprocessing, dynamic feature selection, and explores both classical and deep learning models on the same dataset.

2.2   Limitations in Preprocessing and Analysis Techniques

Thaeler et al. [6] applied Mach-O file analysis and nine machine learning algorithms, but performance suffered from class imbalance and lack of hyperparameter tuning. Pham and Massacci [7] introduced the Mac-A-Mal framework, a dynamic malware framework requiring runtime environments. Unlike them, this study focuses on static feature analysis to ensure lightweight offline detection, supporting by rigorous feature engineering and hyperparameter tuning.

2.3   Deep Learning and Image-Based Detection

Recent studies have explored image-based approaches. Bensaoud and Kalita [8] converted raw binaries into RGB images and used CycleGAN for augmentation, achieving high accuracy on CNNs with Adam optimizer. This study build on that by transforming structured static features into RGB images, which improves interpretability and reduce noise. Aslan and Yilmaz [9] proposed a similar deep learning pipeline for other platforms, but noted challenges in family-level classification due to overlapping features. This study instead targets binary classification and addresses dataset size limitations by using CycleGAN for synthetic augmentation.

2.4   Summary of Literature Gaps

Building on these prior works, this study addresses several recurring limitations. None of the reviewed macOS malware detection studies employed nested cross-validation for model evaluation. Most relied on a simple train-test split or a single round of k-fold cross-validation, which can lead to optimistic performance estimates when hyperparameters are tuned in the same data used for evaluation. This study is the first to apply nested cross-validation on the Cyber-ScienceLab dataset, ensuring an unbiased assessment of generalization performance. In addition, it integrates robust preprocessing, dynamic feature selection, and dataset balancing via SMOTE, alongside deep learning integration through Cycle-GAN-based augmentation, to improve performance and reduce false positives in macOS malware detection.

3   Methodology

This section outlines the methodology used to develop, train, and tune several supervised machine learning models, including **Support Vector Machine (SVM), Decision Tree, Naïve Bayes, Random Forest, Logistic Regression, and a Convolutional Neural Network (CNN)** for macOS malware detection. The pipeline includes data preprocessing, feature engineering, dataset balancing, synthetic image generation, model training and hyperparameter tuning, and evaluation. The purpose is to describe the steps taken to prepare the data and configure each model prior to evaluation, which is detailed in the following section.

3.1   Dataset Selection and Conversion

Several datasets are initially explored to identify the most suitable one for this study. The macOS malware and benign dataset from **CyberScienceLab** [10] is selected, as it is the most recent open source, well-labeled and structured publicly available in a usable format. The dataset is extracted from the static analysis of Mach-O executable files, including their dynamic library dependencies. It contains a total of 611 samples, including 152 malware and 459 benign samples. Although the dataset is imbalanced, this reflects real-world conditions where benign software is significantly more prevalent than malware. The original XLSX dataset is converted to CSV for preprocessing in Python.

3.2   Data Preprocessing

Several preprocessing steps are applied to prepare the dataset before model training. The *name* feature serves only as an identifier and does not contain meaningful information for model training, so it is removed. The *strsize* feature, which represents the size of the string table, is intended to be numerical. However, upon inspection, some values are inconsistently recorded in both hexadecimal and decimal formats, causing the features to be interpreted as an object type. Two functions are implemented to clean and standardise this feature. One converts a hexadecimal value to decimal, and the other removes hexadecimal components from a mixed-format recording, retaining only the decimal value. The cleaned values are then cast as integers.

The *DYLIBnames* feature contains the names of the dynamic libraries that each binary depends on. As a multi-label categorical feature, it is not directly suitable for model training. Several encoding techniques are considered, including one-hot encoding, multi-hot encoding, and labelled encoding [11]. Since each sample is associated with multiple libraries simultaneously, multi-hot encoding is selected as the most appropriate method. This technique maps each library to a fixed-length binary vector, effectively capturing the presence or absence of each library without unnecessarily inflating dimensionality.

Handling the missing value is also an important part of preprocessing, as many models do not support null input. Upon inspection, there are two missing values with each in a different feature. The missing value can be replaced by the mean or median value of the corresponding feature. Before replacing the missing value, histograms and boxplots of the features are plotted, to assess the distribution and skewness of each feature. The *LoadDYLIB* feature follows an approximately normal distribution but contains a few outliers, so the median value is used to replace the missing value. The *strsize* feature is heavily right-skewed, reinforcing the use of the median value as an appropriate replacement.

Several features exhibit high skewness, which can negatively impact the model stability and performance. To address this, a logarithmic transformation of the form $log(1+x)$ is applied to these features. This transformation compresses the range of large values and shifts the distribution closer to a normal distribution, reducing the influence of extreme values during training.

Following the transformation, some features still contained outliers, which are data points that significantly deviate from the overall distribution. These are addressed using the *Interquartile Range (IQR)* method [12]. Samples that fall outside the lower bound $(Q1 - 1.5 \times IQR)$ and the upper bound $(Q3 + 1.5 \times IQR)$ are removed from the dataset to improve data quality.

3.3   Feature Engineering

To improve model performance and reduce overfitting, various feature engineering techniques are applied, including feature selection and feature scaling. These steps help identify the most relevant features and standardize the data before training.

Several feature selection techniques are explored across all models except the CNN model, including **Variance Threshold, Rare Features Removal, Correlation-Based Feature Selection, and Chi-Square Selection** [13–15]. Variance Threshold removes features with low variance across data samples, as they provide little discriminative power. Rare Feature Removal filters out binary features that appear in only a small percentage of data samples, helping to reduce noise. Correlation-Based Feature Selection eliminates features that are highly correlated with others to reduce redundancy. Chi-Square Selection evaluates the dependency between each feature and the target class, selecting those with the highest relevance. These methods are applied to evaluate their impact on model performance and to determine the optimal feature configuration for each model. The effectiveness of each selection method is assessed based on accuracy, and the results are presented in the Evaluation section.

Feature scaling [16,17] is applied to all models except the CNN model. Although certain models, such as Decision Trees and Random Forests, are inherently invariant to the feature magnitudes, all models are evaluated with and without scaling to assess their impact on accuracy. Two scaling methods from Scikit-learn are explored: Standard Scaling, which standardizes the feature to have zero mean and unit variance, and Robust Scaling, which scales features using the median and interquartile range to reduce the influence of outliers.

3.4   Dataset Balancing

The CyberScienceLab dataset used in this study is imbalanced, containing significantly more benign samples than malware samples. To address this issue, the **Sythethic Minority Oversampling Technique (SMOTE)** [18,19] is applied. SMOTE generates synthetic samples for the minority class by interpolating between existing minority data points and their nearest neighbours. This method has been shown to improve the predictive performance for minority classes, as reported in previous studies. Unlike simple oversampling, SMOTE balances the class distribution without duplicating existing data, thereby reducing the risk of overfitting. It is applied after feature selection to ensure that the generated samples reflect the most informative features.

3.5   Synthetic Image Generation

The Synthetic Image Generation is applied only for the CNN model, which is trained on RGB images converted from structured feature vectors. Each sample has 82 features (69 binary, 13 continuous), normalized to [0, 255] via Min-Max scaling. To form the image, features are taken in sequence and grouped in sets of three, where each set becomes the red, green, and blue values of a single pixel. This process produces roughly 28 pixels, which are arranged into a 6×6 grid (36 pixels) by padding with 26 zeros, giving a fixed $6 \times 6 \times 3$ format. This structured image representation allows the CNN to learn spatial patterns from originally tabular data. To increase the amount of training data, CycleGAN is used to perform unpaired image-to-image translation between malware and benign domains, generating synthetic RGB samples.

3.6   Model Training and Validation

Training Strategy. For the five supervised learning models, including SVM, Decision Tree, Naïve Bayes, Random Forest, and Logistic Regression. This study is the *first* to apply **nested cross-validation** [23] on the CyberScienceLab dataset. A 10-fold outer loop estimates generalization performance, while a 5-fold inner loop tunes hyperparameters within the training portion of each outer fold, ensuring the outer test fold remains unseen during model selection.

The CNN model is trained on the RGB-transformed feature representation described in Sect. 3.5, using a compact two-layer convolutional architecture tailored for $6 \times 6 \times 3$ inputs. Training incorporates manual hyperparameter tuning (batch size, epochs, learning rate, dropout, weight decay), early stopping with lowest validation loss checkpointing, and a fixed 64%, 16%, 20% train/validation/test split. These design choices are optimised to capture spatial patterns from structured features while mitigating overfitting.

Hyperparameter Tuning. Hyperparameter tuning is applied to all models, except for the CNN model, which is manually tuned on a validation split due to computational constraints. The hyperparameter explored for each model are summarized in Table 1. Tuning is performed using grid search within the inner loop of nested cross-validation.

3.7   Evaluation Strategy

After the best hyperparameter configurations are selected through the inner loop of nested cross-validation, each final model is retrained on the full outer training set and evaluated on the corresponding test fold. This process is repeated across ten outer folds, ensuring that each fold is used as the test set exactly once. The final performance metrics are averaged across all outer folds to obtain a reliable estimate of generalization performance.

All models are evaluated using several multiple classification metrics, including accuracy, F1-score, confusion matrix, precision, recall, false positive rate (FPR), and area under the ROC curve (AUC score).

Table 1. Hyperparameter tuning ranges

Model	Hyperparameter	Values Explored
SVM	C	0.1, 1, 10, 100
	gamma	scale, 0.001, 0.01, 0.1, 1
	kernel	linear, rbf, poly
Decision Tree	max_depth	None, 5, 10, 15, 20
	min_samples_split	2, 5, 10
	min_samples_leaf	1, 2, 4
	criterion	gini, entropy
Naïve Bayes	var_smoothing	10^0 to 10^{-9}
Random Forest	n_estimators	100, 200
	max_depth	None, 10, 20
	min_samples_split	2, 5
	min_samples_leaf	1, 2
	max_features	sqrt, log2
Logistic Regression	C	0.01, 0.1, 1, 10, 100
	solver	saga, liblinear, lbfgs

Note: `scale` automatically calculates the gamma value based on feature variance.

`None` allows unlimited tree depth.

All solvers in Logistic Regression are used with L2 regularization.

The CNN model is evaluated using a separate held-out test set that remains unseen during training and validation. The best-performing model checkpoint, selected based on validation loss with early stopping, is used for final testing. In addition, several optimizers, including **Adam, SGD, Adagrad, and RMSprop**, are compared to assess their effect on performance.

Model comparisons are conducted in two parts. First, all models developed in this study are evaluated against one another using metrics such as accuracy, precision, recall, F1-score, AUC score, and false positive rate (FPR). Second, all models except the CNN model are compared with the corresponding models reported in prior studies on the same dataset, using only accuracy since other performance metrics are not consistently reported in literature.

4   Experimental Evaluation

This study evaluates six machine learning models for macOS malware detection. All models are assessed using a consistent set of evaluation metrics. Feature engineering significantly affects model performance, with the largest relative gain observed in Naïve Bayes, while Random Forest remains largely unaffecred due to its ability to handle redundant features via ensemble learning. The effectiveness of these techniques varies by model, as detailed in Table 2.

Table 2. Accuracy improvement from feature engineering techniques

Model	Feature Engineering Method	Before (%)	After (%)	Gain (%)
SVM	Rare Features Removal	98.56	98.88	+0.32
	Robust Scaling	98.40	98.88	+0.44
Decision Tree	Correlation-Based Selection	97.27	97.43	+0.16
	Robust Scaling	96.95	97.43	+0.48
Naïve Bayes	Correlation-Based Selection	93.40	95.17	+1.77
	Rare Features Removal	92.44	95.17	+2.73
Random Forest	Rare Features Removal	97.75	97.75	+0.00
	Variance Threshold	97.75	97.75	+0.00
	Correlation-Based Selection	97.75	97.75	+0.00
	Chi-Square Selection	97.75	97.75	+0.00
Logistic Reg.	Variance Threshold	97.59	97.91	+0.32
	Correlation-Based Selection	97.43	97.91	+0.48
	Robust Scaling	97.27	97.91	+0.64

For the CNN, four optimizers are compared under identical hyperparameters with **Adam** performing the best, achieving 96.21% accuracy, an AUC score of 0.9936, with the lowest FPR. The model also showed good generalization, misclassifying only six malware samples as benign in the test set. Feature maps and learned filters from the final model are examined to sanity-check what the network learned.

4.1   Models Comparison

All six supervised models developed in this study are evaluated using consistent experimental settings, allowing for direct comparison across multiple performance metrics. Among them, the Support Vector Machine (SVM) model achieves the highest accuracy of 98.88% with AUC score closes to 1. After the inspection, only one outer fold misclassified two benign samples as malware, while the rest achieved 100% accuracy. This result is likely due to its ability to create optimal boundaries to handle high-dimensional data with the help of SMOTE and advanced comprehensive workflow.

Logistic Regression and Random Forest also perform strongly, both exceeding 97% in accuracy. After applying Variance Threshold and Correlation-Based Feature Selection to remove redundant features, the Logistic Regression model benefited from stronger linear relationships among retained features. The Random Forest model outperformed the Decision Tree model even without scaling and feature selection used by Decision Tree model, likely because its ensemble learning structure helps reduce the variance and overfitting.

Naïve Bayes achieves the lowest accuracy of 95.17% among all models. Although Correlation-Based Feature Selection was applied to support the algorithm assumption and improve its performance by approximately 3%, it remains less effective than other models. This may be due to its underlying assumptions: Naïve Bayes presumes feature independence and Gaussian distribution, which are often violated in real-world malware datasets. In particular, the transformed numerical features derived from a categorical feature do not follow a normal distribution, potentially biasing the model's probability estimates. Furthermore, malware data frequently exhibits complex interdependencies, making Naïve Bayes less suitable for such detection tasks.

The CNN model, trained on RGB-transformed feature images, achieves an accuracy of 96.21% and an AUC score of 99.36%. While this indicates strong discriminative capability, its accuracy remains slightly below that of the top-performing models trained directly on structured data. This outcome suggests that, despite the use of image transformation and synthetic augmentation via CycleGAN, the spatial structure inferred from tabular features may not retain sufficient spatial correlations for CNNs to fully exploit.

Nevertheless, this study demonstrates that deep learning remains a viable approach even for limited datasets, provided that appropriate augmentation techniques are employed. CycleGAN proves effective in generating synthetic data to support CNN training. However, further exploration of alternative generative models may yield more diverse or semantically meaningful augmentations. Additionally, the dataset used is dated, which may affect the generalisability of results to newer macOS threats. Updating the dataset to reflect modern attack patterns would be a valuable direction for future research. These results suggests that well-optimized models trained on structured features can outperform more complex image-based classifiers when feature engineering and validation are rigorously applied. A summary of all models is presented in Table 3.

Table 3. Comparison of all models evaluated in this study

Model	Accuracy (%)	F1 (%)	Precision (%)	Recall (%)	FPR (%)	AUC	Rank
SVM	98.88	98.89	98.88	99.36	1.60	0.9995	1
Decision Tree	97.43	97.42	97.46	97.43	2.41	0.9741	4
Naïve Bayes	95.17	95.19	94.77	95.82	5.46	0.9851	6
Random Forest	97.75	97.77	97.54	98.07	2.57	0.9899	3
Logistic Regression	97.91	97.91	97.50	98.40	2.56	0.9973	2
CNN (Adam)	96.21	96.21	95.70	96.70	4.32	0.9936	5

Second comparison between all models except the CNN model against prior work using the same dataset. All models in this study outperformed previously reported. For example, the SVM model improves upon prior accuracy by over 5%, while Decision Tree and Naïve Bayes models also show meaningful gains. These improvements are attributed to the systematic application of feature selection techniques, robust preprocessing, and nested cross-validation with hyperparameter tuning. A summary of comparative results is presented in Table 4.

Table 4. Comparison of models between this study and prior studies

Model	Average Accuracy (%)	Best Accuracy from Prior Studies (%)	Improvement (%)	Prior Study Ref.
SVM	98.88	93.60	+5.28	[3]
Decision Tree	97.43	96.62	+0.81	[4]
Naïve Bayes	95.17	93.00	+2.17	[5]
Random Forest	97.75	95.00	+2.75	[5]
Logistic Regression	97.91	96.00	+1.91	[5]

Compared to Pajouh et al. [4], who reported increased false positive rates when using large synthetic datasets generated through SMOTE, this study achieves improved performance by integrating SMOTE with a comprehensive pipeline. These include outlier removal, skewed features transformed, Correlation-Based Feature Selection, and Robust Scaling, all of which help reduce noise and enhance generalization. As a result, the Decision Tree model in this study achieves a lower false positive rate of 2.57% and a higher overall accuracy. While there are slightly difference between the Decision Tree-J48 used by Pajouh [4] and the Decision Tree from the Scikit-learn library used in this study, the main difference is that Decision Tree-J48 allows splitting into more than two branches, while the Decision Tree from Scikit-learn only allows splitting into exactly two branches.

Similarly, although Bensaoud and Kalita [8] reported a CNN accuracy of 99.97% using RGB images derived from raw binary malware code, this study demonstrates that CNNs trained on structured static features converted into RGB format can also achieve competitive performance, as it reaches an accuracy of 95.21%.

5   Conclusion

In this study, six supervised machine learning models are developed using Cyber-ScienceLab macOS dataset. The models consist of Support Vector Machine (SVM), Decision Tree, Naïve Bayes. Random Forest, Logistic Regression, and Convolutional Neural Network (CNN), trained through comprehensive data pre-processing, feature engineering, balancing the dataset using SMOTE, and a nested cross-validation application. Their performance are compared with the same models reported in four previous studies using the same dataset [2–5]. This study shows that all models achieved improved accuracy compared to previous studies.

Among all models, SVM achieves the highest accuracy and AUC score. This highlighted that SVM can effectively handle high-dimensional malware data. The following models in performance are Logistic Regression, Random Forest, Decision Tree, CNN, and finally Naïve Bayes. Although Naïve Bayes achieves the lowest accuracy of 95.17%, it still has strong malware detection capability with an AUC score of 0.9851. Naïve Bayes' assumption of feature independence and Gaussian distribution has made it less effective than other models.

Structured static features were converted into RGB images for CNN model training. The CNN model achieves slightly lower accuracy compared to the SVM model. This indicates that the transformation of structured features into RGB images may not fully capture the complex patterns for CNN to train.

Several limitations identified in previous studies are addressed in this study. These include the feasibility of deep learning models on small dataset by applying cycleGAN to generate synthetic images, the absence of hyperparameter tuning, and the lack of a combination of several feature selection methods for every model.

Overall, this study highlights that a well-performed machine learning pipeline, combined with robust data preprocessing and feature engineering, can outperform deep learning approaches in malware detection tasks on structured datasets. Since static analysis with SVM can also obtain a high accuracy above 98%, future research could apply the same data preprocessing and feature selection methodology to newer static macOS malware datasets to evaluate generalization. Additionally, integrating the latest real-world malware samples into the models could further validate these models. Future work could also explore different types of GANs to improve the CNN model's performance on a small dataset, investigate the performance of more traditional image classification neural network architectures on the same task, incorporate time detection to evaluate models' efficiency in real-world deployment scenarios, and introduce additional features to strengthen detection performance while enhancing the novelty of the approach.

References

1. StatCounter Global Stats: Desktop Operating System Market Share Worldwide. https://gs.statcounter.com/os-market-share/desktop/worldwide/#monthly-200901-201909. Accessed 02 Dec 2024
2. Chen, A.C., Wulff, K.: Machine learning for OSX malware detection. In: Choo, K.-K.R., Dehghantanha, A. (eds.) Handbook of Big Data Analytics and Forensics, pp. 209–222. Springer, Cham (2022). https://doi.org/10.1007/978-3-030-74753-4_14
3. Gharghasheh, S.E., Hadayeghparast, S.: Mac OS X malware detection with supervised machine learning algorithms. In: Choo, K.-K.R., Dehghantanha, A. (eds.) Handbook of Big Data Analytics and Forensics, pp. 193–208. Springer, Cham (2022). https://doi.org/10.1007/978-3-030-74753-4_13
4. Pajouh, H.H., Dehghantanha, A., Khayami, R., Choo, K.-K.R.: Intelligent OS X malware threat detection with code inspection. J. Comput. Virol. Hacking Tech. 14(3), 213–223. https://doi.org/10.1007/s11416-017-0307-5
5. Sahoo, D., Dhawan, Y.: Evaluation of supervised and unsupervised machine learning classifiers for Mac OS malware detection. In: Choo, K.-K.R., Dehghantanha, A. (eds.) Handbook of Big Data Analytics and Forensics, pp. 159–175. Springer, Cham (2022). https://doi.org/10.1007/978-3-030-74753-4_11
6. Thaeler, A., Yigit, Y., Maglaras, L., Buchanan, W.J., Moradpoor, N., Russell, G.: Enhancing Mac OS malware detection through machine learning and Mach-O file analysis. In: IEEE 28th International Workshop on Computer Aided Modeling and Design of Communication Links and Networks (CAMAD), pp. 170–175. IEEE. https://doi.org/10.1109/CAMAD59638.2023.10478430

7. Pham, D.P., Vu, D.L., Massacci, F.: Mac-A-Mal: macOS malware analysis framework resistant to anti evasion techniques. J. Comput. Virol. Hacking Tech. **15**, 249–257. https://doi.org/10.1007/s11416-019-00335-w

8. Bensaoud, A., Kalita, J.: Deep multi-task learning for malware image classification. J. Inf. Secur. Appl. **64**, 103057. https://doi.org/10.1016/j.jisa.2021.103057

9. Aslan, Ö., Yilmaz, A.A : A new malware classification framework based on deep learning algorithms. IEEE Access **9**, 87936–87951. https://doi.org/10.1109/ACCESS.2021.3089586

10. CyberScience Lab: macOS Malware and Benign Dataset. https://github.com/CyberScienceLab/Our-Datasets/tree/master/OSX. Accessed 02 Dec 2024

11. Mujacmsigai, M.: Different Types of Encoding Methods for Your Dataset. https://medium.com/@mujacmsigai/different-types-of-encoding-methods-for-your-dataset-4b4f1a3b7823. Accessed 10 Mar 2025

12. Patil, P.: Outlier Detection and Removal using the IQR Method. https://medium.com/@pp1222001/outlier-detection-and-removal-using-the-iqr-method-6fab2954315d. Accessed 03 Mar 2025

13. Scikit-Learn Developers: Feature Selection. https://scikit-learn.org/stable/modules/feature_selection.html. Accessed 22 Feb 2025

14. Scikit-Learn Developers: VarianceThreshold in Feature Selection. https://scikit-learn.org/stable/modules/generated/sklearn.feature_selection.VarianceThreshold.html. Accessed 22 Feb 2025

15. Medium Data Science: Chi-Square Test for Feature Selection in Machine Learning. https://medium.com/data-science/chi-square-test-for-feature-selection-in-machine-learning-206b1f058223. Accessed 24 Feb 2019

16. Pickl, S.: What is Feature Scaling and Why Does Machine Learning Need It? https://medium.com/@shivanipickl/what-is-feature-scaling-and-why-does-machine-learning-need-it-104eedebb1c9. Accessed 27 Feb 2025

17. Mahamulkar, P.: Feature Scaling Using Standardization, Normalization and Robust Scaling. https://medium.com/@prasadmahamulkar/feature-scaling-using-standardization-normalization-and-robust-scaling-cb333f943f70. Accessed 27 Feb 2025

18. Maklin, C.: Synthetic Minority Over-sampling Technique (SMOTE). https://medium.com/@corymaklin/synthetic-minority-over-sampling-technique-smote-7d419696b88c. Accessed 27 Feb 2025

19. Imbalanced-Learn Developers: SMOTE Class for Oversampling in imbalanced-learn: API Documentation. https://imbalanced-learn.org/stable/references/generated/imblearn.over_sampling.SMOTE.html. Accessed 27 Feb 2025

20. Google Developers: Generative Adversarial Networks (GANs). https://developers.google.com/machine-learning/gan. Accessed 02 Dec 2024

21. Viso.ai: CycleGAN Explained: Image Translation with GANs. https://viso.ai/deep-learning/cyclegan/#elementor-toc__heading-anchor-0. Accessed 18 Mar 2025

22. Zhu, J.-Y., Park, T., Isola, P., Efros, A.A.: pytorch-CycleGAN-and-pix2pix. https://github.com/junyanz/pytorch-CycleGAN-and-pix2pix. Accessed 13 Mar 2025

23. Kumar, A.: Python – Nested Cross Validation for Algorithm Selection. https://vitalflux.com/python-nested-cross-validation-algorithm-selection/. Accessed 01 Mar 2025

Insights into Learning Broadcast Protocols
(Short Paper)

Dana Fisman[1], Noa Izsak[1,2](✉), and Swen Jacobs[2]

[1] Ben Gurion University, Beer-Sheva, Israel
`dana@bgu.ac.il`, `izsak@post.bgu.ac.il`
[2] CISPA Helmholtz Center for Information Security, Saarbrücken, Germany
`jacobs@cispa.de`

Abstract. Broadcast protocols (BPs) are a formal model of distributed systems with an unbounded number of processes communicating through broadcasts. We study the problem of passively learning BPs from execution traces, focusing on the class of *fine BPs* which does not have hidden states and admits a cutoff. We present a passive learning algorithm with a constraint-based approach that guarantees consistency with the sample, and returns a minimal equivalent BP if the sample is sufficiently complete (i.e., subsumes a characteristic set). Furthermore, we describe *LeoParDS*, the first tool that implements these techniques, supporting the practical inference of fine BPs, as well as tasks that include sample generation and approximate equivalence checking.

This work was previously published at AAAI'24 [8] and later implemented at ATVA'24 [12]. We summarize its main results here to foster discussion within the cybersecurity and verification community. This short paper is intended as a concise overview for readers unfamiliar with both prior publications.

Keywords: Learning Theory · Broadcast Protocols · Multiagent Systems

1 Introduction

Learning computational models has long attracted interest in artificial intelligence and formal verification, e.g., [1,9,15]. In particular, concurrent computational models pose significant challenges for learning due to their succinctness and the absence of canonical minimal representations. While previous learning techniques have addressed models with a fixed number of processes (such as communicating automata [3], workflow Petri nets [7], and negotiation protocols [14]), they fall short for parameterized protocols, which are required to work correctly for *any* number of processes.

Broadcast protocols (BPs) are an expressive class of concurrent models with synchronous broadcast communication. They have previously been considered in

---

D. Fisman, N. Izsak and S. Jacobs—Contributed equally.

A. Akavia et al. (Eds.): CSCML 2025, LNCS 16244, pp. 306–313, 2026.
https://doi.org/10.1007/978-3-032-10759-6_20

the context of parameterized verification [4,6], where one seeks correctness guarantees for all system sizes. In parameterized verification, the notion of a cutoff provides a promising way to reduce the reasoning about infinitely many system instances to a finite-size representative. However, the application of cutoff concepts within a learning framework for BPs had not previously been explored.

Our work proposes a learning framework for BPs under two conditions: (1) the BP has no hidden states, and (2) there exists a cutoff (i.e., a number beyond which its language stabilizes). We call these *fine* BPs, and note that many broadcast protocols satisfy these constraints, making this a meaningful target class. Our main contributions are as follows.

- A constraint-based passive learning algorithm for fine BPs, using SMT solver to infer models from execution traces.
- Hardness results showing that consistency is an NP-hard problem, characteristic sets may be exponentially large, and fine BPs are not polynomially predictable under standard cryptographic assumptions.
- Implementation of these techniques in the tool *LeoParDS*, supporting sample generation, random BP synthesis, and approximate equivalence checking.

These results extend previous learning frameworks by not requiring a fixed system size or a known cutoff, thus introducing a new way of passive learning for parameterized concurrent models. For complete and detailed proofs, please refer to "Learning Broadcast Protocols" (AAAI 2024) publication [8], and for implementation details, see the "Learning Broadcast Protocols with LeoParDS" (ATVA 2024) paper [12].

2   Preliminaries

This section briefly recalls key definitions from [8,11,12] for self-containment.

Broadcast Protocols (BPs). Broadcast protocols (BPs) [5,6] are finite-state systems that use synchronous broadcast messages. Formally, a BP $\mathcal{B} = (S, s_0, L, R)$ consists of a finite state set S with initial state $s_0 \in S$, a set of labels $L = \{a!!, a??|a \in A\}$ for a finite set of actions A, where $a!!$ is a *broadcast sending transition* and $a??$ is a *broadcast receiving transition* (or *response*), and a transition relation $R \subseteq S \times L \times S$. All processes execute the same protocol, $\mathcal{B}$, and the system with n identical processes is denoted $\mathcal{B}^n$. A global step consists of *one* process broadcasting a (taking an $a!!$ transition) while all others respond simultaneously (taking an $a??$ transition). Processes can always respond, yet at any step only a single action is broadcasted. States with no outgoing sending transitions are called *hidden*; in this work, we focus on BPs without hidden states, which is a mild restriction.

Semantics and Cutoffs. The semantics of $\mathcal{B}^n$ can be expressed by tracking how processes move between the states when a broadcast action occurs. Feasible words in $\mathcal{B}^n$ form the language $L(\mathcal{B}^n)$, and the language of the protocol $\mathcal{B}$ is: $L(\mathcal{B}) = \bigcup_{n \in \mathbb{N}} L(\mathcal{B}^n)$. A word $w \in A^*$ is feasible in $\mathcal{B}^n$ if there exists an execution trace of $\mathcal{B}^n$ based on the sequence of actions w.

A BP, $\mathcal{B}$, has a *cutoff* c if its language stabilizes for all $n \geq c$, that is, $L(\mathcal{B}^n) = L(\mathcal{B}^c)$ for any $n \geq c$. If a BP has a cutoff and no hidden states, we call it a *fine BP*. Two BPs are equivalent if they accept the same language. We note that minimal fine BPs (and thus BPs in general) are not unique up to isomorphism (see Fig. 1 for an example).

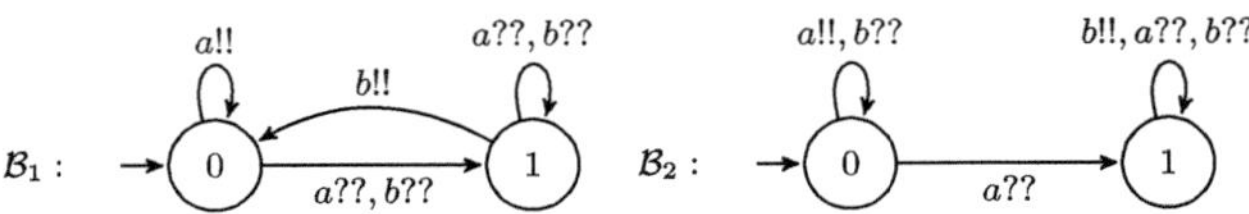

Fig. 1. Two non-isomorphic minimal fine BPs: $L(\mathcal{B}_1) = L(\mathcal{B}_2) = a(a \cup b)^*$.

Learning Problems. We consider the following learning problems for BPs. A *sample* is a set of labeled words that indicates their feasibility/infeasibility in $\mathcal{B}^n$. The key questions are:

- **Inference:** Given a consistent sample, infer a BP consistent with it.
- **Consistency:** Is there a BP with at most k states consistent with a sample.
- **Polynomial Data:** Can characteristic sets be of polynomial size?
- **Polynomial Predictability:** Can a learner classify unknown words with high probability after polynomially many queries?

Further algebraic details of transition matrices and state vectors along with detailed definitions, including the formal language of membership and draw queries, appear in our full version [8].

3   Properties of Broadcast Protocols

This section summarizes key properties of broadcast protocols needed for our learning results. First, note that the language of any BP is prefix-closed, and adding processes can only increase feasible behaviors:

Lemma 1 (Prefix-closedness and Monotonicity [8]). *If $\mathcal{B}$ is a BP, then $L(\mathcal{B})$ is prefix-closed. Moreover, $L(\mathcal{B}^k) \subseteq L(\mathcal{B}^\ell)$ for all $\ell > k$.*

Second, BPs exhibit a type of progressive growth across process counts:

Lemma 2 (Step-by-step Progress [8]). *Let $w \in A^*$, $a \in A$, and $m < n$. If $w \in L(\mathcal{B}^m)$ and $wa \notin L(\mathcal{B}^m)$, yet $wa \in L(\mathcal{B}^n)$, then $wa \in L(\mathcal{B}^{m+1})$.*

Third, even though fine BPs do not have a unique canonical minimal representation (see Fig. 1), there is a consistent correspondence among their states:

Lemma 3 (Relation Between Minimal Equivalent Fine BPs [8]). *Let $\mathcal{B}_1$ and $\mathcal{B}_2$ be minimal fine BPs with $L(\mathcal{B}_1) = L(\mathcal{B}_2)$. Then for every $m \in \mathbb{N}$, it holds that $L(\mathcal{B}_1^m) = L(\mathcal{B}_2^m)$ and there is a bijection between their states that preserve the sets of enabled sending actions, and their reachable configurations are consistent under this bijection.*

These results lay the foundation for the inference algorithm described in Sect. 4.

4   Inferring a BP from a Sample

This section summarizes the inference algorithm developed in our previous work [8, 12] for learning fine broadcast protocols from samples. Full technical details and proofs are given in that extended version.

Given a sample $\mathcal{S}$ of labeled traces, the algorithm $\mathfrak{I}$ constructs a BP $\mathcal{B}_\mathcal{S}$ consistent with $\mathcal{S}$. Its key idea is to encode constraints on partial functions:

- $f^{\mathsf{st}} : A \to S$, mapping each action to the state enabling its broadcast;
- $f^{!!} : A \to S$, giving the post-broadcast state;
- $f_a^{??} : S \to S$ for each $a \in A$, $s \in S$, specifying where receivers go on a.

These functions define the transition relation of $\mathcal{B}_\mathcal{S}$. The sample provides positive and negative examples of feasible words with various amounts of process counts, allowing constraints to rule out inconsistent states and to ensure specification satisfaction. In essence, the algorithm ensures:

- Consistency with positive example (i.e., with feasible words),
- Rejection of negative example,
- No hidden states,
- Partitioning of actions among states to match the observed behavior.

The resulting constraints are encoded in the theory of equality with uninterpreted functions (EUF) and can be solved with standard SMT solvers. A sample-consistent valuation defines a BP consistent with $\mathcal{S}$.

Theorem 1 (Correctness [8]**).** *Let $\mathcal{S}$ be a sample consistent with some fine BP. Then any $\mathcal{B}_\mathcal{S}$ satisfying the constraints is consistent with $\mathcal{S}$.*

The full constraint definitions, the induction-based correctness proof appear in [8] and the SMT encoding appear in [12] for completeness.

Corollary 1 ([8]**).** *Algorithm $\mathfrak{I}$ is a sound inference algorithm for fine BPs and can be implemented using existing SMT tools.*

5   Returning a Minimal BP

This section summarizes how a sufficiently complete sample allows returning a minimal equivalent BP, rather than just any consistent one.

We define a *characteristic set* (CS) for a fine BP $\mathcal{B}$ as a sample (a finite set) rich enough to capture the BP behavioral properties, that is, fully separate its states and transitions. We provide a constructive algorithm $\mathfrak{G}$ that explores a finite unfolding of feasible traces (via a prefix-tree-like exploration) to produce such a CS. Intuitively, $\mathfrak{G}$ explores all feasible words up to the cutoff (which is detected on the fly). It labels each node with reachable state-vectors, and terminates once the exploration stabilizes (i.e., the cutoff is detected).

Theorem 2 (Minimal BP Recovery [8]). *For any minimal fine BP $\mathcal{B}$, there exists a characteristic set $\mathcal{S}_B$ such that an inference algorithm $\mathfrak{A}$, given any sample subsuming $\mathcal{S}_B$, returns a minimal fine-BP equivalent to $\mathcal{B}$.*

Unfortunately, characteristic sets may be exponentially large:

Theorem 3 (CS Lower Bound [8]). *There exists a family of fine BPs with no characteristic set of polynomial size.*

A consequence of this construction is that fine BPs can be exponentially more succinct than the minimal DFA for the same language:

Corollary 2 ([8]). *There exists a family of fine BPs whose minimal equivalent DFA is exponentially larger.*

These results clarify the sample complexity limits to achieve minimal inference of fine BPs. The complete construction details and proofs are given in [8].

6   Consistency is NP-Hard for Fine BPs

We show that deciding BP consistency is NP-hard, even for fine-BPs. While DFA consistency is known to be NP-hard [10], a DFA is not a special case of a fine BP; however, a fine-BP can simulate any DFA with a modest overhead.

Figure 2 illustrates the key construction. It embeds the DFA states into a BP states and uses additional broadcast transitions to capture accepting/rejecting behavior while maintaining no hidden states. Extra symbols (i, \$, $\top$, $\bot$, x) coordinate the simulation, and projections recover the original DFA language.

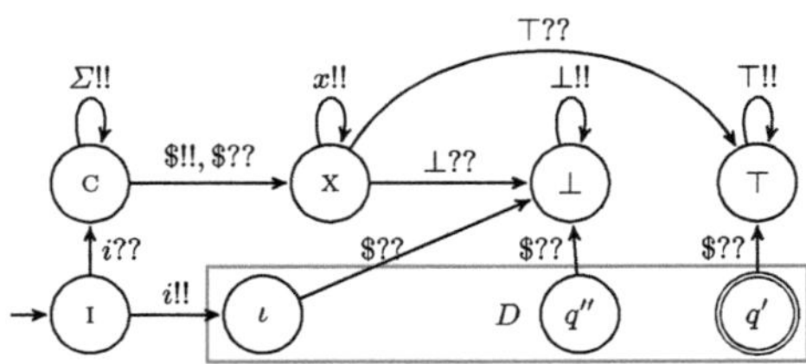

Fig. 2. Reduction from DFA-consistency to BP-consistency.

Lemma 4 (BP Simulation of DFA [8]). *Any nontrivial regular language L over Σ with DFA of n states can be simulated by a fine BP with at most $n + 5$ states so that the feasible BP words project back to L.*

This simulation enables a reduction from DFA-consistency:

Theorem 4 ([8]). *BP consistency is NP-hard.*

The reduction is polynomial and it preserves the feasibility (or infeasibility) of words under the mentioned projection. See the extended version [8] for a full construction and an alternative reduction from all-eq-SAT [13].

Furthermore, since the feasibility of a word $w \in A^*$ in $\mathcal{B}^n$ can be checked in polynomial time, BP-consistency is NP-complete.

Corollary 3 ([8]). *BP consistency is NP-complete.*

7   Polynomial Predictability

Finally, we discuss the predictability of fine BPs under the polynomial-predictability learning paradigm which is an active learning problem. Roughly speaking, a class $\mathcal{C}$ is *polynomially predictable* if there is a learner that, given polynomially many membership or draw queries, can predict the membership of a random test word with high accuracy. See Angluin and Kharitonov [2] for formal background.

We show that under standard cryptographic assumptions, fine BPs are not polynomially predictable. The key idea is a reduction from the intersection of DFAs, known to be polynomially-unpredictable in this sense. Our construction uses a BP that simulates multiple DFAs concurrently, routing one process per DFA to its initial state, while controlling the alphabet via an additional broadcast controller, as shown in Fig. 3.

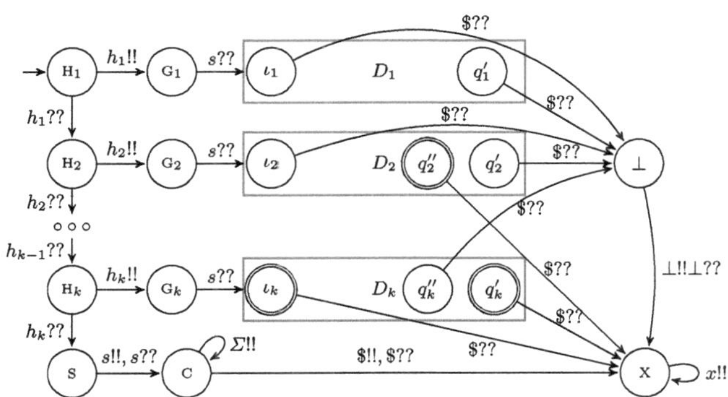

Fig. 3. A BP simulating intersection of k DFAs.

Theorem 5 (Predictability Lower Bound [8]). *Assuming the hardness of quadratic residuosity, RSA inversion, or factoring Blum integers, BPs are not polynomially predictable with membership queries.*

The proof is for *fine*-BPs, but thus follows for broadcast protocols, in general. The reduction follows Angluin and Kharitonov's classical techniques [2], adapting them to broadcast-based models.

8   Conclusion

This paper summarized our investigation into the learnability of fine broadcast protocols, the first framework for learning concurrent models without assuming a fixed number of processes. On the positive side, we presented a passive inference algorithm capable of returning a consistent BP, and even a minimal equivalent BP given a sufficiently complete sample. On the negative side, we showed that consistency is NP-hard, characteristic sets can be exponentially large, and fine BPs are not polynomially predictable.

To bridge theory and practice, we implemented these methods in *LeoParDS*, the first tool for learning broadcast protocols in a parameterized setting. LeoParDS supports characteristic set generation, random sample and BP generation, equivalence checking, and demonstrates that these learning techniques can be applied in practice despite their worst-case theoretical complexity[1]. Full details and experimental results are provided in [12].

Acknowledgment. Noa Izsak carried out this work in part as a member of the Saarbrücken Graduate School of Computer Science.

References

1. Angluin, D.: Learning regular sets from queries and counterexamples. Inf. Comput. **75**(2), 87–106 (1987)
2. Angluin, D., Kharitonov, M.: When won't membership queries help? J. Comput. Syst. Sci. **50**(2), 336–355 (1995)
3. Bollig, B., Katoen, J., Kern, C., Leucker, M.: Learning communicating automata from MSCs. IEEE Trans. Software Eng. **36**(3), 390–408 (2010)
4. Emerson, E.A., Namjoshi, K.S.: Automatic verification of parameterized synchronous systems. In: Alur, R., Henzinger, T.A. (eds.) Computer Aided Verification, pp. 87–98 (1996)
5. Emerson, E.A., Namjoshi, K.S.: On model checking for non-deterministic infinite-state systems. In: LICS, pp. 70–80. IEEE Computer Society (1998)
6. Esparza, J., Finkel, A., Mayr, R.: On the verification of broadcast protocols. In: LICS, pp. 352–359 (1999)
7. Esparza, J., Leucker, M., Schlund, M.: Learning workflow petri nets. Fundam. Informaticae **113**(3–4), 205–228 (2011)
8. Fisman, D., Izsak, N., Jacobs, S.: Learning broadcast protocols. In: Proceedings of the 38th Annual AAAI Conference on Artificial Intelligence, Vancouver, Canada, vol. 11, pp. 12016–12023 (2024)
9. Gold, E.M.: Language identification in the limit. Inf. Control **10**(5), 447–474 (1967)
10. Gold, E.M.: Complexity of automaton identification from given data. Inf. Control **37**(3), 302–320 (1978)
11. Izsak, N.: Learning broadcast protocol. Master's thesis, Ben-Gurion University of the Negev, Beer-Sheva, Israel (2023). https://primo.bgu.ac.il/permalink/972BGU_INST/23v028/alma9927020902704361

---

[1] The tool is available online by GitHub or Zenodo (DOI 10.5281/zenodo.10968037).

12. Izsak, N., Fisman, D., Jacobs, S.: Learning broadcast protocols with leopards. In: Akshay, S., Niemetz, A., Sankaranarayanan, S. (eds.) Automated Technology for Verification and Analysis, pp. 220–234. Springer, Cham (2025)
13. Lingg, J., de Oliveira Oliveira, M., Wolf, P.: Learning from positive and negative examples: new proof for binary alphabets. Inf. Process. Lett. **183**, 106427 (2024)
14. Muscholl, A., Walukiewicz, I.: Active learning for sound negotiations. In: LICS 2022, pp. 21:1–21:12 (2022)
15. Vaandrager, F.W.: Model learning. Commun. ACM **60**(2), 86–95 (2017)

Predictive Enhancement of RBAC Policies Using Access Log Analytics
(Short Paper)

Shmuel Amour[1] and Ehud Gudes[1,2(✉)]

[1] Department of Mathematics and Computer Science, The Open University,
Raanana, Israel
shmuel.amour@openu.ac.il
[2] Department of Computer Science, Ben-Gurion University of the Negev,
Beer-Sheva, Israel
ehudgu@openu.ac.il

Abstract. Access control is vital for protecting organizational resources, with Role-based access control (RBAC) offering a widely adopted framework for managing permissions. However, static role assignments in traditional RBAC systems often become misaligned with evolving organizational structures and user behaviors, leading to inefficiencies and potential security risks. This paper explores a predictive enhancement to RBAC policies by analyzing historical access logs using Hierarchical Clustering (HCL) techniques. The proposed approach uncovers behavioral access patterns to support data-driven refinement of role assignments. By incorporating behavioral clustering into access control workflows, the method helps align permissions with observed usage trends and may reduce excessive privilege assignments. Evaluation on a real-world dataset demonstrates that the model adapts roles based on access behavior, offering a step toward more responsive and behavior-aware access governance.

Keywords: Role-Based Access Control (RBAC) · Predictive Access Control · Hierarchical Clustering · Access Log Analytics · Machine Learning

1 Introduction

Access control ensures that only authorized users can interact with sensitive organizational resources. Among existing models, RBAC is widely adopted for its structured permission assignment via user-role associations. However, static RBAC policies often become misaligned with evolving responsibilities, increasing security risks and administrative overhead.

This work addresses these limitations by proposing a predictive enhancement to RBAC, based on **historical access logs** and **hierarchical clustering**. The approach analyzes user and resource behavior to refine role definitions and access decisions dynamically. By clustering similar access patterns, the model identifies behavior-based groupings and supports threshold-driven approval scoring using the Approval Ratio (APRV).

Key contributions include:

- A predictive RBAC model guided by behavioral clustering of access logs.
- A dual-model approach modeling both managers and resources.
- A threshold-based decision mechanism using APRV scores for access prediction.
- Experimental evaluation on real-world access logs, showing effective role adaptation (Fig. 1).

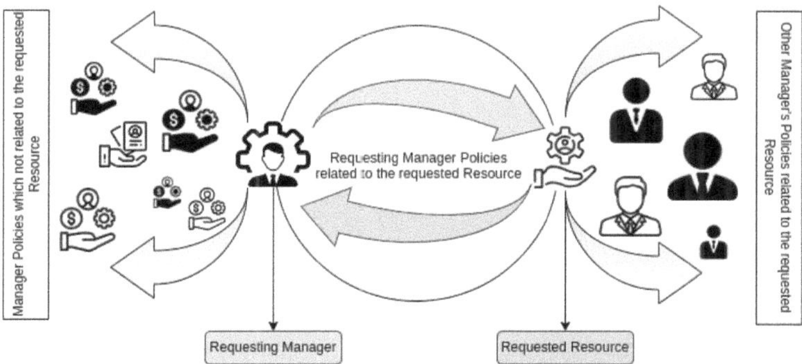

Fig. 1. Manager-Resource Access Policy Model

This research builds on our previous ABAC-focused study [1] and extends the methodology to RBAC, offering a data-driven framework for adaptive role refinement.

Paper Outline: Section 2 discusses related work. Section 3 presents the model. Section 4 evaluates the approach, and Sect. 5 concludes.

2 Background and Related Work

RBAC and Role Mining. RBAC is widely used for permission management but becomes challenging to maintain in dynamic environments. Role Mining (RMin) techniques extract roles from access logs to reduce manual policy engineering. Mitra and Sural [7] categorized key RMin approaches—such as clustering-based, rule-based, matrix factorization, and genetic algorithms—highlighting their tradeoffs and the need for adaptability in evolving organizations.

Hybrid models incorporating Attribute-based access control (ABAC) into RBAC frameworks have been proposed to support more dynamic decisions [3].

Other works emphasize the need for continuous role validation to prevent privilege escalation in large organizations [4].

Predictive Enhancements to RBAC. Traditional RBAC suffers from static role definitions that can result in overprovisioning or underprovisioning. Researchers have proposed machine learning-driven methods to address this. For example, Argento et al. [2] introduced a behavioral model for refining RBAC policies using access patterns. Similarly, Bertino [4] and Sanders and Yue [8] emphasized dynamic policy adaptation and log-based detection of excessive permissions.

Clustering and Role Adaptation. Hierarchical clustering has been explored as a technique for identifying behavioral groups in access control systems [10]. While effective, these methods may struggle with high-dimensional data. Kunz [6] proposed an adaptive identity and access management (IAM) framework where access policies evolve in response to observed behavior. These trends reflect a broader move toward role models that adapt automatically to usage patterns.

This paper builds on these foundations and extends our prior ABAC-focused work [1]. We propose a predictive RBAC model that uses hierarchical clustering of access logs to guide adaptive role refinement.

3   Predictive RBAC Policy Model

Dynamic access environments—where user roles, projects, and resource needs frequently shift—challenge the effectiveness of static RBAC policies. To address this, we propose a behavior-aware model that leverages historical access data to form hierarchical clusters of users and resources. Incoming access requests are evaluated against these clusters using a *default-deny* strategy to minimize over-permission and improve contextual alignment.

Predictive Access Control in RBAC: Our method groups users and resources by behavioral similarity using hierarchical clustering on historical access logs. Each new request is assessed against existing clusters to determine the likelihood of approval. The decision process considers three possible outcomes. A ***Full Match*** occurs when the request fully aligns with a known access pattern, in which case access is granted. A ***Partial Match*** is identified when the request shares key features with previously observed behavior, allowing for conditional approval based on similarity thresholds. If the request does not sufficiently match any known cluster, it is treated as a ***No Match***, and access is denied.

This logic enables adaptive decisions based on empirical usage, allowing RBAC policies to evolve in response to real-world behavior patterns.

RBAC Adaptation with Clustering: We model the organization as a hierarchy of managers, users, and resources, with access events defined by structured actions. To identify behavioral patterns, we apply hierarchical clustering (HCL) to group users and resources based on historical access similarity. The clustering process begins with individual entities and iteratively merges them using a defined distance metric. The resulting dendrograms [5] visualize these behavioral structures, allowing administrators to refine roles based on observed usage rather than predefined assignments.

Each access request is treated as a tuple consisting of manager ID, resource ID, action, and other relevant attributes:

$$Access\text{-}request = (\texttt{mgr\_id, rsc\_id, action, other\_features}\ldots)$$

Clustering is performed using selected features from the labeled Amazon Access Samples dataset [11], as detailed in Table 1. This structure-driven approach enables policy alignment with real-world behavior and supports data-informed adaptation of RBAC roles.

RBAC Model Generation via Clustering: We construct a dynamic RBAC model by applying hierarchical clustering (HCL) separately to manager and resource behaviors. For each axis, unique `Manager-ID` and `Resource-ID` values are extracted from access logs and clustered based on behavioral similarity. The result is a structured forest of hierarchical trees that reflect real-world organizational behavior. All clustering is performed using the labeled Amazon Access Samples dataset [11]. Table 1 lists the core attributes selected for clustering. These features represent both organizational roles and behavioral indicators such as approval trends. The model also derives aggregated cluster-level metrics used for access prediction.

A key component of the model is the Approval Factor (Approval Factor (APRV)), which quantifies the likelihood of access being approved within a given cluster:

$$AF_{cls} = \frac{NGrnt_{cls}}{Size_{cls}} \tag{1}$$

where $NGrnt_{cls}$ is the number of granted requests and $Size_{cls}$ is the total number of requests in the cluster. The APRV score supports threshold-based access decisions and contributes to fine-grained policy adaptation.

Data Preparation for Hierarchical RBAC: Before clustering, we filter and encode access log records to build a structured training set. The process accepts four inputs: a raw training dataset, model type (manager or resource), entity ID, and a selected feature set. Records are filtered by entity ID and reduced to relevant attributes. Categorical features are one-hot encoded to prevent misleading proximities and to enable distance-based clustering.

In addition to input features, derived attributes are initialized to support clustering and prediction. These include `APP_RATIO` (based on access labels), `DISTANCE` (initially zero), and `AUDIENCE` (set to one per entry). The output consists of a feature-rich training dataset and its one-hot encoded version, which are used in subsequent clustering steps.

Algorithm 1 summarizes the full data preparation pipeline.

Table 1. Selected Features for Clustering

Feature Name	Description and Importance	Feature Source
Manager Id (MGR ID)	Unique identifier for the user's manager or supervisory entity	DataSet
Resource Id (RSC ID)	Unique identifier for the resource entity	DataSet
Action (ACT)	Represents the outcome of the access request (granted/denied). Used for model training but excluded from predictions	DataSet
RollUp 1 (R1), RollUp 2 (R2)	Hierarchical groupings that define organizational structures, influencing access policies	DataSet
Department (DEPT)	User's department, relevant for department-specific access control policies	DataSet
Business Title (BT), Business Title Detail (BTD)	User's job title and additional business role details, essential for role-based permissions	DataSet
Job Code (JC)	Job function code, categorizing users into functional roles	DataSet
Company (CO)	Organization affiliation, useful in multi-entity access control settings	DataSet
Job Family (JF)	Job family grouping, capturing broad access patterns	DataSet
Distance (DIST)	A measure of how dissimilar or far apart two data points (or clusters) are, guiding which observations get merged at each step of the hierarchy	Hierarchical Clustering Compute
Audience (AUD)	The size or share of each cluster's data points	Hierarchical Clustering Compute
Approval Factor (APRV)	Measurement of likelihood of granting access	Hierarchical Clustering Compute

---

Algorithm 1. Data Preparation

```
Input   : TrainDataset, ModelType, EntityId, SelectedFeatures
Output: TreeDataset, TreeHotKeyDataset
1  FilterQuery ← "{ModelType } == {EntityId }";
2  TreeDataset ← TrainDataset.filter(FilterQuery);
3  TreeDataset ← TrainDataset.select(SelectedFeatures);
4  SelectedFeaturesHotKey ← SelectedFeatures.remove(ACTION);
5  TreeHotKeyDataset ← get_dummies(TreeDataset, SelectedFeaturesHotKey);
   // We extend 'TreeDataset ' with additional features.
6  TreeDataset ['APP_RATIO'] ← TreeDataset ['ACTION'];
7  TreeDataset ['DISTANCE'] ← 0;
8  TreeDataset ['AUDIENCE'] ← 1;
9  return TreeDataset, TreeHotKeyDataset;
```

Cluster Formation with a Linkage Matrix: Algorithm 2 describes the clustering procedure, which constructs a **Linkage Matrix** from the encoded access dataset. Each row in the matrix represents a merge operation between two clusters, capturing merge distance and resulting cluster size [9]. This structure supports the formation of behavioral hierarchies and enables access policy refinement based on similarity.

We apply average linkage with cosine distance to guide the merging process. The result is a hierarchical clustering tree that reflects similarity in historical access behavior. As clusters are formed, we derive additional metadata—such as approval ratios and match counts—for each internal node. These features are consolidated into the **ExTreeDataset**, which supports downstream decision-making and adaptive policy modeling.

Algorithm 2. Hierarchical Clustering Extended

```
Input  : TreeHotKeyDataset, TreeDataset
Output : ExTreeDataset, LinkageMatrixDataset
1  LinkageMatrix ← linkage.(TreeHotKeyDataset, method='average', metric="cosine")
2  LinkageMatrixDataset ← DataFrame(LinkageMatrix, columns=['node_a', 'node_b', 'dist','audi'])
3  TreeDatasetDict ← to_dict(TreeDataset);
4  foreach entry ∈ LinkageMatrixDataset do
5  |    node_a, node_b, dist, audi ← get_record_data(entry);
6  |      node_a_record ← get_record(node_a, TreeDatasetDict);
7  |      node_b_record ← get_record(node_b, TreeDatasetDict);
8  |      total_audience ← node_a_record["Audience"] + node_b_record["Audience"];
9  |      approved_ratio ← ((node_a_record["Action"] * node_a_record["Audience"]) +
   |      (node_b_record["Action"] * node_b_record["Audience"])) / total_audience;
10 |      shared_attributes := // if the attribute value on both nodes is the same keep it,
   |        otherwise set nan
11 |    shared_attributes["MATCH_COUNT"] := // no' matched nan attr
12 |    shared_attributes["ALLOW_ARRAY"] := // allowed ids
13 |    shared_attributes["DENY_ARRAY"] "= // denied ids
14 |    shared_attributes["APP_RATIO"] ← approved_ratio;
15 |      shared_attributes['QUERY'] ← build_query_string(shared_attributes);
16 |      append_to_dict(TreeDatasetDict, shared_attributes);
17 end
18 ExTreeDataset ← to_frame(TreeDatasetDict)
19 return ExTreeDataset, LinkageMatrixDataset
```

Dendrogram and Data Extraction: Figure 2 illustrates a hierarchical clustering dendrogram generated for MGR_ID = 33634, using the linkage matrix. Each merge step groups access records based on feature similarity, where lower branches indicate tighter behavioral alignment. The x-axis lists records; the y-axis shows the merge distances.

This visual structure helps identify behavioral groupings that support role refinement and anomaly detection. Fully overlapping feature sets are clustered near the base of the tree, while more generalized groupings emerge at higher levels.

Table 2 presents a subset of the resulting **ExTreeDataset**, which summarizes node-level metadata from the dendrogram. Attributes such as APP_RATIO, MATCH_COUNT, AUDIENCE, and the ALLOW_ARRAY/DENY_ARRAY fields reflect both

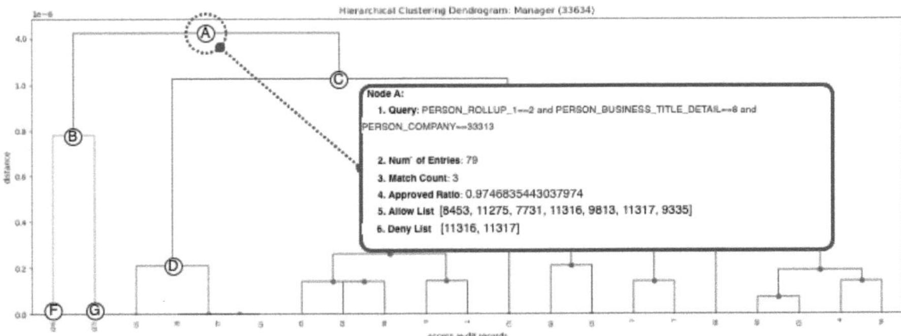

Fig. 2. Dendrogram for MGR_ID = 33634

structure and decision history. Notably, some nodes capture conflicting permissions, indicating policy ambiguity.

Hierarchical Model Construction: Algorithm 3 summarizes the construction of the hierarchical model for managers. For each unique **Manager-ID**, access logs are filtered, encoded, and clustered to form a behavior tree rooted in access activity. Each root node captures structural metadata and decision metrics derived from the ExTreeDataset.

Algorithm 3. Building Managers Model

Input   : TrainDataset
Output: ManagersModel

1 ModelType ← "Manager"; UniqueManagers ← get_unique_mangers(TrainDataset);
2 SelectedFeatures   ←   ['RSC_ID', 'ROLLUP_1', 'ROLLUP_2', 'DEPTNAME', 'BUSINESS_TITLE', 'B_TITLE_DETAIL', 'JOB_CODE', 'COMPANY', 'JOB_FAMILY', 'ACTION'];
3 **foreach** *mgr_id* ∈ UniqueManagers **do**
4 | TreeDataset, TreeHotKeyDataset ← data_preparation(TrainDataset, ModelType, mgr_id, SelectedFeatures); // (Algorithm 1)
5 | ExTreeDataset, TreeHotKeyDataset ← hierarchical_clustering_extended(TreeHotKeyDataset, TreeDataset); // (Algorithm 2)
6 | RootNode ← build_model_entity_instance(ExTreeDataset, TreeHotKeyDataset, ModelType);
7 | append_to_dict(ManagersModel, RootNode);
8 **end foreach**
9 **return** ManagersModel;

A similar procedure builds the **Resources Model**, applying the same logic from the perspective of **Resource-ID**. Both models support prediction by encoding empirical access patterns in a reusable, hierarchical format.

Matching Incoming Access Requests: A *target* is a new access request evaluated against the hierarchical models for managers and resources. Algorithm 4 describes the process of traversing each model to locate the node that best aligns with historical access behavior.

Matching outcomes are classified into three categories. A **Full Match** occurs when the request exactly matches a previously observed pattern. A **Partial**

Table 2. ExTreeDataset for MGR_ID = 33634

R_UP_1	R_UP_2	DPRT	B_TITLE	BIZ_DTL	JB_CD	CMP	JB_FAM	RSC_ID	MGR_ID	ACTN	ALLOW_AR	DENY_AR	RPP_RTO	DIST	AUDI	MATCH_CNT
2	3	33273	33308	8	33309	33313	11	9813	33634	1	[9813]	[]	1	0	1	10
2	3	33273	33308	8	33309	33313	11	11317	33634	1	[11317]	[]	1	0	1	10
2	3	33273	33336	8	33275	33313	11	9813	33634	1	[9813]	[]	1	0	1	10
2	3	33273	33336	8	33275	33313	11	11275	33634	1	[11275]	[]	1	0	1	10
2	3	33273	33489	8	33275	33313	11	9335	33634	1	[9335]	[]	1	0	1	10
2	3	33273	33489	8	33275	33313	11	9813	33634	1	[9813]	[]	1	0	1	10
2	3	33273	33489	8	33275	33313	11	9813	33634	1	[9813]	[]	1	0	1	10
2	3	33273	33489	8	33275	33313	11	9813	33634	1	[9813]	[]	1	0	1	10
2	3	33273	33489	8	33275	33313	11	9813	33634	1	[9813]	[]	1	0	1	10
2	3	33273	33489	8	33275	33313	11	9813	33634	1	[9813]	[]	1	0	1	10
...	...	...	...	...	...	...	...	...	...	...	...	...	...	...	...	...
2	3	33307	33489	8	33275	33313	11	NaN	33634	NaN	[11275, 9813]	[]	1	0	5	9
2	3	NaN	33308	8	33309	33313	11	NaN	33634	NaN	[11317, 8453, 11275, 9813]	[]	1	0	5	8
2	3	NaN	33489	8	33275	33313	11	NaN	33634	NaN	[7731, 11317, 9335]	[11316, 11317]	0.666667	0	6	8
2	3	NaN	33489	8	33275	33313	11	NaN	33634	NaN	[11275, 11316, 9813]	[]	1	0	8	8
2	3	NaN	NaN	8	33275	33313	11	NaN	33634	NaN	[11275, 7731, 11317, 9813, 9335]	[11316, 11317]	0.750000	0	8	7
2	3	NaN	NaN	8	33275	33313	11	NaN	33634	NaN	[11275, 7731, 11316, 11317, 9813, 9335]	[11316, 11317]	0.875000	0	16	7
2	3	NaN	NaN	8	NaN	33313	11	NaN	33634	NaN	[8453, 11275, 7731, 11316, 9813, 11317, 9335]	[11316, 11317]	0.904762	0.000001	21	6
2	3	33273	33489	8	33275	33313	11	NaN	33634	NaN	[11275, 9813]	[]	1	0.000001	51	9
2	NaN	NaN	NaN	8	NaN	33313	NaN	NaN	33634	NaN	[8453, 11275, 7731, 11316, 9813, 11317, 9335]	[11316, 11317]	0.928571	0.000001	28	4
2	NaN	NaN	NaN	8	NaN	33313	NaN	NaN	33634	NaN	[8453, 11275, 7731, 11316, 9813, 11317, 9335]	[11316, 11317]	0.974684	0.000039	79	4

Match is detected when some attributes align but others differ. If no sufficient similarity is found, the request is treated as a **No Match** and denied. This approach enables access decisions to reflect real usage patterns while preserving security through cautious default behavior.

Algorithm 4. Find Matching Node

Input : p (current node), *row_dict* (row to match), *target* (incoming req), *match_mode* (init
mode).

Output: (approved_artio, payload, match_mode, match_count).

1 **if** *is_full_match(row_dict, p.payload)* **then**
2 | **return** $(p.approved\_artio, p.payload, match\_mode \lor FULL\_MATCH, p.match\_count())$

3 **else if** *target.rsc_id* $\in$ *p.deny_list* **then**
4 | *is_match, mismatch_count* $\leftarrow$ is_partial_match(row_dict, p.payload)
5 | **if** *is_match* **then**
6 | | **if** *p.children exists* **then**
7 | | | **if** *target.rsc_id* $\in$ *p.children[0].deny_list* **then**
8 | | | | **return** *find_match_node(p.children[0], row_dict, target, DENY)*
9 | | | **else**
10 | | | | **return** *find_match_node(p.children[1], row_dict, target, DENY)*
11 | | **else**
12 | | | **return** $(p.approved\_artio, p.payload, match\_mode, p.match\_count())$

13 | **else**
14 | | **return** $(p.approved\_artio, p.payload, match\_mode, p.match\_count())$

15 **else if** *target.rsc_id* $\in$ *p.allow_list* **then**
16 | Similar logic as DENY list with ALLOW mode.
17 **else**
18 | *is_match, mismatch_count* $\leftarrow$ is_partial_match(row_dict, p.payload)
19 | **if** *is_match* **then**
20 | | **if** *p.children does not exist* **then**
21 | | | **return** $(p.approved\_artio, p.payload, match\_mode, p.match\_count())$
22 | | **else**
23 | | | Recurse into both children: $(approvedL, payloadL, mmL, mmpL, mcL)$ $\leftarrow$
find_match_node(p.children[0], row_dict, target, -)
$(approvedR, payloadR, mmR, mmpR, mcR)$ $\leftarrow$
find_match_node(p.children[1], row_dict, target, -)
24 | | | **if** *Both children fail to match* **then**
25 | | | | **return** $(p.approved\_artio, p.payload, match\_mode, p.match\_count())$
26 | | | **else if** *One child fully matches* **then**
27 | | | | **return** *Better child result with maximal match or higher approval.*

28 | **else**
29 | | Handle no matches by returning parent context or NONE mode.

Recursive Node Matching Algorithm: The system evaluates access requests
by recursively traversing hierarchical models to find the closest matching node.
It prioritizes exact matches, then nearby branches, selecting the node with minimal mismatches and highest approval score when multiple candidates exist.
This approach balances consistency with flexibility in access behavior. Table 3
illustrates representative outcomes.

Applying the Matching Algorithm: Once the best-matching node is identified, its APRV score is used to determine the final access decision. Algorithm 5 evaluates audit requests in **test_dataset** using the **ManagersModel**
and **ResourcesModel**.

Table 3. Matching Strategies Example

Strategy	Node Definition	Target (Request)	Explanation
Full Match	Mgr_id = 123; Src_id = 345; title = 3567; department = 1863;	Mgr_id = 123; Src_id = 345; title = 3567; department = 1863;	*All features match exactly; request fully aligns with the node*
Partial Match	Mgr_id = 123; title = 3567; department = 1863;	Mgr_id = 123; Src_id = ABC; title = 3567; location = 0000; department = 1863;	*Partial match on Mgr_id, title, and department; other fields differ*
No Match	Mgr_id = 123; title = 3567; department = 1863;	Mgr_id = aaa; Src_id = ABC; title = 3567; location = 0000; department = 1863;	Mgr_id *mismatch on a* key feature results in **No Match**

Algorithm 5. Processing Incoming Audit Requests

Input : DataFrame `test_dataset`, Models `managers_model`, `resources_model`
Output: DataFrame `test_dataset` with updated approved_ratio_avg results

```
 1  foreach row ∈ test_dataset do
 2      row_dict ← convert_to_dict(row); // Convert row to dictionary
 3      rsc_id, mgr_id ← extract_from_dict(row_dict);
 4      rsc_root ← resources_model[rsc_id].get_root();
          mgr_root ← managers_model[mgr_id].get_root();
 5      mgr_approved_ratio ← find_match_node(p = mgr_root, row_dict= row_dict, target=rsc_root);
          rsc_approved_ratio ← find_match_node(p = rsc_root, row_dict= row_dict, target=mgr_root);
 6      if mgr_approved_ratio ≠ None ∧ rsc_approved_ratio ≠ None then
 7          approved_ratio_avg ← (mgr_approved_ratio + rsc_approved_ratio)/2;
 8      else if mgr_approved_ratio ≡ None then
 9          approved_ratio_avg ← rsc_approved_ratio;
10      else if rsc_approved_ratio ≡ None then
11          approved_ratio_avg ← mgr_approved_ratio;
12      else
13          approved_ratio_avg ← None;
14      row["approved_ratio"] ← approved_ratio_avg;
15  return DataFrame test_dataset with approved_ratio_avg predictions;
```

For each request, root nodes are retrieved and scored via `find_match_node`. If both manager and resource scores are available, their average is used; otherwise, the single available score is applied. If neither exists, the request is unapproved. The resulting `approved_ratio_avg` enables automated, behavior-based decisions.

4   Evaluation

We evaluated the model on held-out data from the Amazon Access Samples corpus [11], tuning the `approved_ratio_avg` threshold to balance security and usability. The system favors a conservative default, denying uncertain cases to reduce false positives.

Biased Dataset and Its Implications: With 94.5% of requests approved, class imbalance risks over-permissiveness. We address this by using approval-history thresholding over similarity methods, promoting conservative and interpretable access decisions.

Threshold Selection and Trade-Offs: To balance access flexibility with risk mitigation, we empirically tested a range of thresholds for `approved_ratio_avg`. A value of 0.86 offered the best trade-off: requests below this ratio are denied, while those at or above are approved. This boundary optimally reduced unauthorized approvals while preserving a majority of legitimate access requests. The selected threshold is easily tunable, making the model adaptable to organizational risk tolerance.

Evaluation Metrics and Outcomes: The model achieved 98.53% precision and 79.48% recall, with AUC-ROC 0.79889 and AUC-PR 0.97669, showing strong performance under imbalance. It approved 74.97% of legitimate and denied 4.55% of unauthorized requests, with just 1.12% false approvals. A tuned F2-score and 80% balanced accuracy confirm its security-oriented design.

Security Considerations: While the model generalizes well despite class imbalance, its dependence on historical logs raises vulnerability to policy poisoning, where adversaries inflate approval ratios over time. This underscores the need to pair behavioral clustering with anomaly detection or audit-based safeguards. Future work will explore defenses against tampered logs and adversarial drift.

Limitations and Baseline Comparison: We did not compare against standard role mining methods (e.g., HCL, decision trees), focusing instead on interpretable, real-time policy adaptation. Preliminary tests showed higher false positives in unfiltered unsupervised methods, which to be detailed in future work.

Adapting Role Structures: Approval patterns inform both real-time decisions and role refinement. Only consistently approved resources define a manager's scope, yielding tighter RBAC roles that reflect actual behavior and reduce over-provisioning.

5   Conclusions

The research demonstrates that ontology-based hierarchical clustering enhances access policy management. By leveraging semantic relationships and clustering, organizations better understand their policies. Including factors like Manager-Id and Resource-Id improves prediction accuracy and helps address policy gaps. Further research is needed to assess the method's scalability and applicability across different policy types and organizations.

References

1. Amour, S., Gudes, E.: Access policy prediction via user behavior. In: Dolev, S., Elhadad, M., Kutyłowski, M., Persiano, G. (eds.) CSCML 2024. LNCS, vol. 15349, pp. 257–267. Springer, Cham (2024). https://doi.org/10.1007/978-3-031-76934-4_16
2. Argento, L., Margheri, A., Paci, F., Sassone, V., Zannone, N.: Towards adaptive access control. In: Kerschbaum, F., Paraboschi, S. (eds.) DBSec 2018. LNCS, vol. 10980, pp. 99–109. Springer, Cham (2018). https://doi.org/10.1007/978-3-319-95729-6_7
3. Batra, G., et al.: Deploying ABAC policies using RBAC systems. J. Comput. Secur. **31**(6), 789–823 (2023)
4. Bertino, E., et al.: The challenge of access control policies quality. J. Data Inf. Qual. **10**(2) (2018)
5. Hastie, T., et al.: The Elements of Statistical Learning: Data Mining, Inference, and Prediction, vol. 2. Springer, New York (2009)
6. Kunz, M., Fuchs, L., Hummer, M., Pernul, G.: Introducing dynamic identity and access management in organizations. In: Jajodia, S., Mazumdar, C. (eds.) ICISS 2015. LNCS, vol. 9478, pp. 139–158. Springer, Cham (2015). https://doi.org/10.1007/978-3-319-26961-0_9
7. Mitra, B., et al.: A survey of role mining. ACM Comput. Surv. (CSUR) **48**(4), 1–37 (2016)
8. Sanders, M.W., Yue, C.: Mining least privilege attribute based access control policies. In: Proceedings of the 35th Annual Computer Security Applications Conference, pp. 404–416 (2019)
9. scipy.cluster.hierarchy.linkage. https://docs.scipy.org/doc/scipy/reference/generated/scipy.cluster.hierarchy.linkage.html. Accessed 02 Mar 2025
10. Shang, S., Wang, X., Liu, A.: ABAC policy mining method based on hierarchical clustering and relationship extraction. Comput. Secur. **139**, 103717 (2024)
11. Amazon. UCI. Amazon Access Samples - dataset. http://archive.ics.uci.edu/ml/datasets/Amazon+Access+Samples

Books, Rooms and Searle
(Short Paper)

George Teşeleanu[(✉)] [iD]

Simion Stoilow Institute of Mathematics of the Romanian Academy, 21 Calea
Grivitei, Bucharest, Romania
george.teseleanu@yahoo.com

Abstract. One response to Searle's Chinese Room thought experiment
is the so-called System's Reply, which states that even though Searle
(who executes the instructions) does not understand Chinese, the system as whole does. Searle analyses this response and asserts that, by
internalizing the whole system, he would appear as a native Chinese
speaker to the outside world, yet he would still not understand Chinese. In an effort to challenge Searle's counter-argument against the
System's Reply, Levesque proposes a more easily characterized and analysed setting, called the Summation Room. Within this simplified context,
Levesque argues that the observed behaviour is still sufficiently complex
that it cannot be produced without appropriate mental qualities. While
we acknowledge the validity of Levesque's assertions, in this paper, we
claim that Searle's counter-argument remains robust despite Levesque's
counter-counter-argument.

Keywords: Chinese Room · Summation Room · mental qualities ·
philosophy of mind

1 Introduction

The Turing test [11] is a thought experiment designed to help us understand
the relationship between external behaviour and mental qualities. By external
behaviour we have in mind linguistic responses in an intelligent conversation or
performing a mathematical operation and by mental qualities we mean understanding the conversation or what we are actually computing. Briefly, the Turing
test states that if we are not able to distinguish between an entity and a person,
in an unrestricted conversation, then we should consider that the entity possesses
mental qualities.

Compared to Turing, Searle takes a completely opposite position. He devised
the Chinese Room [10] as a counter-argument to Turing's test. In a nutshell,
Searle is locked in a room and has to reply in Chinese to messages given to
him through an opening. Since Searle is a native English speaker and does not
understand Chinese, incoming messages look like meaningless squiggles to him.
To respond, Searle uses a large book containing symbolic rules for inputs and

A. Akavia et al. (Eds.): CSCML 2025, LNCS 16244, pp. 326–336, 2026.
https://doi.org/10.1007/978-3-032-10759-6_22

outputs, along with several data banks of sets of Chinese symbols. An important feature of the book and data banks is the absence of any English translations, indicating the meaning of Chinese symbols. Using these tools, Searle can answer any question in written Chinese, and the receiver cannot distinguish his replies from a native speaker's. However, Searle does not understand Chinese. Therefore, even if the entity's external behavior is indistinguishable from a human's, we cannot attribute mental qualities to the entity.

As noted in [6], both thought experiments investigate the following fundamental issue

When can we justifiably draw conclusions about mental qualities, given external behaviour that is indistinguishable from that of a person?

Although on opposite sides, both Turing and Searle agree that when we talk about indistinguishable behaviour, we must test it in an unrestricted environment. Otherwise, one can use trickery to get the behaviour right in restricted conversations. For example, ELIZA [12] can pass as a Rogerian psychotherapist, engaging in text-based conversations that mimic therapeutic interactions. Similarly, PARRY [2] is indistinguishable from a real paranoid patient in its responses. These examples highlight the importance of evaluating indistinguishable behavior in a broader and less controlled setting.

When Searle presented his idea to the artificial intelligence community, one of the many critiques he received was the so-called System's Reply. According to this argument, even if Searle himself does not understand Chinese, the whole system[1] does understand Chinese. In response to the System's reply, Searle extends his thought experiment by asserting that he memorizes the rules stated in the book and the data banks of Chinese symbols, and he performs all the calculation in his head. Through this process of internalizing all the components of the system, Searle effectively becomes the system. However, since Searle himself does not understand Chinese, and Searle is the system, the conclusion is drawn that the system does not understand Chinese. An important conclusion of Searle's paper is that

Whatever purely formal principles you put into the computer, they will not be sufficient for understanding, since a human will be able to follow the formal principles without understanding anything.

Levesque [6] challenges one of the premises of Searle's argument. More precisely, he contends that if Searle were to memorizes the book, then he would actually learn Chinese, leading to an understanding of the language. To support his argument, he devises a simplified setting known as the Summation Room. In this scenario, a person lacking knowledge of addition adheres to precise instructions to sum twenty numbers. Subsequently, Levesque shows the physically impossibility of creating a look up table in this context. Thereby arguing that the entity

---

[1] comprised of Searle, the book, the data banks, as well as his pencils and papers used for calculations.

inside the Summation Room possesses genuine knowledge of how to perform addition.

In this paper, our primary focus is on examining Levesque's argument, and we argue that his conclusion is false. We will not delve into the debate surrounding the correctness or fallacies of the Turing test or the Chinese Room. For a detailed discussion on the pros and cons of the Turing test, we refer the reader to [5,9].

Structure of the Paper. In Sect. 2 we provide the technical details of the Summation Room. To counter Levesque's conclusion we first imagine a new room, called the Random Room, and then we discuss its implications in Sect. 3. Related work is provide in Sect. 4 and we conclude in Sect. 5.

2   Preliminaries

2.1   Type 1 and Type 2 Books

If an entity wants to perform a given behaviour, there are two possibilities: either she simulates the behaviour without understanding it, or she learns how to perform it. According to [6], in the former case, she simulates the behaviour using as an aid a *Type 1* book, while in the latter case she learns the behaviour using a *Type 2* book.

A Type 1 book is exactly what Searle uses when locked in the Chinese Room, as he merely simulates Chinese responses without understanding their content.

On the other hand, a Type 2 book, for example, is a textbook from Chinese to English back to Chinese. In this case, Searle first uses the book to translate the question he receives into English, then formulates his response in English, and finally uses the book to translate his response into Chinese. By memorizing this Type 2 book, Searle would understand Chinese because he naturally uses English as an intermediate language[2].

It is important to note that the artificial intelligence community has no use for this kind of Type 2 books, as they assume that the entity already knows English. Therefore, they teach Chinese as a second language. The real challenge for artificial intelligence lies in finding a method to teach Chinese as a first language.

In his paper [6], Levesque argues that

There are no Type 1 books for Chinese!

He claims that this alone is sufficient to refute Searle's argument against the System's Reply. More precisely, if there are no Type 1 books for Chinese, then Searle must resort to using a Type 2 book. Consequently, he learns Chinese, and therefore, understands it.

---

[2] It is crucial to note that Searle is a native English speaker.

2.2 Summation Room

Since we lack knowledge about the structure of a Chinese book, Levesque proposes a simplified thought experiment to overcome this obstacle. If he manages to prove that there is no Type 1 book for summation, then we can infer that there is no Type 1 books for Chinese[3].

According to [6], Levesque is locked into a room where he must add twenty numbers, each composed of ten digits. An important feature is that Levesque does not possess the knowledge of how to perform addition. Similarly to the Chinese Room, the numbers are passed to him on a sheet of paper, and he uses a large book to respond.

The first book Levesque describes is *Book A*, comprised of ten billion chapters, each chapter with ten billion sections, each section with ten billion subsections, and so forth, up to depth twenty. The preface of Book A contains the following guide for processing the input numbers

> *Take the first number in the list of twenty and go to that chapter; then take the second number in the list and go to that section; then take the third number and go to that subsection, and so on until all twenty numbers have been used up. At the end of this process, there will be a number written in the book with at most twelve digits. Write that number on a slip of paper and hand that message back outside the room.*

It is easy to see that Book A is a Type I book. If Levesque memorizes Book A he will only simulate that he is adding the numbers, even though to the outside world his behaviour is indistinguishable from someone who understands how to add twenty numbers. This is Levesque's equivalent to Searle's counter-argument to the System's Reply.

Although from the philosophical armchair Book A is enough to produce indistinguishable external behaviour, in practice Book A cannot exist. To see this, note that Book A has 2^{200} entries, and that our physical universe has about 2^{100} atoms. Hence, each atom has to store 2^{100} entries. It is easy to see that Book A cannot be real.

To overcome Book A's memory requirements, Levesque introduces a new book: Book B. Intuitively, the entity has at its disposal a 10×10 array[4] that it uses to perform the naive algorithm for addition. The exact details are given in [6]. It should be pointed out that the exact size of the array is irrelevant to the discussion as long as it can be easily stored. For example, we could use a 2×2 array to perform binary addition and the outcome would be the same. The main differences between Book A and Book B are that Book B can actually exist and it is easy to memorise. Levesque claims that

> *The person following the algorithm described in Book B is not just looking up answers, but is literally adding numbers. In other words, a person who*

---

[3] Given the greater complexity of Chinese compared to summation.

[4] The array contains on row i, column j the value $i + j$, where $0 \le i, j < 10$.

> *memorizes the book B and learns* Proc 1, Proc 2, Proc 3 *and* Proc 4[5]
> *actually learns how to add.*

and that

> *The person who memorizes Book B does not necessarily realizethat he is
> adding numbers. He may never have heard of addition, and Book B does
> not require him to relate what he is doing to arithmetic or to counting or
> even to numbers. But he still knows how to add.*

and finally that

> *A person who memorizes Book B actually learns addition, and not merely a
> simulation of additionthat happens to produce the right external behaviour*

Note that even though the entity only knows how to add 10-digit numbers,
Levesque extends the courtesy to knowing how to add. That is because it is easy
to adapt Book B to deal with any list of numbers having any number of digits.
In the case of Book A this extension is not possible, and therefore the entity is
not really adding.

Finally, Levesque concludes that is not possible to produce the correct
answers in the case of ten digits numbers without labeling the result as "addition". His arguments are

> *Once we accept that we cannot look up the answer(simply because the mem-
> ory would have to be too large), the only alternative is to operate on the
> numbers by taking them apart, manipulating them, and putting the answers
> together piece by piece. If this procedure uses no other source of informa-
> tion, works for any list of numbers(or can be trivially adapted to do so),
> then I claim we would indeed call it "addition". We might say that the
> procedure in question was roundabout or clever or even bizarre compared
> to addition as we normally understand it, but it would still be addition.*

and

> *The mapping from inputs to outputs for the latter is complex enough that
> there is no plausible alternative but to process the numeric inputs and
> perform what amounts to addition.There are no Type 1 books for the Sum-
> mation Room.*

As far as Searle's argument is concerned, according to [6]

> *The mapping from possible inputs to appropriate outputs in the Chinese
> Room is so complexcompared to the Summation Room that it is ludicrous
> to imagine that this could be the result of fakery, a trick, a simulation, a
> lookup table, while the mapping for the Summation Room could not.*

---

[5] the procedures presented in book B

and

> *You would have us imagine producing behaviour X using a Type 1 book.*
> *But there are no Type 1 booksfor something as simple as the Summation*
> *Room, where the behaviour consists of just a 12-character response to a*
> *single 200-character message. Why should we think your behaviour X is*
> *easier to fake?*

3   Random Room

We agree with Levesque that the entity locked in the Summation Room with Book B knows how to perform addition, although she does not necessarily realize it. But we shall argue against him that, first, there is difference between knowing how to perform a task and learning what you are actually performing; and, second, that books of Type 1 do exist and are practical. As a consequence, even if one memorises a Type 1 book he still does not understand the underlying operation, but simply simulates it. Therefore, Searle's argument holds despite Levesque's counter-argument.

3.1   Description

In the case of the Summation Room, there is a chance that the entity locked inside the room figures out that he is actually adding numbers. To eliminate this possibility, we will generate a random operation that will be performed by the entity. We further introduce a room based on this operation, called the Random Room.

As in the case of the Summation Room, we are locked in a room and we receive on a piece of paper twenty 10-digit numbers written in base b. We have to perform an operation that is described in Book R (described below) and output the resulting number. Note that the challenger will also receive the knowledge needed to check that the answers he receives are correct.

Before writing Book R, the book's author randomly generates b lines with b unique elements from 0 to $b-1$ and assembles them into a table T. Then he writes the following preface

> You will be handed a list of twenty 10-digit numbers written in base b.
> Follow procedure **Proc 3**, described below, on these numbers. Do what it
> says, write down the output number it says on a piece of paper, and hand
> it back.

Before describing the procedures used to compute the output number, he writes table T. On the next page, he presents **Proc 1** that states

> On input two numbers n and m, locate row n and column m in table T, and
> find their intersection. Output the number located at their intersection.

In the next section, he writes **Proc 2** that says

On input two 10-digit numbers a and b, start with the rightmost digits of a and b, and use them as input to `Proc 1`. Set the rightmost digit of the output as the output computed using `Proc 1`. Repeat the process for the ninth digits, the eight digits and so on until you have finished all the digits. Output the computed 10-digit number.

Finally, the author presents `Proc 3` as follows

On input twenty 10-digit numbers $c_1, \ldots, c_{20}$, first use `Proc 2` on c_1 and c_2. Let d_2 be the output of `Proc 2`. Then use `Proc 2` on d_2 and c_3. Let d_3 be the output of `Proc 2`. Then use `Proc 2` on d_3 and c_4. So on, until you used the last number c_{20}. Output the result of `Proc 2` on input d_{19} and c_{20}.

Example 1. Let $b = 10$. We further provide an example of a table T (see Table 1) and how to perform `Proc 2`. Note that `Proc 3` can be easily extrapolated from this example. Suppose that we receive two numbers $a = 7084196325$ and $b = 1487396025$. According to `Proc 2`, we have to use `Proc 1` for each pair of digits from right to left. Hence, we obtain that

$$T[5][5] = 6, \quad T[2][2] = 0, \quad T[3][0] = 9, \quad T[6][6] = 4, \quad T[9][9] = 7,$$
$$T[1][3] = 0, \quad T[4][7] = 1, \quad T[8][8] = 5, \quad T[0][4] = 0, \quad T[7][1] = 7,$$

and the final result is

$$\text{Proc } 2(a, b) = 7051074906.$$

Table 1. Table T

n \ m	0	1	2	3	4	5	6	7	8	9
0	6	1	4	9	0	8	5	3	7	2
1	1	4	9	0	8	5	3	7	2	6
2	4	9	0	8	5	3	7	2	6	1
3	9	0	8	5	3	7	2	6	1	4
4	0	8	5	3	7	2	6	1	4	9
5	8	5	3	7	2	6	1	4	9	0
6	5	3	7	2	6	1	4	9	0	8
7	3	7	2	6	1	4	9	0	8	5
8	7	2	6	1	4	9	0	8	5	3
9	2	6	1	4	9	0	8	5	3	7

3.2   Discussion

It is easy to see that Book R and Book B have the following similarities

- The entity that memorizes Book R or Book B only has access to the book and not to the choices made by the book's writer, nevertheless she knows how to perform the operation.[6]
- The operations described in Book R and Book B can be adapted to deal with any list of numbers having any number of digits.
- Since implementing each of them as a look up table is impossible, "the only alternative is to operate on the numbers by taking them apart, manipulating them, and putting the answers together piece by piece".
- Both operations are complex enough "that there is no plausible alternative but to process the numeric inputs and perform" the real operation.

Since table T is generated at random, the entity inside the Random Room will never learn what she is doing[7], but she will always know how to perform the operation described in Book R. To the outside world, she always provides the correct answers. Thus, the entity has the right external behaviour. But, contrary to Levesque's conclusion, the entity cannot learn to understand what she is doing. Therefore, the entity learns how to perform the operation, but she does not understand it. Hence, Levesque's argument that Searle must use a Type 2 book to respond in Chinese is false.

To further support our claims, we will use Example 1. We claim that the entity inside the room actually performs digit-wise addition modulo 10, denoted $\boxplus$. Note that the writer of Book R made sure that the knowledge written inside the book does not leak any information about that. Hence, the entity locked inside the room cannot actually learn digit-wise addition modulo 10 from Book R. To see why she performs $\boxplus$, he have to know that the writer generated table T as $T[n][m] = \pi(n + m \bmod 10)$, where π is a random permutation given in Table 2. Since, π is random the conditions from Sect. 3.1 hold.

Table 2. Permutation π

i	0	1	2	3	4	5	6	7	8	9
$\pi(i)$	6	1	4	9	0	8	5	3	7	2

As stated in Sect. 3.1 the challenger needs to receive the information needed to check the correctness of the answer. That knowledge is actually a different book, denoted Book D, that states

---

[6] Note that, in the case of book B some entities might deduce that they are doing addition, while this is not true for book R.

[7] since it just jumbles numbers according to an arbitrary operation.

On input a 10-digit number c, start with the rightmost digit c_{10} of c, and set rightmost digit of the output as $\pi^{-1}[c_{10}]$. Repeat the process for the ninth digit, the eight digit and so on until you have finished all the digits. Output the computed 10-digit number.

where π^{-1} is the inverse permutation of π (see Table 3).

Table 3. Permutation π^{-1}

i	0	1	2	3	4	5	6	7	8	9
$\pi^{-1}(i)$	4	1	9	7	2	6	0	8	5	3

Using Book D, we can see that

$$\pi^{-1}[6] = 0, \quad \pi^{-1}[0] = 4, \quad \pi^{-1}[9] = 3, \quad \pi^{-1}[4] = 2, \quad \pi^{-1}[7] = 8,$$
$$\pi^{-1}[0] = 4, \quad \pi^{-1}[1] = 1, \quad \pi^{-1}[5] = 6, \quad \pi^{-1}[0] = 4, \quad \pi^{-1}[7] = 8,$$

which leads to the correct answer

$$7084196325 \boxplus 1487396025 = 8461482340.$$

As a consequence, memorizing book R does not lead to learning addition modulo 10 since the entity will not understand anything, although she will be able to follow the formal principles. The key to achieving this was to encrypt the knowledge used by the entity, while providing the key to the verifier. Therefore, Type 1 books that work in an unrestricted environment and for as long as is necessary do exist. For that reason, we cannot conclude that Searle's argument does not hold.

Remark 1. Note that for simplifying our presentation we used $b = 10$. But, to be secure the writer of Book R should choose $b \geq 35$, since $35! > 2^{132}$ which prevents brute-force attacks. The above arguments can be easily adapted to bases larger than 35.

4   Related Work

A concept similar to the Chinese Room was published in [8]. In this short story, a stadium full of 1400 math students are arranged to function as a digital computer. Each of them follows blindly the instructions given to them before the game. More precisely, they do some computations and pass the result to one of their neighbors. When asked, at the end of the simulation, none of the participants knew what they where actually computing. The conclusion of the story is

We have proven that even the most perfect simulation of machine thinking is not the thinking process itself, which is a higher form of motion of living matter.

Using our approach, even after they are told what they where computing, the students do not gain any insight about the operation described in Book R[8]. The statement is not true for Book B. This was the starting point for our thought experiment.

In [4], French notes that the book used by Searle to respond in Chinese

does not have to be a direct table matching of the string of symbols in the question with symbols in the rule base, but can include any type of look-up program, regardless of its structural complexity.

This is exactly what Book B and Book R do. Internally, both books use a look up table and manipulate symbols such that they match the row and column numbers of the table. French's conclusion matches Levesque's conclusion, but for completely different reasons. He argues in [3,4] that there is no way to simulate a person without simulating all the linguistic and non-linguistic life experiences of that particular person[9]. Hence, both the Turing Test and the Chinese Room are fundamentally flawed. Note that in the cases of the Summation Room and the Random Room there is no need to simulate the life experiences of the person locked inside since neither of them test for linguistic competence[10]. They are more practical tests, but they do not have the same ambition as the Turing Test, *i.e.* to test for human-likeness/human-indistinguishability/linguistic intelligence.

When the entity locked either in the Summation Room or the Random Room successfully simulates the given operation, what the entity actually exhibits is the intelligence of the books' writer and its intelligence of interpreting what is written in the given book. What the entity does not exhibit is understanding what the operation does. The idea of a machine exhibiting the intelligence of its programmers, while the machine's internal process mediates between the programmers and the machine can be found in [1]. Although in a different context, Ben-Yami's conclusion can be easily adapted to our case: the entity is merely reproducing the book writer's answers, while it lacks understanding. If the writer makes a mistake or simply writes silly answers, then the entity will fail to be indistinguishable.

5   Conclusion

In this paper we presented a new thought experiment, the Random Room, and we analyzed its implications. We conclude that Type 1 books that are practical do exist. Therefore, Levesque's conclusion that Searle must use a Type 2 book to converse in Chinese is refuted.

---

[8] The fact that the operation is random tells them nothing about what the operation is actually doing. This is similar to telling them that they are performing a mathematical operation.

[9] A similar line of reasoning can also be found in [7].

[10] which involves embodied experience.

References

1. Ben-Yami, H.: Behaviorism and Psychologism: Why Block's Argument Against Behaviorism is Unsound. Philos. Psychol. **18**(2), 179–186 (2005)
2. Colby, K.M., Weber, S., Hilf, F.D.: Artificial Paranoia. Artif. Intell. **2**(1), 1–25 (1971)
3. French, R.M.: Subcognition and the Limits of the Turing Test. Mind **99**(393), 53–65 (1990)
4. French, R.M.: The Chinese Room: Just Say No!. In: Proceeding of the 22nd Cog. Science Conference, pp. 657–662. Lawrence Erlbaum Associates (2000)
5. Korukonda, A.R.: Taking Stock of Turing Test: A Review, Analysis, and Appraisal of Issues Surrounding Thinking Machines. Int. J. Hum Comput Stud. **58**(2), 240–257 (2003)
6. Levesque, H.J.: Is It Enough to Get the Behavior Right? In: IJCAI 2009, pp. 1439–1444 (2009)
7. Michie, D.: Turing's Test and Conscious Thought. Artif. Intell. **60**(1), 1–22 (1993)
8. Mickevich, A.P.: The Game. Knowledge is. Power **5**, 39–42 (1961)
9. Saygin, A.P., Cicekli, I., Akman, V.: Turing Test: 50 Years Later. Mind. Mach. **10**(4), 463–518 (2000)
10. Searle, J.R.: Minds, Brains, and Programs. Brain Behav. Sci. **3**(3), 417–457 (1980)
11. Turing, A.M.: Computing machinery and intelligence. Mind **59**(236), 433–460 (1950)
12. Weizenbaum, J.: ELIZA - A Computer Program for the Study of Natural Language Communication Between Man and Machine. Commun. ACM **9**(1), 36–45 (1966)

Avatar PLC/SCADA: Cloud Half-Twin for Industrial Control Systems
(Short Paper)

Alon Dankner, Shlomi Dolev[✉], and Ehud Gudes[✉]

Department of Computer Science, Ben-Gurion University of the Negev,
Beer Sheva, Israel
{dolev,ehud}@cs.bgu.ac.il

Abstract. Industry 4.0 drives the ICS and SCADA systems to utilize the cloud for its significant benefits. New models, designs, and applications of traditional ICS systems incorporate the cloud to enhance and streamline industrial processes. In this paper, we propose a novel model that utilizes avatar processes for devices in the ICS system, such as PLCs. The avatar runs on the cloud and executes PLC tasks. The avatar can perform heavy computations that were previously impossible, especially for legacy devices standard in these systems. We also describe a security architecture for our system that thwarts cybersecurity threats that may arise from attackers on the cloud. Furthermore, we introduce a new decentralized architecture that combines blockchain with avatars to secure our ecosystem. In total, our system enhances the industrial process and enables engineers to easily incorporate complex logic into their (potentially heterogeneous and legacy) systems.

1 Introduction

An industrial control system (ICS) is a hardware and software system with network connectivity that automates an industrial process. ICS systems are the core of a country's critical infrastructure, encompassing power generation, water supply, oil and gas processing, manufacturing, transportation, and agriculture. These systems are widely used in factories and critical infrastructure facilities, including power plants, water treatment plants, oil and gas processing facilities, and transportation systems. They monitor and control the industrial processes, and they are vital to modern life.

According to the Purdue model, a traditional ICS system consists of four levels, as seen in Fig. 1.

The model consists of four layers:

1. The Field Layer contains the industrial equipment, e.g., turbines, generators, water pumps, centrifuges, and more.

Partially supported by the Google Research Grant, the Rita Altura Trust Chair in Computer Science, the BGU Data Center, the Frankel Center for Computer Science, and the Israeli Science Foundation (Grant No. 465/22).

A. Akavia et al. (Eds.): CSCML 2025, LNCS 16244, pp. 337–346, 2026.
https://doi.org/10.1007/978-3-032-10759-6_23

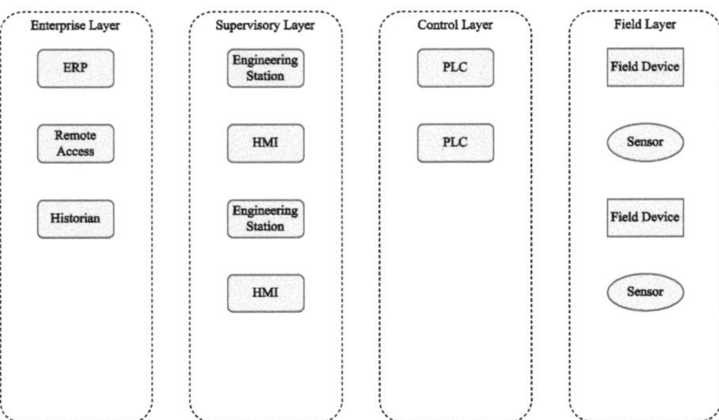

Fig. 1. Purdue Model.

2. The industrial equipment is controlled by the PLCs that reside in the Control Layer.
3. The Supervisory Layer consists of SCADA HMIs and engineering stations. The engineering stations allow the engineers to program and configure the PLCs, while the SCADA HMIs allow the operators to monitor and control the industrial process.
4. The Enterprise Layer is a typical IT network for business systems such as ERP and SAP. It also contains the historian, which stores ICS data.

Note that in most organizations, firewalls (that are not illustrated in Fig. 1) forcibly separate the layers, and certainly between the Enterprise Layer and the Internet.

Nowadays, however, some express reservations about the traditional model. As part of the fourth industrial revolution, also known as Industry 4.0, new technologies for the system are being moved to the cloud [5]. This enables organizations to enhance their industrial processes, increase effectiveness, and stay competitive in the industry. Enhancing the computation and functionality capabilities, rather than replacing the legacy controlled devices and controllers that already exist on the factory floor.

Several models were proposed to define the interactions between the cloud and the ICS system [10]. Some systems, known as open-loop systems, store ICS data in the cloud (e.g., the historian is migrated to the cloud). The more interesting models, known as closed-loop systems, enable the cloud to make decisions that impact the industrial process. We propose a novel approach for a closed-loop system that enables the PLC itself (or parts of it) to run on the cloud.

We propose a new framework for ICS systems that utilizes avatar processes [3, 6]—processes that represent each PLC (and possibly each controlled device on the factory floor) in the cloud. The avatar communicates with the device it represents and may tune or even replace the program running on that device.

We focus on separating the real-time portions of programs to run on the PLCs located on the industrial site, while migrating the non-real-time aspects to avatars that run on the cloud. The cloud avatar can be sophisticated (having cloud computation and communication resources) and may implement complex algorithms and expensive security layers. Avatars can also be created for field devices and sensors (those that use TCP/IP). The avatar of a sensor, for example, may record all the sensor's readings and stop its operation if it is faulty.

This architecture is also helpful in enhancing the computing capabilities of cars or IoT devices. As devices have limited computation power and/or become obsolete, they can be enhanced by offloading tasks to the cloud-based avatar, leaving only the real-time portions on the devices.

The cloud provides substantial benefits for the industry. It contains redundant, expandable hardware and software components that are well-connected and can be programmed to adapt to changing situations (e.g., heterogeneous devices, controllers, and extreme conditions such as disaster recovery). These components have less energy and other limitations compared to devices and controllers on the factory floor. The cloud provider maintains these resources. The use of the cloud reduces an organization's expenses in many aspects.

Another advantage of the architecture is that avatars may communicate with each other in the cloud to form online distributed decisions and adaptations.

Another notable technology is the digital twin [13]. The digital twin is a digital representation of a device, system, or process. It allows organizations to analyze the system, run simulations, and get predictions about the system. The digital twin is inherently different from our avatar PLC, as we do not replicate the entire ICS network or PLC; instead, we move some of the PLC logic to the cloud to achieve better performance and other valuable features. We restrict real-time operations on the production floor and let the cloud assist with system tuning and programming to achieve better performance, security, and more.

2   Avatar PLC

In our new architecture, the local PLCs in the plant are accompanied by avatar PLCs that run in the cloud. Figure 2

illustrates the model. The avatar PLC is an avatar process [3,6] that communicates with the local PLC.

As can be seen in Fig. 3,

a new layer is added to the traditional model, the Cloud Layer. This layer crosses all the layers up to the field layer and may affect each of them. The Cloud Layer contains the following entities:

- The avatar processes for the ICS devices. In this paper, we focus on avatars for the PLCs.
- An application of an engineering station or a SCADA HMI may be added to the cloud if access is needed at any time from anywhere on Earth. Alternatively, it is also possible to program the PLCs and their avatar solely from the plant.
- Additionally, the historian is moved to the cloud to store a massive amount of historical ICS data.

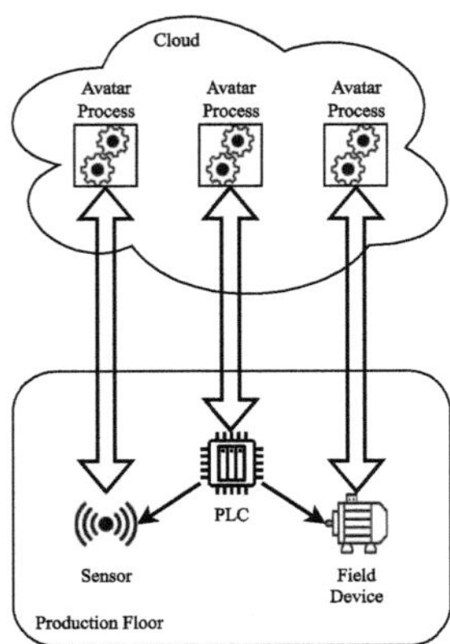

Fig. 2. Avatar PLCs in the Cloud.

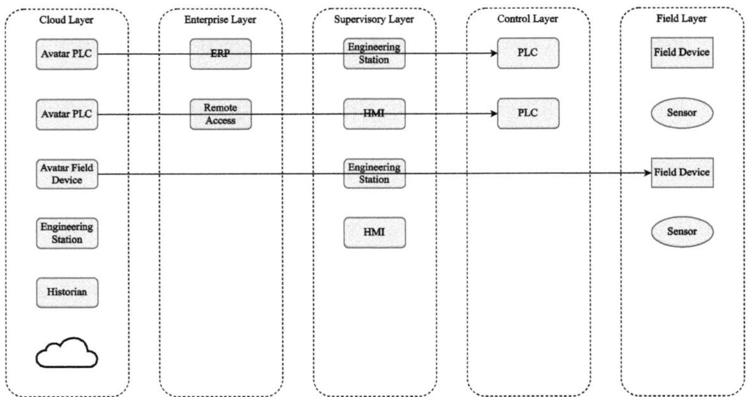

Fig. 3. ICS Topology with Avatar PLCs.

We split the programmable logic of the PLC into two parts. One part consists of critical code snippets that must be executed in real time, and the other part consists of non-critical code snippets. In many cases, it is crucial that parts of the programmable logic run locally at the PLC. These snippets cannot tolerate network latency. Therefore, we suggest only a partial offloading of PLC tasks to the cloud.

An example of such logic is predictive maintenance, which typically uses machine learning techniques. Suppose the PLC needs to analyze the data history and, at runtime, utilize the output of a machine learning algorithm. The part of the program that implements the machine learning algorithm can run as an avatar process and transmit the output to the PLC; there is no need for this code to run locally at the PLC. An example of the use of machine learning in autonomous cars is the implementation of the vision and object identification component, as seen in, e.g., [2].

A major advantage of the avatar PLC is that it can perform computationally intensive tasks, which are not necessarily possible on the standard PLC. Examples include machine learning algorithms, simulations, and intrusion detection. PLCs cannot typically perform complex calculations. To make matters worse, existing ICS deployments often exhibit low replacement and update frequencies. PLCs have a lifetime that can reach decades (unlike devices in standard IT networks). As a result, many legacy PLCs have limited computational power.

Another advantage of Avatar PLC is the cost reduction. Many places offer a discounted rate for electricity during specific times. The avatar PLC can plan when production costs are at their lowest and operate the system accordingly.

Our avatar actually contains a certain percentage of the PLC code. Notice that in the case of 100% of the code, the PLC is essentially a relay for the field devices, making it unnecessary. We introduce a new model of PLC as a Service [8], which is realized through the avatars. It is important to note that in this case, we compromise on the real-time requirement, as all operations originate from the cloud.

In this architecture, the engineering stations and SCADA HMIs are also accessible from the cloud. The PLCs communicate directly with the field devices using the same protocols as before.

Note that communication with the cloud depends on the ISP; however, the industrial process must not be affected by failures such as a loss of communication. For this purpose, the engineer can implement an emergency program that runs in case of a communication failure with the cloud.

2.1   The Role of the Engineering Station

The engineering station enables the user, or the engineer, to implement a control logic program, load it into the PLC, and send various other commands to the PLC. Since parts of the control program run on the cloud in our new system, the role of the engineering station must be adapted and extended accordingly.

The engineering station has a special task during the installation of the avatar, securely coupling the PLC/device to its avatar. Later, the avatar and its coupled PLC/device communicate directly (using an encrypted channel with the private key(s) unrevealed to the engineering station). Thus, following installation, the engineering station communicates only with the avatar, which in turn allows the usage of commands and reports in a high level of abstraction.

Suppose that the engineer implements a control logic program for the PLC and the avatar. The engineering station prepares the running environment for the program as follows:

- Creates a new avatar process if one does not already exist.
- Gives the identification and security information of the PLC to the avatar.
- Loads the program to the avatar.
- Gives the identification and security information of the avatar to the PLC.
- Loads the program to the PLC.

The PLC can then start running the loaded program and communicating with its avatar process.

Communication with the cloud, however, holds various security risks. In the following section, we address these risks and provide a holistic security solution for our new system.

3   Security Architecture

ICS systems are an attractive target for cyber attacks due to their critical nature. Over the years, numerous attacks against ICS systems have been publicly disclosed by the media [1,4,7]. In this section, we describe a security architecture for our new system that enables devices in the plant to communicate securely with their corresponding avatars in the cloud.

A significant difference in our new architecture compared to traditional architecture is the inbound traffic to the industrial network. In traditional architecture, data is only sent out of the network. In this new architecture, messages and commands are transmitted directly from outside the industrial network to the PLCs, similar to other closed-loop systems [10]. This opens a window for previously impossible attacks; the threat model has undergone drastic changes.

This change allows potentially malicious traffic to impact industrial networks, which are inherently insecure. The Modbus/TCP protocol [12], for example, does not provide integrity or confidentiality for the messages. As a result, an attacker can eavesdrop and manipulate sensitive traffic.

Our goal is to limit the broad attack surface created by the transition of the control logic to the cloud.

The communication between the PLC and the avatar is conducted over a secure channel, such as TLS [11] or IPSec [9]. I.e., there is an authenticated and encrypted tunnel between the PLC and the avatar. The tunnel allows the avatar to send commands and control the PLC securely. For this purpose, we use the engineering station to provide the PLC and its avatar with security information. We design a new protocol at the end of which both parties can establish a secure channel using cryptographic keys.

When the engineering station creates the avatar, it sends a pair of public keys and private keys to both the PLC and the avatar. The engineering station also sends the identifying details of the PLC and its public key to the avatar and vice versa. Note, unlike the public key infrastructure, here we use asymmetric encryption capabilities of a well-established security infrastructure, with no certificate authority; mutual authentication is ("manually") established during a setup stage and continuously maintained. This process is illustrated in Fig. 4.

Using the public keys, the PLC and its avatar establish a secure channel for communication. When a PLC wants to communicate with its avatar, it uses a challenge-response protocol to authenticate its identity. Each entity validates the identity of the other with the public key. If the validation is successful, the entity knows that the other party is the real avatar and not an impostor. Then, they use the public keys to agree on a shared symmetric key. This key is a temporary

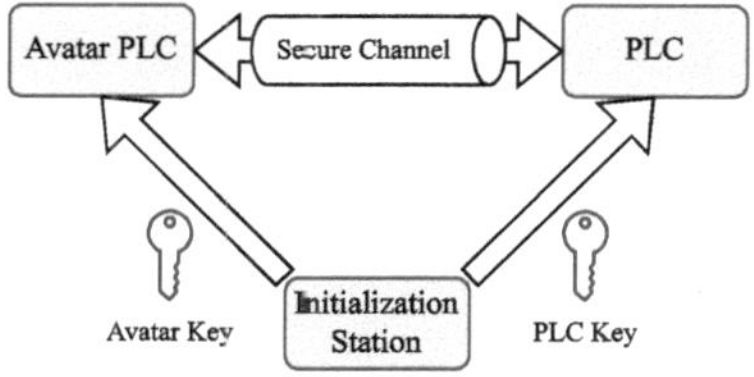

Fig. 4. Key Distribution in High Level.

key used for a limited period. If the PLC and the avatar have already agreed on a key recently, they continue using it without generating a new key.

A public key can be revoked, e.g., if the private key of the entity is compromised. In such a case, the programmer uses the engineering station to load another public key to the PLC and the avatar.

A benefit of this architecture is that the Avatar PLC can run security tools that are not currently available on standard PLCs, such as sophisticated firewalls and anti-virus systems. Nowadays, many attacks against ICS systems explicit takeovers of PLCs that lack such sophisticated tools. We migrate these security tools to the avatar, and therefore, such tools dramatically enhance the security of the whole system.

4   Key Distribution Protocol

The following are details about our new key distribution protocol: a cryptographic protocol between the avatar, its PLC, and the initialization station (which is implemented as part of the engineering station). The protocol is outlined in Fig. 5.

The initialization station, as its name suggests, initiates the protocol and bootstraps the cryptographic keys of the parties.

We assume that both the PLC and the avatar have initial keys installed. These keys are stored outside the system framework, e.g., by the PLC vendor.

Configuration. The protocol starts when the initialization station sends a new configuration for the avatar and the PLC, such as a new logic.

Bootstrapping. The initialization station generates a new symmetric key, $InitKey$, and sends it to the avatar and the PLC. The new key is encrypted together with a random nonce, which is used as a challenge under the receiver's key. The receiver decrypts $InitKey$ and its nonce from the message. Then, it encrypts the nonce under $InitKey$ and sends it to the initialization station. The final task of the initialization station is to ensure that the nonce is returned properly.

Creating a new key. The avatar randomly generates an ephemeral public key pair. It uses $InitKey$ to encrypt the public key with its ID and sends the result to the PLC. The PLC decrypts the received ciphertext and validates the ID

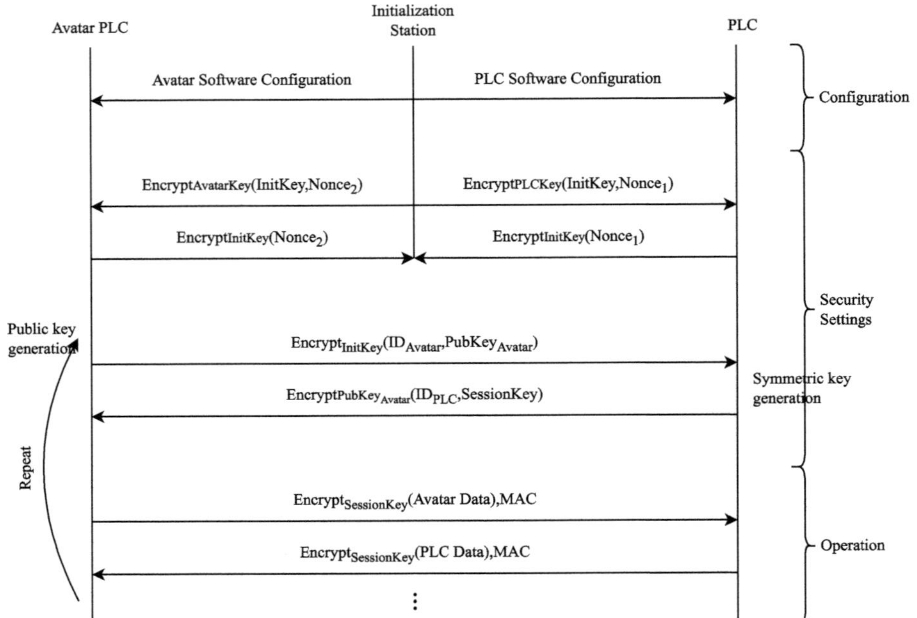

Fig. 5. Key Distribution Protocol.

of the avatar. It then creates a symmetric session key, *SessionKey*, and uses the public key to encrypt it with its ID using quantum-safe encryption. Upon receipt, the avatar decrypts the ciphertext with the private key and validates the ID of the PLC. Moreover, the ephemeral public key pair is removed from the avatar's memory.

Operation. After the message exchange is completed, the avatar and the PLC share a symmetric key that is used to secure the session. The parties use this session key to form a secure channel over which they can send messages securely. Messages are protected using encryption and authentication.

Our security architecture provides various security features:

- **Authentication** Each party knows how to verify the other party's identity. To communicate, each party needs to decrypt *InitKey*, which is encrypted with its secret key. The parties receive it in a message from the initialization station, and they only have to decrypt the message to obtain the key. In the next message exchange between the parties, they both use *InitKey*, which allows them to identify a rogue machine if it exists.
- **Integrity and confidentiality** Secure the transmitted data from malicious modification and reading (respectively) by an attacker by a secure channel that encrypts and authenticates the data.
- **Forward secrecy** The protocol provides forward secrecy because if either of the long-term keys is exposed, *AvatarKey* or *PLCKey*, it will lead to

exposure of $InitKey$, because the attacker can decrypt it from the traffic. Still, the attacker will not be able to decrypt the avatar–PLC data. The ephemeral key, $PubKey_{PLC}$, protects against such an attack because the private key remains secret, even if long-term keys are compromised, as it is not sent over the channel. Therefore, the session key also remains secret, and the traffic is protected.

- **Backward secrecy** In the opposite direction, the protocol provides backward secrecy because the parties replace the session key every once in a while. Therefore, even if long-term keys are compromised, an attacker still fails to decrypt future traffic.
- **Post-quantum safety** The protocol is post-quantum safe because we use post-quantum cryptography. Examples of such primitives are AES-256 for symmetric encryption and lattice-based cryptography for asymmetric encryption.

5   Implementation Concepts for the Avatar PLC/SCADA

Several implementation aspects are omitted from this extended abstract.

- **Real-Time-Oriented Programming** Extensions to common programming languages and compilers that allow the programmer to mark parts of the code as real-time code. We provide an interface for the programmer to instruct the PLC and the avatar on which parts should run locally on the PLC, as they are critical, and which parts may take longer to execute and should be offloaded to the cloud.
- **Real-Time-Oriented Compiler** A compiler that automatically turns a generic program into a real-time-oriented program. The compiler decides which parts run locally and which parts run on the cloud based on program analysis.
- **Adaptive Real-Time Partition** A program that automatically splits a program into a real-time-oriented program. The PLC and the avatar determine which parts must run with real-time restrictions and should be executed locally, and which parts would require more time.
- **Blockchain** Investigate the use of blockchain, a decentralized system, in the environment of ICS systems. Using smart contracts in blockchain to act as distributively implemented avatars. Blockchain provides various security features that allow the secure storage of information on a ledger.
- **Machine Learning Models** Use machine learning algorithms on the data the avatars collect from the sensors. Constantly learning and tuning operations according to the collected data from the controlled production floor, from the PLCs, sensors, activators, cameras, and alike.
- **Distributed Computations** Our architecture enables PLCs to collaborate and perform computations in a manner previously impossible through their avatars.

References

1. Biham, E., Bitan, S., Carmel, A., Dankner, A., Malin, U., Wool, A.: Rogue7: Rogue engineering-station attacks on s7 simatic plcs. Black Hat USA, 2019 (2019)
2. Bochkovskiy, A., Chien-Yao, W., Hong-Yuan, M.L.: Yolov4: Optimal speed and accuracy of object detection. arXiv preprint arXiv:2004.10934 (2020)
3. Borcea, C., Ding, X., Gehani, N., Curtmola, R., Khan, M.A., Debnath, H.: Avatar: Mobile distributed computing in the cloud. In: 2015 3rd IEEE International Conference on Mobile Cloud Computing, Services, and Engineering, pages 151–156. IEEE (2015)
4. Defense Use Case. Analysis of the cyber attack on the Ukrainian power grid. Electr. Inf. Sharing Anal. Center (E-ISAC), **388**, 1–29 (2016)
5. Church, P., et al.: SCADA systems in the cloud. In: Handbook of Big Data Technologies, pages 691–718. Springer (2017)
6. Dolev, S., Kopeetsky, M., Mimran, D.: Avatar process for mobile devices, February 2014. EP2696608 A2
7. Falliere, N., Murchu, L.O., Chien, E.: W32. stuxnet dossier. White paper, symantec corp., security response, **5**(6), 29 (2011)
8. Givehchi, O., Imtiaz, J., Trsek, H., Jasperneite, J.: Control-as-a-service from the cloud: a case study for using virtualized PLCs. In: 2014 10th IEEE Workshop on Factory Communication Systems (WFCS 2014), pages 1–4. IEEE (2014)
9. Kent, S., Seo, K.: Security architecture for the internet protocol. RFC 4301 (2005)
10. Dale Peterson. Securing closed loop ICS cloud services (2020). https://dale-peterson.com/2020/02/13/securing-closed-loop-ics-cloud-services/
11. Rescorla, E.: The transport layer security (TLS) protocol version 1.3. RFC 8446 (2018)
12. Swales, A., et al.: Open modbus/TCP specification. Schneider Electric **29**, 3–19 (1999)
13. Tao, F., Zhang, H., Liu, A., Nee, A.Y.C.: Digital twin in industry: State-of-the-art. IEEE Trans. Indus. Inform. **15**(4), 2405–2415 (2018)

Automatically Reviewing Movie Plots
with LLMs
(Short Paper)

Milka Kaplan[(✉)] [iD], Armin Shmilovici [iD], and Mark Last [iD]

Ben-Gurion University of the Negev, P.O.B. 653, Beer-Sheva, Israel
`milkak@post.bgu.ac.il`, `{armin,mlast}@bgu.ac.il`

Abstract. This study focuses on developing an automated literary criticism (ALC) system using Large Language Models (LLMs). The ALC system aims to analyze the stylistic, structural, and thematic features of short literary texts, particularly movie synopses. By combining quantitative indicators, such as stylistic consistency and consistency of presentation, with qualitative assessments, the system aims to provide authors and researchers with detailed feedback regarding the content.

The ALC goal is to reliably reproduce professional critical assessments by evaluating texts across key narrative criteria such as Character, Conflict, Originality, Logic, and Premise. Focusing on movie synopses and other short literary texts offers an ideal starting point due to their short length, availability of external quality benchmarks, and manageable length for consistent LLM evaluation. Our initial results demonstrate that LLMs, without prior domain-specific fine-tuning or calibration, can distinguish between high-quality and low-quality synopses, as evidenced by statistically significant differences between evaluations scores of Oscar-winning screenplays and Golden Raspberry winners. An automated evaluation system providing objective, structured, and evidence-based critiques aligned with human expert assessments can facilitate rapid pre-evaluation of scripts and literary texts in publishing and media industries, enhancing editorial decision-making processes.

In the future, we plan to extend the proposed framework to broader literary genres and conduct user studies to evaluate alignment with professional critics.

Keywords: Automatic Critic · Movie Plots · LLM

1 Introduction

Large Language Models (LLMs) extend far beyond simple text generation to solve complex cognitive tasks related to literature understanding and analysis.

The aim of this study is to develop an automated literature critic using LLM with an emphasis on reproducing professional assessments and to find out whether LLMs can detect meaningful narrative differences between clearly distinguishable categories without imposing a normative standard. We seek to define the parameters that should govern the evaluation of fiction, emphasizing not only traditional literary elements such

A. Akavia et al. (Eds.): CSCML 2025, LNCS 16244, pp. 347–357, 2026.
https://doi.org/10.1007/978-3-032-10759-6_24

as character development and thematic complexity but also the nuanced interpretations that AI can sometimes provide. ɸSince LLM output quality depends heavily on prompt design and input characteristics [1], we acknowledge ongoing concerns about annotation reliability, reinforcing the need for human oversight.

To our knowledge, no previous work has proposed a system that implements an automated literary critic based on LLMs degrees in a modular and interpretable structure based on explicit criteria of narrative quality (such as character consistency, logical structure, or originality). While recent studies such as [2, 3] have explored literary interpretation with LLMs using emotional modeling or semiotic analysis, they pursue different goals and rely on alternative methodologies. In contrast, our work introduces a complementary framework focused on modular, criterion-based evaluation and statistical validation, aiming to enable reproducible and scalable automated evaluation.

While any automated system must include rigorous checks for compliance with literary standards [1], this study is the first step towards integrating LLMs into literary criticism as a promising way to improve the analytical processes traditionally conducted by expert editors. The integration of LLMs into automated assessment could eventually reduce the reliance on expert opinion for analyzing audience reactions to literature, similar to trends seen in fields like customer feedback analysis [4].

We conducted our study in several stages. First, we explore the quality criteria that allow us to identify the difference between fiction texts and their impact on the overall rating. Simultaneously, we search for the best prompt that allows the model to produce the most relevant answers.

The original contribution of our article to the field of computer narrative understanding is in implement an automatic evaluation of texts without involving the participation of a human expert.

The rest of this paper is organized as follows: Sect. 2 summarizes the definition of ranking criteria; Sect. 3 presents the initial experiments using LLMs to evaluate texts automatically and describes an evaluation case study, the construction of a dataset; Sect. 4 presents the results of the experiments; Sect. 5 concludes the paper with a discussion of the experimental results.

2   Constructing an Automated Literary Critic (ALC)

The concept underlying the Automated Literary Criticism (ALC) system for movie plots is to operationalize narrative evaluation into structured, quantifiable assessments by LLMs. It is based on the assumption that key narrative features – such as character development, conflict complexity, originality, logical coherence, and premise clarity – can be decomposed into discrete evaluative criteria that LLMs can systematically analyze.

In this framework, movie synopses are an ideal text type due to their concise narrative structure and the availability of existing quality ratings. The ALC system automates evaluation by having an LLM answer a list of questions typically considered by human critics [5]. By weighing these answers and aggregating them into a vector score, the system allows for objective measurement and comparison of narrative quality. This approach transforms qualitative literary criticism into a reproducible computational process, laying the groundwork for scalable automated evaluation tools.

To finalize the ALC system and validate its ability to predict perceived literary quality, the following stages were identified (Fig. 1):

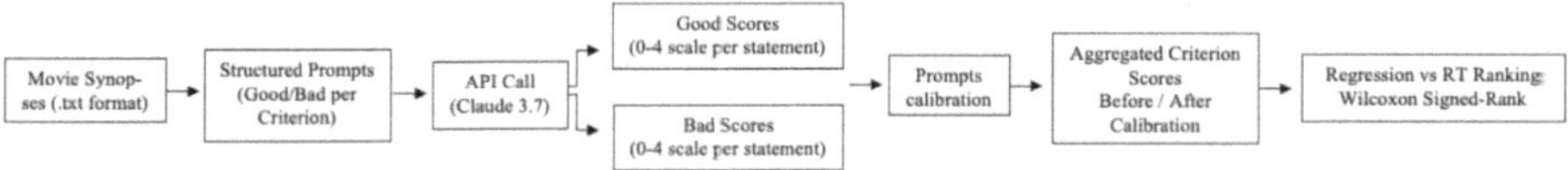

Fig. 1. Pipeline of the overall methodology of the ALC.

Definition of the Evaluation Criteria Identify the most important quality criteria to identify differences between texts of movie synopses and their impact on ratings. This included a review of existing literary screenplay scoring system and critical assessments [5].

Implementation of Each Criterion Using Structured LLM Prompts. For each criterion, a prompt template was developed and tested across tree leading LLMs to ensure consistency. The five core evaluation criteria include few statement questions, divided into positive (Good) and negative (Bad) indicators (subcategories):

Character. The positive aspects include the presence of a clearly formulated dramatic desire or goal for the main character, the sequence of his actions against the background of internal and external conflicts, the presence of emotional needs, balancing secondary characters and the antagonist in relation to the main character, as well as the presence of a convincing character transformation. Negative indicators measure the lack of empathy for the main character, lack of purpose, passivity, implausible behavior and stereotypical images.

Conflict. Positive criteria include the universality of the conflict embedded in the plot, the sufficient complexity of obstacles for the protagonist, the presence of internal and external conflicts that create tension, and the escalation of conflict over time. Negative indicators indicate the lack of a challenge for the main character, the contrivance of the conflict or its complete absence.

Originality. The positive aspects include the presence of a unique element in the basic concept, a successful combination of usually incompatible genres, unusual plot twists, unexpected character characteristics and an innovative representation of archetypes. Negative indicators indicate a lack of original material, excessive similarity to other works, plagiarism, or lack of innovative elements.

Logic. Positive indicators include the consistency of the internal logic of the text, the absence of plot holes and inexplicable coincidences, as well as the creation of a whole exciting experience for the audience. Negative indicators indicate the presence of significant plot contradictions, unclear or unexplained events, as well as inconsistencies in the internal logic of the narrative.

Premise/Concept. The positive subcategory include the clarity and conciseness of the basic concept, the correspondence of each scene to the central idea, the universality of the conflict and the uniqueness of the premise. Negative – the vagueness of the basic concept, the weak connection of the plot with the stated idea, the premature resolution of the main conflict or excessive similarity with the concepts of other works.

Implementing each criteria required repeated refinement of the instructions for the models, careful consideration of the key criterion, the division of criteria into sub criteria, and manual verification of responses to the first preliminary results.

So, for each subcategory we have developed structured prompts for each criterion, containing special leading questions for subcategories designated as «good» and «bad». These tips were designed to get specific answers from LLM and to ensure consistency of grades. For example, for the «logic» criterion, we created a detailed prompt in which we asked the model to evaluate how consistently the text follows its internal logic, addresses problems, explains phenomena, preserves the boundaries of knowledge about characters and avoids plot holes. The sample prompt for the «logic» criterion had the following structure:

Analyze the text and evaluate each statement for compliance with the criteria of logic:

Good:
The movie consistently follows its own logic.
There are no gaping plot holes or coincidences that cannot be logically explained.
The internal logic of the script makes it whole and exciting for the audience.
Bad:
Major plot holes or contradictions
Unclear or unexplained events disrupt immersion in history.
The logic of the world seems contradictory or non-existent.

Similar prompts have been developed for other criteria such as character development, thematic consistency, and stylistic elements.

The three LLMs in Table 1 (GPT-4o-mini, Claude 3.7, and Grok 3) were tasked with evaluating each statement on the following 5-point scale:

4 – («highest score») – the text matches the statement,
3 – («mostly true») – the text matches the statement to a greater extent.
2 – («partially corrected») – the text partially corresponds to the statement.
1 – («disagree, incorrect») – the text minimally matches the statement.
0 – («irrelevant question») – the text is irrelevant to the statement.
Return the result in the following format:
Good: Average score = X, Detailed: [4, 4, 3…].
Bad: Average score = Z, Detailed: [0, 1, 4…].

The Claude 3.7 model provided the most consistent, non-repeating scores compared to the GPT and Grok. This model also distinguishes between «bad» and «good» films most consistently, as indicated by the results of the t-test. At the same time, given the large size of the context window (approximately 150,000 words), including through the Application Programming Interface (API), which is confirmed by the official documentation [6], it is likely that this model will be chosen for evaluation.

Scores and Reports

In turn, the responses of each of the analyzed language models to structured queries are comprehensive analytical reports with quantitative and qualitative components. Thus, each response includes:

Detailed Criteria Analysis: LLM conducts a systematic evaluation for each parameter of a given criterion, accompanying quantitative estimates with detailed justification. For example, when evaluating the «Premise» criterion, the model analyzes the possibility of expressing the main idea in a concise form, the universality of the conflict, the uniqueness of the concept, and other aspects.

Evidence-Based Approach: For each parameter being evaluated, LLM provides specific examples from the analyzed text, demonstrating the depth of the analysis and the validity of the estimates. Thus, justifying the appreciation of the universality of conflict in a work, the model identifies elements that resonate at the universal human level, regardless of cultural or temporal context.

Quantitative Indicator: Each statement is evaluated on a five-point scale (0–4), where 4 means full compliance with the criterion, and 1 means complete non-compliance (0 marks irrelevance). These scores are summarized into the average score for the categories «Good» and «Bad» and are also presented in the form of detailed arrays for subsequent statistical analysis.

The objectivity of this assessment is achieved through explicit reference to textual examples, and a systematic approach allows for intertextual comparisons, minimizing the subjective factor.

Calibration and Expanding Data Corpus. To enhance LLM's discriminative capacity for qualitative assessment differences, criterion-specific prompt calibration was performed. Subsequently, LLM robustness was evaluated under increased sample size conditions.

Predicting Final Quality Assessments. To determine the weight of each criterion, we used regression analysis to understand which aspects most impact perceived quality. This analysis went beyond identifying the strongest individual predictors, like Conflict and Logic. It also examined the interplay between criteria, such as cases where a high Conflict score did not compensate for low Originality or weak Character development, thereby providing a more nuanced model of narrative quality.

3 Experiments with Movie Synopsis Corpus

In order to quantify how well different LLMs can evaluate the quality of synopses according to key criteria, and determine whether these ratings correspond to different models and known ratings of movies, initial testing and analysis of the preliminary rating system was conducted on the basis of a clean data set.

The experiment proceeded in two phases. First, we evaluated 30 movie synopses to calibrate prompts and assess the model's baseline ability to distinguish narrative quality across five criteria. Comparison with Rotten Tomatoes scores showed weak correlation, highlighting the need for refinement. In the second phase, calibrated prompts were applied to a larger set of 231 MPST synopses (600–1200 words). We analyzed the results statistically, using Wilcoxon tests and regression to assess improvements and correlations with critic ratings.

3.1 Movie Synopsis Corpus

We used a clean set of synopses from the MPST corpus, a collection of 14,828 movie synopses with tags [7]. From this corpus - short movie descriptions, selecting only those in the range of 600 to 1,200 words, in total 5,194 synopses. The advantage of using movie synopses lies both in the short text and in the availability of objective quality assessments from sources such as Rotten Tomatoes [8], Metacritic [9], and others, which allows us to correlate our computer analysis with generally accepted quality assessments. Movie synopses usually have a more standard format than literary excerpts, which reduces the variability that can complicate our analysis.

As a test, from this clean set of data we created mini-corpus consisting of 30 movie synopses: 15 synopses of movies winning Oscars for Best Original Screenplay [10], and 15 synopses of movies winning Golden Raspberry Awards for worst movies [11]. In total, our mini-case contains 30 movie synopses.

In this study, the Oscar/Golden Raspberry polarity was selected a clearly distinguishable benchmark to test discriminative capacity. We agree that many valuable or enjoyable texts fall outside award-oriented evaluation. To clarify, the Oscar/Raspberry contrast in our study serve solely as an illustrative benchmark for initial testing.

To test calibrated criteria on larger, diverse data, we built an extended corpus of 231 synopses, excluding the initial 30 used for calibration. This separation ensures evaluation on unseen data, avoiding overfitting and providing robust assessment of criteria generalizability across wider text ranges.

The extended corpus of 231 synopses was balanced across a broad range of film quality, containing 66 low-rated (≤ 40; 28.6%), 72 medium-rated (41–69; 31.2%), and 93 high-rated (≥ 70; 40.3%) synopses.

Using full rating ranges ensures that calibrated prompts will be evaluated at various quality levels rather than focusing only on high- or low-rated films. Almost balanced distribution between low, medium, and high categories allows models to demonstrate whether their scores and ratings on specific criteria remain consistent and reliable at various storytelling [12] and product quality levels.

3.2 Design of Experiments

The automatic evaluation system itself, in turn, consists of 5 criteria in a preliminary form: Character, Conflict, Originality, Logic, and Premise. Each criterion is evaluated according to two parameters: G (Good) and B (Bad). To perform a statistical t-test, the significance level is set at 0.05.

The results of such an initial experiment demonstrate that all three LLMs considered are able to distinguish between high-quality and low-quality this mini data set of movie scripts, which is confirmed by statistically significant differences in ratings between Oscar-winning movies and Golden Raspberry winners. Quantitative measurement of content quality shows, that the average value for Oscar-winning movies significantly exceeds the corresponding values for movies that received the Golden Raspberry, which is confirmed by low p-values. For instance, on the Character criterion, Oscar winners averaged a score of approximately 3.89, whereas Golden Raspberry winners averaged only 1.23. Higher scores according to positive criteria (G) for Oscar-winning movies indicating alignment between LLM assessments and the ranking of movie academics (Fig. 2).

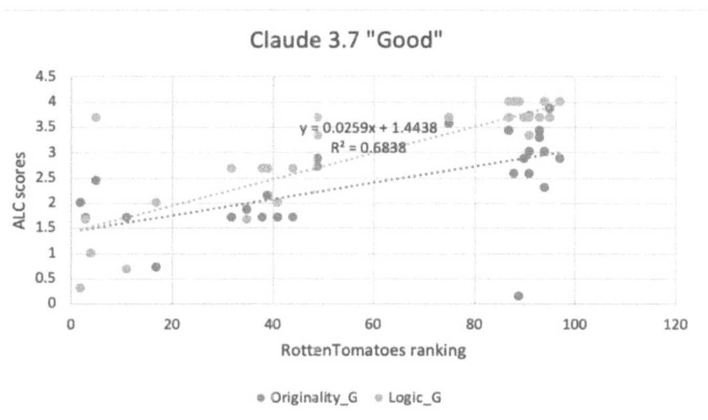

Fig. 2. Automatic Literary Critic Scores vs. Rotten Tomatoes Rankings.

Scatter plots showing the correlation between Rotten Tomatoes rankings (x-axis) and ALC scores (y-axis) for Good substatements under the Logic and Originality criteria. The upward trends—especially for Logic_G ($R^2 = 0.68$) – indicate that the model tends to agree with logical descriptions of high-rated movies and disagree with illogical descriptions of them, demonstrating narrative sensitivity, validating the discriminative capability of the ALC framework.

To assess which of the criteria have a significant impact on the final estimates generated by each model, multiple linear regression was performed separately for each LLM to examine whether the ALC model assigns higher scores for strong narrative features in critically acclaimed movies and lower scores for weak features in poorly rated movies. Rotten Tomatoes ranking scores [8] were used as the dependent variable, and five criteria were used as independent ones: Character, Conflict, Originality, Logic, and Premise. The regression model of ALC scores for each LLM showed statistical significance and statistically significant regression coefficients indicated, that significance of the Conflict and Logic criteria in predicting movie rankings aligned with external ranking scores. Specifically, Conflict criteria emerged as significant in all LLMs, indicating low scores for poorly constructed conflict. Logic criteria was also a statistically significant predictor in all three models, suggesting that narrative coherence plays a central role in LLM judgment (Table 1). It is significant that ALC demonstrates consistency in identifying these differences across all three examined LLM models.

Table 1. Statistically Significant Predictors ($p < 0.05$ marked *)

	GPT-4o-mini	Claude 3.7	Grok 3
Sign F	**0.001**	**0.000**	**0.016**
F-statistic	**4.97**	**16.52**	**3.1**
R-square	**0.32**	**0.60**	**0.22**
Character	0.259	0.057	0.573
Conflict	0.000*	0.040*	0.003*
Originality	0.555	0.576	0.031*
Logic	0.002*	0.000*	0.030*
Premise	0.045	0.094	0.205

3.3 Analysis of Results Before Calibration

The initial analysis before calibration showed that while the LLMs could distinguish between high- and low-quality synopses, their performance had clear limitations. The regression models had only modest explanatory power (F-statistics from 3.1 to 16.52). Furthermore, key literary dimensions like Character and Originality failed to emerge as consistently significant predictors of external ratings, unlike Conflict and Logic. These weaknesses highlighted the need for prompt calibration to improve the precision of the evaluations.

These findings underscored the need to calibrate prompts to reduce ambiguity and improve the statistical significance of key criteria, particularly Conflict and Originality, essential for professional literary evaluation.

3.4 Calibration and Expanding Movie Synopsis Corpus

After a detailed analysis of the obtained scores for 15 synopsis of Oscar-winning films and 15 synopsis of films that received Golden Raspberry awards for worst screenplay, certain inconsistencies were identified.

For example, films such as Jaws: The Revenge, Rocky IV, Rocky V, Speed 2, Cobra, and Rambo III have low overall ratings (ranging from 2 to no higher than 40), yet their scores on the Conflict criterion were high (with average values exceeding 3). Indeed, these films contain a clear conflict involving the main character, and the events are filled with fights, chases, and other forms of action, creating a state of emotional tension for viewers despite the banality of the plot or the flatness of the special effects. In this regard, the Conflict criterion, for instance, was calibrated to focus on the quality of the conflict within the narrative.

Calibration on a small dataset is crucial because initial prompts and evaluation criteria may not fully capture the nuances of narrative quality [13]. With a small number of examples, there is a higher risk that the LLM's assessments will be biased or inconsistent due to overfitting to specific text features or wording styles within that limited sample [12]. By calibrating prompts on the small dataset, we refine the instructions to elicit clearer, more consistent, and more discriminative responses across different criteria, ensuring that each evaluation truly reflects the intended narrative dimension rather than superficial text prompt.

This calibration testing was conducted using a single LLM, namely Claude 3.7, since the goal was not to identify the best-performing LLM, but rather to select a model that provides more diverse and non-repetitive outputs, allows API access, and has a large context window. The latter is particularly important for future analyses involving longer texts, as it enables processing extensive inputs without splitting them into smaller parts.

While calibration on a small dataset optimizes the clarity of prompts and their initial recognition ability, their application on a larger dataset assumes that model responses are stable and reliable in conditions of greater variability in content and structure. In this regard, we compared the results of ALC estimates already on the extended dataset (231 synopses) before calibration (row data) and after calibration of the experiments. As a result, the following results were obtained in Table 2.

Table 2. Statistically Significant Predictors Before and After Calibration ($p < 0.05$ marked *)

	Claude 3.7			
	Row (**Good**)	After calibration (**Good**)	Row (**Bad**)	After calibration (**Bad**)
Sign F	**0.000**	**0.000**	**0.000**	**0.000**
F-statistic	**17.98**	**26.89**	**20.52**	**29.86**
R-square	**0.298**	**0.385**	**0.329**	**0.411**
Character	0.027*	0.419	0.732	0.369
Logic	0.000*	0.000*	0.000*	0.000*
Conflict	0.559	0.006*	0.393	0.092
Originality	0.109	0.019*	0.003*	0.002*
Premise	0.209	0.452	0.163	0.507

Thus, Table 2 presents the regression results for the Good and Bad categories of 231 film synopses before and after calibration.

The F test p-value in all cases is 0.000, indicating the overall statistical significance of the models, and the F-statistic increased after calibration in both categories, suggesting an improvement in the overall explanatory power of the models after calibration.

Calibration increased the number of significant predictors from two to three, with Conflict and Originality gaining importance and Character losing significance. Logic remained a consistent quality predictor. Though numerical gains were modest, calibration notably improved differentiation between Good and Bad substatements, confirmed by Wilcoxon tests. While parameter tuning may further improve results [14], it is not supported by the Claude 3.7 API. Thus, it was not applied in this study, but we plan to explore it in future work with models that allow fine-tuning.

To assess if prompt calibration had a significant impact, we conducted a Wilcoxon Signed-Rank test comparing pre- and post-calibration scores. The test revealed statistically significant improvements across all five criteria (Character, Logic, Conflict, Originality, and Premise) in both "Good" and "Bad" categories ($p < 0.05$). The effect of calibration was very strong, with z-statistics for most criteria exceeding 12.0, which confirmed that our refinements effectively and substantially altered the model's evaluations (Table 3).

Table 3. Wilcoxon Signed-Rank Nonparametric Test for Good and Bad Category ($p < 0.05$)

n = 231						
crit = 1.96						
	Character	Logic	Conflict	Originality	Premise	
sum_max (Good)	25695	10578	24287	25471	24003	
sum_min (Good)	−287	−9221	−783	−894	−633	
T (Good)	287	9221	783	894	633	
z_stat (Good)	**12.894**	**4.108**	**12.407**	**12.297**	**12.554**	
sum_max (Bad)	337	10771	280	0	423	
sum_min (Bad)	−26039	−12361	−23825	−25647	−24910	
T (Bad)	337	10771	280	0	423	
z_stat (Bad)	**12.845**	**2.584**	**12.901**	**13.177**	**12.761**	

The results demonstrated statistically significant differences across all five criteria, leading to the rejection of the null hypothesis. This indicates that prompt calibration effectively produces significant changes in ALC evaluation scores, thereby enhancing the system's discriminative capacity and alignment with narrative evaluation standards.

4   Discussion

The results of both the preliminary and extended corpus analyses show that calibrated prompts significantly improve the ALC system's discriminative capacity. The Wilcoxon Signed-Rank Test confirmed statistically significant differences across all five criteria, indicating meaningful performance gains. Regression analyses revealed Logic as the only stable predictor of external ratings across both Good and Bad categories. After calibration, Conflict and Originality gained significance while Character lost it, suggesting refined prompts better captured narrative tension and uniqueness. These findings support the use of LLMs for structured literary evaluation aligned with established quality standards.

Beyond the entertainment domain, the ALC platform offers a flexible methodological framework potentially applicable to areas such as education, mental health, and safety. For example, the same criteria-driven structure could be adapted to identify signs of emotional distress, social isolation, and adaptation difficulties in online narratives.

Motivated by this idea, we conducted a small-scale exploratory experiment on anonymous Facebook posts by newly arrived immigrants. While the results are not presented in this paper, this initial application suggests that the core principles of the ALC system can be extended beyond literary evaluation and may be valuable in socially meaningful contexts. Future can will aim to formalize and validate this use case more rigorously

5 Conclusion

We demonstrated the feasibility of an LLM-based Automated Literary Critic (ALC) capable of distinguishing narrative quality in movie synopses, with Conflict and Logic emerging as the strongest predictors of external ratings. Our findings show that prompt calibration is crucial for evaluating qualitative depth over surface-level features, highlighting narrative coherence as a key quality metric. While future work should use lesser-known texts to mitigate potential LLM training bias, this criterion-driven framework presents a promising and scalable evaluation tool not only for entertainment domain.

Acknowledgments. This research was partially supported by the Israeli Council for Higher Education (CHE) via the Data Science Research Center, Ben-Gurion University of the Negev, Israel.

Disclosure of Interests. The authors have no any competing interests.

References

1. Pangakis, N., Wolken, S., Fasching, N.: Automated annotation with generative AI requires validation. arXiv preprint arXiv:2306.00176 (2023)
2. Yang, Z., et al.: Analyzing nobel prize literature with large language models. arXiv preprint arXiv:2410.18142 (2024)
3. Dong, F., et al.: Structuralist approach to AI literary criticism: leveraging Greimas semiotic square for large language models. arXiv preprint arXiv:2506.21360 (2025)
4. Katsiuba, D., et al.: Artificially human: examining the potential of text-generating technologies in online customer feedback management (2023)
5. Screenplay scoring system. Accessed 10 July 2025
6. Anthropic, documentation, model comparison table. Accessed 10 July 2025
7. Kar, S., et al.: MPST: a corpus of movie plot synopses with tags. arXiv preprint arXiv:1802.07858 (2018). MPST: A Corpus of Movie Plot Synopses with Tags – RiTUAL (uh.edu)
8. Rotten Tomatoes - source of movie and TV reviews
9. MetaCritic – source for aggregating movie professional reviews
10. Oscar for Best Original Screenplay
11. Golden Raspberry Award
12. Huang, P.-S., et al.: Reducing sentiment bias in language models via counterfactual evaluation. arXiv preprint arXiv:1911.03064 (2019)
13. Zhao, Z., et al.: Calibrate before use: improving few-shot performance of language models. In: International Conference on Machine Learning. PMLR (2021)
14. Parthasarathy, V.B., et al.: The ultimate guide to fine-tuning LLMs from basics to breakthroughs: An exhaustive review of technologies, research, best practices, applied research challenges and opportunities. arXiv preprint arXiv:2408.13296 (2024)

SSPT: Shallowest Shortest Path Tree
(Short Paper)

Omer Asher[1], Shlomi Dolev[1(✉)], and Li-on Raviv[2]

[1] Department of Computer Science, Ben-Gurion University of the Negev,
Beer Sheva, Israel
`omeras@post.bgu.ac.il, dolev@cs.bgu.ac.il`
[2] Gilat, Petah Tikva, Israel
`LionR@gilat.com`

Abstract. This paper introduces a polynomial-time modification to Dijkstra's algorithm aimed at constructing a Shallowest Shortest Path Tree (SSPT) from a source vertex s in a weighted graph. Unlike the standard Dijkstra's algorithm, which prioritizes minimizing path weights without regard for path depths (i.e., the number of edges), this modified approach ensures that among paths of equal weight, the one with the fewest edges is selected. This enhancement is achieved by tracking both path weight and depth during the algorithm's execution. The paper provides formal definitions of key concepts and proves the correctness of the modified algorithm. This work extends the applicability of shortest path algorithms to scenarios where minimizing path depths is also substantial. A formal treatment and proof for the solution are presented.

We apply the SSPT to approximate solutions for the **Directed Steiner Tree Problem** on several graphs, including Erdős-Rényi random graphs with randomly and uniformly selected terminals. In particular, we show that using this tree allows us to notably reduce the number of nonterminal nodes included in the solution. We believe that further development of this method may lead to improved approximation strategies for Steiner-type problems and related optimization tasks.

1 Introduction

Given a graph with non-negative edge weights and a source vertex s, a Shortest Path Tree (SPT) is found by the classic algorithm Dijkstra [4]. We consider the enhanced problem setting where the path depths in SPT, as the second criterion, should be minimized at every vertex in the graph; we call such a tree Shallowest Shortest Path Tree (SSPT). We suggest a modified version of Dijkstra's algorithm computing SSPT for an arbitrary given graph, with the same time complexity as Dijkstra's algorithm. This algorithm is useful in cases

Partially supported by the Rita Altura trust chair in computer science, the SATELLITE project of the Israeli innovation authority, Frankel Center for Computer Science, BGU-NJIT grant, the Israeli Smart Transportation Research Center (ISTRC), and Israeli Science Foundation (Grant No. 465/22).

where, among paths of equal length, the one with fewer edges is preferred. The standard Dijkstra's algorithm computes the shortest path distances but does not prioritize minimizing the number of edges in the case of ties. In this modified approach, we introduce a depth tracking mechanism to achieve this additional criterion. For a similar approach to prioritized multi-criteria tasks, see [5]. There, the *lexicographic priority* for several criteria is used, meaning: 1) to minimize the first criterion, and 2) while keeping it fixed, to minimize the second criterion, and so on.

Finding a shallowest tree among all shortest path trees is useful in various domains where both path weight and depth need to be considered simultaneously. This makes the algorithm applicable to problems where traditional shortest path algorithms fall short, such as when there is a need to optimize not only the cost of traversal but also the number of edges traversed. We further apply the SSPT as a heuristic for approximating the Directed Steiner Tree problem on Erdős-Rényi random graphs with randomly and uniformly selected terminals. This suggests that the SSPT structure may be advantageous in Steiner-type problems where reducing non-terminal nodes is beneficial. We believe that further developing this direction could lead to improved approximation techniques for such combinatorial optimization problems.

Related Work. Variants of the classical shortest path problem that incorporate multiple optimization criteria have received significant attention. In the Multi-Criteria Shortest Path problem, each edge may have multiple weights corresponding to different objectives, such as cost, delay, or reliability. A path is considered Pareto optimal if no other path improves at least one criterion without worsening any of the others. Martins [9] observed that even simple instances of the MCSP can yield a large number of efficient solutions, highlighting the difficulty of identifying all Pareto optimal paths in practice.

As an alternative, prioritized or lexicographic approaches have been proposed. These methods impose a fixed order over the criteria and seek paths that are optimal with respect to the first, breaking ties using the second, and so on. Dinitz et al. [5] developed polynomial time algorithms for computing k-shortest and disjoint paths under such lexicographic priorities by encoding multiple weights into a single composite value (or vector of values compared lexicographically). The bit packing technique proposed in their work assumes distinct weight functions for each objective. In contrast, our method remains within the classical single weight model and enforces shallowness by modifying the path selection rule itself. [[As a side note, we demonstrate that Dijkstra's algorithm extends naturally to use ordered sets of weights rather than only weights represented as numbers]].

A related line of research is the restricted shortest path problem, where the goal is to find a minimum cost path subject to a hard constraint on delay or hop count. This problem arises in scenarios such as network design and quality of service routing, where bounds on latency or the number of hops reflect performance or policy requirements. The restricted shortest path problem is known to be NP hard [7], and approximation schemes have been developed to address it. While our setting does not enforce a strict constraint on hop count, it shares the motivation of favoring shorter paths. Instead of treating hop count as a hard constraint, our approach incorporates path depth lexicographically to prefer shallower paths among those of equal total weight.

2 Shallowest Shortest Path Tree (SSPT)

While classic shortest path trees minimize the distance from the source to each node, they may include deep paths when multiple shortest paths exist. In this section, we study the problem of computing an SPT that, among all shortest path trees, minimizes the number of edges from the source to each node. We call such a tree a shallowest Shortest Path Tree (SSPT) and present an efficient algorithm for computing it.

2.1 Problem Setting and Notations

Consider a directed graph $G = (V, E)$ with a weight function $w : E \to \mathbb{R}$, where $s \in V$ is the source node, and all nodes in V are reachable from s. Note that all results of this paper are correct for the case of undirected graphs, by the known reduction that replaces every undirected edge by two anti-parallel edges between the same nodes. For a path P in G, the weight of P, denoted by $w(P)$, is the sum of weights of all edges in P:

$$w(P) = \sum_{e \in P} w(e).$$

The depth of a path P in G, denoted by $|P|$, is the number of edges in the path. For any $v \in V$, the shortest path distance is denoted as $\beta(v)$:

$$\beta(v) = \min_{P \in \mathcal{P}(v)} w(P),$$

where $\mathcal{P}(v)$ is the set of all paths from s to v. A Shortest Path Tree (SPT) is a tree in G rooted at s where the path from s to any other vertex v in the tree is the shortest path possible in G.

Definition 1 (Path Depth). *Let $T = (V', E')$ be a tree rooted at s and $v \in V$. The **path depth** of v in T is the number of edges in the path from s to v within T.*

Definition 2 (Minimal Path Depth). *For any $v \in V$, the minimal **path depth** among all the paths that weight $d(v)$ is denoted as $\gamma_{d(v)}(v)$:*

$$\gamma_{d(v)}(v) = \min_{P \in \mathcal{P}_{d(v)}(v)} |P|,$$

where $\mathcal{P}_{d(v)}(v)$ is the set of all paths from s to v in G that weight $d(v)$.

Definition 3 (Shallowest Shortest Path Tree (SSPT)). *A Shallowest Shortest Path Tree (SSPT) is a Shortest Path Tree T, such that for any vertex $v \in V$, the path depth of v in T is minimal over all possible shortest paths from s to v in G.*

2.2 Algorithm

Our algorithm (see its pseudo-code in Algorithm 1) uses $(d(v), \ell(v))$ records to maintain the current parameters of the best known path from the source vertex to each other vertex $v \in V$. The $d(v)$ component stores the cumulative weight of the shortest currently known path from s to vertex v, while the $\ell(v)$ component tracks the currently known minimal number of edges (depth) in a path of weight $d(v)$. This dual representation allows resolving ties in path weight by preferring the path with fewer edges. As the algorithm progresses, both components are updated for each vertex. Additionally, the algorithm uses an array `prev[]` to store the predecessor of each vertex on its currently shortest path of the shallowest from the source s. For a given vertex v, `prev[v]` indicates the vertex immediately preceding v on such a path. This array is crucial for reconstructing the shortest path after the algorithm has completed its execution.

Routine 1. Relax(u,v)

1: **if** $d(u) + w(u, v) < d(v)$ **then**
2:     $d(v) \leftarrow d(u) + w(u, v)$
3:     $\ell(v) \leftarrow \ell(u) + 1$
4:     `prev[v]` $\leftarrow u$
5: **else if** $d(u) + w(u, v) = d(v)$ **then**
6:     **if** $\ell(u) + 1 < \ell(v)$ **then**
7:         $\ell(v) \leftarrow \ell(u) + 1$
8:         `prev[v]` $\leftarrow u$
9:     **end if**
10: **end if**

The `Relax(u,v)` method evaluates whether updating the distance to vertex v via edge (u, v) is advantageous. It updates the distance if a path with less weight is found, or if a shallower path with the same weight is discovered.

The priority queue is ordered first by $d(v)$ (shortest distance) in ascending order, and among vertices with equal distance, by $\ell(v)$ (path depth) in ascending order. This ordering is equivalent to lexicographic comparison of the pairs $(d(v), \ell(v))$. At each iteration, the algorithm selects and removes the vertex with the minimal pair $(d(v), \ell(v))$ according to the lexicographic ordering. Once all nodes are processed, the queue becomes empty, and the algorithm concludes with the shortest path information stored in the distance records and `prev[]`.

2.3 Algorithm Correctness

We are given a graph $G = (V, E)$ with non-negative edge weights and a source vertex s. The objective is to formally verify that the algorithm correctly computes $d(v) = \beta(v)$, $\ell(v) = \gamma_{d(v)}(v)$, for all $v \in V$, and that the array `prev[]` defines a Shallowest Shortest Path Tree (SSPT).

Algorithm 1. SSPT Finding

Require: Graph $G = (V, E)$ with non-negative edge weights, source vertex s
1: **initialize:** distance $d(v) \leftarrow \infty$, $\ell(v) \leftarrow \infty$ and `prev[v]` $\leftarrow$ `null` for all $v \in V$
2: $d(s) \leftarrow 0$, $\ell(s) \leftarrow 0$
3: $Q \leftarrow$ priority queue ordered by $(d(v), \ell(v))$ lexicographically
4: $S \leftarrow \emptyset$
5: **while** $Q \neq \emptyset$ **do**
6:     $u \leftarrow pop(Q)$ // node with smallest $(d(v), \ell(v))$
7:     $S \leftarrow S \cup \{u\}$
8:     **for** each neighbor $v \in Q$ of u **do**
9:         Relax(u, v)
10:     **end for**
11: **end while**
12: **return** `prev[]`

Lemma 1. *Once a vertex is added to S, its distance and prev records remain unchanged.*

Proof. The *dist* and `prev[]` records of a vertex v can only change during a relaxation step, where a shorter or shallower path to v is found. However, the algorithm only relaxes edges to nodes that are in the priority queue Q (which contains nodes that have not yet been added to S). Once a vertex u is added to S, it is removed from Q, and no further relaxation involving u occurs. Therefore, distance records of u cannot change after it is added to S. $\square$

Lemma 2. *After the i'th step of the algorithm, for any $v \in V$, $\beta(v) \leq d(v)$ and $\gamma_{d(v)}(v) \leq \ell(v)$ is satisfied, and if $d(v) < \infty$, there exists a path from s to v with weight $d(v)$ and depth $\ell(v)$.*

Proof. We prove this by induction on the number of relaxations.

Base case: At the start of the algorithm, we initialize $d(s) = 0$, $\ell(s) = 0$ for the source vertex s, and $d(v) = \infty$, $\ell(v) = \infty$, for all $v \neq s$. Since $\beta(s) = 0, \gamma_0(s) = 0$, it follows that $\beta(s) \leq d(s)$, $\gamma_0(s) \leq \ell(s)$, and for all other nodes v, $\beta(v) \leq \infty = d(v)$, $\gamma_{d(v)}(v) \leq \infty = \ell(v)$.

Inductive Hypothesis: Assume that after the $i-1$'th relaxations, for all nodes $v \in V$, $\beta(v) \leq d(v)$, $\gamma_{d(v)}(v) \leq \ell(v)$, and if $d(v) < \infty$, there exists a path from s to v with weight $d(v)$ and depth $\ell(v)$.

Inductive Step: During the i'th relaxation, the algorithm ensures that $d(v)$ is updated to the minimum of its current value and $d(u) + w(u, v)$. If $d(v)$ changes to $d(u) + w(u, v)$, then $\ell(v)$ is updated to $\ell(u) + 1$. By the inductive hypothesis, $d(u)$ is the weight of a path to u of depth $\ell(u)$. Thus, $\ell(u) + 1$ is the depth of a path to v of the currently optimal weight $d(u) + w(u, v)$.

Otherwise, if $d(v)$ does not change, $\ell(v)$ is updated to $\min(\ell(v), \ell(u) + 1)$. If $\ell(v)$ changes to $\ell(u) + 1$, then by the inductive hypothesis, the record of $\ell(u)$ is the length of a path to u that weights $d(u)$. Thus, $\ell(u) + 1$ is the length of a path to v through u that weights $d(v) = d(u) + w(u, v)$. If no changes occurred, the lemma holds by the inductive hypothesis. Since each value corresponds to a specific path, and since we defined $\beta(v)$ as the shortest path weight to v, we conclude $\beta(v) \le d(v)$. Similarly, $\ell(v)$ is the depth of a path that weighs $d(v)$, thus it cannot be smaller than $\gamma_{d(v)}(v)$, which is the minimal depth among all the paths that weights $d(v)$. Therefore, $\gamma_{d(v)}(v) \le \ell(v)$.

$\square$

Lemma 3. *Let S_i denote the set of nodes selected after i steps. After the i'th step of the algorithm, for any $v \in S_i$, $d(v) = \beta(v)$, $\ell(v) = \gamma_{\beta(v)}(v)$ are satisfied, and the array* **prev[]** *restricted to S_i defines an SSPT for S_i.*

Proof. **Base Case:** Initially, $S_0 = \{s\}$, and the source vertex s has $d(s) = 0$, $\ell(s) = 0$. This case trivially holds, as the shortest path from s to itself is of distance zero and depth zero, and the array `prev[]` restricted to $\{s\}$ defines a tree that includes only s, which is an SSPT.

Inductive Hypothesis: Assume that after the $i - 1$'th iteration, for all nodes $v \in S_{i-1}$, $d(v) = \beta(v)$, $\ell(v) = \gamma_{\beta(v)}(v)$ and the array `prev[]` restricted to S_{i-1} defines an SSPT.

Inductive Step: Let v_i denote the vertex added to S by the algorithm during the i-th iteration. From Lemma 1, we know that the distance records of all nodes in S_i, except for v_i, remain unchanged. So, our objective is to establish that $d(v_i) = \beta(v_i)$, $\ell(v_i) = \gamma_{d(v_i)}(v_i)$, and that the `prev[]` array, when restricted to S_i, defines an SSPT. The distinction between the tree defined by `prev[]` for S_{i-1} and S_i lies in the inclusion of the vertex v_i and its associated edge $(\text{prev}[v_i], v_i)$. Thus, we must also verify that the weight of the path from s to v_i in T_i equals $\beta(v_i)$, and its length is $\gamma_{\beta(v_i)}(v_i)$.

Lemma 2 states that after the ith iteration:

$$\beta(v_i) \le d(v_i), \tag{1}$$

$$\gamma_{d(v_i)}(v_i) \le \ell(v_i). \tag{2}$$

Let P be a shortest path from s to v_i that has minimal depth, that is:

$$w(P) = \beta(v_i), \tag{3}$$

$$|P| = \gamma_{\beta(v_i)}(v_i). \tag{4}$$

Note that since P is a shortest path with the minimal depth from s to v_i (a lexicographically minimal path), any prefix of P leading to any intermediate vertex is also a shortest path with the minimal depth. Indeed, if this was not the case, we could replace the prefix either with a shorter path or one with the same length and lesser depth, which would contradict the lexicographic minimality of P.

In P, $s \in S$, $v_i \notin S$. Let (x, y) denote the first edge in P such that $x \in S$ and $y \notin S$. Let $P^{(1)}$ denote the part of P from the start up to x, and $P^{(2)}$ denote the rest of the path after (x, y). From now on, we consider the variable values at the moment of the beginning of the ith iteration since the distance records of v_i do not change during the current iteration. In particular, $S = S_{i-1}$. Since $x \in S$, by the inductive hypothesis, $d(x) = \beta(x)$ and $\ell(x) = \gamma_{\beta(x)}(x)$. Moreover, by Lemma 1, these values remain unchanged during the current iteration.

$$d(x) = \beta(x), \tag{5}$$

$$\ell(x) = \gamma_{\beta(x)}(x). \tag{6}$$

When x was added to S, the algorithm considered updating $d(y)$ using $d(y) \leftarrow d(x) + w(x, y) \overset{(5)}{=} \beta(x) + w(x, y)$. Since then, the record of $d(y)$ can only decrease. Thus, after the current iteration,

$$d(y) \leq \beta(x) + w(x, y). \tag{7}$$

Since $\beta(x)$ is the shortest path distance from s to x, P is a lexicographically minimal path, and $P^{(1)}$ is its prefix:

$$\beta(x) = w(P^{(1)})$$
$$\beta(x) + w(x, y) = w(P^{(1)}) + w(x, y)$$
$$\beta(x) + w(x, y) \leq w(P^{(1)}) + w(x, y) + w(P^{(2)}).$$
$$\beta(x) + w(x, y) \leq w(P). \tag{8}$$

Since $\gamma_{\beta(x)}(x)$ is the minimal depth among the shortest paths from s to x (of weight $\beta(x)$), and $P^{(1)}$ is a shortest path of the minimal depth to x as a prefix of P:

$$\gamma_{\beta(x)}(x) = |P^{(1)}|$$
$$\gamma_{\beta(x)}(x) + |w(x, y)| = |P^{(1)}| + |w(x, y)|$$
$$\gamma_{\beta(x)}(x) + |w(x, y)| \leq |P^{(1)}| + |w(x, y)| + |P^{(2)}|$$
$$\gamma_{\beta(x)}(x) + 1 \leq |P| \tag{9}$$

At the beginning of the current iteration, v_i was removed from the queue, while y was a candidate. Given the ordering in the priority queue, we have:

$$d(v_i) \leq d(y), \tag{10}$$

Combining these results, we get:

$$\beta(v_i) \overset{(1)}{\leq} d(v_i) \overset{(10)}{\leq} d(y) \overset{(7)}{\leq} \beta(x) + w(x, y) \overset{(8)}{\leq} w(P) \overset{(3)}{=} \beta(v_i) \overset{(1)}{\leq} d(v_i).$$

Thus $\beta(v_i) = d(v_i)$, as we wanted to prove, and

$$d(v_i) = d(y). \tag{11}$$

$$d(v_i) = \beta(x) + w(x, y). \tag{12}$$

Equations (11) and (12) imply that:

$$d(y) = \beta(x) + w(x, y). \tag{13}$$

Recall that when x was added to S, the algorithm considered updating $d(y)$ using $d(y) \leftarrow d(x) + w(x, y) \overset{(5)}{=} \beta(x) + w(x, y)$. From (13) we know that $d(y)$ remains unchanged from the iteration where x is inserted into S up to the beginning of the current iteration. Thus, since $x \in S$,

$$\ell(y) \leq \gamma_{\beta(x)}(x) + 1. \tag{14}$$

Recall that v_i was selected for processing before y was. According to the lexicographic ordering in the priority queue, and the knowledge that $d(v_i) = d(y)$ (Eq. 11):

$$\ell(v_i) \leq \ell(y), \tag{15}$$

$$\gamma_{\beta(v_i)}(v_i) = \gamma_{d(v_i)}(v_i) \overset{(2)}{\leq} \ell(v_i) \overset{(15)}{\leq} \ell(y) \overset{(14)}{\leq} \gamma_{\beta(x)}(x) + 1 \overset{(9)}{\leq} |P| \overset{(4)}{=} \gamma_{\beta(v_i)}(v_i).$$

Thus $\gamma_{\beta(v_i)}(v_i) = \ell(v_i)$, as required.

Now, we demonstrate that the path from s to v_i in the tree that `prev[]` restricted to $\{S_i\}$ defines has a weight of $\beta(v_i)$ and a depth of $\gamma_{\beta(v_i)}(v_i)$. The vertex v_i is added to the set S in this algorithm iteration. Consequently, the tree that `prev[]` defines is updated to include the edge $(prev[v_i], v_i)$. Recall that we have already proved that $\beta(v_i) = d(v_i)$, $\gamma_{\beta(v_i)}(v_i) = \ell(v_i)$. Since the last vertex that updated $d(v_i)$ is $prev[v_i]$,

we have the relations $d(prev[v_i]) + w(prev[v_i], v_i) = d(v_i)$, and $\ell(prev[v_i]) + 1 = \ell(v_i)$ because after $prev[v_i]$ updated them, these values remained unchanged. Thus,

$$\beta(v_i) \overset{\text{proved}}{=} d(v_i) = d(prev[v_i]) + w(prev[v_i], v_i) \overset{\text{I.H.}}{=} \beta(prev[v_i]) + w(prev[v_i], v_i),$$

$$\gamma_{\beta(v_i)}(v_i) \overset{\text{proved}}{=} \ell(v_i) = \ell(prev[v_i]) + 1 \overset{\text{I.H.}}{=} \gamma(prev[v_i]) + 1.$$

(I.H. stands for inductive hypothesis).

This completes the proof that the path from s to v_i in the tree that `prev[]` restricted to $\{s\}$ defines has weight of $\beta(v_i)$ and depth of $\gamma_{\beta(v_i)}(v_i)$. $\square$

Theorem 1. *At the completion of the algorithm, for every $v \in V$, we have $d(v) = \beta(v)$, $\ell(v) = \gamma_{d(v)}(v)$, and the array* **prev[]** *defines a Shallowest Shortest Path Tree (SSPT).*

Proof. At the end of the algorithm, $Q = \emptyset$ and $S = V$. Therefore, by Lemma 3, the conditions of this theorem are satisfied. $\square$

2.4 Running Time Analysis

This algorithm differs from the original Dijkstra's algorithm only in the `relax` method and in the selection rule used to prioritize vertices. Since the running times of these operations remain unchanged, the overall running time of the algorithm is equivalent to that of the original Dijkstra's algorithm, which is $O(|E| + |V| \log |V|)$ when implemented with Fibonacci heap (see, e.g., [3]).

3 Trimmed SSPT as Steiner Shortest Path Tree Simple Approximation

We use SSPT trimming as a simple heuristic for approximating the Directed Steiner Tree (DST) problem: given a root and a terminal set, we build the SSPT from the root and remove every non-terminal vertex that does not lie on a root-terminal path. Assuming each node is a terminal independently with probability q, even a trivial algorithm that returns the entire SSPT achieves a $1/q$ approximation in expectation, under the pessimistic assumption that the optimal solution includes only the terminals. This follows from observing that the expected size of such a solution is n, while the expected number of terminals is qn:

$$\frac{\mathbb{E}[\text{Trivial Algorithm}]}{\mathbb{E}[\text{OPT}]} = \frac{n}{qn} = \frac{1}{q}.$$

Since this ratio is trivially achieved by taking the whole tree, we focus instead on improving the quality of the solution by reducing the number of non-terminal nodes. For each instance, we use a different connected graph sample and choose a terminal set uniformly at random. One terminal is selected as the root, and the SSPT is constructed. All non-terminal vertices in the SSPT that are not lying on a rootterminal path are removed, producing a subgraph that still spans all terminals while typically discarding a large fraction of non-terminal vertices. In our experiments, we observed that the number of non-terminal nodes removed is typically close to $(1 - q)n$. As a side note, there are indications of the relation between the SSPT and the optimal directed Steiner trees, e.g., when the input graph is a star topology with the root being at the center, or a complete graph with uniform weights, the SSPT trimming coincides with the optimal directed Steiner tree. In both cases, all terminals are already directly connected to the root, and no non-terminal vertices are required.

We evaluate the heuristic of SSPT trimming on both synthetic and real-world networks. Our synthetic suite includes ErdősRényi $G(n, p)$, WattsStrogatz small world, and BarabásiAlbert scale-free graphs; the real-world suite includes Email-Enron and roadNet-PA. The reported values are averages over 1000 independent trials. A summary of all datasets appears in Table 1, and trends for ErdősRényi are shown in Fig. 1. The implementation of our experiments is available at [1].

3.1   Structured Synthetic Graph Models

We complement ErdősRényi with two structured models that capture common network features observed in practice, providing a broader perspective on SSPT trimming performance. These models, representing small world connectivity and scale free degree distributions, allow us to examine how the heuristic performs across varied graph structures.

Erdős–Rényi Random Graphs. We first evaluate SSPT trimming on the classical Erdős–Rényi model $G(n, p)$ [6], varying the edge probability p with $n = 1000$.

Across trials, the number of removed nodes was approximately $(1 - q)n$ for terminal probability q, with the variance decreasing for larger p. Table 1 lists the average removed ratios for different (p, q) pairs, and Fig. 1 illustrates how the average removal count changes with p for several fixed q values. These results confirm that in Erdős–Rényi graphs, trimming can eliminate a substantial portion of non-terminal vertices while maintaining terminal connectivity.

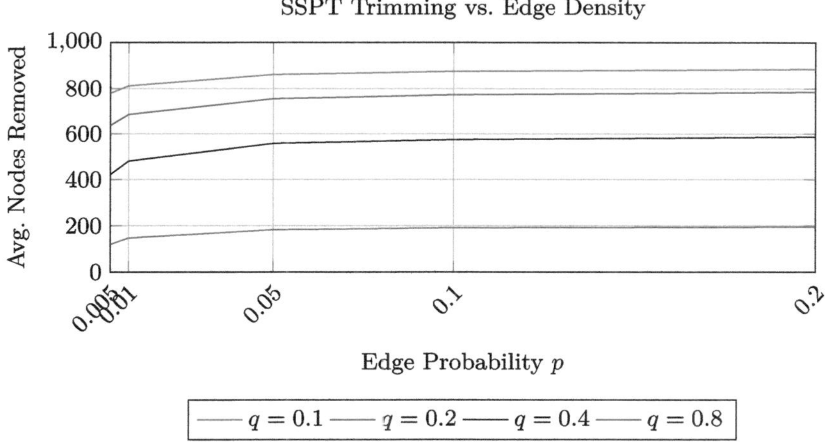

Fig. 1: Average number of non-terminal nodes removed through SSPT trimming on Erdős–Rényi graphs with $n = 1000$, plotted against the edge probability p for different fixed values of terminal probability q. Each point represents an average over 1000 trials.

Watts-Strogatz Small World Graphs. The Watts-Strogatz model [10] generates graphs that combine properties of regular lattices and random graphs, a structure often referred to as "small world". In many real-world networks, most vertices can be reached from every other by a short sequence of edges, and neighbors of a vertex are often connected to each other. The model starts with a k-regular ring lattice on n vertices, where each vertex is connected to its k nearest neighbors. Then, with probability β, each edge is rewired to connect to a randomly chosen vertex. This process introduces shortcut edges that shorten the average path length while preserving much of the original local connectivity. In our experiments, we vary the neighborhood size k, the rewiring probability β, and the terminal probability q, while fixing the graph size to $n = 1000$ vertices. For each parameter set, we generate 100 connected instances and report the average removed ratio and variance when applying the SSPT trimming heuristic.

Barabási Albert (Scale Free) Graphs. The Barabási–Albert (BA) model [2] generates scale free networks by sequentially adding vertices, where each new vertex connects to m existing vertices with probability proportional to their degrees. We evaluate the SSPT-based trimming heuristic on BA graphs for varying terminal probabilities q and attachment parameters m, reporting the average removed ratio and variance over 100 runs.

3.2   Real World Network Datasets

We also evaluate the SSPT trimming heuristic on several real-world network datasets. These datasets differ substantially in topology and density, enabling us to study the heuristic's behavior in practical scenarios.

Email-Enron Dataset. The Email-Enron dataset is a real-world communication network derived from email exchanges within the Enron corporation [8]. It is a directed graph where the vertices represent email addresses and the edges correspond to sent messages. We evaluate the SSPT-based trimming heuristic on randomly selected connected components of this graph for different terminal probabilities q.

RoadNet-PA Dataset. The roadNet-PA dataset is part of the SNAP road network collection, representing the road topology of the state of Pennsylvania, USA [8]. Vertices correspond to intersections and road endpoints, while edges represent undirected road segments between them. We evaluate the SSPT-based trimming heuristic on randomly selected large connected components for various terminal probabilities q.

Table 1: Merged SSPT trimming results across all experiments. For undirected graphs, similar results were obtained when edges were assigned random directions to form a directed version.

Hyperparameters	q	Avg. Removed Ratio
Erdős-Rényi $G(n, p)$ (directed; 1000 trials)		
$p = 0.005$	0.1	0.779
$p = 0.010$	0.1	0.812
$p = 0.050$	0.1	0.860
$p = 0.100$	0.1	0.875
$p = 0.200$	0.1	0.885
$p = 0.005$	0.2	0.637
$p = 0.010$	0.2	0.685
$p = 0.050$	0.2	0.755
$p = 0.100$	0.2	0.772
$p = 0.200$	0.2	0.784
$p = 0.005$	0.4	0.422
$p = 0.010$	0.4	0.480
$p = 0.050$	0.4	0.557
$p = 0.100$	0.4	0.575
$p = 0.200$	0.4	0.586
$p = 0.005$	0.8	0.120
$p = 0.010$	0.8	0.148
$p = 0.050$	0.8	0.183
$p = 0.100$	0.8	0.191
$p = 0.200$	0.8	0.195
Watts Strogatz Small World (undirected; 1000 trials)		
$k = 8,\ \beta = 0.05$	0.2	0.613
$k = 8,\ \beta = 0.20$	0.2	0.642
$k = 10,\ \beta = 0.05$	0.2	0.634
$k = 10,\ \beta = 0.20$	0.2	0.657
$k = 14,\ \beta = 0.05$	0.2	0.663
$k = 14,\ \beta = 0.20$	0.2	0.679
$k = 8,\ \beta = 0.05$	0.4	0.406
$k = 8,\ \beta = 0.20$	0.4	0.430
$k = 10,\ \beta = 0.05$	0.4	0.431
$k = 10,\ \beta = 0.20$	0.4	0.448
$k = 14,\ \beta = 0.05$	0.4	0.455
$k = 14,\ \beta = 0.20$	0.4	0.469
Barabási–Albert Scale Free (undirected; 1000 trials)		
$m = 6$	0.2	0.745
$m = 10$	0.2	0.759
$m = 6$	0.4	0.540
$m = 10$	0.4	0.558
$m = 6$	0.6	0.355
$m = 10$	0.6	0.370
Email Enron Communication Network (directed; 1000 trials)		
—	0.2	0.770
—	0.4	0.560
—	0.6	0.370
roadNet PA Road Network (undirected; 1000 trials)		
—	0.2	0.490
—	0.4	0.303
—	0.6	0.177

4   Discussion and Conclusions

We presented a simple and efficient heuristic for approximating the Directed Steiner Tree problem based on trimming a Shallowest Shortest Path Tree. The method is easy to implement and inherits the fast runtime of Dijkstra's algorithm, making it practical for large-scale graphs. By retaining only the paths from a fixed root to terminals, the algorithm often discards a significant number of non-terminal nodes. Our empirical results suggest that the method performs well in practice. Beyond its practical utility, this work also demonstrates that Dijkstra's algorithm extends naturally to settings where path weights are structured objects rather than simple scalars. In our case, each path weight is a pair $(d(v), \ell(v))$, representing the total distance and the number of edges, compared lexicographically. More generally, the algorithm remains correct as long as path weights belong to an ordered set with an addition rule that preserves the ordering.

Our experiments are performed across a variety of graph models, including ErdősRényi, Watts Strogatz small world, and BarabásiAlbert graphs, as well as real world networks such as Email-Enron and roadNet-PA, consistently resulting in approximately $(1 - q)n$ number of non-terminal nodes removed, where q is the terminal probability. This behavior persists not only in purely random graphs but also across various network structures, including clustered, small-world, scale-free, and real-world graphs. Across all datasets, the effect of q on the removal ratio dominates structural variations, indicating that the trimming heuristic adapts robustly to diverse topologies. Note that the SSPT tree structure is not a function of the terminal assignment; the probability q is applicable to the tree nodes as well, thus, our experiments reflect the SSPT number of leaves and depth (recall the star optimality).

Future work may explore the following directions:

- Deriving worst-case or average-case approximation guarantees for specific classes of graphs (e.g., bounded degree, planar).
- Combining SSPT-based trimming with MST or LP-based Steiner heuristics to create hybrid methods that leverage the structure of both metrics and path depths.

Overall, we believe that our algorithm offers a new and intuitive angle for Steiner tree (approximation), a version that combines shortest path computation with depth minimization. The algorithm's simplicity, scalability, and empirical performance suggest that it is a valuable direction for further study in both theory and practical applications.

Acknowledgments. We thank Yefim Dinitz and Baruch Schieber for contributing much to the paper.

References

1. (2025). https://github.com/Account0715/SSPT-Trimming-Experiment
2. Barabási, A., Albert, R.: Emergence of scaling in random networks. Science **286**(5439), 509–512 (1999)
3. Cormen, T.H., Leiserson, C.E., Rivest, R.L., Stein, C.: Introduction to Algorithms, 3rd edn. MIT Press (2009)
4. Dijkstra, E.W.: A note on two problems in connexion with graphs. Numer. Math. **1**(1), 269–271 (1959)
5. Dinitz, Y., Dolev, S., Kumar, M.: Polynomial time k-shortest multi-criteria prioritized and all-criteria-disjoint paths - (extended abstract). In: Dolev, S., Margalit, O., Pinkas, B., Schwarzmann, A.A., (eds.) Cyber Security Cryptography and Machine Learning - 5th International Symposium, CSCML 2021, Be'er Sheva, Israel, July 8–9, 2021, Proceedings, vol. 12716 of Lecture Notes in Computer Science, pp. 266–274. Springer (2021)
6. Erdos, P., Rényi, A.: On the evolution of random graphs. Publ. Math. Inst. Hung. Acad. Sci. **5**, 17–61 (1960)
7. Hassin, R.: Approximation schemes for the restricted shortest path problem. Math. Oper. Res. **17**(1), 36–42 (1992)
8. Leskovec, J., Lang, K.J., Dasgupta, A., Mahoney, M.W.: Community structure in large networks: natural cluster sizes and the absence of large well-defined clusters. Internet Math. **6**(1), 29–123 (2009)
9. Martins, E.Q.V.: On a multicriteria shortest path problem. Eur. J. Oper. Res. **16**(2), 236–245 (1984)
10. Watts, D.J., Strogatz, S.H.: Collective dynamics of 'small-world' networks. Nature **393**(6684), 440–442 (1998)

PQ-STAR Post-quantum Stateless Auditable Rekeying
(Short Paper)

Shlomi Dolev[1], Avraham Yagudaev[1(✉)], and Moti Yung[2]

[1] Department of Computer Science Ben-Gurion University of the Negev,
Beer Sheva, Israel
`avraamy@post.bgu.ac.il`
[2] Google, New York, NY, USA

Abstract. Rekeying is an effective technique for protecting symmetric ciphers against side-channel and key-search attacks. Since its introduction, numerous rekeying schemes have been developed [40]. We introduce *Post-Quantum Stateless Auditable Rekeying* (*PQ-STAR*), a novel post-quantum secure [12] stateless rekeying scheme with *audit* support. PQ-STAR is presented in three variants of increasing security guarantees: (*i*) *Plain PQ-STAR* lets an authorized auditor decrypt and verify selected ciphertexts; (*ii*) *Commitment-based PQ-STAR* with the additional binding guarantee from the commitments, preventing a malicious sender from potentially claiming a random or wrong session key. (*iii*) *Zero-knowledge PQ-STAR* equips each session key with a signature-based zero-knowledge proof (ZKP), which proves that the session key was derived honestly, without ever revealing the secret preimage. We provide informal arguments that all variants achieve *key-uniqueness*, *index-hiding*, and *forward-secrecy*, even if a probabilistic polynomial-time (PPT) adversary arbitrarily learns many past session keys. PQ-STAR provides a verified, stateless, and audit-capable rekeying primitive that can be seamlessly integrated as a post-quantum upgrade for existing symmetric-key infrastructures.

Keywords: Post-Quantum Cryptography · Stateless Rekeying · Side Channel Resistance · Symmetric-Key Updates · Zero-Knowledge Proof · Auditability

1 Introduction

Side-channel attacks [33] endanger practical cryptographic implementations by exploiting physical leakages, such as timing, power consumption, or electromagnetic emissions. A well-established countermeasure is rekeying, i.e., updating

Partially supported by the Google Research Grant, the Rita Altura Trust Chair in Computer Science, the BGU Data Center, the Frankel Center for Computer Science, and the Israeli Science Foundation (Grant No. 465/22).

A. Akavia et al. (Eds.): CSCML 2025, LNCS 16244, pp. 372–381, 2026.
https://doi.org/10.1007/978-3-032-10759-6_26

cryptographic keys at sufficiently short intervals so that an adversary observes only negligible leakage for any single key.

Rekeying [2] can be categorized as either *stateless (parallel)* or *stateful (sequential)*. Stateless rekeying—also called *parallel rekeying* [1,2]—derives every session key directly from a long-term master key, which must withstand both Simple Power Analysis (SPA) and Differential Power Analysis (DPA) [25,26]. In contrast, stateful rekeying maintains a mutable state for generating subsequent keys and was popularized by Kocher's index-based scheme [27].

Recently, Chang *et al.* [10] introduced HOP-1 and HOP-2 as refinements of Kocher's design. Whereas the original permits up to three encryptions per session key, HOP-1 restricts a key to two uses, and HOP-2 forbids any reuse.

In a related direction, Dolev *et al.* proposed HBSS [17], a post-quantum, hash-based stateless signature scheme. HBSS combines Lamport signatures, Merkle trees, and Bloom filters to authenticate many messages without maintaining state. Although HBSS addresses digital signatures rather than key evolution, its stateless, hash-based nature motivated the design choices of PQ-STAR.

Our Contributions. We introduce PQ-STAR, the first rekeying primitive that unifies post-quantum security, stateless fresh rekeying, and an explicit audit mechanism. Auditability is beneficial in various social contexts, as it can provide (sampled) evidence of correct and lawful actions, see, e.g., [16].

We present three progressively stronger variants: plain, commitment-based, and zero-knowledge proof, and argue informally that each satisfies *key-uniqueness*, *index-hiding*, and *forward-secrecy*. We also provide parameter choices and resource costs for PQ-STAR. Some of the details and proofs are omitted from this short version; see [18] for additional details.

Related Work. Since its introduction, numerous rekeying schemes have been developed [1,2,25–27,34,35,40,42]. The description of these works follows.

• **Rekeying and Side-Channel Security.** Rekeying was first studied to extend the secure lifetime of symmetric keys. Abdalla and Bellare [2] formalized this idea, showing that deriving short-lived session keys from a long-term master key can *increase the lifetime of a key* and mitigate classical cryptanalysis limits such as differential or linear attacks [31] and birthday collisions. Independently, Kocher's introduction of Differential Power Analysis (DPA) in 1999 [25] noted that simply updating the secret key frequently would render many power-analysis attacks ineffective. As [2] observes, Kocher et al. proposed changing the key *for each or after a small number of encryptions* âĂŞ a method known as *rekeying*. Later research confirmed its efficacy against side-channel adversaries when combined with a secure key-update function [1].

Rekeying complements masking, which injects randomness into intermediate values to decorrelate power consumption from secrets [13]; leakage-resilient designs that bound the total information extracted by an adversary [20]; and hardware-level hiding techniques such as balanced dual-rail logic and noise injection, which reduce observable side-channel signals at the circuit level [41].

•Rekeying Variants and Recent Work. Research on rekeying has progressed steadily: early key-derivation proposals of the 2000s evolved into recent leakage-resistant designs that rely on frequent key rotation to blunt side-channel attacks [1,34]. The idea of fresh (frequent) rekeying has continued to attract attention. Medwed *et al.* [34] formalized fresh rekeying for lightweight protocols in 2010, and later papers introduced more efficient instantiations together with complete security proofs. For instance, Mennink [35] presents generalized rekeying constructions that, for the first time, achieve beyond-birthday-bound security against side channels. [42] proposes an LR4 rekeying mode with a formal leakage-resistant proof.

•Indexed Rekeying Schemes (Kocher, HOP-1, HOP-2). A concrete approach to rekeying is *indexed sequential rekeying*, developed by Kocher [27]. Kocher's scheme requires the sender to maintain a secret current key, updating it after every message, while the receiver remains stateless by deriving any session key directly from the message index. Subsequent work [10] refines the traversal. *HOP-1* prevents session-key reuse by introducing a composite update; *HOP-2* strengthens the guarantee to single-use keys.

•Post-quantum Signatures and Stateless Schemes. We have concentrated on symmetric and key-exchange primitives. Concurrently, the cryptography community has turned its attention to quantum adversaries. According to NIST's assessment [12], large-scale quantum computers would endanger many existing public-key systems, motivating the search for post-quantum alternatives. In the post-quantum setting, symmetric primitives and hash functions remain secure— Grover's algorithm [21] offers only a quadratic speed-up, which doubling key lengths can counter—so schemes that depend solely on hashes look promising.

A prominent family of post-quantum signatures is the hash-based family. Hash-based signatures build on one-time signing techniques such as Lamport's scheme [30] and typically employ a Merkle tree to enable many signatures. Because the security argument requires only collision-resistant hashes, no number theoretic assumptions arise. The primary drawback is statefulness: the signer must track whether signatures have been issued. Recent work removes this restriction by designing stateless hash-based signatures [6,17].

2   Plain PQ-STAR

Construction. PQ-STAR is a stateless rekeying scheme that supports message auditing by a third party. The scheme relies on a large shared secret array from which ephemeral session keys are derived. By design, each encrypted message can be independently verified by an auditor without revealing any long-term secret.

Let $m \geq 1$ and let $A = (a_1, a_2, \ldots, a_m)$ be an array of m secret values shared between Alice and Bob (e.g., via an initial key exchange). The array A functions as a large shared secret key that must remain confidential at all times (like any long-term symmetric key). Because A may be very large, it is practical to generate each a_i pseudorandomly from a short seed (or seeds) instead of storing the entire array. For example, given two seeds $seed_l$ and $seed_r$, one may set

$$a_i := \mathrm{SHA}^i(seed_r) \oplus \mathrm{SHA}^{(m-i+1)}(seed_l),$$

so that each a_i is derived from both seeds (the left seed $seed_l$ is iterated forward and the right seed $seed_r$ is iterated backward), this construction behaves like a "lock": with only a single seed, once one preimage is exposed, subsequent preimage values can be computed by iterative hashing. This obviates the necessity to store the full array A; any entry can be recomputed on demand from the seeds. This approach is similar to standard techniques for expanding a one-time pad from a short seed in a post-quantum setting [4,15,17]. A time-memory trade-off (e.g., precomputing $O(\sqrt{m})$ intermediate values) can further reduce the computation cost. This construction ensures that reconstructing any a_i requires both seeds. Note that a similar locking can be based on a single seed, as follows, $a_i := \mathrm{SHA}^i(seed) \oplus \mathrm{SHA}^{(i+1)}(seed)$. Another approach for deriving each a_i from a single seed and its index i is based on *key-derivation function* (KDF) [11,24,28,29]. One may simply use $a_i = \mathrm{AES}(seed \parallel i)$ in contexts where the risk of breaking the cipher is considered small [3,7,8,37].

In PQ-STAR, each session (each message sent between Alice and Bob) uses a fresh session key derived from A. At a high level, the process is as follows:

1. Alice and Bob establish the shared master array A (or equivalent seeds).
2. For every new message, Alice (or Bob) selects k random indices (with repetition allowed) to assemble an index tuple $\mathcal{I} = (j_1, \ldots, j_k)$ from $[m]$. She then computes the session key

$$sk = H(a_{j_1} \parallel a_{j_2} \parallel \cdots \parallel a_{j_k}),$$

where H is a cryptographic hash function (e.g., SHA-256). Bob (or Alice), who also knows A, can derive the identical sk from the shared tuple $\mathcal{I}$. We intentionally use a one-way hash to derive sk rather than a reversible block cipher: symmetric block ciphers instantiate pseudorandom permutations, which are invertible given the key, so an adversary with the encryption key could invert the mapping and recover the secret inputs used to derive sk. A cryptographic hash compresses its input and resists preimage and collision attacks, guaranteeing that the selected array entries remain confidential.

3. Alice uses sk to encrypt the message, and she includes $\mathcal{I}$ in the transmission (in plaintext) so that Bob knows which a_i's were used. An authorized auditor can later verify the ciphertext using $\mathcal{I}$ and sk

An alternative scheme (proposed by an anonymous reviewer) is based on AES as follows. To encrypt a message M, Alice randomly selects a nonce r and uses AES with the master key A to encrypt r, obtaining a session key sk for M. She then sends r concatenated with $\mathrm{AES}_{sk}(r \parallel M)$, namely,

$$r \parallel \mathrm{AES}_{sk}(r \parallel M).$$

In the sequel, during the audit process, we require authentication of Alice and Bob, and the resulting schemes are more involved.

PQ-STAR also supports an *audit* mechanism to prove the origin and correctness of an encrypted message. If an authorized auditor needs to verify a ciphertext C and its claimed plaintext M, Alice (or Bob) can reveal the corresponding session key sk without exposing any part of the master key A. Concretely, Alice provides the auditor with the tuple $(C, \mathcal{I})$ and the session key sk used for C. The auditor decrypts C with sk, obtaining $M' \parallel \mathcal{I}' = \mathrm{DEC}_{sk}(C)$. If $\mathcal{I}' = \mathcal{I}$ (we conclude that then M' matches the claimed M), then C is confirmed as the encryption of M under the key derived from $\mathcal{I}$. This audit procedure confirms the authenticity of M without revealing any long-term secret in A (only the one-time key sk). Even a malicious auditor learns nothing beyond the disclosed sk, which does not compromise the scheme.

Security Analysis

The next proofs holds for large enough parameters; for instance $n \geq 256$, $k \geq 16$, and $m \geq 2^{20}$.

Theorem 1 (Key-Uniqueness). *With overwhelming probability, distinct sessions produce distinct session keys.*
Proof (Sketch). Two sessions produce the same sk only if they use the same index tuple $\mathcal{I}$ or if H collides on two different inputs. $\qquad\square$

Theorem 2 Index-Hiding). *No PPT adversary has more than a negligible advantage in determining the session key sk from the public index tuple $\mathcal{I}$.*
Proof (Sketch). The adversary sees $\mathcal{I} = (j_1, \ldots, j_k)$ but not the values $a_{j_1}, \ldots, a_{j_k}$ themselves. $\qquad\square$

Theorem 3 (Forward-Secrecy). *No PPT adversary that obtains up to t session keys (and their index tuples) has more than negligible advantage in learning any information about any other session key.*
Proof (Sketch). Suppose the adversary learns $(\mathcal{I}_1, sk_1), \ldots, (\mathcal{I}_t, sk_t)$ for some sessions. These give no direct information about any a_i, since each $sk_j = H(a_{j_1} \parallel \cdots \parallel a_{j_k})$ is a one-way hash. $\qquad\square$

Our security proofs implicitly assume that the authenticated encryption primitive binds each ciphertext to a unique key. This assumption does not hold for many widely deployed *authenticated encryption with associated data* (AEAD) modes, for example, AES-GCM [19] and ChaCha20-Poly1305 [36] can decrypt a single ciphertext under multiple keys, enabling *partitioning-oracle attacks* [23,32]. To prevent this, the encryption algorithm used with Plain PQ-STAR must be *key-committing*: for any fixed ciphertext and associated data, at most one key yields a valid decryption. Key-committing AEAD mitigates this risk [9]. Some modern designs provide forms of committing security under specific conditions [14]. Alternatively, one can enforce key commitment by including a commitment tag in the plaintext or by computing a separate hash-based MAC over the ciphertext and associated data. In particular, the commitment-based and zero-knowledge variants inherently provide such binding information; therefore guarantee the key-commitment property and are robust against partitioning-oracle attacks.

3 Extensions and Conclusions

We first describe two additional schemes, commitment-based PQ-STAR, zero-knowledge-based PQ-STAR, then performance and parameter selection, and finally conclude.

Commitment-based PQ-STAR

- **Construction.** The commitment-based variant of PQ-STAR differs from the plain scheme only in the *Setup* and *Audit* phases. As before, Alice and Bob share a secret array $A = (a_1, \ldots, a_m)$ of random n-bit values. In *Setup*, they derive a *commitment* array $Cmt = (c_1, \ldots, c_m)$ by setting

$$c_i = SHA(a_i),$$

where SHA is a cryptographic hash function (e.g., SHA-256). The Cmt is published publicly, while the values a_i remain secret. These commitments bind Alice and Bob to their chosen preimages (the a_i): once c_i is public, neither party can later claim a different a_i without detection (this is the *binding* property of a hash-based commitment).

- **Security Analysis** Note that in 2 we assumed no preimage values were ever revealed (since there was no audit). In the commitment variant, each audit reveals the specific a_i values used in that session. Thus, the total number of sessions derived from a single master key must be further limited to preserve the unpredictability of new session keys. In practice, one can adopt the technique from HBSS [17] where the parameter α represents the fraction of total array entries that have been exposed so far. This maintains the scheme's index-hiding and forward secrecy.

Computational Binding. With negligible probability, a malicious sender can claim a random session key or a different preimage set without being detected. In the plain scheme, a malicious sender could potentially claim a random session key or a different set of preimages without being detected immediately by a third-party auditor. With commitments, this is no longer possible (assuming SHA is collision-resistant).

Zero-Knowledge-Based PQ-STAR

- **Construction.** We now describe a third variant of PQ-STAR that enables an auditor to *validate* every session key in *zero knowledge*. Instead of exposing the preimages $a_{j_1}, \ldots, a_{j_k}$ during the audit, the sender proves possession of the correct secret material using a post-quantum digital signature equipped with a zero-knowledge proof. We instantiate the signature with *FAEST* [5], but any (post-quantum) scheme providing unforgeability and zero-knowledge suffices.

To verify a transcript $(C, \mathcal{I})$, an auditor proceeds as follows:

1. Alice reveals the session key sk.
2. The auditor decrypts C with sk to obtain $(M', \mathcal{I}', \sigma')$ and aborts if $\mathcal{I}' \neq \mathcal{I}$.

3. The auditor checks that $\text{Verify}_{\mathsf{FAEST}}(\mathsf{pk}_{\mathsf{FAEST}}, sk, \sigma') = 1$.

At no point does the auditor learn any a_i; the zero-knowledge property of FAEST guarantees that the signature discloses no information beyond the validity of sk.

- **Security Analysis** The construction inherits key-uniqueness, index-hiding, and forward-secrecy (Theorems 1, 2 and 3) from 2. The additional FAEST signature provides:

Authenticity. No PPT adversary can produce an auditor-accepted transcript $(C, \mathcal{I}, \sigma)$ without knowledge of the real session key sk, except with negligible probability. A forged transcript yields a fresh (sk, σ) signature on a message never queried, violating EUF-CMA.

Zero-Knowledge Privacy. For every PPT auditor $\mathcal{A}$ there exists a PPT simulator $\mathcal{S}$ whose output is computationally indistinguishable from $\mathcal{A}$'s real view of any transcript. Because FAEST is zero-knowledge and the encryption is IND-CPA, the resulting distribution is indistinguishable from a real transcript.

At last, we elaborate on our choice to use FAEST rather than *zero-knowledge middleboxes* (ZKMBs) [22]. In their construction, Grubbs *et al.* demonstrate that while a middlebox can verify a proof of correct TLS key derivation in roughly 2-5 ms, generating the proof on the client side takes several seconds and can require hundreds of megabytes of memory. The FAEST signature scheme, on the other hand, implements a non-interactive zero-knowledge proof of knowledge of the secret session key: the signature on sk is constant-size and can be verified in a few million cycles [5].

Performance and Parameter Selection

PQ-STAR is parameterised by three integers: n, m and k. For example, for post-quantum security, one may choose $n = 256$, so that the session key has 256 bits and offers roughly 128 bits of quantum security [21]. Section 2 explains how to avoid storing this in full by deriving entries from short seeds. Each session independently samples k indices from $[m]$; the probability that two sessions choose the same tuple is m^{-k}. Selecting $k = 16$ and $m = 2^{20}$, for example, yields a negligible chance of any collision even across billions of sessions.

Deriving a session key requires computing a single hash; hashing a few hundred bytes, therefore, takes on the order of microseconds [39], which is negligible compared with the time to encrypt a message. Consequently, the overhead of session-key derivation is constant per message [19].

PQ-STAR can be integrated into existing protocols with minimal changes. The index tuple $\mathcal{I}$ can be sent in the clear or as associated data in the AEAD. PQ-STAR operates at the application layer and can run atop a secure transport such as TLS 1.3; integrating PQ-STAR with TLS 1.3 thus allows for deriving auditable session keys while retaining the confidentiality and integrity guarantees of the transport [38].

To our knowledge, there is no prior work that simultaneously combines stateless rekeying, post-quantum security, and public auditability. Because PQ-STAR introduces new functionality rather than optimizing an existing primitive, our evaluation focuses on qualitative properties (statelessness, post-quantum soundness, and auditability).

Conclusions

We introduced PQ-STAR, a post-quantum, stateless, auditable rekeying scheme. PQ-STAR allows each message to be encrypted with a fresh session key derived from a shared secret array, while enabling an authorized auditor to verify any ciphertext by revealing only the corresponding one-time session key. The scheme utilizes only hash functions, operates without maintaining state between messages, and does not require any synchronization between sender and receiver. We provide informal arguments that all three PQ-STAR variants are secure. The commitment-based PQ-STAR variant augments the plain construction with binding commitments, preventing a malicious sender from later claiming an unrelated session key. The Zero-knowledge PQ-STAR variant equips each session key with a signature-based zero-knowledge proof, which proves that the session key was derived honestly, without ever revealing the secret preimages.

References

1. Abdalla, M., Belaïd, S., Fouque, P.A.: Leakage-Resilient symmetric encryption via re-keying. In: Bertoni, G., Coron, J.-S. (eds.) CHES 2013. LNCS, vol. 8086, pp. 471–488. Springer, Heidelberg (2013). https://doi.org/10.1007/978-3-642-40349-1_27
2. Abdalla, M., Bellare, M.: Increasing the lifetime of a key: a comparative analysis of the security of re-keying techniques. In: International Conference on the Theory and Application of Cryptology and Information Security, pp. 546–559. Springer (2000)
3. Ali, S., Guo, X., Karri, R., Mukhopadhyay, D.: Fault attacks on AES and their countermeasures. In: Secure System Design and Trustable Computing, pp. 163–208. Springer (2016)
4. Barker, E.B., Kelsey, J.M., et al.: Recommendation for random number generation using deterministic random bit generators (revised). US Department of Commerce, Technology Administration, National Institute of (2007)
5. Baum, C., et al.: Faest v2: Algorithm specifications (2025)
6. Bernstein, D.J., et al.: The sphincs+ signature framework. In: Proceedings of the 2019 ACM SIGSAC conference on computer and communications security, pp. 2129–2146 (2019)
7. Biryukov, A., Khovratovich, D.: Related-key cryptanalysis of the full AES-192 and AES-256. In: International conference on the theory and application of cryptology and information security, pp. 1–18. Springer (2009)
8. Biryukov, A., Khovratovich, D., Nikolić, I.: Distinguisher and related-key attack on the full AES-256. In: Annual International Cryptology Conference, pp. 231–249. Springer (2009)
9. Chan, J., Rogaway, P.: On committing authenticated-encryption. In: European Symposium on Research in Computer Security, pp. 275–294. Springer (2022)

10. Chang: Hop (2025), manuscript in preparation
11. Chen, L., Chen, L.: Recommendation for key derivation using pseudorandom functions. US Department of Commerce, National Institute of Standards and Technology (2024)
12. Chen, L., et al.: Report on post-quantum cryptography, vol. 12. US Department of Commerce, National Institute of Standards and Technology (2016)
13. Coron, J.S., Goubin, L.: On boolean and arithmetic masking against differential power analysis. In: Koç, Ç.K., Paar, C. (eds.) CHES 2000. LNCS, vol. 1965, pp. 231–237. Springer, Heidelberg (2000). https://doi.org/10.1007/3-540-44499-8_18
14. Denis, F., Lucas, S.: The AEGIS family of authenticated encryption algorithms. internet-draft draft-irtf-cfrg-aegis-aead-17. Internet Eng. Task Force (2025). https://datatracker.ietf.org/doc/draft-irtf-cfrg-aegis-aead/17/, work in Progress
15. Dolev, S.: System and method for Merkle puzzles symmetric key establishment and generation of Lamport Merkle signatures (2019). US Patent 0140819
16. Dolev, S., Panagopoulou, P.N., Rabie, M., Schiller, E.M., Spirakis, P.G.: Rationality authority for provable rational behavior. Algorithms, Probability, Networks, and Games: Scientific Papers and Essays Dedicated to Paul G. Spirakis on the Occasion of His 60th Birthday, pp. 33–48 (2015)
17. Dolev, S., Yagudaev, A., Yung, M.: HBSS:(simple) Hash-based Stateless Signatures–hash all the way to the rescue! Cryptography and Communications, pp. 1–18 (2025)
18. Dolev, S., Yagudaev, A., Yung, M.: PQ-STAR: Post-quantum stateless auditable rekeying. Cryptology ePrint Archive, Paper 2025/1489 (2025). https://eprint.iacr.org/2025/1489
19. Dworkin, M.J.: SP 800-38d. recommendation for block cipher modes of operation: Galois/counter mode (GCM) and GMAC. National Institute of Standards and Technology (2007)
20. Dziembowski, S., Pietrzak, K.: Leakage-resilient cryptography. In: 2008 49th Annual IEEE Symposium on Foundations of Computer Science, pp. 293–302. IEEE (2008)
21. Grover, L.K.: A fast quantum mechanical algorithm for database search. In: Proceedings of the twenty-eighth annual ACM symposium on Theory of computing, pp. 212–219 (1996)
22. Grubbs, P., Arun, A., Zhang, Y., Bonneau, J., Walfish, M.: {Zero-Knowledge} middleboxes. In: 31st USENIX Security Symposium (USENIX Security 22), pp. 4255–4272 (2022)
23. Grubbs, P., Lu, J., Ristenpart, T.: Message franking via committing authenticated encryption. In: Annual International Cryptology Conference, pp. 66–97. Springer (2017)
24. Kelsey, J., Chang, S., Perlner, R.: Sha-3 derived functions: cshake, kmac, tuplehash, and parallelhash. NIST Spec. Publ. **800**, 185 (2016)
25. Kocher, P., Jaffe, J., Jun, B.: Differential Power Analysis. In: Wiener, M. (ed.) CRYPTO 1999. LNCS, vol. 1666, pp. 388–397. Springer, Heidelberg (1999). https://doi.org/10.1007/3-540-48405-1_25
26. Kocher, P., Jaffe, J., Jun, B., Rohatgi, P.: Introduction to differential power analysis. J. Cryptogr. Eng. **1**, 5–27 (2011)
27. Kocher, P.C.: Leak-resistant cryptographic indexed key update (Mar 25 2003), US Patent 6,539,092
28. Krawczyk, H.: Cryptographic extraction and key derivation: The HKDF scheme. In: Annual Cryptology Conference, pp. 631–648. Springer (2010)

29. Krawczyk, H., Eronen, P.: HMAC-based extract-and-expand key derivation function (HKDF). Technical report (2010)
30. Lamport, L.: Constructing digital signatures from a one way function (1979)
31. Langford, S.K., Hellman, M.E.: Differential-Linear Cryptanalysis. In: Desmedt, Y.G. (ed.) CRYPTO 1994. LNCS, vol. 839, pp. 17–25. Springer, Heidelberg (1994). https://doi.org/10.1007/3-540-48658-5_3
32. Len, J., Grubbs, P., Ristenpart, T.: Partitioning oracle attacks. In: 30th USENIX security symposium (USENIX Security 21), pp. 195–212 (2021)
33. Mangard, S., Oswald, E., Popp, T.: Power analysis attacks: Revealing the secrets of smart cards, vol. 31. Springer Science and Business Media (2008)
34. Medwed, M., Standaert, F.-X., Großschädl, J., Regazzoni, F.: Fresh re-keying: security against side-channel and fault attacks for low-cost devices. In: Bernstein, D.J., Lange, T. (eds.) AFRICACRYPT 2010. LNCS, vol. 6055, pp. 279–296. Springer, Heidelberg (2010). https://doi.org/10.1007/978-3-642-12678-9_17
35. Mennink, B.: Beyond birthday bound secure fresh rekeying: application to authenticated encryption. In: International Conference on the Theory and Application of Cryptology and Information Security, pp. 630–661. Springer (2020)
36. Nir, Y., Langley, A.: ChaCha20 and Poly1305 for IETF Protocols. RFC 8439 (2018). https://doi.org/10.17487/RFC8439, https://www.rfc-editor.org/info/rfc8439
37. Renauld, M., Standaert, F.X., Veyrat-Charvillon, N.: Algebraic side-channel attacks on the AES: Why time also matters in DPA. In: International Workshop on Cryptographic Hardware and Embedded Systems, pp. 97–111. Springer (2009)
38. Rescorla, E.: The Transport Layer Security (TLS) protocol version 1.3. Technical report (2018)
39. Santos Jr, C.E., Silva, L.M.d., Torquato, M.F., Silva, S.N., Fernandes, M.A.: Sha-256 hardware proposal for IoT devices in the blockchain context. Sensors **24**(12), 3908 (2024)
40. Smyshlyaev, S.V.: Re-keying mechanisms for symmetric keys. RFC 8645 (2019). https://doi.org/10.17487/RFC8645, https://www.rfc-editor.org/info/rfc8645
41. Tiri, K., Verbauwhede, I.: A logic level design methodology for a secure DPA resistant ASIC or FPGA implementation. In: Proceedings Design, Automation and Test in Europe Conference and Exhibition. vol. 1, pp. 246–251. IEEE (2004)
42. Ueno, R., Homma, N., Inoue, A., Minematsu, K.: Fallen sanctuary: a higher-order and leakage-resilient rekeying scheme. IACR Trans. Cryptographic Hardware Embed. Syst. **2024**(1), 264–308 (2024)

Author Index